J. S. BACH

The Organ Works

Frontispiece. Dresden, Church of Our Lady (1726–1743): pulpit, baptismal font, altar, and Gottfried Silbermann organ of 1732–1736, played by Bach before an audience of distinguished listeners on December 1, 1736.

J. S. BACH

The Organ Works

GEORGE B. STAUFFER

OXFORD
UNIVERSITY PRESS

OXFORD
UNIVERSITY PRESS

Oxford University Press is a department of the University of Oxford. It furthers
the University's objective of excellence in research, scholarship, and education
by publishing worldwide. Oxford is a registered trade mark of Oxford University
Press in the UK and certain other countries.

Published in the United States of America by Oxford University Press
198 Madison Avenue, New York, NY 10016, United States of America.

Library of Congress Cataloging-in-Publication Data
Names: Stauffer, George B., 1947– author.
Title: J.S. Bach : the organ works / George B. Stauffer.
Description: New York : Oxford University Press, 2024. |
Includes bibliographical references and index.
Identifiers: LCCN 2023054940 (print) | LCCN 2023054941 (ebook) |
ISBN 9780195108026 (hardback) | ISBN 9780197661208 (epub) |
ISBN 9780197661192 | ISBN 9780197661215
Subjects: LCSH: Bach, Johann Sebastian, 1685–1750. Organ music. |
Organ music—Analysis, appreciation.
Classification: LCC MT145.B11 S73 2024 (print) | LCC MT145.B11 (ebook) |
DDC 786.5092—dc23/eng/20231219
LC record available at https://lccn.loc.gov/2023054940
LC ebook record available at https://lccn.loc.gov/2023054941

DOI: 10.1093/oso/9780195108026.001.0001

Printed in Canada by Marquis Book Printing

*To my friends and colleagues who play, study,
and admire Bach and the king of instruments.*

Contents

PART V   THE GRAND SYNTHESIS:
LEIPZIG (1723–1750)

Preface

> We cannot be blamed if we are bold enough to declare that our Bach
> was the greatest organist and clavier player that we have ever had.

Thus ran the claim in the obituary of Johann Sebastian Bach that appeared shortly after his death. In the title, Bach was described as "The World-Famous Organist," and with good reason. Of all his musical accomplishments, it was as an organist that he achieved the greatest acclaim during his lifetime. In organ concerts in Hamburg, Dresden, Potsdam, Leipzig, and elsewhere and in his late publications of organ music he received the broad recognition that escaped him in other endeavors. Not only was he a virtuoso player, with manual and pedal technique that went far beyond that of his predecessors and contemporaries, but his works redefined the very nature of organ music and what could be accomplished on the instrument.

Bach's organ compositions—the tangible results of this playing—were highly valued during his lifetime. Circulated among a small but dedicated group of students and connoisseurs, they were viewed as *exempla classica*—classic pieces to be studied, performed, and preserved. Unlike Bach's vocal and instrumental music, the organ works never went into eclipse after his death in 1750. They continued to be played and disseminated, and in the nineteenth century, when they first appeared in complete editions, they were quickly adopted as the core curriculum for organ playing, the works a professional organist had to know and perform to be considered an accomplished player. They have retained that role to the present day and continue to be the ultimate test of an organist's technique and musicianship.

Bach made many of his strongest musical statements in his organ works. It was there that he evolved his approach to fugue composition, strict part-writing, and the creation of large preludes. It is in his organ works that we see the first evidence of his life-changing encounter with Vivaldi's music. Among his other keyboard pieces there is nothing quite comparable to the unabashed virtuosity of the Vivaldi concerto arrangements or the immense musical journey of the C-Minor Passacaglia. In the realm of the prelude and fugue there are no equivalents in the Well-Tempered Clavier to the monumental proportions of the "St. Anne" Prelude and Fugue in E♭ Major or the modulatory excursions of the "Wedge" Fugue in E Minor. "I wish that you could once hear Mr. Bach on the organ," Georg Ludwig

Heinrich Schwanenberg wrote to his father after hearing Bach play in Leipzig, "for neither you nor anyone else in Braunschweig could hold your head before him. I have never heard anything like it!" Indeed, there was nothing quite like it.

In addition, the organ music is the only repertoire—keyboard, choral, or instrumental—that spans the entire length of Bach's career, from the Neumeister Chorales of his Ohrdruf and Lüneburg years to "Vor deinen Thron tret ich hiermit," refined on his deathbed in Leipzig. In between these markers was a steady flow of organ compositions, in Arnstadt, Mühlhausen, Weimar, Cöthen, and Leipzig. Organ music played a defining role in Bach's development: it was his first and last love, so to speak, and as a consequence, it offers the unique opportunity to trace the complete arc of his growth as a composer, from beginning to end. In the early years, the organ works dominated his output and influenced his approach to vocal and instrumental composition, as seen in the organ-like scoring of the Mühlhausen cantatas and Brandenburg Concertos, with their alternating blocks of sound. From the mid–Weimar years onward, the flow of ideas reversed: Bach's involvement with instrumental and vocal composition influenced his organ writing, as witnessed in the borrowed movements of the Six Sonatas or the *stile antico* idiom of the large "Aus tiefer Not, schrei ich zu dir" setting of Clavier-Übung III. Also coming into play during the Cöthen and Leipzig periods were the shifting tastes in musical styles in Europe as well as the progressive trends in Central German organ building. It was a long road from the Central German pedestrianism of "Erhalt uns, Herr, bei deinem Wort" in the Neumeister Collection to the cosmopolitan urbanity of the pedal setting of "Vater unser im Himmelreich" in Clavier-Übung III.

The goal of the present volume is to trace that journey, to follow the evolution of Bach's organ works within the trajectory of his personal development. The narrative does not provide a blow-by-blow account of each work—ground well covered by Peter Williams in his magisterial (but sometimes maddening) study *The Organ Music of J. S. Bach* and, for the early works, by Jean-Claude Zehnder in his meticulous *Die frühen Werke Johann Sebastian Bachs*. Rather, the approach here is to look at groups of works of the same genre in roughly chronological order, weighing them against broad cultural and stylistic currents and comparing the compositional features of individual pieces, to illuminate Bach's irrepressible invention and relentless drive for improvement.

Bach was a remarkably methodical composer. He seemed to relish focusing on a particular compositional issue and resolving it through a series of works in which he systematically explored various musical and technical possibilities. He espoused this process early on. His exploration of fugal procedures in Arnstadt, for instance, discussed in chapter 6, is well illustrated by placing the four independent fugues from that time side by side and looking at the different directions

Bach took in each. By pursuing this approach more widely, we can see the logic in his stylistic development as a composer of organ music. At the same time, we come to a better understanding of the individual pieces and how they might be performed.

It is to be admitted that the dating of the early organ works, especially, poses challenges. The lack of original source material, discussed in the introduction, makes exact chronological placement of the surviving compositions difficult. However, studies by Christoph Wolff, Werner Breig, and Jean-Claude Zehnder and my own examination of the free preludes have helped in recent years to clarify the dating of the organ works considerably—so much so that it is now possible to place most of the pieces in a limited time frame with a reasonable degree of confidence. Moreover, the recent discovery of the Neumeister Chorales; the Weimar tablatures; copies of the Clavier-Übung III, Schübler Chorales, and Canonic Variations prints with the composer's personal annotations; and previously unknown Leipzig manuscripts of the C-Major Toccata and Pièce d'Orgue have broadened our understanding of Bach's early development in Ohrdruf and Lüneburg and his later use of the organ works for teaching, performance, and publication. The time has never been better for a reappraisal of Bach's organ music.

In this survey the groups of organ works are not approached in the same way. In cases like the "Great Eighteen" Chorales, where a fair amount is known about the context and genesis of the collection, background information is presented and assessed in detail. In instances such as the Canzona in D Minor, where little is known about the origin and evolution of the work, the focus is on stylistic analysis and the insights it can yield.

Another marked difference in this book is the attention given to the early variants of the organ works. While these versions have frequently been marginalized in past studies, here they are examined in depth, since they reflect Bach's initial thoughts on solving particular compositional issues. In many cases the variants contain rough edges that Bach smoothed out in subsequent revisions. As discussed in chapter 17, the recycling and revision of preexisting music was almost as important as new composition during Bach's Leipzig tenure. It came to be part and parcel of his production of sacred works for the weekly services in the St. Thomas and St. Nicholas churches and, from 1729 onward, of secular works for the weekly performances of the Collegium Musicum in Zimmermann's Coffee House and Garden. The organ works benefited from this practice, and many early pieces were refined and reworked during the Leipzig years for teaching, performance, and personal pleasure. The recycling process that produced the Christmas Oratorio, the Mass in B Minor, and the harpsichord concertos played out in Bach's organ music, too, giving us the Six Sonatas, the Schübler Chorales, and the "Great Eighteen" Collection. Thus, in this book, the compositional style of the "Great Eighteen" Chorales, for example, is discussed in chapter 10 as part of Bach's Weimar undertakings, whereas the revision of the settings is discussed in chapter 25, as part of his Leipzig projects.

This survey begins with an overview of the world of Bach's organ works and the culture from which the music arose. It then moves to Bach's early studies in Eisenach, Ohrdruf, and Lüneburg with his brother Johann Christoph Bach and his mentor Georg Böhm and the critical influence of Johann Pachelbel, Johann Adam Reincken, and Dieterich Buxtehude, and other contemporaries. This is followed by a look at the bold experiments of the Arnstadt-Mühlhausen years and Bach's initial adaption of North German style. This style was refined further in Weimar and brought under strict contrapuntal control by the part-writing studies of the Orgel-Büchlein before being fully transformed by Bach's encounter with Vivaldi's concerto-writing. The Cöthen years brought a stepping back from organ composition, since it was no longer allied with Bach's professional duties. But in Leipzig he returned to organ playing and organ composition with renewed zeal, this time drawing on his expanded experience with instrumental and vocal music to create a grand synthesis of national and historical styles. The cosmopolitan idiom of the Six Sonatas, the four large preludes and fugues, Clavier-Übung III, and the Canonic Variations resulted in organ works of unprecedented elegance and grace. The unabashed virtuosity of the Weimar years yielded to broader musical concerns in the Leipzig period, producing masterpieces for the ages.

Finally, there is a certain "Je ne sais quoi" about Bach's organ compositions that separates them from the works of all others. While Bach was a devout, church-going Lutheran, as a performer he was also a showman, and he did not hesitate to draw on every possible means to impress his listeners. We know from a contemporary account that when accompanying congregational singing at a Sunday service on the new organ in the Court Chapel in Altenburg in 1736, Bach modulated the Creed hymn "Wir glauben all' an einen Gott" from its normal key, D minor, to E♭ minor for the second verse and then to E minor for the third verse. He was a player who did not shy away from daring gestures.

These gestures can be observed in his earliest surviving works, the Neumeister Chorales, and in Weimar compositions such as the Fugue in G Minor, BWV 542/2, and Fugue in D Major, BWV 532/2. There is nothing modest about these pieces. One of the most fascinating aspects of the evolution of Bach's organ writing is the way he gradually polished and refined the element of drama. The sudden descent into dark chromaticism in the pedal setting of "Kyrie, Gott heiliger Geist" in Clavier-Übung III on the word "Elend" (misery) or the climactic appearance in augmentation of the long-delayed pedal voice in the Fugue in C Major, BWV 547/2, were sophisticated features calculated to astound. In the complicated and turbulent world of the twenty-first century, this music continues to surprise and delight—just as Bach intended.

+   +   +

There are several highly useful companions for this book: Mark Bighley's *The Chorales of Bach's Organ Works: Tunes, Texts, and Translations*, which includes the texts of all verses of the chorales set by Bach in the organ works, in the original German and English translation; Christoph Wolff and Markus Zepf's *The Organs of Johann Sebastian Bach*, which includes the most up-to-date information on the dispositions and current states of the organs played by Bach; and the Leupold and new Breitkopf complete editions of the Bach organ works, which present texts that reflect the most recent appraisal of the sources of the repertoire. The references to measure numbers in this book reflect the straightforward numbering of those editions rather than the more idiosyncratic numbering of the Neue Bach-Ausgabe.

The translations of Bach documents cited from *The Bach Reader* are those of Hans T. David, Arthur Mendel, and Christoph Wolff, and the translations of chorale texts are adapted from Mark Bighley's *The Chorales of Bach's Organ Works*. Unless otherwise indicated, all other translations are my own.

+   +   +

This book reflects my engagement with the Bach organ works over a period of more than sixty years. I owe a great debt to my principal organ teachers, Milton Gill, Robert Elmore, John Weaver, and Vernon de Tar, for introducing me to many of the works discussed in this survey and patiently guiding me through the challenges of playing them. A number of professional projects also provided the opportunity for immersion in the repertoire and collaboration with colleagues well versed in Bach and Baroque performance practices: the writing of *Organ Technique: Modern and Early* with concert organist George Ritchie; the editing of the Leupold Edition of the complete organ works with the editorial team of Wayne Leupold, Christoph Wolff, and Quentin Faulkner; and the provision of liner notes for the Bach recordings of organists David Higgs, George Ritchie, Joan Lippincott, Kei Koito, and Renée Anne Louprette.

I am also indebted for substantive discussions about the Bach organ works over the years with colleagues Andreas Glöckner, Michael Maul, Hans-Joachim Schulze, and Peter Wollny at the Bach Archive in Leipzig; Alfred Dürr, Dietrich Kilian, and Yoshitake Kobayashi (alas, all deceased) at the Bach Institute in Göttingen; and Gregory Butler, Lynn Edwards Butler, David Higgs, Robert L. Marshall, Annette Richards, David Schulenberg, Russell Stinson, Christoph Wolff, and David Yearsley in the United States and Canada. I am grateful, too, to David Chapman for tracking down the plates; to David Yearsley, once again, for his thorough reading of the final draft and his good suggestions for its improvement; to Norman Hirschy, Executive Editor of Academic and Trade, Rachel Ruisard, Project Editor, and Gwen Colvin, Senior Production Editor, at Oxford University Press for ushering the book through production; to Martha Ramsey for her expert copyediting; to Niko D. Schroeder, for his meticulous engraving of the music examples; to Enid L. Zafran for producing the index; and to the Office of the Dean, Jason Geary, Dean, Mason Gross School of the Arts, Rutgers University, for a subvention to set the music examples.

But the greatest thanks must go to concert organist Renée Anne Louprette, whose elegant performances and recordings of this music have served as a constant reminder of its transcendent beauty and power. It was Renée who encouraged me to finish this project after a hiatus of many years, and I am indebted to her for the helpful feedback and good cheer she provided during the final stages of writing and revision.

George B. Stauffer
New Brunswick, New Jersey
January 2024

Abbreviations and Terms

Reference Works

Bach Compendium   *Bach Compendium. Analytisch-bibliographisches Repertorium der Werke Johann Sebastian Bach*, Hans-Joachim Schulze and Christoph Wolff, eds. (Leipzig: Edition Peters, 1985–89).

BDok   *Bach-Dokumente* (Kassel: Bärenreiter, 1963–).

BG   *Johann Sebastian Bachs Werke* [Bach-Gesamtausgabe], issued under the auspices of the Bach-Gesellschaft (Leipzig: Breitkopf und Härtel, 1851–99).

Breitkopf Edition   *Johann Sebastian Bach: Sämtliche Orgelwerke* (Wiesbaden: Breitkopf & Härtel, 2010–18).

BJ   *Bach-Jahrbuch* (Leipzig: Evangelische Verlagsanstalt, 1904–).

BWV   Unless otherwise indicated, BWV refers to the traditional numbering of BWV^1, BWV^2, and BWV^{2a} that is used in all modern editions of Bach's organ works to date: e.g., BWV 653, BWV 653a, and BWV 653b for the three forms of "An Wasserflüssen Babylon," rather than BWV 653.3, BWV 653.2, and BWV 653.1, for the same three forms, as given in BWV^3. The numbering of BWV^3 is used in the case of new works or arrangements that have been assigned BWV numbers since the appearance of BWV^{2a}.

BWV^1 *Thematisch-systematisches Verzeichnis der musikalischen Werke von Johann Sebastian Bach*, Wolfgang Schmieder, ed. [Bach-Werke-Verzeichnis] (Wiesbaden: Breitkopf & Härtel, 1950).

BWV^2 *Thematisch-systematisches Verzeichnis der musikalischen Werke von Johann Sebastian Bach*, Wolfgang Schmieder, ed., rev. ed. (Wiesbaden: Breitkopf & Härtel, 1990).

BWV^{2a} *Bach-Werke Verzeichnis: Kleine Ausgabe*, Alfred Dürr and Yoshitake Kobayashi, eds. (Wiesbaden: Breitkopf & Härtel, 1998).

BWV^3 Wolfgang Schmieder, *Thematisch-systematisches Verzeichnis der musikalischen Werke von Johann Sebastian Bach*, Christine Blanken, Christoph Wolff, and Peter Wollny, eds., 3rd ed. (Wiesbaden: Breitkopf & Härtel, 2022).

KB   *Kritischer Bericht* (Critical Report of the NBA).

Leupold Edition   *Johann Sebastian Bach: The Complete Organ Works* (Colfax, NC: Wayne Leupold Editions, 2010–).

NBA   Johann Sebastian Bach, *Neue Ausgabe Sämtlicher Werke* [Neue Bach-Ausgabe] (Leipzig and Kassel, 1954–2007).

NBR *The New Bach Reader*, Hans T. David, Arthur Mendel, and Christoph Wolff, eds. (New York: Norton, 1998).

P Partitur (or score) *Mus.ms. Bach P.* in the Berlin State Library.

Peters Edition *Johann Sebastian Bach's Kompositionen für die Orgel* (Leipzig: C. F. Peters, 1844–52).

RV *Antonio Vivaldi. Thematisch-systematisches Verzeichnis seiner Werke*, Peter Ryom and Federico Maria Sardelli, eds., rev. ed. (Wiesbaden: Breitkopf & Härtel, 2018).

TWV *Georg Philipp Telemann. Thematisch-systematisches Verzeichnis seiner Werke*, Martin Ruhnke, ed. (Kassel: Bärenreiter, 1984–99).

Website

Bach digital A collaborative project of the Staatsbibliothek zu Berlin— Preußischer Kulturbesitz, Berlin; the Sächsische Landesbibliothek Staats- und Universitätsbibliothek, Dresden; and the Bach-Archiv, Leipzig (2001–).

Libraries, Archives, and Collections

Austrian National Library	Vienna, Österreichische Nationalbibliothek
Bach Archive	Leipzig, Bach-Archiv
Berlin State Library	Berlin, Staatsbibliothek zu Berlin— Preußischer Kulturbesitz
British Library	London
Darmstadt University Library	Darmstadt, Universitäts- und Landesbibliothek, Handschriften- und Musikabteilung
Göttingen University Library	Göttingen, Niedersächsische Staats- und Universitätsbibliothek Göttingen
Göttweig Benedictine Abbey	Göttweig, Benediktinerstift Göttweig, Musikarchiv
Kaliningrad, University Library	Kaliningrad, Universitetskaya biblioteka
Leipzig State Archive	Leipzig, Staatsarchiv Leipzig
Leipzig Town Library	Leipzig, Städtische Bibliotheken— Musikbibliothek
Princeton University Library	Princeton, NJ, Department of Rare Books and Special Collections
Royal Library of Belgium	Brussels, Bibliothèque royale de Belgique
Sibley Music Library	Rochester, NY, Eastman School of Music, University of Rochester, Sibley Music Library
Württemberg Regional Library	Stuttgart, Württembergische Landesbibliothek

Yale Music Library   New Haven, CT, Yale University, Irving
                                      S. Gilmore Music Library

Terminology
In this book, keys are represented by the standard abbreviations of music theory.
Lowercase equals minor and uppercase equals major, with the roman numerals
i–vii or I–VII representing the steps of the scale of the key in question:

    I = tonic major
    i = tonic minor
    V = dominant major
    v = dominant minor
    V^7 = dominant seventh
    $V°$ = diminished seventh

Pitch is represented by the standard Helmholtz system of c-based octaves:

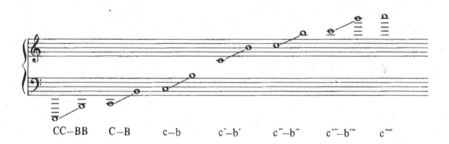

    CC–BB   C–B   c–b   c′–b′   c″–b″   c‴–b‴   c⁗

Parts are indicated by standard organ terminology:

    RH = right hand
    LH = left hand
    Ped. = pedal

In the settings of bar-form chorales, the measure numbers follow those in the
Breitkopf and Leupold editions rather than those in NBA IV/2 and IV/3, where
the measures of the repeated Stollens are counted twice.

Organ dispositions are represented by the use of roman numerals for the number
of manuals and arabic numerals for the number of stops. Thus III/46 indicates a
three-manual organ with 46 stops.

The following specialized terms that occur repeatedly in discussions of Bach's organ music may be unfamiliar to general readers.

Abgesang	The B section of a strophic chorale composed in a bar form: A A B
corta	A dactylic rhythmic figure, found especially in Bach's early keyboard works: ♪ ♫
manualiter	An organ work for manuals alone
passaggio	A section of free passagework, usually of 16th- or 32nd-note scales and arpeggios, commonly occurring at the beginning of North German–oriented organ preludes
pedaliter	An organ work with an obbligato pedal part
Stollen	The A section of a strophic chorale composed in a bar form: A A B; the music is repeated with a different text
suspirans	A rhythmic figure consisting of a 16th-note rest followed by three 16th notes, found especially in Bach's early keyboard works: 𝄾 ♫

Introduction

The World of Bach's Organ Music

Central German Music Culture

Johann Sebastian Bach had the advantage of being born into a family rich in musicians. But he also benefited from being born in Central Germany, a region that fostered a rich music culture. To the north lay Protestant Germany, strict in its abstract religious practices, cold in climate and serious in temperament, an area in which contrapuntal practices and the *stylus fantasticus* held sway. To the south lay Catholic Germany, mystical in its emotional religious practices, warmer in climate and temperament, a region in which flexible counterpoint and melody prevailed.

Thuringia, Saxony, and Anhalt, the areas in which Bach was born, raised, and worked, benefited from their central position. The three regions were part of a cultural crossroads between the North and South as well as the East and West, drawing strongly on artistic practices from the outside. This is evident in the Ohrdruf keyboard albums of Bach's brother Johann Christoph and the Weimar collections of his colleague Johann Gottfried Walther: both contain a wide assortment of pieces from Italy, France, and Bohemia as well as North, Central, and South Germany. As Bach mentioned in his often-cited memorandum of complaint to the Leipzig Town Council in 1730, German musicians were expected to be able to perform "at once and *ex tempore* all kinds of music, whether it comes from Italy or France, England or Poland."[1] Bach, perhaps more than any other composer of his age, took advantage of this eclecticism to forge an international musical language. But the fertile mélange of artistic and musical styles itself was part of Central German culture.

Germany as we know it today did not exist. Rather than a unified country, it was a loosely organized federation of some 350 principalities—kingdoms, duchies, prince-bishoprics, free imperial cities, and other domains—tied to one another by a common language (though with many dialects) and the fading concept of the Holy Roman Empire. Of the three areas in which Bach worked, Thuringia was a Lutheran region, Saxony a Catholic electorate, and Anhalt a Calvinist duchy. Thuringia, consisting of 33 politically distinct territories in 1690,[2] lacked large commercial cities and was relatively unaffected by the territorial conflicts

J. S. BACH. George B. Stauffer, Oxford University Press. © Oxford University Press 2024.
DOI: 10.1093/oso/9780195108026.003.0001

that plagued other areas of Germany and Europe. The political insignificance of Thuringia proved to be of great benefit to artists and musicians, who could work there undisrupted by the strife of war and international intrigue.

Cities in Central Germany differed greatly in nature, and Bach profited from the distinct musical opportunities offered by each. Leipzig was a bustling international trade city, similar to Hamburg in the north and run by a town council of prosperous citizens concerned with supporting the arts as a status symbol. Mühlhausen, as an independent imperial city, had a similar aspiration, sponsoring the only contemporary publications of Bach cantatas.[3] Eisenach, Ohrdruf, Arnstadt, Weimar, Weissenfels, and Cöthen were either primary or secondary ducal or princely residences, with courts that vied with one another to emulate the cultural extravagances of Louis XIV at Versailles. The dukes and princes of Central Germany sought glory, pleasure, and prestige through the splendor of their courts and their patronage of the arts, in the hope, as one historian has put it, that "the glamour of culture would overcome the stigma of isolation."[4] In Saxony and Thuringia these ambitions were fulfilled on a truly monumental scale only in Dresden, through the great building projects of Frederick August I ("Frederick the Strong") and his son Frederick August II.

In Central Germany daily life was constantly punctuated by musical events that occurred on four fronts: town, school, court, and church. Municipal music-making was led by a city director of music and the Stadtpfeiffer, or town pipers, a small group of versatile professional players adept on multiple instruments. The Stadtpfeiffer were often joined by the Kunstgeiger, or art fiddlers, a second tier of full-time professionals, and occasionally by the Bierfiddler, or beer fiddlers, freelance musicians who played on a per-fee basis. Municipal music included daily performances from the tower of the town hall, festive works for the annual change of town council, dedications of new buildings, visits of royalty, and other special occasions. Bach's father, Ambrosius Bach, was head Stadtpfeiffer in Eisenach, allowing Bach to observe the ins and outs of municipal music-making at an early age.

Latin schools were also an important component of music-making in Central Germany, since they offered scholarships to musically talented boys who earned their keep by singing in the school choir. The choirs provided music for worship services in the churches affiliated with the schools and performed at town festivities and sometimes at court events as well. Latin schools were open solely to boys, who ranged in age from seven to early twenties. They were trained and directed by the cantor of the school, a musician with strong academic credentials who was expected to teach academic subjects in addition to overseeing the music program. It was through the Latin-school system that Bach gained not only sound choral training but also an academic grounding sufficiently strong to qualify him for the cantor position at the St. Thomas School in Leipzig many years later.

Courts hosted a wide variety of music events that were often open to townspeople as well as members of the nobility. The music was provided by a court *capelle*, an instrumental and vocal ensemble composed of professional players and singers supplemented by part-time musicians, commonly drawn from the court's staff. The court ensemble supplied daily Tafelmusik, or table music, during or after dinner; dance music for balls; music for worship services if the court included a chapel; accompaniment for operas and ballets; and concerted vocal music for special occasions.

It was the pervasive influence of the Lutheran church, however, and its wholehearted embrace of music and the organ that gave Central Germany and Thuringia their most distinctive cultural stamp. When formulating the principles of Protestant doctrine in the 1520s and 1530s, Martin Luther proclaimed music a "donum Dei," a gift of God that could be used as a force for instilling faith in congregants. "Music alone produces what otherwise only theology can do," Luther claimed, "namely, to instill a calm and joyful disposition."[5] And in a letter to the composer Ludwig Senfl he reiterated: "next to the Word of God, music deserves the highest praise."[6] As a result, music became a central element of the worship service, appearing throughout the rite in the form of chants, Latin motets, German cantatas, congregational chorales, and organ preludes, interludes, and postludes.

The chorale, in particular, was a critical addition to Lutheran worship, drawing the congregation directly into the music-making. Created by Luther and his fellow founders from existing Catholic chants, Latin hymns, retexted popular songs, and new compositions, chorales were, as Luther expressed it, "vernacular psalms for the people—that is, spiritual songs, so that the Word of God even by means of song may live among the people."[7] So popular was this participatory music form that by Bach's time the repertory of chorales had grown to more than 4,500 texts,[8] set to appealing melodies that provided composers with a vast storehouse of material for composition and improvisation.

Church performing forces normally included a choir drawn from an affiliated Latin school and an instrumental band of professionals (the Stadtpfeiffer and Kunstgeiger) and townspeople (students, gifted aristocrats, and others), led by a cantor or adjuvant (assistant). Organ music was supplied by a full-time organist and assistants. Christmas, Easter, Pentecost, and other high feasts were occasions for special music—so much so that large churches such as St. George's in Eisenach, St. Thomas's and St. Nicholas's in Leipzig, and the Church of Our Lady in Dresden became virtual concert halls, attracting 2,000 or more congregants to services to hear festive music as well as the Word of God.

The organ stood at the very center of the sacred music-making. It was used for preludes to the motet, cantata, and hymns within the service; free works before and after the service; accompaniment for congregational singing; and music during Communion. In churches with special instruments or special organists, the organ postludes often evolved into organ recitals, in the manner of the public organ recitals presented in the Netherlands and North Germany. In Thuringia, the feast of St. John (June 24) became a traditional day for the principal organists of churches to present a recital after the service, to demonstrate their continued mastery of the instrument.[9] Such a performance was specified in Johann Pachelbel's contract of 1678 at the Prediger Church in Erfurt,[10] and according to the early biographer Johann Nicolaus Forkel, Bach was often asked to demonstrate the organ outside the worship service—that is, to give public recitals (see chapter 15).[11]

Unlike the town pipers, organists did not belong to a guild, and as a result there was no established apprentice system for learning the trade. The normal course of training was several years of private study—the path taken by Bach's brother Johann Christoph, who took lessons with Pachelbel for three years. Organ students commonly boarded with their teachers and followed them from place to place as they changed jobs. Bach had several such students: Johann Martin Schubart, who received instruction in Arnstadt, Mühlhausen, and Weimar, and Bernhard Christian Kayser, who received instruction in Cöthen and Leipzig, for instance. Bach benefited greatly from the income and the ready assistance such students provided (see chapter 15). Organists gained positions through auditions and letters of recommendation written by their teachers.

The central place of the organ in the Lutheran service is underscored by Luther's ideal design for church architecture, first realized in the Court Church in Torgau, which was completed in 1544 and consecrated by Luther the same year. Luther's plan put the pulpit, altar and baptismal font, and organ at the front of the church, representing the Word, sacrament, and music, respectively, as the essential elements of the Protestant rite.[12] The congregation, in turn, was seated in a series of balconies in the sanctuary, placing them as close as possible to the front of the church and the center of ritual activity. This design became the standard for new Lutheran churches built in Central Germany and was stunningly realized in buildings such as the City Church of 1719–1723 in Waltershausen, where the large organ (III/47) by Tobias Heinrich Gottfried Trost crowns a front ensemble of baptismal font, altar, and pulpit, the whole framed by two sets of balconies (plate I-1). The City Church served as the model for the Church of Our Lady in Dresden, where Gottfried Silbermann's organ (III/43) completed Luther's plan on an even grander scale (see the frontispiece).

Plate I-1 Waltershausen, City Church (1719–1723): altar, pulpit, and Tobias Heinrich Gottfried Trost organ of 1722–1735.
Orgelbau Walterhausen

Two broad societal factors in Germany also affected Bach's musical development. The first was the atmosphere of religious tolerance and cross-fertilization. Catholicism and Calvinism existed side by side with Lutheranism, and it was in Berlin, Leipzig, and other German cities that French Huguenots found refuge after Louis XIV's Edict of Fontainebleau (1685) forced them to leave France. Bach was unshakably Lutheran, but his interactions with Prince Leopold in Cöthen, a Calvinist, led to a concentrated period of secular music-making and composition, and later, in Leipzig, his interactions with Catholic composers and Latin-texted Mass settings in Dresden resulted in an intense interest in Renaissance vocal style. The mix of religions in Central Germany contributed to Bach's mix of musical styles.

Within the Lutheran faith the interplay of Orthodoxy and Pietism helped to create a similarly dynamic atmosphere. Launched around 1675 with Philipp Jacob Spener's *Pia desideria* (Pious desires), Pietism called for a reduction of doctrine and ceremony, daily Bible study, and personal piety. While Bach remained an Orthodox Lutheran, he was clearly attracted to the personalized emotional aspects of Pietism, which seeped into his cantata texts and his organ chorale settings. The crosscurrents within the Lutheran religion influenced Bach in a positive way.

The second broad factor was the emergence of the Enlightenment and Enlightenment thinking. There is no evidence that Bach embraced Enlightenment thought, with its reliance on the reasoning of mankind rather than the Word of God. There were no Enlightenment volumes in his personal library, only religious tracts,[13] and his belief that God controlled the course of humankind remained unshakeable.[14] But Bach seemed attracted by the Enlightenment aesthetic of rational order, as represented in the symmetry of the Zwinger Pavilion of Frederick August I in Dresden (plate I-2) or the terraced gardens of the Sanssouci Palace of Frederick the Great in Potsdam. Bach's late compositions show a shift toward musical symmetries, apparent in organ works such as the Prelude in E♭ Major ("St. Anne"), BWV 552/1, or the Fugue in C Minor, BWV 537/2. The Enlightenment also spurred a delight in systematic, encyclopedic endeavors. Johann Gottfried Walther's *Musicalisches Lexicon* (1732) and Johann Heinrich Zedler's *Grosses vollständiges Universal-Lexicon* (1731–54) find their musical equivalent in Bach's Clavier-Übung series and the Art of Fugue.

It was these varied elements of Central German life—the professional opportunities offered by diverse towns; the central position of music in city, school, court, and church undertakings; the multiplicity of faiths and debates within Lutheranism; and the growing influence of Enlightenment thinking—that created fertile ground for Bach to develop and refine his unique musical style.

Plate I-2 Dresden, Zwinger Pavilion (1710–1728), designed by Matthäus Daniel Pöppelmann for Frederick August I, with St. Sophia's Church in the background.
Deutsche Fotothek, Sächsische Landesbibliothek, Dresden

The Grandest Machine of Them All

It is difficult for us in the twenty-first century, surrounded by loud, complex machines, to think back to the preindustrial age, when the pipe organ was the largest and most technically advanced mechanism in European society. Owned by churches, municipalities, and nobility, it was an object of awe and veneration. Its façade was a feast for the eyes, with a majestic display of pipes (often of silvery tin), intricately painted case, hand-carved pipe shades decorated with gold leaf, and, on larger instruments, coats of arms, frolicking putti, angels blowing trumpets or playing drums, and other figures and decorations. And inside, hidden from view, was a complex maze of machinery: metal and wood pipes, wind-chests, bellows, trackers, roller boards, backfalls, and other devices designed to transform the lowering of a manual or pedal key into a musical tone (plate I-3).

These tones ranged from the soft strains of delicate flute and exotic reed stops to the mighty roar of the *plenum*, which was the loudest sound known to Europeans aside from church bells and cannon fire. In the *Musurgia Universalis*

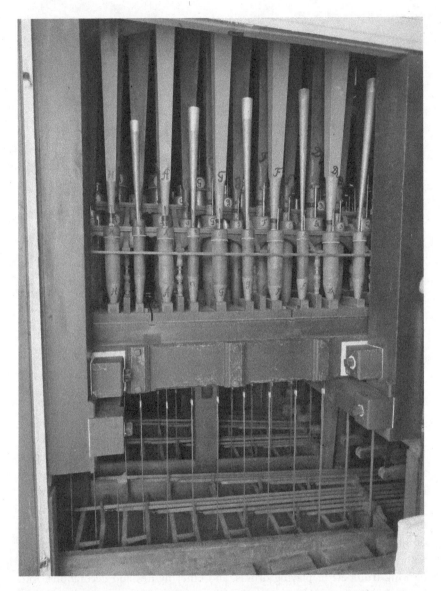

Plate I-3 Waltershausen, City Church (1719–1723): interior of the Trost organ.
Orgelbau Walterhausen

of 1650 the German Jesuit Athanasius Kircher used the organ as an allegory for God's creation of the world, comparing the drawing of single stops to the six days of creation and the combining of the stops into a full ensemble as the moment on the sixth day when God created humankind.[15] According to Michael Praetorius, the organ at St. Peter's Church in Perugia was inscribed with the saying "Hac si continunt terries, quae gaudia Coelo?"—"Since this can take place on earth, how delightful must it be in heaven?"[16] The linking of the organ with God and eternal bliss stemmed in part from the instrument's location in houses of worship. But it also reflected the view that the organ was humankind's ultimate musical and mechanical creation, much as the earth was God's ultimate harmonic and material creation.

Just as Christians journeyed to holy sites, musicians made pilgrimages to see revered organs. In May 1687 Dieterich Buxtehude received funding from his church in Lübeck to travel to Hamburg for four days to view the recently completed organ in St. Nicholas's Church, the largest instrument, with four manuals and 67 stops, from the shop of Arp Schnitger.[17] It was but one of a quintet of large organs in Hamburg that also included the instruments in St. Catherine's (IV/58), St. James' (Jakobikirche; IV/60), St. Peter's (IV/53), and St. Michael's (III/52).[18] Surely Bach's youthful trips to Hamburg from Lüneburg (see chapter 1) were not just to hear Johann Adam Reincken perform at St. Catherine's, as later claimed in the Obituary of 1750,[19] but also to see, hear, and play all five of these splendid instruments.

After the end of the Thirty Years War in 1648, pipe organs became a symbol of economic recovery in Germany, a sign of prosperity and prestige regained. Next to town halls, churches offered the best opportunities for cities to display their wealth, and within the churches, it was the organ that commanded the attention of all who entered.[20] Even in small Central German villages, parishes were eager to impress and often built larger churches with more balconies and grander organs than were needed.[21] Cities competed with one another to obtain the largest and most extravagant instruments, which were commonly the most expensive piece of equipment owned by a church, municipality, or member of the nobility.

In Hamburg, a prosperous Hanseatic city with a population of 70,000, the organs in St. Nicholas's, St. Catherine's, St. James', and St. Peter's each grew from three manuals to four in a flurry of one-upmanship during the second half of the seventeenth century. In the case of St. Catherine's, when Johann Friedrich Besser was commissioned in 1671 to add the fourth keyboard as well as a 32' Principal, 32' Groß-Posaune, and eight new bellows, the stated goal was that "our organ can be at least as good as, if not better than, the large organ at St. Mary's in Lübeck."[22] And in 1689, at St. James' across town, Schnitger was given approval to spend

3,415 marks for sculptures and carvings for the case of the new organ[23]—an immense sum at the time. Such expenditures were a good investment, since these magnificent instruments not only were a source of civic pride but also served as cultural magnets for visitors. An English-language travel guide to Hamburg published in 1688, for instance, highlighted the organs as a "must see" tourist attraction:

> The Churches here are rich in revenues, and ornaments, as Images and Stately Organs wherein they much delight. . . . Their Organs are extraordinarily large. I measured the great pipes in the organs of St. Catharine's and St. James' and found them to be 3 foot and 3 quarters in circumference and 32 foot long. . . . The wealth and trade of this city increases daily.[24]

In small villages and courts, too, organs bestowed a sense of well-being. In Thuringia, approximately 1,800 villages contained churches with pipe organs, constructed by a wide array of local builders.[25] For the citizens of these villages, chorale singing, concerted music, and organ playing in church represented the sole source of musical life. Störmthal and Zschortau, both with populations of fewer than 300 in Bach's time, can only be described as *Dörfer*, or farm villages. Yet each boasted small but distinguished pipe organs: an instrument built by Zacharias Hildebrandt (I/14, 1723) in Störmtal's Town Church, and an instrument built by Johann Scheibe (I/13, 1746) in Zschortau's St. Nicholas's Church. Both were dedicated by Bach.

Organ building required the work of a host of skilled artisans: architects for the design and engineering; cabinet makers for the construction of windchests, toe boards, and other wooden parts (cases were often built by a separate team of wood workers); joiners for the construction of wooden pipes; metal workers for the pouring of metal sheets and the construction of metal pipes and other parts; tanners for curing the leather needed for pallets and bellows; leather workers to outfit the pallets and bellows; mechanics to cut and fit iron springs; wood sculptors to carve pipe shades, figures, and other ornamental work; and painters for the case, statuary, and gold leafing. In large operations, such craftsmen were part of an in-house operation —more than 50 journeymen can be linked to Schnitger's shop in Hamburg.[26] In smaller operations, craftsmen were hired according to need, often from the town in which the organ was to be installed.

Organ projects commonly stretched over centuries. Pipes and components were expensive, and builders faced with renovating or rebuilding an organ normally saved whatever they could from the existing instrument. The result was often a historical compilation, reflecting stylistic and musical tastes of several periods. The organ in the Totentanz Chapel of St. Mary's Church in Lübeck, destroyed in World War II, spanned four centuries, with a Hauptwerk from the fifteenth century, a Rückpositiv from the sixteenth century, a Brustwerk from the seventeenth century, and an enlarged Pedal from the eighteenth century.[27]

The strong presence of the Lutheran religion in Central Germany was a great stimulus for inventive organ building, since the main worship service required a versatile instrument that could fulfill many functions. Chorale preluding called for two manuals and pedal, colorful reed and mutation stops, delicate flute and string stops, and 4' solo pedal registers. Congregational singing required strong principals and mixtures. Continuo-playing required a Brustwerk or Positiv division with an 8' Gedackt (preferably wooden, according to Bach). Cantata performances in provincial areas required imitative flute, oboe, and string registers that could substitute for the real instruments (see chapter 17). And free preluding before and after the service required a full, rich principal chorus and large, impressive pedal stops. Even small one-manual instruments in Central Germany commonly included a 16' Posaunen-Baß in the Pedal.

The competition to provide such organs was keen, and builders vied with one another not only in covering the required bases but in adding exotic elements. For the large organ in St. John's Church in Gera completed in 1725 (III/42), builder Johann Georg Finke provided a 4' Flöte douce containing two ranks, one of stopped metal pipes and one of open pear-wood pipes. Trost subsequently copied this novel register for his instruments in the City Church in Waltershausen (III/47) and the Court Church of St. George's in Altenburg (II/37).[28] The councils of small towns and the nobility of petty courts encouraged cutting-edge organ building. Both wanted musical bragging rights over their neighbors.

The fascination with the mechanical aspects of organs is reflected in the detailed descriptions of organ stops in books such as Arnolt Schlick's *Spiegel der Orgelmacher und Organisten* (1511), Michael Praetorius's *Syntagma musicum* (Part II, *De Organographia*, 1619), or Johann Mattheson's *Der vollkommene Capellmeister* (1739). In addition, a mania developed for distributing the stoplists of famous instruments, as seen in Carl Gottfried Meyer's *Sammlung einiger Nachrichten von berühmten Orgelwerken in Teutschland* (1757) or Jacob Adlung's *Musica mechanica organoedi* (1768). When Mattheson edited Friedrich Erhardt Niedt's highly popular *Musicalische Handleitung zur Variation* in 1721, he added an appendix with 60 organ dispositions for good measure. Summing up the art of German Baroque organ building was Johann Samuel Halle's *Die Kunst des Orgelbaues, theoretisch und practisch beschrieben* (1779), which describes all aspects of the craft, from the specialized shop tools to the construction of keyboards to the alloys necessary for metal pipes (plate I-4). It was the German equivalent of the famous French treatise *L' Art du facteur d'orgues* (1766–1778) by Dom Bédos de Celles.

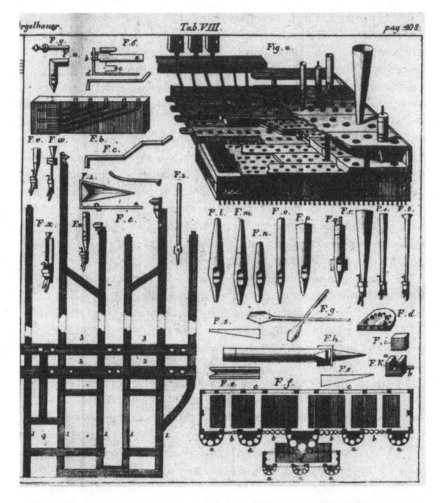

Plate I-4   Table from Johann Samuel Halle's *Die Kunst des Orgelbaues, theoretisch und practisch beschrieben* of 1779.

It is not surprising that the young Bach was attracted to the organ and became an expert on its inner workings at an early age, for at the time it was the grandest machine of them all.

The Transmission of Bach's Organ Works

The Bach organ works originally existed in the form of autograph manuscripts and engraved prints supervised by the composer. During the eighteenth century they were disseminated in a very limited way through the prints and handwritten copies made by members of the Bach family, students, colleagues, and admirers. The organ works did not become readily available to a broad public until the nineteenth century, when publishing firms such as Hoffmeister & Kühnel, C. F. Peters, and G. W. Körner began to issue mass-produced editions.

The original materials for much of the Bach organ repertory have been lost, with the result that many works are known through secondary copies only. Thus, a work's provenance becomes critically important in evaluating its authenticity, text, and chronological placement within the canon. The four modes of transmission, in order of increasing distance from the composer, are autograph manuscripts, original prints, copies made during Bach's lifetime, and copies made after Bach's death. Let us look at each in turn.

Autograph Manuscripts

Only 16 of Bach's autograph manuscripts of organ works have survived. While these manuscripts are not dated, their approximate time of origin can be established through an analysis of Bach's handwriting and the watermarks of the paper used:[29]

Arnstadt:
   "Wie schön leuchtet der Morgenstern," BWV 739 and BWV 764 (fragment), c. 1704
   Prelude and Fugue in G Minor, BWV 535a, c. 1705
   Fantasia in C minor, BWV 1121 (tablature), c. 1708–1709

Weimar:
   Orgel-Büchlein, BWV 599–644, c. 1708–1716
   "Nun komm, der Heiden Heiland," BWV 660a, c. 1714–1717
   Concerto in D Minor (after Vivaldi), BWV 596, c. 1714–1716

Cöthen:
   Clavier-Büchlein for Wilhelm Friedemann Bach of 1720:
       "Wer nur den lieben Gott lässt walten," BWV 691, c. 1720
       "Jesu, meine Freude" (incomplete), BWV 753, c. 1720
   Clavier-Büchlein for Anna Magdalena Bach of 1722:
       "Jesus meine Zuversicht," BWV 728, c. 1722–1723
       Fantasia in C Major (incomplete), BWV 573, c. 1723–1724

Leipzig:
>   Prelude and Fugue in B Minor, BWV 544, c. 1727–1732
>   Prelude and Fugue in E Minor, BWV 548, c. 1727–1732
>   Six Sonatas, BWV 525–530, c. 1727–1732
>   Prelude and Fugue in G Major, BWV 541, c. 1733
>   Fantasia and Fugue (incomplete) in C Minor, BWV 562, c. 1743–1748
>   Leipzig Chorale Portfolio (the "Great Eighteen" Chorales), BWV 651–668,
>   c. 1739–1748

Original Prints

Printing music was an arduous undertaking in Bach's day. The most common process in Germany for printing chamber and keyboard music was engraving, which involved etching the score onto copper plates and then taking the plates to a copper-plate press for printing.[30] Music engraving was time-consuming and financially risky, and it is not surprising that Bach managed to bring only three collections of organ music to print during his lifetime, all during the Leipzig years, when they could be produced by area engravers and printers and sold at the annual trade fairs. The editions appear to have had runs of no more than approximately 200 copies:[31]

>   Clavier-Übung III, 1739
>   Schübler Chorales, c. 1747–48
>   Canonic Variations on "Vom Himmel hoch, da komm ich her," c. 1748

Unlike Telemann, Handel, and Vivaldi, who used major metropolitan publishers with international distributions,[32] Bach relied on local engravers in Leipzig, Nuremberg, and Zella, with mixed results. The texts of Clavier-Übung III and the Canonic Variations are handsome and accurate (see chapters 22 and 23); the text of the Schübler Chorales, by contrast, is amateurish and riddled with errors (see chapter 24). Bach sold his editions locally, for the most part, at the Leipzig fairs and from his home in the St. Thomas School. In addition, his sons Wilhelm Friedemann and Carl Philipp Emanuel and several colleagues served as sales representatives in other German cities.

The Mystery of the Missing Autographs

Taking the contents of collections into consideration, the surviving autograph scores and original prints account for about 130 organ works—approximately half of the repertory. The fate of the autographs of the other half is one of the great unsolved mysteries of Bach research. Unlike the cantatas, which fell from favor after Bach's death, the organ works remained popular and were played widely. The original materials would have been highly valued, and it is difficult to understand why the autographs of so many pieces were lost.

There are several possible explanations. First, late in life Bach may have come to view his pre-Weimar works as "youthful sins" and destroyed most of the original materials, in an act of self-critical editing. As an adult composer, Carl Philipp Emanuel Bach confessed to having destroyed his own early works, and it is possible that he took his cue from his father.[33] Second, many of the earliest pieces were probably written in German tablature, a notation that went out of fashion in the early eighteenth century. Manuscripts of works notated this way would have been of little use to players accustomed to staff notation. Third, other than three prints, three collections, and two family albums, the organ works seem to have been passed down as individual pieces in separate folios, to judge from the way they were listed in Bach's Obituary[34] and the format of the few autographs that have survived outside the collections.[35] The single copies would have been viewed as less substantial than the prints, collections, and albums and discarded with less consequence. Finally, in the distribution of Bach's estate, it is likely that the bulk of the organ works went to Wilhelm Friedemann Bach, the oldest son and the foremost organist in the family.[36] Friedemann lived an unsettled life after giving up his position in Halle in 1764. He was often in dire financial straits and gradually sold off the manuscripts he inherited from his father, including the scores of the chorale cantata cycle, most of which are now lost.[37] If Friedemann inherited autographs of the organ works, he probably squandered them as well.[38]

Copies Made during Bach's Lifetime

Given the grave loss of original materials, the manuscript copies of the organ works made by family members, students, colleagues, and admirers take on the role of primary sources for approximately half the repertory.

Many of Bach's earliest organ works are preserved in the two albums assembled by his brother and first teacher, Johann Christoph Bach (1671–1721): the Möller Manuscript and the Andreas Bach Book. Named after later owners, these albums represent anthologies of the keyboard repertory circulating in the Bach family during the period 1703–1714.[39] They contain a wide range of organ and clavier works and instrumental transcriptions by German, French, and Italian composers, including Pachelbel, Kuhnau, Reincken, Böhm, Buxtehude, Dieupart, Steffani, and the young Johann Sebastian Bach. They also contain ornament tables from several French *Livres de clavecin*. Of the two albums, the Möller Manuscript is the earliest, dating from c. 1703–1707. It contains the Prelude and Fugue in G Minor, BWV 535a, in Bach's youthful hand, as well as four other

Bach organ works, entered by Johann Christoph. The Andreas Bach Book dates from a slightly later period, 1707–1714, and holds seven organ works by Bach, six entered by Johann Christoph, including the earliest copies of the Fugue in G Minor, BWV 578 (plate I-5), the Passacaglia in C Minor, BWV 582, and the Fantasia in C Minor, BWV 1121, entered in tablature by Johann Sebastian.

A large number of Bach's Weimar organ works were written down at the time in three albums assembled by his colleague Johann Gottfried Walther (1684–1748), organist at the City Church, and Johann Tobias Krebs (1690–1762), who studied first with Walther around 1710–1714, and then with Bach around 1714–1717. Residing today in the Berlin State Library as *P 801*, *P 802*, and *P 803*, the three are immense compellations (they total 1,350 pages) of German and French clavier and organ works collected by Walther and Krebs as part of Krebs's study.[40] They contain not only major works by Bach but also important pieces by Buxtehude, Böhm, Bruhns, and others that have not been preserved elsewhere. *P 802*, a bound volume with works entered in chronological sequence, appears to be the earliest, initiated by Walther and then shared with Krebs as he began his studies with Walther. *P 801*, a compilation of individual fascicles, appears to

Plate I-5 Fugue in G Minor, BWV 578: manuscript copy in the hand of Bach's brother, Johann Christoph Bach, in the Andreas Bach Book, c. 1710.
Leipziger Städtische Bibliotheken—Musikbibliothek

have been started next. It contains copies of Orgel-Büchlein chorales, which may stem from the beginning of Krebs's study with Bach. *P 803*, also a collection of individual fascicles, is of a later origin and includes entries by anonymous scribes as well as Krebs's son Johann Ludwig (1713–1780), who studied with Bach from approximately 1729 to 1733 while attending the St. Thomas School.[41] *P 801* and *P 802* contain mostly chorale settings; *P 803* is almost exclusively devoted to free works. In addition to containing the Orgel-Büchlein chorales, the Walther-Krebs manuscripts are the most important source of the Weimar versions of the "Great Eighteen" Chorales (plate I-6).

Organ works from Bach's Weimar years are also reflected in the manuscript collection assembled in the 1740s by Johann Nicolaus Mempell (1713–1747) and Johann Gottlieb Preller (1727–1786) and preserved today as the Mempell-Preller Collection in the Leipzig Town Library.[42] Although there is no evidence that either Mempell or Preller studied with Bach, Mempell seems to have had close connections with his son Carl Philipp Emanuel and may have had contact

Plate I-6 "Fantasia super Komm, heiliger Geist, Herre Gott," BWV 651a: manuscript copy in the hand of Johann Tobias Krebs, in the Weimar compilation *P 803*, c. 1713–1717.
Staatsbibliothek zu Berlin—Preußischer Kulturbesitz, Musikabteilung mit Mendelssohn-Archiv

with Bach himself. Preller, who perhaps studied with Mempell and seems to have taken over the collection after Mempell's death, lived in Weimar from 1744 to 1749 or so. It is possible that he based his copies of the organ works on manuscripts that remained in Weimar after Bach's departure in 1717.[43] Several of Preller's copies—including those of the Canzona in D Minor, BWV 588; Fugue in E Minor ("Cathedral"), BWV 533a/2; and Partita on "Sei gegrüßet, Jesu gütig," BWV 768—display profuse ornamentation and fingering.

During Bach's Leipzig years his organ works were copied from the autograph manuscripts by Johann Peter Kellner (1705–1772). Kellner, who worked as organist and cantor first in Frankenhain and then Gräfenroda, claimed that his relationship with Bach was that of an acquaintance rather than a student.[44] He was an ardent collector of Bach's keyboard and string music, and his fair copy of the Prelude and Fugue in E Minor ("Wedge"), BWV 548,[45] written jointly with Bach, verifies that he had direct access to Bach's scores. His manuscripts of the organ works, written between 1725 and 1735 or so, include the earliest copies of the Pastorella in F Major, BWV 590; the Prelude and Fugue in C Major, BWV 547; and other major works. They are preserved today in *P 804*, *P 274*, *P 286*, *P 287*, and *P 288* in the Berlin State Library. Working in Kellner's circle were Wolfgang Nicolaus Mey (first half of eighteenth century), who may have served as a scribe for Kellner, and Johannes Ringk (1717–1778), who studied with Kellner as well as Gottfried Heinrich Stölzel. Ringk's copy of the Toccata in D Minor, BWV 565, probably derived from a Kellner manuscript, is the earliest source of the famous work (plate I-7).

The copies of the organ works made by students studying with Bach in Leipzig represent some of the most important sources of the repertory, since they often reflect the revised texts of pieces composed earlier in Arnstadt, Mühlhausen, or Weimar. The most important Leipzig student copies were written by the students listed here, with their approximate times of study with Bach:[46]

Johann Caspar Vogler (1696–1763)	1706–1707; 1710–1714[47]
Bernhard Christian Kayser (1705–1758)	1718–1725[48]
Johann Jacob Kieser (1703–1762)	1723–1727[49]
Christian Gottlob Meißner (1707–1760)	1723–1729
Heinrich Nicolaus Gerber (1702–1775)	1724–1727
Samuel Gottlieb Hedar (1713–after 1739)	1725–1734
Carl Gotthelf Gerlach (1704–1761)	1727–1729
Johan Ludwig Krebs (1713–1780)	1729–1733
Johann Georg Heinrich (1721–after 1744)	1734–1744
Johann Friedrich Agricola (1720–1774)	1738–1741
"Anonymous X" (first half of eighteenth century)[50]	1739–1742
Johann Christoph Altnickol (1719–1759)	1744–1750
Johann Christian Kittel (1732–1809)	1748–1750

Plate I-7 Toccata in D Minor, BWV 565: manuscript copy in the hand of Johannes Ringk, in the manuscript *P 595*, c. 1740–1759.

Of these students, Johann Christian Kittel is of special importance. A devoted champion of Bach's music, he assembled a large collection of the organ works that he used for teaching in Erfurt with his wide circle of students.[51] Although most of Kittel's collection itself is lost,[52] the texts of the organ works survive in copies made by four of his students: Johann Nicolaus Gebhardi (1781–1813), Michael Gotthard Fischer (1773–1829), Johann Andreas Dröbs (1784–1825), and Johann Christian Heinrich Rinck (1770–1846).

An outlier collecting the organ works during Bach's time in Leipzig and shortly after his death was Leonhard Scholz (1720–1798), organist at St. Sebald and other churches in Nuremberg.[53] While Scholz's connection with Bach is unclear, and many of his copies are abridged or adjusted arrangements (normally to avoid difficult pedal parts), a number of his manuscripts present versions of Bach's works that seem to reflect now-lost autograph sources.

Copies Made after Bach's Death

In the half century after Bach's death, three cities emerged as centers for the distribution of his organ works: Leipzig, Erfurt, and Berlin.

Although the Bach sons and the manuscripts they inherited were no longer present in Leipzig after 1750, the town continued to be a source for the Bach organ works. The publishing house of Breitkopf sold handwritten copies of Bach's music after his death, produced on demand by professional scribes working from house manuscripts owned by the firm. The organ works offered for sale included early chorale settings that were otherwise unknown: the so-called Kirnberger Collection (BWV 690–713a), which, in truth, Kirnberger obtained from Breitkopf by mail order in 1777.[54] How Breitkopf secured the scores of the pieces remains uncertain. A large portion of Breitkopf's house manuscripts of Bach's music was purchased by the Belgian musicologist François Joseph Fétis in 1836 for the Royal Library in Brussels, where it remains today.[55] Copies of organ works derived from Breitkopf manuscripts are also preserved in the Berlin State Library as part of the Princess Anna Amalia Collection.[56]

In Erfurt Johann Christian Kittel, mentioned earlier, held sway as a master teacher, publishing Der angehende praktische Organist (1801–8), an organ method "grounded in the principles of Bach," and disseminating Bach's organ works through copies made by his pupils. Many of the pieces published by Körner in his important early nineteenth-century editions (see below) appear to have been based on manuscripts connected in one way or another with Kittel.

In Berlin, Bach's second-oldest son, Carl Philipp Emanuel Bach (1714–1788) served as a critical source for those interested in his father's music. Employed as court harpsichordist for Frederick the Great from 1738 to 1768, Emanuel owned copies of his father's organ works that were distributed through manuscripts made by professional scribes—a pattern that continued when he moved to Hamburg for the final twenty years of his life.[57] Also living in Berlin after 1750 were Bach students Johann Friedrich Agricola, who owned copies of a number of important organ works, and Johann Philipp Kirnberger, who served as curator of the immense music collection of Princess Anna Amalia (1723–1787), the music-loving sister of Frederick the Great. Kirnberger probably drew to some extent on his own manuscripts of the Bach organ works, but he also enlisted professional scribes to copy pieces provided by C. P. E. Bach, Agricola, Breitkopf, and other sources.[58] Wilhelm Friedemann Bach also lived in Berlin for the last 10 years of his life and may have made manuscripts of the organ works available to his students.

Standing outside these urban repositories is the Neumeister Collection, a large album of chorale preludes that came to light only in 1984.[59] It contains 38 pieces attributed to Bach that appear to be among his earliest surviving organ works (see chapter 3). It is unclear from what source the compiler of the album, Johann Gottfried Neumeister (1756–1840), derived the text.

Finally, in the 1840s and 1850s two publishers issued editions of Bach's organ music, in some cases utilizing manuscripts that have since been lost. C. F. Peters in Leipzig published the first complete edition of the Bach organ works, *Johann Sebastian Bach's Compositionen für die Orgel*, between 1844 and 1852.[60] Issued in nine volumes, it was edited by Friedrich Conrad Griepenkerl (1782–1849), a student of Bach's first biographer, Johann Nicolaus Forkel, and Ferdinand August Roitzsch (1805–1889), who completed the edition after Griepenkerl's death. Setting the standard for future editions of the organ works, Griepenkerl used modern source-critical methods, deriving the text from a comparative analysis of the sources available at that time. These included the only copy of the early version of the Fugue in D Major, BWV 532/2a, and the alleged autograph of the Passacaglia in C Minor, BWV 582, both no longer extant (see chapters 12 and 13).

Around the same time, Gotthilf Wilhelm Körner (1809–1865) issued a series of editions that featured organ works by Bach: *Der Orgel-Virtuos, Musikalische Aehrenlese*, and *Sämmtliche Orgel-Compositionen von Joh. Sebastian Bach*.[61] Utilizing now-lost manuscripts that appear to have come from Kittel's circle, Körner published important first editions of the Fantasia and Fugue in C Minor, BWV 537, the trios in C Minor, BWV 21/1a, and in G Minor, BWV 584, and other works.

Fortunately, high-resolution scans of almost all the Bach autographs and original prints and many of the secondary manuscript copies of the organ works are available on the Bach digital website. Given the large number of variant readings that resulted from Bach's repeated use of the pieces as teaching and recital material, the scans of the texts represent an invaluable resource for the player, scholar, and admirer of this remarkable music.

Notes

1. NBR, no. 151.
2. Friedrich 2000, 60.
3. Cantata 71, *Gott is mein König*, written for the change of Mühlhausen Town Council in 1708, was printed at the Council's expense. Bach composed two additional works for Mühlhausen Council changes, in 1709 and 1710. Both were printed, but no copies have survived.
4. Rich 2009, 74.
5. *Luther's Works* 1955–1986, vol. 49, 428, as quoted in Leaver 2009, 120.
6. *Luther's Works* 1955–1986, vol. 53, 323, as quoted in Leaver 2009, 121.
7. *Luther's Works* 1955–1986, vol. 53, 221, as quoted in Leaver 2009, 118.
8. Paul Wagner's eight-volume *Andächtiger Seelen geistliches Brand- und Gantz-Opfer— Das ist Vollständiges Gesanguch in Acht unterschiedlichen Theilen*, published in Leipzig in 1697 and part of Bach's personal library, presented the texts to 4,723 hymns.
9. Wolff 2000, 71.
10. Ziller 1935, 172: "every year at the Feast of St. John the Baptist he shall play at the close of the afternoon service for a half hour the full organ with all its stops and voices, in pleasing and harmonious concord, in remembrance of his installation as organist and at the same time to give proof to the whole Christian congregation of how he has improved himself in his office during the year." Translation from Wolff 2000, 479.
11. Forkel 1802, 22.
12. Marshall and Marshall 2016, xx–xxi. See especially the illustration of the Court Chapel in Torgau, xxi.
13. Bach's books were listed in the inventory of his estate. See BDok II, no. 627; NBR, no. 279.
14. See Marissen 2021.
15. Kircher 1650, part 2, 366. See also Snyder 2002, 1–3.
16. Praetorius 1619, part 3, 88, quoting the Italian organist and theorist Girolamo Diruta.
17. Snyder 2007, 87. Upon returning to Lübeck, Buxtehude lobbied with the church directors to hire Schnitger to renovate the main organ in St. Mary's Church. Schnitger subsequently made visits to Lübeck in 1689 and 1702 to see the instrument and make written proposals, which were not accepted by the directors.
18. The organ in St. Michael's was destroyed by fire in 1750; the organs in St. Nicholas and St. Peter's perished in the Great Town Fire of 1842.
19. Bach's Obituary was completed shortly after his death in 1750 by his son Carl Philipp Emanuel Bach and his student Johann Friedrich Agricola but first published in 1754 by Lorenz Christoph Mizler in his periodical *Musikalische Bibliothek* (Leipzig: Im Mizlerischen Bücher-Verlag, 1754), 158–176.
20. Snyder 2002, 10.

21. Friedrich 2000, 62–64.

22. Fock 1974, 57.

23. Edskes 2016, 40.

24. William Carr, *Remarks of the Government of severall Parts of Germanie, Denmark, Sweedland, Hamburg, Lubeck, and Hansiatique Townes . . . with some few directions how to Travell in the States Dominions* (Amsterdam, 1688), 157–158, as quoted in Snyder 2017, 107.

25. Friedrich 2000, 62.

26. Golon 2016, xxv.

27. Stahl, 1942.

28. Wolff and Zepf 2012. The Gera instrument was destroyed by fire in 1780, but the two Trost instruments survive, with their Flöte dolce stops intact. The wooden pipes of the Waltershausen stop are pictured in Friedrich 1989, 204.

29. The classic study of Bach's handwriting is Georg von Dadelsen, *Beiträge zur Chronologie der Werke Johann Sebastian Bachs* (Trossingen: Hohner-Verlag, 1958), updated by Yoshitake Kobayashi in NBA XI/2 (*Die Notenschrift Johann Sebastian Bachs*; 1989). The classic study of the watermarks of the papers used by Bach is Wisso Weiss, NBA IX/1 (*Katalog der Wasserzeichen in Bachs Originalhandschriften*, 1985). The dates given here are those presented in BWV[3] and Bach digital.

30. See the eighteenth-century illustrations of copperplate engraving and copper-plate printing shops in the Leupold Edition, vol. 8, xx.

31. Stauffer 2010, 50–51.

32. Telemann used a variety of publishers in Frankfurt, Hamburg, and Paris for his chamber and keyboard works; Handel used John Walsh in London for his chamber and keyboard works; and Vivaldi used Estienne Roger in Amsterdam for his concerto publications.

33. *The Letters of C. P. E. Bach*, Stephen Clark, ed. and trs. (Oxford: Oxford University Press, 1997), no. 287. See discussion in Wolff 2020, 18.

34. Item 5, "A lot of free preludes, fugues, and similar pieces for organ, with obbligato pedal," and Item 7, "Many preludes on chorales for the organ." NBR, no. 306.

35. The autographs of "Nun komm, der Heiden Heiland," BWV 660a, Concerto in D Minor (after Vivaldi), BWV 596, Prelude and Fugue in G Major, BWV 541, Prelude and Fugue in B Minor, BWV 544, and Prelude and Fugue in E Minor, BWV 548.

36. Johann Christian Bach, allegedly his father's favorite, received "three claviers and a set of pedals" before his father's death, and the autograph score of the Prelude and Fugue in B Minor, BWV 544, and possibly those of the Toccata in E Major, BWV 566, and Prelude and Fugue in G Major, BWV 541, as well (see NBA IV/5–6, KB [Dietrich Kilian, ed., 1978], 223). But if he had received the bulk of the organ works, he probably would have left the scores with his brother Carl Philipp Emanuel when he departed from Berlin for Italy in 1754, and Emanuel most likely would have preserved the materials.

37. At one point Friedemann offered the entire set of scores to Johann Nicolaus Forkel, who could not afford the proposed price. Forkel stated that Friedemann later sold them for a much smaller amount "out of necessity." See NBR, no. 392d.

38. On this point see NBA IV/5–6, KB, 224–227.
39. Berlin State Library, *Mus.ms. 40644*, and Leipzig Town Library, Becker Collection, *III.8.4*. The most important studies of the two albums are NBA IV/5–6, KB, 180–183; Schulze, 1984, 30–56; and Hill 1987. A handy summary of the albums' contents is given in Zehnder 2009, 343–344 and 348–349.
40. The most important studies of the three manuscripts are Zietz 1969 and Daw 1976.
41. Bach rated Johann Ludwig Krebs as one of his best pupils and is reputed to have said: "Es sei in einem Bach nur ein Krebs gefangen worden"—there is only one crab caught in the brook). See Forkel 1802, 43.
42. Leipzig Town Library, *Peters Ms. 7* and *Peters Ms. 8*. The most important studies of the Mempell-Preller collection are Schulze 1974; Schulze 1984, 69–88; and Synofzik 2001.
43. Synofzik 2001, 51–52 and 64.
44. The most important studies of Kellner and his Bach manuscripts are Stinson 1990, Stinson 1992, and Claus 1999.
45. Berlin State Library, *P 274*, fascicle 2.
46. The classic study of Bach's students is Löffler 1953. Löffler's findings and research carried out more recently are summarized in Koska 2019.
47. Although Vogler studied organ with Bach in Arnstadt and Weimar, his copies of the organ works appear to date from c. 1729. See Schulze 1984, 66–69.
48. Kayser seems to have remained in contact with Bach after concluding his studies around 1725 and continued to obtain copies of new works. See Talle 2003, 155–168.
49. Wollny 2018, 82.
50. This unidentified copyist, termed "Anonymous X" in this book for the sake of discussion, seems to have studied with Bach, whose hand appears in his copy of the Prelude and Fugue in G Minor, BWV 535 (Leipzig Town Library, Becker Collection, *III.8.7*). Anonymous X's copies also include an important transitional version of "Allein Gott in der Höh sei Ehr," BWV 664a, and Bach's final version of the Partita on "Sei gegrüßet, Jesu gütig," BWV 768. His manuscripts are preserved mainly in the Becker Collection of the Leipzig Town Library. See Wollny, 2013, 157–158.
51. The best summary of Kittel's manuscript copies of Bach's organ works is NBA IV/5–6, KB, 208–217.
52. According to a letter written by Johann Wolfgang von Goethe to Carl Friedrich Zelter on May 5, 1816, it perished in a fire at the home of J. H. F. Schütz in Bad Berka. See NBA IV/5–6, KB, 210.
53. The most important studies of Scholz and his Bach manuscripts are NBA IV/5–6, KB, 159–160, and Blanken 2013a.
54. BDok III, no. 824. Breitkopf's role in the dissemination of Bach's early chorale settings is discussed in May 1974, May 1996, and Blanken 2019.
55. The Bach holdings of the Royal Library are discussed and cataloged in Leisinger and Wollny 1997.
56. Berlin State Library, *Am.B. 72a* and its copy *Am.B. 72*, which contain the so-called Kirnberger Chorales.
57. The most important of these scribes can be identified by their handwriting only and are known in Bach scholarship as Anonymous 301 and Anonymous 303, working

in Berlin with C. P. E. Bach, and Anonymous 401, working in Berlin for Kirnberger at the Library of Princess Anna Amalia. See Paul Kast, *Die Bach-Handschriften der Berliner Staatsbibliothek* (Trossingen: Hohner-Verlag, 1958), 139.

58. The classic studies of the manuscripts and scribes of Anna Amalia's collection are Eva Renate Blechschmidt, *Die Amalien-Bibliothek* (Berlin: Merseburger Verlag, 1965), and Eva Renate Wutta, *Quellen der Bach-Tradition in der Berliner Amalien-Bibliothek* (Tutzing: Schneider, 1989). A number of the anonymous scribes cited in these volumes have since been identified and listed with the appropriate manuscripts on Bach digital.

59. Krumbach 1985 and Wolff 1991d.

60. The most important appraisal of the Peters Edition is found in NBA IV/5–6, KB, 261–267.

61. A summary of the Körner editions is given in NBA IV/5–6, KB, 257–260.

PART I

LEARNING THE CRAFT

Eisenach, Ohrdruf, Lüneburg, and Weimar (1685–1703)

The love of our little Johann Sebastian for music was uncommonly great, even at this tender age. In a short time he had fully mastered all the pieces his brother had voluntarily given him to learn.

—Obituary of 1750

1

The Young Bach

Eisenach (1685–1695)

We know relatively little about Johann Sebastian Bach's first decade. He was born in Eisenach on March 21, 1685, as the last child of Johann Ambrosius Bach and his wife, Maria Elisabeth, née Lämmerhirt. The Bachs had eight children altogether, four of whom lived to maturity: Johann Christoph (1671–1721), Marie Salome (1677–1728), Johann Jacob (1682–1722), and Johann Sebastian. The name "Johann" was ubiquitous in Thuringia at the time, bestowed in honor of John the Baptist and John the Apostle. "Sebastian," on the other hand, was unusual. In this case it stemmed from Sebastian Nagel, head town piper in Gotha, who served as a godfather at Bach's baptism.

Bach's father, Johann Ambrosius (1645–1695), was also a town piper, working first in Arnstadt and Erfurt before being appointed town music director in Eisenach. The Bach clan was filled with organists, town pipers, music directors, and other such positions—so much so that in Thuringia the name "Bach" became synonymous with "musician." By being born a Bach, Johann Sebastian was preordained to become a musician, as were his brothers—Johann Christoph went on to serve as organist in Ohrdruf and Johann Jacob as oboist in the royal guard of King Charles XII of Sweden. Johann Ambrosius assumed his Eisenach post in 1671 and was soon able to purchase a large house on Fleischgasse with sufficient space to accommodate his family as well as several apprentices, which was customary in the town piper tradition.[1]

Living in the house, Johann Sebastian would have observed the demanding duties of a town piper firsthand, as his father composed new works, prepared performance parts, and led rehearsals for church and town performances. More events were added to this busy schedule in 1672, when Duke Johann Georg I established residency in Eisenach, making it the capital of an independent principality and a center of cultural life. From that point onward, Ambrosius served as a member of the court ensemble as well as head town musician. He was supported in his work by the apprentices living in the house, but he surely turned to his sons as well for help with menial tasks once they reached the age of eight or so.

Johann Sebastian probably attended one of the eight German schools in Eisenach before enrolling in St. George's Latin School, a small but prominent institution devoted to providing a classical Latin/Lutheran education. The

J. S. BACH. George B. Stauffer, Oxford University Press. © Oxford University Press 2024.
DOI: 10.1093/oso/9780195108026.003.0002

academic curriculum included grammar studies in German and Latin and religious instruction taught through biblical passages, the hymnal, and Luther's Large and Small Catechisms. It is likely that Bach sang in the school choir, which performed regularly at church and town functions and occasionally at court events, too. The Eisenach hymnal of the time contained the texts—but not the music—of 612 chorales.[2] Thus Bach started learning a large body of chorale melodies by ear at a very early age.[3]

There is no evidence that Bach studied organ as a young child in Eisenach. He was undoubtedly inspired by an attractive role model, however, in the form of his father's first cousin, Johann Christoph Bach (1642–1703), who served as town and court organist. Johann Christoph was in charge of the organs in Eisenach's three main churches, including the large three-manual instrument in St. George's Church that dated from 1576 and was in constant need of repair.[4] This would have given the young Johann Sebastian the opportunity not only to hear Johann Christoph perform but also to see the interior of an organ and explore its intricate maze of pipes and machinery—knowledge that formed the basis of his lifelong interest in organ construction and design. Johann Christoph's hopes for a thorough renovation and expansion of the St. George organ were finally realized in 1698, when a contract was signed with organ builder Georg Christoph Stertzing. The completed instrument (IV/58) was the largest in Thuringia, but the work was not finished until 1707, four years after Johann Christoph's death and long after Johann Sebastian's departure from Eisenach.

Johann Ambrosius was a skilled violinist rather than keyboard player, and it is probable that he taught Johann Sebastian the fundamentals of violin playing, which helped him win his first position as a court musician in Weimar 10 years later. The valuable seventeenth-century Stainer violin Bach owned at the time of his death may have been inherited from his father.[5] Also formative in Bach's first decade was the local aura of Martin Luther. Luther attended St. George's Latin School in Eisenach as a young boy, and it was in the Wartburg Castle overlooking the town that he translated the New Testament from Greek into German in the winter of 1521–1522. The foundation of Bach's great admiration for Luther and his Reformation chorales was undoubtedly laid during the Eisenach years.

Bach's mother died in May 1694, and within seven months his father married Barbara Margaretha Bartholomaei, née Keul, who was already twice widowed, including a first marriage to Johann Ambrosius's cousin, Johann Günther Bach, organist and instrument-maker in Arnstadt. In February 1695 Ambrosius himself passed away, leaving Barbara Margaretha a widow once again, after just three months of marriage, and the Bach family in a precarious state. Bach's sister returned to her mother's relatives in Erfurt, the Lämmerhirts, and Johann Jacob and Johann Sebastian were entrusted to their older brother Johann Christoph, who was already working as organist of St. Michael's Church in Ohrdruf. If Johann Ambrosius had lived longer, Bach might have followed in his footsteps and become a town piper. But under the tutelage of his brother Johann Christoph he moved in a different direction—that of becoming an organist and clavier player.

Ohrdruf (1695–1700)

The Obituary of 1750 describes Bach's time in Ohrdruf this way:[6] "Johann Sebastian was not yet ten years old when he found himself bereft of his parents by death. He betook himself to Ohrdruf, where his eldest brother, Johann Christoph, was Organist, and under his brother's guidance he laid the foundations for his playing of the clavier."[7]

Johann Christoph had left the family household, one year after Johann Sebastian's birth, to study organ and clavier with Pachelbel in Erfurt (see chapter 2). Following the traditional manner of training for organists, Christoph remained with Pachelbel for three years before entering the profession. He served briefly as organist of St. Thomas Church in Erfurt and then assisted his uncle Johann Heinrich Bach in Arnstadt; he finally won the organist position of St. Michael's Church in Ohrdruf in 1690.

Johann Sebastian attended the Lyceum in Ohrdruf, where he studied Christian doctrine, Latin and Greek, and Roman biographies as part of the Latin school's rigorous curriculum. He also sang in the school choir under the direction of Elias Herda, a capable cantor who led the ensemble in performances of choral repertoire that included sixteenth- and seventeenth-century Latin and German motets from printed collections and probably concerted music by local composers such as Wolfgang Carl Briegel from Gotha, Andreas Christian Dedekind from Eisenach, and several Bachs: Johannes, Heinrich, Johann Christoph (the Eisenach organist), and Johann Michael (Bach's future father-in-law).[8] The young Johann Sebastian did well in his academic studies and must have excelled in the choir as well, given his later acceptance into St. Michael's School in Lüneburg as a chorister. He remained at the Ohrdruf Lyceum until the midwinter of 1700, when the lack of scholarship funds forced him to leave before completing the final two years of work in the *prima* class.

The traditional method of keyboard training in Bach's time called for students first to copy and then to study and play instructive pieces from the existing repertoire, all under the guidance of an experienced player. We will examine Johann Christoph's pedagogical approach in detail in the next chapter, but his younger brother's general desire to learn during his Ohrdruf years can be sensed from an anecdote passed down in the Obituary:

> The love of our little Johann Sebastian for music was uncommonly great even at this tender age. In a short time he had fully mastered all the pieces his brother had voluntarily given him to learn. But his brother possessed a book of clavier pieces by the most famous masters of the day—Froberger, Kerll, Pachelbel—and this, despite all his pleading and for who knows what reason, was denied him. His zeal to improve himself thereupon gave him the idea of practicing the following innocent deceit. This book was kept in a cabinet whose doors consisted only of grillwork. Now, with his little hands he could reach through the grillwork and take up the book (for it had only a paper cover). Accordingly, he would fetch the book out at night, when everyone had gone to bed and, since he was not even possessed of a light, copy it by moonlight. In six months' time he had these musical spoils in his own hands. Secretly and with extraordinary eagerness he was trying to put it to use, when his brother, to his great dismay, found out about it, and without mercy took away from him the copy he had made with such pains. . . . He did not recover the book until after the death of his brother.[9]

The tale of the "Moonlight Manuscript," which surely stemmed from Bach himself, underscores his early zeal for keyboard playing and his exposure to works that went beyond local fare. Carl Philipp Emanuel Bach said later that the training his father received in Ohrdruf "may well have been designed for an organist and nothing more."[10] That may be, but it planted the seed of Bach's lifelong passion for the organ and organ music and provided a strong foundation for the talents he was soon to develop much further.

Lüneburg (1700–1702)

In March 1700, shortly after leaving the Ohrdruf Lyceum, Bach and an older schoolmate, Georg Erdmann, set out for Lüneburg in North Germany, having obtained scholarships to attend St. Michael's School there. Bach's decision to leave Thuringia at age 15 and finish his *prima* studies was unusual. Normally a member of the Bach family would have remained in Thuringia, abandoned academic work, and commenced training for a music position—the path taken by his two brothers. Bach's departure from the normal career trajectory probably stemmed from a combination of factors: his determination to complete Latin school at all costs, his desire to become acquainted firsthand with North German organ music, and his wish to be within traveling distance of Hamburg, with its monumental organs and cosmopolitan music culture.

The path to the St. Michael's School in Lüneburg was probably cleared by Elias Herda, Bach's cantor in Ohrdruf and a St. Michael's alumnus. The school was a distinguished institution, offering a broader range of academic subjects than the Ohrdruf Lyceum, including religion, logic, rhetoric, mathematics, physics, and German literature. Bach sang in the school chorus as part of his scholarship, performing as a soprano in the top ensemble, the Matins Choir, until his voice changed at age 15 or 16.[11] As the Obituary describes it:

> In Lüneburg, our Bach, because of his uncommonly fine soprano voice, was well received. Some time thereafter, as he was singing in the choir, and without his knowledge or will, there was once heard, with the soprano tone that he had to execute, the lower octave of the same. He kept this quite new species of voice for eight days, during which he could neither speak nor sing except in octaves. Thereupon he lost his soprano tones and with them his fine voice.[12]

The Matins Choir provided music for Vespers on Saturdays and Matins and the main service on Sundays. The group was led by Cantor August Braun, a seasoned musician who was able to draw on a rich choral library that included more than 1,000 works[13]—a resource equal at the time to the well-known choral collection of the St. Thomas School in Leipzig.

It has long been conjectured that Bach also studied organ with Georg Böhm, organist of St. John's Church in Lüneburg. Bach never claimed Böhm as a teacher, but as Philipp Spitta first pointed out, Bach's early compositions show the strong influence of Böhm's style,[14] and Bach later turned to Böhm to serve as a northern agent for the sale of Partitas 2 and 3 of Clavier-Übung I. When C.P.E. Bach listed the composers his father had heard and studied, he initially described Böhm as "his teacher" rather than "the Lüneburg organist,"[15] a slip that shows his uncertainty about the relationship. Evidence of a direct tie between Bach and Böhm during the Lüneburg years was finally confirmed in 2005 with the sensational discovery of a tablature copy of Johann Adam Reincken's "An Wasserflüssen Babylon" in Bach's youthful hand. It concludes with the colophon "written down at the home of Georg Böhm in Lüneburg, 1700" (plate 1-1).[16]

Böhm was born and raised in Thuringia before moving to North Germany, and as a fellow Thuringian he surely took Bach under his wing at the very least, providing him with access to northern works in his music library and perhaps opening doors for him in Hamburg, too. At the time Böhm lived directly opposite the St. Michael's Monastery.[17] This would have made it convenient for Bach to drop by for advice, encouragement, and copying music—and perhaps for composition lessons as well.

The organ in St. John's Church was in a poor state of repair at the time of Bach's stay. It lacked the large pedal towers and supplementary stops that were added

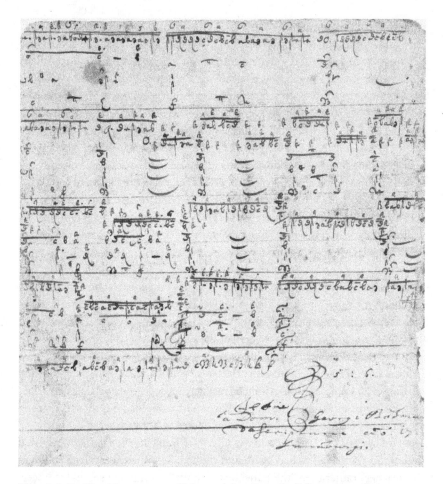

Plate 1-1 Bach's tablature copy of Johann Adam Reincken's Fantasia on "An Wasserflüssen Babylon." The colophon states that it was written in Georg Böhm's home in 1700, when Bach was 15.
Klassik Stiftung Weimar

in 1712–1715 by Mathias Dropa at Böhm's request. It was nevertheless a sizable instrument (III/28) that had been expanded little by little after its installation in 1551–1553 by the Netherlander Hendrik Niehoff and Jasper Johansen,[18] and it would have provided Bach with the opportunity to try the contrasting colors available on a sizeable North German organ in the lush acoustics of a Gothic hall church.[19] Its Rückpositiv included an 8' Regal, 8' Baarpfeiffe, and 4' Schalmey—exotic stops unknown in Ohrdruf.

The Obituary also states that Bach heard the French manner of playing at performances given by the instrumental band of the Duke of Celle, and that he traveled to Hamburg now and then to hear Reincken play the organ at St. Catherine's Church. Böhm may have been helpful with the Hamburg visits, since before moving to Lüneburg he appears to have performed in the orchestra of the Gänsemarkt Opera,[20] an institution with which Reincken was involved as a founder and board member. The organ in St. Catherine's (IV/58) was the third largest instrument in North Germany and was lovingly cared for by Reincken, who is said to have tuned the reed stops himself.[21] Bach returned to play the instrument in 1720 and afterward praised the clarity of its 32' pedal stops (Principal and Groß-Posaun) and Reincken's fastidious tuning of its 15 reed registers.[22] That Bach took repeated trips to Hamburg during his Lüneburg stay suggests that he may have visited the large organs in the town's four other principal churches as well. Each instrument had more than 50 stops (see the introduction).

Bach graduated from St. Michael's school in the spring of 1702, and in late September he competed for the organist position at St. James' Church in Sangerhausen. He won the vote of the Town Council, but their decision was overruled by the reigning duke, Johann Georg of Weißenfels, who appointed Johann Augustin Kobelius instead. Kobelius was eleven years older than Bach and an experienced performer and composer trained in Italy and Weißenfels, where he had served as a member of the court *capelle*. Still, Bach's playing must have greatly impressed the council, and we can only assume that by the age of 17, with experience in North Germany under his belt, the young Johann Sebastian was already a stunning performer on the organ.

Weimar (1702–1703)

After the thwarted attempt to win the organist position in Sangerhausen, Bach worked for a short time at the Weimar Court, hired by Duke Johann Ernst III (1664–1707), the younger brother of Duke Wilhelm Ernst (1662–1728). The two dukes ruled in an awkward coregency (see chapter 7), yet they were both deeply committed to enriching court life with musical activities. Bach's official position was "Lackey," the term used in the court account books, though he himself later referred to his employment as that of a "court musician."[23] The job probably combined playing in the court ensemble as violinist, violist, or continuo keyboardist with carrying out menial domestic tasks. He received quarterly salary payments at the beginning of March and June, implying that he worked at the court approximately six months, from late December 1702 through June 1703.

Bach may have obtained his appointment with the help of Weimar court organist Johann Effler (c. 1635–1711), who had various connections with the Bach family. Effler preceded Johann Michael Bach in Gehren and followed Johannes Bach in Erfurt, where he worked with Johann Christian Bach.[24] In Weimar he was to be succeeded by a Bach once again—Johann Sebastian in 1708. Effler was knowledgeable about organ building, serving as consultant for the Collegiate Church in Jena,[25] and he may have imparted some of this knowledge to his new young colleague at the court. A second critical figure in Weimar at the time was Johann Paul von Westhoff (1656–1705), a virtuoso violinist whose two volumes of unaccompanied violin suites, published in 1682 and 1696,[26] later served as models for Bach's solo violin sonatas and partitas, BWV 1001–1006.

We know no more than this about Bach's brief first stay in Weimar. We can be certain that he did not languish, however, for when the opportunity for a full-time organist position arose again, this time in Arnstadt, he was well prepared for success (see chapter 4). But first we must look at the specific works Bach took as models during his journeyman years, and his own initial efforts at composition.

Notes

1. The house, located at the current site of Lutherstraße 35, no longer exists. The present Johann Ambrosius Bach House, at Ritterstraße 11, is the building in which Ambrosius and his family lived from 1671 to 1674. The present Bach House, at Frauenplan 21, is a museum with instruments, manuscripts, and other artifacts from Bach's time. It was never occupied by the Bach family.
2. *Neues vollständiges Eisenachisches Gesangbuch* (Eisenach: Rörer, 1673). See *Eisenacher Dokumente um Sebastian Bach*, Conrad Freyse, ed. (Leipzig: Neue Bachgesellschaft, 1933), XXXIII/2, 139.
3. Many of the chorale melodies in the Orgel-Büchlein do not line up perfectly with versions printed in contemporary hymnals. Bach may have been citing them from memory, perhaps introducing small variants in the process (see chapter 8).
4. Wolff and Zepf 2012, 20.
5. In the Specification of Bach's estate, the Stainer violin was appraised to be worth four times as much as Bach's second violin (8 taler versus 2 taler). NBR, no. 279.
6. NBR, no. 306.
7. The Obituary is the most important early account of Bach's life and works. It was written toward the end of 1750 by his son Carl Philipp Emanuel and Johann Friedrich Agricola, one of Bach's most eminent students, and published in 1754 by Lorenz Christoph Mizler in his periodical *Musicalische Bibliothek*. C.P.E. is credited with writing the biographical portion and Agricola with writing the general evaluation of Bach's achievements. Mizler added a few sentences at the end. On the division of writing duties see Wolff 2020, 7–8.
8. Wolff 2000, 43.
9. NBR, no. 306.
10. NBR, no. 395.
11. In Bach's time, boys' voices changed at a later age than they do today, sometimes as late as 17 or 18. The accelerated physical maturation of children in modern times

is attributed to better diet. See Herbert Moller, "Voice Change in Human Biological Development," *Journal of Interdisciplinary History* 16, no. 2 (Autumn 1985), 239–253.

12. NBR, no. 306.
13. Max Seiffert, "Die Chorbibliothek der Michaelisschule in Lüneburg zu Seb. Bach's Zeit," in *Sammelbände der Internationalen Musikgesellschaft* 9 (1907–8), 593–621.
14. Spitta 1873–80, vol. 1, 210–217.
15. NBR, no. 395.
16. Maul and Wollny 2007, xxvii–xxx.
17. Böhm lived at Neue Sülze 8 from 1699 to 1711. He later moved to Papenstrasse 13, where he died. The Papenstrasse residence still exists and is marked with a plaque. See Marshall and Marshall 2016, 26.
18. Wolff and Zepf 2012, 64–65.
19. A so-called *Hallenkirche*, with nave and side aisles of approximately equal height.
20. Zehnder 1988, 80.
21. NBR, no. 358a. The organ in St. Catherine's was destroyed in World War II, but sample pipes from many ranks were saved and subsequently used as the basis for the remarkably faithful reconstruction of the instrument carried out by Flentrop Orgelbouw in 2008–2013.
22. As reported by Bach's student Johann Friedrich Agricola in his annotations to Jacob Adlung's *Musica mechanica organoedi* of 1768. NBR, no. 358. On Bach's 1720 visit to St. Catherine's see chapter 14 here.
23. In the genealogy that he drew up in 1735. NBR, no. 303.
24. Jauernig 1950a, 69.
25. Maul 2004, 160. The church was destroyed in World War II.
26. *Erstes Dutzend Allemanden, Couranten, Sarabanden und Giguen Violino Solo sonder Passo Continuo* (Dresden, 1682 and 1696).

2

Study and Models

Bach himself said very little about his early studies. To his friend and colleague Johann Gottfried Walther, author of the *Musicalisches Lexicon*, he seems to have mentioned only that he "learned the first principles of clavier playing from his eldest brother, Mr. Johann Christoph Bach, formerly organist and schoolmaster at Ohrdruf."[1] The same bare description appeared in the Obituary of 1750.

A quarter of a century later, Bach's son Carl Philipp Emanuel elaborated further on his father's training, telling the biographer Johann Nicolaus Forkel that "besides Froberger, Kerll, and Pachelbel"—the composers linked to the "Moonlight Manuscript" his father copied in secret as a boy—"he heard and studied the works of Frescobaldi, the Baden Capellmeister Fischer, Strunk, some old and good Frenchmen, Buxtehude, Reincken, Bruhns, and the Lüneburg organist Böhm."[2] Emanuel minimized the formal instruction his father received in Ohrdruf and portrayed him instead as essentially self-taught, saying "the departed formed his taste through his own effort." But as Alfred Dürr aptly expressed it when discussing the Neumeister Chorales, "no great composer falls out of the sky fully formed."[3] By the age of 18, Bach was an impressive organist and knowledgeable organ consultant, able to win the confidence of church officials in Sangerhausen and Arnstadt. This must have stemmed from intensive study during his youthful years in Ohrdruf and Lüneburg.

Ohrdruf: Johann Christoph Bach and Thuringian Circles

Unfortunately, we know relatively little about the musical skills of Bach's first keyboard teacher, his brother Johann Christoph Bach (1671–1721). There were two other prominent Johann Christophs in the Bach clan at the time—Johann Christoph Bach (1642–1703), organist in Eisenach, and Johann Christoph Bach (1673–1727), cantor in Gehren—and the surviving works passed down under the name "Johann Christoph Bach" or simply "J.C.B." do not stipulate which of the three individuals was the composer. Hence it is difficult to pinpoint which pieces might have been written by Bach's brother.

That said, the training and accomplishments of the Ohrdruf organist Johann Christoph Bach suggest that he was a skilled and well-respected musician.[4] He studied for three years in Erfurt with Johann Pachelbel, who was generally

J. S. BACH. George B. Stauffer, Oxford University Press. © Oxford University Press 2024.
DOI: 10.1093/oso/9780195108026.003.0003

recognized as the foremost keyboard teacher in Central Germany. Pachelbel's students included Nicolaus Vetter, Johann Heinrich Buttstett, Johann Conrad Rosenbusch, and other successful organists, who loyally championed his works and compositional style after his death.

Johann Christoph's training would have included the opportunity to hear Pachelbel's annual recitals in the Prediger Church on St. John's Day, an event to which the entire congregation was invited. As noted in the introduction, Pachelbel was required by contract to observe the anniversary of his employment by demonstrating his professional progress in a half-hour recital at the end of the St. John's Day service, using the entire resources of the organ in "delightful and euphonious harmony."[5] This was one of the most important music events in Thuringia at the time and an opportunity to see and hear some of the most artful organ playing in Central Germany.

After studying with Pachelbel, Johann Christoph attained the organist position at St. Michael's Church in Ohrdruf in 1690 at the age of 18, and in his very first year he was entrusted with overseeing the renovation of the Rückpositiv division of the organ. His letter to the Town Council concerning the repairs shows that he already had a firm grasp of organ construction—much like his younger brother Johann Sebastian in Mühlhausen, many years later:

> It is my obedient duty, in constant anticipation of things that should not go unreported, that the organ builder, with dispatch, is almost finished with the contracted 16' Principal Bass, and that it should be made known next that the Rückpositiv, which is of great help to me in making music as well as to the entire instrument itself, stands, alas, in a fully deteriorated state—so much so that it is completely unusable. However, it could be repaired for a very small commission, and the organ builder could carry out this work while he is here, with little effort and limited cost.[6]

The council accepted the renovation proposal, and upon completion of the project, Pachelbel was commissioned to inspect and approve the work. Two years later Johann Christoph was offered Pachelbel's post of town organist in Gotha when Pachelbel decided to return to his native Nuremberg. The Ohrdruf Town Council responded by making Johann Christoph a counteroffer of increased salary and amenities. He took the offer and remained in Ohrdruf the rest of his life. At the time of his death, he was described in the funeral register as "optimus artifex" (a first-rate artist).[7] All of this points to an accomplished organist whose talents were recognized and rewarded.

No teaching materials survive from Johann Sebastian's study with his brother. It is reasonable to assume that Johann Christoph used the same pedagogical method as his famous teacher, however, and we can gain a good idea of that approach from the tablature book of Johann Valentine Eckelt (1673–1732), who studied briefly with Pachelbel in Erfurt in 1690. The tablature book consists of 73 pieces divided into six parts. When viewed as a whole, it reflects Eckelt's work with Pachelbel as well as his zeal to supplement the instruction with additional material:[8]

Section 1   8 works studied with Pachelbel.

Section 2   5 works by Pachelbel, purchased from Pachelbel.

Section 3   2 capriccios by Johann Jacob Froberger, obtained from "Wunderlescher"(?).

Section 4   22 works obtained from "Krompholtz, who studied them with Pachelbel."

Section 5   11 works obtained from Nicolaus Vetter, another Pachelbel student.

Section 6   25 works, including study pieces that appear to be Eckelt's compositions.

Sections 1, 2, and 4 demonstrate Pachelbel's teaching method. Sections 1 and 4, containing music studied with Pachelbel, consist of short, illustrative examples of the main keyboard genres of the time: prelude, fantasia, toccata, fugue, and chorale prelude. They were composed mostly by Pachelbel, Pachelbel's teacher Georg Caspar Wecker, and Johann Krieger, a Central German composer known especially for his keyboard fugues and ricercars. Many of these works consist of no more than 10 or 20 measures and seem geared toward instruction rather than performance. Interspersed with these pieces are more substantial works by Froberger: a canzona, two fantasias, and a toccata, as well as a canzona and ricercar from Froberger's printed collections of 1649 and 1656. Froberger's multisectional toccatas were as striking as Buxtehude's later multi-sectional praeludia. Also present is a short duo from Guillaume-Gabriel Nivers' *Livre d'orgue* of 1665. The special works in section 2 purchased from Pachelbel consist of three fugues, a toccata, and a ciaccona. Like the Froberger pieces, they stand apart from the shorter compositions and were probably intended as *exempla classica*—classic examples of their genres.[9]

What would the young Johann Sebastian have learned from such material, which was surely used for instruction by his brother Johann Christoph? He would have been introduced to the principal genres then in use in Central and South Germany as well as the meters, tempos, forms, and figurations associated with each. From Pachelbel's compositions, in particular, he would have been presented with examples of clear, carefully crafted counterpoint in three and four parts.

This can be seen, for instance, in the exposition of Pachelbel's Fugue in C Major, one of the purchased pieces (example 2-1). Here an attractive, well-rounded

Example 2-1 Johann Pachelbel, Fugue in C Major: opening exposition.

subject begins with 16th notes, decelerates to a dotted quarter note and 8th note, and concludes with 16th notes that include a 32nd-note "kick." Harmonically, the subject resolves fully in C major only at the end, giving it a dynamic forward thrust. In measure 3 the slow rhythmic movement of the dotted quarter note and 8th note in the tonal answer is accelerated slightly by the ♪♫♩ figure in the countersubject. In measure 4 the third entry of the subject is sharpened by the dissonant suspension in the alto and the syncopation in the soprano. In measure 5 the dotted quarter note and 8th note of the subject are enlivened further by a stream of 16th notes in the alto. And in measure 6, a continuous pulse of 16th notes is produced by distributing the motion among the parts. Measure 6 concludes with an 8th note, however, to prepare for the final entry of the subject, which has been delayed by a measure to create suspense. In this compact exposition, the prescribed dux-comes entries of the fugue subject are enhanced by the increasingly prominent participation of the accompanying voices. There was much to be learned from the close scrutiny of such passages.

Pachelbel's habit of ending fugues with an entry of the subject in the lowest register of the bass is also evident in the C-Major Fugue:[10] the work concludes with a bass entry that descends for the first time to the very bottom of the keyboard, the note C. This, too, was not lost on Bach, who later adopted it to great effect in several *pedaliter* organ fugues.[11]

From exposure to such works the young Bach also would have learned the art of cantabile composition, which was at the heart of Pachelbel's keyboard idiom. As Pachelbel's student Johann Heinrich Buttstett expressed it: "One should write in a cantabile style. This rule I received almost forty years ago from my teacher, the famous Pachelbel, who in turn learned it from his teacher Wecker in Nuremberg, and so forth and so on, from one generation to the next."[12] According to Walther, "cantabile" referred to "a composition, whether set for voices or instruments, in which all parts and sections have a singing quality."[13]

With Pachelbel's music, this effect is achieved by several factors: even note motion, smooth part-writing, motivic consistency, and sonorous harmony.[14] Bach eventually adopted these qualities in his own keyboard compositions after he moved beyond the drama and extravagance of the North German school. The heritage of Pachelbel can be seen in the Inventions and Sinfonias, BWV 772–801, which Bach claimed would teach keyboard players "allermeisten aber eine *cantable* Art im Spielen zu erlangen"[15]—above all, to acquire a singing style in playing. Pachelbel's contract in Erfurt stipulated that works performed be written out rather than improvised (the more common approach to producing service music at the time).[16] This resulted in a very detailed, carefully calculated idiom—another trait bequeathed to Bach.

The Eckelt album focuses on free works and contains only a handful of chorale settings, found mostly in the material obtained from Vetter. Either there once existed a second Eckelt tablature book devoted to chorale preludes, or Pachelbel felt that this skill could be developed later, after a student had mastered the fundamental rules of free composition. Johann Christoph must have introduced his brother to the art of chorale preluding, since the earliest layer of settings in the Neumeister Collection shows that the young Sebastian was quite familiar with Central German traditions (see chapter 3). The most important Central German genres of organ chorales were the chorale fughetta, a manual setting in which the first phrase of the chorale melody is used as the basis for a short fugue, and the fore-imitation chorale, in which each phrase of the chorale melody, normally presented in long notes in the soprano or bass, is foreshadowed by a web of imitative polyphony in smaller note values in the accompanying voices. Pachelbel brought both types of settings to a high state of refinement.[17]

Pachelbel's skill is apparent, for instance, in "Wenn wir in höchsten Nöten sein," a three-part fore-imitation setting in the cantabile style. The fore-imitation begins mostly in slow, stately quarter notes before moving smoothly to quarter and 8th notes (m. 4; example 2-2) and then to syncopations (m. 6). This gradual increase in rhythmic activity prepares the way for chorale melody (m. 7), which appears as a serene half-note cantus firmus in the soprano. The rhythmic pulse of the accompaniment increases further during the first phrase of the cantus

Example 2-2 Pachelbel, "Wenn wir in höchsten Nöten sein": first phrase of the chorale and final measures.

firmus, with the introduction of the figure ♪♫ (m. 9), a much-beloved Central German rhythmic motive called a *corta*,[18] and a final group of four 16th notes (m. 12) that anticipates the 16th-note motion that eventually dominates the setting. Also significant is the nuanced way a fourth voice is introduced in the last two measures of the setting (mm. 37–38) to achieve a graceful thickening of sonority. Bach's own arrangement of this melody in his "death-bed chorale," "Vor deinen Thron tret ich hiermit," BWV 668, displays similar fore-imitation, rhythmic acceleration, and increase in texture at the end. It would seem that for Bach, the lessons learned from Pachelbel were lifelong.

While living in Ohrdruf, Bach was also influenced by the music of two other members of the Bach family, the Eisenach organist Johann Christoph Bach and the Gehren organist Johann Michael Bach, both sons of Johann Heinrich Bach in Arnstadt. Bach later termed the first "a profound composer" and the second "like his brother, an able composer,"[19] and he preserved vocal works of both in the Old

Bach Archive he assembled in the 1730s.[20] Bach later married Johann Michael's orphaned daughter, Maria Barbara.

The keyboard works of Johann Christoph remain elusive, for the reasons mentioned earlier, but the Obituary of 1750 states that "his writing was, so far as the taste of his day permitted, *galant* and *cantabile* as well as remarkably polyphonic. . . . On the organ and the clavier he never played in fewer than five real parts."[21] Such composing and playing undoubtedly impressed the young Bach, who would have heard him perform in St. George's Church in Eisenach as a very young boy. Bach's initial attempts at five-part fugue writing in Arnstadt (see chapter 6) may reflect Johann Christoph's influence.

Johann Michael Bach's importance as a composer of chorale preludes has been recognized only recently with the discovery of the Neumeister Collection, where 25 pieces are handed down under his name, more than tripling his known settings.[22] While his works are cast in the Central German mold, they display a number of distinctive features: simple but effective canonic writing (as in "In dulci jubilo," formerly assigned to Johann Sebastian, as BWV[1] 751), a love of expressive chromatic harmonizations (as in "Jesus Christus, unser Heiland, der den Tod überwand"; example 2-3), free interludes between homophonic phrases of the chorale melody (as in "Allein Gott in der Höh sei Ehr"), and a wide variety

Example 2-3 Johann Michael Bach, "Jesus Christus, unser Heiland, der den Tod überwand": first phrase of the chorale.

Example 2-4 Johann Michael Bach, "Nun freut euch, lieben Christen g'mein": last phrase of the chorale.

of rhythms, deployed in fanciful ways (as in "Nun freut euch, lieben Christen g'mein," in which the deceptive cadence in the penultimate measure subtly enriches the conclusion; example 2-4). Such pieces have a playful spirit of spontaneity and seem less reserved than Pachelbel's chorale settings.

Jean-Claude Zehnder has suggested that the two Bach brothers may have had a greater influence than Pachelbel on Johann Sebastian's initial compositional efforts.[23] Without a doubt Johann Michael and Johann Christoph captured the imagination of the young Bach with their distinctive manner of composing and improvising. But at the same time, Johann Michael's chorale preludes, which are now readily available for scrutiny, fit comfortably into the Central German tradition and adhere to many of the same conventions as Pachelbel's settings. The fact that five of Johann Michael's works were attributed to Pachelbel before the discovery of the Neumeister Collection underscores the general similarity of the two composers' writing.

The style of the earliest layer of Neumeister Chorales suggests that Bach was also familiar with North German organ music during his Ohrdruf years. This suspicion was confirmed recently by the discovery of his tablature copy, dating from c. 1698–1699, of Buxtehude's large fantasia on "Nun freut euch, lieben Christen g'mein," BuxWV 210.[24] His source for this and other northern works may have been his brother Johann Christoph, who not only owned the special portfolio of works by Froberger, Kerll, and Pachelbel that Johann Sebastian copied into the Moonlight Manuscript but also assembled the albums known today as the Möller Manuscript and the Andreas Bach Book (see the introduction). Compiled between 1703 and 1714, the two collections contain more than a hundred free pieces for keyboard, including works by Böhm, Reincken,

Buxtehude, and Bruhns. The North German pieces may have been carried south by Johann Sebastian after his Lüneburg stay or his trip to Lübeck in the winter of 1705–1706, which would place their acquisition after the Ohrdruf years. But the albums point to a tradition within the Bach family of assembling large, diverse collections of keyboard music that included music by northern composers.

A number of related manuscripts support this idea. The Plauen Organ Book of 1708, lost in World War II but preserved in a photocopy,[25] contained almost 190 chorale settings.[26] Most of the pieces were Central German, including three of Bach's earliest *pedaliter* chorale settings,[27] but Böhm and Buxtehude were also represented with 15 works. Within the Bach family two collections once belonging to the Gehren Johann Christoph Bach contain a wide assortment of free pieces and chorale settings by Central German composers such as Wecker, Pachelbel, Zachow, Krieger, and Pachelbel, but Buxtehude is also well represented.[28] And coming very close to Johann Christoph and Johann Sebastian in Ohrdruf is a large portfolio of chorale settings, now lost, acquired from the Bach family by the lexicographer Ernst Ludwig Gerber (1746–1819), whose father, Heinrich Nicolaus Gerber, studied with Bach in Leipzig in the 1720s. The portfolio contained 201 chorale settings, many with 15-20 variations, resulting in more than 500 chorale preludes "from the best masters of the golden years of organ playing, 1680–1720."[29] The composers included four members of the Bach family—Johann Bernhard, Johann Christoph (which one is unclear), Johann Michael, and Johann Sebastian—as well as Pachelbel, Vetter, Buttstett, Zachow, and other Central Germans. Once again settings by Buxtehude and Böhm are present, too.

These diverse collections, both preserved and lost, provide a glimpse of the wide variety of organ music that was circulating in Thuringia during Bach's youth. In nearby Halle, Handel was learning "the different writing manner of the various nations" by copying German and Italian works contained in the collection of his teacher Friedrich Wilhelm Zachow, "so that he would not only play them, but also learn how to compose in a similar manner."[30] In light of this Central German tradition of dissemination, there is good reason to believe that when Bach headed north to Lüneburg at the age of 15, he was not entirely unfamiliar with the repertoire in which he was about to immerse himself.

Lüneburg: Georg Böhm and North German Circles

Bach's decision to leave Thuringia in favor of North Germany in 1700 was unusual but not unprecedented. Matthias Weckmann and Georg Böhm, both native Thuringians, had undertaken similar journeys before him and found work there,[31] and Johann Christoph Graff, who trained with Pachelbel in Erfurt, later traveled north to study with Böhm in Lüneburg.[32]

At 15, Bach could have remained in Thuringia and undertaken the normal course of study for an organist—though a lack of funds might have prevented him from doing so. The Matins Choir in Lüneburg, by contrast, offered employment, schooling, and the opportunity to enter the North German world of magnificent Hanseatic organs and legendary organists. In Hamburg, where four of the five principal churches boasted four-manual organs and 32' stops, one could count three generations of distinguished figures: Heinrich Scheidemann (c. 1595–1663) and Jacob Praetorius (1586–1663), both of whom had studied in Amsterdam with Sweelinck, the "Maker of Hamburg organists,"[33] followed by Matthias Weckmann (1616–1674), followed by Johann Adam Reincken (1643–1722) and Vincent Lübeck (1654–1740). Farther to the north, at St. Mary's Church in Lübeck, Franz Tunder (1614–1667) was succeeded by Buxtehude (who married Tunder's daughter). And in Lüneburg, Christian Flor (1626–1697) was followed by Böhm. Also present in the maritime town of Husum was Buxtehude's brilliant but short-lived student Nicolaus Bruhns (1665–1697). Such a constellation of stars could not be found in Central Germany.

By the end of the seventeenth century, North German organ music represented a blend of styles. The Sweelinck keyboard idiom, carried to Hamburg by Scheidemann, Praetorius, and others, served as the foundation for a new manner of improvising and composing, one that took full advantage of the large metropolitan organs with multiple manuals, bright registers, and well-developed pedal divisions.[34] This resulted in chorale preludes that exploited kaleidoscopic combinations realized on two manuals and pedal and free works written in a daring improvisation style—the *stylus fantasticus* that featured startling changes of color and gesture, held together by the plush acoustics of the large brick Gothic churches. French mannerisms and Italian multisectional formats also came into play in the northern stylistic amalgamation. North German organ music represented a dramatic contrast with the more reserved, balanced writing of the Central German school. It was bold and brash. As Philipp Spitta nicely put it, for the young Bach, the "meandering looseness of form and romantic picturesqueness" of northern works must have contrasted greatly with the "calm severity and sunny cheerfulness" of the music of his native Thuringia.[35]

As noted in chapter 1, Bach received strong support from Böhm during his stay in Lüneburg, copying North German works from his music library and most probably receiving organ instruction from him as well. Böhm may have provided Bach with an entrée to Reincken, too, drawing on ties from his earlier stay in Hamburg.[36] Many of Bach's early keyboard works bear the unmistakable stamp of Böhm's influence (see chapter 3), strongly suggesting a teacher-student relationship. No matter what the precise connection in Lüneburg, Bach and

Böhm remained lifelong friends, with Böhm later serving as an agent for Bach's publications.

Böhm was born in 1661 in the small Thuringian town Hohenkirchen and received his education at Thuringian institutions: the Latin school in Goldbach, the gymnasium in Gotha, and the university in Jena. Nothing is known of his musical training, however. Around 1691 he resettled in Hamburg, where he appears to have played continuo in the orchestra of the famous Gänsemarkt Opera for a time.[37] In 1698 he succeeded Christian Flor as organist of the St. John's Church in Lüneburg, where he remained until his death in 1733.

Böhm's organ music confirms that he was solidly schooled in Central German practices. This is especially evident in his fondness for the manual chorale partita and his inconsistent use of obbligato pedal. At the same time, his music shows him to be an adventurous composer who experimented imaginatively with forms, figurations, and procedures to create highly individualistic works.

It is safe to assume that many of the North German pieces that appeared later in the Möller Manuscript and Andreas Bach Book were acquired by Bach during his stay in Lüneburg.[38] Böhm's compositions figure prominently in the albums and include the Praeludia in D Minor and G Minor, the Capriccio in D Major, and the Partita on "Jesu, du bist allzu schöne" for organ and nine dance suites for harpsichord.[39] These works, together with Böhm's other extant pieces,[40] provide a good sense of his style.

Böhm's blend of diverse elements is especially striking in his chorale settings. The Partita on "Jesu, du bist allzu schöne" might be mistaken for a work by Pachelbel or Johann Michael Bach, with standard Central German devices deployed over the course of 14 variations: *corta* and *suspirans* figures (partitas 2 and 3);[41] animated 16th-note runs, arpeggios, or neighbor-notes in the soprano (partita 4), bass (partita 7), or both (partitas 8, 10, and 14); gigue idioms (partitas 5, 9, and 13); and a general adherence to two- and three-part texture.

Elsewhere, however, Böhm tossed Central German conventions to the wind. The Partitas on "Ach wie nichtig, ach wie flüchtig" and "Gelobet seist du, Jesu Christ" begin with chordal harmonizations of the chorale in five, six, and seven parts. Such writing abandons the clear voice-leading and four-part texture of the standard Central German model in favor of breaking the rules of counterpoint to create a grand effect. In "Ach wie nichtig" the use of dance forms is extended beyond the gigue to the minuet (partitas 6 and 8), showing the strong influence of French harpsichord music. Or in the Partita on "Wer nur den lieben Gott lässt walten," six rather conventional binary variations conclude with a seventh variation that dissolves into a loosely structured *stylus fantasticus* close, with the tempo moving from presto (for a gigue-like figure) to adagio (for an expressive interlude) to presto once again (for the return of the gigue-like figure). A similar mixing of styles appears in the chorale prelude "Nun bitten wir den heilgen

Geist," which opens with Central German fore-imitation before moving to stretto passages and a free close in the North German manner.

Böhm's most distinctive contribution to the chorale partita was his use of the quasi-ostinato and devise. This type of bicinium, or two-part variation, has been linked to continuo arias found in works of Johann Sigismund Kusser that were being performed at the Hamburg Opera during Böhm's time in the orchestra.[42] Such movements begin with an ostinato-like bass figure that appears alone at the outset and then returns in various forms throughout the variation. After the opening bass statement, the treble enters with a few notes of the embellished chorale tune —the "devise" or motto that serves as a "tease" of the chorale melody. The decorated melody then appears in full, phrase by phrase, accompanied freely by the quasi-ostinato bass.

We can see this technique at work in Versus 1 ("à 2 Clavier manualiter") of Böhm's "Vater unser im Himmelreich," a weighty setting of the Lord's Prayer. Here a bass figure, two and a half measures long, leads to the initial notes of the chorale, followed by a repeat of the bass figure and the first phrase of the chorale in full (example 2-5). The chorale melody is decorated with dotted figures and 32nd notes, and in the same manuscript it was embellished further by an

Example 2-5 Georg Böhm, "Vater unser im Himmelreich": opening phrase of the chorale, with quasi-ostinato bass and melodic devise.

early user with trills, appoggiaturas, and other flourishes[43] that reflect the type of French harpsichord ornamentation that commonly appears in Böhm's organ music.[44] French harpsichord idiom is also evident in Böhm's frequent use of *style brisé*, the stroked style derived from lute playing, in his chorale partitas, especially.

Invention abounds in Böhm's chorale settings. In "Allein Gott in der Höh sei Ehr," the Stollen and Abgesang of the chorale are set in different styles: the Stollen is treated as a free fantasy on the first two phrases of the chorale melody, while the Abgesang is set as a stricter imitative treatment of the chorale's final phrases. In the *pedaliter* setting of "Vater unser im Himmelreich," a melody chorale for two manuals and pedal, the last phrase of the chorale is repeated three times for the sake of embellishment: the first and the last iterations are expressive, recitative-like flourishes, while the second is a steady stream of ornamented 16th notes. In "Aus tiefer Not, schrei ich zu dir," versus 2 takes the form of a mirthful dance in 3/8 meter for two manuals and pedal. The chorale melody appears in the left hand in short phrases (with a devise at the start, once again) while the right hand presents a beguiling accompaniment in sweet parallel thirds—perhaps a representation of joyful thanks for the "grace and good will" mentioned in the second stanza of Luther's text. It is quite unusual for an organ setting of Psalm 130 ("Out of the depths have I cried unto Thee, O Lord") to have such charm. Böhm's ability to generate highly attractive material from a single phrase or motive of a chorale tune seems to have been inexhaustible.

This invention continues in his free works. As with the free compositions of Reincken, Buxtehude, and Bruhns, the term "Prelude and Fugue," used by Spitta and continued in modern editions, is inappropriate. The title found most commonly in the manuscripts is simply "Praeludium," or "Praeludium pedaliter," which better accommodates the wide variety of structural designs that resulted from the large-scale expansion of freely developed material. Böhm's Praeludium in G Minor contains four sections: a long introduction of half-note arpeggios, strummed up and down; a short, recitative-like adagio bridge; a lengthy fugue; and a closing section of descending arpeggios, in *style brisé* 16th notes. The limited harmonic scope of the fugue is offset by the unorthodox figurations of the opening and closing sections. The Capriccio in D Major, which seems to have taken its title and sectional design from Froberger, is based on an evolving theme that is first treated diatonically in ₵ meter, then chromatically with a distinctive countersubject in 3/4 meter, and finally as a gigue in 24/16 meter (example 2-6).

While the Praeludium in G Minor and Capriccio in D Major reflect the northern penchant for contrapuntal manipulation and multiple fugues, they also display the southern propensity for tunefulness and figurative play. This is especially evident in Böhm's Praeludium in C Major, with its exuberant opening pedal solo, chordal chitchat, and catchy fugue tune. Böhm had a prolonged influence

Example 2-6 Böhm, Capriccio in D Major: the three fugue subjects.

on Bach, apparent not only in Bach's initial keyboard works in Lüneburg and Arnstadt but also in the cantatas of the Mühlhausen years.[45]

Reincken's role in Bach's early development has also been reconsidered lately, in light of Bach's Lüneburg copy of Reincken's "An Wasserflüssen Babylon." Born in the Netherlands and trained in Hamburg by Scheidemann, Reincken was a larger-than-life figure. He served as Scheidemann's assistant before succeeding him in 1663 at St. Catherine's Church, where he won wide recognition through his improvisations. He supervised the important expansion of the church's organ in 1671, and he was a founding member of the Gänsemarkt Opera. Reincken was a close friend of Buxtehude—the two appear together as "brothers" in the painting of a musical party by Johannes Voorhout of 1674.[46] Reincken was also a bon vivant (he wears a Japanese kimono in the Voorhout portrait), one of Hamburg's most prominent citizens and immensely successful financially. And he enjoyed a long life, living to the age of either 79 or 99, depending on the source of information.[47] By 1700 he was viewed as the dean of North German organists, and it is not surprising that Bach ventured from Lüneburg to Hamburg several times specifically to hear him perform.

Unfortunately, only four of Reincken's organ works survive.[48] The free works, a Toccata in G Major that appears in the Andreas Bach Book and a Fugue in G Minor, display traditional North German characteristics: a five-part structure with two fugues in the Toccata (the first fugue in C meter, the second in 12/8) and long-winded fugue themes in both pieces. It is the two chorale fantasias, "An Wasserflüssen" and "Was kann uns kommen an für Not," that give the best impression of Reincken's extraordinary skills as a composer and improviser. According to his own account, he wrote the "An Wasserflüssen" setting to demonstrate to Scheidemann that he was worthy of serving as his assistant at St. Catherine's Church, knowing full well that another ambitious Scheidemann student, Matthias Weckmann, had improvised impressively on the same chorale to win the organist position at St. James' Church a few years earlier. Reincken included a note with his arrangement: "from this, one can perceive the portrait of an audacious man."[49]

Reincken's setting of "An Wasserflüssen" is about as audacious as one can get. Lasting almost 25 minutes and stretching to 327 measures, it is the largest extant North German fantasia and covers every chorale-preluding gesture imaginable: fore-imitation, florid melody, tierce-en-taille, fugato, Rückpositiv-Oberwerk echoes, expressive sigh motives, diminutions, fantasia passages, and double pedal (to conclude special sections). The chorale is not treated verse by verse but loosely instead, with phrases and motives serving as the basis for passages that alternate between imitative and free writing, in *stylus fantasticus* fashion. The 15-year-old Bach must have been awestruck by this sprawling piece. "Was kann kommen an," handed down in Walther's hand in the Weimar manuscript *P 802*, is shorter, with 222 measures, but equally diffuse.

At a later point, sometime between 1703 and 1713 or so, Bach turned to Reincken's *Hortus musicus*, a collection of North German–style trio sonatas and suites published in 1688, and fashioned three keyboard arrangements: the Sonata in A Minor, BWV 965; Sonata in C Major, BWV 966; and Fugue in B♭ Major, BWV 954.[50] These were not mere transcriptions but, in the case of fugal movements, complete reworkings, in the fashion of the Fugue in C Minor after Bononcini, BWV 574; the Fugue in B Minor after Corelli, BWV 579; and the three Fugues after Albinoni, BWV 946, 950, and 951. Bach used such arrangements as contrapuntal exercises to expand, modify, and refine the counterpoint of the original. The involvement with *Hortus musicus* took place after the Lüneburg years, however.

For Bach the receptive teenager, Reincken probably served mainly as the role model of a composer and improviser of gigantic chorale fantasias that were admired but not imitated, a practitioner of learned counterpoint (especially evident in *Hortus musicus*), an organ expert who was often called upon to test and approve new instruments, and an entrepreneur who played a central role in big-city civic life.[51] When Bach returned to Hamburg in 1720 to audition at St. Catherine's Church in Reincken's presence (see chapter 14), he improvised on "An Wasserflüssen Babylon" for 30 minutes—longer still than the huge fantasia he had copied as a wide-eyed boy. Reincken's subsequent praise was something Bach evidently treasured and later related to his sons, ensuring that it became part of family lore.

Music historians have seen Buxtehude as the most important North German influence on Bach's organ music. This view stems in part from the large body of impressive organ works that have been passed down under Buxtehude's name, and in part from Spitta, who believed that Bach encountered these works for the first time during the Lübeck journey of 1705–1706 and that the experience was transformative.[52] Although Bach would have had the opportunity to hear Buxtehude play the organ and become acquainted with his manner of performance and registration while in Lübeck, the trip most likely represented his introduction to Buxtehude's vocal music, which was being presented in Advent concerts at the time of his visit. It is now apparent from Bach's youthful copy of "Nun freut euch, lieben Christen g'mein," BuxWV 210, and the Neumeister Chorales that Bach was already familiar with Buxtehude's organ music before he made the Lübeck pilgrimage (see chapter 4).

Buxtehude's organ works were well known in Central Germany in the last decade of the seventeenth century, winning public admiration from Pachelbel, for instance, who dedicated the *Hexachordum Apollinis* of 1699 to his North German counterpart. The Möller Manuscript and Andreas Bach Book contain eight free works by Buxtehude that Bach may have acquired during his Lüneburg years:[53] the Praeludia in A Major, BuxWV 151, G Minor, BuxWV 150, and C Major, BuxWV 137; the Toccata in G Major, BuxWV 165; the Fugue in C Major ("Jig"), BuxWV 174; the Ciaconas in C Minor, BuxWV 159, and E Minor, BuxWV 160; and the Passacaglia in D Minor, BuxWV 161. The three large ostinato pieces are preserved in no other source. Bach was surely aware of Buxtehude's chorale settings, too, as the "Nun freut euch" manuscript attests.

Like Reincken, Buxtehude worked very much as an independent artist in North Germany. He trained in his native Denmark before attaining, in 1668, the organist position at St. Mary's Church in Lübeck, where he greatly expanded the series of *Abendmusiken* (evening concerts) that had been initiated by Tunder. Under Buxtehude's direction, the concerts became celebrated public events, featuring monumental ensembles and attracting large audiences. Buxtehude also published and performed North German–style trio sonatas, thus providing chamber music in a town that lacked a collegium musicum ensemble. In addition, Buxtehude worked closely with Andreas Werckmeister (1645–1706),[54] the champion of progressive tuning systems, and his organ works in keys with three or more sharps and flats helped to demonstrate the new tonal regions opened by Werckmeister's well-tempered approach.

Buxtehude's 47 chorale settings represent the largest portion of his organ music. The works can be divided into three categories: chorale fantasias, chorale variations, and chorale preludes.[55] The fantasias were an outgrowth of the North German practice of improvising at great length on a chorale melody, treating its phrases in sharply contrasting ways, much like the different sections of a *stylus fantasticus* praeludium. Although Bach was familiar with Buxtehude's fantasia settings, having copied the 256-measure "Nun freut euch, lieben Christen g'mein" in Ohrdruf, he does not seem to have written such pieces himself. The freewheeling nature of the fantasia may have been incompatible with his desire to compose more tightly constructed works. Buxtehude's chorale variations are less important and less impressive than Pachelbel's carefully organized sets. They appear to have been music to be used for alternatim practice in services, in which the organ alternated with the choir, verse by verse, in the performance of chorales, or for study.

It was Buxtehude's chorale preludes that were of greatest influence on Bach. The most important are the 27 melody settings for two manuals and pedal, with a chorale tune in the soprano highlighted on its own keyboard. The use of two contrasting manuals, one for the solo and one for the accompaniment, and the formal presence of the pedal as an obbligato voice were critical elements for Bach to emulate. Buxtehude handled all aspects of these settings with great skill. The chorale melodies range from unembellished cantus firmi to florid coloratura lines. The manual accompaniments range from homophonic chords to intricate contrapuntal fore-imitation. And the pedal parts range from continuo support to thematic voices that play an integral role in the imitative counterpoint.

Buxtehude's approach to the melody chorale can be seen in "Vater unser im Himmelreich," BuxWV 219. In the opening measures, the first phrase of the chorale appears as a lightly decorated solo in manual I, accompanied by simple chords in manual II and the pedal (example 2-7, a). The syncopated entries (mm. 1–2) and suspensions (mm. 2–4) in the accompaniment provide a gently undulating rhythmic undercurrent. The third phrase is handled quite differently. Here the chorale melody is surrounded by a web of expressive imitative counter-point, whose ascending chromatic lines first adumbrate and then echo the chro-matic ascent of the chorale line (example 2-7, b). The setting concludes with a three-measure cadenza over a tonic pedal point, thus providing a final melodic flourish that resembles the embellished close of an opera aria (example 2-7, c). Buxtehude's other chorale preludes are filled with similarly inventive passages and figurations, which served as a rich resource for Bach as he developed his own concept of the *pedaliter* chorale prelude. It was not long before he expanded the melody chorale to a size that almost matched that of the North German fantasia. "Komm, heiliger Geist, Herre Gott," BWV 652a, written during the early Weimar years, unfolds over 193 measures.

Buxtehude also greatly refined the North German praeludium pedaliter, expanding its multisectional format to five, six, and even seven sections, each marked by a sudden change of *affect*, or mood. At the same time, he brought the praeludium under tighter thematic control by basing the fugues on mate-rial presented in the free introduction. To this he added shocking harmonic surprises, virtuosic pedal passages, recitative-like sections, and distinctive *trillo longo* figures. Buxtehude's dramatic approach is reflected in the bold gestures he used to open the praeludia: virtuosic pedal solos, animated passagework (often over pedal points), hypnotic ostinatos, fugal imitation, and even conversational recitatives.

Example 2-7 Dieterich Buxtehude, "Vater Unser im Himmelreich," BuxWV 219: (a) opening phrase of the chorale, (b) third phrase of the chorale, with imitative accompaniment, and (c) pedal-point close.

Many of these qualities are apparent in the monumental Praeludium in E Minor, BuxWV 142. It unfolds in seven sections over the course of 153 measures. The free introduction of 16 measures is devoted to the development of an arpeggiated theme—first by imitation, then by fragmentation—that consequently serves as the basis for the subjects of three large fugues: an instrumental fugue in 4/4 meter, a chromatic fugue in 3/2 meter (with inversion and stretto), and a jig fugue in 12/8 meter (example 2-8, a). The entire piece is devoted to exploring the motivic potential of the material set forth in the first measure—an approach to creating a highly organic, unified structure that Bach subsequently adopted in many of his own compositions. Also noteworthy in the Praeludium is the series of rich, partly nonfunctional chords that are presented over a dominant pedal point at the end of the first fugue (example 2-8, b). This type of gratuitous harmonic coloring—a dash of *stylus fantasticus* spice—permeates Buxtehude's free works.

Buxtehude's gift for sustaining large, unified structures is also evident in the three ostinato works preserved in the Andreas Bach Book. In the Passacaglia D

Example 2-8 Buxtehude, Praeludium pedaliter in E Minor, BuxWV 142: (a) introductory theme and three fugue subjects, and (b) chords leading to the second fugue.

Minor, BuxWV 161, seven variations in D minor are followed by seven variations in F major, seven variations in A minor, and seven variations in D minor,
once again, with short modulatory passages between each group. This produces
a symmetrical, balanced format while providing harmonic relief from the potential monotony of 28 variations in the same key. The work later served as a structural model for Bach's own Passacaglia (see chapter 13).

Of the fourth North German named as an influence on Bach, Nicolaus Bruhns,
we know little other than the presence of tablature copies of the Praeludia in
E Minor and G Major (in fragmentary form) in the Möller Manuscript. The
Praeludium in G Major, in particular, is a freewheeling, pyrotechnical work
with rapid 16th-note pedal octaves and double pedal passages that must have
impressed Bach greatly.[56] The Hamburg theorist Johann Mattheson reported
that Bruhns was such a gifted violinist and organist that he was able to perform
trio sonatas by himself while seated at the organ, by playing the two treble parts
on a violin through double stops while providing the continuo part on the pedals
with his feet.[57]

Bach chose selectively from North German organ music. He adopted the two-
manual-and-pedal setting for chorale preludes but avoided the unwieldy chorale fantasia. He embraced the concept of large, dramatic free pieces but mostly
rejected the multipartite design of the praeludium pedaliter in favor of the two-
part prelude and fugue. He retained the idea of highlighting special lines of a
chorale text with a sudden change of *affect* but used it very sparingly in his mature works. On the whole, however, Bach opted for North German style, with
its large, bold forms, unabashed virtuosity, and fully obbligato pedal.[58] After
the Hanseatic experience, he became a North German organist with Central
German sensitivities.

Notes

1. Walther 1732, 64.
2. NBR, no. 395.
3. Dürr 1986.
4. The most detailed account of Johann Christoph Bach's life is found in Schulze 1985.
5. The contract is reprinted in full in Hugo Botstiber's introduction to *Denkmäler der Tonkunst in Österreich*, vol. 17, series viii/2, xvii.
6. Cited in Schulze 1985, 69.
7. Schulze 1985, 77.
8. Eckelt's studies began at Easter of 1690, but ended abruptly just 10 weeks later, when Pachelbel left to take up a new position in Stuttgart. See Wolff 1986, 374–387. A catalog of the contents of Eckelt's album, with incipits, concordances, and modern editions of each piece, is presented in Belotti 2001.

9. Modern editions: *Johann Jacob Froberger, Neue Ausgabe sämtlicher Clavier- und Orgelwerke*, Siegbert Rampe, ed. (Kassel: Bärenreiter, 1993–95); *Johann Pachelbel, Complete Works for Keyboard Instruments*, Michael Belotti, ed. (Colfax, NC: Wayne Leupold Editions, 1999–).

10. Kube 1993, 128.

11. The Fugue in F Major, BWV 540/2, or the Fugue in C Major, BWV545/2, for instance.

12. Johann Heinrich Buttstett, *Ut, Mi, Sol, Re, Fa, La, Tota Musica et Harmonia Æterna* (Erfurt: Otto Friedrich Werther, 1717), 58.

13. Walther 1732, 134.

14. See the discussion in Kube 1993, 127–128.

15. The phrase Bach used on the title page. NBR, no. 92.

16. See n. 5.

17. See the discussion in Kube 1994.

18. See the definition in the list of terms.

19. NBR, no. 303. He so described them in the genealogy of the Bach family that he created around 1735.

20. Daniel Melamed, *J. S. Bach and the German Motet* (Cambridge: Cambridge University Press, 1995), 172–173.

21. NBR, no. 306.

22. Modern edition: *Johann Michael Bach: Sämtliche Orgelchoräle*, Christoph Wolff, ed. (Neuhausen-Stuttgart: Hänssler-Verlag, 1987).

23. Zehnder 1999, 186–187.

24. Maul and Wollny 2007, xxiii. The manuscript is a fragment that breaks off after 90 measures.

25. Berlin, Staatliches Institut für Musikforschung--Preußischer Kulturbesitz, *Fot. Bü 129*, 1–2.

26. The contents are described in Seiffert 1920.

27. "Ein feste Burg," BWV 720; "Valet will ich dir geben," BWV 735a; and "Wie schön leuchtet der Morgenstern," BWV 739.

28. Yale Music Library, *LM 4982* (*Ma21.Y11.A35*) and *LM 4983* (*Ma21.Y11.A36*), described in Kobayashi 1983.

29. Ernst Ludwig Gerber, *Neues historisch-biographisches Lexikon der Tonkünstler* (Leipzig, 1812–14), vol. 1, col. 208.

30. John Mainwaring, *Memoirs of the Life of the Late George Frederic Handel* (London: R. and J. Dodsley, 1760; rpt. Amsterdam, F. A. M. Knuf, 1964), 35.

31. As a teenager, Weckmann spent three years in Hamburg studying with Jacob Praetorius and coaching with Heinrich Scheidemann before winning the organist position at the city's famous St. James' Church in 1655. Böhm moved to Hamburg in his thirties before securing the organist post at St. John's Church in Lüneburg in 1698.

32. Walther 1732, 288.

33. Mattheson 1740, 332. Sweelinck also trained Ulrich Cernitz and Johannes Praetorius, who held the other two principal church positions in Hamburg.

34. See Breig 2006, especially 34–36.

35. Spitta 1873–80, vol. 1, 195.

36. It is likely that Böhm knew Reincken from their mutual association with the Hamburg opera. Böhm was also a colleague of Heinrich Elmenhorst, minister of St. Catherine's Church, where Reincken worked, having provided 23 settings for a collection of religious songs published by Elmenhorst in 1700. See Zehnder 1988, 80.

37. Zehnder 1988, 77–78.

38. Wolff 2000, 46–47.

39. Modern editions: *Georg Böhm, Sämtliche Werke—Klavier- und Orgelwerke*, Johannes Wolgast, ed., rev. ed. (Wiesbaden: Breitkopf & Härtel, 1952), and *Georg Böhm, Sämtliche Orgelwerke*, Klaus Beckmann, ed. (Wiesbaden: Edition Breitkopf, 1986), and *Georg Böhm, Sämtliche Werke für Clavier*, Klaus Beckmann, ed. (Wiesbaden: Edition Breitkopf, 1986).

40. These pieces are preserved almost exclusively in sources that can be linked to Bach or his Weimar colleague Johan Gottfried Walther.

41. See definitions in the list of terms.

42. Zehnder 1988, 93–94.

43. Berlin State Library, *P 802*. The text of the piece was written by Johann Gottfried Walther around 1712; the French ornaments were added by Johann Tobias Krebs, who was studying with Walther at the time. The unadorned Walther version is presented in the Beckmann edition; the embellished Krebs version is presented in the Wolgast edition.

44. The Möller Manuscript and Andreas Bach Book contain three French ornament tables that Böhm may have shared with Bach during his Lüneburg stay: one from Nicolas Lebègue's *Les pieces de clavessin* (Paris, 1677), one from Charles Dieupart's *Six Suittes de Clavecin* (Paris, 1701), and one from an anonymous source.

45. Dürr 1977, 92 and 138; Zehnder 1988, 96–102.

46. BDok IX, no. 28. In the portrait, Reincken performs at the harpsichord with other musicians, and Buxtehude appears to sit nearby, listening to a canon dedicated to "Dietrich Buxtehude and Johann Adam Reincken, brothers." Although Buxtehude is sometimes identified as the gamba player in the portrait, that instrumentalist is more likely Johann Theile, a member of the North German circle of contrapuntists (he may be the author of the canon in question) and a skilled gambist.

47. In *Critica musica* (1722), Johann Mattheson stated that Reincken was born in 1623, and the Obituary of 1750 claimed that when Bach performed in St. Catherine's Church in 1720, Reincken was nearly 100 years old. But baptismal records from Deventer, Reincken's home town, contain an entry for "Jan Reinse" in 1643. See Ulf Grapenthin, "Johann Adam Reincken," in *The New Grove Dictionary of Music and Musicians*, vol. 21, 154.

48. Modern editions: *Joh. Adam Reincken: Sämtliche Orgelwerke*, Klaus Beckmann, ed. (Wiesbaden: Breitkopf & Härtel, 1982), and *Johann Adam Reincken: Sämtliche Orgelwerke*, ed. Pieter Dirksen (Wiesbaden: Edition Breitkopf, 2005).

49. Walther 1732, 547–548: "Hieraus könne er des verwegenen Menschen *Portrait* ersehen."

50. See Wolff 1991b and Heller 2006. Wolff dates the Reincken arrangements "certainly before 1710, and possibly much earlier"; Heller dates them "c. 1713."

51. Stauffer 2009, 244–249.

52. Spitta 1873–80, vol. 1, 256–310.

53. An additional manuscript, dated c. 1700, that appears to be in the hand of Johann Christoph Bach contains the Praeludium in G Minor, BuxWV 148. See Schulze 1991.

54. Buxtehude contributed two congratulatory poems to Werckmeister's *Harmonologia musica* (Quedlinburg, 1702).

55. The best discussion in English of Buxtehude's chorale settings is found in Snyder 2007, 260–276.

56. Modern edition: Nicolaus Bruhns, *Orgelwerke,* ed. Michael Radulescu (Vienna: Doblinger, 1993).

57. Mattheson 1740, 26.

58. See the discussions in Breig 2006 and Krummacher 1985.

3

Initial Efforts

The initial efforts of the young Johann Sebastian Bach—the organ works he
produced before taking up his position in Arnstadt in the summer of 1703—
reveal a composer who was not a prodigy in the Mozartian sense, able to write
suave, urbane works at an early age. They show, rather, a composer who was
somewhat unpolished but remarkably bold, daring, and ambitious. Invention
and experimentation outweigh control and discipline in Bach's earliest works.

The Neumeister Chorales

Bach's youthful ambition is nowhere more evident than in the Neumeister
Chorales. They are of critical importance for understanding his early training,
for they provide the only comprehensive look at his compositional efforts during
the Ohrdruf and Lüneburg years.

The settings are preserved in a manuscript album that came to light only
in 1984, when it was discovered, more or less simultaneously, by Wilhelm
Krumbach and Christoph Wolff in the Yale Music Library, where it had resided
unnoticed for more than a century as part of the Lowell Mason Collection.[1]
Compiled in the 1790s by Johann Gottfried Neumeister (1756–1840), a student
of Bach's colleague Georg Andreas Sorge,[2] the album contains 82 small pieces in
the Central German tradition of *fugirte, variirte, und figurirte Choräle* (fugued,
varied, and figured chorales), including 31 previously unknown works attributed
to Bach. The settings are loosely arranged in the order of a German hymnal (seasonal chorales followed by general chorales), and most are for one manual only,
with little or no pedal. Neumeister included an index of the pieces at the end of
the album, suggesting that he intended the contents for practical use in service
playing in Friedberg and Homburg, where he served as a part-time organist.[3]
Nothing is known about the source from which he copied the works.

Aside from five pieces from Sorge's *Erster Theil der Vorspiele* of 1750 and two
Orgel-Büchlein chorales, which appear at the end of the album and seem to be
later additions, the contents are oriented toward the generation of composers
directly before Bach, including Johann Pachelbel, Friedrich Wilhelm Zachow,
Daniel Erich, Johann Michael Bach, and Johann Christoph Bach (probably

J. S. BACH. George B. Stauffer, Oxford University Press. © Oxford University Press 2024.
DOI: 10.1093/oso/9780195108026.003.0004

Johann Michael's brother, the Eisenach organist). The young Johann Sebastian Bach is represented by 38 pieces altogether: the 31 previously unknown settings along with two settings that were partially known and five settings that were fully known from other sources. Both the context of the settings (a collection of small Central German chorales) and the concordances with other sources weigh in favor of Bach's authorship of the entire group:

Previously unknown setttings:

Wir Christenleut, BWV 1090

Das alte Jahr vergangen ist, BWV 1091

Herr Gott, nun schleuß den Himmel auf, BWV 1092

Herzliebster Jesu, was hast du verbrocken, BWV 1093

O Jesu, wie ist dein Gestalt, BWV 1094

O Lamm Gottes unschuldig, BWV 1095

Christ der du bist Tag und Licht, oder Wir danken dir, Herr Jesu Christ, BWV 1096

Ehre sei dir, Christe, der du leidest Not, BWV 1097

Wir glauben all an einen Gott, BWV 1098

Aus tiefer Not schrei ich zu dir, BWV 1099

Allein zu dir, Herr Jesu Christ, BWV 1100

Durch Adams Fall ist ganz verderbt, BWV 1101

Du Friedefürst, Herr Jesu Christ, BWV 1102

Erhalt uns, Herr, bei deinem Wort, BWV 1103

Wenn dich Unglück tut greifen an, BWV 1104

Jesu, meine Freude, BWV 1105

Gott ist mein Heil, mein Hilf und Trost, BWV 1106

Jesu, meines Lebens Leben, BWV 1107

Als Jesus Christus in der Nacht, BWV 1108

Ach Gott, tu dich erbarmen, BWV 1109

O Herre Gott, dein göttlich Wort, BWV 1110

Nun lasset uns den Leib begraben, BWV 1111

Christus, der ist mein Leben, BWV 1112

Ich hab mein Sach Gott heimgestelt, BWV 1113

Herr Jesu Christ, du höchstes Gut, BWV 1114

Herzlich lieb hab ich dich, o Herr, BWV 1115

Was Gott tut, das ist wohlgetan, BWV 1116

Alle Menschen müssen sterben, BWV 1117

Werde munter, mein Gemüte, BWV 1118

Wie nach einer Wasserquelle, BWV 1119

Christe, der du bist der helle Tag, BWV 1120

Partially known settings:

Ach Gott und Herr, BWV 714 (appears here with an additional opening section)

Machs mit mir, Gott, nach deiner Güt, BWV 957 (appears here with additional closing measures)

Fully known settings:

Der Tag, der ist so freudenreich, oder Ein Kindelein so löbelich, BWV 719
Ach, Herr, mich armen Sünder, BWV 742
Vater unser im Himmelreich, oder Nimm von uns, Herr, du treuer Gott, BWV 737
Ich ruf zu dir, Herr Jesu Christ, BWV 639
Herr Christ, der ein'ge Gottes Sohn, BWV 601

Krumbach proposed that Bach's settings, aside from the two Orgel-Büchlein chorales, date from the Arnstadt and Mühlhausen years, 1703–1707 and 1707–1708.[4] Wolff, citing their formative style and lack of obbligato pedal, proposed a much earlier period, 1695–1705.[5] Jean-Claude Zehnder has suggested four specific stages of composition for the pieces: c. 1699, c. 1701, c. 1704, and c. 1706.[6]

What seems certain about the Neumeister Chorales is that they are very early pieces. As Alfred Dürr pointed out in his review of the first edition,[7] several settings contain rudimentary compositional mistakes such as parallel fifths and octaves and strings of consecutive fifths and fourths.[8] In light of this, the settings must be counted among Bach's earliest surviving efforts, certainly preceding by a number of years more broadly conceived *pedaliter* pieces such as "Wie schön leuchtet der Morgenstern," BWV 739, which can be assigned to the period c. 1704–1705 on the basis of Bach's handwritten autograph, or "Christ lag in Todesbanden," BWV 720 (see chapter 5). Both settings appear to stem from Bach's stay in Arnstadt.

The bulk of the Neumeister Chorales appear to have been written before that time, in Ohrdruf and Lüneburg. Viewed as a whole, they show a stylistic evolution that must have taken place over a period of several years. Not surprisingly, a number of settings closely mirror the Central German style of Pachelbel and Johann Michael Bach. Other pieces, presumably written at a somewhat later date, show unconventional combinations of Central and North German elements that distinguish them from all other settings in the collection. And a few works, possibly the latest of all, display refined stylistic syntheses that hint at the remarkable composer Bach was to become. We can trace these developments by looking at representative examples.

"Erhalt uns, Herr, bei deinem Wort," BWV 1103, is an unassuming chorale fughetta with Pachelbel-like features: compositional clarity, smooth counterpoint, and cantabile lines. It displays serene movement in quarter and 8th notes, formulaic but convincing sequences, and consistent three-part texture that expands to four-part with the final pair of entries. The theme is derived from the first phrase of the chorale, and the final entry appears in the bass and descends to the lowest note in the piece, E. It is very much like the pieces Pachelbel used for the instruction of Johann Valentin Eckelt (see chapter 2)—so much so that Zehnder has questioned its attribution to Bach.[9] Yet there are interesting twists that point to an ambitious hand. After the initial exposition, the entries of the theme are strategically prepared by preceding rests (mm. 12, 15, 22, and 27), and near the end of the setting the last phrase of the chorale melody suddenly appears twice, first in augmented half notes (m. 25, soprano) and then in quarter notes (m. 30, tenor). Bach returned to the second gesture many years later in the fugue on "Wir glauben an einen Gott," BWV 680, from Clavier-Übung III, where the last line of the chorale tune suddenly appears in augmented notes in the final measures. Despite these inventive details, however, the prevailing tone is that of Pachelbel.

"Christe, der du bist Tag und Licht, oder Wir danken dir, Herr Jesu Christ," BWV 1096, also underscores the close ties with Pachelbel's style. The piece is a double setting: the first half is a four-part fughetta based on the first phrase of the chorale (mm. 1–26), and the second half is a four-part harmonization of the entire chorale melody (mm. 28–56). Although the complete work is attributed to Bach in the Neumeister manuscript, the first half appears elsewhere under Pachelbel's name.[10] This is probably a misattribution, but it reflects the similarity of Bach's writing to Pachelbel's at this point.

While "Christus, der ist mein Leben," BWV 1112, has a Central German stamp, its variegated rhythmic profile is more characteristic of Johann Michael Bach than Pachelbel. The chorale melody is presented straightforwardly in the soprano as a half-note cantus firmus, but each phrase is accompanied differently: phrase 1 by fore-imitation based on the first two lines of the chorale, phrase 2 by free counterpoint, phrase 3 by fore-imitation based on the third line of the chorale, and phrase 4 by free counterpoint. Johann Michael Bach's influence can be seen in the shift in the accompaniment from steady 8th notes for phrase 1 to *corta* figures for phrases 2 and 3 and back to steady 8th notes for phrase 4. The shift to *corta* figures enlivens the rhythmic pulse in the middle of the setting; the return to smooth 8th notes at the end forms a framing element with the opening.

Bach's assimilation of both Pachelbel's and Johann Michael Bach's writing can be seen in "Was Gott tut, das ist wohlgetan," BWV 1116. The setting relies on the Central German concept of fore-imitation, and through the first 25 measures and the presentation of the five phrases of the chorale in the soprano it maintains the placid 8th-note movement of Pachelbel. In the six-measure coda that follows, however, the movement suddenly takes wing with the emergence of 8th- and 16th-note *corta* figures reminiscent of Johann Michael Bach. The shift is subtly prepared by the final phrase, in the soprano, of the chorale tune, which is decorated with the *corta* figure that subsequently takes charge of the music. In addition, the fore-imitation in the setting is treated in an unorthodox way: in the Stollen of the bar form, the initial fore-imitation, based on line 1 of the chorale, serves for both phrases of the soprano melody, and in the Abgesang, each phrase of the soprano melody is foreshadowed differently; phrase 3, in particular, is preceded by catchy repeated notes in diminution. Peter Williams has termed the setting "a free-for-all contrapuntal tapestry."[11] That it is, with fabric woven from the threads of Bach's Central German predecessors.

The double setting "Als Jesus Christus in der Nacht," BWV 1108, shows a broader amalgamation of styles still, one that combines Central and North German elements. The first movement displays the pure four-part writing of a Central German organ chorale, with the chorale melody appearing in the soprano as a half-note cantus firmus. It is supported by two off-beat 8th-note motives—the first an ascending fourth, the second a repeated-note falling third—that are combined in various ways. The second movement, labeled "Variatio," is a diminution version of the first (that is, it is permeated with smaller note values), with the cantus firmus appearing both in quarter notes (phrases 1 and 3) and half notes (phrases 2 and 4), accompanied by *suspirans* 16th-note figures that are reminiscent of Böhm's partita writing. The four phrases of the cantus firmus migrate from the soprano to the alto to the soprano and finally to the pedal, which enters for the first time to bring the setting to a close. Arpeggiated figures in cross-rhythms appear over the pedal statement. In this modest setting Bach seems to be reinterpreting Central German gestures in light of North German practices.

Böhm's influence is even clearer in "Du Friedefürst, Herr Jesu Christ," BWV 1102. Like "Als Jesus Christus in der Nacht," this is a double setting, but with the two verses combined into one continuous movement. The first verse is a bicinium, or two-part piece, with quasi-ostinato bass in the left hand and decorated chorale in the right. This reflects Böhm's opera-derived technique, but with subtle adjustments. The ostinato appears in many forms: exact repetition (m. 6), transposed to G minor (m. 10), modulating from B♭ major to G minor (m. 13), varied (mm. 16 and 20), and quasi-inversion (m. 23). The first phrase of the chorale initially appears with the ostinato in B♭ major, but when the first phrase appears again, in the repeat of the Stollen, the ostinato is delayed and transposed to G minor (example 3-1, a–b). The fourth and final phrase of the chorale ends in the tonic (m. 24a), but the melody line continues with a florid riff on the third and fourth chorale lines (mm. 24b–29). The second verse is also a bicinium, but

Example 3-1 "Du Friedefürst, Herr Jesu Christ," BWV 1102: embellishment of the first phrase of the chorale melody (a) in the Stollen of Part I, with the basso ostinato (bracketed) in B♭ major, (b) in the repeat of the Stollen of Part I, with the basso ostinato (bracketed) in G minor, and (c) in the Stollen of Part II.

it is marked by a sudden change to a more animated *affect*, emphasized by the al-legro indication. The chorale is now treated in *style brisé*, in the manner of Böhm, once again, with the melody tapped out in the upper voice (example 3-1, c). Each phrase of the chorale concludes with a flourish, in triplets (phrases 1 and 2) or 16th notes (phrases 3 and 4). The sudden arrival of triplets is quite like the out-burst that takes place in the solo organ part of the quasi-ostinato aria "Ich bin nun achtig Jahr" of Cantata 71, *Gott ist mein König*, from 1708. Zehnder sees links between "Du Friedefürst" and the quasi-ostinato movements (verses 2 and

6) of Cantata 4, *Christ Lag in Todesbanden,* and consequently proposes a late date within the Neumeister Chorales of c. 1706 for "Du Friedefürst."[12]

Bach's adoption of broader North German elements is evident in **"Herr Gott, nun schleuß den Himmel auf,"** BWV 1092. In this remarkable setting, the chorale melody appears throughout in the soprano, in unadorned half and quarter notes, in a Central German manner. But the *affect* and texture of the accompaniment changes with each phrase, in the manner of a North German chorale fantasia. The piece begins with an unusual prologue dialogue on the first phrase of the chorale, which appears initially as a two-note chordal echo and then as a full melodic line, all in four-part homophony. The prologue is followed by the seven phrases of the chorale and a *passaggio* close in 32nd notes—a North German gesture. The overall structure looks like this:

Mm. 1–4	Prologue	Dialogue on phrase 1: 2-chord echo, then 4-part chordal homophony
Mm. 5–7	Chorale phrase 1	3-part *style brisé*
Mm. 7–9	Chorale phrase 2	4-part chordal polyphony
Mm. 10–11	Chorale phrase 3	3-part imitative counterpoint on *suspirans* figures
Mm. 11–12	Chorale phrase 4	3-part imitative counterpoint on *suspirans* figures
Mm. 13–15	Chorale phrase 5	4-part chordal polyphony
Mm. 16–18	Chorale phrase 6	3-part imitative counterpoint on *suspirans* figures
Mm. 18–24	Chorale phrase 7	4-part chordal polyphony, in opening dialogue style
Mm. 24–27	Close	32nd-note *passaggio*

The asymmetry of the structure is offset by recurring textures (the imitative counterpoint and chordal polyphony), the framing prologue and close, and the surprising return of the prologue dialogue in the final phrase of the chorale, where it is extended and altered. Werner Breig has suggested that the two opening chords, set to "Herr Gott" of the text, portray an emphatic cry to God to "open the door of heaven"—a cry that echoes down from the sky above.[13] This is quite like the echo passages in Heinrich Schütz's extraordinary setting of "Saul, Saul, was verfolgst du mich?" and points to a young composer filled with adventurous ideas.

"Herzlich lieb hab ich dich, o Herr," BWV 1115, is more North German still and once again shows a multitude of inventive twists. The Stollen portion of the chorale begins with a solo bass theme that has been linked to the opening pedal solo of Buxtehude's Praeludium in C Major, BuxWV 137, a work passed down in the Andreas Bach Book. The theme initially appears to be a quasiostinato, but it serves instead to supply a leaping *suspirans* motive for the two-part imitative counterpoint that accompanies the chorale melody, which appears in the soprano in unadorned half and quarter notes, much like that of "Herr Gott, nun schleuß den Himmel auf." The *affect* changes abruptly in the Abgesang portion of the chorale: the meter switches to 12/8/ℭ, and the chorale melody is decorated with triplets, accompanied by punctuated chords. With the seventh phrase of the chorale (m. 21) the meter shifts subtly back to the opening ℭ, and with the eighth phrase (m. 25) the texture becomes a simple quarter-note cantus firmus accompanied by a single 16th-note line. The ninth and tenth phrases (m. 28f.) are the climax of the piece, with the chorale melody set in augmented half notes accompanied by pairs of 8th-note thirds, much like the keyboard music of Sweelinck. For the close, the last line of the chorale tune (m. 33) is decorated once again, now with 16th notes rather than triplets. This setting, too, represents a compilation of many ideas, assembled in a *stylus fantasticus* sort of way.

"**Wir Christenleut haben jetzund Freud**," BWV 1090, is similarly eclectic and brimming with stylistic invention. The Stollen of the chorale is set straightforwardly, with the melody appearing in the soprano as a half-note cantus firmus accompanied by two-part imitative counterpoint based on a driving, off-beat figure (example 3-2, a). This figuration can be found in the Central German settings of Bach's contemporaries as well as in Bach's chorale partitas and Orgel-Büchlein chorales. The rhythmic intensity increases for the conclusion of the Stollen (mm. 14–16), along with the addition of a fourth part. The Abgesang begins with a complete change of *affect* (m. 16). The meter shifts to 12/8 and the idiom switches to that of a dance accompanied by gentle triplets (example 3-2, b). The cantus firmus remains the same, in half notes that would be the equivalent of those in the Stollen (verified by the mixed-meter signature 12/8/ℭ). For the final phrase of the chorale the *affect* changes once again, to that of a French overture, with a rising motive in dotted rhythm (probably double-dotted), presented in imitation and based on the chorale melody (example 3-2, c). After a cadence in F major (m. 27), the three phrases of the Abgesang appear once again, one by one, first abstractly (phrase 5: m. 27; phrase 6: m. 30) and then in clear quarter notes in the soprano (phrase 7, m. 31 to the end).

The unambiguous statement of the final phrase of the chorale at the end of the setting may reflect the last line of Caspar Füger's sixteenth-century text, which states that whoever believes firmly in Christ's redemptive power "shall not be lost." In Bach's setting, it is the chorale tune that is not lost. Zehnder has pointed to two works in the Möller Manuscript as possible models for Bach's use of French style for the last section: Böhm's Prelude in F Major, a keyboard overture, and Steffani's Overture from *Briseide*.[14] French overture style appears nowhere

Example 3-2 "Wir Christenleut," BWV 1090: (a) the first phrase of the chorale, (b) the fifth phrase of the chorale, and (c) the seventh phrase of the chorale.

else in the settings of the Neumeister album. Bach, alone, adopted it here to expand the vocabulary of the chorale prelude. He returned to the idiom in a similar way many years later, in the *manualiter* setting of "Wir glauben all an einen Gott," BWV 681, in Clavier-Übung III.

The many strands of experimentation converge in what might be the most astonishing Neumeister chorale, **"Jesu, meine Freude,"** BWV 1105. During the course of just 18 measures, Bach presents a multitude of compositional devices, setting each of the chorale's six phrases in a different way. The Stollen features a migrating cantus firmus (example 3-3). For phrase 1, the chorale melody appears in the soprano in quarter notes, in a four-part chordal harmonization. The penultimate note is decorated with a *corta* figure, which then serves as the basis for the

Example 3-3 "Jesu, meine Freude," BWV 1105: the first three phrases of the chorale.

imitative counterpoint that rises through the voices surrounding phrase 2. The melody now appears in the tenor, with the penultimate note decorated with the *corta* figure once again and the ultimate note with a neighbor-note flourish. For phrase 3, the melody shifts to the bass, accompanied by rising imitative counterpoint like that of phrase 2, but now based on a *suspirans* figure.

After the repeat of the Stollen, the Abgesang begins with phrase 4, presented as chordal fragments that echo back and forth in a North German manner (example 3-4). This material, which is not unlike the opening dialogue of "Herr Gott, nun schleuß den Himmel auf," cadences firmly in F Major. A cadenza-like flourish leads to phrase 5, where the melody continues in the soprano against animated counterpoint in the lower voices. This is the most intense section of the setting, and the distinctive four-part texture—quarter-note melody, lively 16th-note middle voices, continuo bass (probably taken by the pedal)—resembles the dense idiom of the Orgel-Büchlein chorales. A virtuosic glissando, similar to that found in Böhm's Praeludium in F Major, leads to the concluding phrase of the chorale, presented in detached chords in five and six parts that break the rules of counterpoint with direct octaves and doubled thirds. This, too, is a Böhmian feature. The homophonic chords hark back to phrase 1; the detachments reflect

Example 3-4 "Jesu, meine Freude," BWV 1105: phrases 4 and 5 of the chorale.

phrase 4. The forceful harmonies and suspended final note make for a dramatic close.

Zehnder has suggested that the rhetorical pauses in the Abgesang represent the phrase "Earth and the abyss must be silent, even if they grumble ever so much" in the third verse of Johann Franck's 1653 text.[15] Possible word-painting aside, Bach took special steps in "Jesu, meine Freude" to unite the potentially disparate phrases, through figural cross-references (the *corta* figure, the detached chords, the chordal texture) and through connective links (the cadenza, the glissando), avoiding the abrupt changes of meter and tempo found in many of the other Neumeister settings. As Werner Breig has pointed out, here is a composer consciously striving to be original—and doing so with great success.[16] Diversity and unity are in perfect balance. It is no exaggeration to say that the multiplicity of gestures in this tiny piece matches that of the magnificent *pedaliter* setting of "Vater unser im Himmelreich," BWV 682, written many years later for Clavier-Übung III (see chapter 22), but on a miniature scale.

The remaining Neumeister settings exhibit similar diversity, and "**Ach Gott und Herr**," BWV 714, and "**Machs mit mir, Gott, nach deiner Güt**," BWV 957, with their additional segments, suggest that even at an early age Bach did not view composed settings as sacrosanct creations but rather as malleable material that could be expanded and revised at a later point. Viewed as a whole, the chorales reveal the compositional curiosity and extraordinary evolution of the young Bach. The most advanced settings are highly individualistic, displaying unconventional combinations of idioms and styles drawn from North and Central Germany. They are quite unlike the pieces written by other composers in the collection, which are more parochial and written along conventional lines. Bach's works present multiple solutions to writing a short chorale prelude. Indeed, no two pieces are alike. In most cases the changes of *affect* within settings are not motivated by the text of the chorale, but rather by Bach's desire to try different effects, to "shake things up." The modest size of the settings and the concentration of material ally them with the chorales of the Orgel-Büchlein, in which Bach focused on the issues of strict part-writing and obbligato pedal within pieces that each display a single *affect*.

We don't know the original context of the Neumeister Chorales—whether they were part of a much larger, diverse collection or whether they were a single project, like the Orgel-Büchlein. The relative unity of size and setting—that is, short, essentially *manualiter*, and mostly for one keyboard—suggests the latter, that they might have been conceived as a single undertaking. The imitative counterpoint in settings such as "Wir Christenleut" and "Jesu, meine Freude" points to the intense contrapuntal idiom of the Orgel-Büchlein. This, together with the seemingly inexhaustible imagination of the pieces, foreshadows the highly diverse organ chorales that emerge in Arnstadt, Mühlhausen, and Weimar.

Free Works

Four free works can be assigned to Bach's Ohrdruf and Lüneburg years with a good degree of certainty:

Fantasia in C Major, BWV 570
Praeludium in A Minor, BWV 551
Prelude and Fugue in C Major, BWV 531
Prelude and Fugue in D Minor, BWV 549a

The **Fantasia in C Major, BWV 570**, may be Bach's earliest surviving free organ work. It is transmitted in the Andreas Bach Book in the hand of Johann Christoph Bach, and it may have been an Ohrdruf compositional exercise carried out by the young Sebastian under his brother's guidance. It fulfills Central German expectations with its *manualiter* setting, consistent 4-part texture, and spinning out of the *corta* rhythmic figure that was so beloved in Thuringia (in the main section of the piece, the figure appears on every beat save one). The music meanders in an unmemorable way, however, without compelling harmonic goals. Several dominant pedal points are squandered without forceful outcomes (mm. 16–18, 31–33, 35–37), and the only truly effective elements are the increase to 16th-note motion over the final dominant pedal point, creating an intensified close, and the piece's expansive length of 42 measures.

The C-Major Fantasia is much like the pedagogical studies undertaken by Johann Valentin Eckelt with Pachelbel (see chapter 2). Specific models appearing in the Eckelt's tablature workbook are Pachelbel's short Fantasia in G Minor and Froberger's lengthy Capriccio in C Major,[17] both of which explore the potential of the *corta* figure. Idioms similar to that of the Fantasia also appear in the Neumeister Chorales, in pieces such as "Christus, der ist mein Leben," BWV 1112, and "Was Gott tut, das ist wohlgetan," BWV 1116 (from m. 29 to the end). The chorale settings are more focused and carefully organized, however, and the Fantasia seems to predate them.

The **Praeludium in A Minor, BWV 551**, is labeled "Præludium con Fuga pedaliter" in its earliest source, a manuscript from the 1730s or 1740s in the hand of Johannes Ringk,[18] who is also responsible for the earliest copy of the famous Toccata in D Minor, BWV 565. The work is not a Central German prelude-fugue pair, however, but rather a North German multisectional praeludium with a well-defined five-part structure: introduction (mm. 1–12), fugue 1 (mm. 12–28), interlude (mm. 29–39), fugue 2 (mm. 39–74), and conclusion (mm. 75–89). It also displays many features characteristic of Buxtehude: introductory passage-work in two parts, the motivic evolution of the fugue subjects, a chordal interlude, a *trillo longo* (m. 84), a shocking harmonic lurch (to C minor, in m. 63), and gratuitous virtuosic pedal passages in the introduction and conclusion.

Like the Neumeister Chorales, the Praeludium reveals a young composer filled with ambitions that sometimes outstrip his compositional abilities. For instance, the first fugue is based on a subject rich with motivic possibilities: the leap of a

Example 3-5 Praeludium in A Minor, BWV 551: (a) subject of fugue 1, (b) two subjects of fugue 2, and (c) new subject that appears in fugue 2.

fourth, animated 16th notes, and a rising chromatic line (example 3-5, a). The subject appears in two expositions, the first with five entries (mm. 12–21), the second with four entries (mm. 21–27). But the number of parts rarely exceeds three,[19] and the fugue's conclusion in C major, emphasized by four cadences, seems overblown. The short *durezza e ligature* interlude (a seventeenth-century Italian style calling for dissonances and suspensions) that follows mirrors that in Buxtehude's Praeludium in A Major, BuxWV 151, passed down in the Möller Manuscript as a fragment. Here, however, Bach thickened the texture to five parts, perhaps under Böhm's influence.

The second fugue (mm. 39–75) ups the ante of the first by having two subjects, both derived from the theme of fugue 1: the first extends its chromatic line, while the second varies its animated 16th notes (example 3-5, b). The two ideas are presented in well-worked-out invertible counterpoint. Here, too, however, the texture rarely goes beyond three real parts. In time a fourth subject appears (mm. 63–64), one that presents the animated 16th notes and rising chromatic line in yet another form (example 3-5, c). The new theme appears in stretto—a climactic gesture—but the part-writing is mostly two-part and lacks a clear textural buildup to three or four voices. The closing section is filled with North German figuration unleashed in an almost random way: two-part *passaggio* passages, pedal solos, 16th notes in parallel thirds and sixths, and a double trill thrown in for good measure. One senses that Bach was attempting to cover all the North German bases in the Praeludium in A Minor and show off his expertise at motivic development and invertible counterpoint. He was unable at this moment to provide the textural control and sectional unity necessary to create a convincingly

Example 3-6 Prelude and Fugue in C Major, BWV 531: (a) opening pedal fanfare of the Prelude, and (b) Fugue subject derived from the octave of the pedal fanfare.

cohesive piece, however. He would return to the multipartite praeludium later with better success, in the Toccata in E Major, BWV 566.

The Prelude and Fugue in C Major, BWV 531, and Prelude and Fugue in D Minor, BWV 549a, are often discussed together, since they both appear in the Möller Manuscript in Johann Christoph Bach's hand. Both are termed "Præludium Pedaliter," in the North German locution, even though they have a clear Central German prelude-and-fugue design. The erratic part-writing and limited harmonic schemes of the fugues mark them as early pieces, and roughly contemporaneous.

The **Prelude and Fugue in C Major, BWV 531**, is a wild work—Bach's ambitious effort to capture North German virtuosity. The Prelude begins with an energetic pedal solo based on an animated, triadic fanfare motive (example 3-6, a). This motive is then picked up in the manuals in various forms, interrupted by a dash of pedal solo here and there. The texture intensifies in the manuals from measure 30 onward with the introduction of triplets and descending octaves in contrary motion. The octave figuration is quite unorthodox, like the opening unison octaves of the Toccata in D Minor, BWV 565, and one has the sense, as in the Neumeister Chorales, of a young composer striving to be original at all costs. Thick chords with doubled thirds lead to concluding 32nd-note flourishes, in the North German manner.

The octave in the fanfare motive of the Prelude is picked up in the Fugue, whose subject is appropriate neither for a tonal answer nor for pedal performance (example 3-6, b). The first issue resulted in an odd opening exposition in which two statements in the tonic are answered by two statements in the subdominant, as in the fugue of the D-Minor Toccata, once again. All subsequence entries of the subject are in the tonic save for one in the dominant, and even the liveliness and bustle of the 16th-note figuration can't overcome the static nature of the harmonic scheme. In addition, the exposition hints at a four-part fugue, but the writing is almost exclusively two- and three-part, and the pedal enters just once with the subject, for two measures (mm. 23–24), with a modified form of the subject.[20] The fugue concludes, like the Prelude, with 32nd-note figuration, this time over a dominant pedal point. In his later years, Bach referred to this kind of piece as the creation of "clavier hussars," who "let their fingers first play for them what they are to write, instead of writing for the fingers what they shall play."[21] As a youthful sin, perhaps, the C-Major Prelude and Fugue fits comfortably into this category. That said, one can imagine the members of the Church Consistory in Arnstadt being astounded by the pedal work in the Prelude, if Bach happened to play the piece in 1703 to demonstrate the Wender organ in the New Church there.

The **Prelude and Fugue in D Minor, BWV 549a**, is the initial version of the Prelude and Fugue in C Minor, BWV 549, a later arrangement transposed down a step, most probably to avoid the note d' that appears in the pedal in the Prelude.[22] Titled "Præludium ô Fantasia Pedaliter ex D♭" in the Möller Manuscript, it is shorter than the Prelude and Fugue in C Major and less virtuosic. It is more tightly organized, however. The Prelude opens with a North German pedal solo, more carefully arranged harmonically than that of the C-Major Prelude. The mordent and upward leaps of the 3rd and 4th in the pedal solo are then transferred to the manuals and used for imitative counterpoint (example 3-7, a), much as the opening mordent and descending scale are spun out in the Toccata in D Minor. This leads to several linear motives, featuring the same *suspirans* rhythm, over a series of pedal points. And this is followed by grandiose chords with the thirds, sometimes doubled and sometimes not. As in the Prelude in C Major, unprepared triplets appear briefly (m. 21)—there is no unity of figuration yet.

The Fugue features a long, tuneful subject derived from the mordent of the Prelude (example 3-7, b). The opening exposition, which features a series of entries in ascending order, suggests a four- or even five-part fugue, but the texture is mainly two- and three-voice, like that of the Fugue in C Major. All entries of the subject are in the tonic or dominant, and a stab is made at a countersubject, which appears in various guises. The pedal, long delayed, enters dramatically in measure 40, accompanied by six- and seven-part chords. The theme is extended by two measures and reaches a climax with a chordal "tremulant" (example 3-7, c)[23]—an audacious, unconventional gesture calculated to capture attention. As with the opening octaves of the Toccata in D Minor or the octaves in contrary motion in the Prelude in C Major, one suspects that the young Bach was determined to impress with exotic, virtuoso elements, and it is noteworthy that he dropped the tremulant when he fashioned the C-minor arrangement years later.

Example 3-7 Prelude and Fugue in D Minor, BWV 549a: (a) opening theme of the Prelude, first in the pedal (m. 1) and then in the manual voices (m. 6), (b) Fugue subject based on the Prelude theme, and (c) chordal tremulant in the Fugue.

The theme then spins out in manual passagework, a pedal solo, and pedal points that hark back to those of the Prelude. The Fugue concludes with free, recitative-like 32nd notes, like the close of the Prelude and Fugue in C major. In this case, they reflect motives found earlier in the piece, however: the upward leaps of the 3rd and 4th that mark the beginning of both the Prelude and the Fugue.

Of the four free works from Bach's early years, the Prelude and Fugue in D Minor is perhaps the most impressive. In Leipzig Bach returned to the idea of an organ fugue with a delayed pedal entry, in the Prelude and Fugue in C Major ("9/8"), BWV 547, treating the fugue and the gesture with much greater maturity. But the seed of the idea was planted here.

Bach's initial efforts, then, reflect a young, ambitious composer overflowing with ideas and determined to explore and experiment. Cohesion of form and unity of idiom are yet to come.

Notes

1. Yale Music Library, *Ma21.Y11.A30* (formerly *LM 4708*). The Lowell Mason Collection, obtained by Yale in 1873, includes manuscripts from the estate of Christian Heinrich Rinck, the most famous student of Johann Christian Kittel, who in turn had studied with Bach. Rinck received the album in question as a gift from Johann Gottfried Neumeister. See Krumbach 1985, Wolff 1991g, and *The Neumeister Collection of Chorale Preludes from the Bach Circle: A Facsimile Edition*, Christoph Wolff, ed. (New Haven, CT: Yale University Press, 1986).
2. Bach and Sorge were fellow members of Lorenz Christoph Mizler's Corresponding Society of Musical Sciences (see chapter 23).
3. Wolff 1991g, 109.
4. Krumbach 1985, 7–8.
5. Wolff 1991g, 121.
6. Zehnder 2009, 9–236.
7. Dürr 1986, a review of *Johann Sebastian Bach: Orgelchoräle der Neumeister-Sammlung* (New Haven, CT: Yale University Press, and Kassel: Bärenreiter-Verlag, 1985). The works have since been issued in the NBA, as volume IV/9 (Christoph Wolff, ed., 2003).
8. See the examples in Dürr 1986, 310–311.
9. Zehnder 2009, 358.
10. Königsberg University Library, Gotthold Collection, *Mus.ms. 15839* (lost but preserved on film), in the hand of Johann Gottfried Walther.
11. Williams 2003, 570.
12. Zehnder 2009, 224.
13. Breig 1990, 174.
14. Zehnder 2009, 165.
15. Zehnder 2009, 74.

16. Breig 1990, 176.
17. Nos. 15 and 20 in the album. Belotti 2001, 28 and 30.
18. Berlin State Library, *P 595*. Ringk studied with Bach's colleague Johann Peter Kellner, and it is likely that he copied the Praeludium in A Minor from a manuscript in Kellner's possession.
19. Despite the Neue Bach-Ausgabe's attempt to account for a fourth voice with editorial rests. See NBA IV/6 (Dietrich Kilian, ed., 1964), 63–64.
20. In NBA IV/5 (Dietrich Kilian, ed., 1972) the manual bass is incorrectly assigned to the pedal in mm. 36–42. The text is presented correctly in the Breitkopf Edition, vol. 1.
21. Forkel 1802, 23. The comparison used here is drawn from Breig 1999, 645.
22. While the authenticity of the C-minor version has been questioned, the improved readings in the Prelude point to Bach as the arranger.
23. In the *Musicalisches Lexicon* Bach's Weimar Colleague Johann Gottfried Walther explained that on the organ, a tremulant should imitate the shaking of a string tremolo. See Walther 1732, 614.

PART II

THE "FIRST FRUITS"

Arnstadt and Mühlhausen (1703–1708)

He has been in Lübeck in order to comprehend one thing or another about his craft.

—Proceedings of the Arnstadt
Consistory (February 1706)

4

Bach in Arnstadt and Mühlhausen

Organist at the New Church

Bach's appointment as Organist of the New Church in Arnstadt was the result of remarkably fortuitous circumstances. At that point he was young, unknown, and inexperienced, and the position had not been advertised. How, then, did he land the job?

Arnstadt is the oldest city in Thuringia, chartered in 1266 but with roots that can be traced back to the beginning of the eighth century. Its location at the entrance to the Thuringian forest made it an economic crossroads, and by the time of Bach's arrival in 1703 it boasted an expanding population of 3,800 citizens and growing ambitions for music in its churches. Arnstadt was also the residence of Count Anton Günther II (1653–1716), who ruled the Schwarzburg district from the Neideck Castle, where he employed a court theater company and a music ensemble of 22 players.[1]

Arnstadt's religious life was centered in three churches: the Upper Church, the Lower Church, and the New Church. The Upper Church (or Church of the Barefoot Friars), a large Gothic structure completed in 1250, was the principal house of worship. The nobility and leading citizens attended services there, including a Sunday *Hauptgottesdienst* that featured concerted music performed by the best students from the Lyceum, the town's Latin school. On high feasts the student ensemble was supplemented with players from the court.[2] The Upper Church was staffed by the Superintendent of the Lyceum, the City Cantor, and the Town and Court Organist. The Lower Church (or the Church of Our Lady or the Morning Church), one of the most important medieval structures in Thuringia, built over a 150-year period from 1180 to 1330, was used mostly for secondary worship services.

The New Church (or St. Boniface's Church or Sophia's Church; now the Bach Church) was the newcomer, as its name suggests, and the lowest in rank of the three churches. It was built as a hall church in 1676–1683 with funds provided by Princess Sophia to replace St. Boniface's Church, which had been destroyed by fire in 1581. The edifice was restored to life to handle the overflow from the Upper Church, where attendance increased greatly after the Thirty Years War. The upper crust of Arnstadt society worshiped at the Upper Church; the less illustrious citizens attended services at the New Church. On Sundays, choral and

J. S. BACH. George B. Stauffer, Oxford University Press. © Oxford University Press 2024.
DOI: 10.1093/oso/9780195108026.003.0005

concerted works were presented in the New Church by an ensemble of second-tier students from the Lyceum—an aspect of the music-making that was to become a point of contention during Bach's tenure. Organ music was initially provided in a makeshift way on a small portative instrument.

In 1699, driven by the desire to improve the state of music in the New Church, the Arnstadt Consistory commissioned instrument builder Johann Friedrich Wender of Mühlhausen to construct a permanent organ for the sanctuary. By the summer of 1703 the organ was complete and in place, in the rear of the nave in the third gallery, just underneath the barrel vault (plate 4-1, a). This should have been a cause for celebration; instead, it posed a personnel problem. Before the

Plate 4-1, a Arnstadt, New Church: sanctuary, with reconstruction of the Johann Friedrich Wender organ by Hoffmann Orgelbau, 1997–1999.
Bach-Archiv (Beyer Foto, Weimar).

Plate 4-1, b Original key desk and bench of the Wender organ (1699–1703).
Bach-Archiv (Schlossmuseum Arnstadt)

installation of the Wender organ, music in the New Church had been handled by
Andreas Börner (1673–1728), a keyboardist capable of playing the portative organ.
But Börner was not trained to play a large instrument, and he was unqualified to
oversee its tuning, maintenance, and repair.[3] In addition, the Consistory hoped
that once music in the church was enhanced by the Wender organ, the quality of

the choral performances might be improved as well. But here, too, Börner was of no help, since he had little experience with choral music. The Consistory therefore needed different leadership for music in the New Church, a musician who could play the new organ, oversee its care and maintenance, direct a vocal and instrumental ensemble, and, on occasion, compose choral music.

Into this situation walked the eighteen-year-old Johann Sebastian Bach, to examine and approve the new Wender organ. Although Bachs were a well-known commodity in Arnstadt during Count Günther's time—Heinrich Bach, Johann Christoph Bach (1645–1693), and Johann Michael Bach had worked there—it was highly unusual to entrust the inspection of the organ to Johann Sebastian, an individual with no organ position and no credentials as an organ examiner. The most logical explanation for the irregular commission is that Weimar Court Organist Johann Effler, who would have known Bach's talents from his short stay at the court, either recommended Bach or sent Bach to examine the organ on his behalf. The Arnstadt pay records give Bach's title as "Court Organist to the Prince of Saxe-Weimar"—a title that belonged to Effler rather than Bach, who was no more than a lackey musician, as we noted earlier. The mistaken ledger-listing suggests that Bach may have visited Arnstadt in Effler's place.

No matter what the case, Bach came, inspected the organ, and played an inaugural recital the first week in July 1703. His appraisal of the organ and his performance so impressed the Consistory that they shifted Börner's duties to playing at the Lower Church and assisting at the Court Chapel, and they immediately hired Bach to take charge of music in the New Church, at a salary of 50 florins—more than twice Börner's pay. The entire sequence of events took place within a six-week period: on July 3 Bach submitted his appraisal of Wender's work; on July 13 he was paid for testing and playing the organ "for the first time"; and on August 14 he was installed as Organist. It is not difficult to imagine how greatly Bach must have impressed the Consistory with his apparently thorough report[4] and his performance of pieces such as the Prelude and Fugue in C Major, BWV 531, or Prelude and Fugue in D Minor, BWV 549a, with their dazzling display of North German virtuosity and pedal playing. The Consistory had probably seen and heard nothing like it.

Bach's duties at the New Church were light. He was required to play for just four services per week: the main service on Sundays at 8 am, a prayer service on Mondays at 7 a.m., a Vespers service on Wednesdays at 2 p.m., and an early morning service on Thursdays at 7 a.m. Within the service he was responsible for leading and accompanying the congregational singing, providing an organ prelude for each chorale, presenting organ preludes and postludes, and providing communion music, which was usually chorale-based. What was unclear, and later led to disagreements, was his role in working with the second-string student choir from the Lyceum.

Bach also taught his first students in Arnstadt: Johann Martin Schubart (1690–1721) and Johann Caspar Vogler (1696–1763),[5] both of whom followed him to Mühlhausen, and possibly Salomon Günter John (1695–after 1745).[6] Bach may have taken part in the court ensemble in the Neideck Castle as well, as a violinist or continuo player.

The presence of a brand-new organ in the New Church represented a great opportunity for Bach. Many organs at the time were decades or even centuries old and in a bad state of repair. Organists such as Johann Christoph Bach in Eisenach and Georg Böhm in Lüneburg spent much of their careers battling for funds to keep their deteriorating instruments in playing condition. Full access to the Wender organ, plus the modest requirements of the New Church position, created an ideal environment for Bach in which he could study, practice, and compose organ music. As the Obituary later noted:

> Here he really showed the first fruits of his application to the art of organ playing and to composition, which he had learned chiefly by the observation of the works of the most famous and proficient composers of his day and by the fruits of his own reflection upon them. In the art of the organ he took the works of Bruhns, Reincken, Buxtehude, and several good French organists as models.[7]

The Wender organ on which he produced the first fruits was a modest-sized but adequate two-manual instrument of 21 stops. The manual compass was CD–c‴; the pedal compass was CD–d′:[8]

Oberwerk	Brustwerk/Positiv	Pedal
Principal 8'	Stillgedacktes 8'	Sub Baß16'
Viola di Gamba 8'	Principal 4'	Principal 8'
Quintadehna 8'	Spitzflöte 4'	Posaunen Bass 16'
Grobgedacktes 8'	Nachthorn 4'	Cornet Bass 2'
Gemshorn 8'	Quinta 3'	
Offenne Quinta 6'	Sesquialtera doppelt II	
Octava 4'	Mixtur III	
Mixtur IV		
Cymbel II		
Trompete 8'		

The keydesk (or console, in modern terminology), pedalboard, and bench from Bach's time have been preserved and can be viewed today in the New Palace Museum in Arnstadt (plate 4-1, b, above).[9] The Wender organ itself was altered many times after Bach's death, but 10 stops have survived and have been incorporated into a modern reconstruction of the original instrument completed in 1999 by Hoffmann Orgelbau.

Bach's dealings with the Arnstadt Consistory were not the smoothest. In the summer of 1705 he complained that while walking home late at night he had been set upon by Johann Heinrich Geyersbach, a bassoon player in the New Church student ensemble, who claimed Bach had insulted him. Bach drew his sword and the two scuffled, but neither was seriously injured. Bach demanded that Geysersbach be punished and the five other students with him apologize. After listening to testimony from the participants of the incident and interviewing an eyewitness (Barbara Catharina Bach, the sister of Bach's future wife Maria Barbara Bach), the Consistory discussed the matter but apparently took no action.[10]

In February 1706 Bach was chastised by the Consistory on several counts: for overstaying the four-week absence granted for visiting Buxtehude (see below); for his unwillingness to accompany the student ensemble in the performance of choral and concerted music; for introducing strange tones and variations into the chorales; and for making the prelude before the choral music too long and then, after being reproached by the Superintendent, for making it too short.[11] We will look at the Consistory's remarks about Bach's hymn accompaniments in detail when we examine Bach's congregational chorales (see chapter 11), but it is obvious from the general criticism that he was departing from traditional Thuringian practices by presenting longer, more complex chorale preludes, probably based on North German rather than Central German practices, and by accompanying the congregation with bold harmonizations and interludes that went beyond the expected norm. Clearly something was afoot in the organ loft.

Nine months later, in November 1706, the Consistory asked Bach once again if he was willing to work with the student choir, as instructed, and issued a veiled threat of reducing his salary if he was not.[12] It also criticized him for bringing an "unknown woman" into the choir loft and allowing her to make music there. This was probably not his future wife, Maria Barbara Bach, with whom the Consistory would have been acquainted.

The ongoing litany of complaints, which foreshadow the squabbles years later with the Town Council in Leipzig, must have been discouraging for Bach, and when a position opened in Mühlhausen in the spring of 1707, he applied for the job.

The Lübeck Pilgrimage

Before this, however, in the fall of 1705, Bach gained permission from the Consistory for a four-week absence to visit Dieterich Buxtehude in Lübeck. He arranged for his cousin Johann Ernst Bach to cover his duties at the New Church and then set out for Lübeck, probably in early November. The Obituary states that he made the journey on foot, which would have required approximately 15 days each way,[13] and the frigid weather in North Germany would have made the going difficult.

As we noted in chapter 2, Bach was already familiar with Buxtehude's organ music. A visit to Lübeck would have allowed him to obtain additional works, but it also would have provided the opportunity to observe Buxtehude's manner of playing on the magnificent organs of St. Mary's. While Reincken was the senior organist in North Germany, Buxtehude enjoyed a greater reputation in Thuringia, where his music circulated widely in manuscript form. George Frideric Handel and Johann Mattheson had made a similar trip from Hamburg to meet Buxtehude in the summer of 1703 and returned greatly impressed.[14]

The timing of Bach's visit suggests that he was particularly interested in observing the special Abendmusiken concerts that Buxtehude presented each winter during Advent, when organ and concerted music was omitted from the worship service. The concerts had been initiated by Buxtehude's illustrious predecessor, Franz Tunder, as a means of providing music for the public during the Advent hiatus. Buxtehude developed them further, turning them into festive events featuring large, concerted works. On December 2, 1705, Bach had the opportunity to hear "Castrum doloris," BuxWV 134, a memorial anthem for Emperor Leopold I. The next day he could hear "Templum honoris," BuxWV 135, a celebratory piece for Leopold's successor, Joseph I. The music to both works is lost, but the surviving printed texts indicate that the pieces were conceived on a grand scale.

"Templum honoris," for instance, called for two vocal choirs, two vocal soloists, two choirs of brass and timpani, two choirs of horns and oboes, 25 violins, and two organs[15]—forces beyond the imagination of a provincial organist from Arnstadt working with a ragtag student ensemble. It is possible that Bach not only attended the Abendmusiken performances but also played in the ensemble as a continuo keyboardist or violinist, since it is unlikely that Buxtehude would not have put his young visitor to work. During the stay Bach also would have benefited from hearing and undoubtedly playing the Schnitger organ (III/45) in the Cathedral as well as the three organs in St. Mary's: the large main organ (III/54), the organ in the "Dance of Death" Chapel (III/40), and the rood screen organ (disposition uncertain).[16]

Bach remained in Lübeck for almost three months,[17] possibly assisting Buxtehude during church services in return for the opportunity to make copies of his organ and choral works. When the Consistory questioned Bach about the trip upon his return to Arnstadt, he responded that he had undertaken the journey so that he could "comprehend one thing or another about his craft."[18] The Lübeck pilgrimage represented the final lesson of his tutorial on North German music.

Organist at St. Blasius's Church

Less than a month after Bach was reprimanded for a third time in November 1706 by the Arnstadt Consistory, the position of Organist at the St. Blasius Church in Mühlhausen opened with the death of Johann Georg Ahle, who had held the post since 1673. Johann Gottfried Walther, Bach's future colleague in Weimar, later mentioned that he himself applied for the job by submitting two church works of his own composition but then withdrew his application for one reason or another. Bach apparently applied after Walther, and that may have been the reason Walther changed his mind. No matter what the actual circumstances, by April 1707 Bach seems to have been the only viable candidate for the position, and on Easter Sunday that month he formally auditioned by performing a cantata within the worship service. The cantata was presumably one of his submission pieces, and it may well have been Cantata 4, *Christ lag in Todesbanden*, an Easter work that dates from around that time.[19] Bach was offered the job, and he began his duties in June 1707 after resigning in Arnstadt, where he was replaced by his cousin Johann Ernst Bach, who had filled in for him during the Lübeck trip.

Mühlhausen was the second largest city in Thuringia after Erfurt. An Imperial Free City, it was the Central German equivalent of Hamburg or Lübeck, with a town council that reported directly to the emperor in Vienna. Mühlhausen had experienced difficult times in the 1680s, losing more than 4,000 citizens to the plague of 1682–1683 and more than 500 buildings to the Great Fire of 1689.[20] But it had quickly recovered, and by 1707 it enjoyed a robust population of 7,000. Although it had suffered a devastating fire in May of that year, just before Bach's arrival, it was a bustling, prospering city.

Of the thirteen churches within the city wall, St. Mary's and St. Blasius's were the most prominent. St. Mary's was the home of the City Council and civic government and featured one of the largest organs (III/60) in Thuringia, complete with a 10-rank mixture and 32' Sub-Baß and 32' Groß-Posaune in the pedal. St. Blasius's was the home of the church government and the superintendent of the Latin School. It contained a much smaller organ (II/29) that had recently been refurbished and enlarged by Wender. The manual compass was CD–c'''; the pedal compass was CD–d'.[21]

Hauptwerk	Rückpositiv	Pedal
Quintatön 16'	Gedackt 8'	Principal 16'
Principal 8'	Quintatön 8'	Subbaß 16'
Gemßhorn 8'	Principal 4'	Octave 8'
Octave 4'	Salicional 4'	Octave 4'
Gedackt 4'	Quintflöte 4'	Rohrflötenbaß 1'

Hauptwerk	Rückpositiv	Pedal
Quinte 3'	Sesquialtera II	Mixtur IV
Sesquialtera II	Octave 2'	Posaunbaß 16'
Octave 2'	Spitzflöte 2'	Trompete 8'
Mixtur IV	Cymbel III	Cornetbaß 2'
Cymbel II		
Trompette 8'		

Bach's duties at St. Blasius included providing organ music for the services on Sundays, Feast Days, and Holy Days; accompanying congregational singing; and providing preludes, fugues, and chorale elaborations before the singing of chorales and during Communion.[22] This was similar to his responsibilities in Arnstadt. In Mühlhausen, however, he was also expected to collaborate with the town musicians and the chorus and instrumental ensemble of the Mühlhausen Gymnasium, the Latin school that provided student musicians for both churches. Bach was also required to play, in weekly alternation with the organist of St. Mary's, at Mary Magdalene's Church in the Augustinian Convent and the churches of St. Kilian's, All Saints, and Holy Cross in town. Most important, perhaps, he was also granted the opportunity to occasionally compose and perform his own church works. Although Bach's salary was roughly the same as that in Arnstadt (he later cited this as a reason for leaving), his position in Mühlhausen represented a professional step upward.

On October 17, 1707, Bach married his second cousin Maria Barbara Bach (1684–1720), whom he had courted in Arnstadt. The wedding took place in the ancient Church of St. Bartholomew in Dornheim, a small village just outside Arnstadt, and was officiated by Lorenz Stauber, who soon married Maria Barbara's aunt, Regina Wedemann. Bach may have composed Cantata 196, *Der Herr denket an uns*, for the Dornheim nuptials.[23]

After just seven months in his new post, Bach submitted a proposal to the Town Council to refine and significantly expand the organ in St. Blasius's, most probably to bring it into line with the much larger instrument in St. Mary's. The proposal is a remarkable document, for it shows that at age 22, Bach already had a deep understanding of the mechanics and tonal design of organs.[24] He recommended that the pedal division be strengthened through the addition of a 32' Untersatz and larger resonators and new shallots for the 16' Posaunbaß, that a 16' Fagotto be added to the Hauptwerk, for use in concerted music and improvisations, and that the Gemshorn 8' on the Hauptwerk be replaced by a Viol di Gamba 8', a more fashionable stop. He also proposed the addition of an entirely new seven-stop Brustwerk, with a wooden Gedackt 8' for choral accompaniment and a Terz

1 3/5' that could be used to create yet another Sesquialtera (both the Hauptwerk and Rückpositiv already had Sesquialtera mixtures). And he supported the addition of a Glockenspiel of 26 bells "desired by the parishioners" and purchased at their expense. Oddly, he placed the Glockenspiel in the Pedal rather than the manuals. The Council approved the plan within a few days and allotted funds for carrying it out—a remarkable vote of confidence for their new young organist.

While in Mühlhausen Bach also composed his first datable cantatas: Cantata 71, *Gott ist mein König*, for the change of the Town Council in 1708, and Cantata 131, *Aus der Tiefen rufe ich, Herr, zu dir*, composed at the request of Archdeacon Georg Christian Eilmar, pastor of St. Mary's Church. Cantata 106, *Gottes Zeit ist die allerbeste Zeit*, and Cantatas 4 and 196, already mentioned, also appear to have been written for Mühlhausen performances. Of these works, Cantata 71 is especially impressive. Scored for four instrumental choirs (trumpets, violins, oboes, and recorders, each with a bass component), two vocal choirs (SATB solo, SATB ripieno), and organ, it reflects Bach's great ambitions as a vocal composer as well as his Lübeck experience with Buxtehude's large *Abendmusiken* works. When Bach resigned from his Mühlhausen position, he stated that he had already assembled a "good store" of church pieces "acquired from far and wide, not without cost."[25] These pieces may have included Buxtehude cantatas obtained during his Lübeck trip, especially since Cantata 71, in particular, displays so many Buxtehudian traits.

Bach's treatment of the organ in Cantata 71 is telling, for it reveals his youthful writing for the instrument at a precise point in time—February 1708. In the Air "Ich bin nun achtzig Jahr," Bach features the organ as an obbligato instrument, first echoing the tenor with short interjections but then presenting longer embellishments in florid triplets that eventually take over the melodic content and round out the movement (example 4-1, a). The great mix of rhythmic figures—*corta* motives, triplets, slurred 16th notes—suggests that Bach had not yet fully adopted a more unified, homogeneous approach to motivic elaboration. And in the last movement, "Das neue Regiment," Bach uses the organ for a single obbligato flourish (mm. 30–33) before requiring it to play an unusual drum-like chord in the lowest octave of the keyboard at the conclusion of the two festive "Glück, Heil und großer Sieg" sections (example 4-1, b). This type of truly original figure parallels other brash early experiments like the chordal tremulant in the Prelude and Fugue in D Minor, BWV 549a, or the opening octaves in the Toccata in D Minor, BWV 565. The young Bach seems to have been determined to try every possible organ sonority.

In June 1708, just a little more than a year after taking the job, Bach resigned from his position at St. Blasius Church to accept a post at the Weimar court. In a long letter he thanked the members of the Town Council for the opportunity to work in Mühlhausen but expressed concern about his modest salary and the lack

Example 4-1 Cantata 71, *Gott ist mein König*: (a) Air "Ich bin nun achtzig Jahr," mm. 39–47, with obbligato organ part, and (b) Arioso "Das neue Regiment," mm. 100–103, organ part, with unusual bass chords.

Example 4-1 *continued.*

of prospects for a "well-regulated church music." The latter may have referred to the animosity between the ministers of St. Mary's and St. Blasius's, who feuded over clashing theological views.[26]

The Council granted Bach's dismissal but expressed the hope that he would oversee the completion of the organ project he had initiated. He apparently did, and he may have dedicated the instrument in February 1709 or February 1710, when he returned to Mühlhausen to direct performances of cantatas he had composed for the change of the Town Council.[27] He may have played the chorale setting "Ein feste Burg ist unser Gott," BWV 720, to demonstrate the expanded resources of the new organ (see chapter 5). Whether or not this was the case, Bach clearly left Mühlhausen on good terms, and he returned once again in June 1735 to accompany his son Johann Gottfried Bernhard during Bernhard's successful audition for the organist position in St. Mary's Church.

Notes

1. Schiffner 1985, 15.
2. Schiffner 1985, 15.
3. Wollny 2005, 89.
4. The report is lost, but Bach's detailed proposal for the rebuilding of the St. Blasius organ in Mühlhausen five years later gives a good idea of his youthful expertise.
5. Koska 2019, 26–27.

6. Koska 2012, 228–230.
7. NBR, no. 306.
8. Wolff and Zepf 2012, 9–10.
9. The keydesk has been restored several times since it was removed from the organ in 1864. The latest iteration, pictured here, appears to be the most historically accurate.
10. NBR, no. 19, a–d.
11. NBR, no. 20.
12. NBR, no. 21.
13. Marshall and Marshall 2016, 165.
14. Mattheson 1740, 94. Mattheson reported that they were invited by the president of the Lübeck Town Council to explore the possibility of succeeding Buxtehude, who was 67 at the time. Both lost interest when they discovered that the position required marrying Buxtehude's daughter Anna Margareta.
15. The work is discussed in detail in Wolff 1991d, 47–51.
16. Mattheson mentioned that during his visit in 1703, he and Handel "played almost all the organs" in Lübeck. The instruments in St. Mary's and the Cathedral are described in Wolff and Zepf 2011, 58–62 and 119–121.
17. The Consistory in Arnstadt complained that Bach had been away for four months, while the Obituary states that he tarried in Lübeck for almost three months. The difference in the two figures can be explained by the month required for travel by foot.
18. NBR, no. 20.
19. Dürr 1977, 167–168.
20. Marshall and Marshall 2016, 41.
21. Wolff and Zepf 2012, 71–72.
22. Ernst 1987, 77.
23. Mary Greer, "From the House of Aaron to the House of Johann Sebastian: Old Testament Roots for the Bach Family Tree," in *About Bach*, Gregory G. Butler, George B. Stauffer, and Mary Dalton Greer, eds. (Urbana: University of Illinois Press, 2008), 24–25. Spitta, on the other hand, proposed that the work was written for Stauber's wedding. Spitta 1873–80, vol. 1, 371.
24. Bach's proposal is reproduced in full in Wolff and Zepf 2012, 141–142. The translation, by Lynn Edwards Butler, is more accurate in terms of organ terminology than that in NBR, no. 31.
25. NBR, no. 32.
26. Johann Adolf Frohne, stationed at the St. Blasius Church, and Georg Christian Eilmar, stationed at St. Mary's Church, quarreled over the proper interpretation of the Bible. See Martin Petzoldt, *Bachstätten aufsuchen* (Leipzig: Verlag Kunst und Touristik Leipzig, 1992), 133–135.
27. The music and texts of both works are lost, but their one-time existence is confirmed by honorarium and printing payments. See NBA I/32.1, KB (Christine Fröde, ed.; 1992), 85–88.

5

Chorale-Based Works

Chorale Settings

Not surprisingly, the "first fruits" of Bach's chorale-prelude-writing in Arnstadt
and Mühlhausen form a natural extension of the Neumeister Chorales. Some
settings are solidly Central German in style; others are solidly North German
in style. Still others show a bold blending of the two idioms, which are sometimes juxtaposed in unconventional ways that produce abrupt changes of *affect*.
The Arnstadt and Mühlhausen pieces are more expansive than the Neumeister
Chorales, however, and more commonly feature the use of obbligato pedal. At
the same time, the settings display few signs of the influence of Italian instrumental music that later characterizes the Weimar organ chorales. During the
Arnstadt/Mühlhausen years Bach continued looking northward for external inspiration, as is confirmed by the North German nature of the vocal works from
this time, such as Cantata 196, *Der Herr denket an uns*; Cantata 106, *Gottes Zeit
ist die allerbeste Zeit*; and Cantata 71, *Gott ist mein König*.

A good number of chorale settings from this general period are passed down
in the sources under Bach's name. The authenticity of some can be confirmed
through the existence of autograph manuscripts or reliable early copies and
through the general acceptance of a work's compositional style. The authenticity
of other pieces is less firmly established and remains open to question. To explore Bach's chorale writing in Arnstadt and Mühlhausen, we will look at a select
group of compositions—settings that are included in BWV[3] and whose authenticity is broadly acknowledged:[1]

Erbarm dich mein, o Herre Gott, BWV 721
Wie schön leuchtet der Morgenstern, BWV 739
Wie schön leuchtet der Morgenstern (fragment), BWV 764
O Lamm Gottes, unschuldig, BWV 1085
Wir glauben all an einen Gott, BWV 765
Christ lag in Todesbanden, BWV 718
Ein feste Burg ist unser Gott, BWV 720
Valet will ich dir geben, BWV 735a
Herr Christ, der einig Gottes Sohn, BWV[3] 1170 (formerly BWV[1] Anh. 55)

J. S. BACH. George B. Stauffer, Oxford University Press. © Oxford University Press 2024.
DOI: 10.1093/oso/9780195108026.003.0006

"Erbarm dich mein, o Herre Gott," BWV 721, is a stylistic unicum. There is nothing else like it among Bach's other organ works, and if it were not attributed to Bach in a reliable source, Johann Gottfried Walther's copy from c. 1710–1714,[2] we might suspect that it was written by another composer. The text of the chorale, published by Erhart Hegenwalt in 1524 and based on Psalm 51 ("Have mercy upon me, O God"), was described in a Dresden hymnal of 1727 as "a penitential prayer for merciful forgiveness of original and actual sins."[3]

Bach arranged this beseeching prayer as an unadorned, half-note soprano cantus firmus with interludes, accompanied by three-, four-, and even five-part 8th-note chords that are steadily repeated in the manner of an expressive string tremolo. Similar homophonic textures appear in two North German cantatas: a setting of "Erbarm dich mein" in *Erbarm dich mein, o Herre Gott*, BuxWV Anh. 9, once attributed to Dieterich Buxtehude but now assigned to his pupil Ludwig Busbetzky,[4] and a setting of "Aus tiefer Not, schrei ich zu dir" in *Ach Herr, komme hinab und hilfe meinem Sohne* by Georg Böhm.[5]

Closer to home is the section "The trembling of the Israelites at the sudden appearance of the giant, and their prayer made to God" from Johann Kuhnau's first Biblical Sonata, "The Combat between David and Goliath," a harpsichord work published in 1700 and copied into the Andreas Bach Book.[6] In this sonata, the chorale "Aus tiefer Not" is set as a half-note soprano cantus firmus accompanied by repeated 8th-note chords with string-like slurrings (example 5-1). The accompaniment fluctuates between three and four parts, and expressive chromaticism captures the despair of the text, which is based on Psalm 130, "Out of the depths have I cried unto thee, O Lord."

Bach's setting of "Erbarm dich mein" has the same character, produced in the same way. Like Kuhnau's movement, it resembles an instrumental transcription, and the 8th-note chords should probably be similarly slurred as pairs, to create a throbbing pulse. Bach's chromaticism is more nuanced than Kuhnau's, and 7th and 9th chords enrich the harmony in a more subtle way. The choice of F♯ minor, the Baroque key of melancholy, also heightens the penitential nature of the music. It is noteworthy that Bach turned to F♯ minor in his organ chorales just two other times, for the melody chorale "Herzlich tut mich verlangen," BWV 727, of Weimar, and the manual setting of "Aus tiefer Not, schrei ich zu dir," BWV 687, in Clavier-Übung III of 1739.

How "Erbarm dich mein" is to be performed is not fully clear. The work can be played comfortably on one manual without pedal, in the same manner as Kuhnau's movement and Bach's *manualiter* "Aus tiefer Not," both of which treat the chorale melody as a half-note cantus firmus. But "Erbarm dich mein" can also be played effectively on one manual and pedal or on two manuals and pedal, with the chorale highlighted on a second keyboard with a solo stop. The latter might be imposing a North German "á 2 Clavier e Pedal" interpretation on a Central German piece,

Example 5-1 "The trembling of the Israelites at the sudden appearance of the giant, and their prayer made to God," mm. 1–9, from Johann Kuhnau, Biblical Sonata I, "The Combat between David and Goliath."

however, and detract from its natural simplicity. It may be significant that Walther's manuscript—the only early source of the work—lacks manual and pedal indications altogether, implying a purely *manualiter* performance, on one keyboard.

"**Wie schön leuchtet der Morgenstern**," BWV 739, holds a special place among Bach's organ works, since it is the earliest of his compositions to be preserved in his own hand—a fair-copy autograph dating from c. 1704–1705.[7] It is also passed down in the Möller Manuscript, in a copy made by Bach's brother Johann Christoph before 1707, and in the Plauen Organ Book, in an anonymous copy from 1710 or so.

The setting is a restless mix of styles, like many of the Neumeister Chorales. The Stollen of the chorale is treated in a Central German way. The melody appears as an unadorned, half-note cantus firmus, first in the soprano (for phrases 1–3 of the chorale) and then in the pedal (for the repeat of phrases 1–3). The cantus is accompanied by two manual parts in animated 16th notes. There is some fore-imitation in the initial run-through of the Stollen; in the repeat the counterpoint is mostly free. All this follows Pachelbelian principles.[8]

An echo passage between the Oberwerk and Rückpositiv (mm. 36–40) serves as a bridge to the Abgesang, where the cantus firmus continues to sound in half notes in the pedal but with diverse accompaniments. Phrase 4 of the chorale is accompanied by syncopated chords, phrase 5 by 32nd-note flourishes, phrase 6 by half-note fore-imitation in the tenor and soprano and Böhm-like, off-beat, triadic figures (much like variation 9 of the Passacaglia in C Minor, BWV 582), and phrase 7 by a half-note fore-imitation in the tenor amid abundant free counterpoint. All of this is rounded off by a final outburst of manual fireworks: rapid scales and 32nd-note anapest figures (which hark back to phrase 5 of the setting but also resemble the seemingly improvised figures in the Prelude of the Prelude and Fugue in G Minor, BWV 535a, a work that also appears in the Möller Manuscript in Bach's hand). The echo bridge, the virtuosic play, and the sudden changes of figuration in the Abgesang mirror North German chorale-fantasia style, writ small.

The presence of the "Wie schön leuchtet" setting in three important early sources—Bach's autograph, the Möller Manuscript, and the Plauen Organ Book—and its very specific performance instructions (carefully annotated manual changes and left- and right-hand indications)[9] suggest that the piece may have been intended for a special event. In addition, the page turn alerts—"volti presto" (Turn quickly!) —in Bach's manuscript hint that the score was used for public performance. Jean-Claude Zehnder has proposed that Bach may have played the setting at the inauguration of the Wender organ in Arnstadt in July 1703.[10] This could well be, and it would place the setting at the very beginning of Bach's Arnstadt stay, a dating that would make it a companion of "Erbarm dich mein," which appears to be very early as well.

In Bach's autograph, "Wie schön leuchtet" leads directly to a second setting of the tune **"Wie schön leuchet der Morgenstern,"** BWV 764, labeled simply "a 4." Like the first setting, the second is a fair copy autograph, with just a few compositional revisions here and there. The "a 4" arrangement breaks off after 23 measures, followed by almost two pages of empty staves.

This second setting, an "alio modo" (another manner) piece of sorts, is much more disciplined than the first. Like the first, it features an unadorned half-note cantus firmus in the soprano, with short interludes. But the cantus firmus is accompanied by a single off-beat *corta* figure that evolves with each line of the Stollen:

Phrase 1	Off-beat *corta* figure, in 3-part fore-imitation
Phrase 2	Off-beat *corta* figure, upright and inverted, in 3-part fore-imitation
Phrase 3	Off-beat *corta* figure, upright and inverted, in 3-part fore-imitation
Phrase 1a	Off-beat figure, filled in with 16th notes, in 4-part fore-imitation

The setting breaks off abruptly in the repeat of the Stollen, after three notes of the cantus firmus.

The half-note cantus firmus, fore-imitation, strict adherence to four-part texture, and homogeneous nature of the accompanying parts are characteristic of Central German style. But the use of one motive for all phrases of the cantus firmus is not. It foreshadows the more unified writing of the Orgel-Büchlein, where each setting is built upon a single motive, creating a single *affect*. At the same time, the evolution of the motive during the course of the Stollen points to Bach's early obsession with compositional variety.

Whether or not Bach finished the second setting of "Wie schön leuchtet" cannot be determined. It appears that the music was copied from another source, and in that source the text may have been complete. It is unfortunate that the piece is transmitted in a partial form, for it has a forward-looking idiom and the same off-beat energy and drive as "Valet will ich dir geben," BWV 736, a more highly unified work from the Weimar years. Unless additional sources emerge, the "a 4" arrangement of "Wie schön leuchtet" must remain an intriguing fragment.

"O Lamm Gottes, unschuldig," BWV 1085, preserved in copies by Johann Gottfried Walther from c. 1710–1714[11] and the Gehren Johann Christoph Bach from around the same time,[12] is a three-part, *manualiter* spinoff of a Central German fore-imitation chorale. Bach's handling of the fore-imitation for the first three phrases of Nicolaus Decius's Agnus Dei hymn is straightforward, but his treatment of the chorale melody is not. The tune appears in the soprano as a half-note cantus firmus embellished with 8th notes. In phrase 4 the embellishments become more florid, however, and the phrase is not preceded by fore-imitation, giving it greater urgency. The sudden appearance of chromaticism and the movement toward C minor seem to reflect the anxiety expressed in Decius's text: "Otherwise we would have to despair." Phrase 5 is preceded by free counterpoint in the form of leaping 8th notes that migrate into the chorale melody itself, which is loosely outlined in the animated figures taken over from the accompaniment (example 5-2). The melody concludes on the downbeat of measure 36, followed by a short coda and a turn to the subdominant. The setting ends in a Central German manner, with the sudden addition of a fourth voice in the final two measures. While the use of fore-imitation is reminiscent of Pachelbel and Johann Michael Bach, the metamorphosis of the chorale melody from embellished cantus firmus to 8th-note figuration is highly irregular. We can credit it once again to Bach's youthful quest for new ideas.[13]

"Wir glauben all an einen Gott," BWV 765, adheres more closely to Central German style. Subtitled "à 4" in Johann Tobias Krebs's copy from c. 1714–1717,[14] it is a four-part *manualiter* fore-imitation setting of the first four phrases of

Example 5-2 "O Lamm Gottes, unschuldig," BWV 1085, mm. 31–36: last phrase of the chorale tune (above) and its appearance in the upper voice of Bach's setting (below).

Luther's eleven-phrase hymn on the Creed. The similarity between the fourth and the last phrases of the chorale allowed Bach to present an abridged version of the melody that nevertheless has a sense of closure.

Bach cast the music in alla breve style, in ¢ meter with predominantly white-note motives. The *corta* rhythm so beloved by Central German composers is present here but expressed in quarter and 8th notes. The phrases of the chorale are preceded by a decreasing number of fore-imitation entries:

Phrase 1   4 entries (soprano, alto, tenor, bass)

Phrase 2   3 entries (tenor, bass, alto)

Phrase 3   1 entry (bass) together with a second imitative motive (tenor, alto) that appears upright and inverted

Phrase 4   Free counterpoint

"Wir glauben all" resembles "O Lamm Gottes" in a sense, since both rely on the gradual transformation of an aspect of the traditional fore-imitation chorale: in "O Lamm Gottes" it is the cantus firmus that evolves; in "Wir glauben all" it is the fore-imitation accompaniment that changes. Both works point to Bach's desire to create dynamic chorale settings that avoid both the static nature of the Central German fore-imitation chorale and the abrupt shifts of the North German chorale fantasia. That said, the sudden flurry of 8th and 16th notes in "Wir glauben" at the end of the final phrase of the cantus firmus, presented over the concluding tonic pedal, reminds one of Buxtehude's melody chorales.[15]

No early chorale setting better illustrates Bach's full familiarity with the works of Böhm, Buxtehude, and Reincken than **"Christ lag in Todesbanden,"** BWV 718. Scored "à 2 Clavier et Pedal," it represents a succinct survey of chorale preluding techniques according to the North German playbook. The piece opens with a bicinium in the Böhmian manner, with the two lines of the Stollen presented as a florid melody on the Rückpositiv over a descending quasi-ostinato bass on the Oberwerk. The bass theme, filled with *corta* figures, is varied (m. 3), inverted (mm. 6 and 9), and transposed (m. 9). In an early copy of the setting in the hand of Johann Ludwig Krebs (son of Johann Tobias Krebs and likewise a Bach student), the bass is heavily ornamented.[16] In the repeat of the Stollen, the two lines of the florid chorale melody, now supplemented here and there by a second part, are preceded by segments of two-part fore-imitation. Both melodic phrases in the Stollen repeat dissolve into ornamental triplets, much like those that emerge in the organ obbligato part of the air "Ich bin nun achtzig Jahr" from Cantata 71, *Gott ist mein König*, of 1708 (see example 4-1). The cantata movement is also cast as a quasi-ostinato form, marked "Andante," which is probably the appropriate tempo for the opening section of the "Christ lag in Todesbanden" setting.

The tempo changes to allegro for the Abgesang of the chorale, probably to reflect the third line of Luther's text: "For this we should be glad." Line 3 of the chorale tune is treated abstractly (marked *x* in example 5-3, a), surrounded by active counterpoint below and above (a semitone motive, derived from the opening three notes of the chorale; *y* in example 5-3, a). Line 4 is embellished by triplets, much in the fashion of the 12/8-meter dance section of Buxtehude's chorale fantasia "Gelobst seist du, Jesu Christ," BuxWV 188.[17] After the appearance of the chorale tune, the triplets lapse briefly into a canon at the fifth (mm. 37–39). Line 5 brings North German echo exchanges, through changes of manual, from Oberwerk to Rückpositiv, and changes of octave. This section is long and diffuse, much like the echo passages in Reincken's "An Wasserflüssen Babylon" and Buxtehude's "Nun freut euch, lieben Christen gemein," the two North German chorale fantasias Bach wrote out as a young boy (see chapter 2). Line 6, the concluding Alleluia, appears first in diminutions as an animated stepwise figure (example 5-3, b) before emerging from the two-part counterpoint as an unembellished half-note cantus firmus, first in the tenor, then the soprano, and finally the bass, now taken by the pedal. The setting concludes with a blitz of 16th-note flourishes.

"Christ lag in Todesbanden" is a freewheeling piece in the Böhm, Reincken, and Buxtehude vein. As Michael Kube has nicely put it, the setting "encapsulates

Example 5-3 "Christ lag in Todesbanden," BWV 718: (a) third phrase of the chorale melody (above) and, in decorated form (marked x) in the upper voice of Bach's setting, accompanied by a motive (y) derived from the first phrase of the chorale, and (b) the Alleluia phrase of the chorale in Bach's setting, first in embellished diminutions and then as a cantus firmus in the tenor.

everything that the young Johann Sebastian Bach learned in Lüneburg, Hamburg, and Lübeck."[18]

As was the case with "Wie schön leuchtet der Morgenstern," BWV 739, the presence of **"Ein feste Burg ist unser Gott," BWV 720**, in several important early sources, the Plauen Organ Book, two manuscript copies by Johann Gottfried Walther, and a manuscript copy by Johann Tobias Krebs,[19] and the work's explicit performance indications—"à 3 Clav. et Ped." and manual and stop indications—suggest that it was intended for a special event. Ever since Philipp Spitta, in fact, it has been associated with the dedication of the expanded Wender organ in St. Blasius Church in Mühlhausen,[20] a project that was completed shortly after Bach's departure for Weimar in July 1708. There is no documentary evidence of an inaugural recital, but as we noted in chapter 4, Bach returned to Mühlhausen in February 1709 and February 1710 to direct cantatas he had written for the annual change of Town Council, and he could have examined the enlarged instrument and demonstrated its resources to the public on either of those occasions. Although Luther's 1527 chorale, a paraphrase of Psalm 46, is often linked with Reformation Day, in October, it was more commonly classified as "Christian Church" and "Word of God" in early hymnals;[21] thus it would have been liturgically acceptable as part of an organ dedication in February.

Like "Christ lag in Todesbanden," "Ein feste Burg" is a display piece showing multiple improvisatory gestures. The Stollen of the chorale is set as a bicinium, with the lightly embellished chorale lines appearing first in the right hand and then the left. The Stollen breaks into three-part texture as it concludes. The Abgesang begins as a trio, with a florid version of line 3 of the chorale in the right hand, with *suspirans* hiccups, accompanied by mirroring counterpoint in the left hand and a continuo-like pedal line. The chorale tune then moves to the pedal for lines 4 and 5, where it appears as unadorned half notes accompanied by imitative counterpoint in the hands. Line 6 is presented as a florid melody in the soprano. And for the final phrase, line 7, the chorale appears as an undecorated half-note cantus firmus, first in the soprano, as part of a duet, and then, for the finale, in the alto against imitative counterpoint in the soprano and tenor and a continuo bass in the pedal. The setting concludes with flourishes of 16th notes and finally 32nd notes over a tonic pedal.

Peter Williams described "Ein feste Burg" as "a tapestry of paraphrases,"[22] and the setting certainly reflects the adventurous if not fully disciplined spirit of the Arnstadt and Mühlhausen chorales. The stop indications at the beginning of the score, "Fagotto" for the left hand and "Sesquialtera" for the right hand, passed down in the Plauen album and one of Walther copies,[23] correspond with new registers on the enlarged Mühlhausen organ,[24] as does the unusual designation "à 3 Clav. et Ped.," which appears in the same manuscripts. But the style of the setting points to a period before the Mühlhausen cantatas of 1707 and 1708. Bach may have composed the piece in 1706 or so and subsequently pulled it off the shelf to play in Mühlhausen in 1709 or 1710, just as he used a previously composed piece, the "Dorian" Toccata and Fugue in D Minor, BWV 538, written in Weimar, for an organ dedication in Kassel during the Leipzig years (see chapter 15). He may have added the registration instructions to "Ein feste Burg" in the process, which would explain why they are present in the Plauen and Walther manuscripts but absent in other copies.

In the final two pieces, "Valet will ich dir geben" and "Herr Christ, der einig Gottes Sohn," we find Bach striving to create a more highly unified type of chorale setting, one that foreshadows his Weimar works.

"Valet will ich dir geben," BWV 735a, is handed down in important early sources, too: the Plauen Organ Book, two copies by Walther, and a copy by an anonymous Weimar scribe, most probably one of Bach's organ students.[25] This hints at the piece's importance, as does the fact that Bach revised it at a later point as BWV 735, most probably in Leipzig.[26]

The setting is highly uniform in terms of procedure: each phrase of the chorale is treated with embellished fore-imitation in quarter notes and animated counterpoint, leading to the unembellished cantus firmus in the pedal, also in quarter notes. While the various expositions are irregular, there is no change of *affect*. An ongoing flow of uninterrupted 16th notes drives the music forward to its pedal-point close. There are fingerprints of Bach's early keyboard style: the broken chord idiom (mm. 50–55) that also appears in the concluding partita of "Christ, der du bist der helle Tag," BWV 766, and several Neumeister Chorales ("Du Friedefürst, Herr Jesu Christ," BWV 1102, or "Jesu, meines Lebens Leben," BWV 1107, for instance) and the sudden outburst of 32nd-note figures in the final measures. And there are signs of Böhm's influence: the use of quarter notes for both the fore-imitation and the cantus firmus, the turn to free counterpoint before the repetition of line 1 of the Stollen (mm. 17–20), and the use of half-phrases as fore-imitation for the penultimate line of the chorale (mm. 42–46), with the Bachian twist of juxtaposing the first half and second half of the line contrapuntally (example 5-4).

But there are also indications of growing maturity: the maintenance of four real parts, including pedal, throughout; the ongoing inversion of contrapuntal motives to create variety within unity; and the convincing reference to the subdominant with the introduction of a♭ over the concluding tonic pedal-point. When revising the setting at a later point, Bach replaced the broken-chord passage with linear counterpoint in contrary motion (example 5-5) and the concluding 32nd-note figures with even 16th-note scales climbing to the highest register of the keyboard. The fact that he returned to the "Valet will ich dir geben"

Example 5-4 "Valet will ich dir geben," BWV 735a: (a) the fifth phrase of the chorale melody, and (b) Bach's fore-imitation, using the first half of the phrase (x) plus the second half (y) as a counter-motive.

setting confirms the value he placed in this "first fruit" from the Arnstadt-Mühlhausen years.[27]

"Herr Christ, der einig Gottes Sohn," BWV^3 1170 (formerly BWV^1 Anh. 55), is handed down without ascription in a Johann Tobias Krebs copy from c. 1714–1717.[28] It can be assigned to Bach with a reasonable degree of certainty on the basis of a title page written by Johann Gottlieb Preller in the 1740s,[29] and in BWV^3 it has been removed from the "Uncertain Works," where it was listed as Anh. 55, and shifted to the "Authentic Works," where it has been given the new number, BWV 1170.

It is an unusually progressive piece. Transmitted with "Wir glauben all an einen Gott," BWV 765, it appears to date either from the final years of the Arnstadt-Mühlhausen period,[30] or the initial years of the Weimar period.[31] It is an organ trio "à 2 Clav. et Ped.," with the right hand presenting a ritornello-like figure, the left hand a lightly embellished chorale cantus firmus, and the pedal a continuo part. Thus, with soprano and tenor parts over a bass, it resembles North German trios such as Buxtehude's opus 1 and opus 2 trios for violin, viola da gamba, and continuo rather than an Italian trio with two violins and continuo. Another sign of its North German orientation is its similarity to versus 3, "Jesus

Example 5-5 "Valet will ich dir geben," mm. 51–53: (a) the initial version, BWV 735a, with broken-chord, *style brisé* texture, and (b) the revised version, BWV 735, with the *brisé* writing replaced by linear counterpoint.

Christus, Gottes Sohn," an aria for unison violins, tenor cantus firmus, and continuo, from Cantata 4, *Christ lag in Todesbanden*, a North German–style work from the late Mühlhausen or early Weimar years. It also owes a debt to versus 2 of Böhm's "Aus tiefer Not schrei ich zu dir," a somewhat incongruously merry quartet with the fragmented melody of the chorale appearing in the tenor (see chapter 2).

The ritornello of "Herr Christ, der einig Gottes Sohn" is derived from the first five notes of the chorale melody, with the final three notes of the chorale phrase, f♯ f♯ e, appearing in the continuo bass (example 5-6). The ritornello appears in the home key at the beginning and end of the setting and in related keys in the interludes between the chorale's five phrases. It is composed of three segments—a, b, and c—and appears in varied and abridged forms:[32]

Example 5-6 "Herr Christ, der einge Gottes Sohn," BWV 1169: the ritornello theme, derived from the first five notes of the chorale melody (above) and composed of three segments, a, b, and c (below).

Mm.	Material	Ritornello segments	Key
1–3	Ritornello	a b c	I
4–6	Chorale, phrase 1		
6–7	Ritornello	b c'	vi
7–9	Chorale, phrase 2		
10–12	Ritornello	a b c	vi
12–15	Chorale, phrase 3		
15–17	Ritornello	a b c	V
17–20	Chorale, phrase 4		
20–23	Ritornello	a' b' c'	ii
22–25	Chorale, phrase 5		
24–27	Ritornello	a' b c	I

The pedal acts not only as a continuo line but also as a distinctive countersubject to the ritornello: it is an important identifier for the ritornello when one of its segments is greatly varied.

"Herr Christ, der einig Gottes Sohn" is an appropriate endpoint for Bach's Arnstadt-Mühlhausen chorale writing, for it represents the culmination of his search for greater means of unification. Although it is still cast in the North German mold, it points forward to the remarkable ritornello trios of the Weimar period: "Trio super Allein Gott in der Höh sei Ehr," BWV 664a, and "Trio super Herr Jesu Christ, dich zu uns wend," BWV 655a.

Chorale Partitas

The chorale partita—a set of variations on a hymn tune—was an organ favorite in Thuringia, where Pachelbel's four works published in the *Musicalische
Sterbensgedanken* (Musical Meditations on Death; 1683) set the standard for
many years. Derived from the variation sets on popular songs of Sweelinck,
Froberger, and others, the Central German chorale versions were similarly
oriented toward *manualiter* performance, with the pedal treated in an ad libitum way.

Bach most probably encountered Pachelbel's chorale partitas during his
Ohrdruf studies with his brother Johann Christoph. Pachelbel's works display
a formalized design: the chorale appears first as a simple four-part harmonization, followed by a series of variations whose rather formulaic binary structures
directly reflect the Stollen-Abgesang design of the hymns upon which the works
are based. The sets include a number of standard variation types: the *suspirans*
variation, which capitalizes on the jazzy snap of off-beat rhythms, in three- or
four-part texture; the diminution variation, which introduces animated 16th- or
32nd-note figures in the right or left hand, in two- or three-part texture; the chromatic variation in three- or four-part texture; the dance variation in 12/8 or 12/
16 meter in three- or four-part texture; the bicinium, or two-part variation; and
the broken-chord variation, with arpeggios divided between the two hands. The
chorale melody appears in each variation, either as an unadorned cantus firmus
in the soprano, tenor, or bass, or as embellished notes within diminution figures.

Bach probably carried the knowledge of Pachelbel's chorale partitas with him
as he traveled north in 1700 to attend St. Michael's School in Lüneburg, where
he was mentored if not instructed by Böhm. As a Thuringian expatriate, Böhm
cultivated the chorale partita, but his approach was quite different from that of
Pachelbel. The chorale, when presented at the beginning, is harmonized in a
thicker texture, in four, five, or six parts. The variations, written under the influence of the North German *stylus fantasticus*, display far greater freedom of form,
which commonly evolves from the spinning out of small motives taken from the
chorale tune. Böhm's chorale partitas also contain imitative variations, variations based on quasi-ostinato and aria forms, and true *style brisé* variations derived from the broken-chord style of French lute and harpsichord music. Böhm
explored the motivic potential of the chorale melody in his partitas through repetition, dissection, modification, and recombination. As Spitta first observed,
Böhm's "ingenious brain" explored musical thoughts "in nimble fancies and
graceful ornamentation."[33] Nothing is predictable or routine in Böhm's chorale
partitas, and the young Bach must have been awed by the richness of invention
and the element of surprise in his compatriot's chorale partita settings. It is significant that Böhm's works are preserved chiefly in manuscripts emanating from

the circles of Bach and Walther. His chorale partitas were obviously admired, studied, and exchanged.

Chorale partitas could have fulfilled a number of functions in Bach's time. As traditionally *manualiter* works, they could have served as music for home devotions. Pointing in this direction are both the works' close stylistic ties with clavier music and the selected chorales' meditative topics: dying, penance, evening prayer, and similar concerns. Within the Lutheran worship service, chorale partitas could have served as organ interludes for congregational singing, with variations performed between verses, or they could have served as Communion music. The meditative quality of many of the chorales would have made the partitas based on them especially appropriate for *sub Communione* use. Chorale partitas also could have been performed in recital, as the virtuoso nature of the pedal variations in Bach's "Sei gegrüßet, Jesu gütig," BWV 768, suggests.

Three chorale partitas are associated with Bach's Arnstadt-Mühlhausen years:

Partita on "Ach, was soll ich Sünder machen," BWV 770
Partita on "Christ, der du bist der helle Tag," BWV 766
Partita on "O Gott, du frommer Gott," BWV 767

"Ach, was soll ich Sünder machen," BWV 770, appears to be Bach's earliest surviving effort at chorale-partita writing. It displays the strong influence of Pachelbel and Böhm and may, in fact, have been composed in Lüneburg under Böhm's supervision.[34] The chorale, written by Johann Flitner in 1659 and listed in early hymnals as a song for affliction and misfortune, sickness, death and dying, and repentance,[35] has seven verses. Bach's 10-variation partita thus appears to be an art piece independent of the chorale's verse structure—an approach taken by Böhm.

Partita 1 is a cross between a thickly harmonized chorale and a passing-tone variation. Partitas 2 and 3 bear a strong resemblance to the initial variations of Böhm's partita on "Ach wie nichtig, ach wie flüchtig" (example 5-7), and it is possible that Bach was modeling his music on Böhm's. This is also true of partita 4, which is written in the *style brisé* that appears in partita 5 of Böhm's chorale partita on "Wer nur den lieben Gott läßt walten." By contrast, partitas 5 and 6 reflect the methodical approach of Pachelbel, with the first variation featuring a chain of 16th notes in the left hand and the second a chain of 16th-note figures in the right hand (in this case arpeggiated figures resembling violin writing). Partita 7, in 12/8 meter, is a gigue-like dance characteristic of both Böhm and Pachelbel, while the 32nd-note figures of partita 8 foreshadow variation 7 of "Sei gegrüßet, Jesu gütig," especially when they alternate between the hands. It is in the final two variations that Bach moves beyond the derivative to display the youthful ingenuity seen in the Neumeister Chorales. Partita 9, an adagio sarabande in 3/4 meter, is

Example 5-7 (a) Georg Böhm, Partita on "Ach wie nichtig, ach wie flüchtig": the first measures of partitas 2 and 3, and (b) Bach, Partita on "Ach, was soll ich Sünder machen," BWV 770: the first measures of partitas 2 and 3.

an extended riff on the chorale melody, with phrases alternating between piano and forte. And partita 10 forms a remarkable *stylus phantasticus* close, featuring contrasting tempos (allegro v. adagio), contrasting manuals (Oberwerk v. Rückpositiv), and varied figurations (duplets v. triplets), with a *passaggio* cadenza in the middle. Although diffuse and challenging to play convincingly in performance, partita 10 is an ambitious attempt to create a new type of climactic chorale-partita finale—an effort that would soon bear fruit in the more tightly structured closing variation of "O Gott, du frommer Gott," BWV 767.

Three additional chorale partitas attributed to Bach—"Herr Christ, der einig Gottes Sohn," BWV[3] 1176 (formerly BWV[1] Anh. 77); "O Vater, allmächtiger Gott, BWV[3] App B 57 (formerly BWV[1] 758); and "Wenn wir in höchsten Nöten sein," BWV[1] Anh. 78—would appear to represent additional early efforts in the genre, if they prove to be authentic. Of these, "Herr Christ, der einig Gottes Sohn" has the best stylistic credentials for acceptance into the Bach corpus.[36]

Sometime after completing "Ach, was soll ich Sünder machen," Bach continued his partita writing with two additional works, the Partita on "Christ, der du bist der helle Tag" and the Partita on "O Gott, du frommer Gott." In each case the number of variations in the partita matches the number of verses in the chorale upon which the setting is based. This suggests that the pieces may have been intended for alternatim performance, played during Communion, perhaps, with the organ presenting the first partita movement, followed by the congregation singing the first verse of the chorale, and so forth in alternation until all verses were performed.

The earlier of the two works, **"Christ, der du bist der helle Tag," BWV 766**, possibly written around 1706,[37] represents a different world from "Ach, was soll ich Sünder machen." The tighter handling of form and the more inventive treatment of motives point to a further stage in Bach's development. The numerous early copies of the work—there are seven in all[38]—suggest that it was popular in Bach's time and the years shortly thereafter. The music is set in F minor, in the dorian notation (three flats) that Bach used up to 1720 or so. The unequal tuning systems of the time favored keys with fewer than three flats or sharps. F minor, with four flats, was viewed as a particularly stirring, gloomy key. Bach's Hamburg colleague Johann Mattheson claimed that it "expressed effectively a dark, helpless melancholy and sometimes caused the listener to shudder or feel a sense of dread."[39] In keyboard works, Bach used F minor sparingly, for the "Lamento" section of the Capriccio on the Departure of a Dearly Beloved Brother, BWV 992; "Ich ruf zu dir, Herr Jesu Christ," BWV 639; and the fragment "O Traurigkeit, o Herzeleid," BWV[3] 1169, from the Orgel-Büchlein. In "Christ, der du bist der helle Tag" F minor lends strength to the somber appeal to Christ for protection from treachery, suffering, and death, as expressed in Erasmus Alber's mid-sixteenth-century adaptation of a medieval Latin text.[40]

We find evidence of Böhm's influence throughout the partita, beginning with the thick five-, six-, and even seven-part chords in the opening harmonization. But there are also signs of restless invention, à la the Neumeister Chorales. Partita 2 is a bicinium with quasi-ostinato bass and opening melodic *devise*. There is no solo introduction of the heavily slurred bass figure, which is quite like the similarly articulated solo cello in the chorus "Du wollest dem Feinde nicht geben" of Cantata 71, *Gott ist mein König*, of 1708. The chorale melody is divided into small fragments that are repeated as piano echoes or as lower-octave displacements in the bass.

In partita 3 the hymn tune is both accompanied and embellished by a *suspirans* figure, which appears upright and inverted. The figuration foreshadows the more systematic treatment of the motive found in the Orgel-Büchlein chorale "Wer nur den lieben Gott läßt walten," BWV 642. Partita 4 appears to be a predictable *perpetuum mobile*–like variation in three parts, in the Pachelbel tradition. But in measure 9 the running 16th-note soprano line suddenly breaks up and descends into the bass before resuming in the treble in the next bar. In partita 5 the cantus firmus appears in the tenor, surrounded by *suspirans* figures, once again, while partita 6 is a typical gigue-like variation in 12/8 meter, but with inventive treatment of the principal leaping motive. Partita 7 serves as a thick-textured climactic finale: it begins in five-part *style brisé* but then moves to syncopated chords before returning to the *brisé* figuration. The chorale appears as a quarternote cantus firmus in the bass, anchoring down the animated counterpoint in the upper voices. The *brisé* idiom reflects Böhm's influence, as does the relaxed partwriting of the earlier variations. Viewed as a whole, "Christ, der du bist der helle Tag" is a North German take on the Central German partita.

"**O Gott, du frommer Gott,**" **BWV 767**, represents the peak of Bach's initial efforts in chorale-partita composition. Unlike "Christ, der du bist der helle Tag," it is transmitted in a single source, a manuscript copy written by Johann Tobias Krebs around 1714–1717,[41] presumably during his time of study with Bach. While the general stamp of Pachelbel and Böhm remains in "O Gott, du frommer Gott," there is much that is new. The opening chorale harmonization displays Böhm's free use of parts and doubled thirds, but the bicinium of partita 2, drawn from Böhm's opera-derived technique (see chapter 2), now begins with a distinctive bass solo derived from the melodic shape of the chorale's first phrase (Example 5-8). The upper voice, fragmented at first but then extended through diminutions, becomes a fanciful riff on the phrases of Johann Heermann's 1630 chorale, a "Daily prayer for divine mercy and aid."[42]

Partita 3 is based on a traditional *suspirans* motive, upright and inverted, that appeared earlier in the Neumeister Chorales and other works. The counterpoint is now tight and concise, however, quite like that of the Passacaglia in C Minor

Example 5-8 Partita on "O Gott, du frommer Gott," BWV 767: first phrase of the chorale (above), with principal motives a, b, and c, and Bach's basso ostinato theme (below), with motives marked.

(mm. 48–72) or the Orgel-Büchlein chorale "Vater unser im Himmelreich," BWV 636. Partita 4 is the obligatory *perpetuum mobile* variation, but with carefully placed chromaticism and a dramatic trailing off at the end, by the upper part. The similarity of the conclusion with the final solo soprano phrase ("Ja komm, Herr Jesu!"--Yes come, Lord Jesus!) in the movement "Es ist der alte Bund" of Cantata 106, *Gottes Zeit ist der allerbeste Zeit,* of 1707 is clear. Partita 5 continues the development of the *suspirans* motive, now combined with *style brisé* in the final measures. Partita 6 features an off-beat leaping bass figure against two-part chords in the right hand. Partita 7, in 3/4 meter, is minuet-like, with a descending line (through two octaves) at the beginning and end that serves to frame the middle material. The intense chromaticism of partita 8 goes beyond anything found in Pachelbel or Böhm. Finally, the last variation shows Bach attempting once again to create a new type of *stylus fantasticus* finale for the partita, one with double echoes created by dynamics and octave displacement. The alternation of tempos—[allegro] → andante → presto—imparts a ternary structure to the phrase-by-phrase treatment of the chorale melody.

Past writers have associated several variations of "O Gott, du frommer Gott" with theological programs. Albert Schweitzer linked partita 7 with death and burial, partita 8 with the sad wait for the signal of the resurrection, and partita 9 with the animated joy of the doxology—all alluded to in verses 7, 8, and 9 of the chorale.[43] Hermann Keller viewed the change from andante to presto in partita 9 as the awakening of the body at the last judgment,[44] whereas Hans Klotz compared the same variation to the concluding dialogues of French classical organ suites, played on the grand jeu.[45] Whether or not these interpretations reflect Bach's thoughts as he composed "O Gott, du frommer Gott," the music shows his youthful mastery of the chorale partita.

He was not finished with the genre, however. In Weimar he would return to it a final time, to create a culminating *pedaliter* masterpiece in the monumental Partita on "Sei gegrüßet, Jesu gütig," BWV 768 (see chapter 10).

The chorale settings of the Arnstadt/Mühlhausen years display Bach's continuing emphasis on variety and invention. Like many of the Neumeister Chorales, the works also show a variegated blend of Central and North German features. Most important, they reflect Bach's growing determination to find a means of unifying his settings—an objective he would finally achieve in the organ chorales of the Weimar period.

Notes

1. Many of the chorale settings of questionable authenticity are included in NBA IV/10 (Reinmar Emans, ed., 2007) and the Breitkopf Edition, vols. 9 and 10 (Reinmar Emans and Matthias Schneider, eds., 2018).

2. Berlin State Library, *P 802*.
3. *Das Privilegirte Ordentliche und Vermehrte Dreßdnische Gesang-Buch* (Dresden and Leipzig, 1727), 291, cited in Bighley 2018, 74.
4. NBA IV/3, KB (Hans Klotz, ed., 1962), 47, and Martin Geck, "Nochmals: Die Authentizität des Vokalwerks Dietrich Buxtehudes in quellenkritischer Sicht," *Die Musikforschung* 16 (1963), 175.
5. As first noted in Zehnder 2009, 152.
6. It appears in the Andreas Bach Book as a fragment (mm. 1–122 are missing), apparently due to lost pages. The other biblical Sonatas copied into the album are complete.
7. Berlin State Library, *P 488*, described in Stinson 1985.
8. See the comments in Kube 2001.
9. The manual indications include "O" (Oberwerk) and "R" (Rückpositiv); the hand signs include "s" (sinistra, or left hand) and "d" (dextra, or right hand). The brackets that appear in the Breitkopf edition are editorial.
10. Zehnder 2009, 163. Zehnder also proposed that Bach might have used the instrument's Cymbelstern to represent the "star" mentioned in Philipp Nicolai's 1599 text. The Wender organ had a Brustpositiv rather than a Rückpositiv, the manual called for in Bach's manuscript. However, it appears to have been a convention in organ manuscripts of the time to call the main manual "Oberwerk" or "Hauptwerk" and the secondary manual "Rückpositiv," no matter what specific divisions were available. See the discussion of manual indications in Bach's concerto arrangements in chapter 9.
11. Berlin State Library, *P 802*.
12. Berlin State Library, *P 802* (Walther) and Yale Music Library, *Ma21.Y11.A36* (formerly *LM 4983*; Johann Christoph Bach).
13. In a manuscript written by the Gehren Johann Christoph Bach (1673–1727) between 1710 and 1720 or so (Yale Music Library, *Ma21 Y11 A36* [formerly *LM 4983*]), "O Lamm Gottes" is followed by a second setting of the chorale, a lightly embellished four-part *manualiter* harmonization labeled "il Chorale, O Lamb Gottes, unschuldig. G. S. Bach." It is not present in the Walther manuscript and may have been a subsequent addition to the first setting by the young Johann Sebastian or by Johann Christoph himself.
14. Berlin State Library, *P 801*, fascicle 2.
15. Williams 2003, 498.
16. Berlin State Library, *Mus.ms. autogr. Krebs, J. L. 2N*. In the copy, many of the ornaments and performance indications appear in a lighter ink than the text of the music, suggesting that they were added at a later point by an owner of the manuscript.
17. Measures 99–139. See Matthias Schneider 1999, 210–211.
18. Kube 1999, 582.
19. Plauen Organ Book: Berlin, Staatliches Institut für Musikforschung, *Fot. Bü 129* (photocopy); Walther copies: Kaliningrad, University Library, *Ms. Gotthold 15830* (photocopy) and The Hague, Gemeente Museum, *Source 3828, Kluis F* (formerly *4.G.14*); Krebs copy: Berlin State Library, *P 802*.
20. Spitta 1873–80, vol. 1, 394–397.
21. Bighley 2018, 71.

22. Williams 2003, 460.

23. Kaliningrad, University Library, *Ms. Gotthold 15830* (photocopy).

24. The specification of the instrument in Adlung 1768, 260–261, lists the Fagotto as extending only from C to c', however.

25. Plauen Organ Book: Berlin, Staatliches Institut für Musikforschung, *Fot. Bü 129* (photocopy); Walther's copies: Königsberg, University Library, *Ms. Gotthold 15839* (photocopy) and The Hague, Gemeente Museum, *Source 3828, Kluis F* (formerly *4.G.14*); Anonymous Weimar scribe (W6 in NBA IX/3 [*Die Kopisten Johann Sebastian Bachs: Katalog und Dokumentation*, Yoshitake Kobayashi and Kirsten Beisswenger, eds., 2007]): Berlin State Library, *P 281*.

26. The authenticity of BWV 735 has been questioned by Heinz Lohmann, *Joh. Seb. Bach, Sämtliche Orgelwerke* (Wiesbaden: Breitkopf), Edition 6589, ix, because of its transmission in post–1750 sources alone (see Bach Digital). But the nature of the revisions in BWV 735, especially the insertion of a new conclusion, points convincingly to Bach's hand.

27. Williams presented the intriguing thought that Bach may have revised the setting with the idea of including it in the Leipzig chorale portfolio as part of the "Great Eighteen" Collection. See Williams 2003, 480.

28. Berlin State Library, *P 801*, fascicle 2.

29. Leipzig Music Library, *Peters Ms. 7*, fascicle 4.

30. Zehnder (Zehnder 2009, 304) dates it c. 1708.

31. In BWV³ it is assigned to "Weimar."

32. Zehnder 2009, 305.

33. Spitta 1873–80, vol. 1, 206.

34. On the authenticity, style, and dating of "Ach, was soll ich Sünder machen" see Dirksen 2019.

35. Bigley 2018, 18.

36. As reflected in its placement in the "Authentic Works" section of BWV³ and the assignment of a new BWV number. On the style of the work, see the commentary in the Leupold Edition, vol. 9, xxiv.

37. Zehnder 2009, 215–219.

38. See Bach digital, under BWV 766.

39. Mattheson 1713, 248–249.

40. Bigley 2018, 39.

41. Berlin State Library, *P 802*.

42. *Das Privilegirte Ordentliche und Vermehrte Dreßdnische Gesang-Buch* (Dresden: Eckels, 1727), 552, cited in Bighley 2018, 189.

43. Schweitzer 1905, 65–66. The complete text of the chorale, in German with a parallel English translation, can be found in Bighley 2018, 190–191.

44. Keller 1967, 180.

45. Klotz 1975, 325.

6

Free Works

Bach's free organ works from the Arnstadt-Mühlhausen years—the other bushel of "first fruits"—display a remarkably wide variety of formats and idioms. Like the chorale settings, some pieces reflect the strong influence of Buxtehude and North German style, while others show the lingering effect of Pachelbel and Central German traditions. The works can be divided into four categories: multisectional praeludia, prelude-and-fugue pairs, independent fugues, and unica. In each case, we see Bach wrestling with the challenge of creating a substantial piece with a cohesive structure.

Multisectional Praeludia

Two works are patterned after the North German multisectional praeludium:

Toccata in D Minor, BWV 565
Praeludium in E Major, BWV 566

The **Toccata in D Minor, BWV 565**, has the distinction of being Bach's best-known organ composition. Its opening mordent and falling scale have come to symbolize Bach, organ music in general, and Halloween horror. At the same time, it is one of Bach's most unusual creations—so much so that in recent times it has been the object of some rather far-fetched theories about its origins and authenticity: that it is not really a work by Bach,[1] that it is derived from a piece for violin,[2] that it is a work by Johann Peter Kellner,[3] that it must have been written by a composer of Bach's sons' generation.[4] These hypotheses have been convincingly refuted,[5] but the very fact that they were proposed underscores the Toccata's unconventional nature.

It does seem odd that this famous work is transmitted in just one eighteenth-century source, a manuscript copy from the 1730s in the hand of Johannes Ringk (see plate I-7).[6] Ringk studied with Kellner, an avid collector of Bach's keyboard and string compositions, and it is likely that Ringk was working from a manuscript in Kellner's possession. Ringk was a reliable copyist—he later served as a professional scribe for the Royal Prussian Opera in Berlin[7]—and there is little reason to doubt his ascription of the piece to Bach.[8] Adding credibility to Bach's

J. S. BACH. George B. Stauffer, Oxford University Press. © Oxford University Press 2024.
DOI: 10.1093/oso/9780195108026.003.0007

authorship is a second copy of the Toccata from the beginning of the nineteenth century in the hand of Johann Andreas Dröbs.[9] Although of late origin, the copy most likely reflects a manuscript owned by Dröbs's teacher, Johann Christian Kittel, one of Bach's last and most faithful students. It, too, unambiguously credits the work to Bach.

In terms of formal design, the Toccata follows the pattern of a North German multipartite praeludium with three sections: a virtuosic opening in free rhythm, a fugue in strict rhythm, and a virtuosic close, again in free rhythm. Although the work is titled "Toccata con Fuge pedaliter" in Ringk's manuscript, no double bar sets off the fugue from the free material, as in Bach's true prelude-and-fugue pairs. One finds comparable continuous three-part structures in Buxtehude's Praeludium in C Major, BuxWV 138, or Böhm's Praeludia in C Major and A Minor.

The similarity ends there, however. The opening section is a series of gestures, seemingly spontaneous, but all derived from the mordent, descending scale, and implied diminished seventh chord of the first measure (example 6-1).[10] Many of the gestures are repeated at the octave, further strengthening their rhetorical effect. The octave doubling in the first 10 measures produces the effect of a plenum based on 16' pitch[11]—a bold, unorthodox device that parallels other experimental figures in Bach's early organ works that we've noted, such as the

Example 6-1 Toccata in D Minor, BWV 565: opening motive, based on a D-minor scale, and figuration derived from its upright and inverted forms.

drum-like chords at the very bottom of the keyboard in the organ continuo of Cantata 71, *Gott is mein König*,[12] or the chordal tremulant in the Prelude and Fugue in D Minor, BWV 549a.[13] Both here and in the closing section of the Toccata, abrupt changes of *affect* are marked by abrupt changes of tempo, another feature of Bach's early keyboard works and cantatas.[14] The string bariolage effect in mm. 12–15, also unusual, most likely stemmed from Bach's personal study of the violin rather than a familiarity with Italian instrumental music at this point. The entire opening section is an imaginative but carefully calculated improvisation on the figures presented in the opening measure.

The subject of the fugue, too, is drawn from the opening mordent, scale, and implied chord. The opening four-part exposition is novel in two regards. First, the tonic entries are answered at the subdominant rather than the dominant, an early feature observed in the Fugue of the Prelude and Fugue in C Major, BWV 531. Second, the third and fourth entries of the subject are preceded by long interludes, of five and ten measures, respectively. This sets the stage for a fugue that is unusually episodic: only one-quarter of its 97 measures are devoted to the subject, suggesting a piece that originated through extemporization rather than composition, much like the three-part ricercar of the Musical Offering.

Other features seem improvised as well: of the 12 entries of the subject, nine are in the tonic or subdominant, two are in the supertonic, and one is in the relative major; the handling of texture is very relaxed, with extended sections in one-, two-, or three-parts; and the pedal is allotted one-third of the subject entries, including a one-part solo (mm. 109–111). All of this points to an improvisational, virtuoso fugue, in which bravura elements trump tight construction. The constant 16th-note pulse holds the fugue together until it reaches a climax in the extraordinary circle-of-fifth progression based on the fugue subject in abbreviated form (example 6-2). This leads directly to the final entry of the theme in full form over a tonic pedal point.

The closing recitative, introduced by a Buxtehude-like jolt of a deceptive cadence to B♭ major (m. 127), is also derived from the opening motives, now decorated with 32nd-note figuration. Such figuration can be found in the early keyboard toccatas, but here it is dispensed with remarkable theatricality, emphasized by the many changes of tempo: recitativo—adagissimo—presto—adagio—vivace—molto adagio—all within 17 measures. The five-part chordal conclusion in the lowest possible range (to create the effect of a 16′ plenum, once again) is so unusual that Peter Williams suggested, improbably, that it was a post-1750 gesture![15]

The overall effect of the Toccata is astonishing. Peters editor Friedrich Conrad Griepenkerl claimed that the work was "not for the church, but rather for concertizing on the organ,"[16] and Christoph Wolff states that it "speaks precisely for the inventiveness of the composer, who conceived the whole work

Example 6-2 Toccata in D Minor, BWV 565; closing measures of the fugue, with subject used for a circle-of-fifths sequence before appearing in full over a tonic pedal point.

as a showpiece of organistic virtuosity, calculated for maximum outward effect."[17] One is tempted to link the Toccata with one of Bach's early auditions, in Sangerhausen or Arnstadt, where he dazzled church officials with performances on organs lacking a 16' manual Principal. The opening octave passages would have produced a grandeur that went beyond the expected capacity of the instruments.

The D-Minor Toccata has been variously dated "c. 1702," "c. 1704," and "after 1708"[18]—another indication of its puzzling nature. It is surely a very early work, closer to the Neumeister Chorales than the Mühlhausen cantatas. Its limited manuscript transmission suggests that Bach may have viewed it as a special display piece he wished to reserve for his own use. Or it could mean that he saw it as a rogue work, a youthful sin that was not to be circulated broadly. Either way, we are fortunate to have it.

As we noted in chapter 3, Bach took a stab at composing a North German praeludium with five sections during the Lüneburg years, in the form of the Praeludium in A Minor, BWV 551. He returned to this format in Arnstadt with the **Praeludium in E Major, BWV 566** (formerly called the "Toccata in E Major"),[19] this time approaching the task with greater ambition and finesse. The work is passed down in C major as well as E major. The E-major version appears to be the original; the C-major version can be traced to Weimar, where it may have been fashioned by Johann Tobias Krebs, writer of the earliest manuscript copy.[20] The C-major version avoids the manual note c$\sharp$''' that appears in the E-major version, and skirts possible tuning issues posed by a key with four sharps. But it also contains rewritings that compromise the score.[21] The key of E major was quite useable on organs employing Werckmeister temperaments (it appears in the works of both Buxtehude and Vincent Lübeck), and in the Toccata it facilitates the performance of the virtuoso pedal passages, which are more easily negotiated in E major than C major.

The Praeludium opens with an energetic burst of North German figures: an animated *passaggio*, thick chordal writing (up to nine parts!) over a double pedal, a virtuoso pedal solo, and a lengthy section of free counterpoint, mostly in five parts, that moves enharmonically through G$\sharp$ minor and D$\sharp$ minor, dwells at length on the dominant, and finally lands in the tonic. All of this is calculated to impress.

The subject of the fugue that follows is constructed on two standard North German figures: a *repercussio*, or repeated-note head motive, and a twisty *Spielmotiv*, or playful 16th-note tail (example 6-3, a, x and y). One can find the *repercussio* figure in Buxtehude's Praeludium in G Minor, BuxWV 148, for instance, and the *Spiemotiv* in Reincken's Sonata in A Minor, which Bach arranged for keyboard as BWV 965. The 16th-note tail of Bach's subject (y) is cleverly constructed, since it contains a figure that combines elements of the *repercussio* and *Spielmotiv* motives (example 6-3, x1 + y1). This figure is repeated five times in an exuberant downward sequence—a gesture that appears in the tail of the subject of the Fugue in D Major, BWV 532, as well (see below).

The fugue proceeds with entries in the tonic and dominant and a single entry in the submediant, C$\sharp$ minor, toward the end (m. 107). The subject is accompanied by two countersubjects: the first (soprano, m. 39) appears with the theme throughout, in the manner of a permutation fugue; the second (soprano, m. 43) appears only in the initial exposition. The fugue is impressively long—88 measures—and four-part texture is retained throughout. But the limited

Example 6-3 Praeludium in E Major, BWV 566: (a) subject of the first fugue, based on similar ideas found in Dieterich Buxtehude's Fugue in G Minor, BuxWV 148, and Johann Adam Reincken's Sonata in A Minor from *Hortus Musicus*, and (b) subject of the second fugue.

harmonic range and unmemorable sequences squander the potential of the strong introduction.

A free interlude with stock North German figures once again—off-beat scales, 32nd-note flourishes, pedal solo with *trillo longo* (punctuated with 8- and 9-part manual chords)—leads to a second fugue, in 3/4 meter. The dance-like theme is derived from the descending fifth of the head motive of the first fugue (example 6-3, b), a transformation common in capriccios and fugues of Froberger, Böhm, Buxtehude, and Bruhns. After a straightforward four-part exposition and additional entries of the subject in the tonic and dominant, the fugue dissolves into free writing, for the most part, with hints of the subject (mm. 206, 218, 225) amid a buildup of 16th- and 32nd-note flourishes. Virtuosity eventually prevails, with a return of the opening pedal-octave-with-manual chords and pedal solo, now in reverse order. The gradual disintegration of the rhythmically strict fugue into free passage work resembles the transition that takes place in the last variation of the early partita "Ach, mich armen Sunder," BWV 770 (see chapter 5).

There is no reason to link the Praeludium in E Major specifically with the visit to Buxtehude[22]—Bach was familiar with the North German gestures it contains before venturing to Lübeck. Still, the work does seem particularly calculated to impress a North German listener. Yet with so much digressive material, it lacks the cohesiveness of Buxtehude's best multi-sectional praeludia. In the early sources the work is passed down in truncated versions that contain either the opening section and first fugue (mm. 1–122)[23] or the middle free section, second fugue, and closing section (mm. 123–229).[24] These abridgements may have stemmed from the work's unwieldy length, which early users sought to remedy by cutting the piece in half. Bach would soon solve the concision problem, but he never returned to the North German multisectional format, preferring instead to focus on the prelude-and-fugue pair.

Prelude-and-Fugue Pairs

Three works from the Arnstadt-Mühlhausen years display the unambiguous stamp of a prelude and fugue:

Fantasia and Imitatio in B Minor, BWV 563
Prelude and Fugue in E Minor ("Cathedral"), BWV 533
Prelude and Fugue in G Minor, BWV 535a

Of the three works, the **Fantasia and Imitatio, BWV 563**, is the oddest and perhaps the oldest as well. It has an excellent pedigree—it appears in the Andreas Bach Book in the hand of Bach's brother Johann Christoph—so there is no reason to question its authenticity. But whether or not it is an organ piece is less clear. Its title in the early sources gives no indication of organ, and its idiom is characteristic of both organ and harpsichord (or clavichord) compositions. It requires pedal, but only for two pedal points at the end of the Fantasia. The second of these calls for C♯, a note not available on Bach's organs until the Weimar years— too late a date for this piece. So the possibility that it was intended for pedal harpsichord or clavichord cannot be discounted.[25]

But to view it as an organ piece: the Fantasia is a free expansion, in four parts, of a *corta* motive, quite like the Fantasia in C Major, BWV 570. With the arrival of a subdominant pedal point (m. 15), the *corta* motive gives way to a second Central German cliché, a *suspirans* motive, first leaping, then moving by step. This is followed by a short cadenza and a sedate conclusion, again in four parts, over a dominant pedal. As with the C-Major Fantasia, there is nothing extraordinary here. The B-Minor Fantasia is best characterized as a relaxed, *manualiter* improvisation in the style of Pachelbel or Johann Caspar Ferdinand Fischer.[26]

The Imitatio, by contrast, is anything but conventional. It begins with motet-like imitation, in four parts, of a concise, off-beat, six-note theme. The theme initially appears in alternating tonic and dominant entries, much like the exposition of a fugue. But this is followed by its extended treatment in diverse shapes and textures: in stretto and contrary motion (m. 19), in inversion and stretto (m. 47), in varied form and contrary motion (m. 54), in fragmented form and stretto (m. 68), in expanded form and stretto (m. 82), and in varied form and parallel motion (m. 99). The writing is not unlike that of the Fantasia in C Minor, BWV 1121, except that new points of imitation are more frequently marked by harmonic arrivals, in D major (m. 19), B minor (m. 47), F♯ major (m. 54), E minor (m. 82), and, in the short coda, B major (m. 99). As the title implies, the Imitatio is a study in imitative counterpoint rather than fugue writing. The most telling element of the Fantasia and Imitatio is its clear prelude-fugue format—the pairing of two autonomous movements, each with its own distinctive idiom, procedure, and meter.

The **Prelude and Fugue in E Minor** ("Cathedral"), BWV 533, displays a similar two-movement structure, with self-contained Prelude followed by self-contained Fugue. Both the Prelude and the Fugue are transmitted singly in a number of early sources,[27] raising the possibility that they were written separately and united at a later point. This would help to explain the stylistic independence of the two pieces.

Whatever its genesis, the Prelude and Fugue has enjoyed a widespread popularity, both in Bach's time and ours, that eclipses its compositional limitations and derivative nature. It is passed down in more than 20 manuscript copies, many written by students of Bach, Kellner, Kittel, and Bach's son Carl Philipp Emanuel.[28] Hence it appears to have served as a favorite teaching piece in the eighteenth century, a role it has retained to the present day.

The Prelude follows a pattern that appears in many of Bach's free preludes written before his encounter with Vivaldi's music: a rhythmically free introduction establishing the tonic leads to a rhythmically strict section of denser material, usually modulatory, which in turn leads to a short conclusion reestablishing the tonic.[29] The Prelude in E Minor opens with a series of North German gestures: a manual *passaggio*, several double *trillo longo* figures, and a pedal solo. This rhythmically free introduction is followed by a middle section in stricter rhythm, with statements of thick five-, six-, and even seven-part declamatory chords alternating with pedal solos. The double *trillo longo* returns at the end, leading to a close that reiterates the tonic several times (mm. 31–32), a gesture found in Böhm's Praeludia in D Minor and G Minor and several Mühlhausen cantatas.[30] The virtuosic use of pedal 10ths before the final cadence is also a North German device, appearing in Buxtehude's Toccata in F Major, BuxWV 156, and Bruhns's Praeludium in G Major. Despite the many borrowings from North Germany, the Prelude creates a unique impression. The repeated chords of the main section, punctuated by the emphatic resolution of diminished-seventh

Example 6-4 Prelude and Fugue in E Minor, BWV 533: fugue subject (mm. 1–2), countersubject (mm. 3–4, upper voice), and sequence leading to the third entry (mm. 5–6), with motives marked.

harmonies, make for an engaging dialogue, fully settled only at the end through the repeated E-minor cadences.

The rhetorical element continues in the Fugue. Its subject is based on the principle of repetition, here taking the form a two-note iambic motive and a four-note triadic motive, both repeated (example 6-4, x and y). This stately theme appears five times in the opening exposition, hinting at a five-part fugue, but the texture never goes beyond three parts. The subject is accompanied by a downward-leaping *corta* countersubject (example 6-4, z) that serves as the material first for a two-part sequence (m. 5) and then, after the exposition, for a two-part episode (mm. 16–18), both with an effective chromatic climb. The falling *corta* figure is reminiscent of similar motives in the Capriccio on the Departure of a Dearly Beloved Brother, BWV 992, of 1704, and the Passacaglia in C Minor, BWV 582, from the early Weimar years.

The two-part episode leads to the abrupt return of the subject, in the tenor, accompanied by four-note chords (m. 19). In the next entry of the subject, in the soprano (m. 24), the two-note iambic figure sounds three times, making the sense of repetition even stronger. This is followed by the return of the leaping *corta* figure for a three-part manual episode and the final entry of the theme in the pedal, in the lowest octave of the bass—a feature characteristic of Pachelbel's fugues, as we noted in chapter 3. The subject never ventures outside the tonic and dominant. While this would appear to be a shortcoming, in this case it seems to unify the fugue, together with manual episodes that are based on the same leaping *corta* figure (with upper and lower parts exchanged).

An analysis of the Prelude and Fugue in E Minor gives little sense of the almost hypnotic effect the work produces. Philipp Spitta viewed the Prelude and Fugue as a masterpiece with "noble melancholy" and consequently assigned it to the first year of the Weimar period,[31] a dating reflected in BWV[1]. In BWV[2] and

BWV³ it has been more appropriately placed in the Arnstadt years. Indeed, it most probably dates from 1704 or so, close to the Capriccio on the Departure of a Beloved Brother, BWV 992, of that year. The work is also passed down in a much-discussed manual variant, BWV 533a, which is now viewed as inauthentic.³²

The **Prelude and Fugue in G Minor, BWV 535a,** is transmitted in only one source, a fair-copy autograph in the Möller Manuscript that can be dated c. 1705.³³ The Fugue breaks off in the middle of measure 65 and appears to have concluded on an inserted leaf, now lost.³⁴ The work is an important gauge of Bach's compositional interests and abilities during the Arnstadt-Mühlhausen years, for it suggests that at this point in time he was more attracted to fugues than preludes, and it confirms that he could write a fugue of considerable length and refinement, thus verifying the statement of Carl Philipp Emanuel Bach to Johann Nicolaus Forkel in 1775 that his father "through his own study and re-flection alone . . . became even in his youth a pure and strong fugue writer."³⁵ Bach apparently viewed the Prelude and Fugue as a meritorious work, for he returned to it at least twice in later years, greatly expanding the prelude (= BWV³ 535.2) and then polishing it further (= BWV³ 535.3) to create a fitting partner for the fugue, which he also refined in matters of detail. The revision process seems to have taken place in Leipzig, where he used the Prelude and Fugue as a teaching piece.

In the initial version of the work, BWV 535a, the Prelude is just 21 measures long—less than a third the length of the Fugue. It seems to have been dashed off quickly to accompany the Fugue, which Bach may have composed first and proudly wished to enter into his brother's album,³⁶ where the available space for the entire piece appears to have been limited to three pages. The Fugue required two of the pages, leaving only one page for the Prelude. The Prelude begins with a short section of passage-work, here specifically labeled "Passaggio" by Bach. The *passaggio* is followed by a middle segment made up of two figures, one imitative and the other arpeggiated. Both emphasize the minor sixth (e♭') and diminished-seventh chords that play a central role in the Fugue. The arpeggiated figure is a single line, but in a reverberant space the slurred notes would blend together like chords, creating the illusion of three-part texture. The outlined chords moving stepwise downward in parallel motion are quite like those in the opening sec-tion of the Toccata in D Minor, BWV 565 (mm. 16–20). The Prelude ends with a dense contrapuntal section in carefully maintained five-part texture. When Bach later expanded the Prelude to 43 measures, he retained elements of the opening and closing sections of the original version but replaced the center material alto-gether (see chapter 17).

The Fugue that follows the short Prelude shows clear signs of an early origin. It is ostensibly a four-part fugue, but four-part texture is not maintained with any consistency until the final pedal entry (and we cannot be sure of this, since the original ending is lost); the modulatory scheme is very limited: all entries of the subject are in the tonic or dominant except for a single entry in the mediant, B♭ major; the episodes are not unified; and the subject is composed of North German clichés.

At the same time, there are also indications of Bach's increasing expertise. First, the subject, while based on the *repercussio* and neighbor-note motives so beloved by Reincken, Buxtehude, and other North Germans (example 6-5, a; x and y), nevertheless shows a carefully calculated sculpting to produce both inner balance (the repetition of both motives a step lower) and a gradual acceleration (quarter notes → 8th notes → 16th notes). The subject may represent Bach's refinement of a Reincken theme elaborated upon by Peter Heidorn in a fugue copied into the Möller Manuscript (example 6-5, b).[37] Second, the pedal now enters only with the fugue subject. Third, the Fugue displays a nicely balanced form: *pedaliter* section—*manualiter* section—*pedaliter* section—*manualiter* section—*pedaliter* section. Each section is marked by an entrance of the subject, and the center of the Fugue, the middle *pedaliter* section, is highlighted by the striking modulation to B♭ major. Third, Bach used almost all possible ranges of the subject, reserving the lowest until the final pedal entry.[38] Fourth, although the two manual episodes are not based on the same material, they both develop a form of the *repercussio* in diminution (example 6-5, c). Finally, if the original Fugue ended in the same way as the revised version, the 32nd notes in the conclusion hark back to the 32nd notes in the Prelude, giving the whole a framing arc.

Bach's twofold return to the Prelude and Fugue in G Minor in later years reflects his admiration for the piece. The fugue, with its impressive structural coherence, was a remarkable early accomplishment.

Example 6-5 (a) Prelude and Fugue in G Minor, BWV 535a: subject of the Fugue, and (b) Fugue in D Minor (here transposed to G minor for comparison) by Peter Heidorn, based on a theme by Reincken.

a)

b)

Independent Fugues

Bach's early passion for fugue-writing is also apparent in four independent fugues, the last of which was later paired with a prelude:

Fugue in C Minor on a Theme of Bononcini, BWV 574b
Fugue in B Minor on a Theme of Corelli, BWV 579
Fugue in C Minor, BWV 575
Fugue in D Major, BWV² 532/2a

As Werner Breig has pointed out, Bach changed the nature of the fugue even in his early works—that is, the pieces written before the critical encounter with Vivaldi's music in Weimar.[39] First, by treating the pedal in a fully obbligato way, Bach altered its role from bit player to leading character. The pedal now commonly serves as the culminating voice of the opening exposition, as the critical marker of modulation to related keys, and as the climactic presenter of the subject at the end of the fugue, often in the lowest octave of the pedalboard. In addition, Bach began to structure the fugue in a more convincing way, presenting the entries of the subject in a logical, four-phase sequence:[40]

Phase 1   Opening exposition, usually in four voices, with subject entries
                in the tonic and dominant
Phase 2   Individual entries of the subject, in the tonic and dominant
Phase 3   Tonal expansion into related keys (usually to vi in major-mode
                works and to III in minor-mode works, together with other
                closely related keys)
Phase 4   A return to entries in the tonic and dominant, commonly
                ending with a tonic entry in the pedal

The dramatic return to the tonic in the final phase gradually replaced the need for rhythmically free, recitative-like material at the conclusion of the fugues.[41]

These phases can be observed in the four independent fugues from the Arnstadt-Mühlhausen years. The first two works reflect Bach's early interest in writing keyboard fugues based on themes from Italian instrumental trios, a repertory that includes five pieces:

From Tomaso Albinoni's *Suonate a tre*, opus 1 (Venice, 1694):
    Fugue in C Major for Harpsichord, BWV 946
    Fugue in A Major for Harpsichord, BWV 950
    Fugue in B Minor for Harpsichord, BWV 951

From Giovanni Maria Bononcini's *Sonate da chiesa*, opus 6 (Venice, 1672):
   Fugue in C Minor for Organ, BWV 574
From Arcangelo Corelli's *Sonate a tre*, opus 3 (Rome, 1689):
   Fugue in B Minor for Organ, BWV 579

The **Fugue in C Minor on a Theme of Bononcini, BWV 574b,** has a complicated history. Its theme was previously attributed to Giovanni Legrenzi, a tradition that apparently began with Bach himself, who seems to have labeled the piece "Thema Legrenzianum. Elaboratum per Joan. Seb. Bach" (Theme of Legrenzi, worked out by Johann Sebastian Bach).[42] Only in recent times has the model been identified as the closing Allegro of Trio Sonata 10 in C Minor from Bononcini's *Sonate da chiesa*.[43] The initial version of the Fugue, BWV 574b (=574.1 in BWV³), dates from the Arnstadt years. Bach returned to the work at a later point, possibly the Weimar years, and fashioned a revised version, BWV 574 (=574.2 in BWV³). Still another variant, BWV 574a, emerged in the 1790s,[44] long after Bach's death. It lacks the closing toccata section and is now viewed as inauthentic.

The Fugue in C Minor is the earliest surviving example of a Bach double fugue. It can be divided into four sections:

Exposition 1 (mm. 1–37)
   Presentation of subject 1, Bononcini's theme, combined in invertible coun-
      terpoint with a countersubject. All entries of the subject are in i and v,
      except for one in III (m. 23).
Exposition 2 (mm. 37–70)
   Presentation of a new subject, composed by Bach. It appears in a simplified
      form in the pedal. All entries of the subject are in i and v, except for for
      one in iv (m. 55).
Exposition 3 (mm. 70–104)
   Subjects 1 and 2 combined in invertible counterpoint. All entries of the
      subjects are in i and v.
Close (mm. 104–118)
   Recitative-like close, initially based on subject 2 (m. 105) but then on un-
      related material. Arpeggiated chords, 32nd-note flourishes in parallel
      motion, 32nd- and 64th-note *passaggio* scales.

In Exposition 1 Bach borrowed the subject and countersubject from Bononcini's trio but revised both themes, making them more concise and har-monically focused (example 6-6). He retained certain elements of the trio's con-trapuntal fabric as well,[45] even as he enhanced the texture with a fourth part, often assigned to the pedal. Despite the Fugue's impressive length—118 meas-ures compared to Bononcini's 31 measures—the work is not fully successful.

Example 6-6 (a) Giovanni Maria Bononcini, Sonata 10 in C Minor, Allegro: theme
and countertheme, and (b) Fugue in C Minor after Bononcini, BWV 574b: subject
(mm. 1–4) and countersubject (mm. 4–7, upper part).

The virtuosic gestures of the conclusion, the deft handling of four-part texture,
and the combining of the two subjects in the third exposition cannot overcome
the static nature of harmonic scheme (which hardly ventures outside the tonic
and dominant), the similarity of the two subjects (both composed solely of black
notes), and the independent nature of the conclusion (set off by a double bar).

When Bach revised the Fugue years later, he added 16th notes to several
passages to create greater forward momentum, but this improved matters only
to a certain degree. Not until he used two subjects of greater contrast in other
works (white note versus black note, for example, in the Fugue in F Major, BWV
540/2, or Contrapunctus 9 of the Art of Fugue, BWV 1080/9) and modulatory
schemes that ranged farther afield did he succeed in writing truly masterful
double fugues.

Bach took a different approach to using Italian thematic material in the **Fugue
in B Minor on a Theme of Corelli, BWV 579**. In this case, he borrowed the
subject and countersubject from the Vivace of Corelli's Trio Sonata No. 4 in B
Minor, opus 3, an intensely contrapuntal movement featuring invertible counterpoint and multiple stretto entries. Bach retained Corelli's compact themes
without change, only transposing them down an octave to make room for a new
fourth voice in the soprano. After that, he limited himself to using fragments of
Corelli's music—a top part here (mm. 6–9), a bass part there (mm. 90–91)—and

he reserved stretto for one grand presentation toward the end (m. 91), with the countersubject appearing in parallel 6ths and 10ths. In addition to adding the fourth voice and assigning the bass part to the pedal, Bach expanded the treatment of Corelli's two themes from 39 measures (the instrumental trio) to 102 measures (the organ fugue). The result, however ambitious, has the character of a dry contrapuntal study, and Bach may have been taking his cue from similar exercises in counterpoint found in North German organ works such as Bruhns's small Praeludium in E Minor or Buxtehude's Praeludium in A Major, BuxWV 151.[46]

In Bach's Fugue, the subject and countersubject appear together throughout, always in the tonic or dominant. As the music progresses, they are joined by new material, making for increasingly dense counterpoint. This progression reaches a climax in the culminating stretto entry. The episodes are the greatest point of interest, since they introduce new, animated 16th-note material (mm. 24–34 and 65–73) that is subsequently mixed with the subject. Some of the episodes are based on the descending half-note tail of the subject, presented three times in syncopated stretto (mm. 44–49, 57–62, 78–82) against a sequential 8th-note motive similar to the figure that dominates the middle section of the Prelude in D Major, BWV 532/1. Although the episodes are not fully coordinated, they are set off by their *manualiter* texture and hint at the future unification of episodic material that takes place in Weimar. The Fugue concludes with an adagio close, a gesture adopted from Corelli's movement but now set off all the more clearly by a short pause in all the parts.

The **Fugue in C Minor, BWV 575**, is an early, whimsical gem. Greatly admired by Spitta for its "uncommon treatment of the subject" and "great harmonic beauty,"[47] it is a *manualiter* fugue written in the spirit of a Buxtehude canzonetta, with a running 16th-note theme not suited for the pedal. The subject itself is playful: it begins ambiguously, in the subdominant rather than the tonic, and its metrical structure does not become fully clear until the fifth measure, when it is joined by the countersubject. One hears the opening notes as being on the beat rather than off the beat (example 6-7, a). The subject is also one of Bach's earliest "gap subjects"—a fugue theme with rests that are filled in by a countersubject, often in a humorous way. Here the countersubject completes the upward leaps of the subject whenever the countersubject appears above it, as in the opening exposition (example 6-7, b). The Fugue in C Minor may have been a dry run for the even more effective gap subjects that appear in the Fugue in D Major, BWV 532/2, and the Fugue of the Toccata in C Major, BWV 564/3.

The entries of the subject in the opening exposition suggest a four-part fugue, but the texture afterward is mostly two- and three-part. In addition, the individual lines sometimes migrate from one voice to another, with the alto becoming the bass (mm. 27–31) or the soprano becoming the alto (mm. 27–30), for

Example 6-7 Fugue in C Minor, BWV 575: (a) subject (as it is written and as it is heard), and (b) subject and countersubject joined.

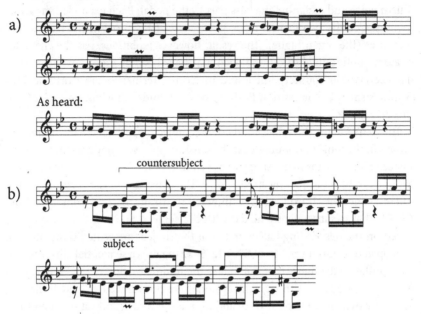

instance. This is not a fugue that one could write out in full score,[48] and it clearly predates the strict part-writing of the Orgel-Büchlein. Aside from the closing section, the idiom resembles that of harpsichord works such as the Toccata in E Minor, BWV 914, or Böhm's Suite in F Minor, which may have been the source for a number of gestures.[49] The entrances of the subject are limited to the tonic and dominant, but this conservative harmonic scheme is counterbalanced both by episodic sequences that touch on F minor (m. 44) and B♭ minor (m. 45) and entries of the subject that are disguised by false starts (mm. 47 and 57–58)—another gesture that may have been borrowed from Böhm.

The Fugue contains many attractive features: a catchy countersubject whose stepwise-moving 8th notes appear in constantly varied form; playful episodes that use sequences from Italian chamber music and broken chords seemingly borrowed, once again, from Böhm; and a final statement of subject and countersubject that simultaneously exploits the highest and lowest registers of the keyboard (mm. 58–61). But the 12-measure, rhythmically free close seems tacked on, like that of the Bononcini Fugue, and the sudden appearance of the pedal (m. 65) bears no relation to what has come before. The 32nd-note scale and the rhythmic figure ♪ ♫♫ ♫ in the concluding section can be found in the free close of Buxtehude's Canzonetta in A Minor, BuxWV 225, and the pedal solo, emerging out of the blue, represents a final token nod to North German practice. Despite the clash of *pedaliter* conclusion with *manualiter* fugue and the presence of many derivative elements, the playful banter of the subject and countersubject result in a work of undeniable charm.

The **Fugue in D Major, BWV² 532/2a** (=532.1 in BWV³) is an early version of the bravura fugue that concludes the Prelude and Fugue in D Major, BWV 532. It is preserved solely in the Peters Edition, whose editor, Friedrich Conrad Griepenkerl, relied on "a very good manuscript," now lost.[50] The Fugue contains 98 measures in its early form, which appears to date from the last Arnstadt-Mühlhausen years or possibly the early Weimar period. Bach later expanded the text to 137 measures by deleting a few short passages and inserting several larger ones. This was quite unusual, since Bach rarely tampered with the structure of a fugue in the revision process, normally limiting the changes to improving matters of detail. In the few cases where he expanded a fugue's form, he most commonly added a single, lengthy section—a new beginning or a new ending, as in Contrapunctus 10, BWV 1080/10, from the Art of Fugue or the fugue of the Prelude and Fugue in A♭ Major, BWV 886, from Well-Tempered Clavier, volume 2. To enlarge a fugue by performing major surgery, as he did here, was a rare undertaking.

The original version, like the later revision, is an unabashed, virtuosic *perpetuum mobile*, with all elements geared to caprice and technical display. Like the Fugue in C Minor, BWV 575, the D-Major Fugue features a gap subject, here filled in with a neighbor-note/octave leap countersubject seemingly inspired by the playful fugue theme of Buxtehude's Praeludium in F Major, BuxWV 145. The head of the subject, the fourfold repetition of a rising and falling third, is perfectly tailored to opposite-toe pedal playing at a fast tempo in sharp keys with two or more accidentals.[51] The tail of the subject, the fivefold sequential repetition of a disjunct 16th-note figure, is derived from a motive occurring frequently in Central and North German works.[52] The presence of so much repetition gives the subject a certain giddy quality.

Bach's Fugue is a breathless sprint from start to finish, reaching a climax with a two-octave closing pedal cadenza that is already present in the early version. Bach toys with the subject and countersubject to an unprecedented degree in a series of unorthodox gestures: at measure 26 the head motive is repeated for a second cadence; at measure 47 the countersubject is replaced by the head motive; at measure 55 the tail of the subject migrates from the tenor to the pedal; at measure 62 the subject and tail begin in the alto, but the tail then migrates to the tenor and pedal; and at measure 81 the head motive and countersubject are tossed about in an almost ridiculous way. The harmonic scheme includes subject entries in B minor and F♯ minor. Although still limited, it is the most advanced plan of the Arnstadt-Mühlhausen fugues. And four-part writing is maintained throughout and even extended to six-part manual chords for the final tonic entry of the subject in the pedal. "With this fugue, one really has to let the feet kick around a lot," the Nuremberg organist Lorenz Sichart noted at the end of his manuscript copy of the revised version of the Fugue.[53] Together with the "Jig" Fugue in G Major, it must be counted as one of Bach's most unabashedly virtuosic organ pieces.

The revised version of the Fugue, BWV 532/2, reveals much about Bach's concern with the limited harmonic scope of his early fugues. His revision involved the refinement or deletion of infelicitous passages (mm. 28–29 and mm. 71–73, for instance, in BWV 532/2a), as we might expect. But it also included, most tellingly, the insertion of two newly composed segments, the first (mm. 76–96 in BWV 532/2) to expand the tonal range of phase 3 of the Fugue to include subject entries in C♯ minor and E major, keys quite unrelated to D major, and the second (mm. 96–137 in BWV 532/2) to expand the return to the tonic in phase 4, most probably to balance the new modulations in phase 3 and to prolong the virtuosic close. The harmonic plans of the two versions can be summarized as follows:

	Phase 1	Phase 2	Phase 3	Phase 4
Original version (BWV 532/2a):	I V I V	I V I	vi iii	V I
Revised version (BWV 532/2):	I V I V	I V I	vi iii vii II	V I

Bach's harmonic expansion of fugues reached its peak in the "Wedge" Fugue in E Minor, BWV 548/2, which includes subject entries on every degree of the scale (see chapter 20).

Unica

Finally, four pieces display formats that are unique within Bach's organ works:

Fantasia in C Minor, BWV 1121
Fantasia in G Major, BWV 571
Praeludium in A Minor, BWV 569
Canzona in D Minor, BWV 588

The **Fantasia in C Minor, BWV 1121**, is transmitted in a single source, a tablature score entered into the Andreas Bach Book around 1706 by Bach himself.[54] Although no composer is mentioned in the title, the Fantasia has been credited to Bach, assigned a Schmieder number (initially Anh. 205 in BWV[2], then BWV 1121 in BWV[3]), and belatedly included in the Neue Bach-Ausgabe.[55]

There are reasons to question this attribution. The first is the source issue. Bach noted his authorship in the two early autographs of his organ works,[56] and within the Andreas Bach Book he is clearly cited (by his brother) as the composer of the Fantasia in C Major, BWV 570, and the Fantasia and Imitatio in B Minor, BWV 563, the two other *manualiter* works written in the style of the Fantasia in C Minor. It seems odd that the tablature lacks Bach's name.

The second problem is the style of the work. The Fantasia is not based on a set theme or motive, like the Imitatio in B Minor or the Fantasia in C Major. It features instead a series of loosely related ideas that unfold casually, sometimes in imitation and sometimes not. While four-part texture is maintained throughout, the chromaticism often fails to move toward compelling goals (mm. 7–9 or 44–46), and the change of meter from 6/4 to 4/4 seems to lack a clear motivation. Both matters are handled more adeptly in the Neumeister Chorales. The harmonic vocabulary is more advanced than that of the Fantasia in C Major,[57] but the music nevertheless unfolds in an unmemorable, meandering way and lacks the structural logic found even in Bach's earliest extant works. The overall impression is that of a Central German *manualiter* improvisation in the style of Johann Kuhnau, Johann Krieger, or Pachelbel's teacher Georg Caspar Wecker. Could this be one of their compositions, presented to Johann Christoph Bach by his younger brother for use in teaching?

Given Bach's restless inventiveness as a youthful composer, we must assume that he wrote a number of organ pieces that defied all conventions. The **Fantasy in G Major, BWV 571**, is such a work. Its three-movement design has traditionally been compared to Buxtehude's Praeludium in C Major, BuxWV 137, with its prelude-fugue-chaconne structure.[58] But it is much closer to Bach's six keyboard toccatas, BWV 910–915, with which it is transmitted in its earliest source, an anonymous manuscript written not much later than 1720.[59] The Toccatas in D Major, D Minor, and E Minor, in particular, have similar idioms and three-movement forms.

The opening movement (presumably allegro) is based on thematic material from the Praeludium of Partita 1 in C Major from Johann Kuhnau's Neue Clavier-Übung of 1689. Bach borrowed the *repercussio* theme, the general shape of the 16th-note countersubject, and the idea of presenting the theme in stretto (example 6-8). In his hands, the theme appears as a motive that constantly spins out in varied forms: extended, inverted, stretto, and parallel 3rds and 6ths. The counterpoint is similar to that of the Fantasia and Imitatio, BWV 563. The pedal does not appear until near the end (a Central German trait) and the movement concludes with a free section (a North German trait). The free section veers off track and cadences in B major, in preparation for the Adagio section in E minor that follows.

Example 6-8 a) Johann Kuhnau, Partita 1 in C Major, Praeludium: section 2, mm. 1–5, and (b) Fantasia in G Major, BWV 571: opening section, mm. 1–5.

The theme of the Adagio is derived from material in the opening movement, and it, too, is manipulated contrapuntally, appearing in imitation, stretto, inversion, contrary motion, and parallel 3rds and 6ths. In the middle, a *corta* motive makes a brief appearance. The closing Allegro is the most masterful of the three movements. It is an ostinato form, with a half-note theme that descends by six steps rather than the usual four-note tetrachord. This theme alternates between the pedal and manual, where it appears in the soprano or alto voice. The variations are generally paired, like those of the Passacaglia in C Minor, BWV 582, but the pairs alternate between G major and its submediant, E minor—a highly original way to structure an ostinato form. Certain gestures in the closing Allegro can be found in the Neumeister Chorales.[60] But the formal concept of an ostinato form with migrating subject in alternating keys cannot be found elsewhere. It is *sui generis*.

To judge from the Andreas Bach Book, Bach and his brother Johann Christoph shared a special fondness for ostinato forms, since the album contains four classic examples of such pieces: Pachelbel's Ciacona in D Minor and Buxtehude's Ciaconas in C Minor and E Minor and Passacalgia in D Minor. As we noted earlier, the Buxtehude entries probably reflect manuscript copies of the works obtained by the young Johann Sebastian during his time in Lüneburg and Lübeck.

An even stronger sign of Bach's interest in ostinato procedure is the remarkable **Praeludium in A Minor, BWV 569**, a work that ostensibly explores the idea of a descending musical line. While the Praeludium has the general features of an ostinato piece—minor mode, triple meter, and variation-like periods—it lacks the four-bar bass theme that characterizes the form. It opens instead with a 13-measure introduction that acts as a type of preamble: the first three measures establish the general idea of downward movement; the next five measures establish the general idea of a syncopated rhythm, ♪ ♩♩ ♩ ♩; and the next five measures present the more concrete idea of an off-beat, stepwise-descending melodic line punctuated by the syncopated rhythm. The preamble is followed by 27 variations that are set off by cadences and changes of figuration. They vary in length from three to nine measures.

More than half of the variations are based on the melody and rhythm presented in the third segment of the preamble, often varied through invertible counterpoint. This is well illustrated by the addition of a falling *saltus duriusculus* (dissonant leap) figure that appears first in the bass (m. 33), then in the soprano (m. 44), tenor (m. 61), alto (m. 93), and bass (mm. 114 and 124), and finally in the bass once again (m. 146) as the upper voice in a double-pedal part that thickens the texture to five parts (example 6-9). There is much cleverness in this work, in the treatment of the preamble material, in the masterful handling of four-part texture, in the intensification of the harmonic scheme (which touches on C major, F major, D minor, and other related keys after m. 54), and in the four highly imaginative variations that suddenly emerge at the end (mm. 133–149).[61]

The Praeludium in A Minor is a large work—152 measures long. But there is no structural logic to the alternation of *manualiter* and *pedaliter* sections, and the variations lack the gradual acceleration of note values that makes ostinato forms so effective. It appears to be an Arnstadt or Mühlhausen improvisation in the *style* of a ciacona or passacaglia—hence its transmission with the more neutral title "Praeludium." The early circulation of the work—a Weimar copy made by Walther and Leipzig copies by Kellner and Kittel[62]—indicates that Bach shared it with colleagues and used it in instruction. He must have felt that the Praeludium had admirable qualities, despite its formal shortcomings, and that there was something to be said for the loose, improvisatory approach it exemplifies.

The **Canzona in D Minor, BWV 588**, is one of Bach's most substantial free works from the Arnstadt-Mühlhausen years and his only essay in this form.

Example 6-9 Praeludium in A Minor, BWV 569: (a) first appearance of the falling dissonant leap, in the pedal, and (b) final appearance of the falling dissonant leap, as top voice of the double-pedal.

It appears as a 16-measure fragment in the Möller Manuscript, where it seems to have been one of the last additions to the album, entered by Johann Christoph Bach shortly before 1707.[63]

While the keyboard canzona enjoyed great popularity in Italy and Germany in the seventeenth century, by 1700 it was considered out of date. In its classic guise, the canzona featured a theme, often with repeated notes, that was treated fugally in a number of sections with different meters. The theme commonly appeared first in duple meter, then triple meter, and then sometimes in duple meter once again, with gradually increasing note motion. Bach's Canzona is often linked with Girolamo Frescobaldi, whose keyboard publications contain classic examples of the genre.[64] But there is no evidence that Bach knew Frescobaldi's music before 1714, when he obtained a copy of *Fiori musicali* in Weimar.[65]

It is more likely that Bach became acquainted with the canzona through German models—works by Johann Jacob Froberger or Johann Caspar Kerll, both named by C.P.E. Bach as writers of music his father "heard and studied," or by Christian Flor, organist in Lüneburg, whose Suite in D Minor in the Möller Manuscript begins with a "Fuga" of three sections that displays the metrical metamorphosis characteristic of a canzona (example 6-10).

Example 6-10 Christian Flor, Suite in D Minor, Fuga: metrical transformation of the canzona-like subject in the movement's three sections: (a) in 𝄴 meter, (b) in 3/2 meter, and (c) in 𝄴.

Bach's Canzona is transmitted in complete form in two important early manuscripts. The original version is preserved in a copy made by Johann Gottlieb Preller[66] around 1745 that includes additional ornaments and fingerings.[67] A slightly revised version of the Canzona is preserved in a copy completed in 1781 by Christian Friedrich Gottlieb Schwencke,[68] who succeeded C.P.E. Bach as Town Music Director in Hamburg and had access to C.P.E.'s collection of his father's manuscripts. The revised version contains several refinements and the marking "Adagio" for the last two measures, apparently added by Bach as a second thought. Although Griepenkerl published the Canzona as a pedal piece in the Peters Edition of 1845, the work is clearly intended for manuals alone, in the *manualiter* tradition of keyboard canzonas. This is verified by the fingering in the Preller copy, which calls for no pedal.

Bach's Canzona is an early study in strict part-writing. The work is titled "Canzona a 4" in the manuscript sources, which underscores its fugue-like, obbligato treatment of the voices. The music could be notated in the four-staff, open-score format that Bach used in the print of the Art of Fugue,[69] and like the Art of Fugue, the Canzona is set in D minor, the traditional key of learned contrapuntal undertakings. The work consists of a series of five expositions distributed across two sections, the first in 𝄴 (mm. 1–70),[70] the second in 3/2 meter (mm. 71–168). The principal subject, a long, mostly step-wise-moving line, is paired with a contrasting countersubject that features a chromatically descending fourth (example 6-11, a). In the 3/2 section, both themes are transformed, with the subject now displaying a sequence of downward-leaping fourths that produce new energy and drive (example 6-11, b). The countersubject retains its chromatic descending fourth, followed by a new circling motive that appears in sequence against the descending fourth of the subject. All forms of the subject and countersubject appear in invertible counterpoint.

Example 6-11 Canzona in D Minor, BWV 588: subject and countersubject in the work's two sections: (a) in **C**, and (b) in 3/2 meter.

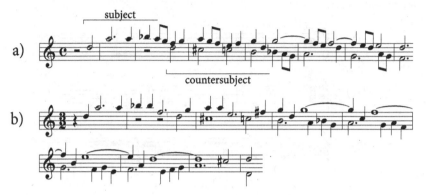

The structure of the Canzona can be outlined as follows:

Part I, in **C** meter
 Exposition (mm. 1–38), entries in i v i v, episode.
 Exposition (mm. 39–70), entries in i i v i, concluding in V.
Part II, in 3/2 meter
 Exposition (mm. 71–101), entries in i v v i, episode.
 Exposition (mm. 102–139), entries in i i i v, episode.
 Exposition (mm. 140–172), entries in iv i i v, dominant pedal-point,
  Adagio close.

The harmonic scheme, like those of other Arnstadt-Mühlhausen works, is very conservative and includes only one entry, in G minor (m. 140), outside the tonic and dominant. Bach created other interest by dressing up the key cadences, changing figuration (mm. 107–110), introducing bold digressions (the abrupt modulation from E major to G minor, mm. 134–140), and finishing with an al-most obligatory but nevertheless compelling dominant pedal-point (mm. 161–164). The Canzona was a noble effort to extend the life of a moribund form.

The free works of the Arnstadt-Mühlhausen period show Bach on the cusp of crafting large, unified forms. The length of many pieces is impressive, even if the harmonic schemes are limited and the episodes digressive and mostly unrelated. Bach's final North German–oriented works, pieces such as the Prelude and Fugue in A Minor, BWV 543, and the Passacaglia in C Minor, BWV 582, were soon to come. And these were followed by compositions influenced by the game-changing idiom of Vivaldi's *L'Estro armonico*. The Arnstadt-Mühlhausen pieces were neces-sary stepping stones leading to Bach's first true masterpieces in Weimar.

Notes

1. Roger Bullivant, *Fugue* (London: Hutcheinson, 1971), 161.
2. Williams 1981.
3. Humphreys 1982.
4. Claus 1995.
5. Most strikingly in Wolff 2002a and Wolff 2002b.
6. Berlin State Library, *P 595*, fascicle 8. A complete facsimile appears in Wolff 2002a and Bach digital, under BWV 565.
7. Wolff 2002a, 90.
8. However, Wolff's claim that Ringk never attributed a work falsely must now be modified in light of the recently discovered copy of the Prelude and Fugue in C Major, BWV 531, in Ringk's hand, in which he wrongly credits the work to "Johann Christ. Bach" rather than Johann Sebastian. See Over 2017.
9. Leipzig Town Library, Becker Collection, *III.8.20.*
10. Example adapted from Wolff 2000, 511–512.
11. Wolff 2002a, 92. For this reason, it is best not to use a 16' registration for the Toccata.
12. In the concluding section "Das neue Regiment," mm. 37–39 and 100–102.
13. Measure 45 of the fugue. See example 3-7, c.
14. As seen in the seven keyboard toccatas, BWV 910–916, the Adagio of the Sonata in D Major, BWV 963, or Cantata 71, *Gott is mein König*, or Cantata 106, *Gottes Zeit is die allerbeste Zeit*, for instance. See Marshall 1989b, 262–269.
15. Williams 2003, 157.
16. Peters Edition, vol. 4, iii.
17. Wolff 2002a, 98.
18. Wolff 2002a, 98; Stauffer 1980, 98–99; Zehnder 2009, 323. In BWV[3] the work is listed as "probably Arnstadt."
19. The "Toccata" title stems from the BG and was consequently adopted in BWV[1]. It does not appear in the sources, however, where the work is called "Praeludium," "Preludium con Fuga," or "Praeludium Concertato con Fuga." In BWV[2] the work was listed as "Präludium und Fuge in E", and in BWV[3] it is more appropriately labeled "Präludium in E."
20. Berlin State Library, *P 803*, fascicle 20, dated 1714–1717.
21. See the discussion in NBA IV/5–6, KB (Dietrich Kilian, ed.; 1978–79), 523–524.
22. As proposed by Zehnder, for instance, who consequently dates the work "c. 1706." See Zehnder 2009, 210.
23. Berlin State Library, *P 320* and *P 557* (in E major) and *P 277* (in C major).
24. Berlin State Library, *P 504* (in E major).
25. That Bach owned a pedal harpsichord or clavichord cannot be doubted. The account of his estate states that during his lifetime he gave "3. *Clavire* nebst *Pedal*" (three claviers with a set of pedals) to his son Johann Christian Bach. See NBR, 256.
26. See comments in Breig 1999, 630.
27. See NBA IV/5–6, KB, 381, or Bach digital, under BWV 533.
28. See Bach digital, under BWV 533.

29. Stauffer 1980, 37–42, where it is termed a "Through-Composed, Sectional Form."

30. Cantatas 71, 106, and 131. See Williams 2003, 46.

31. Spitta 1873–80, vol. 1, 402.

32. NBA IV/5–6, KB, 581–582, and BWV³, 415.

33. Schulze 1984, 46–47.

34. Robert Hill has speculated that the piece following the Prelude and Fugue in G Minor in the Möller Manuscript, the Chaconne in G Major from Jean-Baptiste Lully's opera *Phaëton*, was already in place when Bach entered the Prelude and Fugue. The Chaconne begins on the verso side of leaf 45, which would have prevented Bach from continuing the Fugue, which breaks off at the bottom of the recto side of the same leaf. See Hill 1987, 297.

35. NBR, no. 395.

36. See note 34. Hill has proposed that Bach may have presented the Fugue to his brother as a farewell gift in the summer of 1707 as he left nearby Arnstadt for the more distant Mühlhausen. See Hill 1987, 128.

37. The "Fuga. Thema Reinkianum à Domino Heydornio elaboratum." See Grapenthin 2003, 20–27.

38. See Werner Breig's analysis, in Breig 1999, 652.

39. Breig 1992.

40. Breig 1992, 13–17.

41. However, one must note that Bach continued to use free conclusions in relatively late pre-Vivaldi works, such as the Prelude and Fugue in A Minor, BWV 543, and the Toccata in C Major, BWV 564.

42. This is the title in the Andreas Bach Book, where the work was entered by Johann Christoph Bach.

43. Zitellini 2013, which includes the full text of the Bononcini movement.

44. In the manuscript Berlin State Library *P 207*, written by an anonymous scribe and dated August 21, 1791.

45. See examples in Zitellini 2013, 244–246.

46. Sackmann 2000, 118.

47. Spitta 1973–80, vol. 1, 252–254.

48. As pointed out in Breig 1999, 641.

49. Spitta was the first to note the similarity to the fugue of the E-Minor Toccata. See Spitta 1873–80, vol. 1, 252. On the Böhm connection, see Zehnder 2009, 281.

50. Peters Edition, vol. 4, iii.

51. It may be for this reason that there are no entries of the subject in the subdominant (G major), a key often touched upon in the third phase (tonal expansion) of Bach's early fugues.

52. Pachelbel's Fugue in D Major or Buxtehude's Canzonetta in G Major, BuxWV 172, for instance.

53. Wurttemberg Regional Library, *Cod. Mus. II, fol. 288.*

54. Bach was first recognized as the scribe by Dietrich Kilian, in Kilian 1983. The entry was dated by Hans-Joachim Schulze, in Schulze 1984, 49–50.

55. NBA IV/10 (Ulrich Bartels and Peter Wollny, eds., 2003).

56. The autographs of the Prelude and Fugue in G Minor, BWV 535a, "per Joan. Sebast. Bachium," and "Wie schön leutet der Morgenstern," BWV 739, "di JSB."

57. As noted in Zehnder 2009, 84.

58. In Spitta 1873–80, vol. 1, 320–321, or Stinson 1990, 122–123, for instance.

59. Brussels Royal Library, *Fétis 2960* (*Ms. II 4093*). Dating from Bach digital.

60. See the observations in Zehnder 2009, 112.

61. Breig has proposed the interesting idea that Bach may have added this final group of variations, each four measures long, in the course of revising the Praeludium, since they stand out so starkly from the more pedestrian variations that precede them. See Breig 1999, 631.

62. Berlin State Library, *P 801* (Walther copy, before 1717) and *P 288* (Kellner copy, after 1727). The Kittel copy is lost but reflected in the manuscript Yale Music Library *Ma21.Y11.B12* (formerly *LM 4842*), which was once owned by his student Johann Christian Heinrich Rinck.

63. NBA V/9.1, KB (Peter Wollny, ed., 1999), 64.

64. Such as the "Canzon dopo la Postola" (Canzona on the Epistle) in *Fiori musicali* of 1635, which was first cited as Bach's model for the Canzona in D Minor by André Pirro in Pirro 1907, 216.

65. The copy is lost, but described in Spitta 1873–80, vol. 1, 421. See also Beißwenger 1992a, 284.

66. Leipzig Town Library, *Peters Ms. 7*, fascicle 19.

67. The text of the Preller version in NBA IV/7 (Dietrich Kilian, ed., 1984) includes the ornaments but not the fingerings. The fingering is given in the Breitkopf and Leupold Editions.

68. Berlin State Library, *P 204*.

69. Breig 1999, 636.

70. ¢ in Preller's copy.

PART III
"THE GOLDEN YEARS"
Weimar (1708–1717)

I have seen things by the famous organist of Weimar, Mr. Johann
Sebastian Bach . . . that certainly make one esteem the man highly.
—Johann Mattheson, in the first reference
to Bach in print (1717)

7

Bach in Weimar

Organist and Chamber Musician at the Weimar Court

In July 1708 Bach returned to the Weimar court, where he had worked briefly
as a "lackey musician" in 1703. His new position was that of court organist and
chamber musician, for which he was paid 150 florins annually by the reigning
duke, Wilhelm Ernst. Although Weimar was a small town, with a population of
approximately 4,700,[1] the court itself was a bustling hub (about one-third of the
town's citizens worked there), and it was known for its music activities, which
were supported by a modest-sized but capable instrumental and vocal ensemble.

The court had been governed by a coregency since 1689. In Bach's time, Duke
Wilhelm Ernst (r. 1683–1728) was the senior regent and de facto ruler of Saxony-
Weimar, a duchy of approximately 50,000 inhabitants. He determined the terms
of Bach's employment and the salary increases and changes of position that took
place over time. Widowed, childless, and deeply religious, Wilhelm Ernst resided
in the Wilhelmsburg Palace, a large, Italian- and French-inspired Baroque castle
complex completed in 1658. Duke Ernst August I (r. 1707–1748), Wilhelm
Ernst's nephew, occupied the second position of power. A great champion of
music and the arts, he was later singled out by Carl Philipp Emanuel Bach as
one of the three nobles who "particularly loved" his father and "rewarded him
appropriately."[2] Ernst August lived in the Red Palace, a Renaissance-era building
located close to the Wilhelmsburg Palace.

Relations between the two dukes were strained and resulted in many un-
friendly actions and exchanges. In 1707, just before Bach's arrival, for instance,
Wilhelm Ernst issued an order forbidding court musicians to play in the Red
Palace without his special permission.[3] The rivalry between the two arms of
the ducal family became increasingly contentious during Bach's stay and led to
much squabbling and petty bickering. An ameliorating force was Ernst August's
younger half-brother, Prince Johann Ernst (1696–1715), who resided in the
Yellow Palace, located next to the Red Palace. Johann Ernst was musically pre-
cocious, studying violin with Gregor Christoph Eylenstein within the court and
composition with Johann Gottfried Walther, organist of the City Church of St.
Peter and St. Paul (known today as the Herder Church). Johann Ernst played a
key role in Bach's stay in Weimar, serving as an important source of music and
a force for music-making. His premature death was a blow to court cultural life.

J. S. BACH. George B. Stauffer, Oxford University Press. © Oxford University Press 2024.
DOI: 10.1093/oso/9780195108026.003.0008

Bach seems to have been able to navigate the turbulent waters of the feuding dukes, winning the admiration and support of both regents, who recognized and rewarded his talents. His salary was elevated to 200 florins in 1711, an increase that placed him on the same level as the court's highest-paid musician, Capellmeister Johann Samuel Drese. This compensation, provided by Wilhelm Ernst, was supplemented still further by Ernst August, who paid Bach to provide keyboard instruction to his young page at the Red Palace, Adam von Jagemann.

Bach's official duties in Weimar were light. He was required to play in the Chapel of the Wilhelmsburg Palace for worship services, which consisted of one Sunday and one weekday service per week. Within these rites he was responsible for accompanying the chorales, providing an appropriate prelude for each, and performing a postlude. Given the strong musical interests of the dukes and the prince, the postludes may have evolved into miniature recitals during Bach's tenure. The surviving Weimar organ repertoire includes chorale settings that were too lengthy for church use and free pieces of a nonliturgical nature, such as the concerto arrangements. From this we can assume that Bach also presented frequent concerts outside the worship service for the ducal families and their guests. His admirers may have listened from the organ loft, where they could observe first-hand the extended pedal solos featured in many of the works from the time. Both the exhibitionist quality of the large pieces and Bach's high salary suggest that he was viewed by the dukes as a type of "trophy musician," whose virtuoso performances on the organ were a warmly welcomed feature of court social life.

We know far less about Bach's role as chamber musician. In this capacity he was undoubtedly required to take part in vocal and instrumental music, probably playing the violin or keyboard continuo. He also may have composed instrumental and vocal pieces for the court ensemble during his initial Weimar years, though none of these works has survived aside from the Fugue in G Minor for Violin and Continuo, BWV 1026, and Cantatas 18, 54, and 199, which may have been written before 1714.[4] As the Obituary of 1750 described his employment:

> In the following year, 1708, he undertook a journey to Weimar, had the opportunity to be heard by the reigning Duke, and was offered the post of Chamber and Court Organist in Weimar, of which post he immediately took possession. The pleasure His Grace took in his playing fired him with the desire to try every possible artistry in his treatment of the organ. Here, too, he wrote most of his organ works.[5]

These organ works included the Orgel-Büchlein; more than 50 additional chorale settings, including the large *pedaliter* pieces later incorporated into the "Great Eighteen" Collection, the concerto transcriptions, and a host of free works, including unique pieces such as the Pièce d'Orgue, BWV 572, the Passacaglia in

C Minor, BWV 582, and the three-movement Toccata in C Major, BWV 564. Aside from Bach's autographs of the Orgel-Büchlein, the Concerto in D Minor, BWV 596, and the "Trio super Nun komm der Heiden Heiland," BWV 660a, the original manuscripts of the Weimar organ repertory are lost. The works are preserved mainly in copies written at the time by Walther and Johann Tobias Krebs, who studied with both Walther and Bach, and in copies made later in Cöthen or Leipzig by Bach's sons, students, and colleagues. In addition, Bach improvised much music that was never written down. Despite these gaps, the surviving autographs and copies confirm that Bach flourished as an organ composer in Weimar, producing a large repertory of bold, innovative pieces. Not without reason the great nineteenth-century biographer Philipp Spitta, surveying Bach's organ music as a whole, termed Weimar "Die goldene Zeit"—The Golden Years.[6]

In early December 1713 Bach traveled to Halle, most probably to give advice on the large organ that was being constructed for the Market Church of Our Lady by Christoph Contius.[7] While there, he was invited to apply for the organist position at the church, which had opened recently with the death of Handel's teacher Friedrich Wilhelm Zachow. Bach agreed to take part in the selection process and carried out the requirements by auditioning on the organ and composing a cantata to a text provided by the pastor of the church, Johann Michael Heineccius. On December 13 he was offered the position, which provided greater musical opportunities than he enjoyed in Weimar, including composing and performing concerted vocal works every third Sunday and on high feast days.

Bach voiced his desire to take the position but delayed his formal acceptance in order to use the offer as a bargaining chip back in Weimar. The tactic worked, and on March 2, 1714, Wilhelm Ernst announced that Bach would henceforth serve as concertmaster as well as organist and chamber musician. While the concertmaster position remained below those of capellmeister and vice-capellmeister, it elevated Bach's income to 250 florins, the highest salary of any musician at the court. It also allowed him to compose and perform concerted works on a monthly basis, as he would have done in Halle. In addition, the duke required the court ensemble henceforth to "appear upon [Bach's] demand" and practice in the Palace Chapel, rather than the capellmeister's home, as in the past.[8] This essentially put Bach in charge of the players.

For the next two and a half years, from March 1714 to December 1716, Bach composed a cantata every four weeks or so, beginning with Cantata 182, *Himmelskönig sei willkommen*, performed on Palm Sunday, March 25, 1714. The 20 or so Weimar cantatas that survive are markedly different from the works Bach had composed in Mühlhausen. Instead of a North German orientation, with texts based on biblical citations and strophic hymns, they show Bach's embrace of the "new" German cantata, with Italianate music and texts based on madrigal poetry as well as biblical quotations and hymns. Introduced by Erdmann Neumeister in 1700 and featuring librettos patterned after the texts of Italian secular cantatas, the new German cantata incorporated musical forms associated with Italian opera: recitative, arioso, and da capo aria. This was critical to Bach's musical development.

The new Italianate style appears in full bloom in Cantata 182, and it is uncertain how Bach became acquainted with it during the period 1708 to 1714. A letter written in 1712 by one of his students, Philipp David Kräuter,[9] refers to composing works in "the latest and most artful church mode," which suggests that Bach was familiar with the new German cantata by then. Cantata 208 ("Hunt Cantata"), *Was mir behagt, ist nur die muntern Jagt*, from February 1713, confirms that Bach had fully incorporated the new cantata style into his own writing before seeking the Halle position.

The Weimar cantatas serve as an important gauge of the organ works, for two reasons. First, they can be dated, for the most part, and thus provide a chronological measure of Bach's stylistic development during the last years of his Weimar residency. Second, the cantatas seem to have occupied much of his compositional energy after March 1714, with the result that the steady production of organ music appears to have decreased. Many of the stylistic features Bach adopted from Vivaldi, such as the use of lengthy, segmented ritornellos, appear in the Weimar cantatas but not in full form in the Weimar organ works, suggesting that the latter were no longer his main point of focus. Work on the Orgel-Büchlein project seems to have dwindled significantly after 1714, never to regain the composer's full interest.

During the Weimar period the number of Bach's students greatly increased. At least 11 can be identified by name, including Johann Martin Schubart and Johann Caspar Vogler, who followed him from Mühlhausen, his nephew Johann Bernhard Bach and cousin Johann Lorenz Bach, Tobias Krebs, Kräuter, Johann Gotthilf Ziegler, and others.[10] Kräuter, who was 22 years old at the time, described an intense course of study that involved clavier and instrumental instruction, composition, and the opportunity to copy works from Bach's personal music library.[11]

Kräuter's copies of Bach organ works have not survived, but those of Tobias Krebs remain extant in the form of the three large manuscript collections assembled between 1710 and 1717 in collaboration with Walther: *P 801*, *P 802*, and *P 803* in the Berlin State Library (see the introduction). The manuscripts contain a remarkably wide range of keyboard pieces by German and French composers and represent the most important source of Bach's Weimar organ music. Also surviving are Bernhard Bach's copy of the Concerto in G Major, BWV 592, and Schubart's tablature copies of "An Wasserflüssen Babylon," "Kyrie, Gott Vater in Ewigkeit," and the Fugue in B Minor, all by Johann Pachelbel.[12] After his appointment as concertmaster in 1714, Bach enlisted his keyboard students to help write out the performance materials for his newly written cantatas. It was part of their well-rounded music education.

Johann Samuel Drese, in poor health during much of Bach's tenure, died in December 1716. His capellmeister position was offered not to Bach but first to Georg Philipp Telemann, who declined, and then to Drese's son, vice-capellmeister Johann Wilhelm Drese, who accepted. While Bach's reaction is not recorded, he stopped writing cantatas immediately, and by August 1717 he had accepted the appointment of capellmeister at the court of Prince Leopold in Anhalt-Cöthen. The dukes in Weimar were understandably reluctant to let Bach go, and when he insisted on leaving, he was jailed for a month in the detention room of the Wilhelmsburg "for too stubbornly forcing the issue of his dismissal."[13] His resistance to staying was a brave move, for some years later a horn player who had requested to leave had been given 100 lashes and imprisoned; when he eventually managed to escape, he was hanged in effigy.[14] Bach was finally released on December 2, 1717, but with an "unfavorable discharge." Within two weeks, however, he was productively testing the new Scheibe organ in St. Paul's Church in Leipzig, and by the end of the month he received his first salary payment in Cöthen.

Aside from its bitter conclusion, Bach's stay in Weimar was remarkably productive. His organ music included the first round of his mature works, and his cantata-writing established the stylistic foundation for the cantata cycles of the Leipzig years. In 1717 he also received his initial tributes on a national level. In Hamburg, the eminent critic Johann Mattheson mentioned Bach in print for the first time: "I have seen things by the famous organist of Weimar, Mr. Johann Sebastian Bach, both for the church and for the fist [i.e., cantatas and keyboard works], that are certainly fashioned such that one must esteem the man highly."[15] And in Dresden, Bach experienced his first public triumph in September by vanquishing the French organist Louis Marchand in what was intended to be a duel of playing skills. The two were scheduled to meet before the elector and other nobles in a contest of improvisation, but Marchand failed to show up, and an inquiry to his rooms revealed that he had left Dresden by carriage early that morning.[16] While Bach apparently accepted his victory modestly, he did not refrain from recounting it to his sons and colleagues years later.

The Palace Organ and Other Instruments

As court organist, Bach's principal performance venue was the chapel within the Wilhelmsburg Palace. The palace stood on the site of an earlier edifice, Hornstein Castle, which had been consumed by fire in 1618. Progress on a replacement had been slow, due to the Thirty Years War (1618–1648), but by 1658, during the reign of Duke Wilhelm IV, a new building was finally completed. The rechristened Wilhelmsburg Palace, designed by the architect Johann Moritz Richter, was a large U-shaped complex with a small but magnificent chapel at the southern end of its east wing. Named the "Weg zur Himmelsburg"—the Path to Heaven's Citadel—the chapel's interior embodied the theological theme of the blessed ascending from the secular realm of Earth to the sacred realm of Heaven.

The well-known gouache of the interior by Christian Richter (plate 7-1), made shortly after the chapel's completion, shows a tall, narrow, rectangular structure, approximately 100 feet long by 40 feet wide and 65 feet high, with three stories.[17] The openings to the side aisles of the ground floor were decorated with columns, those to the first gallery with pilasters, and those to the second gallery with pilasters containing busts, thus creating increasing decorative excitement as the eye moved upward from the floor. Rising above the altar at the eastern end of the chapel on an elevated platform supported by stylized palm trees was a narrow stone obelisk decorated with dancing putti, extending upward to an opening in the ceiling, approximately 13 feet x 10 feet, bordered on all sides by a balustrade.

The room above, crowned by a cupola called the "Capelle," 25 feet in height, was a musicians' gallery containing space for performers and the chapel organ. The Capelle was covered by a movable ceiling, painted with images of angels in heaven, that could be lowered by a pulley system to separate the gallery from the main room of the sanctuary. This allowed the Capelle to be closed off and heated independently for rehearsals during winter. But the movable ceiling also must have created a wondrous effect when raised slowly to gradually reveal the sound of playing musicians.[18] Organ and ensemble music thus reached the chapel below through the modest-sized opening in the ceiling, some 65 feet above the floor, creating the effect of ethereal sounds floating down from celestial heights. A local almanac from 1702 describes the setting well:

> One comes now to the most sovereign and magnificently constructed castle and fashionable palace residence known as Wilhelmsburg, whose incomparably commanding great hall, beautiful dining chamber, splendid castle church (known as the Path to Heaven's Citadel), ornate theater, and so forth are viewed as masterpieces of architecture, world-renown[ed] and a blessed memorial to Duke Wilhelm IV.... If one enters the justifiably famous chapel, one hears with greatest delight the most delicate and pleasing music, which is presented by a vocal and instrumental ensemble of talented virtuosos.[19]

Unfortunately, this remarkable chapel perished in 1774 when the Wilhelmsburg suffered the same fate as its predecessor and burnt to the ground. All that remains of the complex today is the castle tower and the Renaissance gatehouse, now named the "Bastille." One can gain a sense of the Chapel, however, by visiting

Plate 7-1 Weimar, Chapel to Heaven's Citadel. Gouache by Christian Richter, c. 1660.
Klassik Stiftung Weimar

the Court Chapel of the Augustusburg Castle in Weissenfels, which was also designed by Richter and completed in 1682. Although the Weißenfels Chapel lacks a musicians' gallery in the roof, its interior dimensions and height are quite similar to those of the Weimar Chapel, and the original organ case of Christian Förner from 1668–1673, located at the very top of the sanctuary, just under the barrel-vaulted ceiling, survives.[20]

The organ in the Weimar Chapel was one of the most important instruments in Bach's professional life, yet its precise makeup during his tenure is not fully substantiated. Two specifications have survived: the disposition of the original organ completed in 1658 by Ludwig Compenius, who added a Seitenpositiv to an existing one-manual-and-pedal organ to create a two-manual, 20-stop instrument; and the stop-list of the organ as it stood in 1737, with two manuals and 24 stops (table 7–1).[21] In between these points, the court ledgers document a series of repairs: Johann Conrad Weißhaupt incorporated the Seitenpositiv into the main organ as an Unterwerk and constructed new bellows, wind-chests, and pedal stops in 1707–1708, just before Bach's arrival; Heinrich Nicolaus Trebs, working under Bach's supervision, improved the bellows and wind-chests and added new stops in 1712–1714; and Trebs made further repairs and renovations after Bach's departure, in 1719–1720 and 1734–1738.[22]

To judge from the two surviving specifications, the Oberwerk remained essentially the same over the nearly 80-year span between the stop-lists. The Unterwerk and Pedal divisions, by contrast, changed considerably, but precisely when those alterations occurred is uncertain. Documents in the Thuringian State Archive in Weimar indicate that Weißhaupt was at work on a new "Subbasso" in the fall of 1707,[23] which probably refers to the Groß-Untersatz 32' that Bach required in the Concerto in D Minor, BWV 596.[24] And the Octava 4' in the Unterwerk and Trompetten-Bass 8' in the Pedal must have been added by Weißhaupt or by Trebs in 1712–1714, since they, too, are required in Bach's Weimar scores.[25] The chronology of the other changes cannot be determined.

Table 7-1 Bach's Weimar Organs
Palace Chapel "Path to Heaven's Citadel," Capelle Organ (Ludwig Compenius 1657–1658; Johann Conrad Weißhaupt 1707–1708; Heinrich Nicolaus Trebs 1712–1714, 1719–1720, 1734–1738)

1658[a] Seitenpositiv →	1737[b] Unter-Clavier	1658 Oberwerk →	1737 Ober-Clavier
	8' Principal	16' Quintadena	16' Quintathön
8' Grobgedackt	8' Gedackt	8' Principal	8' Principal
8' Quintadehna	8' Viol di gamba	8' Gedackt	8' Gedackt
4' Spielpfeife	4' Octava	8' Gemßhorn	8' Gemshorn
	4' Klein Gedackt	4' Octava	4' Octava
2' Spitzflöthe	2' Waldflöt	4' Klein Gedackt	4' Quintathön
Sesquialtera	Sesquilatera IV	Mixtur	Mixture VI
8' Krumbhorn		Cymbel	Cymbel III
8' Trommet	8' Trompette		Glockenspiel
4' Schallmeyen			
Glockenspiel			

Table 7-1 Continued

1658		1737	
Pedal	→	**Pedal**	
		32' Groß-Untersatz	Manual compass: CD → c'''
16' Gedackter		16' Sub-Bass	Pedal compass: C → c'
SubBass		16' Violon-Bass	(1658–1707);
		8' Principal Bass	C → e' (1708 onward)
16' Posaunen Bass		16' Posaun-Bass	UW → OW coupler
		8' Trompetten-Bass	OW → Ped. coupler
		4' Cornett-Bass	Present in 1737: Tremulant and
16' Fagott-Bass			Cymbel-Stern

City Church of St. Peter and St. Paul
(Christoph Junge 1685)[c]

Rück Positiv	Oberwerk	Pedal
8' Grobgedackt	16' Quintadehna	16' Sub-Baß
8' Quintadena	8' Principal	16' Posaunen
4' Principal	8' Grobgedackt	8' Trompet-Baß
4' Klein Gedackt	8' Gemßhorn	2' Cornet-Baß
4' Spill-Flöten	8' Viol di Gamba	
4' Viol di Gamba	4' Octava	
2' Octava	3' Qunita	
1' Sifflöth	2' Octava	Manual tremulants
Sesquialtera II	Mixtur IV	RP → OW coupler
Cymbel Mixture III	Cymbel III	OW → Ped. coupler
Cymbelstern	8' Trompeta	RP → Ped. coupler

[a] State Archive, Weimar, *B. 8 888*, cited in Schrammek 1988, 100–101.
[b] Gottfried Albin Wette, *Historischen Nachrichten von der berühmten Residentz-Stadt Weimar* (Weimar, 1737), 174, cited in Schrammek 1988, 103.
[c] Wolff and Zepf 2012, 94–95.

No matter what the precise dating of the stop-list, the overall evolution of the Palace organ reflects contemporary trends in Central German organ building. The addition of the Principal 8' and Octava 4' on the Unterwerk and the Groß-Untersatz 32', Violon-Bass16', and Principal Bass 8' in the Pedal reflect a new concern for gravity, and the addition of string stops—the Viol di gamba 8' in the Unterwerk and Violon-Bass 16' in the Pedal—stem from the growing desire to replicate the sounds of chamber music. As we shall see in chapter 17,

both were tenets of the progressive Central German organ, as was the reduction of manual reed stops to a single 8' Trompette. The strengthening of the
Pedal division, including the addition of a 4' Cornett-Bass, a stop especially
useful for carrying the cantus firmus of chorale settings, may have stemmed
from Bach's recommendations to Trebs for the 1712–1714 repairs. The disposition Bach drew up 30 years later for a two-manual instrument of roughly the
same size in Bad Berka calls for a similarly well-balanced Pedal division (see
the appendix here).

The Trebs repairs rendered the Weimar Chapel organ unplayable or only
partially playable for almost two years, from June 1712 until May 1714.[26] This
coincided with the period when Bach first became familiar with the works of
Antonio Vivaldi and began to incorporate Vivaldi's style into his own organ
music. During the two-year hiatus at the chapel, he may have turned to the organ
of the City Church of St. Peter and St. Paul, which would have been available to
him through his friendship with Walther. All of Bach's concerto transcriptions
and the Toccata in D Minor ("Dorian"), BWV 538/1, call for "Oberwerk" and
"Rückpositiv"[27]—a combination that in Weimar was only available on the City
Church organ. Built by Christoph Junge in 1685, the instrument was approximately the same size as the Palace organ: 25 stops distributed over two manuals
and pedal (table 7–1). It is likely that the City Church organ was an important
factor in Bach's creative activities in Weimar.

We must also take into consideration the organs Bach played in other cities
during his Weimar tenure. The Toccata in F Major, BWV 540/1, and "Gott,
durch deine Güte," BWV 600, require a pedalboard that extends upward to f',
a highly unusual feature available on instruments in St. Michael's Church in
Buttstädt (II/23), which belonged to the duchy of Weimar, and the Palace
Chapel in Weißenfels (II/30), which Bach visited in February 1713 to perform
Cantata 208, *Was mir behagt, ist nur die muntre Jagd*, for the birthday of Duke
Christian. Bach also played the large organ in the Market Church of Our Lady
in Halle (III/65) during visits in 1713 and 1716, and he tested the large organ
in St. Augustine's Church in Erfurt (III/39) in 1716 and smaller instruments in
St. Ursula's Church in Taubach (I/11) in 1710 and possibly in the Church of St.
Vitus in Ammern (I/13) in 1708.[28] He probably played dedicatory recitals on
many of those occasions.

New Connections, New Influences

Although Weimar was a provincial town, about the same size as Arnstadt and
smaller than Mühlhausen, it provided Bach with significant connections to
the world of music beyond Germany. This was due mainly to the presence of

individuals who provided him with access to works from France and Italy that greatly broadened his horizons.

At the court, Duke Wilhelm Ernst, Duke Ernst August, and Prince Johann Ernst assembled what must have been a well-stocked library of old and new music. Although the court collection is lost, we can assume that it contained prints and manuscripts of a wide range of vocal and instrumental works and that its holdings were frequently replenished. In 1702 Wilhelm Ernst granted permission to Johann Wilhelm Drese, son of the court capellmeister Johann Samuel Drese, to travel to Italy for music study.[29] The younger Drese undoubtedly returned with copies of the latest Italian sonatas and concertos. Four years later Ernst August, before succeeding his father as coregent, visited Brussels, Paris, and Amsterdam while on a European grand tour and surely came back to Weimar with newly acquired music in print and manuscript form.[30] And in 1712, Prince Johann Ernst made a similar musical pilgrimage to the Netherlands, returning in the spring of 1713 with a large cache of new works, most probably including prints obtained from the publishing firm of Estienne Roger in Amsterdam.[31] Court ledgers from this time show expenditures for binding the music and the construction of shelves to hold the new acquisitions, as well as similar outlays for music obtained in Halle.[32] Such infusions, plus exchanges of music with other local courts, provided a steady influx of new instrumental, vocal, and keyboard repertoire that Bach could hear, perform, and study.

Walther was also an invaluable colleague. An enthusiastic organist, composer, and theorist and an indefatigable collector, Walther assembled an immense collection of music and theoretical treatises that culminated in his publication in 1732 of the *Musicalisches Lexicon*, the first music dictionary in German and the first in any language to include biographical entries as well as terminological definitions. Its more than 3,000 entries and citations from more than 250 authors attest to the breadth of Walther's knowledge and the depth of his personal library. In 1729 he confirmed to his colleague Heinrich Bokemeyer:

Now I have to add that in addition to the French keyboard pieces contained in the packet I sent you, I can also provide to an enthusiast, in a manner already mentioned, works by Messrs. Anglebert, Begue, and German organists, especially by the famous Buxtehude and Bach, since I have a great deal written by the two—indeed, I estimate that I possess more than 200 pieces. The ones from first I obtained mostly from the late Mr. Werckmeister, in Mr. Buxtehude's own hand in German tablature; the ones from the second I received directly from the author himself, my cousin and godfather to my son, while he served as court organist here for nine years.[33]

Bach surely turned to Walther as a musical resource, discussing, sharing, and copying new pieces,[34] and engaging in friendly competition in the writing of canons, canonic organ chorales, and keyboard transcriptions. Walther served as a critical sounding board and stimulus for Bach.

Also present in Weimar as a frequent visitor was Telemann, who as a prolific, progressive composer was always abreast of the latest national styles. C.P.E. Bach listed Telemann as one of the composers his father "esteemed highly" and added that his father "in his younger days saw a good deal of Telemann, who also held me at my baptism."[35] Bach and Telemann were close friends during Bach's Weimar years, when Telemann held positions in Eisenach and Frankfurt (am Main) before moving north to Hamburg in 1721. Bach wrote out performance parts for Telemann's Concerto in G Major for Two Violins, Strings, and Continuo, TWV 52: G2, around 1709,[36] and transcribed his Concerto in G Minor for Violin, String, and Continuo (TWV 51: g21) as the Concerto in G Minor for Clavier, BWV 985. There is also evidence that Bach arranged a Telemann concerto for organ, as the Concerto in F Major, BWV 1168, now lost.[37] Telemann's forward-looking instrumental works and his keen interest in French, Italian, and Polish styles were critical models for Bach during his Weimar years.

Finally, it was in Weimar that Bach first met Johann Georg Pisendel, the sixth key figure in his Weimar circle of patrons and colleagues. A virtuoso violinist, Pisendel studied with Giuseppe Torelli in Ansbach and first met Bach in March 1709 on his way to Leipzig, where he successfully auditioned with the collegium musicum (playing a Torelli violin concerto) before enrolling in the university to study law.[38] In 1712 Pisendel joined the court orchestra in Dresden and gradually rose to the position of concertmaster, replacing Jean-Baptist Volumier in 1728 as the court transitioned from French to Italian music practices. Pisendel became Bach's principal connection to the Dresden court ensemble of lavishly paid professional musicians. The close collaboration between the two men is reflected in the fact that Pisendel added duplicate parts to Bach's performance materials of the Telemann Concerto in G Major, most probably to accommodate a performance in Dresden, where the manuscript became part of the court music library.[39] As a member of the Electoral Prince's entourage, Pisendel toured in France (1715) and Italy (1716–1717), studying with Vivaldi while the group was in Venice. Pisendel was Bach's direct connection to French and Italian instrumental and vocal style, as practiced by the professional musicians of the Dresden court.

Through these relationships, Bach became acquainted with a wealth of new music and musical ideas. Although he was already familiar with the North German organ school from his time in Lüneburg and Lübeck, he undoubtedly encountered still more representative works through Walther's rich collection of keyboard music. Many of Bach's early Weimar organ works are an extension of North German style (see chapter 12). The music in Walther's collection may well have served as a catalyst for Bach, inspiring him to expand upon the North German idiom for a final time before embracing French and Italian styles.

It may have been through Walther, too, that Bach first became familiar with Johann Theile's *Musicalisches Kunst-Buch* (Book of Musical Art), an important seventeenth-century counterpoint treatise that circulated in Germany in manuscript form.[40] Theile was the most fervent of several North German musicians committed to contrapuntal investigations, a group that included Reincken, Buxtehude, Matthias Weckmann, and Christoph Bernhard, in addition to Theile. Known as "the father of contrapuntists," Theile was obsessed with invertible counterpoint and wrote several treatises concerning its composition and manipulation. The *Musicalisches Kunst-Buch* of 1691 was the most important of these, summarizing rules of invertible counterpoint that can be traced back to Gioseffo Zarlino's famous work *Le istitutioni harmoniche* of 1558. Theile updated and expanded Zarlino's principles, presenting the results in the *Kunst-Buch* in the form of 15 puzzle pieces, each illustrating a different aspect of invertible counterpoint through a musical example with poetic couplet hinting at the example's resolution. In Piece 7, for instance, Theile presented a five-measure segment of two-part counterpoint that could be: (1) inverted at the octave and tenth, (2) subjected to melodic inversion, retrograde, and retrograde inversion, and (3) expanded to three and four parts by adding additional voices in parallel thirds.

Walther's copy of the *Kunst-Buch*, preserved in the Berlin State Library,[41] shows that he devoted many hours to solving Theile's contrapuntal riddles. For Piece 7, for instance, Walther wrote out 32 two-part permutations, 68 three-part permutations, and 56 four-part permutations of Theile's original five-measures.[42] The examples of canon and invertible counterpoint presented in the *Kunst-Buch* would have been of great interest to Bach, who applied the illustrated principles in Weimar organ works. Canon appears in the Toccata in F Major, BWV 540/1, as well as the eight canonic chorales in the Orgel-Büchlein, for instance, and the exchange of parts through invertible counterpoint appears in the Toccata in C Major, BWV 564, and the "Trio super Herr Jesu Christ, dich zu uns wend," BWV 655a.

Of equal significance in the *Musicalisches Kunst-Buch* was Theile's treatment of permutation fugue—that is, a fugue in which blocks of music containing the subject and countersubjects written in invertible counterpoint are repeated over and over in varied combinations, in the tonic and dominant, with little or no episodic material in between.[43] Although Bach used a preliminary form of the permutation fugue in Mühlhausen, he brought the genre to a high level of refinement during the Weimar years, applying it in large cantata choruses such as "Lob, und Ehre, und Preise und Gewalt" from Cantata 21, *Ich hatte viel*

Bekümmernis, of c. 1713, and "Himmelskönig, sei willkommen" from Cantata 182, *Himmelskönig, sei willkommen,* of 1714. Permutation technique, developed by the North Germans and codified by Theile, who presented examples of quadruple invertible counterpoint with exchangeable parts in the *Kunst-Buch* (plate 7-2), stands behind the voice-exchange of Weimar organ fugues such as the Fugue in G Minor, BWV 542/2, and the Fugue of the Passacaglia in C Minor, BWV 582 (see chapters 12 and 14). Permutation technique provided Bach with a new way of expanding fugal material while maintaining a high degree of thematic unity.[44]

C.P.E. Bach said that his father heard and studied the music of some "old and good Frenchmen."[45] This encounter appears to have taken place in Weimar, where Bach gained access to French keyboard music in printed and manuscript form, perhaps through Walther, Duke Ernst August, or Prince Johann Ernst. The manuscript copies of French keyboard music made by Bach, Walther, and Bach's student Johann Caspar Vogler give a sense of the repertory circulating in Weimar during Bach's stay (table 7-2). The copies encompass a wide range of organ and harpsichord works, from old-fashioned pieces by Jacques Boyvin, Gabriel Nivers, and André Raison to intense, idiosyncratic works by Nicolas de Grigny, and to more fashionable compositions by Pierre Du Mage, Louis Marchand, and Gabriel Le Roux. The collections titled *Livres d'Orgue,* in particular, were of special significance to Bach's organ writing, both in Weimar and later in Leipzig, where they served as a model for Clavier-Übung III of 1739 (see chapter 22).

Bach's copies of music by Jean-Henri d'Anglebert, Charles Dieupart, and Grigny, contained in a single manuscript now located in Frankfurt,[46] date mostly from the period 1709–1713; his copy of Raison's *Livre d'Orgue,* now lost but whose existence was recently verified by a citation in an auction catalog, bore the date "1709." Walther's copies of various clavier pieces appear in the Weimar compilation *P 801* and stem mostly from 1712 or so. And Vogler's copy of Boyvin's two *Livres d'Orgue* dates from around the same time as Bach's copies of d'Anglebert, Dieupart, and Grigny.[47] All this suggests that Bach's study of French keyboard music took place mainly during his initial years in Weimar and that by 1714 or so he was well-schooled in French keyboard style. Vogler's Boyvin manuscript also implies that Bach included French classical repertory as part of organ instruction during the Weimar years.

Bach's use of French elements in his organ works was selective. *Style brisé,* or the stroked style of French harpsichord playing (derived, in turn, from the French style of lute playing), appears in "Nun komm, der Heiden Heiland," BWV 599, the opening setting of the Orgel-Büchlein, and variation 16 of the Passacaglia in C Minor, where it leads to a buildup of six-part chords. But these seem to have been experiments in Weimar, and aside from embellishing

Plate 7-2 Johann Theile, *Musicalisches Kunst-Buch* (1691): "Vier Contra Subjecta, welche auf viererlei Art verweckselt werden" (Four countersubjects, which can be exchanged in four ways). An example of quadruple invertible counterpoint, which could serve as the basis for a permutation fugue.

Staatsbibliothek zu Berlin—Preußischer Kulturbesitz, Musikabteilung mit Mendelssohn-Archiv

Table 7-2 French Keyboard Music Available to Bach in Weimar

Composer	Work	Scribe	Date
Livres d'orgue			
Jacques Boyvin (1653–1706)	*Premier Livre d'Orgue* (Paris, 1689)	Vogler	c. 1710–1715
	Second Livre d'Orgue (Paris 1700)	Vogler	c. 1710–1715
Nicolas de Grigny (1672–1703)	*Premier Livre d'Orgue* (Paris, 1699)	Bach	c. 1709–1712
	Premier Livre d'Orgue (Paris, 1699)	Walther	after 1717?
Pierre Du Mage (c. 1676–1751)	*Livre d'Orgue* (Paris, 1708)	Bach[a]	unknown
Guillaume Gabriel Nivers (c. 1632–1714)	*Livre d'Orgue* (Paris 1665)		
	Prelude and Fugue on 4th tone	Walther	c. 1712
André Raison (before 1650–1719)	*Premier Livre d'Orgue* (Paris, 1688)	Bach	1709[b]
Livres de clavecin			
Jean-Henri d'Anglebert (1635–1691)	*Pièces de Clavecin*, Livre 1 (Paris 1689)[c]	Bach	c. 1709–1712
	Ornament table	Walther	c. 1712
	Suite 1 in D Minor	Walther	c. 1712
Jean-François Dandrieu (1682–1738)	Suite in G Minor (no printed source)		
Charles François Dieupart (?–1740)	*Six Suittes de Clavessin* (Amsterdam, 1701)		
	Entire collection	Bach	c. 1709–1712[d]
			c. 1713
			c. 1714–1716
	Suite 1 in A Major	Walther	c. 1712

Nicolas Antoine Le Bègue (1630–1702)		
Les pièces de Clavecin (Paris, 1677)		
Suite 2 in G Minor	Walther	c. 1712
Gaspard Le Roux (?–1700)		
Pièces de Clavecin (Paris, 1705)		
Suite 1 in D Minor and Suite 3 in G Minor	Walther	c. 1712
Louis Marchand (1669–1732)		
Pièces de Clavecin, Livre 2 (Paris, 1714)		
Entire collection?	Bach[e]	unknown
Suite in G Minor	Walther	after 1714

[a] Johann Abraham Birnbaum, in his 1738 defense of Bach over attacks from Johann Adolph Scheibe, mentions that Bach owned Du Mage's *Livre d'Orgue*, which Bach presumably copied in Weimar. NBR, no. 344.

[b] Lost, but described as containing the copy date of 1709. Wollny 2015, 122–123.

[c] D'Anglebert's *Livre* also contains five fugues for the organ.

[d] Bach appears to have copied out Dieupart's collection in three stages: 1709–1712 (Suites in A Major, D Major, and E Minor), 1713 (Suite in F Minor), and 1714–1716 (Suites in B Minor and F Major). Beißwenger 1992a, 282.

[e] Jacob Adlung reported Bach in Erfurt playing pieces from Marchand's collection, presumably copied in Weimar. BDok III, no. 696.

cadences, Bach seldom used *style brisé* elsewhere, probably because it is less effective on the organ than on the harpsichord.

By contrast, he used French embellishments ubiquitously,[48] especially in florid
chorale settings written in the French organ manner of *Tierce en taille* and *Cornet
de dessus*, two genres appearing for the first time in his organ works in Weimar.
The *Tierce en taille*, which features the melody in the tenor, is represented by
pieces such as "An Wasserflüssen Babylon," BWV 653a (transformed during
the Weimar years from a North German double-pedal setting, BWV 653b, with
the melody in the soprano, to a French piece, with the melody in the tenor) and
"Allein Gott in der Höh sei Ehr," BWV 663a. The *Cornet de dessus*, which features
the melody in the soprano, is represented by pieces such as "Komm, heiliger
Geist, Herre Gott," BWV 652a; "Fantasia super Schmücke dich, o liebe Seele,"
BWV 654a; and "O Mensch, bewein dein Sünde groß," BWV 622, from the
Orgel-Büchlein. In some cases, Bach even used French embellishments in pieces
that were traditionally German, such as the manual fughetta on "Christum wir
sollen loben schon," BWV 696, where the ornaments seem tacked onto the subject in an almost whimsical way.

In some instances, Bach also utilized French five-part texture, which stemmed
from the French instrumental practice of using split violas in string ensembles.
It appears most strikingly in the Orgel-Büchlein setting "Liebster Jesu, wir sind
hier," BWV 633; the Fantasia in C Minor, BWV 562/1; the middle section of the
Pièce d'Orgue in G Major, BWV 572; and even the closing section of the Prelude
in D Major, BWV 532/1. All four works show ties to the music of Grigny, whom
Bach must have viewed as a kindred spirit—a very special composer fond of
five-part fugues, five-part chant arrangements on two manuals and pedal, and
harmonically bold, almost mystical *tierce en taille* settings. Grigny's influence
on Bach's organ composition, felt first in Weimar, was long-lasting, resurfacing
in the five-part *pedaliter* setting "Vater unser im Himmelreich," BWV 682, in
Clavier-Übung III.

Finally, the elusive but palpable presence of French style can be felt in the
Passacaglia in C Minor, where Bach not only borrowed the theme from the
"Christe eleison" of the *Messe du Deuzième Ton* in Raison's *Livre d'Orgue* but
also the dramatic buildup of the lengthy chaconne dances that represented the
musical high point of French Baroque operas. One such chaconne, from Jean-
Baptist Lully's *Phaëton*, appears in the Möller Manuscript, assembled by Bach's
brother Johann Christoph around 1703–1707.

Even greater, and longer lasting, than the effect of French music on Bach's
organ writing in Weimar was the influence of Italian music. Aside from Girolamo
Frescobaldi's 1635 collection of liturgical organ settings, *Fiori musicali*, which
Bach acquired in 1714,[49] Italian influence came mainly in the form of trend-
setting instrumental works. We can divide Bach's encounter with these works

into two phases: pre-Vivaldi and post-Vivaldi, with the demarcation line drawn around the summer of 1713, when Bach appears to have encountered the concertos of Vivaldi's *L'Estro armonico* for the first time.

We can confirm Bach's acquaintance, by the initial Weimar years, with trio sonatas and concertos by Tomaso Albinoni, Giovanni Maria Bononcini, Arcangelo Corelli, Giuseppe Torelli, and Telemann, who by this time was writing in a fully Italianate style (table 7-3). Walther's organ transcriptions suggest that the instrumental music of other Italian composers—Giorgio Gentili, Giovanni Lorenzo Gregori, Luigi Mancia, and Giulio Taglietti—was available at the Weimar court as well.[50]

This music had a significant effect on Bach's writing. In terms of structure, it resulted in his adoption of a short ritornello form, with thematic expositions of modest length alternating with equally modest episodes, sometimes derived from motives presented in the expositions. The use of the short ritornello form allowed Bach to create longer, more highly unified works, with themes that returned periodically in related keys. Among the organ works, we can observe this format in pieces such as the Toccata in F Major, BWV 540/1, the Prelude in G Major, BWV 541/1, and the "Trio super Allein Gott in der Höh sei Ehr," BWV 664a. Torelli and Telemann's influence appears in the designs of the "Trio super Herr Jesu Christ, dich zu uns wend," BWV 655a, and the opening movement of the Toccata in C Major, BWV 564, whose three-movement format reflects its direct connection with the early Italian concerto.[51]

The smooth sequential movement to clearly established harmonic stations, also borrowed from Italian chamber music and evident in the concerto-derived organ preludes and chorale settings, played a critical role in the Weimar organ fugues as well, in pieces such as the Fugue in G Minor, BWV 578, and the fugue of the Passacaglia in C Minor, BWV 582. Well-worked-out sequential modulation, à la Torelli and company, allowed Bach to expand the structure of organ works by moving to a wide range of keys. Voice exchange, à la Theile and company, allowed him to unify ritornello segments, fugue expositions, and episodes. In combination, these two procedures—Italian and German—provided both coherence (the carefully prepared return of the ritornello or fugue theme and the use of unified episodes) and diversity (the appearance of the themes and episodes in varied forms and related keys).

Italian trio sonatas and concertos also provided a model for clear, consistent part-writing, evident in the works of Corelli, Albinoni, and Torelli, in particular. Bach's turn to real part-writing—that is, the use of two, three, four, or even five voices of equal importance that maintain a designated range and independent trajectory—became a hallmark of his mature style. The transition to disciplined textures took place in Weimar, through his own efforts, seen in the settings of the

Table 7-3 Italian and Italianate Instrumental Music Known to Bach in Weimar

Composer	Work	Evidence
Between 1707 and c. 1713		
Tomaso Albinoni (1671–1751)	Suonate á tre, op. 1 (Venice, 1694)	Bach's clavier fugues (BWV 946, 950, and 951) on themes from Sonatas 3, 8, and 12.
	Sinfonie e concerti, op. 2 (Venice, 1700)	Bach's handwritten continuo part from Concerto 2, c. 1709.
Giovanni Maria Bononcini (1642–1678)	Sonate da chiesa, op. 6 (Venice, 1672)	Bach's organ fugue (BWV 574) on theme from Sonata 10.[a]
Arcangelo Corelli (1653–1713)	Sonate a tre, op. 3 (Rome, 1689)	Bach's organ fugue (BWV 579) on theme from Sonata 4.
Georg Philipp Telemann (1681–1767)	Concerto in G Major for Two Violins, TWV 52:G2	Bach's handwritten parts, c. 1709.
Giuseppe Torelli (1658–1709)	Concerto in C Major?	Played by Pisendel in Leipzig just after his visit with Bach in 1709.
	Concerto in D Minor for Violin, RV Anh. 10	Bach's clavier transcription (BWV 979).
Between c. 1713 and 1717		
Prince Johann Ernst (1696–1715)	Six Concerts, op. 1 (Frankfurt, 1716)	Bach's clavier transcription of Concerto 4 (BWV 987).
	Four unpublished concertos	Bach's organ and clavier transcriptions (BWV 592, 595, 982, 984, and 592a).
Alessandro Marcello (1684–1750)	Concerti a Cinque, op. 1 (Amsterdam, 1717)	Bach's clavier transcription of Oboe Concerto (BWV 974).
Benedetto Marcello (1686–1739)	Concerti a 5, op. 1 (Venice, 1708)	Bach's clavier transcription of Concerto 2 (BWV 981).
Telemann	Concerto in F Major?	Bach's lost organ transcription (BWV 1168).
	Concerto in G Minor for Violin, TWV 51:g1	Bach's clavier transcription (BWV 985).
Antonio Vivaldi (1678–1741)	L'Estro armonico, op. 3 (Amsterdam, 1711)	Bach's organ and clavier transcriptions (BWV 593, 596, 972, 976, 978).
	Concertos circulating in manuscript	Bach's organ and clavier transcriptions (BWV 594, 973, 975, and 980).

Principal source of information: Beißwenger 1992a.

[a] Zitellini 2013.

Orgel-Büchlein, in which both manual and pedal parts are fully obbligato, and through his emulation of the transparent textures of Italian chamber music. The elimination of discontinuous, superfluous parts within the texture of keyboard works was one of the most important steps in the development of Bach's personal idiom. It took place in Weimar, under Italian influence.

It was the encounter with Vivaldi's music, however, that proved to be the most significant stylistic catalyst for Bach. The contact appears to have taken place in the summer of July 1713, when Prince Johann Ernst returned from his study trip to the Netherlands with a large amount of new music that seems to have included *L'Estro armonico*, opus 3, Vivaldi's first published collection of concertos, issued by Estienne Roger in Amsterdam. (We will discuss this in more detail in chapter 9.) From within the confines of the Weimar court, Bach could hear, study, and arrange the works that were responsible for initiating the "Vivaldi fever" that swept through Europe in the second decade of the eighteenth century. For Bach, the experience was transformative.

Forkel, drawing on the reports of the two oldest Bach sons, singled out the *L'Estro armonico* concertos as the music that decisively altered Bach's keyboard style and taught him to "think musically." After describing Bach's youthful dissatisfaction with "clavier hussars"—players who scampered up and down the keyboard, allowing their fingers to dictate musical ideas—Forkel turned to Bach's conversion in Weimar:

> But Bach did not long follow this course. He soon began to feel that the eternal running and leaping led to nothing; that there must be order, connection, and proportion in the thoughts; and that, to attain such objects, some kind of guide was necessary. Vivaldi's concertos for the violin, which were then just published, served him for such a guide. He so often heard them praised as admirable compositions that he conceived the happy idea of arranging them all for his clavier. He studied the chain of the ideas, their relation to each other, the variations of the modulations, and many other particulars. The change necessary to be made in the ideas and passages composed for the violin, but not suitable to the clavier, taught him to think musically, so that after his labor was completed, he no longer needed to expect his ideas from his fingers, but could derive them from his own fancy. Thus prepared, he wanted only perseverance and unremitting practice to reach a point where he could not only create himself an ideal of his art, but might also hope, in time, to attain to it. In this practice he was never remiss.[52]

Forkel may have overestimated the importance of the keyboard transcriptions in the learning process, for Bach's additions to the original scores suggest that he had thoroughly absorbed Vivaldi's style before he set about arranging select concertos for clavier and organ.[53] But Forkel was correct in pointing to "the chain of ideas," "their relation to each other," and "the variations of the modulations" as being the key elements in Vivaldi's music that impressed Bach.[54]

We can see these elements in play in the ritornello of the opening movement of Vivaldi's Concerto in A Minor for Two Violins, Strings, and Continuo, RV 522, the *L'Estro armonico* work Bach arranged for organ as the Concerto in A Minor, BWV 593 (see chapter 9). The 15½-measure ritornello consists of five segments, which for purposes of discussion are labeled here r1–r5 (example 7-1). Segments r1 and r2 represent the introduction of the melodic material, segment r3 its extension, and segments r4 and r5 its conclusion. The first segment, r1 (mm. 1–3), begins with an emphatic, declamatory theme that immediately defines the tonic with three quarter-note chords, tonic-dominant-tonic, and then broadens this harmonically defining sequence, dominant-tonic, to half-bar changes in measures 2–3. Measure 2 is repeated note-for-note in measure 3, thus branding the key rhythmic elements as well as continuing the half-bar harmonic pulse. The r1 segment contains all the material that is necessary for generating the entire movement:

Melodic motives	Rhythmic motives
a: semitone	x: dotted rhythm ♩. ♪
b: descending 16th-note scale	y: dactylic rhythm ♩ ♫ ♪
c: leap of fifth	
d: leap of octave	Harmonic pattern: i–V–i, then V–i

The r2 segment (mm. 4–5) continues the harmonic pulse of mm. 2–3 as well as the octave-leap motive (d) while presenting new variations of the dactylic rhythm (y), one in the bass and the other, presented in imitation in the violins, in which displacement by half a beat shifts the accent and results in an anapestic figure (♪ ♫). The imitation introduces new complexity and energy, which radiates into the r3 segment (mm. 6–9a). R3 begins with an animated extension of the semitone motive (a) in 16th notes, followed by a simplified 8th-note version of the descending 16th-note scale (b) of r1. (It uses just the four even notes of the scale.) Harmonically, the r3 segment is sequential, with the octave motive (d) in the bass leading a circle-of-fifths progression over three measures. The harmonic pulse of r1 (mm. 2–3) and r2—a change every half measure—remains the same.

This harmonic pulse slows dramatically in r4 (mm. 9b–13), which rests on the dominant (with added 7th) for three measures before cadencing in the tonic. The sustained notes in the lower strings are shocking after the animated movement of the earlier segments, and the first violin presents an augmented variant of the

Example 7-1 Antonio Vivaldi, Concerto in A Minor, RV 522, movement 1: ritornello, with segments r1–r5; melodic figures a, b, and c and rhythmic figures x and y marked.

Example 7-1 continued

semitone motive (a), now expanded outward, wedge-like, to the interval of the sixth. The final segment, r5 (mm. 14–15½), displays a melodic variation of the augmented variant of r4, now falling by semitone steps over a chromatically descending bass. As a whole, r5 is a compressed variant of r4 (two and a half measures rather than four), producing a rush to the cadence. The melodic notes of the cadence are the same as that of r4, but an octave lower, producing both unity and variety. The solo that follows immediately picks up the dotted-note rhythm (x), the fifth motive (c), and then the dactylic rhythm (y) of the initial ritornello segment.

The "order, connection, and proportion" of such writing, as Forkel put it, made a profound impression on Bach as he searched for new means of organizing and unifying his compositions. From this time forward, his personal idiom became a rich tapestry of Vivaldi's structural, motivic, and harmonic principles and his own unique approach to counterpoint and part-writing.

The Vivaldi encounter cemented Bach's conversion to Italian style rather than French style as the foundation for his writing. This change is symbolized in the Weimar cantatas around 1715 by Bach's decision to shift the makeup of his string ensemble from five-part French texture, with two violins, two violas, and continuo, to four-part Italian texture, with two violins, viola, and continuo. In the organ music, it is symbolized by the form of attribution that appears in many copies of the Weimar works: "Sig^{re} Giovanni Sebastiano Bach."

Eclectic Blends and Hybrid Forms

If there is a predictable characteristic of Bach's Weimar compositions in general, it is their unpredictability. As Alfred Dürr demonstrated in his groundbreaking study of the Weimar cantatas,[55] the choruses and arias of the works are oriented toward Italian rather than North German practice, but they rarely follow expected patterns. The choruses exhibit an exceedingly wide array of formal structures: fugue (Cantata 182/2), chaconne (Cantata 12/2), concerto (Cantata 172/1), bipartite form (Cantata 63/1), tripartite form (Cantata 31/2), motet (Cantata 21/2), choral motet (Cantata 182/7), French overture (Cantata 61/1), and others. And the arias, while clearly Italianate, rarely follow the normal da capo model. In both instances one finds eclectic blends and hybrid forms, with elements drawn from different national styles, sometimes juxtaposed in startling ways.

For instance, the opening chorus of Cantata 61, *Nun komm der Heiden Heiland*, written for the first Sunday in Advent, 1714, is laid out in a French overture format (surely to symbolize the beginning of the church year). It starts with a section of five-part material in dotted rhythm for orchestra in ¢ time (French style), with the chorus singing the chorale, line-by-line, as a unison cantus firmus (German style). This leads to a fugue-like section for chorus with doubled orchestra (French style with Germanic *colla parte* scoring) and a return of the dotted material (French style), this time with the chorus singing the last phrase of the chorale, fully harmonized (German style). Or the bass aria "Seligster Erquickungs-Tag" of Cantata 70a, *Wachet! betet! betet! wachet*, written for the second Sunday in Advent 1716, has an unusual tripartite design, with a molt'adagio continuo arioso serving as introduction (Italian style), followed by a *presto* middle section for trumpet and strings (German scoring), followed by an adagio return of the continuo arioso (Italian style).

Similarly shocking appositions of German, Italian, and French elements appear in the Weimar organ works, in the Toccata in C Major, BWV 564; *Pièce d'Orgue*, BWV 572; Prelude in D Major, BWV 532/1; "Trio super Herr Jesu Christ, dich zu uns wend," BWV 655a, and other unique pieces. The eclectic blends and hybrid forms of Bach's Weimar organ music hark back to the daring, heterogeneous designs of the Neumeister Chorales. While the Weimar compositions lack the suave syntheses of the Leipzig works (see chapter 17), they succeed in part because of their shock value. In Weimar, Bach seems to have been driven to experiment with exotic mixtures of the new styles that he encountered there, applying diverse elements—native and foreign—in unconventional ways. Through these stylistic amalgamations, Bach redefined the nature of organ music. At the same time, by expanding the proportions of pieces and enriching them with unparalleled virtuosity, he established a new role for Central German organists, transforming them from humble church musicians to brash recital players.

We will examine these developments as we look at the individual works.

Notes

1. Marshall and Marshall 2016, 50.
2. NBR, no. 395. The two other supporters were Prince Leopold of Anhalt-Cöthen and Duke Christian of Weissenfels.
3. Wolff 2000, 119.
4. Dürr 2005, 13.
5. NBR, no. 306. To whom "His Grace" refers is not entirely clear. Most biographers have assumed it means Ernst August, who was singled out by Carl Philipp Emanuel Bach as being especially supportive of his father. But within the context of the statement, it seems to refer to "the reigning duke"—that is, Wilhelm Ernst. What is certain is that Bach's organ playing was greatly admired and nurtured at the court.
6. Spitta 1873–80, vol. 1, xxiv.
7. Wolff 2000, 152.
8. NBR, nos. 51 and 52.
9. BDok V, B54a.
10. A nearly complete list of Bach's students can be found in NBR, 315–316. Hans Löffler's classic study "Die Schüler Joh. Seb. Bachs," BJ 40 (1953), 5–28, has been updated in Koska 2019.
11. See the quotations of Kräuter's remarks in chapter 9.
12. The Pachelbel copies were discovered only recently and are reproduced in facsimile in Maul and Wollny 2007.
13. NBR, no. 68.

14. Andreas Glöckner, "Gründe für Johann Sebastian Bachs Weggang von Weimar," in *Bericht über die Wissenschaftliche Konferenz zum V. Internationalen Bachfest der DDR*, Winfried Hoffmann and Armin Schneiderheinze, eds. (Leipzig: VEB Deutscher Verlag für Musik, 1988), 141.

15. Mattheson 1717, 222.

16. NBR, no. 67 (Johann Abraham Birnbaum account) and no. 306 (Obituary account).

17. The description of the Chapel here is based on the specifications presented in Jauernig 1950b, 60.

18. This was not unlike the appearance of theater organs rising slowly from a pit in American theaters in the 1920s and 1930s. A similar, lower-able Baroque gallery ceiling can be seen today in the Sommersaal of the eighteenth-century Bose House in Leipzig, home of the Bach Museum and the Bach Archive.

19. *Das Fest-lebende Weimar . . . im Jahr 1702* (manuscript in the State Archive, Weimar), quoted in Schrammek 1988, 99.

20. See the illustration in Wolff and Zepf 2012, 97.

21. Schrammek 1988, 100.

22. Schrammek 1988, 101–104.

23. Schrammek 1988, 109.

24. Where Bach uses the same term as Weißhaupt: "Sub.B." 32 Fuß.

25. In the Concerto in D Minor, BWV 596 ("Octava 4 Fuß") and "Gott, durch deine Güte," BWV 600, from the Orgel-Büchlein ("Tromp. 8 Fuß").

26. Jauernig, "Bach in Weimar," 73–75.

27. In the Concerto in D Minor after Vivaldi, BWV 596, Bach's terminology changes from "Brustpositiv" to "Rückpositiv" between the first and last movements; in the "Dorian" Toccata in D Minor, the manual indications are "Oberwerk" and "Positiv," but in Walther's manuscript copy of the work, written between 1710 and 1717 (Berlin State Library, P 803, fascicle 21), the indications turn to "O" (Oberwerk) and "R" (Rückpositiv) as the piece progresses. One must also take into account that "Rückpositiv" seems to have been the generic term for a second manual in German organ scores from Bach's time.

28. See Wolff and Zepf 2012 for the specifications of these instruments.

29. Küster 1996, 190.

30. Wollny 2015, 125–126.

31. Schulze 1984, 156–163.

32. Schulze 1984, 159.

33. Letter of August 8, 1729, to Heinrich Bokemeyer, in *Johann Gottfried Walther: Briefe*, Klaus Beckmann and Hans-Joachim Schulze, eds. (Leipzig: VEB Deutscher Verlag für Musik, 1987), 62–63.

34. In one instance, Bach and Walther collaborated on copying a Mass by Johann Baal, with Bach writing the Kyrie and Walther the remaining portions. The manuscript, *Mus.ms. 30091* in the Berlin State Library, dates from the period 1714–1717.

35. NBR, no. 395. In the same account C.P.E. also crossed out a statement that his father esteemed Telemann "very highly, particularly in his instrumental things."

36. Schulze 1983, 73–74.

37. See Beißwenger 1992a, 378–379, and BWV[3], 442.

38. BDok III, no. 735.
39. Schulze 1983, 75.
40. Modern edition: *Johann Theile: Musicalisches Kunstbuch*, Carl Dahlhaus, ed., in *Denkmäler norddeutscher Musik* (Kassel: Bärenreiter, 1965), vol. 1.
41. Berlin State Library, *Mus.ms. theor. 913*.
42. Samples of Walther's solutions are reproduced and discussed in Yearsley 2002, 76–82.
43. Neumann 1953 and Walker 1989, 21–41.
44. Bach's interest in theoretical counterpoint is also confirmed by his handwritten copy of Angelo Berardi's *Documenti armonici* (Bologna, 1667), once owned by his student Johann Christian Kittel but now lost. See Beißwenger 1992a, 341.
45. NBR, no. 395.
46. Frankfurt, City and University Library, *Mus. Hs. 1538*.
47. It's written on the same type of paper. See Horn 1986, 259.
48. Employing the symbols outlined in d'Anglebert's *Marque des Agréments*, which Bach copied between 1709 and 1712. A facsimile of d'Anglebert's ornament table with modern realization is given in the Leupold Edition, vol. 1B. It is noteworthy that Bach's older brother Johann Christoph entered ornament tables by Dieupart and LeBègue into the Möller Manuscript around 1710–1713.
49. Bach's copy of the 1635 print, described in Spitta 1873–80, vol. 1, 421, was lost in World War II.
50. See table 9–1 and the discussion in chapter 9.
51. Discussions of Torelli's influence, in particular, can be found in Stauffer 1980, 104–106; Zehnder 1991; and Hill 1995.
52. Forkel 1802, 23–24; translation from NBR, 441–442.
53. This is well demonstrated in Klaus Hofmann's detailed analysis of the changes, in Hofmann 1995, 198–199, in particular.
54. See the discussion in Wolff 1991h.
55. Dürr 1977, especially 211–216.

8

The Orgel-Büchlein

Little Organ Book, in which a beginner at the organ is given instruction in developing a chorale in many diverse ways, and at the same time in acquiring facility in the study of the pedal, since in the chorales contained therein the pedal is treated as wholly obbligato.

> In Praise of the Almighty's will
> and for my neighbor's greater skill
> Composed by Johann Sebastian Bach
> p.t. Capellmeister to the Serene Reigning
> Prince of Anhalt-Cöthen

Thus reads the title page of the Orgel-Büchlein, Bach's first organized collection of keyboard music and a pivotal project of the Weimar years.[1] The term "little" most certainly alludes to the diminutive size of the original manuscript, a small volume in landscape format measuring approximately 7½ inches wide and 6 inches high. Bach used the term *Büchlein*, "little book," for family albums of similar dimensions: the Clavier-Büchlein for Wilhelm Friedemann Bach of 1720 and the two Clavier-Büchlein for Anna Magdalena Bach of 1722 and 1725. In this case, "little" might also refer to the modest size of the pieces, for many are no more than a dozen measures long, and all occupy no more than one or two manuscript pages. This does not diminish the importance of the collection, however, for by any standard the Orgel-Büchlein was an extraordinarily ambitious undertaking, calling for the composition of 164 organ chorales. It was Bach's first attempt at compiling an encyclopedic compendium, and it stands as a worthy predecessor to the carefully organized collections of the Cöthen and Leipzig periods.

Compositional History

In Bach's time, organists in Central Germany commonly assembled large collections of organ chorales for study and practical use. The now-lost Plauen Organ Book of 1708 contained some 280 Thuringian organ chorales, and Bach's industrious Weimar colleague Johann Gottfried Walther compiled several large

J. S. BACH. George B. Stauffer, Oxford University Press. © Oxford University Press 2024.
DOI: 10.1093/oso/9780195108026.003.0009

manuscripts of organ chorales, including the important "Frankenberger auto-graph,"[2] which served as a repository for 196 chorale settings. Bach, too, surely possessed numerous portfolios of miscellaneous organ chorales that are now lost (including, perhaps, an album from which the Neumeister Chorales were drawn). These collections would have contained his own works as well as those of contemporaries and predecessors. The Orgel-Büchlein represents Bach's de-sire to assemble a diverse collection of newly composed pieces and arrange them in a systematic way.

There were numerous models for this. Bach may have been familiar with two manuscript collections circulating in Thuringia at the time: the 44 chorale settings credited to the Eisenach Johann Christoph Bach (1642–1703), *Choraele welche bey wärenden Gottesdienst zum Praeludiren gebrauchet werden können* (Chorales that can be used to prelude during the Sacred Church Service),[3] and Pachelbel's *Choral-Fugen durchs gantze Jahr* (Chorale-Fugues for the entire Church Year).[4] Both present small chorale settings in orderly formats.

In addition to these manuscripts, several published collections were also available: Johann Philipp Treiber's *Der accurate Organist im General-Baß* (The Organist Diligent in Continuo Playing; Jena, 1704, and reprints) and Elias Nicolaus Ammerbach's *Orgel oder Instrument Tabulatur* (Organ or Instrumental Tablature; Leipzig, 1571), for instance. Ammerbach served as organist of the St. Thomas Church in Leipzig from 1561 to 1595, and Bach owned at least three copies of his important collection,[5] perhaps for use in teaching. When formulating a title for the Orgel-Büchlein, Bach may have turned to Ammerbach's print for guidance, since its title has a similar didactic turn of phrase: "A useful little book, in which necessary explanation of organ or instrumental tablature . . . is to be found . . . for the benefit of young people and of beginners in this art."[6]

The presence of two Orgel-Büchlein pieces in the Neumeister Collection suggests that Bach may have begun developing the special type of concise, *pedaliter* setting that appears in the Orgel-Büchlein some years before arriving in Weimar—perhaps in Arnstadt or Mühlhausen or even earlier. A recently dis-covered Orgel Büchlein–like setting of "Es ist das Heil uns kommen her," BWV[3] 1175, with accompanimental figuration resembling that of "Herr Christ, der ein'ge Gottessohn," BWV 601, also hints at an extended period of development.[7] But the handwriting and watermark of the Orgel-Büchlein album confirm that Bach formally started the collection and assembled the bulk of its contents in Weimar, adding the title at a later point, in Cöthen.[8] Bach initiated the project by laying out space for 164 chorales in the small album that is preserved today in the Berlin State Library as *P 283*. He ruled each page with three two-staff systems (or four, on two occasions) and wrote in the titles of the chorales to be set (plate 8-1). Having made the decision from the start to compose small, compact settings, he allocated only a single page for most melodies, using two in just a few cases.

Plate 8-1 Autograph manuscript of the Orgel-Büchlein: the first of two empty pages laid out for the chorale "An Wasserflüssen Babylon."
Staatsbibliothek zu Berlin—Preußischer Kulturbesitz, Musikabteilung mit Mendelssohn-Archiv

When laying out the chorales, Bach followed the general order of hymnals of the day. He began by designating spaces for 60 *de tempore* chorales—that is, hymns for the church year, commencing with Advent and ending with Trinity and special feast days (see table 8-1, at the conclusion of this chapter). He then marked pages for 104 *omni tempore* chorales—hymns for general use, commencing with chorales associated with Luther's Catechism and continuing with chorales associated with aspects of Christian life.

Bach did not follow the precise order and contents of either of the two hymnals in use at the Weimar court chapel at the time—*Auserlesenes Weimarisches Gesangbuch* (Select Weimar Hymnal) of 1681 (2nd ed., 1713) and *Schuldiges Lob Gottes, oder: Geistreiches Gesang-Buch* (Praise of God by the Guilty, or Spiritually Rich Hymnal) of 1713—or of any other known hymnal from the time.[9] His choice of chorales was decidedly old-fashioned,[10] raising the possibility that he was working from a now-lost hymnal from c. 1675 or so, perhaps a volume in the Bach family.[11] The absence of a section for Epiphany and the presence of an "appendix" of later hymns suggest a personal approach to the contents of the album.

Bach's selection of chorales was retrospective, indeed: 70% date from the sixteenth century, and most of the remainder were written before 1650. There are very few chorales from after 1650, and contemporary hymns from Bach's era are not present at all. The works of the prolific Paul Gerhardt (1607–1676), for instance, who wrote more than 130 hymn texts, are represented only once, in the form of "Nun ruhen alle Wälder." Such popular Gerhardt creations as "Wie soll ich dich empfangen?" (1653) and "O Haupt voll Blut und Wunden" (1656), which appear later in the St. Matthew Passion and Christmas Oratorio, are nowhere to be found in the Orgel-Büchlein. The emphasis rather is on the chorales of the Reformation, the founding period of the Lutheran church—an interest to which Bach returned some 30 years later in the third part of the Clavier-Übung. The retrospective nature of the Orgel-Büchlein chorales is underscored by Bach's addition of eight "newer" hymns from the 1660s and 1670s at the end of the collection, seemingly as an afterthought.

With titles and staves in place, Bach began to fill in the music, eventually completing 45 of the planned 164 settings.[12] In many cases he drew on a sketch or preexisting version and entered the setting into the Orgel-Büchlein album in the form of an elegant fair copy. In other instances, he composed the setting directly on the page, revising and correcting the text as he worked. In still other cases it is unclear what process he was following: the entries have a rushed, compositional appearance but display very few mistakes or none. Such entries could be either a hurried fair copy or an accurate composition score.

Quite often Bach could not fit the work into the allotted space. When this occurred, he finished the music at the bottom of the page in tablature or let the text run onto the next page or wrote out a small insert. In the case of the late entry "Hilf, Gott, dass mir's gelinge," BWV 624, he notated the entire pedal line in tablature. The diverse nature of the entries, the makeshift spacing of the conclusions, and the many empty pages give the Orgel-Büchlein the appearance of a work in progress rather than a polished collection.[13] The album is quite different from the neat and carefully laid-out autographs of the Inventions and Sinfonias or the first volume of the Well-Tempered Clavier. It represents a chorale workbook, offering a rare peek into Bach's composition studio in Weimar.[14]

We don't know why Bach completed certain chorales and neglected others. He does not seem to have entered the pieces in a systematic way, aside from attempting to fill the *de tempore* section first, entering settings for 26 of the initial 27 chorales. After that, the gaps between settings become increasingly larger, and by the end of the album, only three of the last 64 proposed pieces stand complete. Albert Schweitzer suggested that Bach focused on chorales that offered special opportunity for expressive writing.[15] While settings such as "Durch Adams Fall,"

BWV 637, and "Wenn wir in höchsten Nöten sein," BWV 641, seem to point in that direction, other chorales appear to have been selected for different reasons, such as the melody's potential for canonic treatment or the text's potential for generating an image-filled contrapuntal fabric.

Bach worked on the Orgel-Büchlein intermittently during his Weimar tenure, adding settings little by little and completing all entries before departing for Cöthen in December 1717, save two: "Helft mir Gotts Güte preisen," BWV 613, and the fragment "O Traurigkeit, o Herzeleid, BWV³ 1169, which were added in Leipzig. He appears to have started the album soon after arriving in Weimar in the summer of 1708 and then proceeded to enter settings in three general phases: c. 1708–1711, c. 1711–1713, and c. 1714–1716 (see table 8-1).[16] It is likely that he composed the bulk of the Orgel-Büchlein chorales before March 1714, when he took up his duties as concertmaster and shifted his creative energies from writing organ music to producing sacred vocal works.

Several factors point to the 1708 start. There is an unbroken link between the Orgel-Büchlein settings and the organ chorales that preceded them in Arnstadt and Mühlhausen. In many cases the figuration is the same, though now employed more artfully. In addition, the seventeenth-century notational practices in the Orgel-Büchlein pieces seem closer to the older North German orientation of the Mühlhausen cantatas than to the more progressive Italian orientation of the Weimar cantatas.[17] It is interesting to note, too, that Bach introduced new compositional types in the third phase of entries, seemingly in an effort to escape the rigid prototypes of phases 1 and 2 (see discussion below). Soon after phase 3, he broke off work on the project and moved to other things.

Bach returned briefly to the Orgel-Büchlein album in Cöthen to add the title that describes the music's pedagogical function. This may have taken place in December 1722, in conjunction with his application for the position of cantor at St. Thomas in Leipzig. The Inventions and Sinfonias and Well-Tempered Clavier, volume I, have similar titles outlining a didactic purpose, and Bach may have wanted to add the Orgel-Büchlein to his group of instructional collections, to bolster his portfolio as a teacher.[18] He returned to the collection again in Leipzig, to enter "Helft mir, Gotts Gütes preisen" and the incipit of "O Traurigkeit, o Herzeleid" and to revise "Christus, der uns selig macht," BWV 620a, and "Komm, Gott Schöpfer, heiliger Geist," BWV 631a, writing directly over the original texts. He also clarified the distribution of parts in "Christe, du Lamm Gottes," BWV 619, by adding brackets and voice-leading lines.[19] These changes were probably made in conjunction with organ instruction. Despite these modifications, there is no evidence that Bach ever considered completing the Orgel-Büchlein.

Function in Weimar

What moved Bach to compile the Orgel-Büchlein during his Weimar years? There are several possible reasons.

A strong factor may have been the practical need for weekly service music. His employer Duke Wilhelm Ernst, a devout Lutheran, required regular attendance at the services in the Court Chapel, and his enthusiasm for organ music, together with that of Duke Ernst August, spurred Bach to explore new compositional possibilities for the instrument. Among these possibilities could have been the intricately worked-out chorales of the Orgel-Büchlein. As we noted earlier, chorale settings were used within the worship service as preludes or interludes for congregational hymn singing, as preludes or postludes before or after the service, and as communion music during the Eucharist. Such pieces were normally improvised, but Bach may have wanted to present especially fine examples for his discerning patrons. The Orgel-Büchlein settings would have served this purpose. At the same time, their contrapuntal intricacy and canonic play would seem to have precluded their use as accompaniments to congregational singing (see chapter 11).

The sophisticated Orgel-Büchlein settings, with their obbligato pedal parts, would have illustrated Bach's organ-playing at its finest, and the theological exegesis of the music would not have been lost on the devout Wilhelm Ernst. The presence of registration indications, tempo markings, and manual-distribution brackets here and there in the settings and the pragmatic layout of the album, in which page turns are avoided, point to the use of the Orgel-Büchlein in performance. The unorthodox repeats in several of the chorales also hint at Bach's desire to "stretch out" the music of the brief settings[20]—a factor pointing once again to practical use in church services, perhaps during Communion, when musical "fill" was required.

As we noted in chapter 7, the Palace Chapel organ was at least partly inaccessible from June 1712 to May 1714. Yet there is no reason to believe this would have curtailed Bach's work on the Orgel-Büchlein, as some authors have suggested. Carl Philipp Emanuel Bach stated that his father normally composed at the desk and later tried completed works at the keyboard.[21] During the renovation of the Chapel organ, Bach could have tested newly written Orgel-Büchlein chorales on the organ of the City Church or the still smaller instrument of St. Jacob's Church (II/18).[22]

The short but intricate settings could also have been part of Bach's recital repertoire, in Weimar or Taubach, Halle, Erfurt, and other locations where he was called upon to examine and demonstrate new organs during his Weimar years. Settings such as "In dir ist Freude," BWV 615"; "O Mensch, bewein dein Sünde groß," BWV 622; and the three-verse "Christ ist erstanden," BWV 627, are certainly substantial enough to have been played in a public concert.

Although the title page proclaiming the collection's pedagogical function was not added until the Cöthen years, the Weimar copies of Johann Tobias Krebs confirm that the Orgel-Büchlein was used at for instructional purposes from the very start. Krebs studied in Weimar first with Walther (from 1710 to about 1714) and then with Bach (from about 1714 to 1717). Several of his copies of Orgel-Büchlein chorales date from the time of his instruction with Walther,[23] and his copy of "Es ist das Heil uns kommen her," BWV 638a, represents a version of the setting that predates the more refined arrangement, BWV 638, that appears in the Orgel-Büchlein as a fair copy. Thus, Bach may have used certain settings as teaching pieces even before entering them into the album.

Bach's decision to assemble a group of organ chorales composed in a markedly methodical way suggests a purpose beyond practical music-making and teaching, however. It points rather to the use of the album as a workbook that offered Bach the opportunity to focus on compositional issues such as motivic development, part-writing, harmony, and musical expression. By limiting the size of the pieces, Bach was able to explore these matters in a highly concentrated way. The different types of autograph entries reflect the different stages of the work process: composing scores reflect the invention of new pieces, revision scores reflect the refinement or expansion of drafts or sketches, and fair copies reflect the appropriation of pieces carefully worked out elsewhere.

Russell Stinson, in his full-length study of the Orgel-Büchlein, has demonstrated the intensity of Bach's compositional work within the collection.[24] The composing score of "O Mensch, bewein dein Sünde groß," for example, with its revisions, scratch-outs, insertions, and added embellishments, reveals Bach striving to develop an organ idiom that is more concise, more expressive, and more highly disciplined than his previous mode of writing (plate 8-2). The small chorales of the Orgel-Büchlein were the perfect vehicle for such a course of rigorous self-improvement.

The compilation of the Orgel-Büchlein album during the Weimar years represents a new phase in the evolution of Bach's compositional idiom. After the Orgel-Büchlein, his keyboard music takes on a discipline, refinement, and efficiency that culminates in the teaching collections of the Cöthen years: the Inventions and Sinfonias, the English and French Suites, and the first book of the Well-Tempered Clavier. In these works, all notes count, and all parts have obbligato roles. The Orgel-Büchlein was the turning point in this development.

The chorale settings of the Orgel-Büchlein, then, could have served as music for the worship service, as pieces for organ recitals, as material for teaching, and as trial works for a new compositional style. It was the last function that had the most far-reaching consequences.

Plate 8-2 Autograph manuscript of the Orgel-Büchlein: composing score of "O Mensch, bewein dein Sünde groß," BWV 622, showing Bach's insertion for the revision of m. 21.

Staatsbibliothek zu Berlin—Preußischer Kulturbesitz, Musikabteilung mit Mendelssohn-Archiv

Musical Style

The signs of intense compositional activity in the Orgel-Büchlein reflect Bach's determination to explore the organ chorale "in many diverse ways." He carried out this exploration by creating a special type of succinct, highly unified organ chorale, one that featured the full hymn tune with no or very little space between phrases, real part-writing, obbligato pedal, and bold, expressive musical language. One can see the roots of the Orgel-Büchlein settings in the concise partita variations of Johann Pachelbel and Georg Böhm and the florid-melody chorales of Dieterich Buxtehude. But there was nothing quite like the concentrated chorale that Bach developed for the Orgel-Büchlein.

Bach poured his ideas into three basic molds: the melody chorale, the canonic chorale, and the florid-melody chorale. The most common by far is the melody chorale, in which the chorale tune is set forth in the soprano with very little embellishment and no interludes between phrases.[25] Thirty-two settings in the Orgel-Büchlein fall into this category:

Nun komm der Heiden Heiland, BWV 599

Herr Christ, der ein'ge Gottessohn, oder Herr Gott, nun sei gepreiset, BWV 601

Lob sei dem allmächtigen Gott, BWV 602

Puer natus in Bethlehem, BWV 603

Gelobet seist du, Jesu Christ, à 2 Clav. et Ped., BWV 604

Der Tag, der ist so freudenreich, à 2 Clav. et Ped., BWV 605

Vom Himmel hoch, da komm ich her, BWV 606

Vom Himmel kam der Engel Schar, BWV 607

Lobt Gott, ihr Christen, allzugleich, BWV 609

Jesu, meine Freude, largo, BWV 610

Wir Christenleut haben jetzund Freud, BWV 612

Helft mir, Gotts Güte preisen, BWV 613

Mit Fried und Freud ich fahr dahin, BWV 616

Herr Gott, nun schleuß den Himmel auf, BWV 617

Da Jesus an dem Kreuze stund, BWV 621

Wir danken dir, Herr Jesu Christ, daß du für uns gestorben bist, BWV 623

[O Traurigkeit, o Herzeleid (fragment), molt' adagio, BWV³ 1169]

Christ lag in Todesbanden, BWV 625

Jesus Christus, unser Heiland, der den Tod überwand, BWV 626

Christ ist erstanden, BWV 627

Erstanden ist der heilge Christ, BWV 628

Heut triumphieret Gottes Sohn, BWV 630

Komm, Gott Schöpfer, heiliger Geist, BWV 631

Herr Jesu Christ, dich zu uns wend, BWV 632

Dies sind die heilgen zehn Gebote, BWV 635

Vater unser im Himmelreich, BWV 636

Durch Adams Fall ist ganz verderbt, BWV 637

Es ist das Heil uns kommen her, BWV 638

Ich ruf zu dir, Herr Jesu Christ, à 2 Clav. et Ped., BWV 639

In dich hab ich gehoffet, Herr, alio modo, BWV 640

Wer nur den lieben Gott lässt walten, BWV 642

Alle Menschen müssen sterben, alio modo, BWV 643

Ach wie nichtig, ach wie flüchtig, BWV 644

The second-most common type is the canonic chorale, in which the chorale tune is presented in canon with a very short interval between the *dux*, the

canonic leader, and the *comes*, the canonic follower. Bach composed eight canonic chorales for the collection:[26]

> Gott, durch deine Güte, oder Gottes Sohn ist kommen, BWV 600
> In dulci jubilo, BWV 608
> O Lamm Gottes, unschuldig, Canon alla Quinta, BWV 618
> Christe, du Lamm Gottes, à 2 Clav. et Ped., in Canone alla Duodecima,
>   BWV 619
> Christus, der uns selig macht, in Canone all'Ottava, BWV 620
> Hilf, Gott, dass mir's gelinge, à 2 Clav. et Ped., BWV 624
> Erschienen ist der herrliche Tag, à 2 Clav. et Ped., in Canone, BWV 629
> Liebster Jesu, wir sind hier, à 2 Clav. et Ped., in Canone alla Quinta, BWV 633

The third-most common setting is the florid-melody chorale, in which the
chorale melody, highlighted on a separate keyboard, is greatly embellished with
coloratura flourishes and ornaments. Accompaniment is provided on a second
keyboard and in the pedal. As with the melody chorale, there are no interludes
between phrases of the hymn tune. There are three florid-melody chorales in
the Orgel-Büchlein:

> Das alte Jahr vergangen ist, à 2 Clav. et Ped. BWV 614
> O Mensch, bewein dein Sünde groß, à 2 Clav. et Ped., adagio assai, BWV 622
> Wenn wir in höchsten Nöten sein, à 2 Clav. et Ped., BWV 641

Two additional settings, entered into the album at a late point, are unique:

> Christum wir sollen loben schon, Choral in Alto, adagio, BWV 611
> In dir ist Freude, BWV 615

By focusing on these chorale types and eliminating extraneous material
such as interludes and structural digressions, Bach was able to focus fully on
accompanimental fabric, canonic elaboration, and melodic embellishment. He
probably drafted a number of "test pieces" to work out the fundamental tenets of
his new chorale style before laying out the album itself. These pieces might have
included the two settings that appear in the Neumeister Collection, "Ich ruf zu
dir, Herr Jesu Christ," BWV 639, and "Herr Christ, der ein'ge Gottessohn," BWV
601a, and the two settings that are transmitted separately as early variants, "Heut
triumphieret Gottes Sohn," BWV 630a, and "Es ist das Heil uns kommen her,"
BWV 638a. All four exhibit the basic features of the melody chorale—the type of
setting that would come to dominate the collection.

Example 8-1 Orgel-Büchlein, colliding parts: (a) "Gott, durch deine Güte," BWV 600, (b) "Puer natus in Bethlehem," BWV 603, and (c) "Lobt Gott, ihr Christen, allzugleich," BWV 609.

The Orgel-Büchlein settings display a new approach to part-writing. All voices are ongoing and accounted for, in a basic soprano-alto-tenor-bass texture. Bach's commitment to real part-writing causes linear collisions here and there, as voices bump and cross, and it outweighs his concern for the hymn cantus firmus, which is often interrupted by a neighboring part (example 8-1). This type of uncompromising counterpoint requires unusual finger dexterity and concentration on the part of the performer, and it is a defining characteristic of Bach's keyboard writing at this time.[27] After the encounter with Vivaldi's concertos, he moved to a smoother, less "snarly" idiom.

In the Orgel-Büchlein chorales, the pedal emerges as an equal partner with the manual voices, leaving the ad libitum practice of the Neumeister Chorales to the past. Bach's commitment to obbligato pedal-writing resulted in the creation of pedal figures that were carefully coordinated with the manual voices, either joining them in imitation or providing an independent line. The net result was a fully integrated organ score.

The Orgel-Büchlein chorales also exhibit a new approach to rhythm. The settings display a continuous, driving, Italianate instrumental pulse, created by a single part ("Herr Gott, nun schleuß den Himmel auf," BWV 617) or by the accumulative effect of subunits within four or five voices ("Nun komm der Heiden

Heiland," BWV 599). In 4/4 meter, the underlying pulse is the 16th note; in 3/2 meter, the 8th note. The Orgel-Büchlein settings represent a transitional stage in Bach's shift from seventeenth-century vocal style to eighteenth-century instrumental style: in the settings in duple meter, the chorale melody appears in quarter notes, a change from the Neumeister Chorales, where the tune often appears in half notes. It foreshadows instead the black-note, four-part harmonizations of the chorale settings in the Leipzig cantatas. The triple-meter pieces, by contrast, remain conservative, set in a vocal-oriented 3/2 with the chorale moving in half notes. The one exception is **"Wir danken dir, Herr Jesu Christ,"** BWV 623, a late entry set in more modern 3/4 time, with the chorale moving in quarter notes. It is also significant that more progressive chamber meters such as 3/8 or 2/4 have no place in the Orgel-Büchlein, underlining once again its retrospective nature and its inception during the early Weimar years.

Within the Orgel-Büchlein settings, strategically placed chromaticism, unprepared dissonance, and clashing contrapuntal lines produce an unprecedented degree of tension and liveliness. Syncopated motives and across-the-beat ties also contribute to rhythmic and harmonic vibrancy, as do compelling harmonic progressions and strategically placed deceptive cadences. One can see these elements at work in the famous conclusion of **"O Mensch, bewein dein Sünde groß,"** BWV 622, which features chromaticism, unprepared dissonances, syncopated motives, across-the-beat ties, and a shocking movement through a C♭ major chord, emphasized by the slowing of tempo to an expressive adagissimo (example 8-2). All this, to portray the anguish of original sin and the momentary glimpse of hope (the C♭ major chord) offered by salvation.

Example 8-2 Orgel-Büchlein, "O Mensch, bewein dein Sünde groß," BWV 622: expressive elements in the closing measures: (a) chromaticism, (b) unprepared dissonances, (c) syncopated motives, (d) across-the-beat ties, and (e) sudden appearance of a C♭ major chord.

The Melody Chorales

Perhaps the most important change in the Orgel-Büchlein is Bach's treatment of accompanimental motives, seen especially in the melody chorales. The motives do not vary from chorale phrase to chorale phrase, in conjunction with the shape of the chorale tune. Rather, they remain the same throughout each setting, creating a single *affect*, or mood. This is quite different from the approach taken in earlier works such as the Neumeister Chorales, in which the accompanimental motives commonly change from chorale phrase to chorale phrase. As we noted in chapter 3, in the Neumeister setting of "Wir Christenleut haben jetzung Freud," BWV 1090, the seven phrases of the chorale are distributed among three sections, which are differentiated by meter, texture, and figuration. In the Orgel-Büchlein setting of **"Wir Christenleut,"** BWV 612, Bach establishes an accompanimental texture at the outset—an imitative ♩ ♫ figure in the alto and tenor and an ostinato-like 8th-note figure in the bass—and maintains it throughout the piece. Thus the localized word painting of the Mühlhausen cantatas and early organ chorales is abandoned in favor of creating a single generalized mood, unified through motivic material stated in the opening measure.

This also distinguishes Bach's settings from those of his predecessors. In Buxtehude's setting of "Durch Adams Fall ist ganz verderbt," BuxWV 183, a falling bass highlights the text phrase, "Through Adam's fall," and a chromatic line emphasizes the phrase "the same poison." Bach uses these very motives in his setting of **"Durch Adams Fall ist ganz verderbt,"** BWV 637, but they are presented simultaneously in the first measure and form the accompanimental fabric for the entire piece. This approach foreshadows the highly unified settings of Clavier-Übung III and the Schübler chorales.

The distribution of the accompanimental motives differs from setting to setting. Sometimes the same motive is used in the alto, tenor, and bass (**"Herr Christ, der ein'ge Gottessohn,"** BWV 601, and **"Jesus Christus, unser Heiland, der den Tod überwand,"** BWV 626). Other times the alto and tenor share the same motive, and the bass has a continuo-like part (**"Lobt Gott, ihr Christen, allzugleich,"** BWV 609, and **"Komm, Gott Schöpfer, heiliger Geist,"** BWV 631). And sometimes the alto, tenor, and bass each have different material (**"Der Tag, der ist so freudenreich,"** BWV 605, and **"Hilf, Gott, dass mir's gelinge"** BWV 624). Here, too, Bach seems to have been systematically exploring the various contrapuntal permutations.

Many of the accompanimental motives in the Orgel-Büchlein display close ties with figures that were linked with classical rhetoric by theorists of the day. Three treatises known to Bach, Friedrich Erhard Niedt's *Musicalische Handleitung* (1706–13) and Walther's *Praecepta der musicalischen Composition* (1708) and

Musicalisches Lexicon (1732), describe the use of motivic and melodic figures to enhance the content of musical works. We encountered two of these motives in earlier works: the *corta* figure, which Walther described as "three swift notes, the first of which is as long as the two others, and the *suspirans* figure, which Walther said was "like the *corta* figure except that the initial long note is divided into a rest and a short note" (example 8-3, a and b).[28] Bach used both motives in the Orgel-Büchlein, to enliven and unify the contrapuntal fabric of accompaniments in new ways. The middle parts of "**Mit Fried und Freud ich fahr dahin**," BWV **616**, for instance, are based on the *corta* figure in diminution, and the three lower parts of "**Alle Menschen müssen sterben**," BWV **643**, are derived from a neighbor-note form of the *suspirans*, presented in consonant thirds and sixths in the manuals and with accented eighth notes in the pedal (example 8-3, c and d).

Elsewhere Bach employed pictorial figures to emphasize aspects of the chorale texts: the *passus duriusculus* (dissonant step) and the *saltus duriusculus* (dissonant leap) in "**Durch Adams Fall ist ganz verderbt**," once again, to portray the fall of Adam; the *anabasis* (rising figure) in "**Erstanden ist der heilge Christ**," BWV **628**, to describe Christ's resurrection; the *catabasis* (falling figure) in "**Es ist das Heil uns kommen her**," BWV **638**, to paint the gift of salvation radiating downward from heaven; the *repetitio* (repeated figure) in "**Dies sind die heilgen zehn Gebote**," BWV **635**, to emphasize the steadfast nature of the Ten Commandments; and the weeping figure of slurred seconds in the canonic chorale "**O Lamm Gottes, unschuldig**," BWV **618**, to portray lamentation over Christ as the sacrificial lamb. Whether Bach consciously thought of these figures in terms of classical rhetoric is uncertain. Quintilian's views on the power of

Example 8-3 Johann Gottfried Walther, *Musicalisches Lexicon*: (a), *Figura corta*, and (b) *Figura suspirans*; Orgel-Büchlein: (c) "Mit Fried und Freud fahr ich dahin," BWV 616, with *corta* in diminution, and (d) "Alle Menschen müssen sterben," BWV 643 (accompanimental parts), with *suspirans* in reinterpreted form.

rhetoric were much in vogue among scholars and theologians in Bach's time,[29] but Carl Philipp Emanuel Bach also said that his father was "no lover of dry, mathematical stuff."[30] The formulaic application of rhetorical figures may have fallen into this category. But a gesture such as accelerating the pace of the dissonant leaps in the pedal for climactic effect at the conclusion of "Durch Adams Fall" went far beyond the prosaic use of rhetorical figures by Bach's contemporaries.

In other instances, the accompanimental motives are more abstract. In the melody chorale "Herr Jesu Christ, dich zu uns wend," BWV 632, the alto and tenor exchange in contrary motion a *suspirans*-like arpeggiated triad derived from the opening melodic fifth of the hymn tune. The pedal picks up the motive in augmentation but then continues with the chorale melody itself, in quasi canon with the soprano. In "Komm, Gott Schöpfer, heiliger Geist," BWV 631, the accompanimental alto, tenor, and bass remain syncopated throughout, coming together rhythmically only to punctuate cadences. In "Nun komm der Heiden Heiland," BWV 599, all four parts work in concert to create the broken style, or *style brisé*, of French lute and harpsichord music, which Bach studied intensely during his initial years in Weimar. Or in "Ich ruf zu dir, Herr Jesu Christ," BWV 639, the only three-part setting in the Orgel-Büchlein, the ongoing 16th notes of the left hand and 8th notes of the pedal form a placid background for the unadorned melody of the chorale, presented in the right hand.

The fragment "O Traurigkeit, o Herzeleid," BWV[3] 1169, entered into the Orgel-Büchlein album in Leipzig, offers a look at Bach's method of composing melody chorales. Only two measures long, the incipit contains all the material needed for a four-part setting: a lightly embellished melody, a more animated alto voice in 16th notes based on an ascending arpeggiated chord, and imitative pedal and tenor voices in 8th notes based on a descending chordal figure (example 8-4). Bach appears to have created the four parts simultaneously, as a contrapuntal fabric, rather than one-by-one, as single lines. The key, F minor, described as "lugubrious and sad" by Jean-Jacques Rousseau,"[31] and the tempo indication "molt' adagio" help to create an appropriately expressive *affect* for Johann Rist's Passiontide hymn from 1641: "Oh sadness, oh heartache! Isn't this something to lament? That the only son of God the Father is carried into the grave." Bach may have abandoned the setting for unknown compositional reasons. But it is also possible that he left it unfinished on purpose, in the fashion of incomplete pieces in the Clavier-Buchlein for Wilhelm Friedemann Bach and Anna Magdalena Bach, as an improvisation or composition exercise for his Leipzig organ students.

Johann Gotthilf Ziegler, who studied with Bach in Weimar, later stated: "with regard to the playing of chorales, I was instructed by my then-living teacher, Capellmeister Bach, not to play the songs merely in an offhand way, but rather

Example 8-4 "O Traurigkeit, o Herzeleid," BWV 1169: unfinished incipit.

according to the *affect* of the words."[32] In modern times Robert L. Marshall has said of the Orgel-Büchlein chorales that the accompaniment, while almost always unrelated to the melodic substance of the chorale, is suggested by the emotional or theological symbolism of the text: "in effect, the chorale text, silent but implied by the traditional melody, is presented simultaneously with its exegesis by the counter-voices."[33]

The Canonic Chorales

The canonic chorales show a special degree of invention, since Bach was compelled to work under additional contrapuntal constraints. The settings may have been stimulated by Walther, who exhibited a keen interest in canonic writing. In three instances Bach and Walther set the same melody as a canon, as if in competition: "Erschienen ist der herrliche Tag," "In dulci jubilo," and "Gott, durch deine Güte." There does, indeed, seem to be an element of gamesmanship to Bach's approach to the canonic chorale, for he addresses a different compositional issue in each setting. It is as if he wished to demonstrate the full range of canonic art within the confines of small *pedaliter* pieces. While Walther limited himself to canons at the octave, with the *dux* and *comes* assigned almost exclusively to the soprano and bass, Bach composed canons at the octave, fifth, and twelfth, and he chose a great variety of canonic combinations: soprano and bass: **"Christus, der uns selig macht,"** BWV 620, and **Erschienen ist der herrliche Tag, BWV 629,** the most obvious choice; but also soprano and alto: **"Hilf, Gott, dass mir's gelinge,"** BWV 624, and **"Liebster Jesu, wir sind hier,"** BWV 633; soprano and tenor: **"Gott, durch deine Güte,"** BWV 600, and **"In dulci jubilo,"** BWV 608; soprano and tenor 2: **"Christe, du Lamm Gottes,"** BWV 619; and even alto and tenor: **"O Lamm Gottes, unschuldig,"** BWV 618.

Bach seems to have posed a special compositional goal for each setting. For instance, in the first canon in the album, **"Gott durch deine Güte, oder Gottes Sohn ist kommen,"** BWV 600, he assigned each voice a clearly defined role: the soprano sets forth the cantus firmus *dux*, in whole- and half-note rhythm; the tenor (here taken by the pedal) presents the *comes*, an octave lower than the soprano and one measure later; the bass (here taken by the left hand) presents a walking bass in quarter notes, on a theme derived from the opening rising sixth of the chorale tune; and the alto consists of an independent descending chain of 8th notes. The setting has a hierarchy of note values—white note, quarter note, 8th note—as well as a hierarchy of connections to the cantus firmus: direct quote (soprano and tenor), paraphrase (bass), free voice (alto). The unceasing rhythmic pulsations, shimmering on three levels, create the subliminal *affect* of eager anticipation for Christ's arrival. The treatment of the pedal part shows further inventiveness: Bach notated the part in the tenor range, at 8' pitch. But because the written range exceeded the upper compass of most eighteenth-century pedalboards, which extended only to c' or d', most performers had to play the part an octave lower, on a 4' stop. The carefully calculated craft of "Gott, durch deine Güte" reflects Bach's determination to take the musical artistry hinted at in the Neumeister Chorales to a new level, and to bring it under tight compositional control.

Greater compositional ambition still can be seen in **"In dulci jubilo,"** BWV 608. By the first decade of the eighteenth century, the tradition of setting this Christmas chorale as a pastoral canon was well established in Central Germany, and Bach surely knew the contribution to the genre by his father-in-law Johann Michael Bach that appears in the Neumeister Collection and was formerly credited to Bach as BWV[1] 751. Bach's Orgel-Büchlein arrangement is far more complex. The cantus firmus is presented as a canon at the octave, presented at the distance of one measure by the soprano and the tenor (here taken by the pedal, played an octave lower with a 4' stop, once again). But the accompanimental parts form a secondary canon at the octave, presented at the distance of one measure by the alto and the bass (here taken by the left hand). The musette drone associated with the pastoral is created by the repeated a's in all four voices rather than a straightforward pedal point, as in Johann Michael's setting or the first movement of Bach's own Pastorella, BWV 590. And the a's are in half notes in the principal canon, followed by quarter notes in the secondary canon, suggesting an imitative diminution. The secondary canon breaks off in m. 25, but in the concluding measures the triplets fall into imitation once again. The double canon, the simulated drone, and the lush textures created by the implied 2 against 3 show Bach striving to take the "In dulci jubilo" canonic tradition to a higher plain, to up the ante with his fellow composers. The many scratch-outs and revisions in the autograph manuscript suggest that this was not accomplished without considerable labor.

Bach's eight canonic settings foreshadow the two *pedaliter* octave canons of Clavier-Übung III, "Die sind die heiligen zehen Gebot," BWV 678, and "Vater unser im Himmelreich," BWV 682. Although the Orgel-Büchlein chorales are much shorter, they present the same type of contrapuntal challenges posed in the later works. We might even view them as a trial run for the monumental Clavier-Übung pieces, which unlike the Orgel-Büchlein settings were offered to the public in printed form.

The Florid-Melody Chorales

Bach's passion for multiple layers of complexity surfaces as well in the florid-melody chorales, all designated for two manuals and pedal. The model in this case was the expressive florid-melody chorale developed by Buxtehude. Buxtehude's settings are longer than the Orgel-Büchlein pieces, and they contain interludes between phrases of the hymn tune. Bach adopted Buxtehude's decorated cantus firmus but retained the concision of his own melody chorales by eliminating the interludes between melodic phrases. In addition, he gave the accompaniment parts a more significant motivic role. In **"Wenn wir in höchsten Nöten sein,"** BWV 641, he subjected the hymn tune to extreme embellishment, through diminutions (dividing the half notes and quarters of the chorale melody into 8ths, 16ths, 32nds, and even 64ths) and French ornaments, including the *port de voix en montant* (ascending appoggiatura) and *port de voix en descendant* (descending appoggiatura) that appear in the "Marques des Agrements" from Jean-Henri d'Anglebert's *Pièces de Clavecin*, which he copied out around 1709–1712 (see chapter 7).

Moreover, the accompanimental voices are now subjected to the rules of real part-writing: the alto, tenor, and bass are obbligato throughout and based on the imitative treatment of a motive derived from the first four notes of the chorale tune (example 8-5, x). The motive appears both upright and inverted, and in measures 7-8 it even appears in augmentation in the tenor against inverted forms in the alto and bass, in stretto. It is not altogether surprising that Bach later returned to the contrapuntal possibilities of this motive in his so-called deathbed chorale, "Vor deinen Thron tret ich hiermit," BWV 668, derived from BWV 641 (see chapter 25). But in the nine measures of this tiny Orgel-Büchlein setting, we sense Bach striving to outdo Buxtehude while imposing new contrapuntal standards on his own writing.

Example 8-5 "Wenn wir in höchsten Nöten sein": (a) first phrase of the chorale tune, and (b) opening measures of Orgel-Büchlein setting, BWV 641.

The Unique Settings

Finally, two settings from the last layer of entries push the limits of the Orgel-Büchlein chorale and suggest that Bach was ready to move on to new things. The first, **"Christum wir sollen loben schon,"** BWV 611, is a melody chorale. However, as Bach highlighted in the title, the hymn tune is now located in the alto, a most unusual placement for a cantus firmus in an organ chorale. The soprano voice, while serving an accompanimental function, is embellished in the manner of a florid melody chorale. And the manual tenor and pedal bass exchange a running, syncopated motive in contrary motion. The feet are required to play scalar 16th notes, pointing beyond the disjunct opposite-toe figurations of the North German school, and in the concluding measures the pedal divides into two parts, in the virtuoso manner of the Prelude in D Major, BWV 532/1, or Passacaglia in C Minor, BWV 582.

Example 8-6 Orgel-Büchlein, "In dir ist Freude," BWV 615: elaboration of the chorale tune.

a) Phrase 1

b) Phrases 4 and 5

c) Phrase 6

Bach went still further in **"In dir ist Freude," BWV 615.** Here the part-writing is free throughout, varying from one to six voices—the only such case in the Orgel-Büchlein. The chorale melody is split up and presented phrase by phrase in small fragments, sometimes unadorned, sometimes slightly adorned, and sometimes highly adorned (example 8-6). The melody normally appears in the soprano, but it also migrates to the pedal (m. 34) and through all four voices (mm. 44–49). The pedal features a carillon-like figure that recurs in the manner of an ostinato, and in the final measures the figure evolves into a virtuosic trill-and-turn that requires even greater dexterity than the concluding bars of "Christum wir sollen loben schon."

The high degree of motivic unity, the emphatic off-beat motives (permutations of the *suspirans* motive), and the powerful rhythmic drive of "In dir ist Freude" reflect Orgel-Büchlein principles. But the formal structure is quite unlike that of any other piece. Russell Stinson has termed it a "chorale fantasia,"[34] and Peter Williams a "re-imagining of the melody chorale."[35] No matter what one calls it, it is a breakout piece, inspired either by the blithe dance qualities of Giovanni Giacomo Gastoldi's balletto of 1591, on which the Lutheran hymn

was based, or by Bach's personal exhilaration at having mastered the compositional goals he had set for himself in the Orgel-Büchlein. The procedure of dividing up a hymn tune and treating it phrase by phrase with lengthy interludes,
in a varied yet unified manner, foreshadows the large chorale fantasias of the
opening choruses of Bach's second annual cantata cycle, written a decade later in
Leipzig.

In sum, the Orgel-Büchlein is the first concrete manifestation of Bach's interest in exploring a single genre in a concentrated, encyclopedic way. All three
types of settings—the melody chorale, the canonic chorale, and the florid-
melody chorale—reflect his ongoing search for new compositional possibilities.
Although the collection lacks the type of sophisticated, multilayered organizational scheme that emerged in the keyboard and instrumental compendia of
the Cöthen and Leipzig years, it established a new standard for Bach's keyboard
writing and prepared the way for the stylistic explorations that were yet to come
in the Weimar, Cöthen, and Leipzig organ works. For Bach the composer, the
Orgel-Büchlein was a transformative undertaking. It is likely that he did not return to the album to complete the remaining 119 settings because he felt that
he had accomplished what he set out to do: develop a new, highly unified organ
idiom with fully obbligato manual and pedal parts.

Notes

1. Translation adapted from NBR, No. 69. The abbreviation "p.t." appears to mean either
   pleno titulo (with full title) or *pro tempore* (at present).
2. The Hague, Gemeente Museum, *4.G.14*.
3. Berlin, Universität der Künste, *Ms. Spitta 1491*. Johann Christoph Bach's authorship
   is questioned in Kaiser 2001.
4. Weimar, Herzogin Anna Amalia Bibliothek, *Q 341 b*, described in Eggebrecht 1965.
5. Beißwenger 1992a, 226–227.
6. The original German reads: "Ein nützlichs Büchlein, in welchem notwendige
   erklerung der Orgel oder Instrument Tabulature . . . zu befinden . . . der Jugend und
   anfahenden dieser Kunst zum besten in Druck vorfertiget." As Peter Williams (2003,
   227) noted, the use of the antiquated word "anfahenden" (instead of "anfangende") in
   both Ammerbach's print and the Orgel-Büchlein is striking.
7. The setting, reproduced in NBA IV/10, is handed down solely in a manuscript of
   Orgel-Büchlein chorales written by Johann Ernst Gebser around 1840. See NBA IV/
   10, KB (Reinmar Emans, ed., 2008), 131–132.
8. It was Philipp Spitta who first proposed that the Orgel-Büchlein originated in Weimar
   rather than Cöthen. See Spitta 1873–80, vol. 1, 647–649. Spitta's supposition was confirmed in the twentieth century by the handwriting studies of Georg von Dadelsen, in
   Dadelsen 1963.

9. The most important seventeenth- and eighteenth-century German hymnals within Bach's circle are listed in Bighley 2018, v–vi, which also includes sample pages from many volumes in facsimile.

10. On Bach's choice of hymns, see Leaver 1985.

11. NBA IV/1, KB (Heinz-Harald Löhlein, ed., 1987), 103. All the chorales set by Johann Christoph Bach in the *Choraele welche bey wärenden Gottesdienst zum Praeludiren* appear in the Orgel-Büchlein, suggesting the possibility of a common hymnal.

12. Bach wrote two settings of "Liebster Jesu, wir sind hier," making a total of 46 entries. The second setting of "Liebster Jesu," BWV 633, is a refined version of the first, BWV 634, which consequently stands as an early variant.

13. See the facsimile edition, *Johann Sebastian Bach: Orgelbüchlein . . . Faksimile der autographen Partitur*, Heinz-Harald Löhlein, ed. (Kassel: Bärenreiter, 1981), or Bach digital, under BWV 599–644.

14. For a detailed account of Bach's compositional process in the Orgel-Büchlein, see chapter 2, "Compositional Process," in Stinson 1999, 35–58, or section II.2, "Ein Lehrwerk?," in Hiemke 2007, 57–74.

15. Schweitzer 1905, vol. 1, 287–288.

16. While there is general agreement among scholars that Bach entered the settings in phases, there is much disagreement on the timing of the phases and the precise contents of each. Christoph Wolff (Wolff 2000, 130–132) and Russell Stinson (Stinson 1996, 15–17) have proposed that Bach began the Orgel-Büchlein in 1708, soon after his arrival in Weimar. This assessment makes sense in light of the retrospective nature of much of the figuration and the conservative meters of many of the settings. By contrast, Heinz-Harald Löhlein (NBA IV/1, KB, 91–93) has suggested that Bach began the album only in the fall of 1713, as he competed for the organist position at the Church of Our Lady in Halle, and then entered groups of settings annually in conjunction with his composition of a new cantata each month in Weimar between 1714 and 1716. The Wolff-Stinson chronology, in its updated form in BWV[3], is used here.

17. This can be seen, for instance, in Bach's strong preference for 3/2 rather than 3/4 meter in the Orgel-Büchlein. The 3/2 meter points back to movements such as "Tag und Nacht" (Cantata 71/4) and "Der Herr segne euch" (Cantata 196/4) from the Mühlhausen cantatas, written in 3/2, rather than forward to movements such as "Jesu, laß durch Wohl und Weh" (Cantata 182/6) and "O Seelenparadies, das Gottes Geist" (Cantata 172/4) of the initial Weimar cantatas, written in 3/4. It is significant that the single *Orgel-Büchlein* setting in the more modern 3/4 meter, "Wir danken dir, Herr Jesu Christ," BWV 623, belongs to the last phase of works added in Weimar.

18. Wolff 2000, 226. One must question, however, whether it would have made sense to submit an incomplete project in support of his application.

19. Stinson 1996, 25.

20. That is, the repeat of the Abgesang as well as the traditional repeat of the Stollen, which takes place in "Herr Christ, der ein'ge Gottessohn," "Wir Christenleut," "In dir ist Freude," "Herr Jesu Christ, dich zu uns wend," and "Liebster Jesu, wir sind hier" (both original and revised versions). In "Puer natus in Bethlehem," Bach indicated that the entire setting should be repeated.

21. NBR, no. 395.

22. The specification of the St. Jacob's organ is given in Wolff and Zepf 2012, 95.

23. Those in the manuscript album Berlin State Library, *P 802*, in particular. See NBA IV/ 1, KB, 46–50.

24. Stinson 1996. See especially chapter 2, "Compositional Process."

25. The term "melody chorale" appears to have been coined by Willi Apel in the *Harvard Dictionary of Music* (Cambridge, MA: Harvard University Press, 1944).

26. Here I am once again considering "Liebster Jesu, wir sind hier," BWV 634, as an early variant of "Liebster Jesu, wir sind hier," BWV 633, rather than a separate piece.

27. Zehnder 1995, 321.

28. Walther 1732, 244.

29. Including individuals close to Bach. The description of Johann Matthias Gesner, rector of St. Thomas from 1730 to1734, of Bach leading a group of singers and instrumentalists during a cantata performance appears in a footnote to his 1738 edition of Quintilian's *Institutione Oratoria*. See NBR, no. 328.

30. NBR, no. 395.

31. Jean-Jacques Rousseau, *Dictionnaire de musique* (Paris, 1768), cited in Rita Steblin, *A History of Key Characteristics in the Eighteenth and Early Nineteenth Centuries* (Ann Arbor, MI: UMI Research Press, 1983), 265.

32. NBR, no. 340.

33. Marshall, 2001, 759.

34. Stinson 1996, 75.

35. Williams 2003, 267.

Table 8-1 Orgel-Büchlein
Layout and Contents of Bach's Autograph Manuscript (Berlin State Library, *P 283*)

Order	Page or pages	Title	Liturgical function	BWV (if set)	Period of entry[a]	Type of entry
		(Composed chorales in bold, uncomposed in normal type)				
		CHURCH YEAR (de tempore)				
1	1	Nun komm der Heiden Heiland	Advent	599	Weimar II	Composing score
2	2–3	Gott durch deine Güte, oder Gottes Sohn ist kommen	"	600	Weimar II	Composing score
3	4	Herr Christ der ein'ge Gottessohn oder Herr Gott, nun sei gepreiset	"	601	Weimar I	Fair copy
4	5	Lob sei dem allmächtigen Gott	"	602	Weimar II	Composing score
5	6–7	Puer natus in Bethlehem	Christmas	603	Weimar II	Composing score
6	7	Lob sei Gott in des Himmels Thron	"	Not set	—	—
7	8	Gelobet seist du, Jesu Christ	"	604	Weimar II	Composing score
8	9	Der Tag, der ist so freudenreich	"	605	Weimar II	Fair copy
9	10	Vom Himmel hoch, da komm ich her	"	606	Weimar I	Fair copy
10	11–10	Vom Himmel kam der Engel Schar	"	607	Weimar II	Composing score
11	12–13	In dulci jubilo	"	608	Weimar II	Revision score

12	14	Lobt Gott, ihr Christen, allzugleich	"	609	Weimar II	Composing score
13	15	Jesu, meine Freude	"	610	Weimar II(?)	Fair copy
14	16	Christum wir sollen loben schon	"	611	Weimar III	Fair copy
15	17	Wir Christenleut haben jetzund Freud	"	612	Weimar II(?)	Composing score
16	18	Helft mir Gotts Güte preisen	New Year	613	Leipzig c. 1740	Composing score
17	19	Das alte Jahr vergangen ist	"	614	Weimar II	Fair copy
18	20–21	In dir ist Freude	"	615	Weimar III[b]	Fair copy
19	22	Mit Fried und Freud ich fahr dahin	Purification of the Virgin	616	Weimar III	Fair copy
20	23–23a	Herr Gott, nun schleuß den Himmel auf	"	617	Weimar III	Fair copy
21	24–24a	O Lamm Gottes, unschuldig	Passiontide	618	Weimar III	Fair copy
22	25	Christe, du Lamm Gottes	"	619	Weimar III	Fair copy
23	26	Christus, der uns selig macht	"	620a / 620	Weimar III(?) / Leipzig c. 1726	Fair copy / Revision of 620a
24	27	Da Jesus an den Kreuze stund	"	621	Weimar II	Composing score
25	28–29	O Mensch, bewein dein Sünde groß	"	622	Weimar II	Composing score

(continued)

Table 8-1 Continued

Order	Page or pages	Title	Liturgical function	BWV (if set)	Period of entry[a]	Type of entry
26	30	Wir danken dir, Herr Jesu Christ, dass du für uns gestorben bist	"	623	Weimar III	Fair copy
27	31–30a	Hilf Gott, dass mir's gelinge	"	624	Weimar III	Fair copy
28	32	O Jesu, wie ist dein Gestalt	"	Not set	—	—
29	33	O Traurigkeit, o Herzleid (fragment)	"	1169	Leipzig c. 1740	Composing score
30	34–35	Allein nach dir, Herr Jesu Christ	"	Not set	—	—
31	36	O wir armen Sünder	"	Not set	—	—
32	37	Herzliebster Jesu, was hast du verbrochen	"	Not set	—	—
33	38	Nun gibt mein Jesus gute Nacht	"	Not set	—	—
34	39	Christ lag in Todesbanden	Easter	625	Weimar I	Fair copy
35	40	Jesus Christus, unser Heiland, der den Tod überwand	"	626	Weimar II	Fair copy
36	41–43	Christ ist erstanden (3 verses)	"	627	Weimar II	Revision and composing score
37	44	Erstanden ist der heilge Christ	"	628	Weimar II	Composing score
38	45	Erschienen ist der herrliche Tag	"	629	Weimar II	Composing score
39	46–47	Heut triumphieret Gottes Sohn	"	630	Weimar I	Fair copy
40	48	Gen Himmel aufgefahren ist	Ascension	Not set	—	—
41	49	Nun freut euch, Gottes Kinder, all	"	Not set	—	—

42	50–51	Komm, heiliger Geist, erfüll die Herzen deiner Gläubigen	Pentecost	Not set	—	—
43	52–53	Komm, heiliger Geist, Herre Gott	"	Not set	—	—
44	54	Komm, Gott Schöpfer, heiliger Geist	"	631a	Weimar II	Fair copy
				631	Leipzig, c. 1726	Revision of 631a
45	55	Nun bitten wir den Heil'gen Geist	"	Not set	—	—
46	56	Spiritus Sancti gratia oder Des Heil'gen Geistes reiche Gnad	"	Not set	—	—
47	57	O heilger Geist, du göttlichs Feuer	"	Not set	—	—
48	58	O heiliger Geist, o heiliger Gott	"	Not set	—	—
49	59	Herr Jesu Christ, dich zu uns wend	"	632	Weimar II	Fair copy
50	60	Liebster Jesu, wir sind hier	"	634	Weimar II	Composing score
51	61	Liebster Jesu, wir sind hier, distinctius	"	633	Weimar II	Composing score
52	62–63	Gott der Vater wohn uns bei	Trinity	Not set	—	—
53	64	Allein Gott in der Höh sei Ehr	"	Not set	—	—
54	65	Der du bist drei in Einigkeit	"	Not set	—	—
55	66	Gelobet sei der Herr, der Gott Israel	St. John the Baptist [June 24]	Not set	—	—
56	67	Meine Seele erhebt den Herren	Visitation [July 2]	Not set	—	—
57	68	Herr Gott, dich loben alle wir	St. Michael [Sept. 29]	Not set	—	—

Table 8-1 Continued

Order	Page or pages	Title	Liturgical function	BWV (if set)	Period of entry[a]	Type of entry
58	69	Es stehn vor Gottes Throne	"	Not set	—	—
59	70–71	Herr Gott, dich loben wir	Apostle Days [October 28]	Not set	—	—
60	72	O Herre Gott, dein göttlich Wort	Reformation [October 31]	Not set	—	—
			GENERAL USE (omni tempore) Catechism			
61	73	Dies sind die heilgen zehn Gebote	Ten Commandments	635	Weimar II	Composing score
62	74	Mensch, willst du leben seliglich	"	Not set	—	—
63	75	Herr Gott, erhalt uns für und für	"	Not set	—	—
64	76–77	Wir glauben all an einen Gott	Creed	Not set	—	—
65	78	Vater unser im Himmelreich	Lord's Prayer	636	Weimar II	Fair copy
66	79	Christ, unser Herr, zum Jordan kam	Baptism	Not set	—	—
67	80	Aus tiefer Not schrei ich zu dir	Penance	Not set	—	—
68	81	Erbarm dich mein, o Herre Gott	"	Not set	—	—
69	82	Jesu, der du meine Seele	"	Not set	—	—
70	83	Allein zu dir, Herr Jesu Christ	"	Not set	—	—

71	84	Ach Gott und Herr	"	Not set	—	—
72	85	Herr Jesu Christ, du höchstes Gut	"	Not set	—	—
73	86	Ach Herr, mich armen Sünder	"	Not set	—	—
74	87	Wo soll ich fliehen hin	"	Not set	—	—
75	88	Wir haben scherlich	"	Not set	—	—
76	89	Durch Adams Fall ist ganz verderbt	Justification	637	Weimar II	Composing score
77	90	Es ist das Heil uns kommen her	"	638	Weimar I	Fair copy
78	91	Jesus Christus, unser Heiland, der von uns den Gotteszorn wandt	Lord's Supper	Not set	—	—
79	92–93	Gott sei gelobet und gebenedeiet	"	Not set	—	—
80	94	Der Herr ist mein getreuer Hirt	"	Not set	—	—
81	95	Jetzt komm ich als ein armer Gast	"	Not set	—	—
82	96	O Jesu, du edle Gabe	"	Not set	—	—
83	97	Wir danken dir, Herr Jesu Christ, daß du das Lämmlein worden bist	"	Not set	—	—
84	98	Ich weiss ein Blümlein hübsch und fein	"	Not set	—	—
85	99	Nun freut euch, leben Christen g'mein	Praise	Not set	—	—
86	100–101	Nun lob, mein Seele, den Herren	"	Not set	—	—

(continued)

Table 8-1 Continued

Order	Page or pages	Title	Liturgical function	BWV (if set)	Period of entry[a]	Type of entry
			Christian Life			
87	102	Wohl dem, der in Gottes Furcht steht	Christian Life and Conduct	Not set	—	—
88	103	Wo Gott zum Haus nicht gibt sein Gunst	"	Not set	—	—
89	104	Was mein Gott will, das gescheh allzeit	"	Not set	—	—
90	105	Kommt her zu mir, spricht Gottes Sohn	"	Not set	—	—
91	106–107	Ich ruf zu dir, Herr Jesu Christ	"	639	Weimar I	Fair copy
92	107	Weltlich Ehr und zeitlich Gut	"	Not set	—	—
93	108	Von Gott will ich nicht lassen	"	Not set	—	—
94	109	Wer Gott vertraut		Not set	—	—
95	110	Wie's Gott gefällt, so gefällt mir's auch	"	Not set	—	—
96	111	O Gott, du frommer Gott		Not set	—	—
97	112	In dich hab ich gehoffet, Herr	Cross, Persecution, and Temptation	Not set	—	—
98	113	In dich hab ich gehoffet, Herr, alio modo	"	640	Weimar II	Fair copy
99	114	Mag ich Unglück nicht widerstahn	"	Not set	—	—
100	115	Wenn wir in höchsten Nöten sein	"	641	Weimar II	Composing score
101	116–117	An Wasserflüssen Babylon	"	Not set	—	—

102	118	Warum betrübst du dich, mein Herz	"	Not set	—	—
103	119	Frisch auf, mein Seel, verzage nicht	"	Not set	—	—
104	120	Ach Gott, wie manches Herzeleid	"	Not set	—	—
105	121	Ach Gott, erhör mein Seufzen und Wehklagen	"	Not set	—	—
106	122	So wünsch ich nun eine gute Nacht	"	Not set	—	—
107	123	Ach lieben Christen, seid getrost	"	Not set	—	—
108	124	Wenn dich Unglück tut greifen an	"	Not set	—	—
109	125	Keinen hat Gott verlassen	"	Not set	—	—
110	126	Gott ist mein Heil, mein Hülf und Trost	"	Not set	—	—
111	127	Was Gott tut, das ist wohlgetan, kein einig Mensch ihn tadeln kann	"	Not set	—	—
112	128	Was Gott tut, das ist wohlgetan, es bleibt gerecht sein Wille	"	Not set	—	—
113	**129**	**Wer nur den lieben Gott lässt walten**	**"**	**642**	**Weimar II**	**Fair copy**
114	130	Ach Gott, vom Himmel sieh darein [Psalm 12]	Christian Church	Not set	—	—
115	131	Es spricht der Unweisen Mund wohl [Psalm 14]	"	Not set	—	—
116	132	Ein feste Burg ist unser Gott [Psalm 46]	"	Not set	—	—

(continued)

Table 8-1 Continued

Order	Page or pages	Title	Liturgical function	BWV (if set)	Period of entry[a]	Type of entry
117	133	Es woll uns Gott genädig sein [Psalm 67]	"	Not set	—	—
118	134	Wär Gott nicht mit uns diese Zeit [Psalm 124]	"	Not set	—	—
119	135	Wo Gott der Herr nicht bei uns hält	"	Not set	—	—
120	136–137	Wie schön leuchtet der Morgenstern	"	Not set	—	—
121	138	Wie nach einer Wasserquelle	"	Not set	—	—
122	130	Erhalt uns, Herr, bei deinem Wort	"	Not set	—	—
123	140	Laß mich dein sein und bleiben	"	Not set	—	—
124	141	Gib Fried, o frommer, treuer Gott	War and Peace	Not set	—	—
125	142	Du Friedefürst, Herr Jesu Christ	"	Not set	—	—
126	143	O grosser Gott von Macht	"	Not set	—	—
127	144	Wenn mein Stündlein vorhanden ist	Death and Burial	Not set	—	—
128	145	Herr Jesu Christ, wahr Mensch und Gott	"	Not set	—	—
129	146–147	Mitten wir im Leben sind	"	Not set	—	—
130	148	Alle Menschen müssen sterben	"	Not set	—	—
131	149	Alle Menschen müssen sterben, alio modo	"	643	Weimar II	Composing score
132	150	Valet will ich dir geben	"	Not set	—	—
133	151	Nun laßt uns den Leib begraben	"	Not set	—	—

(continued)

Table 8-1 Continued

Order	Page or pages	Title	Liturgical function	BWV (if set)	Period of entry[a]	Type of entry
153	171	Nun laßt uns Gott dem Herren	"	Not set	—	—
154	172	Lobet dem Herren, denn er ist sehr freundlich	"	Not set	—	—
155	173	Singen wir aus Herzensgrund	"	Not set	—	—
156	174	Gott Vater, der du deine Sonn	Good Weather	Not set	—	—
		Appendix (of newer hymns, written in 1660s and 1670s)				
157	175	Jesu, meines Herzens Freud	Jesus Hymn	Not set	—	—
158	176	Ach, was soll ich Sünder machen	Penance and Confession	Not set	—	—
159	177	**Ach wie nichtig, ach wie flüchtig**	**Death and Burial**	644	**Weimar II**	Fair copy
160	178	Ach, was ist doch unser Leben	Death and Dying	Not set	—	—
161	179	Allenthalben, wo ich gehe	"	Not set	—	—
162	180	Hast du denn, Jesu, dein Angesicht gänzlich verborgen, oder Soll ich denn, Jesu, mein Leben in Trauern beschließen	Cross and Comfort	Not set	—	—
163	181	Sei gegrüßet, Jesu gütig, oder O Jesu, du edle Gabe	Passiontide	Not set	—	—
164	182	Schmücke dich, o liebe Seele	Lord's Supper	Not set	—	—

[a] BWV³. Weimar I = c. 1708–1711 (or earlier); Weimar II = c. 1711–1713; Weimar III = c. 1714–1716.
[b] BWV³ lists "In dir ist Freude" as Weimar I, but it clearly belongs to Weimar III.

9

The Concerto Transcriptions

The five concerto transcriptions for organ provide a true sense of the remarkable feats of extravagant playing that Bach achieved in Weimar. They exhibit unorthodox figurations, gymnastic manual-changes, and registrational wizardry that sets them apart from all other organ music of the time. They also reflect Bach's contrapuntal mind at work, as he added obbligato lines to enhance and further unify the music in front of him. Performed in a nonliturgical setting, as music "for the enlightenment of the spirit" (to use the phrase appearing in Bach's keyboard publications), the organ transcriptions were pure concert fare, the product of a composer freed from the constraints of the worship service. They were extraordinary pieces in Bach's day, and they remain so in ours.

Incomparable Things

The presence at the Weimar court of a small chamber ensemble and two dukes and a prince deeply committed to music resulted in the performance of hundreds of instrumental works, unfortunately no longer extant.[1] The performances appear to have spurred a friendly competition between Bach and Walther to transcribe favorite pieces from the sessions for keyboard. Walther's 14 surviving organ transcriptions—a small remnant of the 78 keyboard arrangements he later claimed to have made—show that he set pieces by an eclectic mix of Italian and German composers, many from an earlier generation, such as Arcangelo Corelli, Giulio Taglietti, and Giuseppe Torelli (table 9-1).[2] Bach's 23 transcriptions—17 for clavier and 6 for organ—suggest that he was more interested in the latest cutting-edge works, turning mostly to music by progressive Italian composers and contemporary Germans writing in an Italianate style. Striking among Bach's transcriptions is the abundance of concertos by Antonio Vivaldi (nine works) and Prince Johann Ernst (six works, and possibly the three anonymous clavier arrangements as well).

Hans-Joachim Schulze has proposed that the transcription activity came to a head during the period immediately following Johann Ernst's return to Weimar in the summer of 1713, and there is much to be said for this hypothesis.[3] As noted in chapter 7, the young prince arrived home in July after two years of study in

J. S. BACH. George B. Stauffer, Oxford University Press. © Oxford University Press 2024.
DOI: 10.1093/oso/9780195108026.003.0010

Table 9-1 Walther and Bach: Weimar Keyboard Transcriptions

Johann Gottfried Walther

Organ transcriptions

After Tomaso Giovanni Albinoni
(1671–1751):

Concerto in G Major, op. 2, no. 8	Concerto in F Major
Concerto in C Major, op. 2, no. 10	Concerto in Bb Major

After François Colin de Blamont (1690–1760):

Concerto in A Major	Concerto in A Major

After Arcangelo Corelli (1653–1713):

Prelude, Sonata in E Major, op. 5, no. 11	Concerto in E Major

After Giorgio Gentili (1669–1737):

Unidentified model	Concerto in A Major

After Christoph Graupner (1683–1760),
but attributed to "sign[r] Megck":

Sinfonia in D Major, GWV 528[a]	Concerto in C Major

After Giovanni Lorenzo Gregori (1663–1745):

Concerto in Bb Major, op. 2, no. 3	Concerto in Bb Major

After Luigi Mancia (c. 1665–1708):

Sinfonia to the aria "Qui dove il fato rio lunghi"[b]	Concerto in G Minor

After Giulio Taglietti (1660–1718):

Concerto in Bb Major, op. 11, no. 2	Concerto in Bb Major

After Georg Philipp Telemann (1681–1767):

Largo from Concerto for Winds and Strings in C Minor, TWV 52:c1	Concerto in C Minor

After Giuseppe Torelli (1658–1709):

Concerto in D Minor for Violin, op. 8, no. 7	
Concerto in G Minor for Violin, op. 8, no. 8	Concerto in A Minor
Sonata in D Major for Two Violins	Concerto in Bb Major

After Antonio Vivaldi (1678–1741), but
attributed to "Sign[r] Meck":

Concerto in B Minor for Violin, RV 275	Concerto in B Minor

Johann Sebastian Bach

Clavier transcriptions

After Prince Johann Ernst (1696–1715):

Unidentified concerto	Concerto in C Major, BWV 984
Concerto in D Minor for Violin, op. 1, no. 4	Concerto in D Minor, BWV 987
Concerto in G Major for Violin	Concerto in G Major, BWV 592a
Concerto in Bb Major for Violin, op. 1, no. 1	Concerto in Bb Major, BWV 982

Table 9-1 Continued

After Alessandro Marcello (1684–1750):	
Concerto in D Minor for Oboe	Concerto in D Minor, BWV 974
After Benedetto Marcello (1686–1739):	
Concerto in E Minor for Violin, op. 1, no. 2	Concerto in C Minor, BWV 981
After George Philipp Telemann (1681–1767):	
Concerto in G Minor for Violin, TWV 51:g1	Concerto in G Minor, BWV 985
After Antonio Vivaldi (1678–1741):	
Concerto in G Major for Violin, op. 3, no. 3	Concerto in F Major, BWV 978
Concerto in D Major for Violin, op. 3, no. 9	Concerto in D Major, BWV 972
Concerto in E Major for Violin, op. 3, no. 12	Concerto in C Major, BWV 976
Concerto in G Major for Violin, op. 7, no. 8	Concerto in G Major, BWV 973
Concerto in B♭ Major for Violin, RV 381	Concerto in G Major, BWV 980
Concerto in G Minor for Violin, RV 316	Concerto in G Minor, BWV 975
Concerto in D Minor for Violin, RV 813	Concerto in B Minor, BWV 979
Anonymous:	
Unidentified model	Concerto in C Major, BWV 977
Unidentified model	Concerto in G Minor, BWV 983
Unidentified model	Concerto in G Major, BWV 986
Organ transcriptions	
After Prince Johann Ernst (1696–1715):	
Concerto in G Major for Violin	Concerto in G Major, BWV 592
Unidentified concerto, movement 1	Concerto in C Major, BWV 595
After Georg Philipp Telemann (1681–1767):	
[Concerto in F Major for Violin, TWV 51:F3?	Concerto in F Major, BWV³ 1168]
After Antonio Vivaldi (1678–1741):	
Concerto in C Major ("Grosso Mogul"), RV 208	Concerto in C Major, BWV 594
Concerto in D Minor for Two Violins, op. 3, no. 11	Concerto in D Minor, BWV 596
Concerto in A Minor for Two Violins, op. 3, no. 8	Concerto in A Minor, BWV 593

[a]Eleanor Selfridge-Field, "The Concerto Transcriptions of J. S. Bach and J. G. Walther," paper presented at the Biennial Meeting of the American Bach Society, Stanford University, February 14, 2020.
[b]Selfridge-Field, "The Concerto Transcriptions of J. S. Bach and J. G. Walther."

Utrecht, bringing with him a large amount of new music obtained in Amsterdam, at that time one of the most important centers of music publishing and distribution in Europe. The works most probably included the concertos of Vivaldi's *L'Estro armonico*, opus 3, issued in Amsterdam by Estienne Roger, and possibly

Roger's reprints of Albinoni's *Sinfonie e Concerti*, op. 2, and Corelli's *Sonate*, op. 5, as well. All three collections contained pieces set by Walther or Bach.

It is also possible, however, that the Roger prints were obtained from Halle, where the bookseller Adam Christoph Sellius served as an agent for Roger.[4] Bach himself was in Halle during the first two weeks of December 1713, to audition for the organist position in the Market Church of Our Lady, and he could have purchased the Roger prints from Sellius at that time.[5] The Weimar court ledgers mention the purchase and binding of "Musicalia von Halle" three months later, in March 1714.[6] This was yet another way the Roger publications could have reached the Wilhelmsburg Palace.

No matter what the case, the arrival of the new works appears to have spurred a burst of musical activity at the court: the acquisitions were performed, admired, and transcribed; Prince Johann Ernst started to study instrumental composition with Walther; and Bach began to adopt elements of Vivaldi's style.

It is likely that Walther and Bach received special encouragement to fashion organ transcriptions from the prince, who during his visit to Amsterdam may have encountered Jan Jacob de Graaf (1672–1738), the famous blind organist of the New Church there.[7] Known in Germany as Johann Jacob Grave, de Graaf specialized in performing fashionable Italian and French instrumental music on the organ, a feat mentioned by Johann Mattheson in a discussion of orchestral music in 1717:

> That this type of music also allows itself to be performed *zur Curiosité* on an instrument such as the organ or clavier with full harmony is shown by, amongst others, the famous but blind organist of the Nieuwe Kerk auf dem Damm in Amsterdam, Msr. de Grave, who knows by heart all the most recent Italian concertos, sonatas, etc. with three to four parts and played them in my presence on his wonderful instrument with uncommon accuracy.[8]

Johann Ernst may have been eager to import this "curiosity" to Weimar, especially since the repairs and improvements to the Palace Chapel organ, begun in 1712 by the Court's organ builder, Heinrich Nicolaus Trebs, were nearing completion. The great anticipation of this event and its convergence with the prince's return is evident in the request of Bach's Weimar student Philipp David Kräuter to his Augsburg sponsors in April 1713, asking for an extension of his stay so that he could be present not only for the prince's arrival with new music but also for Bach's inauguration of the refurbished organ:

> Because the Weimar Prince here, who is not only a great lover of music but himself an incomparable violinist, will return to Weimar from Holland after Easter and spend the summer here, I could hear much fine Italian and French

music, particularly profitable to me in composing concertos and overtures. By Whitsuntide the castle organ here will be in as good a condition as possible; hence I could familiarize myself more completely with the structure of an organ, in order to be able to judge if this or that would be useful for an organ, if all repair work were executed well and not superficially, and at the same time how much, approximately, one or two ranks of pipes would cost, all of which I consider rather worthwhile. Also, especially after the new Weimar organ is ready, Herr Bach will play incomparable things on it, and thus I shall be able to see, hear, and copy a great deal.[9]

The organ was not fully ready until the spring of 1714, however, when a thorough two-week tuning of the entire instrument took place in May.[10] It was then that Bach would have been able to perform his organ transcriptions in the Palace Chapel for the ducal court, presenting arrangements of concertos by Vivaldi and Telemann and works recently composed by Johann Ernst under Walther's tutelage. But by this time the prince was increasingly hampered by health problems and on July 4, 1714, departed for Bad Schwalbach in an unsuccessful attempt to find a cure. He died a year later, on August 1, 1715, in Frankfurt am Main, at the age of 18.

It seems likely, then, that the bulk of the clavier and organ transcriptions—and the arrangements of works by Vivaldi and Johann Ernst, especially—were composed during the prince's final year in Weimar, that is, between July 1713 and July 1714. The sources of the transcriptions support this chronology. The only surviving autograph from the time, Bach's neatly written copy of the Concerto in D Minor, BWV 596 (plate 9-1), can be dated 1714–1716.[11] Cantata 21, *Ich hatte viel bekümmernis*, which is transmitted on the same paper as Bach's transcription, was first performed on June 17, 1714. And the earliest source of Bach's clavier arrangements (and the Concerto in G Major, BWV 592), a manuscript in the hand of Bach's nephew and Weimar student Johann Bernhard Bach (1676–1749), can be dated c. 1715,[12] confirming that most of the pieces were composed by that time. Court ledgers also show payment in April 1714 for "improvements to a Clavcymbel."[13] These repairs may well have been carried out in conjunction with Bach's fashioning of the clavier transcriptions.

If the organ in the Palace Chapel was not fully playable until May 1714, Bach may have joined Walther at the City Church of St. Peter and St. Paul and played his organ transcriptions composed up to that point there. Weighing in favor of this option is the disposition of the church's 25-rank, two-manual organ constructed by Christoph Junge in 1685 (see table 7-1). It contained an Oberwerk, Rückpositiv, and Pedal, the divisions consistently stipulated in the surviving sources of both Walther's and Bach's transcriptions.[14] In addition, the compass of its pedalboard was C–d', to judge from Walther's organ works. This

Plate 9-1 Concerto in D Minor after Vivaldi, BWV 596: first page of Bach's autograph score.

would have accommodated all of Bach's arrangements except the Concerto in A Minor, BWV 593, which requires the pedal note e' that in Weimar was found only on the pedalboard of the Palace Chapel organ.[15] Thus it is possible that Bach played the two Johann Ernst transcriptions and the Vivaldi C-Major and D-Minor arrangements on the City Church organ, as a stopgap until Trebs's work on the Palace Chapel instrument was completed.

Walther's organ transcriptions have been eclipsed by Bach's in modern times, but they were special pieces in their day. Passed down in a single autograph manuscript dating from after 1726,[16] they may have been assembled as a group and selected for survival by Walther, who was forced in old age to sell most of his personal collection of instrumental pieces and transcriptions.[17] His clavier arrangements, which may have been among this lost material, were probably intended for private use by Johann Ernst, as part of his studies with Walther.[18] The organ transcriptions, which survive in part, at least, were public pieces and rank among Walther's finest keyboard works. While they lack the virtuosity of Bach's organ arrangements, they contain inventive, unorthodox figurations that accommodate string writing to the keyboard as well as rapid manual changes that highlight tutti-solo contrasts (albeit it in a more straightforward way than in Bach's works; example 9-1). The best of Walther's transcriptions, pieces such as the Concerto in G Major after Telemann or the Concerto in B Minor after Vivaldi, must have impressed Weimar audiences.

That said, Bach's arrangements went far beyond Walther's. As noted in chapter 7, the early biographer Johann Nicolaus Forkel proposed that Bach used

Example 9-1 Johann Gottfried Walther, Concerto in G Major after Telemann, section 3, showing the composer's use of brackets and broken flags to notate manual-change.

the transcriptions to acquaint himself with Vivaldi's style.[19] Although that was surely part of the learning process, Bach would have initially studied Vivaldi's music through the ensemble performances that took place at the court and from the scores that he had to fashion from the performance parts to make his transcriptions. The transcriptions suggest that by the time Bach composed them, he understood Vivaldi's style well and was able to take the next step of enhancing the music with his own counterpoint.[20]

Schulze has proposed that the transcriptions may have been commissioned by Johann Ernst,[21] but there is no evidence of payments for such a transaction. It is just as likely that the Walther and Bach organ arrangements were a normal part of the celebrations that surrounded the arrival of the prince and the sudden influx of new music at the court.[22] Bach's transcriptions of Johann Ernst's works would have curried favor with the ducal family while demonstrating to the young prince how his music might be improved (see discussion below). Vivaldi's *L'Estro armonico* concertos, on the other hand, were all the rage in Europe, and Bach's transcriptions, as bravura extravaganzas, would have demonstrated the use of manual-change, double pedal, crossed-hands, and other virtuoso techniques. A sixth organ transcription of a Telemann concerto, no longer extant but recently assigned the Schmieder number 1168 in BWV[3], would have brought Bach's Eisenach/Frankfurt colleague into the circle of composers whose new works were featured in the Weimar organ recitals.[23] It may have been performed in the early spring of 1714, when Telemann was in Weimar to serve as godfather for the baptism of Carl Philipp Emanuel on March 10.

One wonders if the ducal family listened to the pieces from the main floor of the Palace Chapel or City Church or if they ascended to the gallery to watch Bach perform up close. The surviving autograph of the Concerto in D Minor hints at a vigorous performance: "Volti presto"—"Turn quickly!"—reads the score, for a page turn in the last movement. The Vivaldi concertos were the latest thing in Europe. Bach's arrangements, which add still more animation to the music through the addition of new contrapuntal lines, make it more exciting still. For Weimar audiences, the organ transcriptions may have been more than substitutions played *zur Curiosité*. With their technical high-jinks and embellishments, they may have been better than the real thing!

The Challenges of the Transcribing Process

The string idiom of the Vivaldi, Telemann, and Ernst concertos presented Bach with special challenges as he worked to fashion transcriptions for the organ. He not only had to deal with the issue of compensating for the natural expressivity of string instruments and the great agility of the violin and cello but also had to solve the problem of recreating tutti-solo contrasts and the simultaneous occurrence of solo instruments against the full ensemble. In addition, he had to find equivalents for rapidly moving continuo lines and characteristic string gestures that did not readily translate to the keyboard: rapid leaps and repeated notes, bariolage (the playing of two strings in rapid alteration, one open, one stopped), tremolos, and other figures.

While the organ lacked the dynamic sensitivity of the clavichord, which Bach was able to exploit in his clavier arrangements,[24] it offered certain advantages for transcriptions. The presence of multiple keyboards—manuals and pedal—and the ability to manipulate pitch through stop selection allowed the reproduction of continuo lines with 16' pitch, the mimicking of solo-tutti contrasts, the accommodation of crossing or juxtaposed contrapuntal lines, and the reproduction of violin pitches above c''' (the conventional top note of German keyboards at the time) by notating passages an octave lower than originally written and using a 4' registration.

Although certain concertos could be readily transcribed for either clavier or organ, such as the two works by Prince Johann Ernst that Bach arranged as BWV 592a/592 and BWV 984/595, other pieces, especially those with multiple soloists, could be transferred to the organ alone. As Werner Breig has convincingly shown, Vivaldi's Concerto in D Minor from *L'Estro armonico*, with two solo violins and solo cello, required resources that were available only on the organ.[25] Bach's brilliant handling of the opening canon in his transcription, BWV 596, in which he used pedal at 8' for the repeated note d' and two manuals at 4' pitch to cover the remainder of the violin lines (see discussion below), would not have been possible on the harpsichord or clavichord.

Faced with the challenge of arranging the Vivaldi and Ernst concertos for the organ, Bach explored new ways of playing the instrument altogether, in some cases devising novel methods of notation as well. As a result, the transcriptions display a number of performance and notational techniques for the first—and in some cases, only—time within Bach's organ works. They include the following devices:

- Notated stop changes in the middle of a movement (Concerto in D Minor, BWV 596, first movement). Such changes do not appear again until the Canonic Variations on "Vom Himmel hoch."
- Broken-flag notation and brackets, to show the precise point of manual change and which notes are involved (all five transcriptions). The use of broken flags appears later in the Toccata in D Minor ("Dorian"), BWV 538/ 1, and the Italian Concerto and French Overture of Clavier-Übung II.

- Thumbing—that is, playing on two manuals simultaneously with one hand (Concerto in A Minor, BWV 593, first movement). This technique, notated through the use of double stems (mm. 16, 25, and 65 of the same movement), appears later in "Meine Seele erhebt den Herren," BWV 648, of the Schübler Chorales.
- Contrapuntal lines moving rapidly against one another on different keyboards, in a nontrio context (all transcriptions). This appears later in the "Dorian" Toccata and the works of Clavier-Übung II, III, and IV.
- Double pedal used in a new way, to cover multiple instrumental lines simultaneously (continuo + violin 3 and 4, Concerto in A Minor, last movement; continuo + violin 2 ripieno and viola, Concerto in G Major, BWV 592, first movement).
- Using octave transpositions to create contrast between two violins of equal timbre (Concerto in A Minor, movement 2; Grosso Mogul Concerto, movement 1).
- Relying on acoustics—"the most important stop on the organ"—to support and create harmonies in lengthy one-part passages (the two solo cadenzas of the Grosso Mogul Concerto). The closest later analogy would be the works for unaccompanied violin, BWV 1001–1006; cello, BWV 1007–1012; and transverse flute, BWV 1013.

Of these techniques, only broken flags and brackets were used by Walther in his transcriptions (see example 9-1). The rest were unique to Bach.

In addition to using the organ in a new way, Bach had to create alternate motives for string figures that were awkward or unplayable on the keyboard. Rapid repeated notes, comfortably executed on the violin, were a special problem. Walther often retained such figures, making for unidiomatic performance on the organ (example 9-2). Bach sought more inventive solutions to such passages. In the Grosso Mogul Concerto and the Concerto in A Minor he changed solo lines with repeated notes to semitone figuration (example 9-3, a), and in the Concerto in A Minor and Concerto in G Major he used chords in opposite hands (and on different manuals, in the case of the Concerto in A Minor) to realize rapidly moving triadic string figures with repeated notes (example 9-3, b). And in the Concerto in G Major, he replaced Johann Ernst's inventive triadic string figures moving in contrary motion through the octave with smaller, playable triadic figures moving in contrary motion in the two hands (example 9-3, c). Klaus Hofmann has pointed out that Bach altered solo violin lines in his transcriptions not only to make the parts more playable on the keyboard but also to create variety in passages he deemed too repetitive or prosaic.[26]

In these and many other passages, we can see Bach's creative imagination at work, finding solutions to specific problems encountered in the transcribing

Example 9-2 Walther, (a) Concerto in C Major after Graupner, movement 1, and (b) Concerto in F Major after Albinoni, movement 1, both showing the composer's literal transcription of idiomatic violin figures in the right hand.

process. The Italian string concertos expanded his concept of the organ idiom and provided him with new ideas that he soon applied to his free works and his chorale settings. As Forkel noted, they taught him "to think musically" (see chapter 7).

The Music

Vivaldi Transcriptions

After using Venetian printers for opus 1 and 2 and being displeased with their work, Antonio Vivaldi decided to take his opus 3, *L'Estro armónico*, to the highly respected publishing house of Estienne Roger in Amsterdam. Roger not only provided a more attractive and accurate edition but also opened the door to a broader European market. Appearing in the last months of 1711, *L'Estro armonico* swept through Europe like a musical tsunami, and the Roger firm became the publisher for all of Vivaldi's subsequent concerto editions, including the immensely popular concerto collection *Il cimento dell'armonia e dell'inventione* (The Contest between Harmony and Invention), op. 8, which included the "Four Seasons."[27]

The demand for *L'Estro armonico* (The Harmonic Invention, or The Harmonic whim; plate 9-2) was unprecedented. The Roger firm issued reprintings at least twice between 1713 and 1743,[28] and pirated editions appeared simultaneously in London and Paris. As was typical of instrumental music at the time, *L'Estro armonico* was issued in performance parts rather than score. Roger's

Example 9-3 Three of Bach's solutions to transcribing idiomatic string figures: (a) Antonio Vivaldi, "Grosso Mogul" Concerto in D Major, RV 208 (transposed to C major for comparison), and Bach, Concerto in C Major after Vivaldi, BWV 594 (with Rückpositiv at sounding pitch, with a 4' stop), movement 1, and (b) Vivaldi, Concerto in A Minor, RV 522, and Bach, Concerto in A Minor after Vivaldi, BWV 593, movement 3, and (c) Johann Ernst, Concerto in G Major, and Bach, Concerto on G Major after Ernst, BWV 592, movement 3.

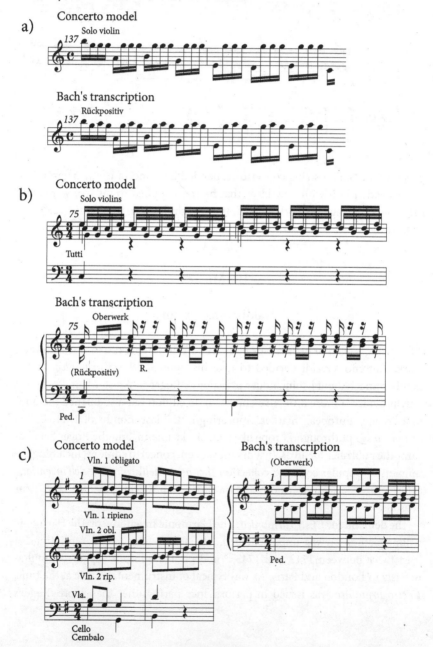

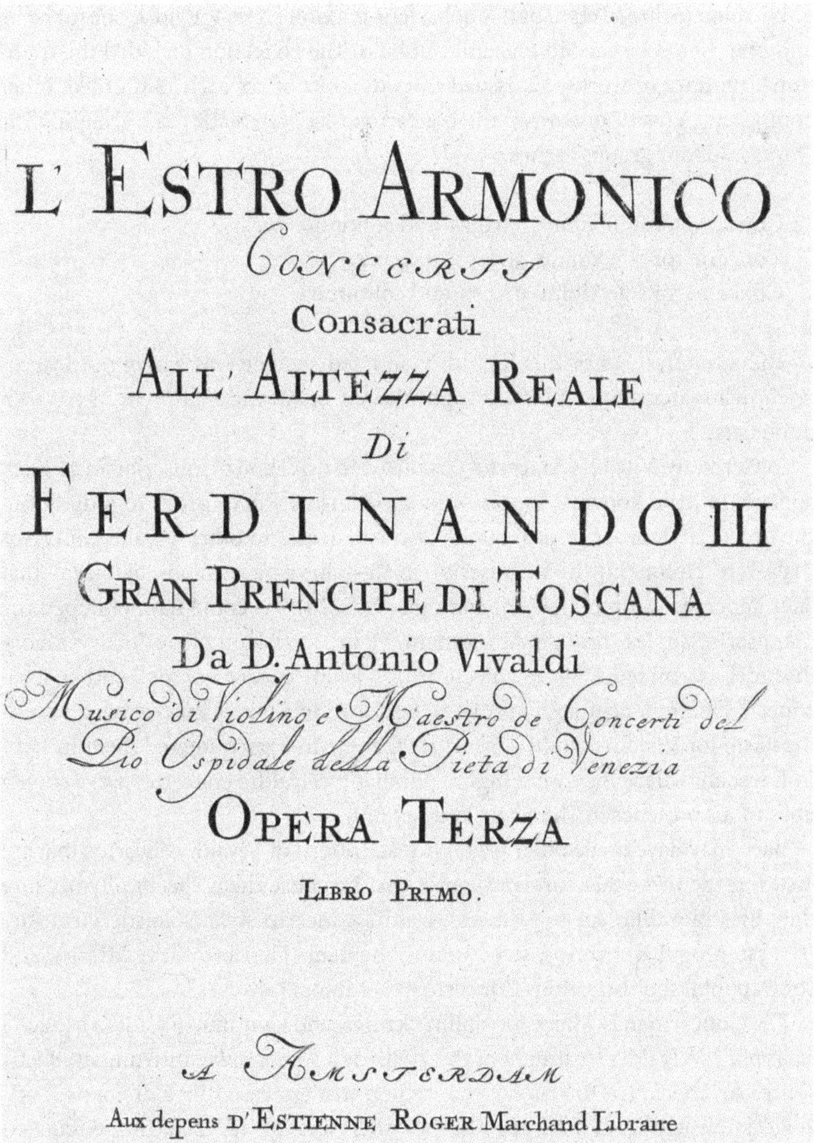

L' ESTRO ARMONICO

Concerti

Consacrati

ALL' ALTEZZA REALE

Di

FERDINANDO III

GRAN PRENCIPE DI TOSCANA

Da D. Antonio Vivaldi

Musico di Violino e Maestro de Concerti del Pio Ospidale della Pieta di Venezia

OPERA TERZA

LIBRO PRIMO.

A Amsterdam

Aux depens D'ESTIENNE ROGER Marchand Libraire

N° 5°

Plate 9-2 Antonio Vivaldi, *L'Estro armonico*, op. 3: title page of the first edition, published by Estienne Roger, Amsterdam, 1711.

Bibliothèque Nationale de France

publication included eight part-books: four for violin, two for viola, one for cello, and one shared by the violone and cembalo. The collection included the traditional number of works, 12, issued in two books of six each. But unlike other composers, Vivaldi organized the concertos in a systematic way, grouping the works into four groups of three:

> Concerto for four violins, strings, and continuo
> Concerto for two violins, strings, and continuo
> Concerto for solo violin, strings, and continuo

The attractiveness of this logical, graduated scheme was surely not lost on Bach, who later adopted highly sophisticated organizational plans in his own publications.

In Germany, Vivaldi's concertos circulated in print and manuscript form. Bach appears to have known *L'Estro armonico* from the Roger print, to judge from the text of his transcriptions, but he also had access to other Vivaldi concertos that were circulating in manuscript form—alternate versions of pieces that later appeared in opus 4 (1716) and opus 7 (1720). He could have obtained the manuscript copies through Amsterdam, Halle, Dresden (where Johann Georg Pisendel assembled a large collection of Vivaldi concertos), or another local court.[29] Johann Joachim Quantz later described to Charles Burney his great enthusiasm for Vivaldi's violin concertos when he first encountered them in 1714 in Dresden, where they were highly popular.[30] Vivaldi's concertos were soon a ubiquitous presence in Thuringia and Saxony.

Bach may have made other organ transcriptions of Vivaldi concertos that are lost. But the three that survive suggest that he chose them specifically because they illustrate different aspects of Vivaldi's concerto style: soloistic virtuosity (Grosso Mogul Concerto), structural refinement (Concerto in A Minor), and contrapuntal sophistication (Concerto in D Minor).

The Concerto in D Major for Violin, Strings, and Continuo ("Grosso Mogul") exemplifies Vivaldi's treatment of the violin as a solo-display instrument. Bach's source for the concerto was not the version that appeared Vivaldi's opus 7, RV 208a, published in 1720, but rather another version, RV 208, that circulated solely in manuscript form.[31] The manuscript version contains an entirely different middle movement, an unusual "Grave— Recitativo," that was thought to have been composed by Bach until Vivaldi's autograph score came to light in the 1960s.[32] Vivaldi's manuscript contains no cadenzas for the outer movements but indicates where they may be placed, through the remark "Qui si ferma à piaci[men]to" (Here one can close as one wishes).

Bach's source for his organ transcription, the **Concerto in C Major after Vivaldi, BWV 594,** is represented in a set of manuscript performance parts copied by Schwerin Court Organist Peter Johann Fink and preserved in the Mecklenburg-Vorpommern State Library in Schwerin.[33] The Schwerin parts contain the cadenzas that Bach included in his arrangement, and it is the only source to bear the epithet "Grosso Mogul," which may refer either to the emperor of India and the land he ruled or to a contemporary opera libretto of the same name.[34]

To accommodate Vivaldi's work to the organ, Bach transposed the music down a step to C major, to avoid the frequent occurrence of d''' in the original score, and he assigned the solo violin part mostly to the Rückpositiv. Luigi Ferdinando Tagliavini has shown that Bach intended the Rückpositiv to be registered at 4' pitch throughout the transcription, since the solo violin line is consistently notated down an octave when it appears on the Rückpositiv but at pitch when it appears on the Oberwerk (mm. 63–81 or 118–126 of movement 1, for instance).[35] By using a 4' registration, Bach was able to preserve the original pitch of solo violin passages that soared as high as b''' (a''' in his transcription).

The middle movement of the Grosso Mogul Concerto, "Recitativo—Grave" (changed to "Recitativo—Adagio" in Bach's transcription), is a unicum in Vivaldi's music: a deeply expressive secco recitative for solo violin. Vivaldi notated the accompanying bass line (played in unison by the cello and cembalo) in long-held notes—the notational convention for secco recitatives in the eighteenth century. In his transcription, Bach replaced the sustained notes with intermittent quarter-note chords (example 9-4, a), reflecting the convention of performing secco recitatives with short chords that allowed for great freedom of the solo voice while still providing harmonic support at critical junctures.[36] Bach's most significant change to Vivaldi's text in the "Recitativo" occurs at the final cadence, where he added florid diminutions to the original violin line and inserted a new obbligato part altogether (example 9-4, b). Although Bach had limited exposure to opera in Weimar, he was clearly familiar with the operatic convention of embellishing the final cadence of a solo recitative or aria.

The outer movements of the Grosso Mogul Concerto are straightforward ritornello forms, with tutti ritornello segments alternating with solo-violin episodes. Bach's treatment of the solo violin line in the episodes is the most striking feature of his transcription. In the opening Allegro, for instance, he handled each episode differently:

Episode 1:
> Mm. 26–39: the solo violin double-stops are replaced with scalar and arpeggiated 16th-note figures.
>
> Mm. 40–58: the solo violin line is transcribed note-for-note (mm. 40–50), and the repeated-note figures and shifts in the continuo theme are transposed to treble range.

Example 9-4 Vivaldi, "Grosso Mogul" Concerto in D Major, RV 208 (transposed to C major for comparison), and Bach, Concerto in C Major after Vivaldi, BWV 594 (right hand at sounding pitch, with 4' stop), movement 2: (a) opening measures, and (b) closing measures.

Episode 2:

> Mm. 63–81: the solo line is moved to the Oberwerk, where it sounds at pitch, parallel 6ths are added on the Rückpositiv, and the accompanimental chords are articulated by changing them from quarter notes to 8th notes and 8th-note rests.

Episode 3:

Mm. 93–104: triplets are interpreted as 16th-note figures, keeping the general shape of the solo violin line but a repeated-note motive is added.

Mm. 105–111: Vivaldi's triplet figures are finally adopted, but the original continuo chords are dropped in favor of a new treble accompanimental triplet motive in parallel 6ths and 3rds.

Episode 4:

Mm. 118–126: the solo line is moved to the Oberwerk, once again, in its proper range. A 32nd-note left-hand glissando figure is inserted to animate Vivaldi's simple continuo line.

Mm. 127–133: the solo moves back to Rückpositiv, with the double stops of the original violin line retained.

The raison d'être of the Grosso Mogul transcription is Bach's further treatment of the solo violin part in the immense outer-movement cadenzas that appear in the Schwerin performance materials—a bravura feature that must have stirred his imagination. The cadenzas that were typically added to Vivaldi's violin concertos at the time can be divided into two categories.[37] The first was the integrated cadenza, which drew on themes from the movement and thus was closely associated with its music. The 34-measure cadenza in the first movement of the Grosso Mogul (Bach expanded it to 36 measures) falls into this category.

The second type of cadenza, the insertion cadenza, contained stock virtuoso violin figures that had nothing to do with the music into which it was placed. Rather, the insertion cadenza was designed solely to showcase the technical prowess of the soloist. Such cadenzas were the instrumental equivalent of the "arie di baule"—the "suitcase arias" that were carried around by star opera singers in the eighteenth century and inserted into whatever work they were performing, even if the language did not match.[38] The 103-measure cadenza in the third movement of the "Grosso Mogul" in the Schwerin parts belongs to this group. We might call it a "suitcase cadenza," which explains why its meter, ¢, does not agree with that of the movement, 3/4. The Schwerin cadenza appears elsewhere, both in a longer, 126-measure form within a set of Grosso Mogul Concerto performance parts now located in Cividale del Friuli[39] and a shorter form within materials located in Dresden for a different Vivaldi concerto.[40]

The Schwerin version of the third-movement cadenza systematically works its way through the customary gestures of virtuoso violin playing: rapid leaps and arpeggiated figures (mm. 180–197 in Bach's transcription), double and triple stops (mm. 198–209), trills and bird-call effects (mm. 210–217), rapid scales (mm. 218–222), *galant* triplets (first alone and then with pedal tone; mm. 222–234), and finally a climactic flurry of extravagant gestures—wide leaps, rapid repeated notes, and triadic motives moving to a dominant pedal point (mm. 234–282).[41] Bach adjusted several of the solo violin figures in the cadenza and inserted additional flourishes here and there (the 32nd-note glissandos in m. 226, for instance). But he retained the solo line throughout and did not add a continuo element. His most shocking change is the alteration of the falling major seconds in measures 246–267 to minor seconds, giving the cadenza an exotic Middle Eastern sound that he and his listeners might have associated with music from India. In an organ performance of the Grosso Mogul transcription, the cadenza makes sense only if it is performed with great freedom, like a violin piece.

A note within the Cividale parts states that its last-movement cadenza was commissioned directly from Vivaldi by a local patrician, Leonardo Giorgio Pontotti.[42] Such claims by local figures are often suspect, but given the stylistic affinities with Vivaldi's writing, it is possible that all versions of the last-movement cadenza—Schwerin, Cividale, and Dresden—can in some way be traced to Vivaldi or his circle. Whether or not this is true, the last-movement cadenza reflects Vivaldi's own practice of concluding solo violin concertos with pyrotechnical display, as witnessed by the Frankfurt traveler Johann Friedrich Armand von Uffenbach during a visit to Venice in 1715:

> Toward the end Vivaldi played a solo accompaniment—splendid—to which he appended a cadenza that really frightened me, for such playing has never been nor can be. He brought his fingers up to only a straw's distance from the bridge, leaving no room for the bow—and that on all four strings with imitations and at incredible speed. With this he astounded everyone, but I cannot say that it pleased me, for it was not so pleasant to listen to as it was skillfully executed.[43]

The return of the ritornello at the end of the last movement of the Grosso Mogul Concerto, in the form of a short seven-measure segment in 3/4 meter, seems anticlimactic. And it should be, for this version of the work is about cadenzas and solo virtuosity rather than ritornello segments. It was the excitement of bravura violin-playing that Bach sought to capture in his transcription. And he must have been deeply impressed by the oversized, outlandish cadenza of the final movement, since he later indulged in an oversized, outlandish cadenza himself in the first movement of Brandenburg Concerto No. 5.

Vivaldi's Concerto in A Minor for Two Violins, Strings, and Continuo, RV 522, from L'Estro armonico, is a very different piece. The solo writing, in this case for two violins, is much more subdued than that of the Grosso Mogul Concerto. What stands out instead is the magnificent handling of ritornello form, which Bach preserved and highlighted in his transcription, the **Concerto in A Minor after Vivaldi, BWV 593.**

Vivaldi's ritornellos normally follow a three-step pattern. They begin with material that emphatically establishes the tonic. This leads to a series of sequences, which are then followed by closing material that reestablishes the tonic. Wilhelm Fischer, in discussing forms that led to the Viennese Classical style, called the three segments "Vordersatz," "Fortspinnung," and "Epilog,"[44] useful terms that we will translate as introduction, extension, and conclusion. This method of constructing a ritornello, with three distinct portions, each well-defined by harmonic function, became a fundamental part of Bach's compositional style after his encounter with Vivaldi's works.

In the Concerto in A Minor, Vivaldi demonstrated that the three portions of the ritornello could be altered and rearranged, much like the blocks of a Lego set. As we noted earlier, the ritornello of the first movement consists of five segments—we will term them "r1–r5"—that evolve naturally out of one another (see chapter 7). The first two segments represent the introduction and define the tonic. The third segment represents the extension and moves through a series of sequences. And the last two segments represent the conclusion and reestablish the tonic with full cadences. In diagram form:

Mm.	Segment	Function
1–3	r1	Introduction: defines tonic
4–5	r2	Introduction: further defines tonic
6–9a	r3	Extension: sequential
9b–13	r4	Conclusion: cadential, reestablishing the tonic
14–16a	r5	Conclusion: cadential, further reestablishing the tonic

During the movement, the ritornello segments are both reinvented and reshuffled and used together and separately. The episodes, a series of violin duets here termed "e," consist of variations of the anapestic rhythmic motive of the second ritornello segment, r2:

Mm.	Material	Segment	Harmonic station
1–16a	Ritornello	r1, r2, r3, r4, r5	i
16a–22	Episode (violin duet)	e1	
23–25a	Ritornello	r5	i
25b–36	Episode (violin duet)	e2	
37–47	Ritornello	r2', r3, r1' (reshaped)	III → iv

Mm.	Material	Segment	Harmonic station
48–51a	Episode (violin duet)	e3	
51b–54	Ritornello	r1	iv
55–62a	Episode (violin duet)	e4	
62b–65a	Ritornello	r4	i
65b–67	Episode (violin duet)	e1	
68–71a	Ritornello	r1	i
71b–78a	Episode (violin duet)	e4'	
78b–86a	Ritornello	r2, r3, r5	i
86b–90a	Episode (violin duet)	e3	
90b–93	Ritornello	r5	i

A recapitulation of sorts occurs from measure 62b onward, with the return to the tonic and the opening material, including the first episode. But the ritornello segments are broken up and presented in a new order, and the final cadential segment, r5, is repeated.

Bach underscored Vivaldi's design in his transcription by enriching the ritornello segments through the addition of a new imitative line in the r3 segment (example 9–5) and by thickening the textures in the r4 and r5 segments from four to six and seven parts. For the arrival of the ritornello in D minor (m. 51b), he dropped Vivaldi's contrapuntal bass line in favor of presenting the head motive (r1) dramatically in unison, marked "O. plen." in the earliest surviving source of the transcription.[45]

Bach enhanced the episodes (assigned mostly to the Rückpositiv) by adding new contrapuntal lines (mm. 19–20, 30–34) and rewriting the repeated–note violin figure in e4' (mm. 71b–78a). But on the whole, this movement is a much more straightforward arrangement than either of the outer movements of the Grosso Mogul transcription. The balance, unity, and motivic development of Vivaldi's model were to become critical elements of Bach's vocal, instrumental, and keyboard works. His transcription of the first movement of the A-Minor Concerto honors and enhances these features.

In the second movement ("Larghetto e spirituoso" in Vivaldi's score, a more neutral "Adagio" in Bach's arrangement), Bach preserved Vivaldi's quasi-ostinato bass line but used octave transposition in the violin parts—played together on the forte keyboard—to provide contrast between the two instruments (violin 2, mm. 9–12, violin 1, mm. 32–33 and 37–41) as well as to avoid d''' (violin 1, mm. 25–31). Otherwise, his transcription reproduces the music without change.

Example 9-5 Vivaldi, Concerto in A Minor, RV 522, and Bach, Concerto in A Minor after Vivaldi, BWV 593, mm. 6–7, showing new alto part.

And in the final movement, Bach enlivened the bass in the initial solo episode (mm. 13–24) and added a pedal motive to fill in Vivaldi's silences (mm. 59–63; example 9-7, below) that subsequently evolves into a critical manual motive (mm. 66–74). The *passage de résistance* in the transcription is Bach's interpretation of Vivaldi's episodic duet at measure 86, where the hands play the solo violin parts on two manuals, cross-handed in the highest register, while the right foot plays the unison violin 3 and 4 line and the left foot plays the unison cello, violone, and cembalo part. Nothing else in the Bach organ repertory illustrates quite so starkly the composer's creative genius and astonishing technique as these 28 mesmerizing measures!

Of the three Vivaldi works that Bach transcribed for organ, the Concerto in D Minor for Two Violins, Cello, Strings, and Continuo, RV 565, from *L'Estro armonico*, surely offered the greatest challenge. Written for three soloists—Violino concertante 1 and 2 and Violoncello principale—and containing a canon, a fugue, and an imitative ritornello movement, the D-Minor Concerto must have intrigued Bach while also forcing him to find unprecedented solutions to translating complex string counterpoint to the organ.

This is apparent in the opening canon for the two solo violins. In the organ arrangement, the **Concerto in D Minor after Vivaldi, BWV 596,** Bach transformed

Example 9-6 a) Vivaldi, Concerto in D Minor, RV 565, movement 1, and (b) Bach, Concerto in D Minor after Vivaldi, BWV 596, movement 1 (manual parts at sounding pitch, with 4' stop), showing Bach's transformation of the opening canon.

the duo into a trio by extracting the note d' from the violin lines and assigning it to a new part, a hypnotic, repetitive pedal tone played in the Pedal with an 8' Principal (example 9-6). He then presented the now-fragmented and playable violin lines on the two manuals an octave lower, with 4' Octava stops that allowed the highest note in Vivaldi's original, d''', to sound. Finally, he embellished the original violin lines with animated 16th notes in parallel motion and expanded the music by inserting a new measure (m. 8 in the organ score). All this in the first 20 measures!

At measure 20 in Vivaldi's score, the cello begins a solo against a pulsating continuo bass. Bach already anticipated this passage in his transcription with his newly fashioned pulsating bass for the violin canon. He continued the bass line in the pedal without pause but indicated that a 32' Subbaß should be added to the registration on the downbeat of measure 21, to simulate the 16' violone that enters at that point in Vivaldi's score. He assigned the cello solo to the Oberwerk, played at pitch with an 8' Principal added to the 4' Octava, and he added repeated chords, played on the Brustpositiv, ostensibly providing the continuo support of the instrumental version. But he enriched the chords with 7ths on each downbeat and added an entirely new line, in contrary motion, in the final three measures, to create a more emphatic cadence. The continuo chords anticipate the repeated 7th chords of the upcoming Grave, now expanded from four parts (Vivaldi's score) to seven (Bach's arrangement).

Bach treated the Fuga that follows (labeled simply "Allegro" in Vivaldi's score) much like a German organ fugue, dropping the distinction between tutti and solo and assigning the entire movement to one-manual and pedal, *organo pleno*. He preserved Vivaldi's magnificent four-part invertible counterpoint with little change by assigning the pedal a practical line and shifting fast-moving parts to the manuals, making octave adjustments wherever necessary to allow them to be played by two hands. This could be accomplished only because of the invertible nature of Vivaldi's lines. Bach heightened the drama of the final return of the tutti (m. 53) with its long pedal point (m. 55) by adding an animated tenor line here and there and maintaining the original rapidly moving parallel 3rds and 6ths, despite the fact that they are almost impossible to play at a fast tempo on the organ (especially on a tracker instrument with a plenum registration). At the end, he thickened the texture to five parts (mm. 67–68) and then six (m. 69–70) and brightened Vivaldi's concluding D-minor chord with a Picardy third.

Bach transcribed the Largo e spiccato movement with very little change, adjusting the spacing of the accompanimental chords so that they could be played on a single manual, but otherwise making only cosmetic additions to the text, mostly in the form of ornaments to the violin solo, played on a second manual, forte.

Bach's arrangement of the final movement is a tour de force, the true culmination of his entire series of organ transcriptions. He maintained the
solo-tutti structure of the original but used the two manuals to represent it
in a creative way. The unaccompanied violin and cello trios are presented
on the Rückpositiv, while the accompanied solos, both violin and cello, are
presented on the Oberwerk or a combination of Oberwerk and Rückpositiv.
The tutti cadences are presented on the Oberwerk, as would be expected:

Element/ Mm.	Vivaldi's score	Bach's transcription	Harmonic station
Ritornello			
1–6	Solo trio: violins 1 & 2, cello	Rückpositiv	
7–11a	Solo cello, tutti accompaniment	Oberwerk	
11b–13	Tutti cadence	Oberwerk	i
Episode			
14–22	Solo trio: violins 1 & 2, cello	Rückpositiv	
23–27a	Solo violin, tutti accompaniment	Oberwerk	
Ritornello			
27b–29	Tutti cadence	Oberwerk	v
Episode			
29–34	Violin duet, tutti accompaniment (piano)	Oberwerk	
35–42	Violin solo, string accompaniment (pp)	Oberwerk/ Rückpositiv	
Ritornello			iv → v
43–46a	Tutti	Oberwerk	
Episode			
46b–50	Solo trio: violins 1 & 2, cello	Rückpositiv	
50–53	Solo trio alternating with tutti interjections	Rückpositiv + Oberwerk	
53–59	Solo trio: violins 1 & 2, cello	Rückpositiv	
59–68	Solo violin, continuo	Rückpositiv/ Oberwerk	
Ritornello			
68–73	Tutti cadence (piano, then forte)	Oberwerk	i

Of the many extraordinary aspects of this movement, three are especially noteworthy. The first is the intricacy with which Bach indicated manual change, using broken flags for individual notes and brackets for chords to clarify precisely where the transfer is to take place and which notes are involved. In two instances (mm. 14 and 23) the change occurs on a downbeat, with one hand playing on the Oberwerk and the other on the Rückpositiv. Brackets show which notes go where. The second aspect is the "organ-izing" of Vivaldi's tutti cadences with string tremolos (mm. 11b, 27b, and 68). Bach replaced the unidiomatic tremolos with a keyboard-friendly triadic 16th- and 32nd-note figure in the left hand and a descending chromatic quarter-note scale in the pedal. Finally, in the last episode Bach inserted a new alto part, in imitation of the off-beat continuo figure appearing in the bass (mm. 59–67). This creates a fiendishly difficult passage to play, and one wonders if Bach added it as a final display of technical bravado, much in the fashion of the double-pedal, crossed-hand passage that concludes his A-Minor Concerto, but more challenging still. We can see why Wilhelm Friedemann Bach was eager to later claim this transcription as his own work![46]

The opening canon and two allegro movements of Vivaldi's D-Minor Concerto must have made a great impression on Bach as he worked through the music for his transcription. A variation of the last movement's main theme appeared in the opening chorus of Cantata 21, *Ich hatte viel Bekümmernis*, performed on June 17, 1714, and the canon may have influenced the pedal-point canons that appear at the beginning of the Toccata in F Major, BWV 540/1,[47] a work probably written around this time as well. And a version of the Fuga subject appeared years later in Cöthen, in the Fuga of Sonata 1 in G Minor for Unaccompanied Violin, BWV 1001, a movement to which Bach returned twice in Leipzig, arranging it for organ (BWV 539/2) and lute (BWV 1000). This was music of far-reaching impact.

Johann Ernst Transcriptions

To judge from the surviving repertoire, Prince Johann Ernst was a gifted composer of instrumental music, highly attuned to the latest stylistic trends. Of the 19 concertos credited to him by Walther, six appeared in print in 1718 in a posthumous edition overseen by Telemann, two survive in the form of manuscript performance parts, and one additional piece, now lost, is reflected in Bach's transcriptions. The remaining 10 concertos are no longer extant.

Bach's six arrangements of Johann Ernst's concertos show significant changes to the original music—changes that hint at a didactic purpose. Walther mentioned only himself as the prince's composition teacher, but it was Bach who fashioned keyboard arrangements of Johann Ernst's works, in two cases going so far as to make organ and clavier transcriptions of the same piece. And it was Bach who was working with Vivaldi concertos that the prince clearly mimicked.[48] While there is no conclusive proof that Johann Ernst studied with Bach,[49] Bach's transcriptions of his music point in that direction.

The model for the **Concerto movement in C Major after Johann Ernst, BWV 595**, does not survive. Bach's clavier arrangement of the entire work, the Concerto in C Major, BWV 984, confirms that the organ transcription is the first movement of a three-movement piece, most probably a concerto for two violins, strings, and continuo. The first movement may represent one of Johann Ernst's earlier compositional efforts, since its use of a short, two-measure ritornello, rigidly maintained throughout, is closer in style to the music of Torelli and Albinoni than that of Vivaldi. The organ transcription is 15 measures longer than the clavier arrangement, which led both Philipp Spitta and Karl Heller, the editor of the organ and clavier transcriptions for the Neue Bach-Ausgabe, to propose that the clavier version represents the prince's original concerto and the organ version Bach's expansion of it.[50]

More recently, David Schulenberg and Dominik Sackmann have suggested that the opposite is true. In their view, the clavier transcription's more highly embellished cadences and tighter harmonic plan, which eliminates the unorthodox redundancies of the organ version, point to a later origin.[51] There is much to be said for this. When Bach revised the Pièce d'Orgue, BWV 572, he shortened the first section by eliminating a redundant return to the tonic (see chapter 13). He appears to have followed the same procedure even further here. He deleted redundant ritornello segments that touched on keys represented elsewhere (I, V, iii, and ii) and composed new bridges to connect the material that remained (figure 9-1). The result was a more concise and finely focused movement. The carpentry of the clavier transcription makes sense only in the context of composition instruction—formal or informal—between Bach and the prince.

The organ transcription appears to represent the public version of the Prince's movement, retaining the full structure of the music but disguising its weaknesses through the distraction of virtuosic manual changes between the Oberwerk (for the tutti, with continuo) and Rückpositiv (for the two solo violins). There are 60 manual changes in the course of 81 measures—far more than in any other Bach organ work—and most take place within the span of a 16th note. The manual changes and their precise designation with broken-flag notation may have served as a dry run for the "Dorian" Toccata in D Minor, BWV 538/1, which contains very similar writing.

The clavier arrangement, by contrast, contains no manual changes and can be played by a keyboardist of moderate ability. It may have been the private version of the concerto, created by Bach to show the Prince how the movement might be improved through careful editing. There is no evidence in the sources that Bach made organ arrangements of the two remaining movements of Johann

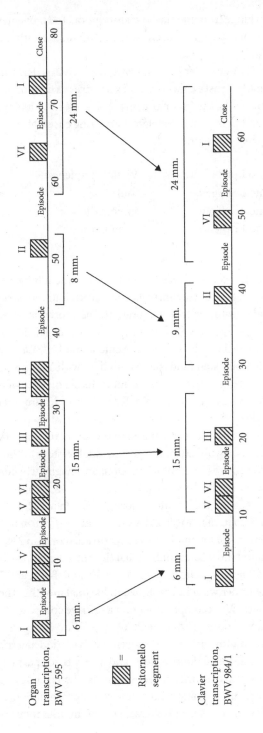

Figure 9-1 Bach's abridgement of the Concerto movement in C Major after Johann Ernst, BWV 595, for organ, to produce the first movement of the Concerto in C Major after Johann Ernst, BWV 984, for clavier.

Ernst's concerto. To judge from the clavier transcription, the movements are un-distinguished, and Bach may have deemed them too uninteresting for further attention.

The **Concerto in G Major after Johann Ernst, BWV 592**, is derived from very different music. Johann Ernst's concerto model survives as a set of performance parts that can be traced to the Weimar court.[52] A work in G major for violin, strings, and continuo,[53] it is written for eight-part string ensemble in the manner of Vivaldi's *L'Estro armonico* scoring:

Violino 1 principale	Violino 2 ripieno
Violino 1 obligato	Viola
Violino 2 obligato	Violoncello
Violino 1 ripieno	Cembalo

It is a very advanced piece, stylistically. The first movement is based on a well-rounded, Vivaldi-like, 14-measure ritornello that returns four times, separated by clear-cut solo episodes featuring triplet figuration. The conservative modulatory scheme (I → V → I → I → vi/I) is offset by the progressive expansion of the ritor-nello in its last two instances. The second movement, marked *Adagio*, features a middle section with violin solo (and then violin duo, with Violino 1 obbligato) framed by a six-measure unison tutti theme, much in the manner of the middle movement of Vivaldi's Concerto in A Minor, RV 522, from *L'Estro armonico*. The last movement, marked "Presto e staccato" in Johann Ernst's score, is the most original, with a 12-measure ritornello alternating with increasingly demanding solo interludes (the last two featuring vigorous double-stops). The ritornello features triadic string figures in contrary motion, an imaginative contrapuntal texture that comes closer to Bach's writing in Weimar works such as the Sinfonia in F Major, BWV 1046a, or the opening chorus of Cantata 172, *Erschallet, ihr Lieder, erklinget, ihr Saiten!* than to Vivaldi's scoring in *L'Estro armonico*. Finally, the two outer movements of Johann Ernst's concerto are scored in 2/4, a progres-sive, *galant* meter found most commonly at that time in Telemann's works. All of this points to new influences in the Prince's music: Vivaldi, Bach, and Telemann, who took the Prince under wing in Frankfurt, in his final months. The G-Major Concerto was a remarkable accomplishment for a teenage composer.

Bach's organ transcription further enhances Johann Ernst's score while preserving its general outline. In the first movement, Bach added a triadic 16th-note figure to further animate the ritornello and a new tenor part (realized via double pedal) to give the ritornello more weight. In the episodes he replaced the prince's simple accompaniment with a new contrapuntal line that becomes increasingly complex as the piece progresses. In the middle movement, Bach created a climax in the final measures of the middle section (mm. 23–38 of the transcription) by introducing the pedal for the first time and increasing the texture from two and three parts to four and then five parts. In the last movement, Bach rewrote the ritornello altogether, replacing Johann Ernst's inventive string figuration with a new motive in contrary motion, one that could be played more easily by the hands (example 9-3, c, above). He also grounded the ritornello with a new diatonic pedal theme that anticipates the rising fifth in the continuo of the first episode. He rounded off the opening ritornello with a descending two-octave glissando that expands to three octaves at the end of the movement.

The third movement is an inspired transformation, and Bach retained a number of its unusual features when he reworked it for the more straightforward clavier transcription, BWV 592a, which contains no manual-changes throughout its three movements. The organ transcription placed Johann Ernst's impressively progressive concerto in the best possible light, and it surely made a great impression on the entire ducal family when Bach brought the music to life for a second time in the Palace Chapel.

Bach versus Vivaldi

Bach returned to his organ transcriptions during the Leipzig years, sharing them with colleagues and using them for instructional purposes. At one point Bach's follower Johann Peter Kellner owned copies of all five arrangements,[54] and Johann Christian Kittel, one of Bach's last students, owned copies of four transcriptions, now lost.[55] The extant manuscripts of Wilhelm Friedemann Bach and Johann Friedrich Agricola show that Bach not only used the concertos for teaching but also made small improvements to the texts during the Leipzig years.[56] Wilhelm Friedemann's fragmentary copy of the Grosso Mogul transcription from c. 1730/1731[57] suggests that the work was part of his advanced organ study with his father, together with the Six Sonatas, which were composed specifically for that purpose.[58] It is also possible that Friedemann received his father's autograph manuscript of the Concerto in D Minor in the summer of 1733, in order to have it in his dossier with the Prelude and Fugue in G Major, BWV 541, for his successful organ audition at the St. Sophia's Church in Dresden (see chapter 12). In a city obsessed with Vivaldi's music, the transcription would have made a great impression, especially if it was thought to be a work of Friedemann's own composition, as he claimed on his father's manuscript.[59]

Bach may also have used the concerto arrangements himself in Leipzig, for public organ recitals presented during the three annual trade fairs. Such recitals would have taken place outside the worship service, much in the manner of De Graaf's programs in Amsterdam, and the transcriptions would have afforded fair visitors the opportunity to hear music similar to the lively instrumental concertos that were being played down the street at the coffeehouse concerts of the city's two collegium musicum ensembles. It was for a collegium performance at Zimmermann's Coffee House that Bach arranged Vivaldi's Concerto in B Minor for Four Violins from *L'Estro armonico* as the Concerto in A Minor for Four Harpsichords, BWV 1065, an extravaganza work by any measure. The "over-the-top" organ transcriptions would have astounded audiences in the same way as the quadruple concerto.

The unorthodox nature of the organ transcriptions did not meet with universal admiration after Bach's death, however. Ferdinand Roitzsch, who edited the works for the Peters Edition in 1852, voiced concern that, as organ adaptations rather than original compositions, they contained "runs and arpeggios that normally would not be acceptable to present-day audiences."[60] Johannes Schreyer, writing in 1912, went further and called the Grosso Mogul transcription a "musical monstrosity" that sounded to him like the "pitiful piping of a barrel organ."[61] And even Hermann Keller, normally a staunch admirer of Bach's organ music, found the use of double pedal in the first movement of the Concerto in G Major "unnecessary."[62]

Which brings us to Vivaldi himself. What would the Venetian composer have thought of Bach's organ transcriptions of his works? One suspects that Vivaldi might have found Bach's additions to the musical texts overly intrusive, introducing elements that distracted from the spontaneous drama and unaffected nature of the original scores. For instance, Vivaldi often used silence as a dramatic gesture in his works—"pregnant pauses" that whet the listener's appetite for the return of sound. Bach seemed uncomfortable with such pauses and, more often than not, filled them in with newly composed lines. In the last movement of the Grosso Mogul Concerto, for example, he inserted glissandos to fill in the rests that occur in the ritornello theme in measures 24 and 174 (example 9-7, a). And in the last movement of the Concerto in A Minor he inserted a new contrapuntal line—a virtuoso pedal figure—into the echo sequence at measures 59–63 (example 9-7, b). For Vivaldi, the moments of silence in his scores allowed the music to breathe; for Bach, they represented opportunities to insert bravura gestures. Vivaldi might have found Bach's contrapuntal additions overly artful.

In the last movement of the Concerto in A Minor, once again, Vivaldi created a powerful ritornello theme that utilizes a descending 8th-note scale played in unison, first by two violins (mm. 1–3) and then by all eight instruments (mm. 82–86, 114–118, and 142–144). Its force comes from its unified unison declamation, first by two members of the ensemble, then by everyone. Bach embellished the unison effect, however, initially through the addition of a 16th-note countersubject (mm. 82–86 and 114–118) and then through the addition of parallel 3rds and 6ths at the close, to thicken the texture (mm. 142–144; example 9-8). Vivaldi might have

Example 9-7 (a) Vivaldi, Grosso Mogul Concerto in D Major (transposed to C Major for comparison), RV 208, and Bach, Concerto in C Major after Vivaldi, movement 3, mm. 23–25, and (b) Vivaldi, Concerto in A Minor, RV 522, and Bach, Concerto in A Minor after Vivaldi, BWV 593, movement 3, mm. 59–61.

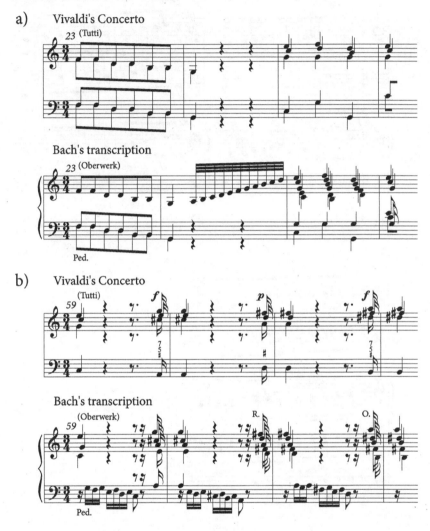

felt that the bare "hammerstrokes" of his original music were more straightforward and hence more effective. Or, finally, in the unusual Recitativo movement of the Grosso Mogul Concerto, Vivaldi concluded the music with a theatrical trailing-off of the solo violin in an ascending arpeggio. Bach, in his transcription, added a second obbligato line in contrary motion, turning the expressive solo into a contrapuntal duet (example 9-4, b, above).[63] Here, too, Vivaldi might have objected,

Example 9-8 (a) Vivaldi, Concerto in A Minor, RV 522, and (b) Bach, Concerto in A Minor after Vivaldi, BWV 593, movement 3, showing the evolution of the ritornello theme.

finding the new line too "learned" and detrimental to the carefully calculated—yet seemingly natural—fading of sound before the final movement.

In 1737 Bach was publicly criticized by Johann Adolph Scheibe for darkening the natural beauty of music with "an excess of art"—that is, for writing lines that were too contrapuntal and, in Scheibe's view, too artificial. "This great man would be the admiration of whole nations," Scheibe said, "if he had more amenity, if he did not take away the natural element in his pieces by giving them a turgid and confused style, and if he did not darken their beauty by an excess of art."[64] Bach's supporters quickly came to his defense in a long series of polemics.[65] But we can sense Scheibe's concern in the Vivaldi organ transcriptions. As Rudolf Eller once expressed it, from a German standpoint, Bach's additions to Vivaldi's text strengthen the music and increase its profundity. From an Italian standpoint, the additions seem antithetical to the music's natural *affect*.[66] Just as Goethe appeared to prefer the simple settings of his poetry by Johann Friedrich Reichardt and Carl Friedrich Zelter to the more sophisticated arrangements of Franz Schubert,[67] Vivaldi might have preferred his concertos in their original, unadulterated form to Bach's Germanized reimaginings.

Whether overly artful or not, the Vivaldi and Ernst concerto transcriptions have remained staples of the organ repertory and invaluable evidence of the inventive fervor Bach brought to the task of transferring finely nuanced string music to the medium of the pipe organ. They were, and remain, incomparable things.

Notes

1. The scores and performance materials for the music appear to have been lost in the great fire that destroyed the Wilhelmsburg Palace in 1774.
2. Modern editions include *Denkmäler Deutscher Tonkunst* (Leipzig: Breitkopf & Härtel, 1892–1927), vol. 27 (1906), and *Johann Gottfried Walther: Sämtliche Orgelwerke*, Klaus Beckmann, ed. (Wiesbaden: Breitkopf & Härtel, 1998), vol. 1, nos. 9–22. Walther described his transcriptions in an autobiographical sketch in Mattheson 1740, 389.
3. Schulze 1972, 7–10, and Schulze 1984, 156–163.
4. Rasch 2019, 77, and Górny 2019, 362–364.
5. The fact that Bach later arranged the Concerto in B Minor for Four Violins from *L'Estro armonico* as the Concerto in A Minor for Four Harpsichords and Strings, BWV 1065, in Leipzig suggests that he possessed his own copy of Vivaldi's collection, perhaps in the form of the Roger print.
6. Schulze 1984, 159.
7. Schulze 1972, 7.
8. Mattheson 1717, 129–130. Walther, later citing Mattheson, added that de Graaf had "rothe triessende Augen"—red runny eyes (Walther 1732, 289–290).
9. NBR, no. 312c.
10. Jauernig 1950b, 74–75.
11. Berlin State Library, *P 330*. Dating from Dadelsen 1958, 79, and NBA IX/2 (*Die Notenschrift Johann Sebastian Bachs*; Yoshitake Kobayashi, ed., 1989), 207.
12. Berlin State Library, *P 280*. Dating from Kaiser 2000, 312.
13. Schulze 1984, 159.

14. With the exception of Bach's Concerto in D Minor, BWV 596, which calls for a Brustpositiv and Oberwerk in the first movement (but Rückpositiv and Oberwerk in the last).

15. Wolff and Zepf 2012, 93.

16. Berlin State Library, *Mus.ms.22541 IV*. Dating from Beißwenger 1992b, 29.

17. *Johann Gottfried Walther: Briefe*, Klaus Beckmann and Hans-Joachim Schulze, eds. (Leipzig: Deutscher Verlag für Musik, 1987), 234. On September 19, 1740, Walther wrote to Heinrich Bokemeyer that "the lack of funds forces me to part with what is dear to me. Enclosed please find a detailed list of the various instrument pieces by various composers which I must sell, most of which are, with the necessary changes having been made, transcribed for keyboard. From these I will take away little more than the memory of much toil."

18. Klaus Beckmann, *Johann Gottfried Walther: Sämtliche Orgelwerke* (Wiesbaden: Breifkopf & Härtel, 1998), vol. 1, introduction, 7.

19. Forkel 1802, 23–24.

20. On this point see Hofmann 1995, 198–199.

21. Schulze 1972, 10.

22. On the infusion of new music, see Wolff 2000, 134.

23. An 1810 auction catalog in Erfurt lists "Telemann, Concerto appropriato all'organo di J. S. Bach, f-dur, geschr[ieben]." Beißwenger 1992a, 378–379.

24. This is most apparent in a passage such as mm. 37–42 and 45–47 of the third movement of the Concerto in C Minor after Benedetto Marcello, BWV 981, where dynamic changes from forte to piano appear in the midst of tied notes. The notated dynamics can only be realized on a clavichord.

25. Breig 1999, 668.

26. Hofmann 1995, 182–183.

27. The Roger firm was run from 1695–1716 by Estienne Roger (c. 1665–1722), then by his daughter Jeanne (1701–1722) from 1716–1722, and finally by Michel-Charles Le Cène (c. 1783–1743) from 1723–1743. Rasch 1996, 89.

28. Rasch 1996, 118.

29. Amsterdam and Halle have been discussed earlier as distribution points. Bach's Weimar student Philipp David Kräuter, in a letter to his patrons dated December 1, 1712, describes obtaining new music from "one of the other courts." BDok V, B 54a.

30. *Dr. Burney's Musical Tours in Europe*, Percy A. Scholes, ed. (London: Oxford University Press, 1959), vol. 2, 185.

31. Rudolf Rasch, in Rasch 1996, 105, suggests that RV 208a is the earlier version, composed by 1712–1713, and that RV 208 represents Vivaldi's second thoughts on the work.

32. Turin, Biblioteca Nazionale Universitaria, *Giordano 29*, fols. 167–181. Vivaldi's autograph was first described by Peter Ryom in "La comparaison entre les versions différentes d'un concerto d'Antonio Vivaldi transcript par J. S. Bach," *Dansk Aarborg for Musikforskning* 5 (1966–67), 91–111.

33. Schwerin, Landesbibliothek Mecklenburg-Vorpommern Günther Uecker, *Mus. 5565*. On the scribe see NBA IV/8, KB (Karl Heller, ed. 1980), 48.

34. *Il gran Mogol* by Domenico Lalli. The concerto might have been played as an intermezzo during a production of one of the operas using the libretto. See Michael Talbot, *The Vivaldi Companion* (Woodbridge, Suffolk, UK: Boydell Press, 2011), 92.

35. Tagliavini 1986, 245–248.

36. Composers appear to have notated secco recitatives with long notes because it was quicker and easier than writing quarter notes and rests. It also allowed the musicians greater freedom to determine how much accompanimental support was needed for a particular performance. Bach's transcription of Vivaldi's "Grave-Recitativo" movement is an important performance practice document, showing his approach to the unwritten convention.

37. Eller 1957, 83–84.

38. Insertion arias were written by Haydn (the duet "Quel cor umano e tenero," for Anna Morichelli and Giovanni Morelli), Mozart (the aria "Alma grande e nobil core," K 578, for Louise Villeneuve), and many other composers. See "On Aria Insertion: Satirists, Insiders, Singers, and Composers," in Hilary Poriss, *Changing the Score: Arias, Prima Donnas, and the Authority of Performance* (New York: Oxford University Press, 2009), 15–24.

39. Cividale del Friuli, Archivio Capitolare, without signature no., described in Grattoni 1983. The beginning and end of the Cividale cadenza are similar to that of the Schwerin cadenza, but the middle section is different.

40. Dresden, Saxon State Library, *Cx 1062 = 2389/0/94*, in a set of parts for Vivaldi's Concerto in D Major for Violin, 2 Oboes, 2 Horns, Strings, and Continuo. Cited in Eller 1957, 83.

41. The Schwerin text is reproduced, together with that of the first-movement cadenza, in NBA IV/8, KB, 100–104.

42. Grattoni 1983, 17.

43. Eberhard Preussner, *Die musicalischen Reisen des Herrn von Uffenbach* (Kassel: Bärenreiter, 1949), 67. Translation from Michael Talbot, *Vivaldi* (New York: Schirmer Books, 1992), 42.

44. Fischer 1915, 28.

45. *P 400b* in the Berlin State Library, written by Johann Friedrich Agricola between 1738 and 1741. The abbreviation "O. plen." surely indicates "Oberwerk pleno," not "Organo pleno" as interpreted in the Peters Edition and Neue Bach-Ausgabe.

46. Friedemann was given or inherited his father's autograph manuscript, *P 330* in the Berlin State Library, and wrote at the top "di W. F. Bach, manu mei Patris descript." (by W. F. Bach, written down by my father; see plate 9-1). The manuscript itself dates from c. 1714–1716, when Friedemann was four to six years old.

47. Wolff 2000, 126.

48. In the inclusion of a recitative movement in the Concerto in D Minor, op. 1, no. 4 (borrowed from Grosso Mogul Concerto) and the rapid alternation of two solo violins and tutti in ritornello of the first movement of the lost model for BWV 984 and 595 (borrowed from the first-movement ritornello of the Concerto in A Minor, RV 522, from *L'Estro armonico*, mm. 39–42).

49. Christoph Wolff has pointed to occasional undesignated payments to Bach from the treasury of the Red Palace, however, as possible evidence that Bach provided the Prince with private instruction. See Wolff 2000, 176.

50. Spitta 1873–80, vol. 1, 415–416; NBA IV/8, KB, 76, and NBA V/11, KB (Karl Heller, ed., 1997), 121–122.

51. Schulenberg 2006, 136; Sackmann 2003, 138–140.

52. The concerto is preserved in two sets of parts from the first half of the eighteenth century. The most important set, Rostock, Wilhelm Pieck University Library, *Musica Saec. XVIII, 66.*[39], was written by a number of copyists, including Johann Döbernitz, who was active as a tenor at the Weimar Court from 1713–1716. Döbernitz's hand also appears in the performance parts of Cantatas 172, 21, 199, and 185 from 1714–1715. See NBA IV/8, KB, 64, and NBA IX/3 (*Die Kopisten Johann Sebastian Bachs: Katalog und Dokumentation*, Yoshitake Kobayashi and Kirsten Beisswenger, eds., 2007), 5.

53. The score is reproduced in full in NBA IV/8, KB, 105–122.

54. His copies of the Johann Ernst transcriptions and the Grosso Mogul transcription are extant; the others are lost. See NBA IV/8, KB, 26, 34, 44, 61, and 74.

55. Kittel owned copies of the three Vivaldi arrangements, BWV 593, 594, 596, and the lost Telemann transcription, BWV[3] 1168. See NBA IV/8, KB, 34, 47, 26, and Beißwenger 1992a, 378–379.

56. W. F. Bach: Leipzig, University Library, *N.I. 5138* (BWV 594); Agricola: Berlin State Library, *P 400b* (BWV 593) and *P 400c* (BWV 594).

57. Dating proposed by Peter Wollny, cited by Pieter Dirksen in the Breitkopf Edition, vol. 5, 25.

58. It is noteworthy that Friedemann's copy of the Grosso Mogul Concerto (Leipzig University Library, *N.I. 5138*) and his copy of the Six Sonatas (Berlin State Library, P 272) appear on the same type of paper, one bearing the middle-sized MA watermark from 1727 to 1731 (NBA IX/1 [*Katalog der Wasserzeichen in Bachs Originalhandschriften*, Wisso Weiss and Yoshitake Kobayashi, eds., 1985], no. 122). This implies a close chronological proximity.

59. See n. 46.

60. Ferdinand Roitzsch, Peters Edition, vol. 8, i.

61. Johannes Schreyer, *Beiträge zur Bach-Kritik*, vol. 2 (Leipzig: Carl Merseburger, 1913), 23. Schreyer's term was "erbärmliche Leierkasten-Dudelei."

62. Keller 1967, 85.

63. Bach created a very similar effect in the opening section of the Concerto in D Minor, BWV 596, by inserting a new line moving in contrary motion into the end of the cello solo (mm. 30–32).

64. NBR, no. 343.

65. The exchanges between Scheibe and Bach's defenders Johann Abraham Birnbaum, Lorenz Christoph Mizler, and Christoph Gottlieb Schröter are reprinted in NBR, nos. 343–348.

66. Eller 1957, 85.

67. See the chapter "Schubert, Goethe, and the Development of the Nineteenth-Century Lied," in Lorraine Byrne, *Schubert's Goethe Settings* (Burlington, VT: Ashgate, 2003), 25–56.

10

Large Chorale Settings

The large chorale settings of the Weimar period stand at the very heart of Bach's accomplishments as a Lutheran church organist. Unlike the small but seminal pieces of the Orgel-Büchlein, they do not signify a new type of organ chorale. They represent instead the fertile extension of traditional chorale-preluding practices, brought forward by new means in a highly refined way. It is not surprising that Reincken praised Bach's chorale improvisation in the famous 1720 Hamburg encounter. And it is equally significant that when Bach began to consider his place in the long musical history of the Bach family, in Leipzig in the 1730s and 1740s, he turned to the large, retrospective chorale settings from the Weimar years to create a collection of his favorite organ works.

The large Weimar settings brought the "first fruits" of the Arnstadt and Mühlhausen years to full maturity. Bach continued to have an eye on Central and North German models of chorale elaboration, but he now interpreted the existing prototypes in his own way, in a unique musical language developed from a rich blend of increasingly disciplined part-writing and new musical elements from Italy and France. Several specific factors account for the change in his chorale settings:

1) The use of an increasingly integrated musical fabric, with attractive motives that generate both unified contrapuntal textures and well-rounded florid melodies. Musical motives no longer simply "spin out" in a conventional way; they now have distinctive, appealing rhythmic and melodic profiles that give each work a stamp of individuality. And strict part-writing becomes the norm.

2) The expansion of forms through the use of (a) Italianate harmonic schemes with compelling sequences and distinct harmonic stations, and (b) the repetition of large segments of material in transposed form, often with voice-exchange to create variety.

3) The appropriation of the Italian instrumental trio, with two treble parts and continuo bass, for chorale trios performed "à 2. Clavier et Pedal."

4) The reduction or elimination of digressive sections found in North German works, especially the chorale fantasia, and the creation of more homogeneous settings with highly unified structures. The use of short, contrasting sections, seen in Bach's North German–oriented Mühlhausen cantatas, gives way to

J. S. BACH. George B. Stauffer, Oxford University Press. © Oxford University Press 2024.
DOI: 10.1093/oso/9780195108026.003.0011

fully rounded, fully integrated movements, seen in Bach's Italian-oriented Weimar cantatas.

5) The use of French style mainly for special colorings: ornamentation, *style brisé* passages, and tierce-en-taille settings.

6) The gradual replacement of localized effects (the sudden, brief appearance of chromaticism in "O Lamm Gottes, unschuldig," BWV 656a, or "Jesus Christus, unser Heiland," BWV 665a) with a single general *affect* (the rushing wind in "Fantasia super Komm, heiliger Geist, Herre Gott," BWV 651a, or the ubiquitous turning motive in "Trio super Herr Jesu Christ, dich zu uns wend," BWV 655a).

The result of these measures was an updating and reimagining of the conventional *pedaliter* chorale prelude. Later, in Leipzig, Bach singled out his favorite Weimar settings by choosing them for inclusion in a chorale portfolio, the "Great Eighteen" Collection. We will discuss his revision of those select works in chapter 25, but it is important to first view them in their original Weimar context, among pieces that were not chosen for the Leipzig portfolio. Only then can one fully appreciate the extraordinary accomplishment that they represent.

Fore-imitation Settings

The element of individuality is striking even in Bach's fore-imitation chorales, perhaps the most traditional type of Central German chorale setting. Each work displays a conscious effort to reinterpret Pachelbel's basic fore-imitation template, in which the chorale melody is divided into individual phrases, with each phrase preceded by a web of imitative counterpoint based on a motive that foreshadows it. Bach's six Weimar settings show a concentrated effort to try something new:

Jesus Christus, unser Heiland, der von uns den Gotteszorn wand, BWV 665a
Jesus Christus, unser Heiland, der von uns den Gotteszorn wand, alio modo,
  BWV 666a
Komm, heiliger Geist, Herre Gott, BWV 652a
Nun danket alle Gott, BWV 657
Fantasia super Schmücke dich, o liebe Seele, BWV 654a
Valet will ich dir geben, BWV 736

The two earliest fore-imitation settings may be the arrangements of "Jesus Christus, unser Heiland," BWV 665a and 666a, which are consistently handed down as a pair in the early sources, with BWV 666a labeled "alio modo" or "auf andere Art"—in another manner.

In **"Jesus Christus, unser Heiland,"** BWV 665a, the four phrases of Luther's chorale unfold in the same way, but with different figuration in each case. The fore-imitation begins with a motive in the tenor based on the upcoming chorale phrase, accompanied by a countermotive in invertible counterpoint. The main motive appears next in the alto and then, in unadorned quarter and half notes, in the pedal. This entry, which constitutes the cantus firmus voice, is followed by the main motive in the soprano and a short coda, in four parts. Thus for each phrase of the chorale, the cantus firmus is decorated by fore- and after-imitation, with all entries accompanied by the countermotive.[1]

The countermotive of the third phrase (mm. 27–38) is a chromatic descending scale that is immediately presented against itself in contrary motion, creating a sense of anguish and tension to highlight the line of Luther's 1524 text, "durch das bitter Leiden" (through [Christ's] bitter suffering). In the one-measure coda (m. 37) the texture expands to five parts—descending parallel sixths against ascending parallel thirds over a pedal point on G. This passage is quite similar to the climactic portrayal of "sonst müsten wir verzagen" (otherwise we would have to despair) in "O Lamm Gottes, unschultig," BWV 656a. In the fourth and final phrase, the writing becomes more animated, with the addition of 32nd-note figuration. And in the last three measures the texture thickens to five, six, seven, and finally eight parts.

The part-writing of this first setting of "Jesus Christus, unser Heiland" is not fully disciplined (the roles of the bass and tenor are not clear), and Bach soon abandoned the technique of treating each phrase of a chorale with a different *affect*—a North German custom. The piece makes a striking impression, however, when played as indicated, "in pleno Organo."[2] Philipp Spitta viewed it as one of Bach's "grandest creations": "how profound is the impression produced each time, when, after the entrance of the cantus firmus, the melody is repeated in the upper part!"[3]

The second setting, **"Jesus Christus, unser Heiland,"** alio modo, BWV 666a, is a dance variation of the first setting, somewhat in the manner of a chorale partita set. The 12/8 meter and gigue-like opening motive (slurred ♪♪♪ in Johann Gottfried Walther's Weimar copy)[4] confirm the piece's dance roots. Here each line of the chorale is treated differently, in sections separated by *passaggio* interludes, much like those in a congregational chorale. In line 1, the fore-imitation is carried out in the lower voices with stretto entries of a motive derived from the first phrase of the chorale. The appearance of the cantus firmus in the soprano is marked "Choral" in the manuscript sources.

For line 2, the motive from phrase 1 is inverted and presented in stretto once again. But now the soprano cantus firmus is foreshadowed in the tenor, which presents the chorale melody note for note. In line 3, the fore-imitation is provided by a 16th-note motive, in normal and inverted forms, that seems to spring naturally from the earlier *passaggio* bridges. Once again the tenor presents the cantus firmus before the soprano entry. In the final phrase, the longest and most elaborate of the setting's four sections, the fore-imitation continues to be generated by the 16th-note motive. But the cantus firmus is foreshadowed not only in the tenor, once again, but also in the alto and bass, before it finally sounds in the soprano. This leads to a closing section consisting of a free *passaggio* (marked with right- and left-hand designations in Walther's score) followed by *style brisé* chords over a pedal point, much like the conclusion of the Fugue from the Toccata in C Major, BWV 564. The metamorphosis of the dance figuration in this setting is attractive, and the gradual increase in note motion as well as cantus firmus foreshadowing helps to make up for the somewhat rigid, sectionalized structure.

Jean-Claude Zehnder assigns the second arrangement of "Jesus Christus" (BWV 666a) to Bach's Arnstadt tenure, c. 1706, on the basis of its early counterpoint, and the first arrangement (BWV 665a) to Bach's Mühlhausen stay, c. 1708, on the basis of its similarity to the Mühlhausen cantatas.[5] But the two settings seem to have been written simultaneously as an "alio modo" pair, with the quarter-note cantus firmus of the first setting related to the dotted-quarter-note cantus firmus of the second. Both pieces may well be a product of the Arnstadt years, when invention still outweighed unity in Bach's writing.

In "**Komm, heiliger Geist, Herre Gott,**" BWV 652a, Bach pursued a more homogeneous approach to fore-imitation writing. The setting is much earlier than the "Fantasia super Komm, heiliger Geist, Herre Gott," BWV 651a, and unlike that work includes all nine phrases of Luther's Pentecostal hymn. Moreover, each phrase is presented in the same way: the fore-imitation appears first in the tenor, then the alto, and finally in the pedal before the cantus firmus, replete with French embellishments, appears in the soprano on a second manual. The note-motion in the pedal generally accelerates beneath the cantus firmus, rounding out each phrase. The work concludes, after 180 measures, with an animated 13-bar coda based on a 16th-note motive derived from the rising fourth of the closing "Hallelujah" of the chorale. It is quite analogous to the "Hallelujah" coda of the tenor aria (versus 3) of Cantata 4, *Christ lag in Todesbanden*, written in Mühlhausen or early Weimar. Both reflect the North German practices of Buxtehude and Böhm.

The uniform treatment of the fore-imitation sections and the profuse French ornamentation of "Komm, heiliger Geist" point to the early Weimar years, perhaps during the period of Bach's encounter with French keyboard music. The leisurely pace of the 3/4 sarabande idiom and the Brucknerian proportions of the work make it one of Bach's longest chorale settings—Peter Williams termed it "mesmeric."[6] Bach went to great lengths to unify the cadences for phrases 2, 3, and 7 when revising it for the Leipzig chorale portfolio, to give it greater cohesion still (see chapter 25). The treatment of all nine phrases of the chorale may have spurred him to do likewise in the great expansion of its companion piece, the "Fantasia super Komm, heiliger Geist," BWV 651a, many years later.

"**Nun danket alle Gott**," BWV 657, for two manuals and pedal and with "Canto fermo in Soprano," is ostensibly an animated version of "Komm, heiliger Geist," BWV 652a, since every entry of the cantus firmus (here in unadorned half notes) is preceded by a web of three-part fore-imitation. But the idiom is very different, and the setting shows an inventiveness that goes far beyond the Pachelbel model. The fore-imitation is subject to various types of stretto from the start; the pedal acts like an instrumental continuo when it is not presenting pre-imitation motives; and the accompanimental fabric is filled with constantly changing motives that are tossed back and forth between the middle voices (such as the *suspirans* figures that suddenly pop up in measures 39–41 and 46–48).[7] As with both "Jesus Christus, unser Heiland" settings, the writing becomes more animated at the close, with a continuous stream of 16th notes taking over the accompaniment. In this case, the conclusion evolves naturally from the final phrase of the chorale melody, since its last note becomes the sustained pedal tone that closes the work.

The instrumental idiom of "Nun danket" resembles that of the Orgel-Büchlein chorales, but the setting lacks their refined motivic and rhythmic integration. Still, Bach must have had a high opinion of the work, for he entered it into the "Great Eighteen" Collection with very little change—the only setting, in fact, admitted without noticeable revision.

The "**Fantasia super Schmücke dich, o liebe Seele**," BWV 654a, represents yet another stage of Bach's engagement with the fore-imitation chorale. His use of the term "Fantasia," which he removed from this and two other Weimar settings,[8] when he revised them for the Leipzig portfolio, seems to refer not to the free idiom of the *stylus fantasticus* but rather to the development of good ideas, as in the three-part Fantasias, BWV 787–801, in the Clavier-Büchlein for Wilhelm Friedemann Bach of 1720, whose titles Bach subsequently changed as well.[9]

We might call the fore-imitation of "Schmücke dich" "imitative homophony," since it is suffused with "sweet" parallel thirds and sixths that make it sound more homophonic than polyphonic. The initial motive is developed from a rich embellishment of the first phrase of the chorale, and toward the end of the setting it is recapitulated, first in the dominant, in parallel thirds (m. 78), and then in the tonic, in parallel sixths (m. 82; example 10-1). So transformed is the accompanimental material that it seems more like an aria duet accompanied by continuo bass than fore-imitation. The cantus firmus is embellished with French ornaments, once again.

Example 10-1 "Schmücke dich, o liebe Seele," BWV 654a: (a) first phrase of the chorale melody, (b) fore-imitation motive derived from it, (c) return of fore-imitation motive in the dominant, and (d) return of fore-imitation motive in the tonic.

The key of "Schmücke dich," E♭ major, was described at the time by Johann Mattheson as "beautiful, majestic, and honest."[10] It was used sparingly for organ works because of the tuning systems then in use, which generally favored the sharp side of the scale. Yet Bach, in his setting, ventured still further into flat territory, touching on F minor (m. 23), A♭ major (m. 65), and B♭ minor (m. 74). It may have been these adventurous harmonic excursions that prompted Schumann to characterize the setting as "priceless, deep, and [as] full of soul as any piece of music that ever sprang from a true artist's imagination" in his review of Mendelssohn's historic benefit concert in the St. Thomas Church in 1840.[11] The soprano aria "Tief gebückt und voller Reue" (Deeply bowed and filled with sorrow) from Cantata 199, *Mein Herze schwimmt im Blut*, of c. 1712–13, displays the same key, meter, and sarabande idiom as "Schmücke dich."[12] It is marked "Andante," which is probably the appropriate tempo for the organ setting.

The last fore-imitation setting, **"Valet will ich dir geben," BWV 736**, with the "Choral in Pedal," is a large and impressive work that Bach nevertheless did not select for the Leipzig portfolio. It appears in a single anonymous copy from c. 1750,[13] and then reemerges fifty years later in the manuscripts of two Kittel students, Johann Nicolaus Gebhardi and Johann Andreas Dröbs, and an anonymous Breitkopf copyist.[14] Its idiom is that of an animated instrumental gigue in 24/16 meter, an exotic time signature that Bach used against 4/4 and 12/8 in the Orgel-Büchlein chorale "Herr Gott, nun schleuß den Himmel auf," BWV 617.

Bach's treatment of fore-imitation technique here is more unorthodox than in any other large Weimar setting. The piece begins with a lengthy soprano theme that paraphrases lines 1 and 2 of the chorale melody (example 10-2). The theme is suffused with a catchy six-note motive (example 10-2, x) that is quickly echoed in an imitative dialogue in the alto and tenor. This dense web of polyphony leads to the appearance of the cantus firmus in the pedal, in lengthy dotted half notes. Phrase 2 of the Stollen continues in much the same way.

Bach maintained this procedure in the Abgesang, first presenting a paraphrase of line 5 of the chorale in the alto, echoed freely by animated motives in the tenor and soprano. The paraphrase theme and its accompanying voices all rise upward, in the manner of the inversion that normally takes place in the second half of a gigue in binary form. The seminal six-note motive returns for line 6 of the chorale in inverted form (m. 24), as the melody is paraphrased once again in the alto. Lines 7 and 8 are also preceded by segments of fore-imitation, but the references to the chorale become more and more vague. It is as if the rollicking triplets take over the piece, to the point of overruling the fore-imitation process. And the piece ends on a single 16th note, much like the trailing off of the soprano solo at the end of the section "Es ist der alte Bund" of Cantata 106, *Gottes Zeit ist die allerbeste Zeit*, of c. 1707–1708, or the quiet conclusion (two recorders, only) of the opening chorus "Gott is mein König" of Cantata 71 of 1708.

"Valet will ich dir geben" is a highly innovative work—perhaps the most path-breaking of the Weimar fore-imitation settings—and the opening six-note motive is impressively developed in various forms: upright, inverted, modified, extended. The piece also has remarkable vigor and rhythmic drive. But strangely, the writing seems more mechanical than musical, perhaps because the six-note

Example 10-2 "Valet will ich dir geben," BWV 736: first phrase of the chorale and fore-imitation motive derived from it.

motive does not evolve in a natural way, and the accompaniment is neither fish
nor fowl—that is, it is neither readily recognizable fore-imitation nor a tightly
knit fabric, as in Orgel-Büchlein settings. "Valet will ich dir geben" resembles
many North German settings: technically impressive, but emotionally un-
moving. It may be for this reason that Bach left it on the shelf in Leipzig when he
selected Weimar pieces for his portfolio of favorite chorale settings.

Florid-Melody Settings

In Weimar Bach also focused on the florid-melody chorale—a setting for two
manuals and pedal, "à 2 Clavier et Pedal," with the hymn tune played in an
adorned fashion on one keyboard, highlighted by a solo stop or solo combination, and the accompaniment played on a second keyboard and pedal. Here
Bach could turn for inspiration to Buxtehude, whose 47 chorale settings include 31 florid-melody arrangements. Of these, 27 are written for four voices
with the hymn tune in the soprano. Bach would have known "Es ist das Heil, uns
kommen her," BuxWV 186, "Vater unser im Himmelreich," BuxWV 219, and
other illustrative models, either from his stay in Lüneburg with Böhm or from
manuscript copies in Walther's possession. And as was the case with canonic
chorales and concerto transcriptions, it seems that Walther and Bach worked in
friendly competition as they composed florid-melody settings, since several of
Walther's arrangements appear side-by-side with Bach's in the chorale collection
assembled in Weimar by Walther and Johann Tobias Krebs.[15]

In reimagining Buxtehude's favorite chorale-prelude genre, Bach strove to
give the embellished hymn tune a more carefully calculated shape and the
accompaniment a greater degree of unity and contrapuntal substance. This
resulted in florid-melody chorales that were less spontaneous than the works of
his predecessors but more musically compelling, as can be seen in the six large
settings from the Weimar years:

Liebster Jesu, wir sind hier, BWV 731
Herr Jesu Christ, dich zu uns wend, BWV 709
An Wasserflüssen Babylon, BWV 653b
An Wasserflüssen Babylon, BWV 653a
Allein Gott in der Höh sei Ehr, BWV 662a
Fantasia super Nun komm der Heiden Heiland, BWV 659a

What appears to be the earliest piece, **"Liebster Jesu, wir sind hier," BWV 731,**
is handed down as a two-manual "alio modo" variant to the more straightforward
one-manual cantus-firmus setting of the same chorale, BWV 730 (see below). In

the most important early source, a Kittel-derived manuscript from 1803,[16] BWV 730 and 731 appear side-by-side with a set of Orgel-Büchlein chorales. This may not be a coincidence, since both "Liebster Jesu" arrangements have Orgel-Büchlein qualities: strict four-part writing, no pauses between phrases of the chorale, and rhythmically animated accompaniment. The florid-melody setting, BWV 731, seems to be a spinoff of the first *Abgesang* phrase of BWV 730 (mm. 6–7), where the soprano melody suddenly takes flight with a flurry of ornaments and diminutions before returning to placid quarter notes.

In BWV 731 the ornaments and diminutions are transformed into a florid melody that becomes increasingly melismatic as the piece progresses. The accompaniment consists of a continuo-like pedal part and two nonthematic manual voices that serve as a rhythmic foil to the soprano melody: when the melody moves to 16th- and 32nd-note flourishes, the manual accompaniment slows to 8th notes; when the melody moves to simple quarter notes (mm. 3 and 7), the accompaniment accelerates to 16th notes. This creates a sense of ongoing rhythmic momentum, but it also gives the setting a certain mechanical quality, with the left-hand parts acting as contrapuntal fill rather than foreshadowing or reinforcing motives in the florid melody. The inventive embellishments of the chorale tune make this arrangement of "Liebster Jesu" effective (it is sometimes played as an encore, in modern times), but it lacks the finely nuanced integration of solo and accompaniment found in later settings.

"Herr Jesu Christ, dich zu uns wend," BWV 709, also exhibits early qualities. While it does not appear in the Walther-Krebs collection, a copy made by Anonymous X in the early 1740s[17] confirms that Bach valued it sufficiently to use it for teaching purposes in Leipzig. It is also transmitted in a Christian Friedrich Penzel manuscript that contains additional ornamentation.[18] Musically, "Herr Jesu Christ, dich zu uns wend" is short, concise, and intense—that is, Orgel-Büchlein-like. But here the phrases of the chorale melody are separated by short, half-measure pauses, and the accompaniment consists of several independent motives, loosely developed. The florid melody is permeated by a turning figure, derived from the opening manual accompaniment, that seems to echo the plea of the chorale's text: "Lord Jesus Christ, turn to us." The melodic phrases are also nicely rounded: each is framed by long notes and moves to a sweeping flourish just before the concluding cadence, much like the phrases in "Nun komm der Heiden Heiland," BWV 659a.

The accompaniment is less cohesive. The initial nine measures are devoted to the imitative treatment of the turning figure and its distinctive rhythm ♫ ♫♫ (transformed in the pedal to ♫♫ ♪). But this soon yields to the development of more conventional motives: the slurred second (ascending, m. 11, and descending, m. 16), the *suspirans* (m. 13), and the *corta* (mm. 8–9, 11–14, and 17–19). The animation of the accompaniment reminds one of the

Orgel-Büchlein, but the multiplicity of motives, not fully coordinated, suggests that this is an earlier effort.

"An Wasserflüssen Babylon" is a chorale with a Hamburg history, as Bach surely knew from his youthful trips to the city during his Lüneburg years. Wolfgang Dachstein's 1525 setting of Psalm 137, "By the Waters of Babylon," was a particular favorite of Hamburg organists, who in accordance with a long tradition improvised on the melody during the Saturday Vespers service. Matthias Weckmann treated it "fugally and through all transpositions" during his successful audition for the organist position at St. James' Church in 1655,[19] and Reincken wrote his enormous fantasy on the tune, copied by Bach in Böhm's home in 1700, to demonstrate his worthiness to succeed Heinrich Scheidemann as organist of the St. Catherine's Church in 1663.[20] And it was on "An Wasserflüssen Babylon" that Bach improvised for "almost a half hour" during his audition in St. Catherine's before Reincken and town officials in 1720, to show that he, too, had the "right stuff" to enter into Hamburg's circle of elite organists (see chapter 14). It is no surprise, then, that Bach devoted special attention to his only written-down arrangement of the chorale,[21] an extravagant piece in North German style (BWV 653b) that he subsequently revised twice, first in Weimar (BWV 653a) and then in Leipzig (BWV 653).[22]

In the initial setting, "An Wasserflüssen Babylon," BWV 653b, "à 5 con 2 Clavier e doppio Pedale," Bach paid homage to Buxtehude's florid-melody style but went beyond it by adding a second pedal part, "a la Tunder," to thicken the traditional four-voice texture to five parts. The double pedal gave the setting a distinctly North German stamp. The sarabande idiom (3/4 meter, with recurring accents on the second beat), also appearing in "Komm, heiliger Geist, Herre Gott," BWV 652a, and "Schmücke dich, o liebe Seele," BWV 654a, is especially appropriate here, since it helps to create a somber "dance of mourning," analogous to the final choruses of the St. John and St. Matthew Passions. In converting the music of the chorale from its traditional duple meter to triple meter, Bach was able to preserve the iambic character of Dachstein's poetry by positioning the florid melody so that the accents of the text aligned with the accents of the sarabande, which shift from the second beat to the first beat in alternate measures (example 10-3).

The decorated chorale tune, assigned to the right hand, is accompanied by dense four-part counterpoint, evenly distributed between the left hand and the feet. The accompaniment is based on two themes that appear in one form or another in 68 of the setting's 77 measures. Derived from phrases 1 and 2 of the chorale (example 10-3, x and y), the motives sometimes appear back-to-back in one long phrase that anticipates the decorated chorale melody (mm. 1–8, 12–20) or marks the arrival of a new key in the fashion of a ritornello (mm. 43–50, D major, then E major; mm. 58–65, A minor). Elsewhere the motives appear as

Example 10-3 "An Wasserflüssen Babylon," BWV 654b: first two phrases of the chorale and fore-imitation motives derived from them, with poetic accents marked.

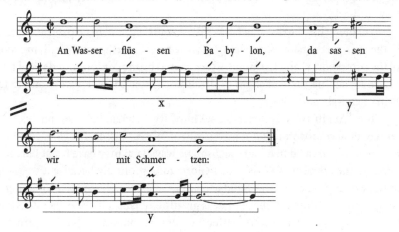

counterpoint against the hymn tune (mm. 43–50, 65–69). In still other spots, the motives are juxtaposed during the course of interludes (mm. 27–33, 61–65). Repeated, superimposed, and manipulated in inventive ways, the motives take on the role, as Werner Breig has expressed it, of a "litany-like lament," constantly intoned against the decorated chorale.[23]

Not long after composing the five-part version of "An Wasserflüssen Babylon," Bach had further thoughts. While still in Weimar he returned to the piece and thoroughly revamped it, eliminating the double pedal by consolidating the two parts into a single line that reduced the texture of the setting to a more modern four-voice idiom but also impoverished the harmony of the original here and there. At the same time, he transferred the decorated melody from the soprano to the tenor, in essence transforming the piece from a retrospective North German florid-melody chorale into a fashionable French tierce-en-taille verset. He also changed details of the embellished chorale and the accompanimental motives, giving each a more distinctive rhythmic profile.[24]

The two versions of "An Wasserflüssen Babylon," BWV 653b and 653a, appear side-by-side in Walther's Weimar manuscript,[25] with the general title "vers. 1 à 5 con 2 Clav: è doppio pedale / vers. 2 à 4 con 2 Clav. è Simp. Ped:" and the heading "alio modo à 4" for the second version inside the score.[26] The two settings are passed down as a pair with the same labels in Johann Gottlieb Preller's early copy as well,[27] raising the possibility that Bach himself viewed the new version as an "alio modo" variation of the original, rather than a "distinctus" revision of it, in the fashion of "Liebster Jesu, wir sind hier," BWV 633 and 634, in the Orgel-Büchlein (see chapter 8). In other words, the two arrangements may have been conceived as equals, rather than one serving as a replacement for the other, suggesting, perhaps, that modern performers should consider playing the two back-to-back.

No matter what the case, Bach was still not satisfied, and in Leipzig he returned to the four-part version, sharpening its rhythms still further and rectifying some of the contrapuntal and harmonic issues caused by the compromised pedal part. We will examine these changes in detail in chapter 25, when we examine the Leipzig chorale portfolio.

While "Allein Gott, in der Höh sei Ehr," BWV 662a, has the same rich interplay of accompanimental motives as "An Wasserflüssen Babylon," the chorale melody is treated in a more melismatic way. Bach may have felt at liberty to decorate the Nicolaus Decius's 1523 Gloria tune profusely because it was sung in the worship service every Sunday and hence extremely familiar to Lutheran congregations. Although the chorale is greatly embellished, the original melody is nevertheless clear in Bach's setting because its main notes fall on principal beats. The melismas are written not in a vocal manner but rather in an instrumental style, much like the oboe solo of the Sinfonia to Cantata 12, *Weinen, Klagen, Sorgen, Zagen*, or the oboe and violin duet of the Sinfonia to Cantata 21, *Ich hatte viel Bekümmernis*, which both conclude with short, temporarily disruptive cadenzas involving diminished seventh chords, similar to the close of "Allein Gott." The two vocal works date from 1714 (or possibly December 1713, for Cantata 21), Bach's first year of cantata-writing in Weimar; "Allein Gott" probably predates that somewhat.

The accompaniment of "Allein Gott" is dominated by a principal motive (example 10-4, x) derived from the opening phrase of the chorale and richly decorated with French *cheutes* (or *ports de voix en descendant*), which may reflect Bach's infatuation with French keyboard music and *agréments* around 1709–1712. This motive is accompanied by a countermotive (example 10-4, y) that contains the rising 4th of the first and second phrases of the Stollen of the chorale. As with the themes of "An Wasserflüssen Babylon," the motive and countermotive appear in a vast number of forms: with x preceding y (mm. 1–2); with x preceding y with the parts exchanged (mm. 3–4); with x, simplified for the pedal, preceding y (mm. 5–6); with y preceding x (mm. 6-7), and so forth. The pedal often presents an unembellished version of the main motive as well as the rising fourth of the countermotive, and it cites the fifth phrase of the chorale as a type of fore-imitation to the Abgesang (mm. 17–19).

There are also elements of cyclical unification in the "Allein Gott" setting: the manual accompaniment that sets the stage for the first phrase of the Stollen (mm. 4–6) returns in more embellished form to prepare for the first phrase of the Abgesang (mm. 17–20). Bach was apparently very proud of this setting, with its eclectic combination of national styles—French (the ornamentation),

Example 10-4 "Allein Gott in der Höh sei Ehr," BWV 662a: (a) first and fifth phrases of the chorale and primary (x) and secondary (y) fore-imitation motives derived from them, and (b) the two fore-imitation motives combined in invertible counterpoint.

Italian (the instrumental treatment of the melismas), Central German (the fore-imitation), and North German (florid melody and concluding cadenza)—and chose it, too, for inclusion in the Leipzig portfolio.

The "**Fantasia super Nun komm der Heiden Heiland,**" **BWV 659a**, represents the culmination of Bach's Weimar florid-melody chorales. Going beyond "An Wasserflüssen Babylon," "Allein Gott in der Höh sei Ehr," and "O Mensch, bewein dein Sünde groß" from the Orgel-Büchlein, it displays new elements of unity, balance, and refinement.

It is grounded by a walking bass that binds the imitative manual accompaniment to the solo flourishes above it. Derived from Italian instrumental practice, the bass serves as a quasi ostinato, with a theme—the rising and falling scale established in the opening measure—that returns to mark the arrival of critical tonal areas: G minor (m. 8), B♭ major (m. 16), and C minor (m. 24). Its continuous chain of 8th notes creates a hypnotic effect quite unlike the bass of any previous chorale setting. The manual accompaniment consists of motives that foreshadow each phrase of the chorale, much in the fashion of fore-imitation. But the motives seem to have a melodic and symbolic life of their own, giving the interludes independent weight. The fore-imitation preceding the final phrase of the chorale, for instance, is based on a motive that features rising and falling seconds (mm. 25–27). The seconds foreshadow the falling second of the chorale melody, but when repeated extensively they also portray the teary sadness over the journey that Christ must take for humankind "below to hell and back to God's seat," as stated in Luther's 1524 text. The course of the harmony is equally subtle: a brush with Neapolitan harmony (m. 22) leads to C minor three bars later (mm. 25–28) for the start of the last phrase of the chorale. The movement to a new key, C minor, plus the appearance of a new motive, the weeping seconds, set up the return to old material, the reprise of the music from the opening phrase.

The embellished hymn tune is closer to violin writing than conventional keyboard figuration, which is reflected in the fact that it is notated in treble clef rather than the normal soprano clef used for the other florid-melody chorales. It is highly expressive, but in a carefully calculated way: each phrase starts slowly, then becomes more animated, and finally concludes with a rush of 32nd notes that ends in a dotted cadential figure that also serves as a unifying device. Luther's 1524 melody, derived from the Ambrosian hymn "Veni redemptor gentium," begins and ends with the same phrase. Bach took advantage of this repetition in his organ setting by bringing back the music—both florid melody and accompaniment—of the opening phrase for the closing phrase (mm. 28–31 = mm. 4–7). This creates a literal recapitulation that gives the arrangement a symmetry and balance that does not appear again in Bach's organ chorales until the ritornello settings of Clavier-Übung III and the Schübler Collection.

When the repeated material concludes the second time around, however, it cadences in G major rather than G minor (not unlike the surprising turn to C major at the end of the Passacaglia in C Minor), opening the door for a short coda. The coda, which features an extended melisma over a tonic pedal point, was surely a nod to the similar two-measure G-major close of Buxtehude's G-minor florid-melody setting of "Nun komm der Heiden Heiland," BuxWV 211. In Buxtehude's coda, the solo line begins with an expressive octave leap upward but then moves to a close with conventional organ figuration and harmony. Bach's florid melody, by contrast, begins with the same octave leap but then circles around a dissonant dominant-ninth chord, jumping upward and downward before ending with the setting's signature cadential figure (example 10-5).[28] The coda sounds dark and mysterious—almost mystical.

Nothing could better illustrate the great distance Bach had traveled from Buxtehude's florid-melody chorale than the coda of this work, with its very distinctive stamp. Bach may have felt he could do no better than this setting, for he did not compose additional florid-melody chorales in Cöthen or Leipzig. "Nun komm der Heiden Heiland" seems to have been his final word on the genre.

Example 10-5 "Nun komm der Heiden Heiland": (a) coda of Dieterich Buxtehude's organ setting, BuxWV 211, and (b) coda of Bach's organ setting, BWV 659a.

Chorale Trios

The improvisation and composition of chorale trios was a well-established tradition in Thuringia. Such settings were normally pieces modest in size, commonly featuring the hymn tune as a cantus firmus in the bass, accompanied by two imitative manual parts. In Weimar Bach transformed the chorale trio into something quite different: a lengthy, virtuosic work for two manuals and pedal, increasingly written in the style of an Italian trio sonata. Three large settings from Weimar show the remarkable evolution of his approach:

Wo soll ich fliehen hin, BWV 694
Trio super Herr Jesu Christ, dich zu uns wend, BWV 655a
Trio super Allein Gott in der Höh sei Ehr, BWV 664a

The earliest of the three, **"Wo soll ich fliehen hin,"** BWV 694, is not transmitted in sources from Bach's lifetime but stems rather from Breitkopf-derived manuscripts and a copy by Leonard Scholz in Nuremberg.[29] This provenance suggests that Bach may not have used the piece for teaching. Although the setting qualifies as a trio, with pedal cantus firmus and two independent manual parts played "con 2. Clav.," it has certain characteristics of a work for one manual and pedal: it is notated on two staves rather than three in the early manuscripts, and the hands never cross. The treble parts, notated in soprano rather than treble clef, show no signs of violin-writing and are not equal: the right hand takes the lead for most of the piece, with the left hand mirroring it in a lower range. Bach's concept of an organ trio with three completely independent parts does not seem to be fully formulated here.

The manual material has the semblance of an eight-measure, harmonically closed ritornello, which initially appears in the tonic (mm. 1–8) and dominant (mm. 17–24) but then never returns in full form. The freely derived ritornello theme (example 10–6), presented first in the right hand, is imitated by the left at the distance of one measure in a series of gradually widening intervals: lower 5th (mm. 1–2, 17–18, 34–35), lower octave (mm. 25–26), lower seventh (mm. 40–41), and lower ninth (mm. 48–49). The theme is inverted (mm. 12, 40, and 45) and varied (mm. 63 and 73) and finally presented in the left hand, without imitation, in highly embellished forms (mm. 73 and 87).

The incessant repetition of the ritornello's opening 16th-note motive and the constant presence of the syncopated figure ♪♩ ♪♩♫ (it occurs in 70 of the setting's 92 measures) successfully portray the frantic searching described in Johann Heermann's 1630 text: "where should I flee, for I am burdened with many and great sins? Where can I find rescue?" Although the two elements are deployed inventively, the result is a somewhat disjointed setting that lacks structural cohesion. The ritornello, which launches into a circle of fifths after just one

Example 10–6 "Wo soll ich fliehen hin," BWV 694: opening ritornello.

measure, never returns at the end to round out the structure, and the syncopation that appears throughout the setting often seems forced. When discussing fugue writing, Bach complained that pedantic composers wrote unsuccessful pieces because they failed to reanimate their fugue subjects with interludes.[30] That appears to be the problem here: there are no contrasting interludes to balance the ritornello material.

For this reason, perhaps, Bach did not include this bold experiment in imitative counterpoint in the "Great Eighteen" Chorales. The Schübler setting of "Wo soll ich fliehen hin," BWV 646, displays a more convincingly shaped ritornello and balanced interludes. And Bach returned to the issue of how to handle ongoing syncopation in the Clavier-Übung III setting of "Jesus Christus, unser Heiland," BWV 688, where he employed off-beat figures in a more artful way.

The "Trio super Herr Jesu Christ, dich zu uns wend," BWV 655a, represents a very different world of trio writing. The setting is now specifically termed a trio, and its instrumental roots are clear from Bach's notation: treble clefs for the two upper parts and bass clef for the bottom part, the standard for an Italian trio sonata with two violins and continuo. And for fifty-one measures, "Herr Jesu Christ" unfolds like a trio sonata, with a three-measure ritornello, derived from the chorale melody, alternating with episodic material. At that point, however, the chorale melody appears in full as a cantus firmus in the pedal, accompanied in the manuals by snippets of ritornello material. The result is a hybrid form— trio sonata followed by cantus firmus trio:

Portion/Mm.	Material	Harmonic station
Trio sonata		
1–3	Ritornello	I
4–6	Episode	
7–9	Ritornello, with upper parts exchanged	V
10–16	Episode	
17–19	Ritornello, with some parts transposed	vi
20–26	Episode	
27–29	Ritornello, embellished	iii
30–39	Episode	
39–42	Episode: ritornello fragment used as a sequence	
43–45	Ritornello, abridged	IV
45–51a	Episode	
Cantus firmus trio		
51b–73	Chorale as cantus firmus in the pedal, with fragments of the ritornello in the manuals	I

The coupling of genres resembles the hybrid opening movement of the Toccata in C Major, BWV 564, whose concerto portion shares a similar short-ritornello design inspired by the instrumental works of Torelli (see chapter 13). In "Herr Jesu Christ," the cantus firmus portion, in the home key of G major, fulfills the dual function of serving as the final ritornello segment of the sonata portion while also confirming for the listener that the setting is, indeed, based on "Herr Jesu Christ, dich zu uns wend,"[31] a popular hymn commonly sung before the sermon each week in Sunday services.[32]

The three-measure ritornello of the setting is a contrapuntal marvel. The main theme, initially played by the right hand, is composed of four motives, which we will label x, y, z, and y^e (an expanded, cadential form of y; example 10-7). The first motive, x, is derived from the first four notes of the first phrase chorale melody, and the third motive, z, from the last three notes. With its repeated turning, z is also a musical pun on the opening phrase of the hymn text: "Lord Jesus Christ, turn to us."[33] This theme is imitated by a countertheme in the left hand containing three of the same motives, but in different order: x, y^e, z. The theme and counter-theme are written in double counterpoint, which becomes evident when the ritornello returns in the dominant three bars later, where the two parts are exchanged. This contrapuntal material is accompanied by a pedal motive, which we will call a, which is a reduction of x. It is immediately repeated in an expanded, cadential form, a^e, much like the y motive of the main theme. The pedal theme returns, ostinato-like, with each appearance of the ritornello, confirming the arrival of a new harmonic station and, symbolically, repeating the appeal to Christ to "turn to us." Bach's miraculous counterpoint is well illustrated by this seemingly unassuming but astonishingly clever ritornello!

The **"Trio super Allein Gott in der Höh sei Ehr,"** BWV 664a, carries Bach's assimilation of the Italian trio sonata still further. As with the "Herr Jesu Christ"

Example 10-7 "Trio super Herr Jesu Christ, dich zu uns wend," BWV 655a: opening ritornello, with manual and pedal motives marked.

setting, it is notated like an Italian trio sonata—upper voices in treble clef, bottom voice in bass clef—and has the same hybrid format: trio sonata followed by cantus firmus trio, this time with the chorale abbreviated. There the similarity ends, however, for the material falls into three large sections: A (mm. 1–35), B (mm. 35–80), A' (mm. 80–96). The A section features the ritornello theme and counter-theme in the tonic (m. 1), dominant (m. 4), tonic (m. 10, with the theme in the pedal, in reduced form), and finally subdominant (m. 26). The B section features a long episodic segment (mm. 35–56), interrupted in the middle with a statement of the ritornello in F♯ minor (m. 44), and a varied repetition of the same episodic segment transposed down a fifth (mm. 57–80), with the upper parts exchanged. It is interrupted in the middle, once again, with a statement of the ritornello, this time in B minor (m. 65).

The recapitulation, A', begins with entries of the ritornello theme in the tonic (m. 80) and dominant (m. 83), as in A. But with the expected answer in the tonic, in the pedal, comes instead the chorale theme, accompanied by motives drawn from the ritornello, often in imitation. With its overall A B A shape and its lengthy, carefully balanced episodic middle section, the "Trio super Allein Gott" foreshadows the large ternary movements of the Six Sonatas (see chapter 19), and the sequence with the long chain of trills (indicated in the revised version; mm. 38–43), repeated later transposed and with parts exchanged (mm. 60–64), closely resembles passages in Sonata 2 (movement 1, mm. 66–70) and Sonata 4 (movement 2, mm. 38–39). The technique of repeating large blocks of material with parts exchanged provided Bach with a new means of expansion and unification. In this regard, the "Trio super Allein Gott in der Höh sei Ehr" was one of his most important Weimar works, the beginning of a journey that would lead to the Six Sonatas and large preludes and fugues 15 years later.[34]

Cantus Firmus Settings

The cantus firmus setting is perhaps the most conventional type of organ chorale, with the hymn melody sounding in long, unadorned notes in the right hand, left hand, or pedal against figurative accompaniment in the remaining parts. Yet it was in this realm that Bach expressed some of his most inventive musical ideas during the Weimar years, in a series of pieces that move from conventional keyboard writing to bold, innovative idioms and procedures:

Liebster Jesu, wir sind hier, BWV 730 ·
Herzlich tut mich verlangen, BWV 727
O Lamm Gottes, unschuldig, BWV 656a
Fantasia super Von Gott will ich nicht lassen, BWV 658a

Meine Seele erhebt den Herren, BWV 733
Komm, Gott Schöpfer, heiliger Geist, BWV 667a
Fantasia super Komm, heiliger Geist, BWV 651a
Nun komm der Heiden Heiland, BWV 661a

"Liebster Jesu, wir sind hier," BWV 730, already mentioned earlier with regard to its "alio modo" variant, BWV 731, is an odd setting that seems to reflect the same restless spirit seen in the Neumeister Chorales. The appearance of the chorale tune in the soprano without pauses and the animated development of small motives in the alto and tenor over a continuo-like pedal in the second half of the piece is Orgel Büchlein-like. But in phrase 5 of the chorale (mm. 6–7) the soprano melody suddenly becomes highly florid, only to return to long notes for phrase 6. The nature of the part-writing also changes, from four parts in phrases 1 and 5 to five parts in phrases 2 and 6. And while the accompaniment is unremarkable in phrases 1 and 2, moving in placid 8th notes, it abruptly changes in phrases 5 and 6, where the pedal assumes the guise of a walking bass in steady 8th notes and the middle voices present two conventional motives in imitation—the *suspirans* in phrase 5 (mm. 6–7) and the *corta* in phrase 6 (mm. 8–10). While the harmonization of the entire setting is ambitious, with dominant 7ths and 9ths, it is also strange—the diminished chord on the last beat of the second ending remains unresolved. The rising pedal in measure 8 may reflect the final lines of verse 1 of Tobias Clausnitzer's 1663 text: "Direct our minds and desires . . . so that our hearts become completely drawn from earth to you,"[35] but the motivation for the changes in texture and note-motion and the constantly shifting motives in this setting is less clear.

"Herzlich tut mich verlangen," BWV 727, designated "à 2 Clav. et Ped.," is a cross between a cantus firmus chorale and a florid-melody chorale. The soprano melody, played on a separate manual, is a mix of 16th-note flourishes and unadorned quarter notes. The famous hymn tune, often called the "Passion Chorale" because of Bach's use of it in the St. Matthew and St. Mark Passions,[36] was immensely popular in Bach's time. Johann Mattheson claimed that it was used for 24 different hymns,[37] and Bach set it in both minor and major modes. As with Orgel-Büchlein settings, the melody is presented here without pauses between phrases, but unlike those pieces and like "Liebster Jesu, wir sind hier," BWV 730, the accompaniment jumps from one idea to the next, phrase by phrase. The setting is effective nevertheless, perhaps because of the expressive *suspirans* "gasps" in the melody line (an *abruptio* or *tmesis*, in classical rhetoric), the effective diminished seventh harmonies in the final phrase, and the overall simplicity of the arrangement.

Despite its ambitious scale, "O Lamm Gottes, unschuldig," BWV 656a, is surely a product of Bach's initial Weimar years, if not earlier still.[38] While it is based on typical seventeenth-century 8th-note figuration in 3/2 meter, its format is impressive: a setting of all three verses of Nicolaus Decius's Reformation hymn on the German Agnus Dei, in which the cantus firmus gradually migrates downward, from the soprano to the alto to the bass. Verses 1 and 2, with three-part *manualiter* texture, are mostly conventional and have literal repeats of the Stollen. In verse 1, the slightly embellished cantus firmus is preceded by a double theme based on the opening line of the chorale, in the manner of fore-imitation. After that, the cantus firmus continues without interruption, accompanied by a steady stream of 8th notes. In verse 2, the stepwise movement of the accompanying voices changes to livelier leaping figures, presented in free imitation. Verses 1 and 2 show solid workmanship on Bach's part, but nothing more.

The setting comes alive in verse 3, with the entrance of the pedal and the shift to 9/8 meter. A new, leaping, dance-like motive, based on the rising third and falling fifth of the first two phrases of the chorale melody, takes over the accompaniment, appearing in diverse imitative combinations against the pedal cantus firmus. The Stollen is now written out, to allow for a varied repeat. With the beginning of the Abgesang (m. 82), the music suddenly shifts from its neutral, motet-like character—maintained throughout all three verses up to this point— to the localized highlighting of *affect*. The chorale phrase "Thou has borne all transgressions" is portrayed with a new, gigue-like theme (m. 82), labeled "vivace" in Preller's manuscript copy from the 1740s.[39] The next line, "Otherwise we would have to despair," is painted with intense chromaticism and the thickening of the texture to five parts. The concluding plea "Grant us Thy peace" is marked by a return to diatonic 8th notes, floating peacefully in ascending and descending scales that mimic the stepwise movement of the final phrase of the chorale.

Spitta was greatly impressed by "O Lamm Gottes," calling it a "sublime composition of masterly construction" and "a marvel of profoundly religious art."[40] Bach, too, must have considered it highly, since he devoted a great deal of attention to its revision when preparing it for the Leipzig chorale portfolio. He altered the first and second endings of the Stollen of verse 2, changed the meter and notation of verse 3, and refined a host of smaller details (see chapter 25). The setting was a tribute to a style from the past, one that Bach would not consider again until the related but very different *stile antico* settings of Clavier-Übung III.

In the **"Fantasia super Von Gott will ich nicht lassen," BWV 658a**, Bach resolved the unification issues raised in "Liebster Jesu, wir sind hier" and "Herzlich tut mich verlangen" by generating the entire accompaniment from a single motive, a memorable figure that combines a rising scale (derived from the opening fourth of the chorale) in a distinctive dactylic rhythm with a falling arpeggio outlining a dominant ninth chord. The motive's persistent appearance (it occurs in every measure except the final three) in dense, three-part imitative counterpoint may well mirror the message of the chorale text, Ludwig Helmbold's 1563 paraphrase of Psalm 73, verse 23: "I will never let go of God for he does not let go of me." Both the Stollen and the Abgesang are preceded by a paraphrase of their first phrase in the soprano, which acts as a type of fore-imitation. The cantus firmus is carried in the pedal by an 8' solo stop[41]—a rare occurrence before the settings of Clavier-Übung III and the Schübler Collection. As if to compensate for the uniformity of the accompaniment, Bach concludes the setting with a two-measure coda composed of new figuration, an undulating figure producing the almost unbearable dissonance of the leading tone against the tonic, doubled in the left hand with repeated notes and in the pedal with a pedal point. This is an odd-sounding North German *stylus fantasticus* type of close.

"Meine Seele erhebt den Herren," BWV 733, is a very unusual cantus firmus setting. Although it is labeled "Fuga Sopra il Magnificat pro Organo pleno con Pedale" in the most important early manuscript source,[42] it doesn't act like a fugue. The main "subject," a metered version of the first phrase of the Magnificat chant (Psalm tone IX, the "tonus peregrinus"),[43] never appears in an opening exposition—that is, it is not presented in each of the four manual voices at the outset, in entrances that alternate between the tonic and the dominant. Rather, it appears first alone (twice in the tonic and once in the dominant) and then in two stretto pairs, sounding more like a chant refrain than a fugue subject. All this leads to the presentation of the complete Magnificat chant, in augmented note values, in the pedal, which enters only toward the end of the setting, as a fifth voice:

Portion/Mm.	Texture	Thematic material	Location	Harmonic station
Fugue	4-part, *man.*			
1		subject	tenor	I
10		subject	soprano	I
30		subject	soprano	V
55		subject in stretto	alto	V
56		subject in stretto	tenor	I
75		subject in stretto	alto	I
76		subject in stretto	bass	IV
Cantus-firmus	5-part, *ped.*			
98		cantus firmus, phrase 1, in augmentation	pedal	I
119		cantus firmus, phrase 2, in augmentation	pedal	vi

This hybrid format—concentrated treatment of material based on the cantus firmus followed by the appearance of the cantus firmus in the pedal—resembles that of the trios on "Herr Jesu Christ, dich zu uns wend," BWV 655a, and "Allein Gott in der Höh sei Ehr," BWV 664a, in which a concluding pedal cantus firmus portion is preceded by a trio sonata movement. But in the Magnificat setting, the initial portion, the four-part manual "fugue," is more loosely constructed, filled with long episodes based on the free treatment of the versatile 8th-note motive that initially appears against the subject in measure 2. The motive appears in upright and inverted forms, in imitation, and in stretto. The melodic limitations of the chant itself, with its reiterated tones, may have restricted Bach's choice of developmental material.

In terms of idiom, "Meine Seele erhebt den Herren" resembles the alla breve writing of the three-part *manualiter* fughetta "Lob sei dem allmächtigen Gott," BWV 704. In terms of procedure, it is similar to the digressive style of the three-part Ricercar from the Musical Offering, which is dominated by lengthy, formulaic digressions. It may be that the Magnificat Fugue, like the three-part Ricercar, stems from an improvisation, since so much of the episodic material has an extemporized feel. Bach's treatment of chant is much tighter in the *pedaliter* Kyrie-Christe-Kyrie settings of Clavier-Übung III, especially the five-part arrangement "Kyrie, Gott heiliger Geist," BWV 671, with the cantus firmus in the pedal.

"**Komm, Gott Schöpfer, heiliger Geist,**" BWV 667a, also has an improvisatory feel. It represents an expansion of the Orgel-Büchlein setting, BWV 631a, with the chorale now migrating from the soprano, where it is accompanied by jazzy off-beat motives in the manual and pedal, to the pedal, where it sounds in a "verse 2" addition at 16' or 32' pitch, organum plenum, against a flurry of 16th-note figures in the manual voices. The new fabric of 16th notes, which may portray the "tongues of fire" described in the second verse of Luther's text, seems to be generated from the 16th-note figures that suddenly appear in measures 6 and 7 of the original Orgel-Büchlein arrangement. Bach subsequently embellished this passage further in the revised version of the Orgel-Büchlein setting, BWV 631, most probably in Leipzig in conjunction with refining BWV 667a for eventual inclusion in the chorale portfolio.

Double settings can be found in the Neumeister Collection: "Ach Gott und Herr," BWV 714, and "Als Jesus Christus in der Nacht," BWV 1108. But here the two verses of the chorale are more organically connected, with the music of verse 2 flowing naturally out of the music of verse 1. The diminished seventh harmony in the final measure of the expanded "Komm, Gott Schöper," just before the concluding tonic chord, is a gesture seen elsewhere in the Weimar chorale settings: "Allein Gott in der Höh sei Ehr," BWV 662a, or "Fantasia super Von Gott will ich nicht lassen," BWV 658a. But nowhere is it more masterfully handled.

That Bach carried out the expansion of "Komm, Gott Schöpfer" in Weimar is confirmed by its presence in the Walther-Krebs Weimar manuscripts.[44] Theodor

Pitschel, a member of Gottsched's circle in Leipzig, reported that Bach would often "set his powers of imagination in motion" by playing something from the printed or written page.[45] The new second half of "Komm, Gott Schöpfer" may reflect the kind of riff Bach performed when using his own music as the basis for improvisation in organ recitals (see chapter 15).

The "Fantasia super Komm, heiliger Geist," BWV 651a, is not as well known as its greatly expanded Leipzig counterpart, BWV 651, which served as the majestic opening of the Leipzig chorale portfolio. It was nevertheless one of Bach's most important Weimar chorale settings, since it demonstrates the full impact of Vivaldi's new concerto idiom on Bach's organ writing. Unlike the Leipzig version, which contains all eight phrases of Luther's Pentecostal chorale, the Weimar version presents the cantus firmus in an abbreviated form: phrases 1, 2, 3, and 8 only, with no "Hallelujah" at the end. A similar abridgement of the chorale appears in the soprano-alto duet "Komm, laß mich nicht länger warten" from Cantata 172, *Erschallet, ihr Lieder*, of May 1714, where the hymn melody appears in decorated form in the right hand of the organ part. The unending chain of cascading 16th notes in the organ Fantasia was surely intended to reflect the nature of the Holy Ghost as described in Acts 2:2:

> And suddenly there came a sound from heaven, as of a rushing mighty wind, and it filled all the house where they were sitting.

The entire accompanimental fabric of "Komm, heiliger Geist" consists of concerto-like material based on an arpeggiated theme derived from the first phrase of the chorale. The theme initially takes the shape of an open triad, but as the music proceeds it is bent into diminished forms. It is also deployed in inventive ways, serving as a critical marker of harmonic stations in the manner of a concerto ritornello (m. 1: tonic; m. 13: dominant; m. 21: tonic, etc.), accompanying the cantus firmus without compromising its shape, and acting as the prime mover of sequences.

Three features of the setting are especially noteworthy. First, the structure consists of two pairs of chorale phrases separated by a modulatory *manualiter* interlude (mm. 21–30). This produces the same type of symmetry that appears in the florid-melody setting of "Nun komm der Heiden Heiland," BWV 659a, and it seems to reflect Bach's growing desire to create balanced structures in chorale preludes, despite the through-composed nature of the texts and tunes of most chorales. Second, the setting begins with a pedal-point on the note F, similar to the opening of the Toccata in F Major, BWV 540/1. For six measures the pedal fulfills the traditional role of a pedal-point—that is, it serves as a harmonic anchor for the music above it. Then, suddenly and unexpectedly, it moves upward to the note c and assumes a new role as carrier of the cantus firmus. The dual function of the pedal resembles a similar practice in the trios on "Herr Jesu Christ, dich zu uns wend," BWV 655a, and "Allein Gott, in der Höh sei Ehr," BWV 664a, and "Komm, Gott Schöpfer, heiliger Geist," BWV 667a. Third, the manual texture is strictly three-part until the end, when it thickens step-by-step to four (m. 45), five (m. 46), and finally six parts (m. 47). This carefully calculated control of parts reflects Bach's study of strict part-writing in the Orgel-Büchlein and his new-found attention to contrapuntal detail.

Both "Komm, Gott Schöpfer, heiliger Geist" and "Fantasia super Komm, heiliger Geist" point to a new type of cantus firmus chorale, one where the accompanimental fabric no longer changes from phrase to phrase, influenced by the chorale's melody or text, but rather remains constant throughout, reflecting a single, broad *affect*, established at the outset. This stems from Bach's work in the Orgel-Büchlein, of course, and similarly resulted in settings that were more homogeneous but at the same time more highly unified.

The final cantus firmus work, **"Nun komm der Heiden Heiland,"** BWV 661a, represents yet another approach to a plenum setting with cantus firmus in the pedal and a general-*affect* accompaniment in the manuals. In this instance, the accompaniment consists of a remarkable three-part fugue based on an angular, disjunct subject, derived from the first phrase of the chorale. The subject appears in upright and inverted forms (example 10–8) in a variety of contrapuntal permutations. The theme is sufficiently elastic not only to generate independent interludes but also to fit with all four phrases of the chorale.

The setting is divided into two nearly equal sections. In the first half (mm. 1–22), which contains the first two phrases of the chorale, the subject appears in upright form. In the second half (mm. 23–46), which begins in the mediant, B♭ major, and contains the last two phrases of the chorale, the subject appears first in inverted form and then, for the final phrase of the chorale and the close, in inverted and upright forms, in stretto. The arrival of bright, sunny B♭ major after a tortuous start in G minor coincides with the transformation of the fugue

Example 10–8 "Nun komm der Heiden Heiland," BWV 661a: (a) first phrase of the chorale, (b) fugue subject derived from it, and (c) fugue subject, inverted.

subject by inversion. And the use of stretto entries uniting the upright and inverted forms of the subject for the final phrase of the chorale aligns the climax of Luther's text ("that God determined such a birth for him [Christ]") with the climax of the counterpoint. Even by Bachian standards, the setting is a remarkable contrapuntal tour de force:

Mm.	Fugue section/chorale phrase	Form and location of fugue subject (S = upright, S^i = inverted)
1–12	Exposition 1 (subject upright)	S (soprano) → S (alto), sequences → S (tenor), sequences
12–15	Chorale: phrase 1	S (alto) → S (soprano)
15–19	Episode	Sequences
20–22	Chorale: phrase 2	S (tenor) → S (soprano)
23–28	Exposition 2 (subject inverted)	S^i (alto) → S^i (tenor), sequences
29–31	Chorale: phrase 3	S^i (tenor) → S^i (tenor)
32–40	Episode	S^i (tenor) → S^i (soprano), sequences
41–43	Chorale: phrase 4	S^i (soprano) + S (tenor) in stretto
43–46	Coda: pedal point close	S^i (tenor) + S (soprano) in stretto → S (alto)

In Leipzig, Bach changed the meter and note values of the setting to 2/2 time with 8th-note motion, doubling the length of the score from 46 measures to 92 measures (see chapter 25). In its Weimar form, in 4/4 time with 16th-note motion, it closely resembles the idiom of the Toccata in D Minor ("Dorian"), BWV 538, which has an equally angular, disjunct theme. "Nun komm der Heiden Heiland" also shows a strong kinship with the second half (that is, the added portion) of "Komm, Gott Schöpfer, heiliger Geist," BWV 667a, and "Fantasia super Komm, heiliger Geist," BWV 651a. All three chorale settings are plenum works with the cantus firmus in the pedal and an ongoing stream of 16th notes in the manner of Vivaldi's instrumental concertos. Viewed as a group, the three pieces demonstrate three approaches to creating a manual accompaniment with a single, general *affect*: free counterpoint ("Komm, Gott Schöpfer"), concerto ("Fantasia super Komm, heiliger Geist"), and fugue ("Nun komm der Heiden Heiland"). With these works, Bach took the traditional cantus firmus chorale and turned it into something new, and brash.

Eclectic Blends

Finally, two large chorale settings combine a number of styles and procedures— so much so that they defy easy categorization. They are best described as eclectic blends:

Allein Gott in der Höh sei Ehr, BWV 663a
Nun komm der Heiden Heiland, BWV 660a

The first setting, **"Allein Gott in der Höh sei Ehr," BWV 663a**, must rank as
one of the most eclectic pieces Bach wrote. On the most fundamental level, it is
a combination of an Italian trio sonata (the two treble parts, notated on the top
staff in violin clef, and pedal) and a French tierce-en-taille setting (the left hand,
notated in tenor clef, carrying the decorated chorale). But it also incorporates an
almost dizzying array of additional elements:

- Ritornello (the return of the accompanimental material in different
  keys)
- Fugato (the imitative treatment of the treble parts)
- Florid melody (the treatment of the chorale melody in the tenor)
- Fore-imitation (the presentation of phrase 1 of the chorale in the pedal be-
  fore the initial entry of the chorale in the tenor)
- Canon (the strict imitation of the pedal by the soprano at the beginning of
  the Abgesang)
- Free cadenza leading to an adagio interruption (in the middle of the
  Abgesang, brought under stricter metrical control in the revised version,
  BWV 663)
- Single-line cantus firmus momentarily breaking into two parts for the last
  phrase (mm. 76–79)
- Long coda, derived from the chorale tune, over a tonic pedal point
- Pedal part that alternates between presenting thematic material and pro-
  viding harmonic support

All this is held together by a steady flow of 8th notes, giving the setting a
placid *perpetuum mobile* feel. Marked "cantabile" ("song-like," according to
Walther)[46] and taken at an andante tempo,[47] the setting unfolds in the same
leisurely manner as "Komm, heiliger Geist, Herre Gott," BWV 652a. The incorporation of so many ideas in one piece reminds one of the youthful Bach of the
Neumeister Chorales, and the occasional addition of an extra part (mm. 15, 69,
71–72) points to the early Weimar years. The imaginative but diffuse nature of
the setting might reflect its origin as an improvisation, much like the Fugue on
the Magnificat, BWV 733.

"**Nun komm der Heiden Heiland," BWV 660a**, is also very eclectic, but
displays more disciplined part-writing and greater organizational control. In this
remarkable setting, Bach amalgamated features of the florid-melody chorale,
chorale trio, and concerto form. The florid melody, assigned as per tradition to
the soprano line, is embellished with ornaments and diminutions. The chorale
tune is unusually clear, due to the fact that its key notes consistently occur on

principal beats. Bach may have deemed this necessary, given the general complexity of the arrangement.

While the setting is a trio, it is not based on the Italian trio sonata for two violins and continuo but on the North German trio sonata for violin, viola da gamba, and continuo—that is, for violin and two bass instruments (or bass lines). Bach may have known the North German tradition through Buxtehude's opus 1 and opus 2 sonatas for violin, viola da gamba, and continuo, published in Hamburg in the 1690s.[48] Bach gave his organ setting a more specific title when he revised the music in Leipzig: "Trio super Nun komm der Heiden Heiland, à due Bassi e Canto fermo." The idiom reflects the work's ties with string writing, with rolled chords in measures 15 and 42 that mimic the rolled chords of a gamba. But at the same time, the ritornello material is deftly fashioned for opposite-toe performance on the pedalboard.

For the first and only time in a Weimar chorale setting, Bach employed here a full-fledged Vivaldian concerto form with a sectionalized ritornello containing the three expected segments: introduction (a thematic segment establishing the tonic but ending on a half cadence, mm. 1–3), which we will call r1; extension (a sequential segment, mm. 4–6a), which we will call r2; and conclusion (a closing segment with full cadence, mm. 6b–7a), which we will call r3. The head motive of r1 is derived from the first phrase of the hymn tune and appears in imitation in the left hand and pedal. It thus acts in the manner of fore-imitation for phrases 1 and 4 of the chorale, which in this case have the same melodic shape.

Following Vivaldi's model, Bach manipulated the three segments in various ways after the opening statement, using them individually, in pairs, in fragmented form, or in reverse order. In "Nun komm der Heiden Heiland" the introduction, extension, and conclusion segments function as the ritornello, while the chorale phrases act as the episodes:

Mm.	Material	Segment	Harmonic station
1–7a	Ritornello	r1, r2, r3	i
7a–11	Episode	Chorale phrase 1, with fragments of r2 and r1	
11–17	Ritornello	r2, r3, r1, with parts exchanged	v
17–20	Episode	Chorale phrase 2, with fragments of r2 and r1	
20–24	Ritornello	r1, r1, with parts exchanged	III
24–27	Episode	Chorale phrase 3, with fragments of r2	
27–33a	Ritornello	r1, r2, r3	iv
33a–38	Episode	Chorale phrase 4, with fragments of r1	
38–42	Ritornello	r2, r3, with parts exchanged	i

Bach's ability to combine the formal gestures of a concerto form (the alternation of ritornello and episode) with the practical requirements of a florid-melody chorale (the intermittent statements of the hymn tune) is uncanny. While all of Bach's organ works are unique, this setting is truly anomalous. It also has the distinction of being the only large Weimar organ chorale to survive in autograph form. Bach's original manuscript is a four-page fascicle with a convenient page-turn for performance.[49] After his death it was added to the compendium that contains the autographs of the Six Sonatas and the Leipzig chorale portfolio.[50] The early copies of the "Nun komm" trio by Walther and Preller[51] reflect Bach's autograph in all important details, suggesting that their copies of other organ works from the time provide an accurate picture of the original materials. A copy by Johann Tobias Krebs[52] transmits a variant of the setting, with the obbligato parts, now an octave higher, transferred to the right hand and left hand and the melody assigned to the pedal, where it appears as a cantus firmus in unadorned half and quarter notes, most probably played at 4' pitch. Krebs may have made the arrangement under Bach's watchful eye. But it is also possible that it stems from Bach himself, and in the most recent Schmieder catalog it is called a "performance variant" and given its own number, BWV[3] 660.2.

Peter Williams has suggested that the three Weimar arrangements of "Nun komm der Heiden Heiland," later grouped together in the "Great Eighteen" Collection, evoke the three roles of Christ portrayed in chorale texts and Luther's Large and Small Catechisms: Jesus "the only beatifier and Saviour," Jesus who "suffered upon the cross," and Jesus who "with his power protects us against all enemies."[53] One also suspects that Bach greatly valued the contrasting nature of the settings and the fact that each broke ground within its genre.

The Apotheosis of the Chorale Partita: "Sei gegrüßet, Jesu gütig"

Bach's transformation of conventional types of organ chorales in Weimar is epitomized by the Partita on "Sei gegrüßet, Jesu gütig," BWV 768. A set of variations in the Pachelbel and Böhm mode, it represents his return to the chorale partita after a pause of several years and his decision to write a final, culminating masterpiece, much in the spirit of the Passacaglia in C Minor for the ostinato variation. Like the Passacaglia, "Sei gegrüßet" appears to date from c. 1711–1713, the last phase of Bach's reimagining of seventeenth-century Central and North German genres. After encountering Vivaldi's concertos in 1713 and taking up the "new" cantata style in the spring of 1714, Bach shifted his focus southward to the progressive musical currents flowing from Italy.

The music of "Sei gegrüßet" is based on Christian Keimann's five-verse Passion text of 1663 (two additional verses were added by an anonymous poet in 1668) set to a melody first printed by Gottfried Vopelius in 1682.[54] The first stanza reads:

Sei gegrüßet, Jesu gütig	Hail to you, kind Jesus
Über alle Maß sanftmütig!	Gentle beyond all measure!
Ach wie bist du so zerschmissen	O, how you are so ripped to pieces,
Und dein zarter Leib zerrissen!	And your fragile body torn apart!
Laß mich deine Liebe erben,	Let me inherit your love
Und darinnen selig sterben.	And through it die blessed.

Bach wrote his partita on this moving chorale in two stages. He began with a short version—preserved in a single manuscript copy written by Tobias Krebs[55]—that contains the chorale and just four variations: variations 1, 2, 4, and 10.[56] Titled "Sey gegrüßet Jesu gütig cum 4 Variat.," this initial version already represented a break with past chorale-partita conventions, since it contained a new type of fully worked-out basso ostinato movement (variation 1, which we will discuss shortly) and concluded with a lengthy finale calling for the use of two manuals and obbligato pedal (variation 10).

Apparently stimulated by the project, Bach took up the pen once again, adding three *manualiter* variations and four *pedaliter* variations to produce an immense, 12-movement work. The expanded setting of "Sei gegrüßet" was most likely intended for organ recitals and study, rather than church services or home devotions, and it is passed down in 16 early manuscripts—a testament to its widespread popularity. The manuscripts also reveal that Bach made adjustments to the expanded version for years, revising variation 3 twice and continuing to ponder the order of the variations into the 1740s.

Manuscripts now located in Kaliningrad, Carpentras, and Leipzig,[57] containing the earliest versions of the 12-movement form, suggest that Bach may have written the new variations out of order, in a workbook or on loose sheets, since the movements appear in various sequences that lack organizational logic: manual and pedal variations are mixed in a haphazard way, and the five-part harmonized chorale (variation 11), seemingly the concluding movement, occurs before the end (see table 10-1).[58] A manuscript produced around 1770 by Johann Nicolaus Schober for the music library of Princess Amalia in Berlin contains the variations in the order generally used today.[59] Written under the supervision of Kirnberger, the Schober copy probably reflects a manuscript owned by Carl Philipp Emanuel Bach and placed at Kirnberger's disposal. The Berlin version presents the variations in a very logical order: first the chorale, then six *manualiter* variations, and then five *pedaliter* variations culminating with the

Table 10-1 Partita on Sei gegrüßet, Jesu gütig, BWV 768

Order of Variations

	Movement sequence[a]											
Early Version (chorale and 4 variations)												
Berlin, *P 802*	Chorale	1	2	4	**_10_**							
Johann Tobias Krebs, c. 1714–1717												
Expanded Version (chorale and 11 variations)												
Kaliningrad, *Gotthold Rfα 6* (variation 3: early version)	Chorale	1	2	5	3	6	**_10_**	7	**_11_**	9	4	**_8_**
Anon. scribe, c. 1760–1789												
Carpentras, *Ms. 1086* (variation 3: early version)	Chorale	1	2	3	4	5	_7_	**_11_**	**_9_**	6	8	_10_
Scribe of Plauener Organ Book, before 1717												
Leipzig, *Peters Ms. 7* (variation 3: middle version)	Chorale	1	2	3	4	5	–	6	**_8_**	7	**_11_**	_10_
Johann Gottlieb Preller, c. 1743–1749												
Berlin, *Am.B. 47* (variation 3: late version)	Chorale	1	2	3	4	5	6	7	**_8_**	9	_10_	_11_
Johann Nicolaus Schober, c. 1770												
Leipzig, Becker Collection, *III.8.17* (variation 3: late version)	Chorale	1	2	3	4	5	7	6	**_8_**	9	_10_	_11_
Anonymous X (Bach student), c. 1740–1742												

[a]Variation numbers from BWV. Normal type = *manualiter* variation; bold, underlined type = *pedaliter* variation

five-part harmonized chorale. This order was adopted by Ernst Naumann for the Bach-Gesamtausgabe in 1893 and consequently by Wolfgang Schmieder for the Bach-Werke-Verzeichnis in 1950. In recent times it has been followed by the Neue Bach-Ausgabe and Breitkopf editions.

But Bach apparently had still more thoughts. Yet another version of "Sei gegrüßet" is preserved in a manuscript written by Anonymous X,[60] the unidentified student working under Bach's supervision in Leipzig in the early 1740s.[61] It follows the Berlin text and format except that variations 6 and 7 appear in reverse order. This disrupts the sequence of manual variations followed by pedal variations, but it places variation 7, with its 32nd-note figuration, next to variation 5, which also has 32nd-note figuration, and variation 6, a dance in 12/8 meter, next to variation 8, a dance in 24/16. In this late form, "Sei gegrüßet" takes on the shape of a monumental, cyclical partita with framing elements (the harmonized chorale) and complementary pairs of variations:

Chorale	¢	Four-part harmonization
Variation 1	¢	Bicinium, basso ostinato
Variation 2	¢	Four-part, *suspirans* figuration
Variation 3	¢	Bicinium, *perpetuum mobile*
Variation 4	¢	Four-part, *suspirans* movement
Variation 5	¢	32nd-note figuration
Variation 7	¢	32nd-note figuration
Variation 6	12/8 meter	Dance idiom
Variation 8	24/16 meter	Dance idiom
Variation 9	3/4 meter	Sarabande idiom
Variation 10	3/4 meter	Sarabande idiom
Chorale (Var. 11)	¢	Five-part harmonization

This compelling sequence, which may have been Bach's last word on "Sei gegrüßet" after a long series of organizational shifts, was used by Friedrich Conrad Griepenkerl in the Peters Edition of 1846. In recent times it has been adopted in the Leupold Edition.

Looking at the individual movements, we see that the advanced style of "Sei gegrüßet" is evident from the start. The opening chorale is set in strict four-part texture, with a natural flow of 8th notes and chromatic passing tones that foreshadows that of the harmonized chorales of the Leipzig cantatas. The spontaneous use of four, five, six, and even seven parts in the harmonized chorales of the earlier partitas has been abandoned. In variation 1, the quasi-ostinato bass, derived from the rising minor third of the chorale melody, is now a well-rounded theme that acts very much like the ritornello of a concerto form, recurring in full to mark principal harmonic stations but also appearing in fragments against the highly embellished chorale melody, which becomes more florid as the music progresses. The result is a well-rounded concerto form with a short ritornello, quite like the designs of the "Trio super Herr Jesu Christ, dich zu uns wend," BWV 655a, or the opening movement of Toccata in C Major, BWV 564—both written around the same time as "Sei gegrüßet":

Mm.	Thematic material	Harmonic station
1–3	Basso-ostinato theme	i
4–12a	Chorale: phrases 1–2	
12b–15a	Basso-ostinato theme	III
15b–21	Chorale: phrases 3–4	
22–24	Basso-ostinao theme	iv
25–33	Chorale: phrases 5–6	
34–36	Basso-ostinato theme	i

In variation 2, the *suspirans* pattern of the tenor is picked up in the three other voices, including the soprano, where it serves to embellish the cantus firmus line. Variation 3 is a *perpetuum mobile* bicinium in the Pachelbel vein, but the upper part, revised and rerevised, is less reliant on the chorale tune and more chromatically intense. Variation 4, which followed variation 2 in the early Krebs version, is a further elaboration of the *suspirans* motive, now converted into an ascending and descending scale and a turning figure against the soprano cantus firmus. Variation 5 is propelled by a snappy, off-beat 32nd-note figure, which evolves into pure 32nd-note runs in the final measures. If one adopts Bach's format and performance indications of the 1740s, the 32nd-note figuration is then continued in the sixth variation (variation 7 in the BWV), now played on two manuals and pedal,[62] with increased note motion in both hands and dramatic ascending and descending leaps in a double-dotted French idiom.[63] Here, too, the note-motion intensifies in the final measures, with simultaneous 32nd notes in both hands.

The seventh variation (variation 6 in the BWV) is then a gentle four-part dance in 12/8 meter, bringing a bit of a respite. The *suspirans*, now converted to triple time, once again plays a role. This leads to variation 8, a remarkable *pedaliter* dance in 24/16 time in which the twisting accompanimental figure, used upright and inverted, is incorporated into the cantus firmus, as in variation 2. The extended pedal point at the end has a certain kinship with those of "Nun komm der Heiden Heiland," BWV 661a, and "Allein Gott in der Höh sei Ehr," BWV 663a. The trio writing in variation 9, in 3/4 meter, is quite like that of the last movement of Trio Sonata 1, BWV 525, for organ. The imitative motives in the manuals are presented upright and inverted and finally in contrary motion at the end (mm. 29–32), while the cantus firmus appears in the pedal as a tenor voice, most probably played with an 8' stop. The idiom is that of a sarabande.

Variation 10, the climactic concluding movement of the early version of "Sei gegrüßet," also has the characteristics of a sarabande in 3/4 meter that Bach used to great effect in "An Wasserflüssen Babylon," BWV 653b, and "Schmücke dich, o liebe Seele," BWV 654a. Its form is unusual, with an opening theme (mm. 1–6) alternating with the chorale melody, presented as a cantus firmus in long notes for the soprano. From bar 75 onward the cantus firmus is intensified through parallel thirds, at first with the two voices moving together and then with them moving through suspensions (mm. 93–99). The final tutti variation, labeled "Variatio 11, overo ultima â 5, in Organo pleno" in the Anonymous X manuscript, presents the simple chorale tune once again, now brilliantly harmonized in five parts, with 16th-note figures in the inner voices. It serves as a perfect bookend with the opening chorale, harmonized more straightforwardly in four parts.

In "Sei gegrüßet" Bach summarized and surpassed his earlier partitas as well as the works of his predecessors, enriching and expanding the form through the addition of pedal variations and the use of Italian ritornello and trio techniques, with a dash of French style thrown in for good measure (in variation 7). With 306 measures of music, it is Bach's largest chorale setting and the apotheosis of a much-beloved Thuringian genre.

Notes

1. The countermotive can be used to accompany the cantus firmus as well as the main fore-imitation motive, since the cantus firmus and main motive share the same note value (the quarter note, in this case)—a technique borrowed from Böhm.
2. Bach changed this indication to "sub Communione" in the revised version, BWV 665.
3. Spitta 1873–80, vol. 1, 613–614.
4. Berlin State Library, *P 802*.
5. Zehnder 2009, 226–228, and 307–309.
6. Williams 2003, 345.
7. Here and elsewhere the measure numbers cited follow those in the Breitkopf and Leupold editions rather than those in the NBA IV/2, where the measures of repeated Stollens are counted twice.
8. "Fantasia super Von Gott will ich nicht lassen," BWV 658a, and "Fantasia super Nun komm der Heiden Heiland," BWV 659a.
9. Bach altered the titles from "Fantasia" to "Sinfonia" in his revised fair copy, which includes the prefatory remark that the pieces were intended to teach the player how to "have good *inventiones* and at the same time to develop the same well." NBR, no. 92.
10. Mattheson 1719, as cited in Rita Steblin, *A History of Key Characteristics in the Eighteenth and Early Nineteenth Centuries* (Ann Arbor, MI: UMI Research Press, 1983), 245.

11. *Neue Zeitschrift für Musik*, August 1840, cited in NBR, 502.

12. Williams 2003, 353.

13. Göttweig Benedictine Abbey, *Mus. Ms. 4662*.

14. Leipzig Town Library, *Poel. mus. Ms. 39*; Berlin State Library, *P 1108*; and Berlin State Library, *P 409*, respectively.

15. Berlin State Library, *P 802*, which contains the early versions of Bach's florid-melody chorales from the "Great Eighteen" Collection as well as Walther's florid-melody settings "Wo soll ich fliehen hin," "Warum betrübst du dich, mein Herz," and others.

16. Leipzig Town Library, *Poel. mus. Ms. 39*, written by Kittel's student Johann Nicolaus Gebhardi.

17. Leipzig Town Library, Becker Collection, *III.8.10.*

18. Berlin State Library, *P 1109*, from the 1760s. Penzel's embellishments are presented without comment in the text of BWV 709 in the NBA. In the Breitkopf Edition they are reproduced in small type.

19. Snyder 2007, 262.

20. As reported in Walther 1732, 547 (entry for Heinrich Scheidemann).

21. The headings in the Orgel-Büchlein album show that Bach intended to compose an unusually long, two-page setting of "An Wasserflüssen Babylon" but never followed through on the idea.

22. Both Spitta (Spitta 1873–80, vol. 1, 616–617) and Williams (William 2003, 349–351) questioned the order of composition of the three settings. Werner Breig, in Breig 1986b, has convincingly demonstrated recently that the sequence is, indeed, BWV 653b → 653a → 653.

23. Breig 1986b, 111.

24. These changes are discussed in detail in Breig 1986b.

25. Berlin State Library, *P 802*.

26. In addition, in the second version the left-hand part is labeled "forte," the right-hand part "piano," and the pedal "pedale."

27. Leipzig Town Library, *Peters Ms. 7*, fascicle 29.

28. The jazzy-sounding figure on the third beat of m. 33 is worthy of George Gershwin—the themes of Prelude 3 in E♭ Minor for Piano or "It Ain't Necessarily So" from *Porgy and Bess*, for example. Bach obviously liked the figure, refining its rhythm in Leipzig to make it more expressive still (see chapter 25).

29. Royal Library of Belgium, *Fétis 2026 [II]* and Berlin State Library, *Am.B. 72a* (Breitkopf sources), and Austrian National Library, *Mus. H. 35149* (Scholz).

30. NBR, no. 357.

31. Breig 1987, 100.

32. Bighley 2018, 116.

33. The text is attributed to Wilhelm II of Saxony-Weimar, the forebear of Bach's Weimar employers the dukes Wilhelm Ernst and Ernst August.

34. Not discussed here is the variant BWV 664b, at one time viewed as the earliest form of the "Trio super Allein Gott in der Höh sei Ehr" and printed as such in BG 25.2 and NBA IV/2. It is now seen as a corrupt version of BWV 664a, with the pedal part transposed at various spots. See Bach digital, under BWV 664b.

35. This idea was first proposed by Jacques Chailley, in Chailley 1974, 185.

36. There is some irony in this, since the tune stems from Hans Leo Hassler's secular song "Mein G'müth ist mir verwirret von einer Jungfrau zart" (My soul is confused by a tender maiden).

37. Mattheson 1739, 473.

38. Peter Williams, in Williams 2003, 357, pointed to similarities between the idiom of verses 1 and 2 and that of the Neumeister chorale "Als Jesus Christus in der Nacht," BWV 1108.

39. Leipzig Music Library, *Peters Ms. 7*, fascicle 36. In this instance "vivace" may indicate a change of articulation rather than a change of tempo.

40. Spitta 1873–80, vol. 1, 612.

41. A manuscript copy of the setting made by a Breitkopf copyist and at one point owned by Johann Christoph Oley (Berlin State Library, *P 1160*) contains the indication "Pedal. 4 Fuß." While the use of a 4' pedal stop allows the cantus firmus to sound out clearly above the manual accompaniment, it brings the part into the alto range, thus producing an arrangement that has two alto parts and no tenor part. It is more likely that the pedal calls for an 8' stop, which puts the cantus into the tenor range.

42. Darmstadt University Library, *Mus.ms. 525a*, a manuscript copy written by "Anonymous O," an assistant, student, or son of Bernhard Christian Kayser, a student of Bach.

43. As classified in the *Liber Usualis*, the book of commonly used Gregorian chants compiled by the monks of the Abbey of Solesmes in France in 1896.

44. Berlin State Library, *P 802*, a complete copy by Walther or Johann Tobias Krebs, and *P 801*, fascicle 31, a fragment (mm. 11–24 only) in the hand of Tobias Krebs.

45. NBR, no. 336.

46. Cantabile: "When a composition, be it set vocally or instrumentally, can be sung in all parts and sections." Walther 1732, 134.

47. So indicated in m. 64, after the adagio cadenza, in the Weimar version.

48. Dietrich Becker, director of the Hamburg municipal musicians from 1674 to 1679, had published a sonata collection with this scoring some 20 years earlier, in 1674. See Snyder 2007, 285.

49. Berlin State Library, *P 271*, fascicle 3, reproduced in facsimile in Bach digital, under BWV 660a, and Wollny 2016a.

50. Berlin State Library, *P 271*.

51. Berlin State Library, *Mus.ms 22541 I* and *Mus.ms. 22541 II* (Walther) and Leipzig Town Library, *Peters Ms. 7* (Preller).

52. Berlin State Library, *P 802*.

53. Williams 2003, 369.

54. Bighley 2018, 214.

55. Berlin State Library, *P 802*. The short version may also be reflected in the initial layer of the Carpentras manuscript (see below).

56. The numbering system used for the variations here and elsewhere is that of the BWV. A number of hymnals from Bach's time omit verses 6 and 7 of "Sei gegrüßet" and present the text in Keimann's original five-verse form. It is possible that Bach

envisioned his initial setting of "Sei gegrüßet" for alternatim performance with the five-verse version of the chorale.

57. Kaliningrad, University Library, *Gotthold Rfα 6* (lost); Library of the Carpentras Museum, Carpentras, France, *Ms. 1086*; and Leipzig Town Library, *Peters Ms. 7*, fascicle 23.

58. Michael Kube discerns certain patterns within the early orders, however, in Kube 1999, 556–557.

59. Berlin State Library, *Am.B. 47*. On recent identification of Schober see Koska 2017, 169.

60. Leipzig Town Library, Becker Collection, *III.8.17*.

61. On Anonymous X see the introduction and Wollny 2013, 157–158.

62. The indication "à 2. Clav." is found solely in the manuscript of Anonymous X and also appears to have been a late second thought on Bach's part.

63. The harmonic structure suggests that the dotted 8th- and 16th-note figures should be double dotted, producing consonant rather than dissonant intervals.

11

Small Chorale Settings

Bach's interest in chorale settings during the Weimar years extended beyond large pedal works to include small pieces, often for manuals alone. This repertoire is difficult to define, for the source material is especially problematic. No original manuscripts survive, and there are very few copies by Bach's students, who seem to have been more interested in the larger *pedaliter* works. As a result, most of the small chorale settings are passed down in a somewhat haphazard fashion, in late sources only—copies from the 1740s by Johann Ludwig Krebs and Johann Gottlieb Preller and copies from the 1760s, 1770s, and 1780s stemming mainly from the sales manuscripts of the Breitkopf firm in Leipzig.[1] One suspects that many pieces have been lost.

Given the poor source transmission, it is hard to establish the context of the small chorale settings and how they might have been organized. As we noted in the introduction, Bach seems to have kept his large Weimar chorale settings in individual folders. In the case of the small settings, eight fughettas and four Christmas interlude chorales are handed down as distinct groups. Otherwise, the small settings, aside from those in the Orgel-Büchlein, appear randomly in the sources, without a perceivable pattern. We are placing them into categories here for the sake of discussion, and, as with the large chorale settings, we will limit ourselves to works assigned to the Weimar period in BWV[3], noting here and there where the chronological placement might, in fact, be different.

Despite the vague profile of the repertoire, the small chorale settings that survive show the same pattern of invention as the large settings: Bach's unquenchable thirst for exploring the widest possible range of compositional techniques in the widest possible range of genres. In many cases this resulted in miniature musical gems.

Miscellaneous *Manualiter* Chorales

Seven settings fall into this category, including several pieces that are transmitted only in post-1750 manuscripts:

Liebster Jesu, wir sind hier, BWV 706
Allein Gott in der Höh sei Ehr, BWV 717

J. S. BACH. George B. Stauffer, Oxford University Press. © Oxford University Press 2024.
DOI: 10.1093/oso/9780195108026.003.0012

Bicinium sopra Allein Gott in der Höh sei Ehr, BWV 711
Nun freut euch, lieben Christen gmein, BWV 734
In dich hab ich gehoffet, Herr, BWV 712
Fantasia super Christ lag in Todesbanden, BWV 695
Fantasia super Jesu, meine Freude, BWV 713

The chorale "Liebster Jesu, wir sind hier," like "Allein Gott in der Höh sei Ehr" and "Herr Jesu Christ, dich zu uns wend," was used as a general hymn in many locations, sung by the congregation each Sunday before the sermon.[2] Bach set it for organ six times: twice in the Orgel-Büchlein, BWV 634, and its revision, BWV 633; twice as modest pedal settings, BWV 730 and 731; and once as a small manualiter chorale, BWV 706, followed by a simple harmonized setting, BWV 706/2, labeled "alio modo" in Johann Tobias Krebs's copy from c. 1714–1717.[3]

The small *manualiter* setting, **"Liebster Jesu, wir sind hier,"** BWV 706, is an embellished version of a simple harmonized chorale, with a soprano black-note cantus firmus accompanied by decorated alto, tenor, and bass lines. The concision of the setting and the lack of interludes between chorale phrases allies it with Orgel-Büchlein settings, but it lacks the spinning-out of motives and obbligato pedal that characterize those works. The gradual acceleration of note motion toward the end of the setting foreshadows Bach's later refinement of this procedure (in the aria of the Goldberg Variations, for instance).

Tobias Krebs entered four of Bach's "Liebster Jesu" settings into his Weimar manuscript as a group, labeling them "Liebster Jesu wir sind hier" (BWV 706); "Alio modo" (BWV 706/2); "Alio modo in Canone all Quinta à 2 Clav. è Ped." (BWV 634); and "Alio modo distinctig" (BWV 633). This grouping appears in later sources as well,[4] hinting at a possible origin with Bach, who may have viewed BWV 706 and BWV 706/2 as *manualiter* alternatives to the *pedaliter* Orgel-Büchlein arrangements.

The two Gloria settings, **"Allein Gott in der Höh sei Ehr,"** BWV 717, and **"Allein Gott in der Höh sei Ehr,"** BWV 711, present a study in "fugirende und verændernde Choraele" (fugued and varied chorales), the phrase used by Telemann for his 1735 collection of 24 chorale settings.[5] In that publication, Telemann presented each chorale tune in a three-part "fugued" version, with cantus firmus accompanied by two "fugued" voices, and a two-part "varied" version, with cantus firmus accompanied by a single "varied" voice. Bach's two *manualiter* "Allein Gott in der Höh sei Ehr" settings follow this pattern.

BWV 717 is a three-part *manualiter* "fugued" setting, with a soprano cantus firmus accompanied by a two-part manual fughetta. The music is cast in the idiom of a gigue in 12/8 meter, and the fughetta subject is derived from the first phrase of the "Allein Gott" melody (example 11-1, a). After appearing in the tonic and dominant in the opening exposition, the subject recurs in single

Example 11-1 "Allein Gott in der Höh sei Ehr," BWV 717: (a) first phrase of the chorale tune and the fughetta subject derived from it, and (b) two mutated forms of the fughetta subject.

Example 11-2 "Allein Gott in der Höh sei Ehr," BWV 711: first phrase of the chorale tune and the ritornello subject derived from it.

entries, somewhat like a ritornello theme, in mutating forms that often contain the wide leaps characteristic of harpsichord gigues (example 11-1, b).[6] Bach also tossed in, seemingly for good measure, two motives derived from intervals in the chorale melody—the rising third and the falling fourth—presenting them in invertible counterpoint between the Stollen and Abgesang (mm. 18–22).[7]

BWV 711 is a two-part *manualiter* "varied" setting, with the "Allein Gott" melody appearing as a cantus firmus in the right hand and a cello-like ritornello figure with arpeggios and wide leaps—derived once again from the first phrase of the chorale—appearing in the left hand (example 11-2). What an extraordinary contrast with the "fugued" setting! In the early sources, BWV 711 is termed "bicinium," which Bach's Weimar colleague Johann Gottfried Walther defined as an Italian term for "a two-part song."[8] The flexible ritornello returns in various guises, in E minor (m. 13), G major (m. 22), A minor (m. 35), and G major (m. 56). The similar use of a string-bass figure for a ritornello occurs in the "Nun komm, der Heiden Heiland," BWV 660a, from Weimar, and "Ach, bleib bei uns," BWV 649, from the Schübler Collection, the latter a transcription of an aria from Cantata 6 of 1725 featuring violoncello piccolo (see chapter 24).

The "fugued" setting of "Allein Gott in der Höh sei Ehr," BWV 717, appears in a manuscript copy by Johann Tobias Krebs from c. 1712–1714,[9] so its Weimar roots are secure. The two-part "varied" setting, BWV 711, is more difficult to date, since it first surfaces in a Breitkopf copy from c. 1740--1745.[10] The similarity between BWV 711 and Telemann's bicinium setting of "Allein Gott in der Höh sei Ehr," TWV 31:4, in his 1735 collection is striking, and this raises the possibility that Bach may have written BWV 711 in response to Telemann's piece. Thus Bach's bicinium could be the product of the Leipzig years, composed after the Unaccompanied Cello Suites of c. 1722, the five cantata arias of 1725 with obbligato violoncello piccolo,[11] and Telemann's bicinium of 1735. At the same time, the notation of the right hand in soprano rather than treble clef weighs in favor of a Weimar origin.

"**Nun freut euch, lieben Christen gmein**," BWV 734, illustrates yet another way to decorate a cantus firmus in a *manualiter* organ chorale. The setting is a *perpetuum mobile*, with a ritornello of ongoing 16th notes in the soprano, an 8th-note continuo bass, and a cantus firmus in the tenor. The exuberant ritornello figure, derived from the first phrase of the chorale and reflecting the rejoicing of the Christian congregation, appears at least five times: in G major (m. 1), E minor (m. 15), D major (m. 21), G major (m. 25), and G major (m. 30). Sometimes it overlaps with the chorale melody, and sometimes it does not.

There is nothing else in the Bach organ repertory quite like this animated piece, though one finds simple harmonized chorales accompanied by *perpetuum mobile*–like instrumental figures in a number of Leipzig vocal works: the concluding choruses (labeled "Corale" or "Choral") of Cantata 22, *Jesus nahm zu sich die Zwölf*, or the Christmas Oratorio, Part VI, *Herr, wenn die stolzen Feinde schnauben*, for instance. Walther wrote a similar organ setting, "Schmücke dich, o liebe Seele," with running 16th notes in the right hand, the chorale in the left hand, and a continuo-like bass in the pedal.[12]

In the earliest source of "Nun freut euch," a copy by Johann Ludwig Krebs,[13] the work is followed by a simple figured-bass setting, implying the sequence: chorale prelude (BWV 734) followed by congregational singing (BWV 734/2). In modern times "Nun freut euch" is often performed with the cantus firmus in the pedal, with an 8' stop. But the indication "manualiter" that appears in an early source,[14] the fact that the tenor cantus firmus can always be played by the left hand together with the continuo bass, and the concluding

16th-note flourish in the cantus firmus all point to a manual performance un-aided by pedal.

"In dich habe ich gehoffet, Herr," BWV 712, a four-part manual setting, is labeled "Fugetta" in several early sources, with good reason. As in the "fugued" version of "Allein Gott in der Höh sei Ehr," BWV 717, a soprano cantus firmus is accompanied by fugal counterpoint. But in this case, the fugal material acts in the manner of a fore-imitation chorale: each phrase of the cantus firmus is preceded by a fughetta based on a subject that foreshadows the upcoming cho-rale phrase and whose last entry serves as the chorale melody itself, which takes the form of the fore-imitation subject. Each exposition concludes with a short closing cadence. And as the piece proceeds, the imitative procedure in the fughettas evolves:

Mm. 1–5   Fughetta with entries on a, e, e', and a' (= chorale, phrase 1), close

Mm. 5–10   Fughetta with entries on a, e', e, and a' (= chorale, phrase 2), close

Mm. 10–15   Fughetta with entries on c♯, f♯, B, and c♯" (= chorale, phrase 3), close

Mm. 15–19   Fughetta with entries on e, b, f♯', and c♯" (= chorale, phrase 4), close

Mm. 19–22   Fughetta with entries on f♯, c♯', g♯', and d" (= chorale, phrase 5), close

Mm. 22–27   Fughetta with subject and countersubject, with entries, in stretto, on f♯', c♯, b, and c♯" (= chorale, phrase 6)

Mm. 27–34   Free close, with phrase 6 of chorale repeated in highly embellished form in the soprano (mm. 30–32)

As this outline shows, "In dich hab ich gehoffet, Herr" is a highly unorthodox piece, with extraordinarily bold chromatic harmonies toward the end. A study in varied fugal expositions, it is similar to "Jesus Christus, unser Heiland," BWV 666a, in terms of its general idiom and free ending. This points to the early Weimar years for both works and the lingering influence of North German style.

The settings of "Christ lag in Todesbanden," BWV 695, and "Jesu, meine Freude," BWV 713, are the most extensive of the miscellaneous *manualiter* works. Bach termed both "Fantasia," not from the North German *stylus fantasticus*, with its unexpected turns, but from the lengthy treatment of the chorale melodies— 144 measures for "Christ lag in Todesbanden" (with the repeat of the Stollen) and 103 measures for "Jesu, meine Freude." In this sense the two works might be viewed as the *manualiter* equivalents of the "Fantasia super Komm, heiliger Geist, Herr Gott," BWV 651, the magisterial, 106-measure *pedaliter* setting that opens the Leipzig chorale portfolio (see chapter 25).

Example 11-3 "Fantasia super Christ lag in Todesbanden," BWV 695: (a) first phrase of the Stollen of the chorale and fughetta subject 1, derived from it, and (b) first phrase of the Abgesang of the chorale and fughetta subject 2, derived from it.

"**Fantasia super Christ lag in Todesbanden, Choral in Alto**" **BWV 695**, is written in the style of a 3/8-meter passepied dance. It is a double fughetta, with subject 1, derived from the first phrase of the Stollen of the chorale, used for the Stollen, and subject 2, derived from the first phrase of the Abgesang, used for the Abgesang (example 11-3), with the chorale appearing as a cantus firmus in the alto throughout.

The work can be analyzed as follows:

Stollen	Two-part exposition on subject 1, with entries in v and i
	Phrase 1 (and 3) of the chorale, followed by subject 1 in i
	Phrase 2 (and 4) of the chorale, followed by subject 1 in i
Abgesang	Two-part exposition on subject 2, with entries in i and v
	Phrase 5 of the chorale, with subject 2 in i, followed by subject 2 in v
	Phrase 6 of the chorale, followed by subject 2, abbreviated, in i and iv
	Phrase 7 of the chorale, with subject 2 in VII, then i
	Interlude, with subject 2 in i
	"Alleluja" of the chorale, with subject 2 in iv
Coda	Subject 1, in i, in alto

"Christ lag in Todesbanden" closes with a series of resolving chords and rests, much like the conclusion of the *manualiter* setting of "Wir glauben all' an einen Gott," BWV 681, from Clavier-Übung III.

Bach used a two-part format in **"Fantasia super Jesu, meine Freude,"** BWV 713, as well, but with significant differences. The Stollen takes the form of a fughetta in 4/4 meter, with a freely derived subject accompanying a slow-moving cantus firmus in half notes. The phrases of the cantus firmus migrate from the soprano to the alto to the bass, and then, in a written-out repeat of the Stollen material, from the alto to the bass and back to the soprano. Phrases 1–3 of the chorale (mm. 1–26) are written in three-part invertible counterpoint; the music is repeated, with parts exchanged, for phrases 4–6 (mm. 26–52).

In the Abgesang, where the text begins "O Lamb of God, my bridegroom," the music changes abruptly in character and procedure. The meter switches to 3/8 meter, marked "dolce," and the texture changes to parallel thirds and sixths, whose pairs of falling seconds are marked with expressive slurs. The texture is now homophonic rather than imitative, and the remaining phrases of the chorale appear one by one in the soprano, in highly decorated, stretched-out versions of each line. The delicate writing is quite like the "Gute Nacht" section of the motet *Jesu, meine Freude*, BWV 227, or the "Adagio e dolce" middle movement (in 6/8 meter) of Sonata 3 in D Minor for Organ, BWV 527.

The fantasias on "Christ lag in Todesbanden" and "Jesu, meine Freude" are both passed down in Breitkopf-derived sources,[15] where they are followed by figured-bass versions of their respective chorales for congregational singing (see below). The original Weimar materials have not survived, and we are fortunate that these two very special pieces were rescued by the Breitkopf firm.

Chorale Fughettas

Eight chorale fughettas ascribed to Bach are transmitted as a group in two post-1750 sources, both associated, once again, with Breitkopf. The first, a manuscript acquired by the Belgian musicologist François-Joseph Fétis for the Brussels Royal Library,[16] dates from c. 1760 and may have served as Breitkopf's house copy, from which sales manuscripts of the settings were made. The second manuscript, titled "Sammlung von varirten und fugirten Choralen vor 1. und 2. Claviere und Pedal von J. S. Bach," was produced in the 1780s by a professional scribe working for Bach's student Johann Philipp Kirnberger at the Amalian Library in Berlin.[17] It, too, has Breitkopf roots[18] and transmits the fughettas with essentially the same text as the Brussels manuscript. There are no earlier copies of the pieces, and the two Breitkopf-derived sources give no hint about the works' date or provenance.

The eight fughettas are based on chorales for Advent, Christmas, and New Year's, though they do not appear in precise church-year order in the Brussels master manuscript:

Christum wir sollen loben schon / Was fürchtest du Feind,
    Herodes, sehr, BWV 696   Christmas

Gelobet seist du, Jesu Christ, BWV 697   Christmas

Nun komm der Heiden Heiland, BWV 699   Advent

Herr Christ, der einig Gottes Sohn, BWV 698   Advent

Gottes Sohn ist kommen, BWV 703   Advent

Lob sei dem allmächtigen Gott, BWV 704   Advent

Vom Himmel hoch, da komm ich her, BWV 701   Christmas

Das Jesulein soll doch mein Trost, BWV 702   New Year's

The obscure lineage of the fughettas has led to a good deal of speculation about their origin. While initial reservations about the authenticity of "Das Jesulein soll doch mein Trost" have been set aside,[19] the date of the works continues to be a topic of lively debate. In an encompassing study, Pieter Dirksen proposed that the eight fughettas represent a closed cycle of settings from Bach's Leipzig years.[20] Comparing them to the fughettas in Clavier-Übung III and viewing them as a collection analogous to the Schübler Chorales, Dirksen claimed to see stylistic similarities with pieces from the Well-Tempered Clavier, volume 2, and the Art of Fugue, both from Bach's last decade. Dirksen's views were challenged by Bernhard Billeter and Jean-Claude Zehnder, who pointed to the fughettas' strong stylistic ties with the Orgel-Büchlein and other Weimar organ works, as well as with cantatas written between 1714 and 1716.[21]

The conservative meters of the fughettas would seem to support a Weimar origin: all but one setting ("Gottes Sohn ist kommen") are written in either C or 3/2, the seventeenth-century-oriented meters that dominate the Orgel-Büchlein (see chapter 8). In addition, the fughettas lack the mix of national styles and the rich influence of dance music that characterizes the manual settings of Clavier-Übung III (see chapter 22). In light of this and their affinity with a number of Orgel-Büchlein settings, most of the fughettas appear to date from the Weimar years, as Billeter and Zehnder have suggested. But as we shall see shortly, the contrapuntal complexity and well-crafted part-writing of several pieces hints at a later origin, perhaps Bach's Leipzig years, as Dirksen proposed. The stylistic disparities of the fughettas suggest that they may have been an ongoing undertaking on Bach's part, rather than a single, concentrated project.

But what sort of project? The eight works could be the remnant of a larger collection of chorale fughettas covering the entire liturgical year, from which Breitkopf extracted settings for Advent, Christmas, and New Year's in the hope that they would have high sales potential. All of the chorales except "Das Jesulein soll doch mein Trost" were broadly popular in the eighteenth century, and short manual preludes on their tunes would have had wide appeal, both to professional organists for church services and to amateur keyboard players for home devotions. A second possibility is that eight settings represent the beginning of a projected full-year cycle of fughettas, which Bach began but then abandoned once he had composed a number of illustrative examples, much in the fashion of the uncompleted Orgel-Büchlein.

No matter what the case, the contrapuntal sophistication and calculated diversity of the eight fughettas point to Bach and his indefatigable desire to try new things. The chorale fughetta was a bread-and-butter piece for Central German organists, who were expected to improvise such settings as a way of preluding on the chorale before it was sung by the congregation, and Bach could draw on a long line of Thuringian examples, such as the collection of 44 "Choräle, welche bey wärenden Gottesdienst zum Prämbulieren gebraucht werden können" (Chorales that can be used for preluding during the course of the worship service) of Johann Christoph Bach (1642–1703), pieces in the Weimar Tablature Book of 1704, or the Magnificat settings of Johann Pachelbel.

These and other collections show that the basic format of the chorale fughetta was well-established in Central Germany: a three- or four-part fugal exposition on a simple subject derived from the first phrase of the chorale is followed by a short episode, one or two additional entries of the subject, and a short close. To this formula Bach added a countersubject that could be combined with the subject in invertible counterpoint, as well as a host of contrapuntal devices that lifted the chorale fughetta to a new level of sophistication.

The three-part settings demonstrate this quite well. **"Gottes Sohn is kommen,"** BWV 703, is perhaps the most straightforward of the group. Here a traditional design (three-part exposition, episode, statement of the subject in the tonic, close) is enriched with a twisty countersubject that appears 17 times in 22 measures. The countersubject is repeated rather than developed, and it forms a continuous, unifying flow of 16th notes that may allude to the excitement produced by Christ's arrival on earth, much like the ongoing flow of 8th notes in the Orgel-Büchlein setting of the same chorale, BWV 600. Bach also enriched the tonal character of the melody by flattening the seventh degree of the scale (E → E♭) here and there in the counterpoint, giving the setting a mixolydian harmonic twist.[22]

"Nun komm der Heiden Heiland," BWV 699, displays the same conventional format as "Gottes Sohn ist kommen." But here the countersubject, derived from the subject, takes over both the episode, where it appears in imitation, and the extended close, where it appears five times, the first four in stretto (example 11-4, a). While some of the figuration is curiously old-fashioned (mm. 10–11), the animated rush to the close and the enriched ninth chords in the final measures speak to Bach's Weimar style. **"Lob sei dem allmächtigen Gott,"** BWV 704, shows a more complex format, with the subject appearing in the tonic (colored with a lydian b natural), dominant, and tonic in the initial exposition, as would

Example 11-4 (a) "Nun komm der Heiden Heiland," BWV 699: countersubject of the fughetta, in four-part stretto at the close, and (b) "Lob sei dem allmächtigen Gott," BWV 704: subject (x) and countersubject (y and z) at the opening of the setting (m. 4) and later (m. 15), with countersubject motives juxtaposed.

be expected, but then in the supertonic and submediant, whose dominant serves as the closing chord. The countersubject consists of two motives that are developed and then juxtaposed (Example 11-4, b). A third motive, a descending fourth derived from the last two phrases of the chorale, appears in measure 17 and proceeds to take over the counterpoint, also producing a gradual sense of acceleration through its continuous 8th notes.

Bach raised the contrapuntal ante in the remaining pair of three-part fughettas. In **"Herr Christ, der einig Gottes Sohn," BWV 698**, a versatile countersubject enters both before and after the subject at various points, at varying distances.[23] Other striking events occur as well: the second phrase of the chorale appears against the subject and countersubject (mm. 11–13), the subject appears in diminution with the countersubject (mm. 15–17), and the subject appears with the second phrase of the chorale in diminution and the first four notes of the countersubject (mm. 17–19; example 11-5, a).

Going even beyond this, **"Vom Himmel hoch, da komm ich her," BWV 701**, is a miniature contrapuntal tour de force, combining all four phrases of Luther's chorale in a format that pushes the boundaries of the chorale fughetta:

Example 11-5 (a) "Herr Christ, der einig Gottes Sohn," BWV 698: subject (x) and motive from the countersubject (y) of the fughetta, with phrase 2 of the chorale (top) in decorated form in the soprano, and (b) "Vom Himmel hoch, da komm ich her," BWV 701: phrase 1 of chorale and subject of the fughetta (x) with phrase 2 (y) and phrase 3 (z, in stretto) of the chorale.

Mm.	Event
1–5	Subject (phrase 1 of the chorale) in I and V, against the countersubject of a falling scale, derived from phrase 4 of the chorale
5–8	Countersubject in augmentation
8–10	Subject in I, with countersubject and first half of the subject in diminution (m. 10)
10–11	Phrase 2 of the chorale, in stretto
12–14	Subject in V, with countersubject, inverted, and phrase 2 of the chorale
14–15a	Subject in I, with phrase 2 of the chorale
15b–19	Subject in vi, with phrase 3 of the chorale, in stretto
20–22	Subject in V, with phrase 2 and phrase 3 of the chorale, in stretto (Example 11–15, b)
23	First half of the subject, in syncopation
24–26a	Subject in I, with phrase 2 of the chorale and countersubject, displaced
26b–27	Simple, seemingly tongue-in-cheek close

The falling scale of the countersubject (surely reflecting the descent of the angel from heaven with the news of Christ's birth), the use of all four chorale phrases, and the intricate contrapuntal combinations—remarkable content for a *manualiter* fughetta—foreshadow the Canonic Variations on Vom Himmel hoch, BWV 769, of c. 1748 (see chapter 23, especially example 23-3). The fughetta, in fact, strikes one as a trial run for the later set of variations.

The masterful handling of complex contrapuntal procedures and figurative play in "Herr Christ, der einig Gottes Sohn" and "Vom Himmel hoch" hints that Bach may have added the two settings to his fughetta collection at a later point than the other pieces, perhaps in Leipzig rather than Weimar. This would have mirrored his treatment of the Orgel-Büchlein, where he assembled most of the contents in Weimar but returned to the album in Leipzig to add "Helft mir Gotts Güte preisen," BWV 613, and the incipit of "O Traurigkeit, o Herzeleid," BWV 1169 (see chapter 8).[24]

Bach explored still other contrapuntal possibilities in the three remaining fughettas within the context of dense, four-part texture. In "**Christum wir sollen loben schon / Was fürchtst du Feind, Herodes, sehr**," BWV 696, the countersubject is derived from the five 8th notes in the subject and appears with the subject at each of its entries. The harmony is spiced with false relations (mm. 4, 6, 10, 11, 15, 18), produced chiefly by the movement of the subject and countersubject in parallel sixths. The phrygian close mirrors that of the dorian-mode chorale melody, which begins on d' but ends on e'.[25] The copious ornamentation that appears in the Neue Bach-Ausgabe text gives the setting a Grigny-like flavor, but it is found only in a third Breitkopf-derived manuscript,[26] rather than the Fétis or Kirnberger copies. The ornaments would thus seem to be a late scribal addition rather than embellishments stemming from Bach or his circle.

In "**Gelobet seist du, Jesu Christ**," BWV 697, a descending countersubject of continuous 16th notes accompanies the subject in each of its 11 entries after the first. The entries can be grouped into three expositions: measures 1–5 (entries in I–V–I–I), measures 6–9 (entries in ii–V–I–IV), and measures 10–14 (entries in V–vi–I–IV). This results in highly concentrated counterpoint. The repeated-note subject and counterpoint resemble the writing in the Orgel-Büchlein setting "Dies sind die heilgen zehn Gebote," BWV 635, which is also set in mixolydian mode. But the texture of "Gelobet seist du" is light and airy—due to the thinning of parts through the placement of judicious rests—and contrasts greatly with the unremittingly dense texture of "Christum wir sollen loben schon." The ongoing 16th notes of "Gelobet seist du" may reflect the fluttering of angel wings, a convention that appears in many other Christmas chorales.[27]

"**Das Jesulein soll doch mein Trost**," BWV 702, is the most adventuresome of the eight fughettas. Rescued from spurious status by Dirksen and added to the Neue Bach-Ausgabe as an afterthought,[28] it consists of the manipulation of two equally important themes: the subject, derived from phrase 1 of the chorale, and the countersubject, derived from phrase 2 of the chorale. The countersubject sounds with the subject from the start, and after appearing in several forms of stretto and an embellished version, it emerges as an independent subject in its own right at the end of the piece, where it is presented in stretto in all four voices, including a bass part assigned to the pedal.

The subject, too, is embellished in this highly complex fughetta, whose proceedings can be summarized as follows:

Mm.	Event
1–2	Subject (in tenor) in I, with countersubject
3–4	Subject (in soprano) in I, with countersubject in stretto
5–6	Subject (in tenor) in I, with countersubject in tighter stretto
7–9	Subject (in bass) in I, subject (in soprano) in I, subject (in alto) in V, in double stretto
9–12	Episode, with countersubject
12–13	Subject (in soprano) in ii, subject (in alto) in vi, in stretto
14–15	Subject (in tenor), embellished, in I, subject (in bass) in V, in stretto, with countersubject, embellished
16–19	Episode, with references to the subject (in soprano)
19–21	Countersubject in all four voices, in stretto

"Das Jesulein soll doch mein Trost" has the appearance of a breakout piece, with its strettos of subject and countersubject, its decoration of both themes, its independent treatment of the countersubject, and its use of pedal for the final thematic entry in the bass. It is much like "In dir ist Freude," BWV 615, in the Orgel-Büchlein—a work that seems to have been added late to the collection that smashes the mold of the earlier entries. Like "Herr Christ, der einig Gottes Sohn" and "Vom Himmel hoch, da komm ich her," "Das Jesulein soll doch mein Trost" may be a product of Bach's Leipzig years rather than a Weimar piece.

The eight chorale fughettas are unjustly neglected works, seldom heard in organ recitals in modern times. When viewed as a group, they show once again Bach's passion for exploration and experimentation, even within the confines of a modest compositional genre. They deserve to be performed more often, as a cycle of eight pieces that lift the art of the chorale fughetta to a new plain.[29]

Congregational Accompaniment: Figured-Bass and Interlude Settings

The communal singing of chorales in the vernacular was a distinguishing aspect of the Lutheran worship service. Congregations participated either by singing a cappella or, more commonly in the eighteenth century, with the support of organ accompaniment. In both cases the singing was preceded by "preluding" on the organ, which served to introduce the chorale and establish the pitch at which it would be sung. Bach's organ chorales serve as classic examples of the preluding tradition.

Organ accompaniment was a widespread practice in Bach's time and a frequent topic of discussion by theorists and church officials, who often voiced concern about organists introducing distracting elements into their hymn-playing. Jacob Adlung's complaint, written in 1758, is typical, warning against organists who, "at the moment when the congregations sings, seek to create variations as if they were preluding on the chorale. One hears 2-voice variations and diminutions, and soon the bass and then the soprano become comical. Then the organist fidgets with his feet, introduces colorful variations, breaks off, chops away, and other such things—so much so that one no longer knows what's happening. Is this truly a proper means of holding the congregation in good order?"[30]

Bach accompanied congregational singing in Arnstadt and mostly likely in Mühlhausen and Weimar as well. Although he did not serve as organist in Leipzig, where support for congregational singing was provided by the organists of the St. Thomas and St. Nicholas churches,[31] he was certainly well acquainted with the art of chorale accompaniment from his early years, and he happily played for the congregational singing of the Creed during his visit to Altenburg in 1739 (see chapter 15).

The simplest type of organ accompaniment took the form of figured-bass settings of the chorale melodies. Such arrangements appear in a number of hymnals from the time, including several from Bach's region: the *Psalmodia Sacra, oder andächtige und schöne Gesänge*, edited by Christian Friedrich Witt (Gotha, 1715), the *Hoch-Fürstliches Sachsen-Weissenfelsisches Vollständiges Gesang- und Kirchen-Buch* (Weissenfels, 1714), and the *Meiningisches Bachisches Choral-Buch*, assembled by Johann Ludwig Bach or his sons (Meiningen, before 1750).[32] The settings typically included the chorale melody, a composed bass, and continuo figures indicating fundamental harmonies (plate 11-1). To judge from annotations in the Meiningen chorale book by one of its early users, organists sometimes realized the continuo figures by grabbing as many notes as possible with the right hand, without regard to voice-leading or consistent texture.[33]

Bach's approach to this type of accompaniment is illustrated by five figured-bass settings that are handed down with corresponding chorale preludes. In each instance the figured-bass arrangement follows the prelude; it is in the same key and labeled "Choral":

Christ lag in Todesbanden, BWV 695/2 (with BWV 695)
Jesu, meine Freude, BWV 713/2 (with BWV 713)

Plate 11-1 The chorale "Christ lag in Todes Banden" as it appears in the Weissenfels hymnal of 1714 (*Hoch-Fürstliches Sachsen-Weissenfelsisches Vollständiges Gesang- und Kirchen-Buch*).

Nun freut euch, lieben Christen gmein, BWV 734/2 (with BWV 734)
Valet will ich dir geben, BWV 736/2 (with BWV 736)
Wer nur den lieben Gott lässt walten, BWV 690/2 (with BWV 690)

A comparison of Bach's figured-bass setting of "Christ lag in Todesbanden" with that in the Weissenfels hymnal shows that Bach updated the chorale to "modern" eighteenth-century instrumental notation (black notes rather than white, regular 4/4 measures), animated the bass with 8th-note figures, and enriched the harmony with 7th and 9th chords, diminished 7th chords, and a bold deceptive cadence before the final "Alleluja" (plate 11-1 and example 11-6). His other figured-bass arrangements show similar refinements.

It is not possible to date the five harmonizations on the basis of the source materials.[34] They are paired with chorale prelude settings from the Weimar years, but they exhibit the smoothly moving bass lines and sophisticated harmonies that are characteristic of Bach's harmonized chorale settings in the Leipzig cantatas. It may be that Bach added them to the chorale preludes during the Leipzig years, perhaps drawing from a now-lost collection of 240 figured-bass arrangements that he assembled at that time.[35] Bach also contributed figured-bass settings to the *Musicalisches Gesangbuch* assembled by Georg Christian Schemelli and published by Breitkopf in 1736.

Example 11-6 Bach: figured-bass setting "Christ lag in Todesbanden," BWV 695/2.

How Bach might have filled in such accompaniments is illustrated by the alio modo setting of "**Liebster Jesu, wir sind hier,**" BWV 706/2, which is a straightforward, four-part harmonization of the chorale. Another possibility is demonstrated vividly by "**Herr Gott, dich loben wir,**" BWV 725, a magnificent five-part setting with obbligato pedal "per omnes versus" of the German Te Deum. The Te Deum arrangement, stretching over 258 measures, makes sense only as a written-out congregational accompaniment, possibly created for a church service celebrating a change of the Town Council in Mühlhausen.[36] It is easy to see from "Herr Gott, dich loben wir" how this type of hymn-playing, with bold, inventive harmonies and constantly changing figuration, would have drawn the often-cited complaints the Arnstadt Consistory expressed about Bach's organ accompaniments a few years earlier:

> Reprove him for having hitherto made many curious *variationes* in the chorale, and mingled many strange tones in it, and for the fact that the Congregation has been confused by it. In the future, if he wished to introduce a *tonus peregrines*, he was to hold it out, and not to turn too quickly to something else, or as had hitherto been his habit, even play a *tonus contrarius*.[37]

The vague terms "tonus peregrines" and "tonus contrarius" suggest that the Consistory members were struggling to describe their discontent while wishing to appear knowledgeable. Both expressions might refer to Bach's ever-varied counterpoint and harmonic colorings, evident in the Te Deum harmonization. What is clear is that Bach was introducing startling complexities into his hymn-playing.

It was also a custom in Thuringia to embellish congregational accompaniments by inserting short interludes between the phrases of the chorale. The interludes normally took the form of one-part cadenzas or "Passagien," leading to the modern German expression "*passaggio* chorale."[38] This tradition can be traced back to 1700 or so, with early examples by Johann Heinrich Buttstedt from 1705 and an anonymous composer in the Plauen Organ Book of 1708.[39] Ostensibly the purpose of inserting the free passage-work was to delight the members of the congregation and allow them to pace themselves during the singing of the chorale. As Johann Carl Voigt remarked at the time: "It has become rather bad taste not to make a few stylish runs, which not only bring pleasure to listeners but also allow them to catch their breath and sing well."[40]

But organists quickly seized the opportunity to use the interludes to show off their artistic and technical skills, tailoring the cadenza-like runs to the *affect* of the chorale on the one hand but making them too elaborate for the congregation to follow on the other. There was much complaining about "abusive" practices. Johann Conrad Rosenbusch, a Thuringian serving as organist in Glückstadt, for instance, confessed in 1718 that he had played many *passaggio* interludes that were "completely unnecessary and inappropriate and had more to do with worldly arrogance than honoring the Glory of God."[41] Rosenbusch pledged that in the future he would play nothing other than an "orderly chorale."

The interlude tradition flourished nevertheless, with printed examples appearing in the *Harmonische Seelenlust* (1733–36) of Buttstett's student Georg Friedrich Kauffmann and in the *Vermischte musikalische Choral-Gedanken* (1737) of Bach's student Johann Caspar Vogler. In Kauffmann's publication, chorale preludes for organ (and sometimes organ with additional instruments) were each followed by a "simple chorale with general-bass figures and a short *passage* between every phrase," as the composer proudly announced on the title page. The settings were intended for "clavier enthusiasts, for private enjoyment, but also for organists in cities and villages, for general use in the church service." In some cases the *passaggio* interludes even contained expressive slurs (example 11-7).

Seven congregational accompaniments with interludes are passed down in Bach's name:[42]

Gelobet seist du, Jesu Christ, BWV 722a
Vom Himmel hoch, da komm ich her, BWV 738a
In dulci jubilo, BWV 729a

Example 11-7 Georg Friedrich Kauffmann, interlude setting "Christ lag in Todesbanden," mm. 1–10, from *Harmonische Seelenlust* (1733–1736).

Lobt Gott, ihr Christen, allzugleich, BWV 732a
Komm, heiliger Geist, erfüll die Herzen, BWV³ 1174
Allein Gott in der Höh sei Ehr, BWV 715
Herr Jesu Christ, dich zu uns wend, BWV 726 (BWV³ App B 52)

The first four are figured-bass settings of Christmas chorales that appear as a group in a manuscript copy made by Johann Tobias Krebs in Weimar around 1714 or so,[43] toward the beginning of his studies with Bach. The notation of the settings—chorale melody in white notes and few or no bar lines—resembles that used for chorales in the seventeenth century and retrospective eighteenth-century hymnals (see plate 11-1).

Bach's arrangements are generally straightforward but hint at innovation here and there. In "Gelobet seist du, Jesu Christ," BWV 722a, the three 32nd-note *passaggio* interludes lead from the last chord of the previous chorale phrase to the first chord of the next, and the harmonic rhythm of the chorale phrases quickens toward the end of the setting. All this is standard practice in Bach's settings. "Vom Himmel hoch, da komm ich her," BWV 738a, shows a similar increase in harmonic rhythm in the last chorale phrase, but the interludes are more complex. The 16th-note *passaggio* passages grow out of 16th-note embellishments in the first phrase of the chorale and begin with falling figures that seem to portray the descent of the angel from heaven bearing good news—a characteristic of Bach's "Vom Himmel hoch" settings in general.

"In dulci jubilo," BWV 729a, is more complex still. Among the chorale phrases, a quarter-note walking bass emerges in phrase 5, perhaps to paint the image in the chorale text of Christ "leuchtet als die Sonne matris in gremio" (shining like the sun in his mother's lap). Among the interludes, the initial three appear in contrary motion, with the first falling, the second rising, and the third falling. Interlude 4 is more animated, with a trill figure toward the beginning, and interlude 5 contains faster-moving triplets, embellishing a falling-fifth motive drawn from phrases 5–6 and 7–8 of the chorale. The exuberance of the *passaggio* writing reflects the joy expressed in the chorale text. "Lobt Gott, ihr Christen, allzugleich," BWV 732a, contains the most nuanced of the *passaggio* interludes, with the 32nd motion modified by 64th, 16th, and quarter notes.

The chords indicated by the general-bass figures of the four arrangements are sophisticated but not as shocking as those in Bach's fully written-out arrangements, which were not limited by the functional nature of figured-bass harmony (we will discuss this shortly). Bach focused rather on the *passaggio* passages, demonstrating four different approaches to creating expressive free interludes. He returned to these figure-bass settings at a later point and fleshed them out, in some cases so elaborately that they became almost unusable as congregational accompaniments. In their figured-bass forms, however, they are eminently singable, especially with appropriate musical cues from the organist to a congregation familiar with the chorale melodies.[44]

The three fully realized interlude settings point to a different compositional goal. **"Komm, heiliger Geist, erfüll die Herzen,"** BWV[3] 1174, passed down in a late manuscript copy by Kittel's student Johann Christian Heinrich Rinck and only recently admitted to the Bach canon,[45] is the most straightforward of the three, with constantly changing 16th- and 32nd-note *passaggio* interludes but an uncomplicated four-part harmonization of the chorale tune.

"Allein Gott in der Höh sei Ehr," BWV 715, and **"Herr Jesu Christ, dich zu uns wend,"** BWV 726 (BWV[3] App B 52), transmitted together in a manuscript written by Bach's friend Johann Peter Kellner around 1727,[46] are more adventurous. The *passaggio* figuration is calculatedly varied, ranging from scales to arpeggios to trill-and-turns to encroachment into the fabric of the chorale harmonization ("Allein Gott," last beat of m. 12), and the chorale phrases show an increase in texture during the course of the settings, beginning in four parts but increasing to five and even six parts toward the end, without concern for strict part-writing or voice-leading. Bach obviously wished to create a grand effect, rather than adhering to a compositionally consistent texture. As we noted earlier, this is a North German trait, passed on to Bach by Georg Böhm.

But most extraordinary in both settings is the bold harmonization of the chorale melody, with colorful, unexpected, unconventional twists. In the last five measures of "Allein Gott in der Höh sei Ehr," diminished seventh chords follow one another without regard to the conventions of traditional linear harmony (example 11-8). Instead, the chords are determined vertically, beat-by-beat, by the note of the choral tune. Bach's brash writing amounts to nonfunctional harmony, used to shock and astound. In "Herr Jesu Christ, dich zu uns wend," the element of astonishment enters even into the *passaggio* figuration, with an unanticipated, unprepared a♭ in the third interlude (m. 6) disrupting the final B-minor arpeggio. No harmonic analysis can account for the resulting dissonance and the subsequent movement to a G[7] chord.

"Allein Gott" and "Herr Jesu Christ," as the Gloria and sermon chorales, respectively, were normally sung in the main church service each week, as part of Lutheran rite. Bach's interlude settings demonstrated ways to grant new life to the weekly singing of these well-known melodies.

Phillip Spitta associated the interlude settings with Bach's return from visiting Buxtehude in Lübeck in the winter of 1705–1706.[47] Hermann Keller later linked them to the complaints of the Arnstadt Consistory about Bach's congregational accompaniments and labeled them "Arnstadt congregation chorales,"[48] a term widely used in the literature until recently. It has now been replaced by the more

Example 11-8 Bach: interlude setting "Allein Gott in der Höh sei Ehr," BWV 715, mm. 13–17.

chronologically neutral German expression "*passaggio* Choräle."[49] "Interlude chorales" might be the best way to describe them in English.

While the four figured-bass interlude chorales are now generally assigned to the Weimar years, the three fully realized settings continue to be linked with Arnstadt.[50] The chronological sequence may be the opposite, however. The old-fashioned white-note notation of the chorale melodies in the four figured-bass arrangements suggests an origin before the Orgel-Büchlein, in which the chorale tunes are written in modern black-note notation. The black-note notation of the three realized passaggio settings suggests an origin around or after the Orgel-Büchlein, as does the bold harmonic vocabulary, which is similar to that of the Fantasia in G Minor, BWV 542/1, and Chromatic Fantasia and Fugue in D Minor, BWV 903, both post-1714 works.

No matter what the precise chronology, Bach may have come to view his interlude settings as youthful sins, for at a later point he seems to have renounced the use of *passaggio* flourishes in hymn accompaniments. Writing in 1770, his student Johann Friedrich Agricola reproached Christian Carl Rolle for including interludes in his recently published organ setting of the Te Deum ("Das Herr Gott dich loben wir"), saying:

> While the melody is set appropriately, we would prefer to send all the interludes back to the composer, even though they are included to give the organist guidance. For these interludes are generally fitting for very few occasions. Johann Sebastian Bach, the greatest organist in all of Europe, valued them little, saying rather: "The organist shows his own art and polish, if he has any, in the prelude. With the singing of the chorale, however, he holds the congregation together

solely through full, clear harmony that supports the true melody. This is how he can show himself to be a talented player.[51]

This apparent change of view may explain Bach's subsequent reworking of the four figured-bass interlude settings, a process that virtually transformed them into chorale preludes:

Gelobet seist du, Jesu Christ, BWV 722
Vom Himmel hoch, da komm ich her, BWV 738
In dulci jublio, BWV 729
Lobt Gott, ihr Christen, allzugleich, BWV 732

The four revised versions are transmitted as a group titled "Four Christmas Chorales" in a manuscript written by Johann Gottlieb Preller around 1740,[52] where they appear in the same order as the figured-bass versions in the Krebs manuscript. There is some evidence that Preller was copying from Weimar sources,[53] and both a complete copy of "Gelobet seist du, Jesu Christ" made by Walther after 1717 and excerpts from "Gelobet seist du, Jesu Christ" and "Lobt Gott, ihr Christen allzugleich" jotted down by Kellner around 1725 confirm that the four revised versions were in place by Bach's early Leipzig years.[54]

In the revamped settings, the chorale melodies appear in modern black-note notation, within metered measures, and the textures have been "contrapuntalized": the original *passaggio* interludes remain intact, but the chorale phrases are now permeated with animated counterpoint, mostly in five parts (example 11-9). The chorale melodies, set forth so clearly in the figured-bass versions, are now either overshadowed by the contrapuntal fabric ("Lobt Gott ihr Christen allzugleich," BWV 732, mm. 6–7), split up ("In dulci jubilo," BWV 729,

Example 11-9 Two settings of "Gelobet seist du, Jesu Christ": (a) figured bass setting, BWV 722a, and (b) harmonized chorale, BWV 722.

mm. 18–20, 26–28), or subsumed into a thick web of motivic counterpoint, complete with obbligato pedal ("Vom Himmel hoch, da komm ich her," BWV 738). With the possible exception of "Gelobet seist du," the new versions are no longer singable.[55] Dressed in thick coats of counterpoint, the settings are closer in style to the chorale preludes of the Orgel-Büchlein than to their original figured-bass forms. One suspects that Bach may have used them as compositional models, to show students how to take a figured-bass interlude arrangement and transform it into a chorale prelude that could be used for preluding on the chorale or as a prelude or postlude to the worship service.

In the most straightforward setting, **"Gelobet seist du, Jesu Christ,"** BWV 722, the distinction between chorale phrase and *passaggio* is clear until the final "Kyrieleise" phrase, where the imitative *suspirans* figuration becomes the focal point of interest. The French ornamentation, more abundant in the Preller manuscript than the Walther copy, also points to the role of the piece as a chorale prelude rather than congregational accompaniment. In the Walther copy, the bass line is marked "man"—that is, *manualiter*.

Bach integrated the *passaggios* of **"In dulci jubilo,"** BWV 729, into the chorale phrases, now harmonized in five parts, and added a four-bar coda, in which the texture increases to six and finally seven parts, prefaced by a new 16th-note *passaggio* interlude. The new interlude adds a third step to the accelerando of the *passaggio* figures during the course of the piece: ♩♪♪♪ → ♪♪.♪♪ → ♫♫♫♫. The progression heightens the sense of rejoicing expressed in the chorale text. The addition of the coda also signals the appropriation of the figured-bass setting for a new purpose, perhaps as a festive postlude to a Christmas Service.[56]

In **"Lobt Gott, ihr Christen allzugleich,"** BWV 732, Bach pushed the limits of congregational accompaniment by starting the setting with an imitative 32nd-note flourish that decorates the initial note of the chorale tune and then descends through the five parts of the harmonization (soprano, alto, tenor I, tenor II, bass) during the first phrase of the melody. In the subsequent phrases the counterpoint becomes increasingly dense, overwhelming the melody in phrase 3, where the accompaniment rises above the chorale tune at the words "He opens today his heavenly kingdom" and provides distracting embellishment in the remaining phrases.

In **"Vom Himmel hoch, da komm ich her,"** BWV 738, Bach converted the bass line of the figured-bass arrangement into an obbligato pedal part and used the 16th-note *passaggio* figuration to create an ongoing motive that permeates the entire piece, much like the intense motivic writing of the Orgel-Büchlein chorales. The resulting idiom is quite like that the second verse of Bach's expansion of the Orgel-Büchlein chorale "Komm, Gott, Schöpfer, heiliger Geist," BWV 631, into the double setting, BWV 667a, a process that took place during his final Weimar years.

With "Lobt Gott, ihr Christen" and "Vom Himmel hoch," especially, Bach wrote the congregation out of the picture. But in doing so, he demonstrated how a conventional improvisatory form—a figured-bass interlude setting—could be used to generate a sophisticated art form—a well-crafted chorale prelude. As Spitta aptly expressed it, Bach displayed "his artistic and creative genius with wonderful freedom and breadth" in these reimagined chorale settings.[57]

Notes

1. See discussion of the Breitkopf firm and the "Kirnberger Chorales" in the introduction.
2. Bighley 2018, 165.
3. Berlin State Library, *P 801*, fascicle 2.
4. In Royal Library of Belgium, *Fétis 2016*, fascicle 2; Berlin State Library, *Am.B. 72a*; Austrian National Library, *Mus. Hs. 35149*, fascicle 13; and Berlin State Library, *Mus.ms. 40037*, a manuscript written in the second half of the eighteenth century by Christoph Sasse (1721–1794), where the group begins with the harmonized chorale (BWV 706/2), followed by BWV 706, BWV 634, and BWV 633, labeled "Var. 1," "Var. 2," and "Var. 3," respectively.
5. *Fugierende und veræendernde Choraele* (Hamburg, 1735), TWV 31:1–48. The phrase is also mirrored in Breitkopf's sales manuscripts of chorale settings, which were often titled "Fugirte und Variirte Choræle."
6. Peter Williams, in Williams 2003, 456, has pointed to the similarity between gigues in the English Suites and the idiom of the "Allein Gott" setting (especially mm. 33–39).
7. Here and elsewhere the measure numbers cited follow those in the Breitkopf and Leupold Editions rather than those in the NBA IV/3, where the measures of repeated Stollens are counted twice.
8. Walther 1732, 94.
9. Berlin State Library, *P 802*.
10. Leipzig, State Archive, *21081/7370*, fascicle 1, written by Johann Ludwig Krebs.
11. The arias appear in Cantatas 41, 68, 85, 175, and 183, all composed in 1725.
12. Found in Berlin State Library, *P 802*.
13. Berlin State Library, *P 1117*.
14. Berlin State Library, *P 1160*, a Breitkopf-derived copy of the work.
15. The most important being Brussels Royal Library, *Fétis 7327 C Mus.*, fascicle 4 ("Christ lag in Todesbanden"), and *Ms. II 3919* (*Fétis 2026 [II]*), fascicle 5 ("Jesu, meine Freude"), both in the hand of Johann Ludwig Krebs. See Leisinger and Wollny 1997, 205–206 and 248–250.
16. Brussels Royal Library, *Ms. II 3919* (*Fétis 2026 [II]*), fascicle 2, described in Leisinger and Wollny 1997, 205–206.
17. Berlin State Library, *Am.B. 72a*.

18. The scribe was apparently copying the chorale settings from a manuscript of Bach works that Kirnberger purchased or borrowed in 1777 from the Breitkopf firm, titled "Sammlung von 110 variirter und fugierter Choräle von 1 u. 2 Cl. u. Pd." See BDok III, no. 824, commentary.

19. By Pieter Dirksen, in Dirksen 2002, 169–174. Doubts about "Das Jesulein" were raised in BWV[1], and it was initially omitted from the NBA (vol. IV/3, Hans Klotz, ed., 1961), It was subsequently added to the edition (vol. IV/10, Reinmar Emans, ed., 2007), in response to Dirksen's study. It is accepted as a Bach work without qualification in BWV[3].

20. Dirksen 2002.

21. Billeter 2007 and Zehnder 2007.

22. Dirksen, in Dirksen 2002, 182, finds this harmonic coloring a late feature and terms it "neo-modal." A similar mixolydian shading of F major appears in the Orgel-Büchlein setting "O Lamm Gottes, unschuldig," BWV 618, however.

23. Before the subject: ½ beat (mm. 11 and 15) and 1½ beats (m. 3); after the subject: ½ beat (mm. 1, 7, 11, and 15) and 4½ beats (m. 8).

24. This point was first made by Jean-Claude Zehnder, in Zehnder 2007, 226, but with regard to "Christum wir sollen loben schon," BWV 696, rather than "Herr Christ, der einig Gottes Sohn" and "Vom Himmel hoch."

25. The same harmonic sequence occurs in the Orgel-Büchlein setting of "Christum wir sollen loben schon," BWV 611.

26. Berlin State Library, P 1119, a manuscript written in the second half of the eighteenth century by an anonymous Breitkopf copyist.

27. "Vom Himmel kam der Engel Schar," BWV 607, or the first variation of the Canon Variations on "Vom Himmel hoch, da komm ich her," BWV 769, for instance.

28. See n. 19.

29. The eight fughettas have been published together as *Leipziger Choralfughetten*, Pieter Dirksen, ed. (Wiesbaden: Breitkopf, 2000) and will be presented as a group in the Leupold Edition, vol. 14 (in progress).

30. Adlung 1758, 822–823.

31. The issue of whether congregations in Leipzig sang chorales with organ accompaniment is controversial. Philipp Spitta (Spitta 1873–80, 278–279) and Arnold Schering (Schering 1926, 242–243) claimed that the singing of chorales was unaccompanied by the organ, a view maintained more recently by Martin Petzoldt (*Die Welt der Bach Kantaten*, Christoph Wolff, ed. [Stuttgart: J. B. Metzler, 1999], vol. 3, 88) and Christoph Wolff (Wolff 2000, 256). None of these writers cites an eighteenth-century source to support this idea, however. By contrast, organists and organ builders from the time referred specifically both to the penetrating tone of the 16' Posaune of the organ in the St. Nicholas Church "during congregational singing" and to the need for a more powerful organ in St. Paul's "to keep order in the congregational singing of chorales" (Edwards Butler 2022, 52–53 and 56). This would seem to indicate that chorale singing was accompanied by the organ in Leipzig, as it generally was elsewhere.

32. Most hymnals from the time contained the texts of the chorales only. A full list of the hymnals from Bach's sphere and the nature of their contents is given in Bighley 2018, v–vi.

33. See the facsimile in the Leupold Edition, vol. 1B, xxxviii.

34. The earliest sources of the "Christ lag in Todesbanden," "Jesu, meine Freude," "Nun freut euch, lieben Christen gmein," and "Wer nur den lieben Gott lässt walten" arrangements are manuscript copies by Johann Ludwig Krebs from c. 1740–1750; the earliest source of the "Valet will ich dir geben" arrangement is an anonymous manuscript copy from c. 1750. See the listings in Bach digital and BWV³.

35. According to Spitta (Spitta 1873–80, vol. 3, 108), the manuscript collection was acquired after Bach's death by the Breitkopf firm, which in 1764 offered copies of it for 10 talers each. The idea that the figured-bass arrangements were added to the chorale prelude settings from a separate source is reinforced by the fact that in three cases ("Jesu, meine Freude," "Valet will ich dir geben," and "Wer nur den lieben Gott lässt walten") the figured-bass arrangement is in a different meter from that of the chorale prelude preceding it.

36. At the service the Te Deum was sung before the sermon. See NBA I/32.1, KB (Christine Fröde, ed., 1992), 59–60, and BWV³, under BWV 725.

37. NBR, no. 20.

38. An early discussion of the art of "Zwischenspiele" or "Passagien" in congregational accompaniments appears in Adlung 1758, pt. II, § 342 (pp. 824–825). The most important recent studies of the *passaggio* chorale are Sackmann 1998, Sackmann 2000, and Zehnder 2013a.

39. Zehnder 2013a, 225–226.

40. Johann Carl Voigt, *Gespräch von der Musik, zwischen einem Organisten und Adjuvanten* (Erfurt: Johann David Jungnicol, 1742), 98. The volume includes a preface added by Lorenz Christoph Mizler in Leipzig.

41. Cited in Kube 1999, 579.

42. The settings are reproduced in NBA IV/3 and the Breitkopf Edition, online resources.

43. Berlin State Library, *P 802*. Dating from Zietz 1969, 99.

44. Such a cue could be, for example, a retard at the end of each *passaggio* and a slight pause for emphasis before the beginning of each chorale phrase.

45. Yale Music Library, *Ma21.Y11.B12* (formerly *LM 4843*). It was added as an afterthought to the NBA, appearing in vol. IV/10, 108–109 and included in BWV³.

46. Berlin State Library, *P 804*. In the manuscript, Kellner credits "Allein Gott in der Höh sei Ehr" to Bach but does not indicate a composer for "Herr Jesu Christ, dich zu uns wend." Perhaps for this reason "Herr Jesu Christ" is consigned to appendix B (works without an eighteenth-century ascription to "J. S. Bach") in BWV³. The context of the setting within Kellner's manuscript and its stylistic similarity to "Allein Gott in der Höh sei Ehr" suggest Bach's authorship.

47. Spitta 1873–80, vol. 1, 318.

48. Keller 1967, 185–189.

49. Used first in Sackmann 1998 and then in Zehnder 2013a.

50. See BWV³, where "Komm, heiliger Geist" is cited as "Arnstadt or earlier" and "Allein Gott" as "Arnstadt or early Weimar."
51. BDok V, no. C760a. See also Czubatynski 1993.
52. Leipzig Town Library, *Peters Ms. 7*, fascicle 24.
53. Synofzik 2001, 49.
54. Berlin State Library, *Mus.ms. 22541 I* (Walther) and *P 274* (Kellner).
55. On this point, see especially Sackmann 1998, 232–237.
56. In recent times it has been used as the signature postlude for the celebrated annual Christmas Eve "Lessons and Carols Service" at Kings College, Cambridge, broadcast internationally on National Public Radio.
57. Spitta 1873–80, vol. 1, 595.

12

Free Works

Prelude-and-Fugue Pairs

The Prelude and Fugue Ideal

Although Bach adopted many aspects of the North German praeludium in his free works, he seemed uninterested in retaining the multi-sectional format favored by Buxtehude and others. As we noted in chapters 3 and 6, Bach courted the multi-sectional praeludium in his early years, in the Praeludium in A Minor, BWV 551; the Praeludium in E Major, BWV 566; and the Toccata in D Minor, BWV 565. But to judge from Lüneburg compositions such as the Prelude and Fugue in D Minor, BWV 549a, and the Prelude and Fugue in C Major, BWV 531, and the Weimar and Leipzig free works, his first and more enduring love was the clear-cut prelude and fugue design that was cultivated in South and Central Germany. Johann Caspar Ferdinand Fischer's *Ariadne Musica* (1702), containing 20 prelude-fugue pairs, each in a different key, and *Blumen-Strauss* (before 1736), containing a cycle of prelude, six fugues, and finale for each of the eight ecclesiastical modes, display in miniature form the format that was to become the principal vessel for Bach's compositional ambitions.

By the time Bach arrived in Weimar, he appears to have settled on the prelude-fugue pair as the ideal vehicle for his free organ works, greatly expanding and transforming the form and filling it first with material derived from North German and French traditions and then with material based on Italian concerto principles.

The Modification of North German and French Idioms

Six free organ works reflect Bach's initial efforts in Weimar to reconcile North German and French stylistic elements with the Central German prelude and fugue format:

Prelude and Fugue in G Major, BWV 550
Prelude and Fugue in A Major, BWV 536
Fantasia and Fugue in C Minor, BWV 562/1a and BWV 546/2a

J. S. BACH. George B. Stauffer, Oxford University Press. © Oxford University Press 2024.
DOI: 10.1093/oso/9780195108026.003.0013

Fantasia and Fugue in G Minor, BWV 542
Prelude and Fugue in D Major, BWV 532
Prelude and Fugue in A Minor, BWV 543

The **Prelude and Fugue in G Major, BWV 550**, features a Prelude with opening manual *passaggio*, dramatic pedal solo (now extended to 10 measures and running from one end of the pedalboard to the other), and a concentrated section in four-part imitative counterpoint. These are obligatory gestures of the North German school, but here they are unified through a steady flow of 8th notes that begins in the Prelude and continues to the end of the Fugue.

The initial four measures of the Prelude display playful rhythmic ambiguity, like the subject of the Fugue in C Minor, BWV 575. Is the Prelude in 3/2 or 2/2 meter? The 3/2 meter becomes clear only as the motive spins out in the measures that follow the opening. In the concentrated section (mm. 23–58), the opening motive is treated imaginatively in an unending chain of small variations. The technique is like that of the Praeludium in A Minor, BWV 569, only more disciplined. And as in that work, the phrases are somewhat square, consisting mostly of three-measure periods that are offset by hemiola passages (mm. 28–29 and 43–44) that hark back to the metrical play of the first measures.

Philipp Spitta compared the "invention and spirit" of the Prelude to Buxtehude's writing,[1] perhaps thinking of the Praeludium in A Minor, BuxWV 153, which exhibits a similar form but contains a mixture of 8th- and 16th-note figuration. Peter Williams saw closer ties with Bruhns's Praeludium in G Major, which is handed down in the Möller Manuscript.[2] The overall gestures in the Bruhns Praeludium are similar to those used by Bach, but the figuration is in 16th notes, once again. If Bach drew on these models, he certainly interpreted them in his own manner.

The structure of the Prelude is logical and marked by increasing intensity:

Mm. 1–23   Manual *passaggio* followed by pedal solo
Mm. 23–47   Concentrated spinning out of the opening motive, in four-part
             counterpoint
Mm. 47–59   Concentrated spinning out of the opening motive, in five-part
             counterpoint

The Prelude concludes with a three-measure bridge, marked "adagio" in two early sources.[3] It serves as a transition to 4/4 meter and the Fugue, and it displays pure five-part texture, like the bridge at the conclusion of the Prelude in D Major, BWV 532/1. It similarly features dark, diminished-seventh chords that set the stage for the bright major-mode of the fugue that follows.

The Fugue is based on a subject built from repeated notes, broken chords, and the repetition of the opening motive a step higher—North German gestures all. The idiom is an unbroken chain of 8th notes, very similar to that of the "Jig" Fugue in G Major, BWV 577, and as in that work, the texture greatly thins out in a manual episode (in this case to two parts, mm. 100–116) before building to dense, four-part writing for an exuberant, almost frenzied close. The opening exposition is unorthodox: it contains five entries of the subject, including a double entry in the pedal at the end, first in the dominant, then immediately in the tonic. The fifth entry implies a five-part fugue, but the texture thins to three parts instead—a mark of Bach's less disciplined, pre–Orgel Büchlein part-writing in Weimar.

The exposition is followed by a lengthy, digressive middle section, first for manuals alone, then with pedal, and then for the manuals alone, once again. The harmonic scheme of this section is adventurous, with entries of the subject in the dominant, submediant, mediant, dominant, supertonic, and subdominant that take it beyond the more limited schemes of the Arnstadt-Mühlhausen fugues. From the second manual section onward, the subject appears in pseudo-stretto, and for its final entry (m. 197) the texture momentarily thickens to five parts. All this adds to the growing intensity of the close. The relentless pedal work also contributes to the dynamic ending, much as it does in the conclusions of the Fugue in D Major, BWV 532/2, and the "Jig" Fugue, once again.

The impressive conclusion cannot dispel the rhythmic monotony of 210 measures of continuous 8th notes, however, interrupted only briefly by the adagio bridge. Bach seems to have valued the Prelude and Fugue in G Major nevertheless, using it late in life as a teaching piece in Leipzig toward the end of the 1730s.[4]

The formal plan of the **Prelude and Fugue in A Major, BWV 536**, is similar to that of the Prelude and Fugue in G Major, but the idiom is entirely different. The declamatory punch of the G-Major work is replaced by gentle arpeggiated chords in the Prelude and a lilting dance subject in the Fugue. The presence of e' in the pedal suggests the extended pedalboard of the Weimar Court Chapel organ and chronological proximity to the G-Major Prelude and Fugue, which contains the same unusual note. The resemblance between the subject of the A-Major Fugue and a theme appearing in the Sinfonia to Cantata 152, *Tritt auf die Glaubensbahn*, of December 30, 1714, first mentioned by Spitta and cited in the Bach literature ever since, seems exaggerated.[5] The two figures are similar, to be sure, but Bach treated them in entirely different ways. If one work influenced the other, it was probably in the direction of the organ fugue affecting the cantata, and most likely at a distance of several years.

The Prelude begins with a variation of the traditional *passaggio*, which in this instance takes the form of a series of broken chords—at first alone, then in a concave arc over a tonic pedal point. A short pedal solo and 32nd-note flourish lead

Example 12-1 Fugue in A Major, BWV 536/2: subject and countersubject.

to a concentrated section in four-part texture. Here the opening chordal material is developed as an imitative *suspirans* motive (mm. 17–27) and a broken chord figure over a dominant pedal point (mm. 28–30). As in the G-Major Prelude, the texture thickens to five parts at the end.

The Fugue is based on an elegant, minuet-like subject, with a rhythmic accent that shifts from the first beat of the measure to the second in alternate measures. A countersubject presents complementary, syncopated rhythms (example 12-1). The Fugue unfolds in units that are very "square," like those of the Prelude in G Major. Here they fall into the periodic pattern of a minuet: 2 + 2 + 4 measures. An initial exposition in four parts leads to an extensive middle section—first *manualiter*, then *pedaliter*, then *manualiter*—with the manual sections featuring false strettos and the pedal section including entries in F♯ minor and B minor.

With the return of the pedal for the final segment of the Fugue, the stretto becomes real (m. 136), and this leads to two final entries in the tonic at the opposite ends of the keyboard: the soprano (m. 145) and the pedal (m. 161). A short coda, in five parts, includes a falling and rising arc like that of the Prelude's opening, a tiny pedal solo, and an abrupt cutoff at the end—a gesture that appears in several works from this period: the Toccata in C Major, BWV 564, and the final chorus of Cantata 71, *Gott ist mein König*, for example. The counterpoint of the Fugue is very well handled—much more adeptly than that of the G-Major Fugue. This may reflect Bach's study of strict part-writing in the Orgel-Büchlein that took place during the initial Weimar years.

The Prelude and Fugue in A Major is an underrated work. It is seldom performed these days, perhaps because it lacks the drama and drive of other free works from the Weimar Period. But it is highly nuanced and dramatic in its own way, building to a carefully crafted conclusion in five parts. It deserves more hearings.[6]

Bach's decision to concentrate on the prelude and fugue in Weimar led to a logical result: the larger and more independent the prelude and the fugue became, the greater the opportunity to pair pieces composed separately or to switch out the prelude or the fugue of a prelude-fugue pair and replace it with a new partner.[7]

We can see the exchange process at work in the **Fantasia and Fugue in C Minor, BWV 562/1a and BWV 546/2a.** Bach appears to have composed this

Example 12-2 Fugue in C Minor, BWV 546/2, mm. 11–17: (a) initial text in BWV 546/2a, and (b) Bach's refinements in BWV 546/2.

fantasia and fugue as a pair during his initial Weimar years,[8] at the time of his concentrated study of French classical organ music and the works of Nicolas de Grigny, in particular (see chapter 7). The pair are transmitted in this form in a manuscript from the circle of Bach's student Bernhard Christian Kayser.[9] Later, in Leipzig, around 1730 or so, Bach appropriated this five-part Fugue for use with the newly composed Prelude in C Minor, BWV 546/1, retaining the Fugue's basic structure but making numerous refinements in its part-writing (example 12-2). At the same time, he seems to have revised the Fantasia as an independent piece, changing its conclusion (which now included a reference in the final measures to the opening theme), improving matters of detail and giving it a new title, "Fantasia pro Organo a 5 Voci," an unusual designation for a prelude that seems to reflect its new stand-alone status. Around 1743–1745, Bach returned to the Fantasia, writing out a fair copy of the revised version.[10] A few years later, around 1747–1748,[11] he returned to the Fantasia a final time, refining measures 61b–62 and adding a new five-part fugue, BWV 562/2, labeled "Fuga a 5," which survives in fragmentary form only (see chapter 21).

The Fantasia and its original Fugue (BWV 546/2a) are a well-matched pair. Both pieces feature five-part texture and somber, expressive themes that are explored in expansive ways. The Fantasia appears to be a tribute to Grigny, whose *Premier Livre d'Orgue* Bach copied out in full between 1709 and 1712. The Fantasia's ornament- and appoggiatura-filled theme resembles the subject of the Gloria fugue in Grigny's collection (example 12-3, a), while the imitative treatment of the theme in five parts resembles the technique Grigny used in his remarkable five-part fugues, where two parts are assigned to the right hand on one manual and two parts to the left hand on a second manual, with the fifth part assigned to the feet on the pedalboard (example 12-3, b). The two manuals were registered with bold, contrasting sounds, typically Cornet in the right hand and

Example 12-3 Nicolas de Grigny, *Premier Livre d'Orgue*: (a) Gloria, theme from the Fugue and the theme from Bach's Fantasia in C Minor, BWV 562, and (b) Verbum supernum, exposition of the Fugue à 5.

Cromorne in the left hand, in the French Classical tradition.[12] The Pedal part was normally played with an 8' Flûte.

In the Fantasia, Bach adjusted this scheme to German practice, taking all four manual parts on one keyboard and the bass part on the pedal, presumably with a 16' foundation (to judge from the many pedal points in the bottom octave). No early source indicates "organum plenum," the normal registration for a free prelude, and it is possible that Bach intended the Fantasia to be played with a French-style registration instead, perhaps with a tierce combination or Krummhorn.

The Fantasia unfolds in a Grigny-like fashion, with dense points of imitation built on overlapping entries of the theme. Six extended pedal points, on the tonic, dominant, supertonic, mediant, subdominant, and tonic, once again, are separated by pedal entries of the theme, initially moving in a circle-of-fifths sequence (mm. 25–31)—a dash of Italian seasoning in an otherwise French recipe. The theme appears with various countersubjects and, toward the end, in parallel sixths (mm. 58–60 and 70–71). But the dominant feature is the ongoing repetition of the theme in imitation, in five-part texture that is maintained throughout. The relentlessly contrapuntal style is reminiscent of Grigny's intense idiom, which must have impressed Bach as he strove to find new ways to construct a free prelude.[13] The serious, melancholy mood reminds one of Grigny's fugues as well. The Fantasia's contrapuntal density is relieved only at the end, where a light conclusion, later replaced, forms a florid *passaggio* bridge to the Fugue (example 12-4).

Example 12-4 Fantasia in C Minor, BWV 562/1a: closing measures.

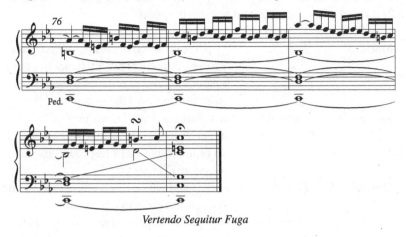

Vertendo Sequitur Fuga

Example 12-5 Fugue in C Minor, BWV 546/2: subject 1 (above) and subject 2 (below).

It is easy to see why Bach temporarily considered the Fantasia, with its unusual French roots, an independent piece, like the equally unusual French-derived *Pièce d'Orgue*, BWV 572. He returned to Grigny's five-part fugue idiom once again, many years later, in the pedal setting of "Vater unser im Himmelreich," BWV 682, of Clavier-Übung III, where he assigned the hands, each playing two parts, to separate manuals, in the true French manner.

The Fugue, BWV 546/2a, has been the object of much criticism, even to the point of having its authenticity questioned.[14] This is mainly due to the fact that it does not measure up to the magnificent Prelude in C Minor, BWV 546/1, the Leipzig work with which it was later paired. When viewed in its original context, as a Weimar experiment in five-part, double fugue-writing, it fares better.

Unlike Bach's earlier attempt at a double fugue, the Fugue on a Theme of Bononcini, BWV 574, in which the two subjects are insufficiently different, the Fugue in C Minor has subjects that sharply contrast with one another: the first, in half and quarter notes, is disjunct and chordal; the second, in 8th notes, is conjunct and scalar (example 12-5).

In terms of structure, the Fugue falls into five clearly defined sections, differentiated by the presence or absence of the pedal:

Mm. 1–59	*Pedaliter*	Five-part exposition of the first subject, with entries in i (manual bass), v (tenor), i (alto), v (soprano), and v (pedal); a second pedal entry in i closes out the section
Mm. 59–86	*Manualiter*	Three-part digressive "exposition" of the second subject, with initial pairs of entries in i and iv followed by free counterpoint based on the subject
Mm. 87–115	*Pedaliter*	Subject 1 and subject 2 combined, in three and four parts; entries in i, v, and III
Mm. 115–139	*Manualiter*	Long episode, beginning with an entry in iv (with second subject inverted), followed by a long digression on a new idea derived from motives from both subjects
Mm. 140–159	*Pedaliter*	Return of subject 1 in i (pedal), followed by quasi-entry in i with Neapolitan-sixth coloring (m. 151) and coda in five parts

This balanced plan is offset by certain asymmetries. The modulation to related keys, the mediant and the subdominant, is divided between the middle *pedaliter* section and the second *manualiter* section, rather than contained in just one or the other. And the second *manualiter* section seems overly digressive and partly superfluous, even though it foreshadows the "music-box" effect that appears more succinctly in the central manual episode of the Fugue in B Minor, BWV 544/2. The use of five-part texture in the outer *pedaliter* sections provides an admirable framing element, but elsewhere the textures shift among two, three, and four parts without convincing logic.

The second subject unfolds in an unorthodox way. It acts more like a countersubject or imitative motive than a subject proper. After it enters in the first *manualiter* section, via imitative, octave pairs in the tonic and the subdominant, it appears in a motivic role for the remainder of the Fugue, acting as an accompaniment for the main subject and providing material for the episodes. Its function and harmonic profile are never clearly defined.

Bach must have admired this early essay in five-part fugue-writing, despite its shortcomings, since he deemed it sufficiently worthy of revision and pairing with the C-Minor Prelude, BWV 546/1. It is unfortunate that the C-Minor Fugue is rarely performed in its original form and context, with the Fantasia in C Minor, to provide a glimpse of Bach's original concept of this well-matched prelude-fugue pair.[15]

The **Fantasia and Fugue in G Minor, BWV 542**, also illustrates Bach's pairing of independently composed pieces. The Fugue was most certainly written first and achieved fame as an independent work. The Fantasia appears to have been composed at a later point and added to the Fugue to create a prelude-fugue pair. This sequence of events is suggested by the separate transmission of the two pieces as well as their different key signatures—the Fugue is handed down in dorian notation (G minor, one flat), the standard for Bach's early works, while the Fantasia is transmitted in modern notation (G minor, two flats), which Bach began to use during the Cöthen years.

The Fugue clearly dazzled players and enjoyed widespread popularity in Bach's time. It is passed down as an independent work in more than 20 early copies,[16] and at an early point it was rewritten in F minor, so that it could be played on organs lacking d' in the pedalboard.[17] This version circulated almost as widely as the original.[18] In addition, Bach appears to have performed the Fugue during his audition recital in 1720 at St. Catherine's Church in Hamburg, where its unprecedented virtuosic demands and subject derived from the Dutch folksong "Ik ben gegroet van" (I am greeted by)[19] would have impressed the audience—especially the resident organist, Johann Adam Reincken, who was born in the Netherlands (example 12-6).

Hamburg officials subsequently used the work's subject and first countersubject for a fugue improvisation requirement during the organist auditions at the Hamburg Cathedral in 1725. The Hamburg composer and theorist Johann Mattheson, reflecting on the cathedral's audition process some years later, quoted the two themes, with the aside: "I knew very well where this subject belonged at home, and who once upon a time had set it artfully to paper. But I wanted to see how this candidate or that would handle it."[20] Such was the reputation of the work and the compositional benchmark it represented. With good reason it was termed "the very best pedal piece by Mr. Johann Sebastian Bach" in two early manuscripts.[21]

The G-Minor Fugue is a *Spielfuge* par excellence. A *Spielfuge*, or instrumental fugue, is characterized by virtuosity and figural play. Its

Example 12-6 (a) Dutch folk song "Ik ben gegroet van," and (b) Fugue in G Minor, BWV 542/2, subject.

Example 12-7 Fugue in G Minor, BWV 542/2: subject, countersubject 1, and countersubject 2.

black-note subject commonly features symmetrical or repetitive elements with accelerating note values, and its episodes are filled with lengthy sequential passages and other animated digressions.[22] The main subject of this fugue—the Dutch folksong, refashioned by Bach—consists of two sequential phrases, the first one-half measure long, the second one measure long (example 12-7, x and y). They are united by a twisting 16th-note motive (example 12-7, z), perfectly tailored for opposite-toe pedal playing, which becomes the object of obsessive development in the episodes (such as mm. 61–63, where it appears in three voices simultaneously, in parallel motion). During the course of the Fugue, Bach embellishes the subject with additional 16th notes, making it more lively still.

The subject is accompanied by two countersubjects. The first contains half notes that move against the subject in syncopation; the second contains animated 16th notes, now tied over the bar (example 12-7). The second countersubject, like the subject, is later decorated in versions suited to the hands as well as the feet.[23] Written in invertible counterpoint, the subject and countersubjects appear together in the six possible contrapuntal combinations outlined by Theile in the *Musicalisches Kunst-Buch* (figure 12-1; see chapter 7). Bach's approach to the permutation fugue is much freer here than in the fugue of the Passacaglia in C Minor (see chapter 13), since he mixes various free voices with the subject and countersubjects and sometimes presents the subject without either countersubject. Still, his contrapuntal manipulations were surely not lost on Reincken and his North German colleagues, who admired Theile as the "father of contrapuntists." In the G-Minor Fugue, Bach brought Theile's theories to life in the most exuberant way.

A fourth theme, an evolving four-note motive derived from the interval of the fourth found in both the subject and the first countersubject, emerges in the first manual episode (mm. 39–41) and proceeds to take over succeeding

Measure	1	4	10	15	22	24	29	37	44	51	55	65	72	80	94	101	103	110	115
Soprano	S	C1	C2	F	S	C1	C2	C1	S	F	C2	C1	S		F	S		F	C2 F
Alto		S	C1	C2	F	S	C1	C2			C1	F		S				S	F
Tenor			S	C1	C2	C2		S	F	S		S	C1	C1	F		S	C1	C2
Bass (pedal)				S	C1		S				S		F	C2					S
Key	i	v		i	v		i	v		i	III	v	v	VII	i	iv	VI	i	i i i

pedaliter — manualiter — pedaliter — manualiter — pedaliter

S = subject; C1 = countersubject 1; C2 = countersubject 2; F = free voice.

Figure 12-1 Fugue in G Minor, BWV 542/2: permutations of the subject and countersubjects.

episodes, eventually appearing in imitation between the hands and feet (mm. 82–93).

The Fugue's large, complex structure can be summarized as follows:

Mm. 1–17   Initial exposition, with subject entries in i, v, i, v

Mm. 18–22   Short episode, based on the x motive

Mm. 22–32   Second exposition, with subject entries in i, v, i

Mm. 32–37   Short episode

Mm. 37–55   Manual episode, with subject entries in III, v, and v; first appearance of the four-note episodic theme

Mm. 55–93   Pedal returns; subject entries in VII, i, iv, and VI alternating with extensive development of the episodic theme

Mm. 93–110   Manual episode (mm. 94–103 = mm. 44–53, transposed), subject entries in i, i, i

Mm. 110–115   Final subject entry, in i, in pedal; short close

The complexity of the design is counterbalanced by the reassuring reappearance of the subject—18 times!—often with disguised beginnings. Despite the Fugue's brilliance, the asymmetry of its structure, the irregular maintenance of four-part texture, the obsessive 16th-note motion (quite like that of the Fugue of the Toccata in C Minor, BWV 911), and the lengthy digressive episodes mark this as a work written before Bach's encounter with Vivaldi in 1713. With its demanding pedal part, it is the apotheosis of North German virtuosic *pedaliter* style.

As Williams pointed out, the two lengthy *manualiter* segments create the sensation of concerto episodes,[24] even though this is not a concerto fugue. But the work is oddly concerto-like in spirit, with its animated motor rhythms. All that is missing is an appropriate prelude.

This came in the form of the Fantasia in G Minor. The origin of the Fantasia rests in the dark. No pre-1750 copies exist, suggesting, perhaps, that the piece was so special that Bach kept it for himself, rather than share it with colleagues and students. The earliest surviving source is a manuscript from the Amalian Library in Berlin, written by an anonymous scribe between 1760 and 1789,[25] in which it is already paired with the Fugue. Both pieces are mysteriously absent from Johann Nicolaus Forkel's 1802 listing of Bach's organ works.[26] Thus the Fantasia's date of composition and pairing with the Fugue are open to conjecture.

The Fantasia's bold chromatic excursions and recitative-like writing link it with the Fantasia of the Chromatic Fantasia and Fugue in D Minor, BWV 903, of the Cöthen years. Similar recitative passages also appear in the opening Adagio movements of Sonatas 1 and 2 for Unaccompanied Violin, BWV 1001 and 1003, which stem from Cöthen as well. The modern notation of the G-Minor Fantasia points to a post-Weimar origin, and it is possible that the piece stems from something Bach improvised before the G-Minor Fugue during the Hamburg audition of 1720. Just as the Fugue is the epitome of the *Spielfuge*, the Fantasia is the epitome of the *stylus fantasticus* praeludium—the two organ genres that would have greatly impressed the North German audience. In addition, the instrument in St. Catherine's Church appears to have been tuned in a temperament approaching meantone.[27] The wild harmonic excursions of the Fantasia, which go as far afield as E♭ minor (m. 21), and the remarkable modulatory sequence in measures 31–34 seem tailor-made to exploit the bold sounds that would be produced when played on an organ tuned in meantone. The Fantasia would have made an ideal, daring companion piece for the G-Minor Fugue at the Hamburg audition. But this is pure speculation.

The structure of the Fantasia combines the predictable with the unpredictable. The predictable element is represented by the two segments of straightforward, four-part imitative writing occurring first in the dominant (mm. 9–14) and then, transposed down a fifth, in the tonic (mm. 25–31). The conventional manual figures, steady rhythmic pulse, and walking bass of continuous 8th notes serve as safe atolls in a sea of harmonic turbulence. The unpredictable element is the free writing that appears in the three fantasy sections, which grow in length and intensity during the course of the piece. The first segment (mm. 1–9) opens with three measures of secco recitative, accompanied by threatening diminished 7th and 9th chords that foreshadow the harmonic turmoil to come. This is followed by five measures of *passaggio*-like material over pedal points in the tonic and then dominant. The second free segment (mm. 14–25) begins with a dialogue of recitative figures before moving from D major to E♭ minor to F minor to G major in the course of four measures. The final free segment (mm. 31–48) begins with the extraordinary chromatic modulatory sequence that starts in D major and travels as far afield as A♭ minor before stopping abruptly on a diminished seventh chord with B♭ in the pedal. From here until the end, all is in a state of flux: the rhythm, the texture, and the harmony. The drama, disruption, and instability are resolved only in the final two chords, root-position dominant to root-position tonic.

Dietrich Kilian, editor of the work in the Neue Bach-Ausgabe, questioned whether the Fantasia and the Fugue were truly paired by Bach, given the pieces' largely independent transmissions.[28] The Fantasia seems to present too much harmonic instability to stand alone, however. The deeply dissonant idiom cries out for more extensive resolution than the work's abrupt conclusion. The Fugue, with nine thematic entries in the tonic, provides such resolution. As Werner Breig has noted, the pairing of the G-Minor Fantasia and G-Minor Fugue is simply too perfect to be happenstance.[29] Surely it was a match made in Cöthen (if not Leipzig).

Prelude and Fugue in D Major, BWV 532. Who but a young, brash Bach could have composed this Prelude and Fugue? With one daring pedal scale he put the North Germans on notice that he was about to take the *pedaliter* Praeludium to a new technical level. And this is to say nothing of the eclectic nature of the Prelude, the heady rush of the Fugue, and the dizzying final pedal cadenza. Although the latest Schmieder catalog speculates that the early version of the Fugue, BWV 532/2a, may go back to Arnstadt,[30] only in Weimar would Bach have had an audience that could fully appreciate this very worldly work.

The Prelude and the Fugue also appear to have had separate origins: they are transmitted mostly as single pieces in the early sources,[31] and the Fugue in its early form, a 98-measure variant, seems to predate both the Prelude and the Fugue in its larger, 137-measure form, BWV 532/2.

The shorter version of the Fugue is preserved solely in the Peters Edition of 1846.[32] The editor, Friedrich Conrad Griepenkerl, stated that he had based the text on a "very good manuscript,"[33] which subsequently disappeared. There are no extant sources that might provide clues to the variant's origin. Spitta believed that the shorter version of the Fugue was an abridgement made by Bach, intended to rectify the excesses of the longer version[34]—a view shared by a number of writers in modern times.[35] More recently, Breig and Jean-Claude Zehnder have convincingly shown that the shorter version is the original, with awkward modulations and a more limited harmonic scheme that Bach expanded and improved when revising the text.[36]

The Prelude was surely written in conjunction with enlarging the Fugue, for Bach seems to have taken carefully calculated steps to coordinate the two pieces: the virtuosic pedal-play of the Prelude's opening foreshadows that of the Fugue; the dissonant, chromatic ending of the Prelude sets up the opening diatonic exposition of the Fugue; and two motives in the Prelude (example 12-8, x and y) anticipate two motives in the Fugue, the first added only in the revision.

Example 12-8 Prelude and Fugue in D Major, BWV 532: motives uniting the
Prelude and the Fugue.

The Prelude has the through-composed, sectional format that Bach used
in earlier preludes: free opening—rhythmically strict, concentrated middle
section—free close. Here, however, he turned to a mix of seemingly disparate national styles for the three segments. The introductory section (mm. 1–16) is filled
with North German gestures: an opening *passaggio*, now distributed between the
feet and the hands; a pedal point on the dominant, with more passage-work; a
second pedal point on the dominant of B minor (an important key in the Fugue),
with a Buxtehudian double *trillo-longo*; and a two-octave manual glissando. All
four gestures stem from the *stylus fantasticus*, which suggests a rhythmically
flexible interpretation. They foreshadow the musical banter that follows in the
middle section.

The middle section (mm. 16–96), marked alla breve, has no clear theme. It
is based rather on two sequences: one built on a descending suspension against
animated 8th notes (example 12-9, a), the other built on two catchy four-note
motives treated in imitation against the animated 8th-note line (example 12-9,
b, x and y). The entire alla breve consists of the repetition, extension, and alternation of these two ideas, in invertible counterpoint. The continuous 8th-note
motion, produced by the playful variations of the animated voice of the suspension sequence, and the harmonic scheme that touches on G major, C major, B
minor, and F♯ minor in addition to the tonic and dominant, reflect Bach's pre-
Vivaldi encounter with Italian instrumental music. Williams claimed that the
suspension figure "looks like a model passage for the learner of figured bass," and
Zehnder finds the alla breve "loose and little organized."[37] They both miss the
point. The sequences are effective, and the seemingly casual structure of the alla
breve gives it an element of wit that complements the playfulness of the Fugue.

In the short close (mm. 96–107), Bach turned again to North German *stylus
fantasticus* elements: glissandi together with jarringly dissonant chromatic
chords in four and five parts, with double pedal. This type of writing, greatly
admired in Bach's time for its shock value, was termed *durezza* (Italian) or *durete*

Example 12-9 Prelude in D Major, BWV 532/1: (a) sequential motive, and (b) four-note motives (x and y).

(French), which Johann Gottfried Walther defined as "extraordinary dissonance of the type that includes diminished and augmented intervals."[38]

Early copyists didn't know what to make of this unusual piece. While most termed it "Preludio" or "Praeludium," one called it "Præludio Concertato" in light of its Italianate alla breve, and another termed it "Pièce d'Orgue," possibly sensing the similarity of the three-part structure with that of the *Pièce d'Orgue*, BWV 572.[39]

The Fugue with which the Prelude was eventually paired is another example of a *Spielfuge*, or animated instrumental fugue. The theme is one of Bach's most ebullient creations. It consists of two parts, separated by a pause: a head motive establishing the tonic, and a tail that begins on the submediant and moves sequentially back to the tonic. Both contain humorous repetitions. Given the rapid toe-crossings required by the head motive, the fugue subject is playable by the feet in keys with scales that contain one or two accidentals in the first notes rather than three naturals. Thus the subdominant, G major, a key that would normally be reached in a fugue in D major, is avoided here, for technical reasons.

Much of the wit in the Fugue comes from the way Bach filled in the pause between the head and tail of the subject. At first, he used a supercilious semitone-and-octave idea (mm. 7–8). But as the Fugue progresses, he filled the gap in other ways, first with the embellished head motive itself (m. 47), then with both the head motive and the semitone idea (m. 54–55), and finally with the head motive, the semi-tone idea, and the first half of the tail motive (mm. 91–93). Elsewhere equally mischievous things happen: the head and tail of the fugue theme migrate to different voices (mm. 80–84, 90–96) and the semitone idea is repeated, first twice, with parts exchanged (mm. 69–71), and then, with its octave, to the point of ridiculousness (mm. 111–117). The whimsical potential of the Prelude is brilliantly fulfilled in the Fugue.

Bach heightened the effect of the whimsical elements when he expanded the Fugue. First, he extended the central modulatory section to include new, exotically distant harmonic stations: C♯ minor (mm. 80–84, in BWV 532/2) and E major (mm. 90–95). Second, he refined awkward spots and added sections of playful figuration (mm. 106–111, for instance). Third, he expanded the coda, inserting a new passage (mm. 124–131) that extends the D major tonality, most probably to balance the enlarged harmonic digression of the middle section. It also increases the virtuosic dialogue between the manuals and the pedal, a gesture that harks back to the beginning of the Prelude.

All this points to Bach's showmanship in Weimar, to his desire to demonstrate to the dukes and the prince just how far he could take bravura playing. The earliest manuscript containing the Prelude and the Fugue as a pair includes a cautionary note for the player: "Nota Bene, in this piece one really has to let the feet kick around a lot."[40] You said it!

The **Prelude and Fugue in A Minor,** BWV 543, may have been the last prelude and fugue that Bach wrote under the direct influence of the North German praeludium, for both the Prelude and the Fugue display northern traits. The Prelude opens with a free manual *passaggio* over a sustained pedal-point followed by a Buxtehudian double trill. This leads to the obligatory pedal solo and a stricter section of concentrated counterpoint. The Fugue shows virtuosic 16th-note figuration and obbligato pedal, and it closes with a pedal solo and free manual *passaggio* that reflect the opening of the Prelude. All this points to the North German school.

But new forces are at work, in the Fugue in particular. The subject has a carefully worked-out sequential pattern, the episodes contain smooth and convincing sequences and modulations, and the overall structure shows a clear division of tutti (the outer *pedaliter* sections) and solo (the middle *manualiter* section), with most of the modulatory activity taking place in the solo portion. All this points to the growing influence of Italian instrumental music.

The earliest copy of the work, an anonymous manuscript from the circle of Johann Tobias Krebs, contains an early form of the Prelude, BWV 543/1a.[41] It includes a few indications for fingering and the distribution of the hands, and it underscores the North German roots of the work all the more. The broken chords over the tonic pedal-point in measure 7 are written as 32nd notes rather than 16th notes, as in the later version, resulting in an abrupt change in figuration that is typical of the *stylus fantasticus*. When revising the Prelude, Bach changed the 32nd notes to 16th-note sextuplets, doubling the length of the section and producing a much more nuanced, graduated transition leading to the pedal solo: ♩♩♩♩ → ♩♩.♩♩ → ♩♩♩♩♩♩. He also refined and expanded the opening sequence and added a measure to the pedal solo, strengthening its effect. But he left the section of concentrated counterpoint essentially unchanged, except to thicken the final chord. The result was a more carefully integrated Prelude, 10 measures longer than the original.

Bach may not have made these revisions until the 1730s or 1740s, since a copy of the work written by Johann Peter Kellner around 1726–1727 still includes the early version of the Prelude.[42] Copies stemming from the circle of Johann Christian Kittel, who studied with Bach from 1748 to 1750, show the revised Prelude in place.[43]

In the revised Prelude, Bach refined the traditional gesture of chromatically descending chords, slowing the rate of descent from the 8th note to the quarter note. The pedal solo, now extended, emerges dramatically out of the double trill and leads to a measure of *style brisé* writing. In the section of concentrated counterpoint (mm. 36–53 in the revised version), the imitation of a *suspirans* figure also moves downward at the start, now through the manual voices to the pedal. And the texture of the final four measures, with the manual and pedal parts in dialogue, closely resembles writing found in the Orgel-Büchlein Chorales "Herr Christ, der ein'ge Gottessohn," BWV 601, and "Alle Menschen müssen sterben," BWV 643, and the Passacaglia in C Minor, BWV 582 (mm. 72–80). Although Bach covered a good number of North German gestures in the Prelude, he nevertheless managed to create a dramatic whole through the strong rhythmic drive of the concentrated section, which sweeps aside the diverse gestures of the opening portion.

The Fugue, by contrast, appears to have pleased Bach from the start. It is a dance fugue—a fugue with the characteristics of a *Spielfuge* but the meter and periodic phrasing of a dance.[44] As Mozart once explained to his sister Nannerl, fugues are much more difficult to compose than preludes.[45] In this case, as with the Prelude and Fugue in G Minor, BWV 535, and Prelude and Fugue in C Major, BWV 545, Bach seems to have invested his initial energies into the composition of the fugue, leaving the expansion and refinement of the prelude until later.

Three aspects of the A-Minor Fugue are especially striking and demonstrate Bach's thinking on fugue-writing around 1713 or so. First, the subject, in a 6/8 dance idiom, consists of three distinct sections: an opening segment that establishes the tonic, a sequential segment that moves through a circle of fifths, and a brief cadential segment that reaffirms the tonic (example 12-10, x, y, and z). This closely resembles the ritornello structure of Vivaldi's concertos and may reflect an early appropriation of the Venetian's technique by Bach for his own purposes.[46]

Example 12-10 Fugue in A Minor, BWV 543/2: subject, with opening segment (x), sequential segment (y), closing segment (z), and implied harmony.

Second, as noted earlier, the Fugue displays a clearly defined tripartite form, with *pedaliter* opening section, *manualiter* middle section, and *pedaliter* closing section:

Mm.	Texture	Event
1–51	*pedaliter*	Exposition in four parts, with entries in i v i v, plus an additional entry in i
51–95	*manualiter*	Episodic material with circle of fifth sequences, entries of the subject in v, III, VII, and iv
95–151	*pedaliter*	Return of the subject in i, with additional entries in v and i, followed by episodic material and concluding pedal cadenza and manual flourish

Unlike the subject entries in the Fugue in C Minor, BWV 546/2a, the subject entries here are fully aligned with the structure of the piece: the tonic and dominant entries take place in the outer sections, and the excursions to related keys take place in the middle section.

Third, like the Fugues of the Fantasia and Fugue in G Minor and the Prelude and Fugue in D Major, the Fugue in A Minor, in addition to its dance idiom, is a *Spielfuge*, a quality that is reflected in Bach's playful handling of the subject. Its entries are sometimes delayed by false and double-false entries (mm. 95 and 113) or disguised by embellished incipits (mm. 51, 61, 71), and toward the end it migrates from voice to voice (mm. 113–119).

And to all this one can add Bach's masterful handling of four-part texture and the climactic conclusion, complete with daring pedal cadenza and dramatic manual flourish (with sextuplets, to match those of the original Prelude).

Where could Bach go with the prelude and fugue after this remarkable work? Beyond German and French style, it would seem.

The Adoption of Italian Concerto Principles

As we noted in Chapter 7, Bach's interest in Italian instrumental music, first evident in Arnstadt through his fugues based on themes by Corelli and Buononcini, reached a peak in Weimar with his encounter with Vivaldi's concertos, most probably in 1713. The engagement with Vivaldi's *L'Estro armónico*, through the performance, study, and the transcription of individual works, was transformative. It opened the door to a new approach to the prelude-fugue pair that can be seen in four works:

> Prelude and Fugue in C Major, BWV 545
> Toccata and Fugue in F Major, BWV 540
> Toccata and Fugue in D Minor ("Dorian"), BWV 538
> Prelude and Fugue in G Major, BWV 541

The **Prelude and Fugue in C Major, BWV 545**, like the Fantasia in C Minor, BWV 562/1, has a complex genesis. It appears to have evolved in three stages. The first, preserved in two eighteenth-century manuscript copies dating from after 1750,[47] consisted of a prelude-fugue pair, BWV 545a, with a Prelude of just 25 measures dwarfed by a Fugue of 111 measures (BWV 545.1 in BWV³). In Leipzig, around 1727 or so, Bach expanded the Prelude to 31 measures by adding a new beginning and end. He also inserted the "Largo" from Sonata 5 between the Prelude and Fugue and refined the Fugue, thus producing a Prelude, Trio, and Fugue (BWV 545.2 in BWV³). This form is reflected in copies by Walther, Kellner, and Johann Caspar Vogler from the late 1720s and early 1730s.[48] Finally, in the late 1740s, Bach removed the Trio movement and returned the work to its prelude-and-fugue format, making small refinements in the Prelude in the process (BWV 545.3 in BWV³). This version was preserved in a now-lost autograph, whose text is reflected in three late copies made by two of Kittel's students.[49]

Even in its initial short form, BWV 545/1a, the Prelude represented a pivotal turning point in Bach's compositional style. Instead of a sectional plan, with multiple opening gestures followed by a section of concentrated counterpoint, the Prelude now unfolds in one continuous stream of 16th notes, in the manner of an Italian instrumental concerto. The Prelude begins with the

North German gesture of a manual *passaggio* over a tonic pedal point, but it is no longer in the free rhythm of the *stylus fantasticus*. Instead, it is in the strict rhythm of a concerto, and the implied harmonic progression of the opening motive, I–V–I–vi–ii^7–V^7–I, gives it a dynamic incisiveness typical of Vivaldi's themes. The obligatory North German pedal solo is also present, at the very end of the Prelude (mm. 21–23 of the early version), but it, too, has been incorporated into the steady flow of ongoing 16th notes. The idiom is that of the Orgel-Büchlein chorales or the preludes of the Well-Tempered Clavier, volume 1.

In addition, Bach replaced the through-composed sectional format of his earlier free organ preludes with a symmetrical design: A B A B Close. The initial A consists of three-part imitation over a tonic pedal, followed by B, a series of sequences modulating to the dominant. The second A consists of three-part manual imitation over a dominant pedal, followed by B, a series of sequences once again, this time leading to the pedal solo and close in the tonic. Bach may have patterned the material in the A section after works by Pachelbel, Fischer, and other Central and South German composers: Pachelbel's Toccatas in C Major and G Minor contain imitative material reiterated over two prolonged pedal points, first in the tonic and then in the dominant, for instance. But the sequences in the B section reflect Italian concerto-writing.

When Bach expanded the Prelude in Leipzig to make a better match for the Fugue, he preserved its symmetrical structure by adding framing segments (X) of equal length and style to the beginning and end: X A B A B Close X. He was able to weave the new material into the fabric of the existing Prelude precisely because of the ongoing flow of 16th notes, which facilitated a smooth and seamless integration (example 12-11).[50]

The Fugue also represents a new direction. It is an alla breve fugue, like the Fugue in C Minor, BWV 546/2a, handled now with great elegance and finesse. An alla breve fugue is an instrumental interpretation of a vocal motet, with roots in the southern keyboard works of Frescobaldi, Froberger, Kerll, and others rather than in Renaissance vocal writing.[51] Its white-note subject, in alla breve meter, moves mostly in conjunct steps, like the theme of a Renaissance motet, and it lacks the repetitive sequences often found in the subjects of instrumental and dance fugues.

In the C-Major Fugue, the suspensions typical of alla breve style emerge in the countersubject, which descends step-by-step, off the beat against the white-note subject. The episodes, which contain mostly black notes, are more subdued that those of *Spielfugen* and dance fugues. It is the presentation of the subject that takes precedence over episodic play. The texture is also thicker than in other fugue types. In this case, after the initial exposition, the texture is never less than

Example 12-11 Prelude in C Major, BWV 545/1: (a) early version, BWV 545/1a, mm. 1–4, and (b) revised version, BWV 545/1, mm. 4–7, showing Bach's carpentry in joining the new opening to the old.

three voices, avoiding the extreme reduction to two parts or even one, seen in earlier fugues. The three final entries of the subject in the tonic (mm. 79, 100, and 105) occur amid four-part texture, which thickens to six- and seven-part chords in the final two measures. Pedal virtuosity is also reduced, in stark contrast to that in *Spielfugen* such as the Fugue in G Minor, BWV 542/2, or the Fugue in A Minor, BWV 543/2.

Breig has pointed out Bach's increased concern for textural and structural balance in the C-Major Fugue.[52] In the opening exposition (mm. 1–20), the four voices enter in the middle range of the keyboard, leaving the higher possibilities (c″, subject, m. 41, and c‴, countersubject, m. 44) and lower possibilities (G, subject, mm. 45 and 73, and C, subject, m. 100) for later development. Of the 16 entries of the subject, 6 are in the tonic, and 6 are in the dominant, creating perfect tonal symmetry. And the excursions to related keys in the modulatory segment (mm. 52–87), now four in number, are anchored by a return to the tonic and dominant in the middle (vi–iii–V–I–IV–ii).

In terms of performance, the alla breve meter, with the eighth note as the smallest note value, points to a somewhat weightier, more earnest articulation that in other fugue types. According to Bach's student Johann Philipp Kirnberger:

It is to be noted about this meter (2/2, or rather alla breve, which is always designated by ₵ or ₵) that it is very serious and emphatic, yet is performed twice as fast as its note values indicate, unless a slower tempo is specified by the adjectives *grave, adagio,* etc.[53]

Bach's decision to temporarily insert the Largo from Sonata 5 between the Prelude and Fugue to produce a concerto-like, three-movement form in Leipzig underscores the Italian instrumental roots of the Prelude and Fugue. But even without the Trio, the Prelude and Fugue in C Major was a pivotal work for Bach, opening a new avenue of exploration that was soon to produce still more fruitful results.

Toccata and Fugue in F Major, BWV 540. The Toccata and the Fugue are transmitted independently in many early sources, and the Toccata calls for an unusual pedal compass, C–f', that is not utilized in the Fugue, which requires a more conventional pedal range, C–c'. These factors point to a separate origin for the two pieces. The earliest evidence of their pairing is found in one of the Krebs family manuscripts, in which Johann Tobias Krebs entered the Toccata around 1714 and his son Johann Ludwig added the Fugue around 1731.[54] Later copies of the complete work from the Berlin circles of C.P.E. Bach and Kirnberger[55] support the idea that the pairing of Toccata and Fugue was made by Bach himself, most probably during the Leipzig years.

The Toccata is Bach's largest organ work, and we are not wrong to see it as a sequel to the opening movement of the Toccata in C Major, BWV 564/1, since it exhibits the same hybrid structure: manual *passaggio*, pedal solo, concerto. But these elements have been fully transformed and tightly unified in the F-Major Toccata. The music is cast in a progressive 3/8 dance meter rather than traditional 4/4 time—itself a sign that new things are afoot—and the *passaggio*, pedal solo, and concerto are united through the use of a principal motive that appears in all three. The motive has Vivaldian features: it is angular and motoric, and in the opening measures it establishes the tonic by emphatically outlining alternating tonic and dominant chords, in a Vivaldi-like manner (example 12-12, a). Bach presents the motive first as a two-part canon over a pedal point, then as a pedal solo, and then as a three-part trio within the concerto section. The motive is joined by two contrasting ideas: detached chords (example 12-12, b) that first appear innocently in the cadence of the initial pedal solo before growing to become a defining factor in the concerto movement, and a triadic sequential motive (example 12-12, c), presented in imitation, that acts in the manner of a modulating ritornello, also in the concerto movement.

From these three ideas Bach spins out 438 measures of music whose forward drive is disrupted (but not stopped!) by three shocking, deceptive cadences, produced through the use of Neapolitan-sixth chords. The immense structure of the Toccata can be outlined as follows:

Example 12-12 Toccata in F Major, BWV 540/1: (a) canonic motive, (b) chordal motive, and (c) sequential motive.

Portion/ Mm.	Material	Harmonic station
Introduction		
1–55	Two-part manual canon on principal motive, tonic pedal point	I
55–82	Pedal solo on principal motive, ending in detached chords	
83–137	Two-part manual canon on principal motive (parts exchanged), dominant pedal point	V
137–176	Pedal solo on principal motive, ending with detached chords	
Concerto movement		
176–219	Sequential motive, detached chords, Neapolitan-sixth disruption	
219–238	Imitative trio on principal motive	vi
238–270	Sequential motive, detached chords	
270–290	Imitative trio (parts exchanged)	iii
290–332	Sequential motive, detached chords, Neapolitan-sixth disruption	
332–352	Imitative trio (parts exchanged)	ii
352–382	Sequential motive, detached chords (both developed)	
382–438	Sequential motive, detached chords (both developed), long dominant pedal point, Neapolitan-sixth disruption, full cadence	I

Bach may have borrowed the idea of using strict canons to replace the traditional free manual *passaggio* from the canonic opening of Vivaldi's Concerto in D Minor, RV 565,[56] which he transcribed for organ around 1714 (see chapter 9). It was also a logical extension of his involvement with canons in the Orgel-Büchlein, in settings such as "Gott, durch deine Güte," BWV 600 (a canon at the octave); "Christe, du Lamm Gottes," BWV 619 (a canon at the twelfth); and "In dulci jubilo," BWV 608 (a double canon). The pedal solos that follow emerge directly from the pedal point of the canons, organically connecting the two elements in a way that did not occur in the C-Major Toccata.

Bach turned concerto convention on its head in the main portion of this long piece, since the sequential motive takes on the characteristic of a ritornello, returning at regular intervals with thick, tutti texture. But at the same time, it also modulates, in the manner of an episode. Zehnder associates the movement's general style with that of Torelli's concertos,[57] but nowhere in those works does one also find trios that provide the element of harmonic stability, as they do here, securely marking the keys of D minor, A minor, and G minor. The trio writing reflects Bach's interest in the Italian trio, which comes to the fore in the aria trios of the initial Weimar cantatas of 1714, such as "Leget euch dem Heiland unter," Cantata 182, or "Seufzer, Tränen, Kummer, Not," Cantata 21. The inclusion of a fully obbligato pedal part in the Toccata's trios, complete with trills (mm. 272 and 336), foreshadows what is to come in the Six Sonatas of Leipzig, as does the exchange of voices through invertible counterpoint. The ongoing manipulation of the principal motive, which resurfaces throughout the Toccata, is similar to Bach's intense treatment of groups of six 16th notes in "Herr Gott, nun schleuß den Himmel auf," BWV 617, a late entry in the Orgel-Büchlein.

Perhaps the most impressive structural feature of the Toccata is its harmonic arc. The tonic and dominant, well established in the introductory canons and solos, do not return until the end of the piece. The concerto movement begins with the resolution of detached C-minor chords into C major (m. 176). From there it begins a long journey through D minor (m. 221), A minor (m. 270), G minor (m. 332), B♭ major (m. 382), and back to F major. Harmonically, neither the concerto movement nor the introductory segments could stand alone, as they can in the first movement of the C-Major Toccata. In the F-Major Toccata, Bach unified the disparate parts of a hybrid form thematically, rhythmically, and harmonically.

No description can convey the hypnotic power of the Toccata, with its forward drive, crashing chords, and final splaying out to the upper and lower extremes of the keyboard (mm. 405 and 417–418). As Felix Mendelssohn said, encountering the piece in 1831: "the F-Major Toccata, with the modulation at the end, sounds as if the church were about to tumble down."[58] And the modern historian

Richard Taruskin, in his compelling reading of the piece,[59] called Bach's use of the Neapolitan-sixth chord to further delay long-expected resolutions "probably the most spectacular 'deceptive cadence' anyone had composed as of the second decade of the eighteenth century."[60]

The Toccata has traditionally been linked with the Palace Church in Weißenfels, where the Christian Förner organ of 1673 (II/30) contained a pedal-board that extended to f'.[61] Bach's first documented visit to the Weißenfels court took place at the end of February 1713, when he performed Cantata 208, *Was mir behagt, ist nur die muntre Jagd*, for Duke Christian's birthday.[62] He returned to Weißenfels several times and served as titular composer there between 1729 and 1736. The Peter Herold organ (II/23) in St. Michael's Church in Buttstädt outside of Weimar also contained a pedalboard rising to f'.[63] As the Weimar Court Organist, Bach probably oversaw the Buttstädt instrument and could have played the Toccata there, as well.

As we noted, the Fugue appears to have been added to the Toccata at a later point, and its concise, well-wrought subjects, highly polished counterpoint, and clearly defined form support the idea that it was written after Bach's Vivaldi encounter. It is a four-part double fugue with two contrasting subjects, first developed separately, then combined. The first subject is an alla breve idea, with slow-moving white notes proceeding mainly by step. The second subject is a more animated instrumental idea, triadic in shape and proceeding mainly by leaping quarter notes and 8th notes (example 12-13). Each subject has its own countersubject, and the two countersubjects provide most of the material for the Fugue's episodes.

The three sections of the Fugue look like this:

Section I (*ped.*):

Mm. 1–23	Four-part exposition of subject 1 with its countersubject: I, V, I, V
Mm. 23–70	Additional entries of subject 1, in I, V, I, I

Section II (*man.*):

Mm. 70–86	Three-part exposition of subject 2 with its countersubject: V, I, I
Mm. 93–128	Additional entries of subject 2, in V, vi, ii, v
Mm. 128–133	Return of subject 1, in I

Section III (*ped.*):

Mm. 134–170	Subjects 1 and 2 combined: V, vi, vi, IV, I, I

The contrast between sections I and II could not be greater: they contain different themes, touch on different keys, and exhibit different textures (*pedaliter* v. *manualiter*). All is reconciled in section III, where the two subjects are joined

Example 12-13 Fugue in F Major, BWV 540/2: the two subjects.

in varying combinations leading to the final entry, in the tonic, at the outer extremes of the keyboard: subject 2 in the top octave of the manual, subject 1 in the bottom octave of the pedalboard. This last gesture, together with the unusual mode-switch to the dominant minor (C minor) in section II and the crescendo effect of growing note motion in section III suggests that Bach may have had an eye on the Toccata as he composed the Fugue.

The **Toccata and Fugue in D Minor ("Dorian"), BWV 538**, is the only Bach organ work for which we have a confirmed place and date of performance. According to a note in a manuscript copy made by Michael Gotthard Fischer toward the end of the eighteenth century,[64] the Toccata and Fugue "was played by Sebastian Bach at the inauguration of the great organ in Kassel." Fischer must have heard this from his teacher, Johann Christian Kittel, who in turn would have learned it directly from Bach during lessons in Leipzig in the late 1740s. The Kassel event took place on September 28, 1732 at the St. Martin's Church, in the presence of the 12-year-old Prince Frederick of Hesse-Kassel.[65] According to an eyewitness, the sound of the organ "penetrated the ears of those present like a thunderbolt" and the prince, greatly moved by the performance, complimented Bach on his pedal playing and, removing a ring "with a precious stone" from his finger, presented it to Bach in gratitude.[66] The organ, a large instrument (III/33) with a 32' Principal in the Pedal, had been expanded by Johann Friedrich Stertzing from an earlier organ and, upon Stertzing's death in 1731, by Johann Nicolaus Becker, Johann Friedrich Wender's son-in-law.

A manuscript copy in Walther's hand,[67] written between 1714 and 1717, confirms that the Toccata and Fugue was composed earlier, in Weimar, most probably in conjunction with the concerto transcriptions that resulted from Bach's encounter with Vivaldi's music. The use of two keyboards and pedal and the intricate indications of manual-change match the setting and notation of the transcriptions. Later manuscripts show that Bach refined the text of the Toccata several times,[68] with Fischer's copy representing the final version. A number of manuscripts, including Fischer's, use the term "Præludium" or "Preludio" rather than "Toccata" for the first movement.

Example 12-14 Toccata in D Minor, BWV 538/1: principal motive and its inversion.

Aside from the Prelude in E♭ Major, BWV 552/1, the Toccata is the only organ prelude with the designated use of two manuals—Oberwerk and Positiv—and manual change. In the E♭-Major Prelude, the manual changes are used solely for an echo passage. In the Toccata, they are an integral part of the work's structural design, and it is clear from the use of the two keyboards simultaneously that the registrational contrast between them should be one of timbre rather than volume.

The entire Toccata is based on a single motive, the opening two-beat figure that appears ubiquitously in German virtuoso keyboard works as well as the violin solos of Vivaldi's *L'Estro armónico* concertos. Presented in various upright and inverted forms (example 12-14), this figure serves as the basis for both ritornello and episode passages. This results in blurred boundaries, so much so that Williams, attempting to find alternate explanations of the Toccata's design, analyzed it by means of Quintilian rhetoric, using *Confutatio* and *Confirmatio* to describe its contrasting sections.[69]

An analysis of the Toccata in more traditional terms reveals the broad outline of a concerto form:

Mm.	Manual	Material
1–13	Ow	Ritornello in i
13–25	Pos→Ow	Episode modulating to v
26–36	Pos→Ow	Ritornello in v (parts exchanged)
37–47	Pos + Ow	Episode: *manualiter* echoes, *pedaliter* echoes
47–66	Ow	Ritornello, modulating from iv→vii→VI, ending on V/i
66–81	Ow + Pos	Episode: *manualiter* echoes (parts exchanged), *pedaliter* echoes (parts exchanged)
81–94	Ow	Ritornello in i, plus extension
94–99	Ow	Close, with pedal point, in I.

While the analysis suggests a well-defined structure, the Toccata is not perceived this way by the listener. The constant presence of the principal motive upright and inverted, the continuous exchange of parts and manuals, the forceful episodic sequences, and the general homogeneity of texture create the sensation of an uninterrupted spinning-out of material, pushed forward by the unending flow of 16th notes and the dynamic resolution of dominant seventh and ninth chords, often highlighted by lengthy trills. The antiphonal passages are similar to those in the Concerto movement in C Major, BWV 595, but employed here with far more sophistication.

In short, the Toccata displays Vivaldian principles, but applied in an intense, Bachian way. As with the Toccata in F Major and several opening movements of the Brandenburg Concertos, Bach defies normal concerto conventions. In the center of the D-Minor Toccata (mm. 47–66), the ritornello modulates through several keys, taking on the character of an episode. And directly after that (mm. 66–81), the initial portion of the earlier episodic material is repeated note-for-note at a different pitch level, taking on the character of a ritornello.

In the Fugue, too, we can observe Bach redefining expected procedures. Of the three alla breve fugues in Weimar works written under the influence of Italian instrumental music, this is by far the longest and most adventurous. The Fugue's white-note subject, echoing the rising minor third of the Toccata's principal motive, is notable itself: it forms a perfect arc, rising a full octave, by step and leap, and then descending back to the first note, step by step. The suspensions that characterize alla breve style pervade the subject. Accompanying this promising theme, in invertible counterpoint, are two countersubjects. The first appears with the subject throughout the Fugue; the second appears only now and then.

The Fugue is divided into seven sections, defined by the presence or absence of the pedal. Subject entries occur in both *pedaliter* and *manualiter* segments, and toward the end, the subject appears twice in stretto for climactic effect. What is most unusual, structurally, is Bach's use of the pedal: after the initial exposition and episode, it marks the beginning of each *pedaliter* section with an entry of the subject in the tonic. These entries serve as harmonic and thematic pillars that hold up the immense, 222-measure structure of the Fugue and constantly pull the episodic meanderings back to the tonic:

Mm.	Texture	Event
1–61	*pedaliter*	Four-part exposition with subject entries in i, v, i, v, plus additional entries in v and i
61–80	*manualiter*	Episodic material, subject entry in v
81–130	*pedaliter*	Subject entry in pedal in i, then entries in III and VII
130–166	*manualiter*	Subject entries in iv and VI
167–188	*pedaliter*	Subject entry in pedal in i, in stretto (pedal and alto)
188–203	*manualiter*	Subject entry in v
204–222	*pedaliter*	Subject entry in pedal in i, in stretto (soprano and pedal), then closing chordal dialogue

Equally unusual is the presence of not one but rather two distinctive contrapuntal procedures: the development of the fugue subject, as would be expected,

Example 12-15 Fugue in D Minor, BWV 538/2: (a) bridge motive, and (b) final appearance of bridge motive in four-part stretto.

but also the development of a bridge motive (example 12-15, a) that first appears between the second and third statements of the subject in the initial exposition (mm. 15–17). This bridge motive enters in stretto from the start, and Bach proceeds to develop it further in a series of *15* stretto entries that fill the space between entries of the main subject. The initial strettos take place between two voices (mm. 15, 26, etc.), but the procedure is soon expanded to three voices (mm. 50, 67, etc.), and finally—following the dramatic appearance of the bridge theme over an extended pedal trill (mm. 178–184) and the second stretto entry of the subject in the tonic (mm. 203–211)—is extended to four voices, with the tenor and pedal sounding just a beat apart and the soprano and alto joining them in the next measure in parallel sixths (mm. 211–212; example 12-15, b). It is this intense, dramatic four-voice entry of the bridge theme that seems to mark the contrapuntal climax of the Fugue, not the stretto entry of the subject eight measures earlier.

What Bach achieved in the Fugue in D Minor was a new type of double fugue, more subtle even than the magnificent Fugue in F Major, BWV 540/1, since the two themes—the Fugue subject and the bridge theme—are integrated from the start, with the "expositions" of each intertwined. The Fugue in F Major features contrasting subjects; the Fugue in D Minor features contrasting procedures, which are united at the end when the main subject joins the bridge theme in the stretto process. It was a new concept of fugue writing. And what is more, the sudden and unexpected chordal dialogue in the last four measures of the Fugue points back to the manual exchanges of the Toccata (mm. 31–33, in particular), uniting the two movements, despite their very different styles, over a vast expanse of musical time. Not only an extraordinary Toccata enthralled Bach's audience in Kassel but also an extraordinary Fugue. It, too, was well worth a prince's ring.

The **Prelude and Fugue in G Major, BWV 541,** represents the final stage of Bach's adoption of Italian concerto principles in his Weimar free organ works. It is difficult to believe that he could surpass the energy of the "Dorian" Toccata and the majesty of its Fugue, but in the G-Major Prelude and Fugue he did just that, with polish and humor.

The surviving sources show that the work went through at least five stages of development. In the initial stage, represented by the manuscript copies of Kellner, Preller, and others,[70] Bach seems to have conceived the Fugue subject as beginning with four 8th notes (♪♪♪♪) rather than a rest and three eighth notes (♪ ♪♪♪).[71] Manuscripts from the circles of C.P.E. Bach and Kittel show that he gradually changed the subject to the off-beat form.[72] In the summer of 1733 Bach appears to have pulled the piece off the shelf once again and proceeded to write a beautiful fair copy for Wilhelm Friedemann, who was auditioning for the organist position of the St. Sophia's Church in Dresden.[73] This version, which Friedemann presumably passed off as his own creation, incorporates refinements that improve the part-writing of the Prelude (see chapter 17). Around this time Bach also considered inserting the last movement, "un poc' allegro," from Trio Sonata 4 between the Prelude and Fugue to produce a three-movement concerto: Prelude, Trio, and Fugue (BWV 541.2 in BWV³). This seems to have been a passing fancy, however, and in the end he returned the work to its original prelude-fugue format. That Bach considered the Prelude and Fugue a new type of "modern" work, based on Vivaldi's fashionable concerto style and capable of sporting a middle movement, may be reflected in his use of "modern" notation— treble and bass clef rather than soprano and bass clef—for the first time in his free organ works.

The Prelude begins with a single-line manual *passaggio*, in the time-honored North German tradition. But the gesture has now been Vivaldized: it has a triadic orientation, clearly outlining the home key of G major, and it is no longer rhythmically free. Instead, it has the forceful motor pulse of a Vivaldi concerto theme, with strategically placed accents and wide-ranging instrumental compass (three and a half octaves). Marked "vivace" in Friedemann's score alone, the *passaggio* serves as the first of four elements that appear throughout the Prelude in various orders, much in the way Vivaldi shifts blocks of ritornello material in his concertos. The other three elements are: (1) an incisive, memorable, triadic tutti figure that appears in thick five-part texture, (2) a 16th-note sequential figure that appears in two forms, one characteristic of violin-writing, the other characteristic of pedal figuration, both accompanied by repeated 8th-note chords, and (3) cadential material, appearing in several forms (example 12-16).

Example 12-16 Prelude in G Major, BWV 541/1: (a) *passaggio* motive, (b) tutti motive, (c) sequential motive, and (d) cadential motive.

These elements are grouped in segments that are defined by emphatic cadences in the tonic, dominant, mediant, and tonic:

Mm.	Harmonic activity	Motivic elements
1–21	Establishment of I	*Passaggio*, tutti figure, sequential figure, cadence
21–29	Modulation to V	Sequential figure, *passaggio*, cadence
29–46	Modulation to iii	*Passaggio*, tutti figure, sequential figure, cadence
46–59	Modulation to I	Snippets of the *passaggio*, tutti figure, and sequential figure, leading to the tutti figure and cadence
59–83	Reestablishment of I	Sequential figure extended over dominant pedal, *passaggio*, cadence

The result is a complete integration of the four elements, with rapid changes of texture but no differentiation of solo and tutti, as in the Toccatas in F Major and D Minor. Instead, the Prelude consists of a continuous unfolding of highly animated figural material, much like the "Dorian" Toccata or the first movements of Brandenburg Concerto No. 1 in F Major or Brandenburg Concerto No. 3 in G Major, with meticulous textural control. It was not until Leipzig that Bach adopted a straightforward tutti-solo concerto design with sectional ritornellos for his organ preludes, filling it, however, with material that was quite different from that of a Vivaldi concerto (see chapter 20).

The Fugue represents an equally remarkable adaptation of Vivaldi's concerto principles. The subject, in its off-beat form, contains both the motto motive that emerges during sequential passages in the Prelude (♪ ♩♩ ♪) and the neighbor-note 16th notes that characterize the Prelude's tutti figure. And once under way, the Fugue continues the motoric 16th-note pulse of the Prelude as well. It also displays a new treatment of modulation and the central episode. Like the Fugue in A Minor, BWV 543/2, and the Fugue in F Major, BWV 540/1, this Fugue is also divided into three sections, distinguished by the presence and absence of the pedal. But the initial *pedaliter* section ends with the first entry of the subject in a related key (E minor), the middle *manualiter* section contains no subject entries whatsoever, and the second *pedaliter* section continues the harmonic meandering with subject entries in the dominant and mediant before darkening with a most unusual entry in the minor tonic (m. 66) and coming to a complete halt on a dominant ninth chord. It then concludes with two stretto entries and a final entry in the subdominant, in a fifth voice. The lighter texture and lack of fugue subject in the middle section gives it the character of a long concerto episode, now assimilated into the structure of a ternary fugue:[74]

Mm.	Section	Texture	Event
1–38	A	*pedaliter*	Four-part exposition, with subject entries in I, V, I, V, then entries in I and vi
38–52	B	*manualiter*	Spinning out of new material, then a motive from the subject
52–83	A'	*pedaliter*	Subject entries in V, iii, and i; fermata; stretto entries I/ii and I/V; final entry in IV in a new, fifth voice

Bach once again reimagined fugal procedure in this movement, throwing convention to the wind and creating a large central "solo" section without subject entries and significantly shifting the weight of the structure to the final *pedaliter* section, with its unorthodox pedal entry in the minor tonic (preceded by three false manual entries), sudden halt, surprising pair of strettos, and unanticipated fifth voice. Bach turned to similar contrapuntal wizardry in the Fugue of the

Prelude and Fugue in C Major ("9/8"), BWV 547. Here he treats them with a light hand, tossing them off in a disconcertingly lighthearted way.

That Bach chose the Prelude and Fugue in G Major for Friedemann's Dresden audition in 1733 is telling. It suggests that of all the organ compositions Bach had written at that point, which included large Leipzig works such as the Prelude and Fugue in B Minor, BWV 544, and the "Wedge" Prelude and Fugue in E Minor, BWV 548, he selected the G-Major Prelude and Fugue as the piece most likely to win over the Dresden jurors. The Prelude, with its snappy, Vivaldian idiom, would have demonstrated that Friedemann was abreast of the most fashionable musical tastes. And the Fugue, with its dramatic and surprising stretto entries of the subject, would have shown that he could turn contrapuntal erudition to humorous purposes. The unveiling of stretto at the end was like a shrewd poker player majestically drawing an ace from his hand at the last moment, to take the game. And take the game it did. Friedemann auditioned at the St. Sophia's Church on June 22, 1733. He was awarded the position the next day.[75]

Notes

1. Spitta 1873–80, vol. 1, 405–406.
2. Williams 2003, 129.
3. Yale Music Library, *Ma21.Y11.B12* (formerly *LM 4839*), fascicle 1, and Salzburg, Dom-Musikarchiv, *MN 104*, fascicle 1.
4. As demonstrated by the manuscript *P 1210* in the Berlin State Library from c. 1735–1740, written by Bach's student Johann Georg Heinrich and containing corrections in Bach's hand. The pedal notes above d' are altered, to accommodate the organs in Leipzig. See Wollny 2016b, 81–83.
5. Spitta 1873–80, vol. 1, 589, and still mentioned in BWV³.
6. A version of the Prelude and Fugue in A Major with the Fugue notated in 3/8 meter, once viewed as an early variant, BWV 536a, and published as such in NBA IV/6, is now accepted as a corrupt arrangement stemming from Leonard Scholz and the Nuremberg School.
7. See "The Pairing of Prelude and Fugue," in Stauffer 1980, 127–136.
8. Kilian 1962, 127–135.
9. Berlin State Library, *P 1104*, written by "Anonymous O," a son, student, or copyist of Kayser. See Talle 2003, 162–163.
10. Berlin State Library, *P 490*.
11. Kilian 1962, 131–133, and Kobayashi 1988, 59.
12. See Douglass 1995, 110–114 and 118 (chart 5, "Trios à trois claviers"), or Ponsford 2011, 175–179.
13. Horn 1986 and Stauffer 1993.
14. By Werner Brieg, in Breig 1995, 17.

15. Although the Weimar versions of the Fantasia and the Fugue are clearly early variants, they are not recognized as such in BWV³, where they are not assigned separate BWV numbers. They are also absent in the NBA. The full texts of both are reproduced in Stauffer 1980, 235–246.

16. See NBA IV/5–6, KB (Dietrich Kilian, ed., 1978–79), 452, and Bach digital, under BWV 542.

17. The dorian notation of the F-minor version (F minor with three flats) points to a pre-Leipzig origin.

18. The F-Minor version is handed down in seven early manuscripts, including copies from the circles of C.P.E. Bach and Bach-student Johann Christian Kittel. This suggests that it may have been made under Bach's supervision.

19. BDok II, no. 302, commentary.

20. Mattheson 1731, 34–35.

21. "Das allerbeste Pedal-Stück vom Herrn Johann Sebastian Bach," in Berlin State Library, *P 287*, fascicle 8, a manuscript written by Johann Stephan Borsch, a copyist working under C.P.E. Bach in Hamburg, and Yale Music Library, *Ma21.Y11.B12* (formerly *LM 4838*), a manuscript written by Johann Christian Heinrich Rinck, a student of Kittel.

22. See the discussion of *Spielfugen* in Stauffer 1986b, 134–138.

23. The decoration of the second countersubject appears to have been an afterthought on Bach's part, added during subsequent refinements of the Fugue. See NBA IV/5–6, KB, 462.

24. Williams 2003, 90–91.

25. Berlin State Library, *AmB 531*, written by "Anonymous 434." Dating from Bach digital.

26. Forkel 1802, appendix, figure 16.

27. *Eine Orgel für Bach in St. Katharinen* (Hamburg: Stiftung Johann Sebastian, 2013). It is also noteworthy that the St. Catherine's organ was originally pitched at a' = 480 Hz.

28. NBA IV/5–6, KB, 456.

29. Breig 1999, 675.

30. BWV³ places the early version of the Fugue "probably in Arnstadt or the early Weimar period." Jean-Claude Zehnder, in Zehnder 2009, 282–289, assigns it to c. 1708.

31. See Bach digital, under BWV 532.

32. Peters Edition, vol. 4, Anhang.

33. Peters Edition, vol. 4, iii.

34. Spitta 1873–80, vol. 1, 406.

35. Schulze 1995, 73, or Williams 2003, 45, for instance.

36. Breig 1992, 19–21, and Zehnder 2009, 285–289.

37. Williams 2003, 42, and Zehnder 2009, 284.

38. Walther 1732, 220.

39. "Præludio Concertato" in Württemberg Regional Library, *Cod. mus. 11*, folio 288, written by Lorenz Sichart in 1740; "Pièce d'Orgue" in Berlin State Library, *P 204*, written by C. F. G. Schwencke in 1781.

40. "Nota Bey dieser Fuge muß man die Füße recht strampfeln laßen," in Württemberg Regional Library, *Cod. Mus. 11*, folio 288.

41. Berlin State Library, *P 803*, fascicle 10. The early form is reproduced in NBA IV/6 and the Breitkopf Edition, vol. 2.

42. Berlin State Library, P 288, fascicle 13.

43. Leipzig Town Library, *III.8.14*, written by Johann Andreas Dröbs, who studied with Kittel, and Berlin State Library, *P 505*, written by Friedrich August Grasnick, who had access to Kittel-circle manuscripts.

44. See the discussion of dance fugues in Stauffer 1986b, 138–142.

45. In his letter of April 20, 1782, where he explains that he composed the Fugue of the Fantasia and Fugue in C Major, K. 394, first, because it was more difficult to write than the Fantasia. He describes how he thought out the Fugue in his head and then wrote it down while thinking out the Fantasia. *The Letters of Mozart and His Family*, Emily Anderson, ed., 3rd ed. (New York: Norton, 1985), 800–801.

46. Breig 1999, 660.

47. Leipzig Town Library, *Poel. mus. Ms. 12*, copied by Carl August Hartung c. 1760–1780, and Berlin State Library, *P 290* (Prelude only), copied by Anonymous 303 (a scribe working with C.P.E. Bach), written around 1760–1880.

48. Yale Music Library, *Ma21.Y.11.B12* (formerly *LM 4718*); Berlin State Library, *P 286*, fascicle 1; and Stockholm, Stiftelsen Musikkulturens Främjande, *MMS 241*, respectively.

49. Berlin State Library, *P 658*, and Yale Music Library, *Ma21.Y.11.B12* (formerly *LM 4839*), fascicle 3, both written by Michael Gotthard Fischer, and Leipzig Music Library, Becker Collection, *III.8.21*, written by Johann Andreas Dröbs. Bach's autograph was used for the editing of the BG in 1867 but disappeared around 1900.

50. A similar process can be observed in the Prelude in D Minor, BWV 875/1, which Bach expanded for volume 2 of the Well-Tempered Clavier by interweaving a new eight-measure segment. See Schulenberg 2006, 252–253.

51. See the discussion of alla breve fugues in Stauffer 1986b, 143–147.

52. Breig 1999, 626–627.

53. Kirnberger 1771–77, pt. II, 118. Translation from *Johann Philipp Kirnberger, The Art of Strict Music Composition*, David Beach and Jurgen Thym, trs. (New Haven: Yale University Press, 1982), 386.

54. Berlin State Library, *P 803*, fascicles 8 and 9. Dating from BWV[3] and Bach digital.

55. Berlin State Library, *P 290*, copied by an anonymous scribe associated with C.P.E. Bach, and *P 277*, copied by an anonymous scribe drawing on a lost Kirnberger source.

56. Wolff 2000, 126.

57. Zehnder 1991, 90–91.

58. Letter of September 3, 1831, in Felix Mendelssohn, *Letters from Italy and Switzerland*, Julie de Marguerittes, trs. (Freeport, NY: Books for Libraries Press, 1970), 243.

59. Richard Taruskin, *Music in the Seventeenth and Eighteenth Centuries: The Oxford History of Western Music* (Oxford: Oxford University Press, 2011), 208–216.

60. Taruskin, *Music in the Seventeenth and Eighteenth Centuries*, 213.

61. Wolff and Zepf 2012, 96.

62. Perhaps it is no coincidence that the instrumental ritornello of the aria "Weil die wollenreichen Herden" from the Cantata bears a close resemblance to the main theme of the Toccata and is also in F Major.

63. Wolff and Zepf 2012, 105.

64. Yale Music Library, *Ma21.Y11.B12* (formerly *LM 4839e*), fascicle 5.

65. NBR, no. 157.

66. NBR, no. 338. The account was written by Constantin Bellermann in 1743.

67. Berlin State Library, *P 803*, fascicle 21.

68. See Breig 1986c for an analysis of the readings.

69. Williams 2003, 66.

70. Berlin State Library, *P 288*, fascicle 8 (Kellner), and Leipzig Town Library, *Ms. 7*, fascicle 15 (Preller).

71. See NBA IV/5–6, KB, 429–431. The subject appears in the four 8th-note form from m. 35 onward.

72. Berlin State Library, *P 290* (Anonymous 303) and *AmB 543* (J. N. Schober) reflecting C.P.E. Bach's Berlin circle, and Berlin State Library *P 320* (J. N. Gebhardi) and *P 557* (F. A. Grasnick) and Yale Music Library, *Ma21.Y11.B12* (formerly *LM 4839*), fascicle 4 (M.G. Fischer) reflecting Kittel's Erfurt circle.

73. Schulze 1984, 17. The extant autograph manuscript, Berlin State Library, *N.Mus.ms. 378*, includes the notation in Friedemann's hand, "per manum Autoris" (in the hand of the composer).

74. On this point see Breig 1986a, 35–36.

75. BDok I, no. 25. Also competing for the job were Bach students Carl Hartwig and Christian Heinrich Gräbner.

13

Free Works

Independent Fugues and Singular Pieces

It is appropriate to end our survey of Bach's Weimar organ music by looking at
five free works that epitomize the growing sophistication and bold experimentation of his compositional style: two highly popular independent fugues, two
pieces with unique formats, and the great Passacaglia in C Minor.

Independent Fugues

The Fugue in G Major, BWV 577, and the Fugue in G Minor, BWV 578, make for
an interesting comparison, not only because of their parallel tonalities and approximately contemporaneous origins but also because of Bach's application of
similar procedures in two very different compositions.

The **Fugue in G Major ("Jig"), BWV 577**, has been a wrongly maligned work.
Its sketchy transmission in the sources—it is handed down in just one reliable
eighteenth-century manuscript[1]—led to its contested acceptance as an authentic
work and its belated publication in both the Peters Edition and the Neue Bach-
Ausgabe.[2] Only with the recent identification of the scribe of the eighteenth-
century manuscript as Johann Jacob Kieser, an organist who studied with Bach
in Leipzig (and possibly Cöthen as well) before taking up a position in Schleiz in
1728,[3] has the Fugue has been unequivocally accepted as a product of Bach's pen.
One wonders why acceptance took so long, since the Fugue shares stylistic qualities with several Weimar organ works written by Bach, and the disciplined part-
writing and demanding pedal part point to him as well. Really, who else could
have written and performed it?

Once Bach had mastered the North German style, he seems to have taken
up the challenge of writing pieces that outdid specific works of Buxtehude, in
particular, in a calculated way. "Nun komm, der Heiden Heiland," BWV 659,
appears to be a response to the North German's setting of the same chorale and
the Passacaglia in C Minor a reply to his three ostinato works. In the case of the
Fugue in G Major, Bach seems to have taken on Buxtehude's Fugue in C Major
("Jig"), BuxWV 174, a *manualiter* work in 12/8 meter passed down solely in

J. S. BACH. George B. Stauffer, Oxford University Press. © Oxford University Press 2024.
DOI: 10.1093/oso/9780195108026.003.0014

the Andreas Bach Book. In a show of one-upmanship, Bach recast Buxtehude's three-part allegro setting in four parts, with a daringly virtuosic pedal line.

Like the themes of several other early Weimar fugues, the subject of the G-Major Fugue is lengthy and consists of distinct components: a head motive in a jig rhythm (example 13-1, v), a disjunct 8th-note motive moving downward four steps (example 13-1, w), a disjunct 8th-note figure expanding upwards (example 13-1, x), a falling scale with initial appoggiatura (example 13-1, y), and a closing figure that cadences in the dominant (example 13-1, z). As if inspired by the blithe spirit of an Irish jig, Bach plays with the subject throughout the piece, altering its shape for pedal playing (m. 28) and pure fun (m. 35), abridging its length (m. 57), extending its length (m. 63), tossing it from one voice to another (m. 35, where it migrates from the soprano to the tenor), and using it to modulate from one key to another (m. 70, where it begins ambiguously in the major supertonic [or V/V?] and ends in the mediant). Jean-Claude Zehnder has pointed to similar liberties Bach took in the closing fugue of Cantata 131, *Aus der Tiefe ruf ich, Herr, zu dir*, written during the Mühlhausen years.[4] The G-Major Fugue may date from soon thereafter.

The contrast with Buxtehude's "Jig" Fugue couldn't be greater. Buxtehude maintained the shape of his subject throughout the piece with little change, and he never presented it beyond the tonic and dominant. Delightful as Buxtehude's fugue may be, the treatment of the subject is wooden, compared to Bach's inventive manipulations. In addition, Bach's Fugue has a very distinct, well-balanced tripartite structure, defined by the presence or absence of the pedal:

Mm.	Nature	Texture	Subject entries
1–35	*pedaliter*	4-part	I, V, I, V
35–57	*manualiter*	1- to 3-part	iii, vi
57–86	*pedaliter*	4-part	I, V, iii, I

The text of the Kieser manuscript raises two performance issues. First, the reentry of the pedal after the manual episode is given as measure 63 rather than measure 57, undoubtedly to avoid the note e' in the pedal, which was available

Example 13-1 Fugue in G Major, BWV 577: subject, consisting of five motives.

on the Weimar Chapel organ but not on the instruments in Leipzig. The part-writing leaves little doubt that measure 57 is the proper entry point for the pedal. Second, the three passages marked with forte and piano echoes (mm. 12, 16–18, and 40) are often discounted as additions made by an overly enthusiastic scribe, but they are characteristic of antiphonal writing in North German works. Since Kieser appears to have been copying under Bach's supervision, the markings may stem from Bach and reflect the same playful spirit as his manipulation of the fugue subject. Like many of Bach's performance indications that appear toward the beginning of pieces, they suggest gestures that could be applied elsewhere (such as the repeated figures in mm. 52–54).

The virtuosic pedal-writing in the "Jig" Fugue tends to overshadow other more nuanced features of the work: the brilliant alterations of the subject, mentioned earlier; the carefully spaced and carefully prepared entrances of the subject; the skillful handling of four-part counterpoint; the harmonic darkening (mm. 73–76) that sets the stage for the startling final appearance of the subject, in G major, in the pedal; and the wonderfully frenetic rush to the close, similar to that of the Fugue of the Praeludium in G Major, BWV 550, but now more succinct and effective. This is a remarkable work, worthy of its secure place, at long last, in the Bach canon.

Unlike the "Jig" Fugue, the **Fugue in G Minor ("Little"), BWV 578**, is extremely well established in the sources. It appears in the Andreas Bach Book in the hand of Bach's brother Johann Christoph, confirming that it was composed before 1714, and in manuscripts written by Bach's students Johann Caspar Vogler and Johann Ludwig Krebs,[5] and numerous other scribes. It is passed down in almost 40 manuscript copies, testifying to its early popularity.

The attractive theme of the Fugue in G Minor may be based on a German folk song. A two-part fugue by Johann Georg Schübler, recently discovered in the Royal Library in Brussels,[6] displays the same subject and countersubject as the G-Minor Fugue and bears the title "Fuga. Lass mich gehn denn dort kommt meine Mutter her" (Fugue. I must go, for my mother is coming this way). Schübler, who studied with Bach and served as the engraver for the prints of the Musical Offering and the Schübler Chorales, appears to have used Bach's subject and countersubject as the basis of his own composition, possibly under his teacher's supervision. His title seems to refer to a folk song—perhaps a nursery tune—that Bach may have cited in the first two measures of his theme (example 13-2).[7] The fact that Bach used a folk song as the basis for the large Fugue in G Minor, BWV 542/2 (see chapter 12), and may have done so in the "Little" Fugue in G Minor as well, raises the question whether other attractive themes in his organ fugues also reflect popular melodies no longer known to us.

Whether or not this is the case here, Bach's Fugue has a song-like quality, even though the subject continues with three additional measures of more typical

Example 13-2 Fugue in G Minor, BWV 578: subject, with the head motive possibly based on the folk song "Lass mich gehn, den dort kommt meine Mutter her" and the tail motive based on a one-measure phrase (x) and its embellished variant (x').

Lass mich gehn, denn dort kommt mei-ne Mut-ter her.

keyboard figuration: the leaping motive of measure 3 is immediately embellished in measure 4, followed by a scalar tail that brings the theme back to the tonic (example 13-2). The subject is accompanied throughout by an equally attractive countersubject whose distinctive trill-and-turn are doubled for the exuberant reentry of the pedal with the theme in B♭ Major (m. 41). These features make the work a *Spielfuge*—an instrumental fugue based on figural play.

Like many compositions from the initial Weimar years, the G-Minor Fugue has early features as well as progressive elements. The early features include the permutation-like treatment of the subject and countersubject, which appear together in invertible counterpoint throughout; the casual part-writing, which never achieves the four-part texture implied in the opening exposition until the final statement of the subject; and the nonthematic entry of the pedal in measure 26 (even though it acts as a quasi–second countersubject).

The progressive elements include the clever false entry of the subject (m. 25), whose head motive first appears in the tenor and then, disguised, in the soprano; the use of thematically related, imitative episodes (mm. 22–23, *manualiter* = mm. 44–48, *pedaliter*); the pleasing Corelli-like circle-of-fifth sequences in the episodes; the carefully prepared entrances of the subject; and the well-balanced form, with modulations to the mediant and subdominant in the middle section. The most telling aspect of the Fugue is the climactic chromatic climb from the lowest octave of the keyboard to the highest (mm. 58–63) that precedes the final entrance of the subject in the pedal, in the highest possible range. This type of dramatic conclusion becomes a hallmark of Bach's mature fugal style. Although the Fugue in G Minor lacks the skilled four-part counterpoint of the "Jig" Fugue, its attractive subject and countersubject appear with utmost clarity throughout the work, explaining in part its continuing popularity today. And a glance at the awkward modulations of Schübler's two-part fugue on the same themes demonstrates how truly suave Bach's fugue writing had become by the early Weimar years.

Experimental Forms

In two instances Bach broke with existing German conventions of free organ music and devised new formats altogether, one patterned after the Italian concerto, the other patterned after the French *plein jeu*. The result was two extraordinary Weimar experiments.

The Toccata in C Major, BWV 564, with its three-movement fast-slow-fast structure, reflects Bach's whole-hearted embrace of the Italian concerto. The opening Toccata is divided into three sections: a manual *passaggio*, a pedal solo, and a concerto movement—the same elements seen in the Toccata in F Major, BWV 540/1. But here the manual *passaggio* and pedal solo are rhythmically free, in the North German *stylus fantasticus* tradition.

The *passaggio* is one of Bach's longest. While it reflects North German practices, it has certain Italianate qualities: a modulatory middle portion (the tug toward the subdominant in mm. 5–10) and a continuous, uniform stream of 32nd notes. Bach also created a sense of rhythmic play through echo-like repetitions (m. 5) and hemiola note groupings (m. 9). It is an effective stage-setter, and we must wonder once again how much the acoustics of the Palace Chapel in Weimar influenced Bach's decision to write such a protracted solo line, extended still further by the pedal solo that follows.

The early sources raise an interesting issue with regard to the performance of the *passaggio*. In the manuscripts of Johann Peter Kellner and Samuel Gottlieb Hedar,[8] copied in the 1720s and 1730s, presumably from Bach's lost autograph, the 32nd notes of the *passaggio* are notated in uniform groups of eight notes each—the notation presented in the Neue Bach-Ausgabe and Breitkopf Edition. In the recently discovered manuscript of Carl Gotthelf Gerlach,[9] copied in the 1720s, most probably under Bach's watchful eye, the *passaggio* contains numerous fingering indications as well as signs showing the distribution of the notes between the hands ("d" for *dextra*, or right hand, and "s" for *sinistra*, or left hand; plate 13-1). In yet another early manuscript, now lost,[10] the 32nd notes of the *passaggio* were written in broken-flag notation to show the distribution of the notes between the hands—the text presented in the Peters Edition. One suspects that Bach's autograph manuscript contained the neutral notation—that of the Kellner and Hedar copies—and that he assigned some students the task of working out a practical method of playing the passage, seen in the Gerlach and lost broken-flag manuscripts (which do not fully agree with one another, in terms of the distribution of the notes between the hands). This was quite like modern teachers requesting students to mark fingering for a difficult passage.

Would that we had such information for pedaling the pedal solo that follows! Unlike pedal solos of the North German Praeludium, the passage here contains not only disjunct, opposite-toe figuration, as expected, but also conjunct melodic

Plate 13-1 Toccata in C Major, BWV 564: manuscript copy of Carl Gotthelf
Gerlach, c. 1725, showing the distribution of the notes between the hands and
fingerings in the opening *passaggio*.

Sächsisches Staatsarchiv, Staatsarchiv, Leipzig

Example 13-3 Toccata in C Major, BWV 564, movement 1: (a) motives from the pedal solo, and (b) use of the motives in the ritornello (m. 32) and episode (m. 36) of the concerto portion.

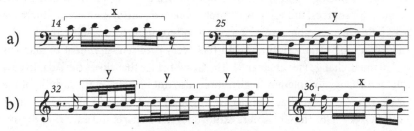

material with triplets and 32nd notes that require great skill to play.[11] Two motives foreshadow themes that appear in the ritornello and episode of the concerto movement (example 13-3), reflecting Bach's determination to place pedal virtuosity at the service of structural unification.

The concerto movement proper, which begins in measure 32, is patterned after the instrumental music of Torelli.[12] The ritornello, a short, four-measure, harmonically closed theme with a head motive of ascending, conjunct *corta* figures (see example 13-3), appears five times, in the tonic (m. 32), dominant (m. 38), submediant (m. 50), mediant (m. 61), and tonic (m. 77). It remains unchanged, except for a one-measure introduction (m. 76) before its final appearance. The episodes are based on a contrasting idea, a descending triadic motive treated in imitation. The episodes are short (2–4 measures) and similar, except for the last (mm. 67–76), which combines and develops the falling pedal octave of the ritornello and the triadic motive of the episode. As it is often pointed out, the opening movement of the harpsichord Toccata in G Major, BWV 916, the most progressive of the seven keyboard toccatas, has a very similar structure. Both works reflect Bach's pre-Vivaldi use of Italian instrumental style, around 1712 or so.[13] This section of the Toccata would be performed *a battuta*, in contrast with the rhythmically free introduction. But the slur and "trillo" indication that appear in the Hedar and Gerlach manuscripts above the pedal 32nd-note motive (mm. 45, 47, and 49) imply that that figure (a remnant of the North German *trillo longo*), at least, is to be played freely.

The Adagio that follows is Bach's organ interpretation of a violin solo with string accompaniment and pizzicato bass. As Jean-Claude Zehnder notes, similar writing appears in Torelli's Concerto Grosso in C Major, op. 8/1,[14] which seems to have been available in Weimar.[15] The Sonata to Cantata 182, *Himmelskönig sei Willkommen*, of March 1714, a duet for violin, recorder, and pizzicato strings, is also quite close in style. The Neapolitan-sixth chord, used dramatically at the end of the Passacaglia in C Minor, appears here frequently as a less-shocking harmonic coloring. Oddly, two-manual performance is not indicated in the manuscript sources, though it was surely expected. This notational indifference may reflect Bach's more casual approach to scoring before writing the Vivaldi and Ernst organ transcriptions, with their very precise assignment of manuals and manual-change (see chapter 9). The Grave bridge that closes the Adagio may call for a change to a plenum registration, also not notated, in the fashion of the Grave, marked *pleno*, that leads to the Fugue in the Concerto in D Minor after Vivaldi, BWV 596. The Grave here exhibits seven real parts and a series of diminished seventh chords, suspended through shockingly delayed resolutions. This intense version of dissonant Italian *durezza*-writing leads to a final resolution in bright C major.

The Fugue, which may have originated as a separate piece, before the other movements of the Toccata,[16] is a rollicking dance in the same spirit as the Fugue in D Major, BWV 532/2. The subject has a head motive with three phrases and three pauses—thrice the fun of the D-Major's subject—and the pauses are similarly filled with a lighthearted countersubject, in this instance a spinning motive that eventually takes over the final manual episode. The tail of the subject consists of continuous 16th notes, modulating to the dominant. The general form of the subject is much like that of the fugue "Lob, und Ehre, und Preis, und Gewalt" of Cantata 21, of c. 1713.

The Fugue unfolds in four phases:

Mm.	Section	Subject entries
1–43	Initial exposition	I, V, I, V
43–78	Second exposition	V, I, V
78–109	"Development"	iii, vii, V/V
109–141	Close	V, plus coda

The appearance of the subject in D major (m. 100), the dominant of the dominant, points to Bach's expanding modulatory horizons. At the same time, the fragmented, syncopated accompaniment (mm. 123–128) of the treacherous final entry of the subject in the pedal harks back to North German style, as does the free close with gradual fade-out, a gesture found at the conclusion of Cantata 71, *Gott is mein König*, of 1708, a North German–oriented work. In short, the Toccata is an eclectic mix of Italian and North German styles. Bach returned briefly to the idea of a three-movement free organ work in the late 1720s in Leipzig, in the Prelude, Largo, and Fugue in C Major, BWV[3] 545.2, and the Prelude, Un poc' allegro, and Fugue in G Major, BWV[3] 541.2 (see chapter 12). But in Weimar, the

C-Major Toccata seems to have been his only excursion into the realm of three-movement concerto design.

The tripartite format seen in the Prelude in D Major, BWV 532/1—three sections with different tempos—came to full fruition in the **Pièce d'Orgue, BWV 572.** How could Bach have dreamed up such a work?! The amalgamation of seemingly disparate material resulted in the ultimate hybrid composition, a piece that is sui generis in Bach's organ music and the organ repertory in general. We see nothing quite as singular as this again until the Leipzig years, in the Allabreve in D Major and the *stile antico* chorales of Clavier-Übung III.

If the Prelude in D Major was Bach's Italian response to the North German praeludium, the Pièce d'Orgue is his French reply to the same. We must assume that Bach composed it as part of his study of French keyboard music in Weimar, and that it is his inventive answer to the *plein jeu* works in front of him. The Pièce has undeniably French features: a French title; French tempo indications; limited use of the pedal in the initial version (we will come back to this); the note B, available on the pedalboards of French organs but not German; a five-part, *plein jeu*-style middle section; and a final segment based on the imaginative expansion of the French *cheute* embellishment. In early copies of the Pièce, the work is cited as "composée par Monsieur J. S. Bach,"[17] and the conventional Italian expression "volti" used for page turns is replaced by the French term "tournez."[18] In two other manuscripts, including a copy from the 1720s written by Kellner,[19] the middle section is powdered with additional French ornaments.

The initial section—"Tres vitement" ("Tres vistement," in eighteenth-century French)—is not French, however; it is an Italianate toccata. It has a breathless quality, with a return of the opening motive in the tonic (m. 5), subdominant (m. 17), and, in embellished form, tonic once again (m. 24). The material in between is an animated spinning out of the initial arpeggiated chord, exuberantly combined with scales. There is much play with the semitone figure that serves as an embellishment of the opening motive. The entire section is a remarkable exercise in one-part writing, like the *manualiter* openings of the Toccata in C Major, BWV 564/1, and Prelude in G Major, BWV 541/1, or the extensive cadenzas of the Grosso Mogul Concerto transcription, BWV 594. In all four cases, Bach was undoubtedly capitalizing on the resonant acoustics of the Weimar Palace Chapel.

The opening toccata leads directly to the heart of the piece, a 185-measure, five-part "Gravement" based on the motive of a rising whole-note scale in the pedal combined with chains of quarter-note suspensions in 3rds and 6ths in the manual. The music touches on a wide range of keys that are temporarily established by full cadences—ironically, a product of Bach's study of Italian harmonic practices:

m. 29	I (from the Trés vitement)	m. 95	vi
m. 49	V	m. 99	I
m. 59	iii	m. 105	IV
m. 68	I	m. 118	ii
m. 76	ii	m. 131	V
m. 87	vi	m. 142	v

It is the deceptive cadences, however, that define the Gravement, creating harmonic ambiguity that drives the music forward with remarkable force. Bach's intentions are clear at the outset, when the opening material fails to cadence in the tonic, as expected, after just six measures, but veers off course with a deceptive cadence (m. 35). The evasion is repeated just six bars later (m. 41), where the dominant is expected but averted, once again with a deceptive cadence. A full cadence is not achieved, in fact, until measure 49—21 bars into the section. After this, the listener's expectations for harmonic resolutions are thwarted time and time again, either with deceptive cadences (mm. 124, 158, 172) or progressions that careen off course (mm. 51, 69, 88, 99, 114, 124, 135). The element of harmonic surprise intensifies in the last third of the section, with dark chromaticism on the flat side of the scale (mm. 127–142) that leads to D minor, via a shocking Neapolitan-sixth chord (m. 139). And it reaches a climax with the final progression that begins at measure 158, where a return to the tonic is anticipated but averted with a deceptive cadence and the rise of the whole-note pedal motive through two octaves. Here the arrival of the tonic is avoided once again at measure 172. Finally, in measure 176, with the arrival of a dominant pedal point, the addition of a sixth voice, and the shift of the rising whole-note motive to the hands in parallel thirds, all seems on course for a conclusion in the tonic. But this is stymied a final time with a jarring diminished seventh chord in the last measure.

In the conclusion of the Gravement, then, arrival of G major is avoided for 28 measures. In the "Lentement," it is delayed yet another 16 measures, until the final bar of the work. This process, of avoiding the harmonic resolution and replacing it with harmonic ambiguity, is the antithesis of Italian concerto style, with its well-defined harmonic stations. Bach correctly viewed it as characteristic of French improvisational style, and we get the impression, listening to the Gravement, that Bach could have extemporized this way for hours.

The Lentement is based on a punctuated pedal part that descends chromatically, note by note, from the final c♯ of the Gravement to a dominant pedal point on D. The figures represent an ingenious filling in of sequential chords, in the same five parts as those of the Gravement, in the manner of a French *cheute* (example 13-4). For this reason, the tempo needs to be slow, so that the listener can perceive the chords the sextuplets outline. The texture (a single manual part, here

Example 13-4 (a) Jean-Henri d'Anglebert: Cheute sur une note (chord and realization), and (b) Pièce d'Orgue, Lentement, m. 186 (hypothetical chord and realization).

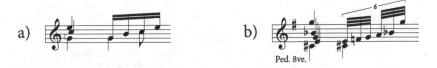

supplemented with pedal), the recurring sextuplets, and the closing scale hark back to the Vitement, now transformed into music that has no clear precedent in the French, Italian, or German repertory. The six-part G-major chord that ends the Lentement provides closure, at long last, to the harmonic quandary initiated in the Gravement.

The Pièce d'Orgue lacks double bars,[20] confirming that Bach viewed it as a single, continuous piece. It was a remarkable accomplishment: the creation of a large free work, held together through harmonic means rather than ritornello procedure or fugal imitation. As Peter Williams expressed it, the three sections of the Pièce d'Orgue represent "a *tour de force* in harmonic manipulation."[21]

Johann Gottfried Walther's copy of the Pièce, written sometime before 1717,[22] captures the work in its initial Weimar form (BWV[3] 572.1), before Bach revised the text, most probably in Leipzig during the course of organ instruction.[23] The first two sections contain variants that are revealing in a number of aspects (the third section remained unchanged). In the early version, the first section lacks a tempo designation and is notated in old-fashioned C 12/8 meter, rather than the straightforward 12/8 that appears in the later version. The principal motive of the first measure is notated differently, implying another type of articulation (example 13-5, a), and the scales in measures 3–12 (of the early version) lack concluding 32nd-note pairs. More important, the original version shows that Bach rewrote measures 13a–17, replacing the original material with figures more closely allied with those that precede and follow the segment and dropping a measure to eliminate a third appearance of the principal theme in the tonic, which he apparently viewed as redundant. Finally, in measure 25, he regularized the flagging (again with implications for articulation) and dropped the momentary addition of a second voice (example 13-5, b). The result was a more concise, more highly unified opening section.

In Walther's manuscript the middle section is labeled "Gayement," a term that appears frequently as a tempo/*affect* indication in the French *Livres d'Orgue* known to Bach. Walther defined *gayement* as "lustig, freudig" (merry, joyous), which seems at odds with the "Gravement" of the revised version, which Walther defined as "ernsthalf, und folglich: langsam" (serious, and therefore slow).[24]

Example 13-5 Pièce d'Orgue, BWV 572: (a) mm. 1–2 of revised version (above) and early version (below), and (b) m. 24 of revised version (above) and m. 25 of early version (below).

Bach improved the part-writing of the middle section here and there when he revised the text. But most significantly, in the initial version he seems to have intended the section to be played *manualiter* until the final 10 bars, where the pedal finally enters for a pedal point on low D.[25] This would have brought the Pièce d'Orgue more firmly into the tradition of French organ music, which commonly used pedal only for concluding pedal points or isolated notes (as in the "Lentement" of the Pièce). In addition, if the middle section was originally conceived as *manualiter*, the mysterious note BB in measure 94 (m. 95 of the early version) finds a possible explanation at long last: the organ in the Village Church of Oßmannstedt bei Weimar reportedly had a manual range of BB to c''', which would have made the note playable on one Central German organ, at least.[26] The middle section can certainly be performed as a manual piece, and Bach changed no bass notes when he later revised the text. The subtitle for the Pièce d'Orgue, "a 5, avec la Pedalle continu," first emerges in Leipzig copies of the work, in which the initial bass note of the Gravement is clearly marked "Ped."

The Great Passacaglia

There is no better way to conclude our survey of "The Golden Years" than to look at the Passacaglia in C Minor, arguably Bach's most important Weimar organ work. It was not his final composition—it was written before his encounter with Vivaldi's *L'Estro armonico*, when he was still focused on Central and North

German styles. But with 302 measures in 3/4 meter, the Passacaglia is his first truly "symphonic" organ composition, and the first work that unquestionably bears the stamp of genius.

It did not break ground in terms of its genre, however. The tradition of ostinato organ works was well established in Germany, and Bach could turn to impressive models among Pachelbel's six ciaconas and Buxtehude's pedal passacaglia and two ciaconas. Although the ostinato variation had begun to fall from favor by the first decade of the eighteenth century because of its limited harmonic scheme, it was still considered a useful vehicle for extemporization. We find it among the audition requirements for the organist position at the Hamburg Cathedral in 1725, for example, when candidates were asked to improvise a "ciacona on a given bass theme."[27]

As a genre, the passacaglia is quite similar to the *ciacona*, the Italian term generally used by German composers for the chaconne. According to Walther, both the passacaglia and the ciacona are in triple meter, with a recurring four-bar theme in the bass.[28] The subject can be altered and presented in smaller notes, but it cannot be lengthened—it must remain four measures long throughout the course of the work. In addition, the music may switch from major mode to minor mode, and vice versa. Both the passacaglia and the ciacona are instrumental pieces, Walther explained, although one finds them in vocal music as well, where they are shorter because of the limitations of the voice. Walther concludes that the passacaglia is, in fact, a ciacona, except that it "normally goes more slowly" and that its "expression is less lively"—features reflecting the fact that passacaglias are invariably in minor mode. The extant examples also suggest that passacaglia themes routinely begin with an upbeat, whereas most chaconnes start on the downbeat. Despite these distinctions, however, the line between passacaglia and ciacona was not entirely clear, even in Bach's time: a copy of the Passacaglia in C Minor written by his student Johann Jacob Kieser bears the title "Ciaccona et Fuga ex C moll."[29]

There seems to have been great interest in ostinato works in Bach's family circle. The Andreas Bach Book contains five ostinato pieces: Buxtehude's Ciacona in C Minor, BuxWV 159; Ciacona in E Minor, BuxWV 160; Passacaglia in D Minor, BuxWV 161; and Praeludium in C Major, BuxWV 137 (which concludes with a spirited ciacona), and J. C. F. Fischer's Chaconne in G Major. The copies of the second two are unique, and possibly stem from manuscripts brought back from the north by Bach himself.[30] The Möller Manuscript, compiled by Johann Christoph a few years earlier, contains yet another ostinato piece, the Chaconne in G major from Jean-Baptist Lully's *Phaëton* (act 2, scene 5) of 1683.[31]

Bach's Passacaglia appears to have enjoyed great popularity in the eighteenth century. It was disseminated broadly, with copies distributed in Thuringia, Leipzig, Berlin, Hamburg, Braunschweig, and Nuremberg. Nine additional copies are known to have existed but are no longer extant.[32] Bach returned to the text several times in Leipzig, making small improvements that resulted in at least three versions of the work. The first is the initial Weimar composition, presumably represented in the Andreas Bach Book by a copy in the hand of Johann Christoph (who apparently liked the work so much that he wrote out a second copy, only partially preserved).[33] The second version, with slight revisions, possibly made by Bach during organ instruction, is represented in the copies of Kieser and Johann Tobias Krebs.[34] The third version, showing final refinements (including the slurs in the first countersubject of the fugue and the adagio indication at the end of the work) is represented in the printed editions of Dunst (1834) and Peters (1844), which relied on a manuscript, now lost, that was owned by Karl Wilhelm Ferdinand Guhr in Frankfurt and was said to be in Bach's hand.[35]

The theme of the Passacaglia is ingeniously constructed. Stretching over eight measures, it is twice as long as a traditional four-bar passacaglia subject. As we noted in chapter 7, the first half represents a four-bar ostinato bass that Bach borrowed from the "Christe eleison" of the *Messe du Deuzième Ton* from André Raison's *Livre d'orgue* of 1688,[36] a collection he encountered and copied out in 1709.[37] In the "Christe," subtitled "Trio en passacaille," the bass theme is foreshadowed by the two upper voices before it enters in measure 3 and takes up its ostinato role (example 13-6, a). It appears six times in the 27-measure piece, sometimes in smaller notes, in the manner described by Walther. The borrowing of Raison's ostinato was similar to Bach's earlier use of themes by Albinoni, Bononcini, and Corelli for organ and clavier fugues—all the more so since Raison's ostinato appears in its original form as the "Thema fugatum" for the Passacaglia's fugue. Bach may have been attracted to Raison's theme because of its potential for expansion and its melodic appeal, which represented an interesting alternative to the often-used descending-tetrachord bass, which had become a cliché in ostinato works by 1700. To Raison's modest, harmonically open-ended idea, Bach added a complementary four-bar period that similarly contains three rising seconds and ends with a falling fifth, which mirrors the rising fifth that opens Raison's theme (example 13-6, b). Bach also transposed the theme from G minor to C minor, so that he could extend the line downward an octave and a half to C, the lowest note on the pedalboard. He concluded the expanded ostinato with a full cadence in the tonic, bringing closure to Raison's half-cadence.

The expanded theme is a miniature hybrid, combining old and new, in the spirit of experimentation that so strongly characterizes the Weimar organ works. Bach also broke with convention by presenting it alone at the beginning. Passacaglias and ciaconas normally began with full texture, as in the Buxtehude, Pachelbel, Fischer, and Lully works in the Andreas Bach Book and Möller

Example 13-6 (a) André Raison: "Christe eleison" from *Messe du Deuxième Ton* (*Livre d'Orgue*, 1688), and (b) Passacaglia in C Minor, BWV 582: theme.

Manuscript and Bach's own opening ostinato choruses in Cantata 12, *Weinen, Klagen, Sorgen, Zagen*, composed in 1714, and Cantata 78, *Jesu, der du meine Seele*, composed 10 years later.[38] Bach was clearly very proud of his newly created passacaglia subject, which could stand alone on its melodic merits.

Much of the figuration in the Passacaglia, especially the use of *corta* and *suspirans* figures, was standard keyboard vocabulary. Similar writing can be found in Pachelbel's organ chorales, Böhm's chorale partitas, and Bach's own Neumeister Chorales, chorale partitas, and Orgel-Büchlein settings. And one can see other links specifically with the Orgel-Büchlein: the disciplined part-writing, the distinguishing of parts through a hierarchy of note values ("Gott, durch deine Güte," BWV 600, and the theme and countersubjects of the Passacaglia fugue), and the overlapping of parts that makes for "snarly" manual playing (mm. 5 or 8 of "Christ lag in Todesbanden," BWV 625; mm. 84 or 181 of the Passacaglia)— a feature of his keyboard idiom that mostly disappeared after the Vivaldi encounter. The old-fashioned figuration confirms that Bach was still attached to his North and Central German roots when he composed the Passacaglia, probably between 1709 (the encounter with Raison's *Livre d'orgue*) and 1713 (the encounter with Vivaldi's *L'Estro armonico*).

It is not the figuration that makes the Passacaglia a great work but its monumental architectural sweep. Buxtehude had set a challenging precedent, with the symmetrical, large-scale design of his D-Minor Passacaglia:

┌── Seven variations, in D minor
│   Manual modulation
├─ Seven variations, in F major
│   Manual modulation
└─ Seven variations, in A minor
     Manual modulation
└── Seven variations, in D minor

The structure of Bach's Passacaglia is much more subtle, and the grouping of the variations has been the subject of various analyses over the years.[39] A straightforward dissection shows that Bach used a combination of symmetrical elements (mirroring groups of two and three variations) and developmental elements (the suspension of the pedal in variations 13–15 followed by the thickening of texture and increased animation of variations 16–20):[40]

Variations 1–2: chordal suspensions, resolved on beat two. Rising melodic arc (variation 1) followed by a falling melodic arc (variation 2).

Variations 3–5: rising and falling melodic line, developed in imitation, first in 8th notes (variation 3), then in *corta* rhythm with conjunct motion (variation 4), then in *corta* rhythm with disjunct motion, with pedal taking part in the imitation (variation 5).

Variations 6–8: continuous 16th-note motion, first rising, in imitative *suspirans* figure (variation 6), then falling, in imitative *suspirans* figure (variation 7), then contrary motion, in imitative *suspirans* figure (variation 8).

Variations 9–10: fragmented theme in pedal, first in chordal *suspirans* figure, imitated in upper parts (variation 9), then in punctuated chords accompanied by running 16th notes (variation 10).

Variations 11–12: theme restored to original form, but transferred to soprano, first accompanied by single line of continuous 16th notes (variation 11), then by dense imitative counterpoint (variation 12).

Variations 13–15: pedal suspended. Theme, embellished, in alto against imitative counterpoint (variation 13), then theme in tenor, in broken chords, in two parts (variation 14), then theme tossed between bass and soprano, in one-part arpeggiated chords (variation 15).

Variations 16–18: theme in original form, in restored pedal, accompanied by six-part *style brisé* chords (variation 16), two-part sextuplets (variation 17), and three-part chordal *corta* figure, with punctuated pedal (variation 18).

Variations 19–20: theme in original form in pedal, accompanied by continuous 16th notes in thick, circular counterpoint, first in four-parts (variation 19), then five parts (variation 20). Concludes with eight-part chord.

Like Buxtehude, Bach created a symmetrical structure, but one that is perceived only subliminally, disguised by the dynamic development of the motivic material.

The fugue, based on Raison's theme without Bach's appendage, emerges suddenly and unexpectedly from the variations. It is not separated by a double-bar (unfortunately introduced into the Peters Edition and Neue Bach-Ausgabe), and its first note is part of the eight-part chord that concludes variation 20.[41] In a broad sense, the fugue serves as the 21st variation of the set and the grandest of all.

Bach combined Raison's four-measure theme, now labeled "Thema fugatum" (theme of the fugue; example 13-7, x), with two contrasting countersubjects: an 8th-note figure with a downward leap followed by the rising second of Raison's tune, and an animated 16th-note figure well suited to pedal playing (example 13-7, y and z).

After adding a fourth free part, Bach proceeded to manipulate the subject, countersubjects, and free voice in the manner of a permutation fugue, using 12 of the 24 possible combinations described for four-part invertible counterpoint in Theile's *Musicalisches Kunst-Buch* (figure 13-1). The result is Bach's most mechanical organ fugue, a permutation fugue that is more rigid than that of the Fantasia and Fugue in G Minor, BWV 542, and one that reflects the strict vocal fugues that appear in Mühlhausen and Weimar cantatas.[42]

In the Passacaglia, Bach relieves the rigidity of the permutation procedure by: (1) inserting interludes of increasing length, based on material from the countersubjects, (2) easing tension by dropping the pedal in a *manualiter* middle section, in major mode, and (3) concluding with a free coda (mm. 276–292) that touches on the subdominant before ending in bright C major. The Passacaglia with its lengthy permutation fugue surpassed anything that had come before. Philipp Spitta may have described Bach's stunning accomplishment best: "it appears as though he had grasped with one clutch all that Buxtehude had laboriously won."[43]

Despite the modern convention of performing the Passacaglia with a registration that begins softly and builds to a mighty fortissimo at the end of variation 20 and the conclusion of the fugue, there is good evidence that ostinato pieces were performed like other free works—that is, *organum plenum* throughout. The 1725 Hamburg audition specified that the ciacona was to be improvised "on the full organ,"[44] and a copy of the Passacaglia in C Minor, written in the 1750s by Johann Christoph Oley, bears the title "Passacaglio con Pedale pro Organo pleno."[45] Bach's nuanced handling of textures, which ebb and flow from four voices to one voice to five voices during the variations and from four voices to three voices to four voices in the fugue, requires no further dynamic adjustment.

Example 13-7 Passacaglia in C Minor, BWV 582, fugue: subject (x) and countersubjects (y and z).

Measure	171	174	181	186	192	198	209	221	234	246	256	272	292
Soprano		S	C1	C2	F	C2	C1	C2		S	F	S	
Alto	S	C1	C2	F	S	C1	S	C1	C2	F	C1	C1	
Tenor	C1	C2	F	S	C1	S	C2	F	S	C1	C2	F	
Bass (pedal)		S		C1	C2			S	C1	C2	S		C2
Key	i	v	i	v	i	III	VII	v	i	v	iv	i	

pedaliter (171–192)   *manualiter* (198–209)   *pedaliter* (246–272)

S = subject; C1 = countersubject 1; C2 = countersubject 2; F = free voice.

Figure 13-1 Fugue of the Passacaglia in C Minor, BWV 588: Permutations of the subject and countersubjects.

The Passacaglia speaks for itself, as a testament to Bach's transformative vision of the organ as a symphonic instrument.

Notes

1. Göttingen, University Library, *Cod. Ms. 2020.21/2.*
2. In the Peters Edition it appeared in vol. 9 (1881; Ferdinand Roitzsch, ed.), 29 years after the publication of the main volumes. In the NBA it appeared in vol. IV/11 (2003; Ulrich Bartels and Peter Wollny, eds.), 31 years after the main volumes of free organ works.
3. Koska 2012, 225–234, and Wollny, 2018, 81–93.

4. Zehnder 2009, 294.
5. Berlin State Library, *Mus.ms 11544*, fascicle 12, and *P 803*, fascicle 14, respectively.
6. Brussels, Royal Library, *25448 MSM*, fascicle 17, described in Leisinger and Wollny 1997, 467.
7. See discussion, facsimile, and transcription of the Schübler fugue in Stinson 2012, 20–27.
8. Berlin State Library, *P 286*, fascicle 5 (Kellner, c. 1726–1727), and *P 803*, fascicle 11 (Hedar, c. 1735).
9. Leipzig State Archive, *21081/7369* (Gerlach, c. 1725), described in Blanken 2013b, 95–105. Gerlach studied with Bach and served both as organist of the New Church and assistant director of Bach's Collegium Musicum ensemble.
10. The "Gleichauf manuscript," used by Friedrich Conrad Griepenkerl to edit the Peters edition. See Peters Edition, vol. 3, iii.
11. Peter Williams, in Williams 2003, 152, rightly questioned whether Bach was beginning to move in the direction of using the heels of the feet in such passages, an issue that surfaces again in Leipzig organ works such as the Fugue in B Minor, BWV 544/2, and the Six Sonatas.
12. Discussions of Torelli's influence can be found in Stauffer 1980, 104–106; Zehnder 1991, 33–95; and Hill 1995, 162–175.
13. See Christoph Wolff's discussion of the G-Major Toccata as Bach's effort to move beyond the North German style of the six earlier keyboard toccatas, in Wolff 2020, 65–70.
14. Zehnder 1991, 47.
15. Johann Gottfried Walther transcribed two concertos from Torelli's opus 8 for organ and therefore must have had access to the collection. See table 9-1 in chapter 9.
16. As Walter Emery first observed, the Toccata calls for the unusual manual note, d''' (mm. 35 and 80), which is specifically avoided in the Fugue (mm. 84–85). See Emery 1966, 600–601. Along similar lines, Zehnder points out that the Fugue utilizes an antiquated form of cadence that does not appear in the two earlier movements. See Zehnder 1995, 336.
17. Berlin State Library, *P 288*, fascicle 3, for instance, written by an anonymous scribe.
18. An indication Boyvin used in his two *Livres d'Orgue*, which Bach apparently held in his music library (see chapter 7).
19. Berlin State Library, P 288, fascicle 2 (Kellner) and fascicle 1 (anonymous scribe).
20. The double bars that appear in the BG, NBA, and other modern editions are editorial.
21. Williams 2003, 168.
22. Berlin State Library, *P 801*, fascicle 5. Dating from Bießwenger 1992b, 27.
23. The earliest copies of the revised version are those of Kellner, Kayser, and Gerlach, copied between 1723 and 1735 or so.
24. Walther 1732, 274 ("gayement") and 290 ("gravement").
25. The Gayement section of BWV³ 572.1, with the entry of the pedal in the final measures, is not included in the NBA. It is reproduced in the Breitkopf and Leupold Editions.
26. Lobenstein 2015, 286–287.

27. Mattheson 1731, 34–35.
28. Walther 1732, 164 ("Ciacona") and 464–465 ("Passacaglio").
29. Göttingen University Library, *Cod. Ms. 2020.21/1*. See Wollny 2018, 83.
30. Schulze 1984, 55–56.
31. A different keyboard arrangement of the chaconne from *Phaëton* appears in Jean-Henri d'Anglebert's *Pièces de Clavecin*, to which Bach had access in Weimar (see chapter 7).
32. Bach digital, under BWV 582.
33. Leipzig Town Library, Becker Collection, *III.8.4* (Andreas Bach Book) and *Peters Ms. R 16* (fragment, mm. 233–292 only).
34. Göttingen University Library, *Cod. Ms. 2020.21/1*, and Berlin State Library, *P 803*, fascicle 11.
35. The "Guhr autograph" disappeared with the owner's death in 1848. It is quite possible that the manuscript was written not by Bach but rather by his student Christian Gottlob Meißner, who served as his principal scribe in Leipzig from 1723 to 1729. Meißner's handwriting greatly resembles that of his teacher. In 1839 Guhr offered Felix Mendelssohn, as a gift, the choice between autograph copies of the Passacaglia or the Orgel-Büchlein. Mendelssohn, who was deeply interested in chorales, chose the Orgel-Büchlein. The Orgel-Büchlein manuscript has survived (Cracow, Jagiellońska Library, *P 1216*), and modern handwriting analysis shows that it was written not by Bach but by Meißner. The same could have been true of the Passacaglia manuscript. See NBA IV/7, KB (Dietrich Kilian, ed.; 1988), 129–130.
36. The discovery was made in 1899 by Alexandre Guilmant and André Pirro as they edited Raison's works for the second volume of *Archives des Maîtres de l'Orgue*.
37. Wollny 2015, 122–123.
38. It is interesting to note that Bach added an ostinato bass introduction to the "Weinen, Klagen, Sorgen, Zagen" chorus of Cantata 12 when he reworked it as the "Crucifixus" of the B-Minor Mass—but only as a second thought. See Stauffer 2003, 122.
39. These include Roth 1915, Tell 1938, Vogelsänger 1967, and Wolff 1991a.
40. This analysis is a modified version of the analysis in Wolff 1991a, 308–313.
41. In a number of early sources, a line connects the c' of the final chord of variation 20 with the g' of the fugue in the next measure. The transition, with the guiding line and without a double bar, is presented correctly in the Leupold and Breitkopf Editions.
42. In choruses such as "muß täglich von neuen dich, Joseph, erfreuen" of Cantata 71 (1708), "Lob, und Ehre, und Preise, und Gewalt" of Cantata 21 (c. 1713), or "Himmelskönig, sei willkommen" of Cantata 182 (1714).
43. Spitta 1873–80, vol. 1, 588.
44. Mattheson 1731, 34.
45. Berlin State Library, *Mus.ms. 10813*. Dating from Bach digital.

PART IV

THE ORGANIST
AS CAPELLMEISTER

Cöthen (1717–1723)

I thought that this art was dead, but I see that in you it still lives.
—Johann Adam Reincken, on hearing
Bach improvise in 1720

14

Bach in Cöthen

Capellmeister at the Cöthen Court

In December 1717 Bach exchanged his position as court organist and concert-master in Weimar for that of capellmeister to Prince Leopold of Anhalt-Cöthen. Leopold's court was Calvinist, and as a result Bach was no longer responsible for Lutheran service music—either organ or vocal. In addition, the town's single Lutheran Church, St. Agnus, at which the Bach family worshiped, had only a modest instrument (II/27) built by Johann Heinrich Müller in 1707–1708.[1] As a consequence of these new circumstances, Bach turned away from organ compo-sition for the next six years, focusing instead on harpsichord and chamber music.

With a population of approximately 3,000, Cöthen was a sleepy town in Bach's time. Like Haydn many years later in Eisenstadt, Bach was compelled to work in isolation and hence forced to be original. At the same time, Prince Leopold was a great champion of music, playing violin, harpsichord, and viola da gamba and singing bass. As part of his training, he had taken a grand tour of Holland, England, France, Italy, Vienna, and Prague, attending performances and assembling a large collection of French and Italian music. Thus Bach had access to a music library that contained the latest works from the Continent and England.

Bach's chief duty in Cöthen was leading Leopold's instrumental band, a small but talented group of professional musicians that was strengthened initially by six virtuoso players recruited in 1713 by Leopold's mother, Gisela Agnes, from the disbanded ensemble of Friedrich Wilhelm I in Berlin. It was augmented by the addition of two more professional musicians when Leopold ascended the throne of Anhalt-Cöthen in 1716. Bach, hired in August 1717, was the capstone appoint-ment. For this able ensemble of 16 players Bach composed a vast amount of in-strumental music for large and small settings: concertos, overtures, trio sonatas, duos, and solos. The Brandenburg Concertos, the violin concertos, and the first three orchestral suites stem from this time, as do the violin and harpsichord sonatas, the unaccompanied violin sonatas and partitas and unaccompanied cello suites. Bookbinding charges and fees for special works and guest artists hint at a large repertory, no longer extant. It has been estimated that Bach may have com-posed for the weekly performances of Leopold's ensemble as many as 200 pieces, most of which are no longer extant or were absorbed into Leipzig works.[2]

J. S. BACH. George B. Stauffer, Oxford University Press. © Oxford University Press 2024.
DOI: 10.1093/oso/9780195108026.003.0015

Bach conducted regular rehearsals that were praised for their rigor: "The princely *Capelle* in this town, which holds weekly music rehearsals, serves as an example that even the most famous virtuosi read through and practice their things together beforehand."[3] It was common at the time for ensembles to sight-read music, but works like the Brandenburg Concertos required both advanced technique as well as practice—a new standard that also applied to Bach's keyboard compositions.

Repertory

Bach was required to provide vocal works for just two occasions: Prince Leopold's birthday on December 10 and New Year's Day on January 1. Traces of 13 such works survive, mostly in the form of texts, and only two pieces have been passed down intact: the birthday serenade *Durchlauchtster Leopold*, BWV 173a, of 1722, and the New Year's Day cantata *Die Zeit, die Tag und Jahre macht*, BWV 134a, of 1719.

At the same time, Bach's production of harpsichord music greatly increased, spurred on the one hand by his growing need for instructional pieces and on the other hand by Leopold's acquisition of a large and magnificent two-manual harpsichord built by Michael Mietke, which Bach picked up in Berlin in March 1719. The Mietke harpsichord was probably brass-strung, in the tradition of Central German instruments, which would have given it an especially broad, rich tone. The purchase was soon followed by a remarkable series of keyboard works: the Two-Part Inventions and Three-Part Sinfonias and the first volume of the Well-Tempered Clavier (both of which first appeared in the Clavier-Büchlein vor Wilhelm Friedemann Bach of 1720), the French Suites (which first appeared in the Clavier-Büchlein vor Anna Magdalena Bach of 1722), and most probably the bulk of the English Suites and the Chromatic Fantasia and Fugue in D Minor, BWV 903, as well. The Chromatic Fantasia and Fugue would have exhibited the full resources of the Mietke harpsichord, while the instructional pieces would have covered Bach's growing pedagogical needs as his sons Wilhelm Friedemann, Carl Philipp Emanuel, and Johann Gottfried Bernhard came of age and his coterie of keyboard students expanded.

New Stylistic Developments

Bach's compositions from the Cöthen period show three stylistic aspects that eventually led to new directions in his organ music. The first is the influence of fashionable dance music. Social dance played a central role in the activities of the Cöthen court, as witnessed by the presence of a dance master, Johann David Kelterbrunnen. The presence of court dancing enabled Bach to supplement the traditional keyboard dances set by his predecessors—the allemande, courante, sarabande, and gigue—with the new *galant* dances that were sweeping through aristocratic circles in Europe: the minuet, bourrée, gavotte, musette, air, passepied, and polonaise. The result was an explosion of new dance types in Bach's music, not only in expected vehicles such as the English and French Suites for keyboard and the orchestra suites for chamber ensemble but also in new areas such as vocal music. The two surviving Cöthen cantatas, written specifically for the house of Prince Leopold, are filled with dance music:[4]

Die Zeit, die Tag und Jahre macht, BWV 134a
  2. Aria: "Auf, Sterbliche, lasset ein Jauchzen ertönen"—passepied in 3/8 meter
  4. Aria (duet): "Es streiten, es prangen die vorigen Zeiten"—bourrée in ¢
  8. Chorus: "Ergetzet auf Erden, erfreuet von oben"—passepied in 3/8

Durchlauchtster Leopold, BWV 173a
  4. Aria (duet): "Unter seinem Purpursaum" (Al tempo di minuetto)— minuet in 3/4
  6. Aria: "So schau dies holden Tages Licht"—bourrée in ¢
  7. Aria: "Dein Name gleich der Sonnen geh"—bourrée in ¢
  8. Chorus: "Nimm auch, großer Fürst, uns auf"—minuet in **3**

The effect of the new fashionable dances on Bach's organ music was a lightening of textures, an increased use of balanced phrasing, and a profusion of dance meters such as ¢, 2/4, 3/4, 3/8, and 12/8. This is especially evident in the Six Sonatas, Clavier-Übung III (the *manualiter* chorale settings and duets, in particular), and the Schübler Chorales. For instance, the lilting, airy, 6/8-meter Clavier-Übung III setting of "Vater unser im Himmelreich," BWV 683, written in Leipzig, is a far cry from the intense, almost turgid, 4/4-meter Orgel-Büchlein setting of the same chorale, BWV 636, written in Weimar, before Bach's Cöthen experience. The fundamental procedure is the same in both pieces: a soprano cantus firmus is presented phrase by phrase, without pause, supported by three-part imitative counterpoint. In the Orgel-Büchlein setting, the imitation is immediate, dense (almost stretto-like), and unrelenting (example 14-1, a). In the Clavier-Übung setting, by contrast, the imitative voices enter more slowly at the beginning of each line of the chorale, allowing the parts to breathe (example 14-1, b). In addition, key phrases are rounded off with groups of three 8th notes (as in m. 3), whose natural dance articulation (♩♪♪) creates an elegant close, much like a *reverence* in ballet.

Example 14-1 Two settings of "Vater unser im Himmelreich": (a) BWV 636, from the Orgel-Büchlein, and (b) BWV 683, from Clavier-Übung III.

The second aspect of the Cöthen experience that influenced Bach's organ music was his involvement with chamber music. There can be no question that Bach composed and performed chamber music in Weimar—the Fugue in G Minor for Violin and Basso Continuo, BWV 1026, and his manuscript copy of Telemann's Concerto in G Major for Two Violins, Strings, and Continuo, for example, date from that time. But these seem to have been occasional pieces only. In Cöthen, by contrast, his participation in chamber music-making was concentrated and continuous. As capellmeister, he was obligated to provide chamber pieces at a steady pace for the weekly performances of Prince Leopold's instrumental ensemble, not only the known concertos, orchestral suites, and unaccompanied violin and cello pieces, but dozens of compositions now lost or absorbed into works produced in the 1730s and 1740s for Bach's Collegium Musicum in Leipzig. We can assume that trios and solo sonatas played a vital role in the Cöthen repertoire, especially when Leopold traveled to Carlsbad in the summers of 1717, 1718, and 1720, taking with him a reduced retinue of players to provide musical entertainment.[5] The Sonata in G Major for Two Flutes and Continuo, BWV 1039, and the fragment of the oboe version (in G minor) of the Sonata in B Minor for Flute and Harpsichord, BWV[3] 1030.1, hint at what must have been a rich repertory of Cöthen trios and duos.

The intense involvement with chamber music expanded Bach's compositional vocabulary in a number of critical ways. Writing works with continuo resulted in simplified bass lines with vertical rather than horizontal harmonic considerations and a slower harmonic pulse. And trio texture allowed for duet writing, both imitative and homophonic (especially in the form of consonant parallel thirds or sixths), over the bass. These idioms gave Bach new compositional options, and changes in Central German organ building, which we will discuss in chapter 17, reflected the growing desire to bring the organ into line with instrumental practice, allowing instrumental genres such as trios to be readily performed on the organ. The fruits of Bach's experience with chamber music in Cöthen played out in Leipzig, in works such as the miscellaneous trios, the Six Sonatas, the *pedaliter* trio "Allein Gott in der Höh Sei Ehr," BWV 676, of Clavier-Übung III, the Schübler Chorales, and variation 5 of the Canonic Variations on "Vom Himmel hoch, da komm ich her," with its walking bass pedal line (example 14-2). Nothing quite so directly derived from chamber music appears among the Weimar organ works.

The third aspect of Bach's Cöthen endeavors that was critical to his organ works was his growing interest in pedagogy. With a rising reputation as an organ virtuoso, Bach began to attract keyboard students in Weimar. But it was during his Cöthen years, perhaps motivated by the addition of his sons Wilhelm Friedemann, Carl Philipp Emanuel, and Johann Gottfried Bernhard to the group, that Bach began to assemble collections of pieces that could be used for instructional purposes. It is not surprising that the Five Short Preludes (BWV 924, 926–929), Inventions and Sinfonias, French Suites, and preludes from

Example 14-2 Canonic Variations on "Vom Himmel hoch, da komm ich her," BWV 769, variation 5, mm. 1–6.

the Well-Tempered Clavier, volume 1, initially appeared in the albums Bach assembled for his family.

"Since he himself had composed the most instructive pieces for the clavier, he brought up his pupils on them," C.P.E. Bach later explained to Johann Nicolaus Forkel, his father's first biographer.[6] In the realm of organ instruction, this resulted initially in the appropriation of the preexisting Orgel-Büchlein for teaching and then in the composition of the Six Trio Sonatas, written around 1727 to give final polish to the organ technique of Wilhelm Friedemann, then 17. This was followed by the four duets of Clavier-Übung III, organ updates of the Two-Part Inventions. We will return to Bach's method of organ teaching and examine it in detail in chapter 15.

Organ Inspections and Performances

During the Cöthen years Bach's professional organ engagements were limited. In December 1717 he inspected the new organ (III/48) in St. Paul's Church (also known as the University Church) in Leipzig, most probably on the journey from Weimar to take up his new position in Cöthen. The St. Paul's organ was the largest in Electoral Saxony at the time, expanded from an earlier instrument by University Organ Builder Johann Scheibe in Leipzig.[7] And in the early summer of 1721 Bach traveled to Gera to examine and approve the new organs in St. John's Church (III/42) and St. Salvator's Church (disposition unknown), both constructed by Johann Georg Finke.[8]

Yet despite Bach's preoccupation with other activities, he still experienced one of his greatest triumphs as an organist while in Cöthen: his audition performance in St. Catherine's Church in Hamburg. Although Bach later claimed that he was blissfully happy working for Prince Leopold, he nevertheless entered the competition for the organist position of the St. James' Church (Jakobikirche) in Hamburg, an opening created by the death of the church's organist, Heinrich Friese, in September 1720. In November 1720 Bach traveled to Hamburg, where he performed on the large and magnificent organ of St. Catherine's Church (IV/57) as part of the audition process. The Obituary of 1750 describes the event in considerable detail:

He made a journey to Hamburg and was heard for more than two hours on the fine organ of St. Catherine's before the Magistrate and other distinguished persons of the town, to their general astonishment. The aged organist of this church, Johann Adam Reincken, who at the time was nearly one hundred years old, listened to him with particular pleasure. At the request of those present, Bach performed extempore the chorale An Wasserflüssen Babylon at great length (for almost half an hour) and in different ways, just as the better organists of Hamburg in the past used to do at the Saturday vespers. Particularly on this, Reincken made to Bach the following compliment: "I thought that this art was dead, but I see that in you it still lives." This verdict of Reincken's was all the more unexpected since he himself had set the same chorale, many years before, in the manner described above, and this fact, and that normally he had always been somewhat inclined to be envious, was not unknown to our Bach. Reincken thereupon pressed him to visit him and showed him much courtesy.[9]

Reincken's compliment probably referred not only to Bach's extraordinary improvisatory skills but also to his decision to improvise a chorale fantasia, a genre that had fallen out of favor by 1720. The recent discovery of Bach's tablature copy of Reincken's grand, 328-measure fantasia on "An Wasserflüssen Babylon," written out in Georg Böhm's house in 1700 when he was just 15 years old, shows that he had been long familiar with Reincken's treatment of the chorale.[10] And the related discovery of an early tablature copy from Bach's library of Pachelbel's setting of the same melody confirms his early interest in treating this particular hymn.[11] Bach's performance in St. Catherine's Church twenty years later in front of the idol of his youth must have been immensely satisfying—so much so that he appears to have related the story to his family and students, who recorded it in the obituary some thirty years after the event. Bach's improvising for "almost a half hour" on "An Wasserflüssen Babylon" (the obituary report is unusually specific on this point) represented a certain amount of gamesmanship on his part, since he publicly surpassed the great length of his famous host's impressive setting.

As noted in chapter 12, Bach may also have played an earlier piece from score, the Fantasia and Fugue in G Minor, BWV 542, since the subject and countersubject of the Fugue were later cited by the Hamburg composer and theorist Johann Mattheson in 1731.[12] Although the Fugue, at least, was written during the Weimar years, it would have been especially appropriate at the St. Catherine's performance, since its theme was based upon a Dutch folksong, "Ik ben gegroet van" (I am greeted by; see chapter 12),[13] and hence would have curried favor with Reincken, who was born in the Netherlands.

At an even later point Johann Friedrich Agricola recalled Bach's observations on the organ in St. Catherine's:

In the organ of St. Catherine's in Hamburg there are 16 reeds. The late Capellmeister, Mr. J. S. Bach in Leipzig, who once made himself heard for two hours on this instrument, which he called excellent in all its parts, could not praise the beauty and variety of tone of these reeds highly enough. It is known, too, that the famous former organist of this church, Mr. Johann Adam Reincken, always kept them in the best tune.

The late Capellmeister Bach in Leipzig gave assurance that the 32-foot Principal and the pedal Posaune in the organ of St. Catherine's in Hamburg spoke well and quite audibly, right down to the lowest C. But he also used to say that this Principal was the only one of that size with these good qualities that he had ever heard.[14]

Bach was apparently offered the position at St. James' but declined when he learned that the appointee was expected to make a monetary contribution to the church—a local custom in Hamburg. In the end, the post was awarded to Johann Joachim Heitmann in return for a gift of 4,000 marks, a sum far beyond Bach's means. Mattheson, reporting on the incident, described the appointee as "the son of a well-to-do artisan, who was better at preluding with his talers than with his fingers." He added that Erdmann Neumeister, minister of the church and a dissenting member of the evaluation committee, declared in his Christmas sermon that year that "even if one of the angels of Bethlehem should come down from Heaven, one who played divinely and wished to become organist of St. James' but had no money, he might just as well fly away again."[15]

Notes

1. Wolff and Zepf 2012, 43.
2. Wolff 2000, 196.
3. BDok II, no. 91, commentary.
4. The effect of dance on Bach's vocal works in Cöthen is discussed in Doris Finke-Hecklinger, *Tanzcharaktere in Johann Sebastian Bachs Vokalmusik* (Trossingen: Hohner-Verlag, 1970), 134–136.
5. Maria Hübner, "Neues zu Johann Sebastian Bachs Reisen nach Karlsbad," *Bach-Jahrbuch* 92 (2006), 93–107.
6. NBR, no. 395.
7. On Scheibe and the construction, inspection, and tonal character of the St. Paul's instrument see Edwards Butler 2022, 88–149.
8. Wolff and Zepf 2012, 23–25.
9. NBR, no. 306.
10. Maul and Wollny, 2007.
11. The copy is in the hand of Bach's Weimar student Johann Martin Schubart. See Maul and Wollny 2007, ix–x.
12. Mattheson 1731, 36. Elsewhere (Mattheson 1722–25, 368) Mattheson also discussed the text of Cantata 21, *Ich hatte viel Bekümmernis*, which suggests that it, too, may have been performed during the 1720 audition process.
13. BDok II, 302, commentary.

14. NBR, no. 358. Agricola recorded these remarks in his annotations to Jacob Adlung's *Musica mechanica organoedi* of 1768. The organ in St. Catherine's was destroyed in World War II, but samples of pipes were preserved, and on the basis of these pipes and the original specifications, the instrument was reconstructed by Flentrop Orgelbouw of Zaandam, Netherlands, and dedicated in 2013. See Wolff and Zepf 2012, 34–36, and *Eine Orgel für Bach in St. Katharinen* (Hamburg: Stiftung Johann Sebastian, 2013).

15. Mattheson 1728; trs. NBR, no. 82.

15

Organ Teacher, Consultant, and Recitalist

With Bach's new responsibilities as capellmeister in Cöthen, the steady flow
of organ works of the Weimar years came to a halt. We can nevertheless observe a number of small pieces that were written in Cöthen, all having a didactic function. Bach's repurposing of the Orgel-Büchlein during the Cöthen
years suggests that he was beginning to consider the need for teaching material for the organ as well as the clavier—a need that culminated in the
composition of the Six Sonatas a decade later. As we noted in chapter 8, the
Orgel-Büchlein initially served primarily as a composition workbook and repository for short chorale settings. It was not until the Cöthen period that
Bach added the well-known title that proclaimed the album's new goal of
offering instruction in the development of organ chorales as well as in the
art of playing the pedal, which was "treated as wholly obbligato" throughout
each piece.[1]

Didactic Works: Miniature Chorale Settings and
an Unfinished Fantasia

A similar pedagogical intent appears in the organ pieces that can be assigned
with certainty to the Cöthen years: the miniature chorale preludes "Wer nur den
lieben Gott lässt walten," BWV 691, and "Jesu, meine Zuversicht," BWV 728, and
the fragmentary works "Jesu, meine Freude," BWV 753, and Fantasia in C Major,
BWV 573. Like the initial versions of the Inventions and Sinfonias, the Well-
Tempered Clavier I, volume 1, and the French Suites, all four are passed down
in the albums that Bach started for his family, the Clavier-Büchlein vor Wilhelm
Friedemann Bach of 1720 and the Clavier-Büchlein vor Anna Magdalena Bach
of 1722 and 1725.

"Wer nur den lieben Gott lässt walten," BWV 691, an eight-measure long
florid-melody chorale entered into Wilhelm Friedemann's album around 1720,[2]
illustrates Bach's instructional aims especially well. The richly embellished chorale melody appears phrase by phrase, without interludes, above an accompaniment in two real parts (example 15-1). One might view it as a *manualiter*
version of an Orgel-Büchlein florid-melody chorale. Here the accompaniment is unrelated to the hymn tune and not developed in any way. Although it

J. S. BACH. George B. Stauffer, Oxford University Press. © Oxford University Press 2024.
DOI: 10.1093/oso/9780195108026.003.0016

Example 15-1 "Wer nur den lieben Gott lässt walten," BWV 691, mm. 1–4.

contains syncopations and diminutions that enliven the rhythmic flow of the setting, it serves mainly as harmonic background for the melodic line, which contains an abundance of both Italian and French ornamentation. The Italian embellishments are written out, in the form of 32nd-note diminutions, while the French embellishments are presented as symbols, drawn specifically from the ornament table at the beginning of Friedemann's album. Titled "Explication unterschiedlicher Zeichen, so gewiße manieren artig zu spielen, andeuten" (An explanation of the various signs that indicate how to play certain ornaments elegantly), the table represents a condensed version of the larger ornament table Bach copied in Weimar from Jean-Henri d'Anglebert's *Pièces de Clavecin* of 1689.

Bach seems to have gone out of his way to include as many of the French ornaments from the condensed table as possible in "Wer nur den lieben Gott," using 9 of the 13 symbols it contains:

Bach's term in the "Explication"	Realization
trillo	trill
mordant	mordent
doppelt-cadence	turn from below and trill
doppelt-cadence	turn from above and trill
doppelt cadence und mordant	turn from below and mordent
accent steigend	upward-resolving appoggiatura
accent fallend	downward-resolving appoggiatura
accent und mordant	upward-resolving appoggiatura and mordent
accent und trillo	downward-resolving appoggiatura and trill

It is often debated whether the heavily ornamented versions of several organ works passed down in copies made by Johann Peter Kellner, Johann Gottlieb Preller, and Berlin scribes working under Carl Philipp Emanuel Bach and Johann Philipp Kirnberger represent Bach's own practice.[3] The profusely embellished text of "Wer nur den lieben Gott" suggests that they might, at least in a pedagogical context. This is also demonstrated by the heavily ornamented versions of several of the Three-Part Sinfonias transmitted in the manuscript copies made by Bach's students Heinrich Nicolaus Gerber and Bernhard Christian Kayser.[4] For organ study, Bach may have used short, uncomplicated florid-melody chorales to teach the art of ornamentation.

The melody "Wer nur den lieben Gott lässt walten" was associated with "Affliction, Persecution, and Temptation," "Christian Life," and "Divine Serenity" in German hymnals of the time.[5] The meditative nature of its text would have made Bach's expressive setting appropriate for domestic devotions, too, and it was probably for this reason that Anna Magdalena Bach entered it into her second Clavier-Büchlein of 1725, copying the c. 1720 text without change. But the setting is also a concise study in the embellishment of a chorale melody and the realization of French ornament symbols. As was so often the case, Bach fulfilled didactic and musical goals in one and the same piece.

"Jesu, meine Freude" (fragment), BWV 753, also entered into Wilhelm Friedemann's album around 1720,[6] and "Jesu, meine Zuversicht," BWV 728, entered into Anna Magdalena's 1722 album around 1722 or 1723,[7] follow similar lines. They both feature highly embellished chorale melodies with coloratura flourishes and Italian and French ornamentation floating over neutral, two-part accompaniments. "Jesu, meine Freude" breaks off in measure 9, just after the beginning of the Stollen of the chorale. Bach may have intended the fragment to serve not only as an exercise in embellishing a chorale tune but also as a study in composition, with the incomplete incipit to be finished by the young Friedemann. "Jesu, meine Zuversicht" goes beyond the other two settings in using profuse Italian diminutions and a tenth French symbol, the "trillo und mordant" (trill and mordent).

Instructional goals also seem to stand behind the intriguing **Fantasia in C Major, BWV 573**, a short draft Bach entered into Anna Magdalena's 1722 album around 1723 or 1724.[8] Labeled "Fantasia pro Organo," a title that confirms that the three small chorale settings could have been intended for organ as well as harpsichord or clavichord, the piece breaks off after 12 measures (plate 15-1), followed by empty space on the page and then a page of empty staves. Bach cast the Fantasia in five parts, with an angular pedal motive and ongoing note-motion that harks back to the Vivaldi-derived idiom of the Concerto movement in C Major (after Johann Ernst), BWV 595, and the Prelude in C Major, BWV 545/1a. But the melodious nature of the upper voices, the embellished suspensions, and

Plate 15-1 Fantasia in C Major, BWV 573: Bach's autograph entry of c. 1723 in Anna Magdalena Bach's Notebook from 1722.

Staatsbibliothek zu Berlin—Preußischer Kulturbesitz, Musikabteilung mit Mendelssohn-Archiv

the rising imitative sequence in mm. 8–9 point ahead to the more fluid writing of the Prelude and Fugue in B Minor, BWV 544, and the Prelude and Fugue in E Minor ("Wedge"), BWV 548, of the Leipzig years.

The form of the Fantasia is unorthodox:

Mm. 1–2   Ritornello-like figure, establishing the tonic, C major
Mm. 3–4   Transition, modulating to the dominant, G major
Mm. 5–7   Sequence 1, remaining in the dominant, G major
Mm. 8–12   Sequence 2, modulating to the mediant, E minor

How is the piece to proceed? Without a repetition of the opening theme in the dominant it is neither a concerto form nor an A B A B form, Bach's two favorite templates for free preludes in Weimar. Its distinctive opening segment is surely intended to return at some point—perhaps in E minor at the break-off point or in C major at the end. The explanation of its ambiguous form may rest in the term "fantasia," which Bach also used for the first version of the Three-Part

Sinfonias in Wilhelm Friedemann's album. It hints that this music, too, reflects the "good inventions" a performer must conjure up to compose—or to complete, in this case—a successful piece. Thus the form may have been purposefully open-ended, to stimulate the player's improvisatory imagination.

No matter how it is to be finished, the Fantasia in C Major provides us with an important, dateable measure of Bach's *pedaliter* organ-writing as he took up his duties as St. Thomas Cantor in Leipzig in 1723. The masterful handling of five-part texture, the rich contrapuntal play of the inner voices, and the lyrical nature of the melodic material hint at the free prelude-writing that will soon take flight on a grand scale.

Organ Pedagogue

Unlike Handel or Telemann, Bach had a steady stream of keyboard students throughout his career. Beginning with just a few documented pupils in Arnstadt and Mühlhausen, his "studio" grew to a dozen or so students in Weimar, as his reputation increased, but then fell to just a few pupils once again during the Cöthen years, when he worked in a town that was not Lutheran-church-oriented and he was no longer a church or court organist. Finally, the number climbed to more than 70 students in Leipzig, where the St. Thomas School and the university provided a steady supply of young men eager to learn clavier and organ and Bach's renown as the best organist in Germany attracted still others from the surrounding area.[9]

Bach was as successful and methodical in his teaching as he was in other musical endeavors, and over the years he trained almost single-handedly the next generation of prominent German organists: Johann Friedrich Agricola, Johann Christoph Altnickol, Johann Friedrich Doles, Heinrich Nicolaus Gerber, Carl Gotthelf Gerlach, Gottfried August Homilius, Johann Philipp Kirnberger, Johann Christian Kittel, Johann Tobias and Johann Ludwig Krebs, Johann Gottfried Müthel, Johann Schneider, and Johann Caspar Vogler, together with Bach's own sons Wilhelm Friedemann, Carl Philipp Emanuel, Johann Gottfried Bernhard, Johann Christoph Friedrich, and Johann Christian.

Many of these students and sons won positions at churches with which Bach had professional ties: Altnickol became the organist at St. Wenceslas Church in Naumburg, Christian Heinrich Gräbner and Homilius at the Church of our Lady in Dresden, Gerlach at the New Church in Leipzig, Johann Ludwig Krebs at the Palace Church in Altenburg, Schneider at St. Nicholas's Church in Leipzig, Vogler at the Palace Church in Weimar, Wilhelm Friedemann Bach at the Market Church in Halle and then St. Sophia's Church in Dresden, and Johann Gottfried Bernhard Bach at St. Mary's in Mühlhausen and then St. James' Church in

Sangerhausen. Bach's students clearly benefited not only from the technical and musical instruction they received but also from their teacher's extensive network of church-music connections.

Study with Bach was intense. Students sometimes received room and board and lived with the Bach family, either paying for food and accommodations or helping with domestic chores. Johann Elias Bach, for instance, a son of Bach's first cousin Johann Valentin Bach, lived in the Bach household from 1737 to 1742 and served as Bach's personal secretary, handling written correspondence on his behalf. Several students remained with Bach as he moved from one position to another: Vogler studied with Bach in Arnstadt and Mühlhausen; Johann Martin Schubart in Arnstadt, Mühlhausen, and Weimar; and Bernhard Christian Kayser in Cöthen and Leipzig.[10] Clearly Bach was a teacher to whom one wanted to remain attached.

Bach apparently charged a hefty fee for instruction. Johann Heinrich Gräbner, organist of the Church of our Lady in Dresden, emphasized to church officials there, when seeking an assistant position for his son Christian Heinrich, that he had sent the candidate to study clavier with Bach in Leipzig for two full years "at no small cost."[11] Christian Heinrich obtained the assistantship in 1733 and inherited the head position when his father died six years later. When Johann Georg Voigt, Jr., applied for an organist post in Ansbach in 1751, he stressed above all that he had received three years of music instruction from the "virtuoso Bach in Leipzig," which his father had financed "at great expense."[12] He, too, received the appointment.

As we noted in the introduction, printed music was very costly at the time, and most music compositions circulated in manuscript form only. Bach's students were granted the privilege of copying works contained in his library, both his own pieces and those of other composers. The Well-Tempered Clavier, for instance, was not published until the nineteenth century. During Bach's lifetime, if one wanted a copy, one had to obtain it directly from the composer himself or from one of his students. The experience of studying with Bach is vividly described in a letter Philipp David Kräuter sent in 1712 from Weimar to his patrons back in Augsburg:

> I shall report, according to your kind instruction, how I have used these funds and how I have duly arranged with my new teacher, Mr. Bach in Weimar, for a year's board and tutelage. The traveling expense was between 25 and 26 florins since the roads were very bad and I had to give the coachman almost twice the normal compensation. I gave 4 florins to Mr. Bach for half the month of April, since I was concerned that he might count the entire month as part of the year that now is to commence with the month of May. He had initially asked for 100 reichstaler to cover the year, but I was able to lower it to 80 taler, against which he will offer me board and tuition. He is an excellent and sterling man, both in composition and in instruction on keyboard and other instruments. It is assuredly six hours per day of guidance that I am receiving, primarily in composition

and on the keyboard, at times also on other instruments. The rest of the time I use by myself for practice and copying work, since he shares with me all the music I ask for. I am also at liberty to look through all of his pieces.[13]

A few months later Kräuter wrote again, stressing the intensity of his studies and the need to work even at night, by candlelight:

No day goes by that I fail to compose something new, or industriously prac-tice the clavier or other instruments, both of which are equally important. Whenever I can obtain something new and really good here or from another court, I don't let it out of my hands until I have made a copy of it. I must often do this by candlelight, since during the day I need to remain unencumbered so that I can carry out my other work.[14]

As we noted in Chapter 9, Kräuter wrote to his benefactors once again in the spring of 1713, requesting permission to extend his stay because he would have the opportunity to "see, hear, and copy a great deal" in the coming months, when Prince Johann Ernst returned from the Netherlands and Bach would perform on the newly restored organ in the Palace Chapel.[15] A manuscript copy of Jacques Boyvin's two *Livres d'orgue* in the hand of Vogler and tablature copies of Johann Pachelbel's Fugue in B Minor, "An Wasserflüssen Babylon," and "Kyrie, Gott Vater in Ewigkeit" in the hand of Schubart provide a glimpse of this type of stu-dent copying activity in Weimar, for they seem to reflect prints and manuscripts once contained in Bach's library.[16]

We know a fair amount about Bach's approach to clavier instruction. The lex-icographer Ernst Ludwig Gerber, whose father, Heinrich Nicolaus, had studied with Bach in Leipzig from 1724 to 1727, reported that Bach started his students off with the Two-Part Inventions and the Three-Part Sinfonias.[17] When these were thoroughly learned, he moved his students to a series of dance suites, drawn mostly from the French and English Suites, and then to the Well-Tempered Clavier.[18] Clavier study culminated in thorough-bass exercises, taught through the use of Albinoni violin sonatas. The early biographer Johann Nicolaus Forkel claimed that Bach saved a great deal of time by playing through assigned pieces, to show students how they were to be performed.[19] In Gerber's case, Bach, "under the pretext of not being in the mood to teach," played through the entire Well-Tempered Clavier, volume 1, altogether three times!

Unfortunately, we know far less about Bach's organ teaching. He used his own compositions, once again, as verified by the numerous copies of the organ works passed down in handwritten manuscripts made by his students. But he does not seem to have assigned the pieces in a systematic way. Free works and chorale settings are transmitted singly, for the most part, in an almost random way. The

Orgel-Büchlein, which might be viewed as the organ equivalent of the Inventions and Sinfonias or the Well-Tempered Clavier, is preserved in incomplete student copies only. The Six Sonatas, written to give final polish to Wilhelm Friedemann Bach's technique, was used solely with selective students, and there are no student manuscripts of Clavier-Übung III at all. In terms of pedal-playing, we have the Pedal-Exercitium, BWV 598, but it may be the work of Carl Philipp Emanual Bach rather than his father (see chapter 21).

Bach appears to have taught clavier and organ in distinctly different ways.[20] When teaching clavier, he first concentrated on the student's basic keyboard skills, honing them in a very methodical manner through the use of instructional collections. When teaching organ, he appears to have assigned a few representative organ pieces in order to develop touch, manual-pedal coordination, and a sense of style. He used early as well as late works for this purpose. The Prelude and Fugue in E Minor ("Cathedral"), BWV 533, and the Passacaglia in C Minor, BWV 582, for example, are each transmitted in a multitude of manuscript copies. In the case of the Prelude and Fugue in G Minor, BWV 535, and the Prelude and Fugue in G Major, BWV 550, early pieces once again, we find Bach seizing the pen from student copyists to write out short passages that apparently were unclear in the original materials.[21] The free works, the Weimar versions of the "Great Eighteen" Chorales, and the miscellaneous chorales were used for instruction, but on a piece-by-piece basis.

The Pedal-Exercitium, whether by Bach or Carl Philipp Emanuel, provides a rare look at pedal training. But otherwise, there are almost no pedaling indications in the organ manuscripts of Bach or his students. An illuminating exception is Johann Tobias Krebs's pedaling for the carillon-like ostinato pedal theme in "In dir ist Freude," BWV 615, from the Orgel-Büchlein (example 15-2).[22] Krebs's markings point to the use of toes only, with opposite toes for notes within the beat (thus creating the possibility of slurs) and the toe of a single foot between beats (thus creating the possibility of agogic accents). The construction of pedalboards and key desks in German organs of the time weighed against

Example 15-2 "In dir ist Freude," BWV 615, mm. 39–40, pedal part: (a) with pedaling indications of Johann Tobias Krebs (d = dextra, or right foot; s = sinistra, or left foot), and (b) modern equivalent.

the routine use of heels in pedal-playing.[23] But the pedal lines of many of Bach's Leipzig organ works show a marked increase of diatonic scale-writing. That Bach might have turned to the use of heels here and there in such pieces to achieve a more cantabile style of playing is not beyond the realm of possibility.

Fingering also occurs rarely in the early sources of the organ works. It is unlikely that the fingering indications of Johann Gottlieb Preller in his manuscript copy of the Canzona in D Minor, BWV 588,[24] for instance, stem from Bach, but they give an idea of the principles in force at the time. As we noted in chapter 13, the Carl Gotthelf Gerlach copy of the Toccata in C Major, BWV 564/1, contains *dextra* (right hand) and *sinistra* (left hand) indications in the opening manual *passaggio* (see plate 13-1). Similar indications appear in Johann Gottfried Walther's Weimar copy of "Jesus, Christus, unser Heiland," BWV 666a,[25] for the free cadenza near the end (mm. 35–36), and in many other early manuscripts.

In other instances, the use of the right hand and left hand in passage work was notated through the use of broken flags. In the closing recitative of the Toccata in D Minor, BWV 565, the distribution of the hands is quite clear from the flagging of the notes. Or in the Passacaglia in C Minor, BWV 582, Bach's flagging of the arpeggios in variation 15 (m. 120) indicates that each arpeggio is distributed between the hands, with a repositioning of the hands every octave (example 15-3).

In light of the paucity of pedaling and fingering indications in the early scores, it would seem that Bach conveyed instructions on such performance matters verbally.

With regard to the playing of chorales, Bach's Weimar student Johann Gotthilf Ziegler stated that he was instructed "not to play the tunes merely offhand, but according to the sense of the words"[26]—an approach seen in "O Lamm Gottes, unschuldig," BWV 618; "Durch Adams Fall ist ganz verderbt," BWV 637, and many other chorale settings.

Aside from teaching the technical aspects of playing the organ, Bach probably focused on the skills most frequently demanded of the organists of the day: improvisation and continuo realization. For an examination administered to applicants for the organist position at Hamburg Cathedral in 1725, candidates were asked to improvise: (1) a short free prelude, (2) a trio on "Herr Jesu Christ, du höchstes Gut," (3) a fugue on a given theme, (4) a ciacona on a given bass theme, and (5) an artful accompaniment for an aria (that is, a continuo realization).[27] The candidates were also required to compose, within two days of the test, a well-worked out piece in written form. What they weren't asked to do was play a work from the written or printed page. Bach taught well-advanced technical skills, and to judge from the many student copies of his works, his students could play written pieces. But it was improvisation that won jobs, and on that count, too, he must have been an extraordinary teacher.

Example 15-3 Passacaglia in C Minor, BWV 582, mm. 120–123: (a) broken-flag notation indicating notes taken by left hand and right hand, and (b) modern interpretation (l = left hand; r = right hand).

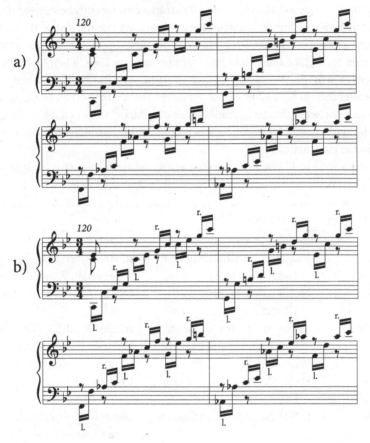

It is interesting to note that in Bach's time, technique alone did not always win the day. Vogler, who benefited from many years of study with Bach, boasted in an application letter for an organist position in Görlitz that he had studied with the famous Mr. Bach in Leipzig, and "as regards virtue on the organ and speed of hands and feet, I come closest to him here in Saxony, which can best be demonstrated by an actual presentation."[28] Vogler received that chance in Leipzig, where he competed for the organist position at St. Nicholas's Church in 1729. He was not chosen, however, because, according to the minutes of the Town Council, "he irked the church people and played too fast."[29]

Organ Examiner and Consultant

Bach served as an organ examiner and consultant throughout his life. He was only 18 when he was called to Arnstadt to inspect the recently completed instrument in the New Church—a circumstance that surely was not lost on the builder, Johann Friedrich Wender, who was 47 at the time. Bach's last documented inspection took place more than four decades later, in 1746, when he examined the organ in the St. Wenceslas's Church in Naumburg. But Bach remained active even after that: in June 1749 he was consulted about a new organ being planned for the Franciscan Church in Frankfurt an der Oder,[30] and in October 1749, just eight months before his death, he was proposed as a consultant for a new organ project in Hartmannsdorf.[31]

Over a span of 43 years Bach served as an advisor or inspector for at least 21 instruments:[32]

Date	Location and church	Builder
1703	Arnstadt, New Church	Johann Friedrich Wender
1706	Langewiesen, Church of Our Lady	Johann Albrecht and Johann Sebastian Erhardt
1708	Mühlhausen, St. Blasius's Church	Johann Friedrich Wender
c. 1708	Ammern, St. Vitus's Church	Johann Friedrich Wender
1710	Taubach, St. Ursula's Church	Heinrich Nicolaus Trebs
1712–1714	Weimar, Palace Church	Heinrich Nicolaus Trebs
1716	Halle, Market Church of Our Lady	Christoph Cuncius
1716	Erfurt, St. Augustine's Church	Georg Christoph Stertzing and Johann Georg Schröter
1717	Leipzig, St. Paul's Church (or University Church)	Johann Scheibe
1723	Störmthal, Town Church	Zacharias Hildebrandt
1725	Gera, St. John's Church	Johann Georg Finke
	Gera, St. Salvator's Church	Johann Georg Finke
1726–1728	Sangerhausen, St. James' Church	Zacharias Hildebrandt
1731	Stöntzsch, Town Church	Johann Christoph Schmieder
1732	Kassel, St. Martin's Church	Nicolaus Becker
1735	Mühlhausen, St. Mary's Church	Christian Friedrich Wender

Date	Location and church	Builder
1739	Altenburg, Palace Church	Tobias Heinrich Gottfried Trost
c. 1742	Berka, St. Mary's Church	Heinrich Nicolaus Trebs
1743	Leipzig, St. John's Church	Johann Scheibe
1746	Zschortau, St. Nicholas's Church	Johann Scheibe
1746	Naumburg, St. Wenceslas's Church	Zacharias Hildebrandt

Undoubtedly there were other organ examinations for which the documentation is lost.

Bach probably gained his early knowledge of organ construction from observing the ongoing repairs to the instrument in the St. George's Church in Eisenach carried out by Johann Christoph Bach; from his own youthful observations of organs in Ohrdruf, Lüneburg, and Hamburg; and from reading Werckmeister's two well-known treatises on organ building, the *Orgelprobe* of 1681 and the *Erweiterte und verbesserte Orgel-Probe* of 1698. So great was Werckmesiter's influence on organ building and maintenance that Bach and his fellow inspectors borrowed terminology and organizational elements from his publications when formulating examination reports.[33]

Carl Philipp Emanuel Bach described his father's skill as an organ examiner in a letter to Forkel:

Never has anyone undertaken organ examinations so strictly and yet so fairly. He understood to the highest degree everything about organ building. If a builder worked honestly, and yet lost money on the project, he would persuade the patron to make a subsequent payment . . . The first thing he did at an organ examination was this: He said, in fun, "Above all I must know whether the organ has good lungs," and in order to test this he would pull on every speaking stop and play as full-voiced as possible. At this point organ builders often became pale with fright.[34]

Agricola also commented on the rigor of Bach's examinations, noting that when Bach and his fellow inspector Zacharias Hildebrandt carried out the 1743 inspection of the new organ built by Johann Scheibe for the St. John's Church in Leipzig, they declared the instrument well constructed only after "the strictest examination of an organ that perhaps ever was undertaken."[35]

Unfortunately, only seven reports from Bach's organ consultancies and examinations survive, those for Mühlhausen (St. Blasius's Church), Taubach, Halle, Erfurt, Leipzig (St. Paul's Church), Zschortau, and Naumburg.[36] Viewed as a whole, they show a number of recurring concerns. First and foremost, Bach wanted an organ to have sufficient wind, especially for 32' and other pedal stops. In describing the particulars of rebuilding and expanding the organ in St. Blasius's Church in Mühlhausen, Bach devoted four points to winding issues, underscoring that "the lack of wind must be remedied" by adding three well-constructed bellows. In Halle he and his fellow examiners (Johann Kuhnau, who wrote the report, and Christian Friedrich Rolle) pointed out that the wind did not push the liquid in the wind gauge to the proper level, with the result that the bellows shook when one played on the Hauptwerk. In Leipzig he praised the builder Johann Scheibe for constructing a new wind-chest for the Brustwerk division, so that its wind supply was sufficient for the expanded range of the keyboard and matched those of the other manuals. These reports mirror C.P.E. Bach's description that the first thing his father tested in an organ was its "lungs"—that is, its winding system.

In the Mühlhausen and Halle documents Bach stressed the need for the 32' pedal stops to be adequately winded and appropriately voiced, so that they would provide the gravity desired from such registers. This parallels his comments to Agricola about the extraordinary clarity of the 32' Principal and 32' Posaune of Reincken's organ in St. Catherine's Church in Hamburg. Bach also emphasized the importance of accurate tuning (Mühlhausen, Halle, and Leipzig), the proper adjustment of tremulants (Mühlhausen), audible and clear voicing (of reed stops, especially; Halle, Leipzig, and Naumburg), and keyboard action that was light, even, and not too deep (Halle, Leipzig, and Naumburg). He also expressed concern that the toy stops that were popular with Central German congregations— Glockenspiel, Cymbelstern, Vogelgesang, and a movable sun (in the case of Halle)—work properly (Mühlhausen and Halle). Finally, he emphasized the need for an organ chamber to be protected from the elements (Leipzig) and sufficiently capacious that all the pipes could be reached easily (Halle and Leipzig).

In sum, Bach's chief concern about the organs he examined was that they functioned well. There is little mention in his reports of aesthetic matters such as the quality of individual registers or the blending of stops in the plenum, one of the most important sounds produced by German pipe organs. In the Mühlhausen report he mentioned that a wooden 8' Gedackt is better than a metal one for continuo-playing, and the dispositions he drew up for the Mühlhausen instrument and a smaller organ in Berka[37] show a desire for the availability of a Sesquialtera sound on every manual. But otherwise, Bach steered clear of analyzing the merits of specific stops and combinations in his reports. As with many aspects of organ registration and playing, he seems to have believed this element was best discussed verbally rather than put into writing—an unfortunate loss for posterity.

Organ Recitalist

Bach presented organ recitals in a number of contexts. When he examined and approved new organs, he often concluded his visits with a dedicatory recital. Such recitals can be documented for the New Church in Arnstadt (1703), St. Ursula's in Taubach (1710), the Town Church in Störmtal (1723), St. John's in Gera (1725), and St. Martin's in Kassel (1732). On other occasions he presented recitals as part of a job application (St. Catherine's in Hamburg, 1720, and most probably the Market Church in Halle, 1713); as part of his successful appointment as "Electoral Saxon and Royal Polish Court Composer" (Church of Our Lady in Dresden, 1736); and as part of his visits to imperial cities (St. Sophia's Church in Dresden, 1725 and 1731; Church of the Holy Spirit and others in Potsdam, 1747). We can also assume that he presented regular concerts in Weimar for the reigning dukes and in Leipzig for visitors to the three annual trade fairs.

What did he perform on these occasions? The most detailed description comes from Forkel:

> When Johann Sebastian Bach seated himself at the organ when there was no divine service, which he was often requested to do, he used to choose some subject and to execute it in all the various forms of organ composition so that the subject constantly remained his material, even if he had played, without intermission, for two hours or more. First, he used this theme for a prelude and a fugue, with the full organ. Then he showed his art of using the stops for a trio, a quartet, etc., always upon the same subject. Afterward followed a chorale, the melody of which was playfully surrounded in the most diversified manner by the original subject, in three or four parts. Finally, the conclusion was made by a fugue, with the full organ, in which either another treatment only of the first subject predominated, or one or, according to its nature, two others were mixed with it.[38]

The same organizational approach—free work on the full organ, smaller pieces (duets, trios, quartets, chorale settings) with more varied registrations, free work on the full organ—appears in Clavier-Übung III, and it seems likely that this type of balanced, symmetrical design was one of Bach's programming principles. It can also be seen in the late version of the partita "Sei gegrüßet, Jesu gütig," BWV 768, where the opening four-part harmonized chorale and the closing five-part harmonized chorale serve as plenum bookends for 10 variations with diverse registrations, and in Bach's Leipzig cantatas in general, where the opening chorus and closing chorale commonly serve as tutti framing pieces for recitatives and arias with smaller forces.[39]

In terms of specific pieces, Bach probably improvised most of the music in his recitals, in the manner of his almost 30-minute extemporization on "An Wasserflüssen Babylon" in Hamburg. But written pieces seem to have played a role as well. As we noted earlier, he appears to have played the Fugue in G Minor, BWV 542/2, for his Hamburg audition in 1720, and the Toccata and Fugue in D Minor, BWV 538, for the inauguration of the Kassel organ in 1732. A year later he wrote out a fair copy of the Prelude and Fugue in G Major, BWV 541, for Wilhelm Friedemann to use in his Dresden audition. And the page-turn instructions in the manuscripts of Leipzig works such as the Prelude and Fugue in B Minor, BWV 544; the Prelude and Fugue in E Minor, BWV 548; and the "Great Eighteen" Chorales suggest that they, too, were used as recital fare. In his later years, Bach's drive for perfection may have led him to use more written works in public concerts than in earlier years—compositions in which all details had been worked out to the highest degree of refinement.

Even within the church service Bach did not hesitate to move those present with his brilliant organ-playing, to judge from an incident that occurred during his 1739 visit to the Court Chapel in Altenburg to examine the new Trost organ,[40] an instrument that apparently incorporated a well-tempered tuning system that allowed the use of all major and minor keys. A later account reported that Bach took part in the Sunday service during his stay and greatly impressed the congregants with the modulations in his organ accompaniment to the Creed chorale "Wir glauben all an einen Gott":

> Few are in a position to guide a congregation as old Bach could do, who one time on the large organ in Altenburg played the creedal hymn in D minor but raised the congregation to E♭ minor for the second verse, and on the third verse even went to E minor. Only a Bach could do this, and only the organ in Altenburg.[41]

Notes

1. For the full title see chapter 8.
2. NBA V/5, KB (Wolfgang Plath, ed., 1963), 63, and NBA IX/2, 207.
3. See the heavily embellished versions of the Canzona in D Minor, BWV 588, Pièce d'Orgue, BWV 572, and Passacaglia in C Minor, BWV 582, in the NBA, Breitkopf, and Leupold Editions.

4. See NBA V/3, 68–81.

5. Bighley 2018, 238.

6. Dating from NBA V/5, KB, 63; NBA IX/2, 207.

7. Dating from NBA V/4, KB (Georg von Dadelsen, ed., 1957) 20, NBA IX/2, 207.

8. Dating from NBA IX/2, 206.

9. The classic study of Bach's students, Löffler 1953, has been greatly updated and expanded by Berndt Koska, in Koska 2019. A useful chronological list, though in need of updating, is given in NBR, 315–317.

10. The life and studies of Schubart and Kayser have been clarified only recently. On Schubart, see Maul and Wollny 2007; on Kayser, long known as "Anonymous 5" in Bach research, see Talle 2003, 155–168.

11. BDok II, no. 319.

12. BDok III, no. 641.

13. Letter of April 30, 1712. NBR, no. 312b.

14. Letter of December 1, 1712. BDok V, no. B 54a.

15. NBR, no. 312c.

16. Horn 1986, 257–258, and Maul and Wollny 2007, xxiii–xxiv.

17. NBR, no. 315.

18. The sequence described by Gerber was confirmed by Alfred Dürr in "Heinrich Nicolaus Gerber als Schüler Bachs," *Bach-Jahrbuch* 64 (1978), 7–18.

19. Forkel 1802, 38.

20. Much of the material here is drawn from Stauffer 1994.

21. In these manuscripts: Leipzig Town Library, Becker Collection, *III.8.7*, and Berlin State Library, *P 1210*, respectively.

22. The indications appear in Berlin State Library, *P 801*, fascicle 2.

23. The pedalboards were flat, and there was very little room under the keyboards, which prohibited the players' knees from being fully bent and the feet to be flat on the keys. See the illustration of the original keydesk and pedalboard of the 1713 organ in the Town Church of Marienhafe, in George Ritchie and George Stauffer, *Organ Technique: Modern and Early* (New York: Oxford University Press, 2000), 261.

24. Leipzig Town Library, *Ms. 7*, fascicle 21, reprinted in the Leupold and Breitkopf Editions.

25. Berlin State Library, *P 802*.

26. NBR, no. 340.

27. Mattheson 1731, 34–35.

28. NBR, no. 313.

29. BDok II, no. 266; NBR, no. 313.

30. BDok V, no. A90a.

31. BDok V, no. B586b.

32. Stauffer 1980, 145–147, and Wolff and Zepf 2012, 139.

33. Williams 1982.

34. Forkel 1802, 23; translation from Wolff and Zepf, 140.

35. Johann Friedrich Agricola, commentary in Adlung 1768, 251. A full description of the St. John's organ is given in Edwards Butler 2022, 196–214.

36. The original German texts are reproduced in BDok I, nos. 83–90. The English translations in NBR are not fully accurate, in terms of organ terminology; those of Lynn Edwards Butler in Wolff and Zept 2012, 141–148, are much more reliable.
37. See the specification in the appendix and discussion in chapter 16.
38. Forkel 1802, 22; translation from NBR, 440.
39. This was especially true in Bach's time, when full-sized organs served as continuo instruments for the cantatas, and manual principals and pedal 16' stops could be drawn for the closing chorales.
40. See the specification in the appendix.
41. BDok V, no. C1005a; translation from Wolff and Zepf 2012, 5.

16

Bach's Art of Registration

The German Tradition

The only firsthand description of Bach's method of registering the organ appears in a 1774 letter from Carl Philipp Emanuel Bach to Johann Nicolaus Forkel, the early biographer of Bach:

> No one knew how to register an organ as well as he. Often he shocked organists when he wanted to play their instruments, for he drew stops in his own manner, and they believed it was impossible that the way he wanted it would sound well. But afterward they heard an effect that astonished them. These arts died with him.[1]

Unfortunately, there is very little information in the surviving sources of Bach's organ music to supplement Emanuel's account. The general descriptions "in organo pleno" (or similar expressions indicating the use of the full organ), "a 2 Clavier et Pedal" (or similar phrases calling for the use of two manuals and pedal), and "forte" and "piano" (to establish manual priorities) appear commonly. But indications of specific stops are few and far between.

For the Orgel-Büchlein chorale "Gott, durch deine Güte," BWV 600, Bach indicated Principal 8' in the manual and Trompette 8' in the pedal. In the first movement of the Concerto in D Minor after Vivaldi, BWV 596, he indicated Principals at various pitches, changed during the course of the music, and the addition of a pedal Subbaß 32'. In the Schübler Chorales he indicated the pitch of manual and pedal stops in four of the six pieces. And in "Vom Himmel hoch, da komm ich her," BWV 769a, the manuscript version of the Canonic Variations, he indicated that stops are to be added at two points in variation 3 ("Canto fermo in Canone"). That's it from Bach's own hand, for a repertory of more than 250 pieces!

While the paucity of specific registrations may be perplexing for the modern player, it reflects conventional practice in Germany in Bach's time. German registration is best understood by comparing it with practices in France and England, where organs tended to be constructed along standard lines dictated from Paris and London, respectively. Composers could write works for specific stops, knowing that those stops would be available throughout the land. Thus in France, a composer could write a piece entitled *Récit de Cornet*, knowing that organists there could rely on the Cornet mixture found in the treble range of almost every French Classical

J. S. BACH. George B. Stauffer, Oxford University Press. © Oxford University Press 2024.
DOI: 10.1093/oso/9780195108026.003.0017

instrument. Or in England, a composer could write a piece titled *Voluntary for the Diapasons*, knowing that organists there could turn to the 8' Open Diapason and 8' Stopped Diapason found on the Great of nearly every English instrument.

Such uniformity did not exist in Germany. Regional traditions were much stronger, and organs were built to suit local tastes rather than those emanating from a central metropolis. The great diversity of instruments prevented German composers from adopting registrational systems as codified as those in France or England. Still, several basic precepts obtained, and there is no reason to believe that they were not generally followed by Bach, even when he "drew stops in his own manner."

The most important precept was the fundamental division of registrations into two broad categories: the full organ, and all the remaining, more colorful combinations. As Bach's Hamburg colleague Johann Mattheson explained:

> In general, organ registrations can be divided into two families. To the first belongs the full organ. To the second belong all the remaining diverse varia-tions, which can be realized especially through the use of several manuals and weaker but nevertheless carefully selected stops.[2]

Let us look at each.

The Full Organ

Bach and other German organists used the full organ first and foremost for free pieces, such as preludes, toccatas, fantasias, and fugues. The description of Johann Adolf Scheibe, the son of Bach's Leipzig colleague, organ builder Johann Scheibe, is typical:

> I have yet to speak of the second kind of preluding, namely when one improvises freely without reference to a chorale. This is usually done on the full organ and principally depends on the organist's liveliness of invention and on a splendid, well-developed fugue. This kind of preluding belongs both at the beginning and end of the service, where there is sufficient time for an organist to play some-thing substantial to demonstrate the extent of his inventiveness and skill.[3]

Even ciaconas and passacaglias fell into the full-organ category, as con-firmed by an early copy of the Passacaglia in C Minor, BWV 582, bearing the title "Passacaglio con Pedal pro Organo pleno."[4] The Allabreve in D Major, BWV 589, is labeled "pro Organo pleno," as well.[5] Indeed, the custom of sitting down at the organ and improvising a free piece on the full organ, practiced by Bach himself when testing new instruments, appears to have continued all the way into the nineteenth century. Franz Liszt complained about the practice's lack of registrational color after hearing his student Alexander Wilhelm Gottschalg perform the Toccata in D Minor, BWV 565, on the full organ, on one manual throughout.[6] So ingrained was the practice in Germany.

Bach also used full organ for chorale fugues (such as "Fuga sopra il Magnificat," BWV 733), chorale fantasias (such as "Komm heiliger Geist, Herre Gott," BWV 651), chorale preludes with a tutti instrumental texture (such as "Komm, Gott Schöpfer, heiliger Geist," BWV 667), and chorale settings written in motet style— the *stile antico* of Palestrina (such as "Aus tiefer Not, schrei ich zu dir," BWV 686). In some cases, works requiring full organ are marked "in organo pleno," "pro organo pleno," or simply "pleno." But more commonly they are not, leaving it to the player to determine that they are to be registered for the full organ.

Mattheson, Jacob Adlung, Friedrich Erhard Niedt, and others described the contents of the plenum in detail.[7] It did not call for the indiscriminate use of all the stops of the organ but rather implied a carefully selected and balanced group of registers. Here is Mattheson's description, for example:

> To the full organ belong the Principals, the Sorduns, the Salicionals or Salicets, the Rausch-Pfeiffen, the Octaves, the Quints, the Mixtures, the Scharfs (small mixtures with three ranks of pipes), the Quintades, the Zimbels, the Nasats, the Terzians, the Sesquialteras, the Superoctaves, and the Posaunes in the pedal, not in the manual, for the Posaunes are reed pipes which are excluded in the manual for the full organ. This is done because the Posaune rattles too much on account of its pitch. On the other hand, when there is proper wind, it sounds splendid in the pedal because of the depth of its tone.[8]

The advice of Mattheson and others can be summarized as follows:

In the manuals:
1. The Principal chorus (all pitches) and Mixtures are to be drawn, plus any other stops that add gravity or brightness to the total ensemble. Terzes at 1⅗' pitch were included in the plenum, whether as independent stops or part of a Sesquialtera or other mixture.
2. Reed stops are generally excluded from the manual plenum.
3. The plenum is concentrated in the sound produced on one manual (the Hauptwerk or Oberwerk, in most cases); the other manuals serve to add strength or brightness to the main manual through coupling. Occasionally they also serve as a second manual in echo passages. Among Bach's plenum free organ works, only the Fugue in G Major ("Jig"), BWV 577, Toccata in D Minor ("Dorian"), BWV 538/1, and Prelude in E♭ Major ("St. Anne"), BWV 552/1, contain indications calling for the use of a second manual.

In the pedal:

1. The Principal chorus (all pitches) and mixtures are to be drawn, plus any other stops that add gravity. If the pedal line does not move too quickly, 32' stops may be used. Bach appears to have admired 32' stops as long as they were winded properly (as per his instructions for the 32' Subbass in St. Blasius's Church in Mühlhausen) and spoke clearly down to the lowest C (as per his praise for the 32' Principal and 32' Posaune in St. Catherine's Church in Hamburg).
2. Reed stops may be employed in the pedal plenum.
3. The manual divisions should not be coupled to the pedal division unless the pedal division is deficient in some regard.

All the Remaining Diverse Variations

The second category of registration included all the nonplenum possibilities. As Mattheson explained, these registrations are best realized through the use of different manuals and softer "but nevertheless carefully selected stops." They encompassed an almost limitless variety of Principal, Flute, String, and Reed combinations, used soloistically on two or more manuals, or as a small ensemble on one. The variegated registrations were employed for two-part pieces (bicinia), trios, chorale partita variations, and chorale settings of many types: duets, trios, canons, and works with a cantus firmus or heavily embellished melody.

On rare occasions Bach's German contemporaries wrote specific registrations into the manuscripts or printed editions of their chorale settings, most notably Johann Gottfried Walther, Daniel Magnus Gronau, and Georg Friedrich Kauffmann. And on some occasions organ builders such as Gottfried Silbermann or organists such as Christian Ludwig Boxberg or Johann Friedrich Walther described the nature and use of specific stops on specific instruments.[9] These sources provide a glimpse of the imaginative ways stops were employed in the smaller combinations.

Kauffmann's *Harmonische Seelenlust* (Leipzig, 1733–1736) is perhaps the most informative, containing 98 chorale preludes with detailed suggestions for registration. For instance, Kauffmann's indications show that the Fagot 16' found on the Hauptwerk of many German organs was often used, together with a Principal 8' and Kleingedackt 4' (or similar stop), for the left hand in duets in which the right hand presented a cantus firmus, outlined with a Sesquialtera or similarly bold sound. This corresponds with Bach's description of the Fagot's function in his recommendations for rebuilding the organ in the St. Blasius Church in Mühlhausen ("The Fagotto sounding at 16' pitch . . . is useful for all kinds of new ideas")[10] and the left-hand registration that is passed down with his chorale prelude "Ein' feste Burg ist unser Gott," BWV 720.[11] Kauffmann also displayed a special affection for 16' registrations, especially for *manualiter* pieces with both hands on the same manual, and for gap registrations calling for high- and low-pitched stops, with a "gap" in the middle.

Hymn Accompaniment

Several accounts give an idea of the registrational practice for accompanying chorales. The closest to Bach appears in the contract drawn up for the organist position at the Market Church of Our Lady in Halle that Bach declined in January 1714. Among the various duties is a description of hymn accompaniment. The organist was required

> To take care to accompany attentively the regular chorales and those prescribed by the Minister, before and after the sermon on Sundays and feast days, and during Communion and also at Vespers and times of meditation, to play slowly and without special embellishment, in four and five parts using the Principal, to change to other stops with each verse, also to use the Quintade and reeds, the Gedackt, as well as syncopations and suspensions, in such manner that the Congregation can take the organ as the basis of good harmony and unison tone, and thus sing devoutly and give praise and thanks to the Most High.[12]

In Halle, therefore, the organist was to begin the chorale with a principal chorus and then change stops during succeeding verses, using colorful registers such as quintadenas, flutes, and reeds. This method of accompaniment mirrors the descriptions of Jacob Adlung:

> In playing chorales it is customary to vary the stops regularly—there is little more to mention than this. One need only observe the above precepts [on the fundamental rules of combining registers], so as not to use the stops in a way contrary to their nature. Moreover, whether a player uses a soft or loud registration depends upon his fancy and upon other circumstances such as occasion, *Affect*, and place. Anyone who uses stops that are simply too high pitched, even though they are octave-sounding stops, provides no satisfaction, since it is necessary to give some consideration to gravity and charm.[13]

And

> In a small church a Gedackt or Quintatön 8' can keep the congregation together as they sing hymns. . . . Furthermore, since larger forces usually provide the

music in large churches, the foundation must inevitably be stronger, i.e., one must draw more bass stops on the organ, especially if there are no other bass instruments at hand.[14]

From these accounts, it appears that changing stops between verses of chorales was a common practice and that using foundation stops (seemingly without mixtures) in the manuals and 16' registers in the pedal (reenforced by 16' continuo instruments, if possible) was highly desirable, to support the congregation with "gravity and charm." One cannot help but wonder if Bach changed stops as he modulated the verses of the Creed hymn in Altenburg (see chapter 15).

Bach's Use of Particular Stops and Stop Combinations

The degree to which the contemporary descriptions of specific stops and stop combinations correspond with Bach's own practice remains unclear. We can assume that Bach was extraordinarily imaginative in using stops in unorthodox ways and in selecting colorful registrations, and it was probably these skills that C.P.E. Bach meant when he said his father registered "in his own manner." Forkel, relying on C.P.E.'s letter of 1774 and possibly additional discussions with C.P.E. and his brother Wilhelm Friedemann, wrote the following in his biography of Bach of 1802, after discussing the composer's obbligato treatment of the pedal:

> To all this was added the peculiar manner in which he combined the different stops of the organ with each other, or his mode of registration. It was so uncommon that many organ builders and organists were frightened when they saw him draw the stops. They believed that such a combination could never sound well but were much surprised when they afterward perceived that the organ sounded best just so, and had now something peculiar and uncommon, which never could be produced by their mode of registration.
>
> This peculiar manner of using the stops was a consequence of his minute knowledge of the construction of the organ and of all the single stops. He had early accustomed himself to give to each and every stop a melody suited to its qualities, and this led him to new combinations which, otherwise, would never have occurred to him. In general, his penetrating mind did not fail to notice anything that had any kind of relation to his art and could be used for the discovery of new artistic advantages.[15]

As we noted in chapter 15, Bach served as an organ examiner and advisor throughout his life, and it was from this experience, then, that he gained a thorough knowledge of organ stops, old and new, which he consequently carried into his registrations. The reports of his inspections, consultations, and performances reveal his thoughts on a number of registers and combinations.

His instructions for expanding the Wender organ in St. Blasius's Church in Mühlhausen indicate that the Viol di Gamba 8' "blended admirably" with the Salicional 4', and that the Fagotto 16' could be used not only for "new ideas," as mentioned earlier, but also would sound "quite delicate" in concerted music—that is, for the continuo bass line in cantatas, where the Posaunenbaß 16' in the Pedal would be too heavy. It is also evident from the Mühlhausen proposal that Bach placed great value on the Sesquialtera. Even though the Hauptwerk and Rückpositiv divisions of the Wender organ already contained Sesquialtera mixtures, he indicated the inclusion of a Terz 1⅗' on the newly proposed Brustwerk, from which a "complete and beautiful Sesquialtera" could be formed by drawing it with other appropriate stops—most probably the Stillgedackt 8', Fleute douce 4', Quinta 2⅔', and Octava 2'. Thus on the newly designed organ, Bach wished to have a Sesquialtera sound available on every manual. In the opening chorus of the St. Matthew Passion and the opening aria of the Weimar version of Cantata 161, *Komm, du süße Todesstunde*,[16] Bach specified that the Sesquialtera should be used to highlight the chorale cantus firmus that is played on the organ. The Sesquialtera appears to have been one of his favorite stop combinations for solo chorale melodies.

From Bach's praise of the 16 reeds of the St. Catherine's Church organ in Hamburg, which Johann Adam Reincken kept in "the best tune," we can assume that he admired the beauty and variety of tone they offered. In addition to a full complement of chorus reeds (Trommete 16', 8', and 4' in the manuals; Groß-Posaune 32', Posaune 16', and Tommete 8' in the pedal), the Hamburg instrument included a host of solo reeds: Dulcian 16', Regal 8' (two stops, on different keyboards), Baarpfeiffe 8', Zincke 8', and Schallmey 4' in the manuals; Krummhorn 8', Schallmey 4', and Cornet-Baß 2' in the Pedal.[17]

And from Bach's retention of the Glockenspiel "desired by the parishioners" in the St. Blasius's Church organ and the 26 bells in the Weimar Court Chapel instrument, it would seem that he was not opposed to the toy stops that were highly favored in Central and South Germany. It is interesting to note his recommendation that the Glockenspiel in the St. Blasius's Church organ be placed in the Pedal division. Would he have played chorale melodies on the pedal with the Glockenspiel, as a cantus firmus?[18]

From a number of works we can assume that Bach commonly used octave transposition and unconventional stop pitches to obtain new sounds or to bring parts into the range of a keyboard or pedalboard. For instance, he may have intended the octave doubling in the opening of the Toccata in D Minor, BWV 565, to simulate the effect of a 16' manual Principal on a small organ that did not have one.[19] In the opening section of the Concerto in D Minor (after Vivaldi), BWV 596, he notated the right-hand and left-hand parts an octave lower than Vivaldi's original and indicated that they should each be performed on a 4' Octava, to accommodate the note d''', which did not exist on his keyboard. In the Concerto in C Major (Grosso Mogul), BWV 594, and the first two obbligato organ movements of Cantata 146, *Wir müssen durch viel Trübsal in das Reich eingehen*, he notated the right-hand of the original models an octave lower and presumably performed them on 4' stops, also to avoid the high d'''.[20] And in "Komm du nun, Jesu, vom Himmel herunter" from the Six Schübler Chorales, he indicated that the cantus firmus could be played on the pedal "with a 4' stop, an octave lower," to bring it back into its normal tenor range.[21] It is likely that Bach commonly used octave transpositions not only to accommodate the range of violin parts in transcriptions but also to make the performance of left-hand parts in trios more convenient (by playing them an octave lower, at 4' pitch), to expand the use of 4' and 16' reeds in the manuals (by playing down or up an octave), and other purposes.

It is also evident that in some instances Bach changed or added stops during the course of a movement. In the opening section of the Concerto in D Minor, once again, he indicated that stops should be added to the Oberwerk and Pedal in measure 21—a registrational change that could be accomplished only with the aid of an assistant. And, as mentioned earlier, in the manuscript version of the Canonic Variations on "Vom Himmel hoch," BWV 769a, he indicated that a stop or stops should be added twice during the course of the third variation, first to manual I in measure 27 ("forte"), at the beginning of the canon at the second, and then to manual II in measure 39 ("forte"), at the beginning of the canon at the ninth. These registrational additions, together with the thickening of texture to four parts, create a graduated crescendo effect.

The fragmentary stop indications, octave transpositions, and stop changes in the original manuscripts hint at Bach's remarkably inventive approach to registration. We can only speculate about the varied combinations he must have used. The development of improved bellows and wind-chests during his lifetime allowed for the use of multiple stops of the same pitch to produce new, exotic sounds—a progressive Central-German practice that we will explore in the next chapter. We can assume that Bach embraced this new possibility and many others, and that his approach to registration paralleled his approach to composition, which is to say that he must have constantly sought novel sounds in his unending quest for artistic perfection.

Notes

1. BDok III, 284; translation from Wolff and Zepf 2012, 140.
2. Mattheson 1739, 467.
3. Scheibe 1745, 159; translation from Faulkner 2008, 19.
4. Berlin State Library, *Mus.ms. 10813*, written by Johann Christoph Oley in the 1750s. Dating from Bach digital.
5. In Berlin State Library, *P 1106*, written by "Anonymous O" (a student, assistant, or son of Bach's student Bernhard Christian Kayser) before 1768, and *P 917*, written by Friedrich August Grasnick in the nineteenth century.
6. As recounted by Gottschalg in the *Neue Zeitschrift für Musik*, November 15, 1899.
7. See Faulkner 2008, 14–31, and Stauffer 1986a, 198–200.
8. Mattheson 1739, 467.
9. Silbermann suggested registrations for his organs in Grossharmannsdorf (1741) and Fraureuth (1742); Boxberg described the stops on the new organ in the Church of St. Peter and St. Paul in Görlitz (1704); and Walther appraised the stops on the new organ in the Garrison Church in Berlin (1726), The registrational recommendations are discussed in Gotthold Frotscher, *Geschichte des Orgelspiels und der Orgelkomposition*, 3rd ed. (Berlin: Merseburg, 1966), 605–614 and 1028–1032, and the texts of the original documents are reproduced and translated in Faulkner 2008.
10. NBR, no. 31.
11. The indication appeared in the now-lost manuscript copy of Johann Gottfried Walther, University Library, Kaliningrad, *Mus. ms. Gotthold 15839*, preserved in part on a microfilm owned by Winterthur Town Library and described in BG 40.
12. NBR, no. 48.
13. Adlung 1768, Kapitel VIII, § 237 (p. 172); translation from Faulkner 2008, 28.
14. Adlung 1758, Kapitel VIII, § 205 (p. 487); translation from Faulkner 2008, 30.
15. Forkel 1802, 20; translation from NBR, 439.
16. Fassung A in NBA I/23.
17. The complete disposition is given in Wolff and Zepf 2012, 35.
18. Jacob Adlung (in Adlung 1758, Kapitel VIII, § 206) noted: "I seldom use the Glockenspiel for obligato purposes, even if the style of the setting might allow it, although it is not improper to use it to make festival days more splendid than ordinary Sundays." Translation from Faulkner 2008, 31.
19. Wolff 2002a, 92.
20. Bach indicated a 4' Octava in the autograph manuscript of the Concerto in D Minor. In the two other works the use of a 4' stop is implied by the lower-octave transposition of the right-hand part. See Tagliavini 1986, 243–248.
21. This may have been an alternative to performing the cantus firmus as notated in the score—that is, by the left hand at its written 8' pitch. See the discussion in chapter 24.

PART V
THE GRAND SYNTHESIS
Leipzig (1723–1750)

The former style of music no longer seems to please our ears.
—Johann Sebastian Bach, Memorandum
to the Leipzig Town Council (1730)

17

Bach in Leipzig

St. Thomas Cantor and Town Music Director

On April 22, 1723, Bach accepted the appointment of cantor of the St. Thomas School and town music director in Leipzig. He won the position only after Georg Philipp Telemann and Christoph Graupner had turned it down, a fact that strikes us as ironic today. The other two composers had far more experience writing cantatas, however, and Telemann, in particular, was a favorite of the Leipzig town officials, having served as director of the opera and energetic founder of a local collegium musicum some two decades earlier. Still, Bach stepped into the vacant position and quickly set about establishing new standards for a "well-regulated church music," a desire he had expressed many years before, when resigning from his organist post in Mühlhausen.[1]

Leipzig was a sea change from Cöthen. A center of learning and trade, with a population of 32,000, it featured one of Germany's oldest universities, founded in 1409. It also hosted three annual trade fairs that each attracted thousands of visitors: the New Year's Fair, the Easter Fair, and the St. Michael's Fair in the fall. Leipzig was a bustling commercial city, with a tree-shaded promenade on its periphery, beautiful parks outside the town walls, and private art collections containing works by Rembrandt, Titan, Rubens, and other Renaissance and Baroque masters. A building spree during the first decades of the eighteenth century, fueled by the ambitions of prosperous merchants, resulted in a modern, forward-looking city whose tall town-palaces greatly impressed the young Johann Wolfgang von Goethe when he studied law at the university in the 1760s.[2] Whereas Cöthen was a sleepy backwater, Leipzig bore the epithet "Little Paris."

As cantor of the St. Thomas School, Bach was answerable to the Town Council and responsible for overseeing the music programs in Leipzig's four main churches: St. Thomas, St. Nicholas, the New Church, and St. Peter's. He also conducted festal services in St. Paul's Church (also known as the University Church) at Easter, Pentecost, Christmas, and Reformation, and in St. John's Church (the burial church outside the city walls) for funerals. Working with the Rector and Conrector of the School, Bach was obligated to provide musical training to the 55 young boys enrolled there, who received an education, room, and board in return for singing at the various services in the four churches. Like

J. S. BACH. George B. Stauffer, Oxford University Press. © Oxford University Press 2024.
DOI: 10.1093/oso/9780195108026.003.0018

his predecessor Johann Kuhnau, Bach hired an assistant to teach the Latin classes that were part of his duties.

As town music director, Bach was also charged with overseeing municipal music activities in Leipzig, which included performances for the annual change of Town Council members, visits of the Saxon Elector, building dedications, and other special events. Leipzig's two collegium musicum ensembles, composed mostly of university students who read through music in coffeehouses (in winter) and coffee gardens (in summer), were also under his purview. The opera house in Leipzig had closed in 1720, three years before Bach's arrival, and the collegium performances helped to fill the gap in the realm of secular music-making. The Town Council hoped that Bach, as a virtuoso performer and experienced capellmeister, would revivify musical life in the city, in both the sacred and secular spheres.

Bach initially approached his cantorial duties with great energy and ambition. His principal obligation was to provide an anthem approximately 30 minutes long for *Hauptgottesdienst*, the main Sunday church service, which alternated each week between the St. Thomas and St. Nicholas Churches. To fulfill this task, Bach set the personal goal of compiling annual cycles of his own cantatas, each set containing approximately 60 works for the Sundays and Feast Days of the church year. According to the Obituary of 1750, Bach compiled five such cycles,[3] and it appears that he assembled them almost entirely during the first seven years of his Leipzig tenure at the blistering pace of one work per week. Of these 300 cantatas, approximately 200 survive today.[4]

There was little time for organ composition during this period of intense cantata production, when Bach had to write, prepare performance parts, coach the vocal soloists, and rehearse the ensemble for a new work each week, plus provide additional pieces such as the Magnificat, the St. John Passion, and the St. Matthew Passion for special services. Nevertheless, between May and November 1726, while compiling the third annual cycle, Bach suddenly introduced the organ as an obbligato instrument in his cantatas, using it as a melodic voice in 17 movements—a phenomenon we examine in chapter 18. Only a handful of solo organ works date from the first seven Leipzig years: a series of miscellaneous trios and the Six Sonatas, BWV 525–530, both written for instructional purposes, and the Prelude and Fugue in B Minor, BWV 544, and Prelude and Fugue in E Minor ("Wedge"), BWV 548, possibly composed for specific events such as the important public organ recitals in St. Sophia's Church in Dresden in 1725 and 1731 or the large memorial service for Electress Christiane Eberhardine in St. Paul's Church in Leipzig on October 17, 1727.[5]

After 1730 or so Bach moved away from church composition. In March 1729 he took the unprecedented step, as St. Thomas cantor, of assuming the directorship of the collegium musicum ensemble founded by Telemann in 1701. By the following year he was at odds with the Town Council over conditions for church music-making, showing "little inclination to work"[6] and submitting a long and detailed memorandum of complaint, the "Short But Most Necessary Draft for a Well-Appointed Church Music, with Certain Modest Reflections on the Decline of the Same."[7] He also voiced his frustration to his boyhood friend Georg Erdmann in Danzig in a letter expressing interest in finding another job.[8]

Disillusioned with the lack of support for his church ensemble, Bach channeled his energies into the weekly performances of the Collegium Musicum in the 1730s, providing more than 1,200 hours of music during the two periods when he was in charge: 1729 to 1737 and 1739 to 1741, the year Gottfried Zimmermann, the proprietor of the coffeehouse and coffee garden where the group performed, passed away.[9] The concertos for one, two, three, and four harpsichords; the gamba sonatas; the Orchestral Suite in B Minor; the second volume of the Well-Tempered Clavier; Cantata 211, *Schweig stille, plaudert nicht* (the "Coffee Cantata," a singing commercial of sorts for Zimmermann's emporium), and other secular works stem from Bach's collegium activities.

During the 1730s, too, Bach's involvement with organ music was limited. He presented important recitals in Kassel (1732), Dresden (1736), and Altenburg (1739), and his organ teaching flourished, which resulted in the revision of pieces from Arnstadt, Mühlhausen, and Weimar that he now used for instruction. He also seems to have refined the Prelude and Fugue in G Major, BWV 541, and composed the Pastorella, BWV 590; the Prelude and Fugue in C Minor, BWV 546; and the Prelude and Fugue in C Major ("9/8"), BWV 547, at this time. But only twice during this decade did he focus on organ composition in a concentrated way, issuing Clavier-Übung III in the fall of 1739 for the bicentennial of Luther's visit to Leipzig and launching a portfolio of revised chorale settings (the "Great Eighteen" Collection) around the same time.

In the 1740s Bach withdrew still further, stepping down from directing the collegium and turning over his church duties to assistants. In a document discovered only recently,[10] a prefect from the time claims to have led the cantata performances in St. Thomas and St. Nicholas "for two full years" in Bach's absence, confirming that the aging cantor more or less abandoned his post after 1740. The members of the Town Council complained,[11] and they exacted a bit of revenge by auditioning a successor while Bach was still alive.[12] But as the titular composer for the Saxon Elector in Dresden, an honor received in 1736, Bach was untouchable and couldn't be fired.

· Bach used this time to work on private projects such as the Musical Offering, the Art of Fugue, and the Mass in B Minor. In his final years he also returned with great vigor to organ music, reworking the incomplete Fantasia and Fugue in C Minor, BWV 562; publishing the Schübler Chorales and Canonic Variations on "Vom Himmel hoch"; adding settings, little by little, to the chorale portfolio; and most probably composing the Fantasia and Fugue in C Minor,

BWV 537. Bach died on July 28, 1750, of complications from two unsuccessful eye operations for cataracts. He left the chorale portfolio as well as the Art of Fugue unfinished.

Although Bach was not expected to compose or perform organ music as part of his employment as St. Thomas cantor, Leipzig offered opportunities that turned his years there into his third productive period of organ writing. First and foremost was the stimulation of the trade fairs, which allowed him to present organ recitals before sophisticated audiences of cosmopolitan visitors. We know relatively little about these events aside from Georg Heinrich Ludwig Schwanberg's report to his father in the fall of 1727 about having heard Bach play recently in Leipzig, most probably during the St. Michael's Fair:

> I wish that you could once hear Mr. Bach on the organ, for neither you nor anyone else in Braunschweig could come close to matching him. I never heard anything like it, and I must completely change my whole style of playing, for it is worth nothing. And in thorough bass, too. I will, if God pleases and keeps me healthy, be uncommonly industrious, for I am eager to learn his style.[13]

On such occasions Bach most likely performed on the instrument in St. Paul's Church (III/48) that had been completed by the Leipzig organ builder Johann Scheibe in 1716.[14] One of the largest organs in Saxony (plate 17-1; table 17-1), it was inspected by Bach the following year. The organs in St. Thomas (III/35 and II/21), St. Nicholas (III/36), the New Church (II/21), and St. John's (II/22, built from pipes of the dismantled small organ in St. Thomas in 1742) were more modest in size and, with the exception of the St. John's organ, older than the St. Paul's instrument. All were well maintained by Scheibe during Bach's lifetime, however.[15]

The fairs also provided the ready availability of the latest printed music and treatises, such as Johann Gottfried Walther's *Musicalisches Lexicon* (Leipzig, 1732) or Lorenz Christoph Mizler's German translation of Johann Joachim Fux's *Gradus ad Parnassum* (Leipzig, 1742). In addition, Bach could publish his own works, calling on the music engravers who resided in Leipzig as well as those who visited during the fair periods. The engravers could handle not only modest-sized organ publications such as the Canonic Variations (7 printed pages) or the Schübler Chorales (15 pages) but also a substantial print such as Clavier-Übung III (78 pages). These editions were sold during the fairs, and their availability was announced in local newspapers. The Schübler Chorales, based on arias from the chorale-cantata cycle, and Clavier-Übung III, spurred by the Luther bicentennial celebration in Leipzig, would not have been composed if Bach had remained in Cöthen.

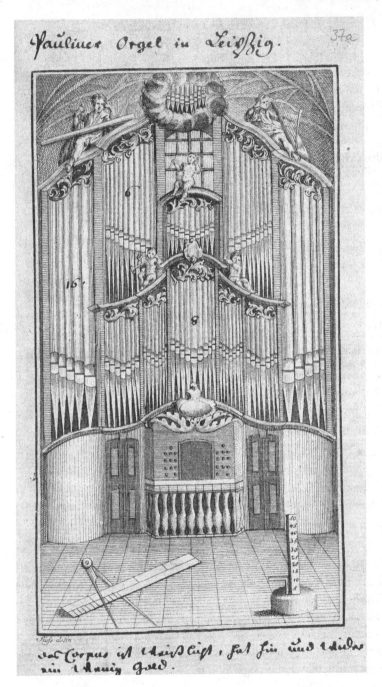

Plate 17-1 Johann Scheibe Organ in St. Paul's Church, Leipzig. Engraving from c. 1720 with comments in the hand of Johann Andreas Silbermann, who noted that the case was painted white with a bit of gold leaf here and there.

Deutsche Fotothek, Sächsische Landesbibliothek, Dresden

Table 17-1 Leipzig, St. Paul's Church (University Church)

Sanctuary Organ (disposition of 1717)[a]
(Josias Ibach, 1626–1627; Heinrich and Esaias Compenius,
1710; Johann Scheibe, 1716)

Hauptwerk (CD-?)	Brustwerk (CD-?)	Hinterwerk (CD-?)
*16' Groß-Principal	8' Principal	8' Lieblich getackt
*16' Groß-Quinta-Tön	8' Viol di Gamb naturell	8' Quinta-Tön
*8' Klein Principal	8' Grob getackt	4' Fleute deuce
8' Fleute Allemande	4' Octav	4' Quinta decima
8' Gems-Horn	4' Rohr-Flöte	3' Decima nona
*4' Octav	3' Nassat	2' Holl-Flöte
*3' Quinta	2' Octav	2' Viola
3' Quint-Nasat	1⅓' Largo [Larigot]	1½' Vigesima nona
2' Octavina	1' Sedecima	1' Weit-Pfeiffe
2' Wald-Flöte	1' Schweitzer-Pfeiffe	III Mixtur
*V-VI Große Mixtur	III Mixtur	II Helle Cymbal
III Cornetti	II Helle Cymbal	8' Sertin [Sordun]
II Zinck		
8' Schalmo [Chalumeau]		

Pedal (CD-c')

16' Groß Principal-Bass		*4' Nacht-Horn-Bass		Cymbelstern
*16' Groß-Principal-Bass		*3' Quint-Bass		Manual tremulants
16' Sub-Bass		**2' Octav-Bass		Ventils for manuals, pedal,
*16' Groß-Quinta-Tön		1' Holl-Flöten-Bass		and cymbelstern
*8' Octav-Bass		IV Mixtur-Bass		
**8' Jubal-Bass		*V-VI Mixtur-Bass		
**6' Groß hell-Quinten Bass		16' Posaunen-Bass		
*4' Octav-Bass		8' Tompeten Bass		

*Pedal transmission
**On the small Brust-Pedal chests
[a]Wolff and Zepf 2012, 49. A contemporary drawing of the layout of the stop jambs is reproduced in BDok IX, 137.

Finally, Bach's retreat from his formal duties as cantor and collegium director in his last decade and a half in Leipzig allowed him to travel repeatedly to Dresden and Berlin, where he had the opportunity to hear the latest fashionable music and play large, magnificent pipe organs built by Gottfried Silbermann and Joachim Wagner. The professional freedom of his final years gave him the opportunity to return to organ composition and to focus once again on the music that had brought him fame in Arnstadt, Mühlhausen, and Weimar.

The Fusion of Styles

In "A Short but Most Necessary Draft for a Well-Appointed Church Music," the letter of complaint sent to the Leipzig Town Council in 1730, Bach made a telling observation about the state of music at the time:

> Now, however, that the state of music is quite different from what it was, since our artistry has increased very much, and the taste has changed astonishingly, and accordingly the former style of music no longer seems to please our ears, considerable help is therefore all the more needed to choose and appoint such musicians as will satisfy the present musical taste, master the new kinds of music, and thus be in a position to do justice to the composer and his work.[16]

Bach emphasized that the music program in the Leipzig churches suffered not only from the insufficient size and quality of the choral and instrumental forces but also from the circumstance that music itself had changed. The singers and players had to cope with the "new kinds of music" that had come into fashion. A critical factor behind the change in taste was the growing awareness and exploitation of national elements. Specific styles and genres were emerging in Europe, linked to the countries of their origin. Italy excelled in opera, with da capo arias and expressive, often virtuosic vocal parts, and in string composition, with the solo sonata, trio sonata, and concerto as prominent forms. France was known for courtly dance music, where binary dance movements were commonly grouped into suites prefaced by an overture. Poland developed the polonaise and colorful folk dances, and England won distinction for its church anthems and string fantasias. Germany earned respect for its keyboard music and contrapuntal arts, especially canons and fugues. But Germany was also recognized as a musically eclectic nation, where composers freely borrowed styles and genres from other countries and combined them in inventive ways.

Georg Philipp Telemann confessed as much, in the autobiographical account he provided to Walther for the *Musicalisches Lexicon*:

> What [Telemann] has accomplished with the styles of music is well known. First it was Polish style, followed by French style, church-chamber-and-operatic styles, and then what is called Italian style, which presently occupies him more than the others.[17]

Telemann's *Musique de Table* series, published in 1733, a year after the appearance of the *Lexicon*, presented audiences with an international mélange of overtures, quartets, concertos, trios, and solo sonatas.

In the "Short but Most Necessary Draft" Bach pointed directly to the national styles and the particular challenges they posed for German musicians, who were expected to master them all:

> It is, anyhow, somewhat strange that German musicians are expected to be capable of performing at once and *ex tempore* all kinds of music, whether it comes from Italy or France, England or Poland, just as may be done, say, by those virtuosos for whom the music is written and who have studied it long beforehand, indeed, know it almost by heart, and who, it should be noted, receive good salaries besides, so that their work and industry is thus richly rewarded.[18]

Bach was working up to requesting additional financial support for his church musicians. But it is also obvious that he had a very clear sense of the role of national music styles in Germany. This was obvious in Clavier-Übung II, published in 1735 and sold at the Easter Fair, in which he presented a concerto "nach Italiænischen Gusto" (in the Italian taste) and an overture "nach Französischer Art" (in the French manner), separating the two harmonically by a tritone (F major for the concerto, B minor for the overture) to emphasize the dichotomy they represented. And in Clavier-Übung III, issued at the St. Michael's Fair in 1739, national styles came to the fore in his organ music: the pedal setting of "Allein Gott in der Höh sei Ehr," BWV 676, is an Italian trio with two treble parts and bass; the pedal setting of "Christ, unser Herr, zum Jordan kam," BWV 684, is cast in the form of an Italian concerto with recurring ritornello; the manual setting of "Wir glauben all an einen Gott," BWV 681, exhibits the dotted rhythms of a French overture; and the manual setting of "Jesus Christus, unser Heiland," BWV 689, is a fugue in the time-honored German tradition (see chapter 22).

From the 1720s onward, however, German composers went further and began to combine aspects of national styles within single pieces. Bach's Dresden colleague Johann David Heinichen pointed to this possibility in his general bass treatise of 1728: "a felicitous mix of Italian and French taste would affect the ear most forcefully and must succeed over all the taste of the world."[19] Years later, Johann Joachim Quantz described this type of synthesis in greater detail and termed it "vermischter Geschmack"—mixed style:

> If one has the necessary discernment to choose the best from the styles of different countries, a *mixed style* results that, without overstepping the bounds of modesty, would well be called the *German style*, not only because the Germans came upon it first, but because it has already been established at different places in Germany for many years, flourishes still, and displeases in neither Italy or France, nor in other lands.[20]

Bach was not the most progressive composer in Germany in this regard. Telemann introduced Italianate episodes into his French overtures and composed Italian concertos "alla francese" at a very early point.[21] He also claimed in his autobiography of 1718 that he had clothed the Polish style "in an Italian dress," incorporating polonaise and mazurka rhythms and melodies into his Italian instrumental pieces."[22] All this blending took place before 1720 or so. Bach's cousin Johann Bernhard Bach (1676–1749) also mixed national styles in his Overture in G Minor, a suite of French orchestral dances featuring solo violin in the manner of an Italian concerto. Bach wrote out Bernhard's work around 1730 for a performance with the Collegium Musicum,[23] and it may well have been this encounter that spurred him to compose his own concerto-like Orchestral Suite in B Minor, BWV 1067, some years later.

As we observed in Part III, Bach became fully aware of national styles during the Weimar years and used them as the basis for innovative organ works such as the Toccata in D Minor ("Dorian"), BWV 538/1, and "Trio super Allein Gott in der Höh sei Ehr," BWV 664a, which reflect Italian prototypes, and the Pièce d'Orgue, BWV 572, and "Allein Gott in der Höh sei Ehr," BWV 662a, which reflect French models. And in certain instances, he joined together segments in different national styles to create unique hybrid works: in the Pièce d'Orgue, the five-part French middle section is preceded by an Italianate toccata.

It was in Leipzig, however, that Bach began to combine national styles in a more cohesive way, blending them within single pieces to achieve the mixed idiom described by Quantz. In the Fugue in E Minor ("Wedge"), BWV 548/2, for example, he joined German fugal procedure with Italian ritornello form, while in the Fugue in C Minor, BWV 537/2, and the Duet in F Major, BWV 803, from Clavier-Übung III, he united German fugal procedure with Italian da capo form. Or in the Prelude in E♭ Major ("St. Anne"), BWV 552/1, he combined the five-part, dotted-rhythm idiom of the French overture while casting the music in the form of an Italian concerto with recurring ritornello sections. By fully integrating the French overture with the Italian concerto in this extraordinary work, he resolved the stylistic conflict presented in Clavier-Übung II.

With such amalgamations, Bach achieved Quantz's "mixed" or "German style." It was more consequential than that, however, for Bach's sophisticated merging of multiple elements from France, Italy, and other countries resulted in a truly international musical language. This is especially evident in what is possibly his most cosmopolitan organ work, the pedal setting of "Vater unser im Himmelreich," BWV 682, from Clavier-Übung III, in which he combined eight stylistic gestures from three countries (see chapter 22).[24] It was this sort of genre-bending, border-crossing synthesis that resulted in an international style, one that pointed ahead to the classical idiom of Haydn, Mozart, and Beethoven. This synthesis elevated the organ works of the Leipzig years to a new level of urbanity and broad appeal.

But Bach did not stop there. During the last fifteen years of his life, he achieved a second synthesis, one that brought together the historical styles of the past, present, and future.[25] In the late 1730s and 1740s he became increasingly interested in both the *stile antico*, the Renaissance vocal style of Giovanni Pierluigi da Palestrina and his forebears, and the *style galant*, the progressive, fashionable style of Giovanni Battista Pergolesi and the generation of Bach's sons and students.

Bach examined the *stile antico* through the Latin-texted church works of Palestrina, Marco Guiseppe Peranda, Giovanni Battista Bassani, and other Catholic composers, and through Fux's *Gradus ad Parnassum*, first published in Latin in 1725 but also available in German in Lorenz Christoph Mizler's 1742 translation.[26] These studies, which coincided with Bach's involvement with the Catholic court in Dresden, ultimately resulted in the *stile antico* sections of the Mass in B Minor: the "Credo in unum Deum" and "Confiteor" movements, in particular. But the *stile antico* first emerged in full form in Bach's music in the "organ motets" of Clavier-Übung III: the Mass settings "Kyrie, Gott Vater in Ewigkeit," "Christe, aller Welt Trost," and "Kyrie, Gott heilger Geist," BWV 669–671, and the Catechism setting "Aus tiefer Not, schrei ich zu dir," BWV 686. "Aus tiefer Not," especially, with its six-part texture and tenor cantus firmus as the upper of two pedal parts, brought the early vocal music of the Christian church to the organ in a way that had never been attempted before.

Bach studied the fashionable *style galant* through the progressive works of his two oldest sons Wilhelm Friedemann and Carl Philipp Emanuel and Berlin composers such as Johann Gottlieb and Carl Heinrich Graun. The Dresden opera, too, provided him with forward-looking models, in the form of Johann Adolf Hasse's *Cleofide* and *Alfonso*, both of which he most probably heard during trips to the Saxon center.[27] In the 1740s Bach also encountered Pergolesi's music, transforming his famous *Stabat mater* into a German motet, *Tilge, Höchster, meine Sünden*, BWV 1083. In the late organ works, the *style galant* surfaces in Clavier-Übung III, in the pedal setting "Vater unser im Himmelreich," as mentioned earlier, but also in the manual settings "Dies sind die heiligen zehn Gebot," BWV 679, and the Duet in F Major, BWV 803, where the playful, forward-looking harmonies and unorthodox melodic intervals point to the playful whimsy of the preclassical style.

In summing up the accomplishments of organ playing in Germany, Quantz noted in 1752:

> The organists and clavier players—among the latter especially Froberger and after him Pachelbel, and among the former Reincken, Buxtehude, Bruhns, and some others—were almost the first to contrive the most tasteful instrumental compositions of their period for their instruments. But particularly the art of organ playing, which had to a great extent been learned from the Netherlanders, was already at this time in a high state of advancement, thanks to the above-mentioned and some other able men. Finally, the admirable Johann Sebastian Bach brought it to its greatest perfection in recent times.[28]

Bach achieved this perfection most distinctly in his Leipzig organ works, through his grand synthesis of national and historical styles. We will examine this phenomenon in greater detail as we look at individual works.

The New Role of Revision and Recycling

A second critical development in Bach's organ-writing in Leipzig was his new reliance on revision and recycling. This, too, reflected broad trends in the eighteenth century, when composers were expected to produce vast quantities of music on a monthly, weekly, or even daily basis. To meet the demands, they commonly turned to existing pieces—their own or someone else's—and recycled them by making necessary changes in the music or the text or both. When text changes were involved—for instance, transforming a secular birthday cantata, used only once, into a sacred cantata, performable on an annual basis, by altering the words—the process was called "parody technique." Bach's contemporary Johann Mattheson, when describing the practice of recycling existing works, stated that "borrowing is an acceptable thing, but one must repay the loan with interest."[29]

We might say that Bach repaid the loan with compound interest. During his first 15 years in Leipzig, he was under extraordinary pressure to produce music, first as St. Thomas cantor compiling annual sets of cantatas, and then as collegium director presenting weekly concerts with his ensemble.[30] In the first cantata cycle of 1723–1724, Bach recycled 20 Weimar and Cöthen pieces, revising the music and texts as necessary to fit into the series of 63 works. The second cantata cycle of 1724–1725, by contrast, consists almost entirely of newly composed pieces. But the third cycle of 1725–1727 displays some of Bach's most inventive borrowing, including the transformation of preexisting instrumental movements into cantata sinfonias for obbligato organ.

The ongoing demands for new music continued when Bach assumed the directorship of the Collegium Musicum in 1729. For the weekly two-hour performances of the student group, he reworked a multitude of existing instrumental and keyboard compositions from Weimar and Cöthen, giving the pieces new life. The concertos for one, two, three, and four harpsichords are derived almost completely from preexisting works for violin or oboe d'amore and strings, and the second volume of the Well-Tempered Clavier, passed down in a series of performance sheets, draws heavily on earlier preludes and fugues that Bach revised, expanded, and transposed as necessary.

By the 1730s, revision and recycling had become deeply ingrained in Bach's compositional process. It was far more than a practical expedient, however, for it also offered him the opportunity to improve works and take them to an even higher level of refinement. The St. Mark Passion, Christmas Oratorio, Four Short Masses, and B-Minor Mass stemmed mostly from existing music that Bach reshaped, refined, and distilled (in the case of the B-Minor Mass) through parody technique.

The organ works benefited greatly from this process. The revision of the Prelude and Fugue in A Minor, BWV 543, the Fantasy in C Minor, BWV 562/1, the Canonic Variations on "Vom Himmel hoch," BWV 769, the "Great Eighteen" Chorales, BWV 651–688, and many other compositions reflect Bach's passion during the Leipzig years for reworking and refining earlier pieces. Within the organ repertory, the revision process can be observed on several levels: refinement of details, structural expansion, reordering of material, and transcription.

The refinement of details was one of Bach's main concerns when he reworked the Prelude and Fugue in G Major, BWV 541, around 1733, most likely in conjunction with the application of his son Wilhelm Friedemann for the organist position at St. Sophia's Church in Dresden.[31] Bach pulled the Weimar work off the shelf and wrote out a clean copy,[32] apparently for Friedemann's use during the audition. Bach made virtually no changes in the Fugue, but he revised numerous details in the Prelude, refining the counterpoint and clarifying aspects of performance. In measures 35 and 37, for example, he altered the downbeat chords in the manual from quarter notes to 8th notes, producing a more articulated release, and in measure 36 he improved the part-writing of the lowest manual voice and sustained the three middle manual parts through ties, creating a momentary *style brisé* effect (example 17-1). These types of finely nuanced improvements appear throughout the Prelude.[33] Similar changes of detail appear in many other organ works during the Leipzig years, such as the sharpening of dotted figures in "An Wasserflüssen Babylon," BWV 653, or "Kommst du nun, Jesu, vom Himmel herunter," BWV 650, or the further animation of the cantus firmus through diminutions in "Allein Gott in der Höh sei Ehr," BWV 663. Bach may have made small changes of this sort when he used the pieces for teaching or concerts.

Example 17-1 Prelude in G Major, BWV 541/1, mm. 34–37a: (a) Weimar version, c. 1716, and (b) Leipzig version, c. 1733.

The expansion of existing works called for a very different compositional process—a rethinking of the formal structure of the music rather than an editing of details. This rethinking is well illustrated by Bach's revision of the Prelude and Fugue in G Minor, BWV 535a. As we noted in chapter 6, the work appears in Bach's youthful hand in the Möller Manuscript, the album of keyboard music assembled by his brother Johann Christoph, and it is most likely a product of the Arnstadt years. The Fugue is substantial: 77 measures long, with carefully worked-out expositions, episodes, and modulatory scheme. The Prelude, by contrast, is cursory: 21 measures long, and essentially a series of improvisatory gestures. It was probably composed on the spot, as it was entered into the album, to accompany the previously worked-out Fugue.

When Bach returned to the piece during the Leipzig years,[34] he subjected the Fugue to a thorough editing, embellishing and refining its counterpoint while retaining the movement's general structure. He completely reimagined the Prelude, however, using the original material as a point of departure for expanding and thoroughly recasting each of the movement's three sections (figure 17-1). The loosely structured introduction, labeled "passaggio," became a more tightly organized development of the initial rising third of the Fugue theme, with syncopated accompaniment, first in four parts, then in five. The middle section, a series of simple chords and arpeggios in the early version, became an extended chromatic fantasy with animated 32nd-note figuration. And the contrapuntal five-part close became a more highly refined conclusion, with walking bass, continuous 16th-note motion, and newly imitative manual voices. The result, BWV 535 (= BWV³ 535.3), was an entirely new Prelude, a 43-measure piece that could serve as a worthy partner for the weighty fugue.

Additional expansions appear in the "Fantasia super Komm heiliger Geist, Herre Gott," BWV 651, "Komm heiliger Geist, Herre Gott," BWV 652, and other settings in the "Great Eighteen" Collection. In the case of "An Wasserflüssen Babylon," BWV 653, Bach added a new six-measure coda that contains a reference to the initial phrase of the chorale tune, first in the pedal and then in the soprano, thus uniting the end of the work with the beginning (example 17-2, x).

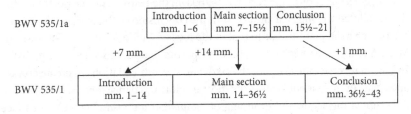

BWV 535/1a	Introduction mm. 1–6	Main section mm. 7–15½	Conclusion mm. 15½–21
	+7 mm.	+14 mm.	+1 mm.
BWV 535/1	Introduction mm. 1–14	Main section mm. 14–36½	Conclusion mm. 36½–43

Figure 17-1 Prelude in G Minor, BWV 535/1a and BWV 535/1: Bach's expansion of the work.

Example 17-2 "An Wasserflüssen Babylon," BWV 653: new coda, with added references to the first phrase of the chorale tune (marked "x").

During the Leipzig years Bach also became interested in altering the structure of existing compositions by adding additional movements or by changing the order of sections. Within the organ works, he toyed with the idea of inserting the Largo from Sonata 5 into the Prelude and Fugue in C Major, BWV 545, and the Un poc' allegro from Sonata 4 into the Prelude and Fugue in G major, BWV 541, to create three-movement, concerto-like forms (BWV³ 545.2 and 541.2).[35] In both instances, Bach seems to have had second thoughts and eventually restored the works to their earlier prelude-fugue formats. In the case of the Canonic Variations on "Vom Himmel hoch" he moved the most complex movement, variation 5 of the printed version, BWV 769, from the end of the work to the middle when writing out a fair copy of the text, BWV 769a, in the Leipzig chorale portfolio. The change shifted the musical climax from the conclusion of the work to the center, creating an axial plan similar to that of the revised Credo portion of the B-Minor Mass. And in a late revision of the chorale partita "Sei gegrüßet, Jesu gütig," BWV 768, Bach reversed the order of the sixth and seventh variations to create contiguous pairs of movements with 32nd-note motion and dance meters, even though it disrupted the sequential grouping of *manualiter* and *pedaliter* variations (see chapter 10).

These types of large-scale changes show Bach rethinking his works in the broadest possible terms, exploring how the insertion or shifting of discrete segments of musical material could produce alternative architec-tonic designs.

Finally, in several instances Bach produced new organ trios by transferring in-strumental or vocal music directly to the organ. In some cases he borrowed music from his own cantatas: the Adagio-Vivace of Sonata 4 in E Minor, BWV 528, from the Sinfonia to Part II of Cantata 76, *Die Himmel erzählen die Ehre Gottes*; the Trio in C Minor, BWV 21/1a, from the opening Sinfonia of Cantata 21, *Ich hatte viel Bekümmernis*; and the Trio in G Minor, BWV 584, from the tenor aria "Ich will an den Himmel denken" from Cantata 166, *Wo gehest du hin*.[36] Three additional trios were derived from the works of Bach's contemporaries or from lost music: the Trio in C Minor, BWV 585, from an instrumental trio by Johann Friedrich Fasch; the Aria in F Major, BWV 587, from an instrumental trio by François Couperin; and the Adagio e dolce of Trio Sonata No. 3 in D Minor, BWV 527, from an earlier instrumental movement, now lost.[37] The Leipzig organ-trio movements based on preexisting works are note-for-note transcriptions. This procedure was facilitated by the new chamber-music qualities of the Central German organ, which we will examine shortly.

Bach's increased reliance on revision and recycling during his last two decades in Leipzig raises the question of whether he was experiencing a creative crisis. Did he have difficulty writing entirely new works? In 1741 Theodor Leberecht Pitschel, a poet in Johann Christoph Gottsched's circle in Leipzig, noted Bach's need to play existing music before improvising something of his own composition:

> You know, the famous man who has the greatest praise in our town in music, and the greatest admiration of connoisseurs, does not get into condition, as the expression goes, to delight others with the mingling of his tones until he has played something from the printed or written page, and has thus set his powers of imagination in motion.... The able man whom I have mentioned usually has to play something from the page that is inferior to his own ideas. And yet his superior ideas are the consequences of those inferior ones.[38]

It may be that the revision and recycling of earlier compositions served a sim-ilar purpose, functioning as a catalyst to get Bach's creative juices flowing. Bach was obviously capable of writing new works in his later years: Clavier-Übung III, the Goldberg Variations, the Art of Fugue, and other pieces composed after 1730 show that his powers of invention remained undiminished. There can be no question, however, that he took special pleasure in reviewing music that he had written earlier and revising its contents to bring it closer to his ideal of perfection. The Leipzig organ works benefited greatly from the revision process and display a degree of refinement that contrasts with the more spontaneous nature of the pre-Leipzig pieces. If the pre-Leipzig works are characterized by astonishing boldness and invention, the Leipzig works are characterized by suave coolness and urbanity.

The Central German Organ

The shift in musical taste that Bach mentioned in the "Short But Necessary Draft" affected not only music performance and composition in Central Germany but organ building as well.

In North Germany, organ builders seemed stuck in the Arp Schnitger mold, constructing instruments that adhered to the classic principles of organ design that Schnitger and others had brought to a high degree of perfection in the seventeenth century. By contrast, in Central Germany, Thuringian and Saxon builders seemed less interested in past tradition. They concentrated instead on creating forward-looking, utilitarian organs that were increasingly allied with instrumental music. Unlike the northern commercial cities in the Hanseastic League, the provincial towns and courts of Central Germany lacked the financial resources for music-making provided by wealthy merchants. They needed organs that could take part in the instrumental ensemble when players were missing, much in the manner of Bach's cantata movements with obbligato organ, where the organ assumes a solo part that might otherwise be assigned to a violin, oboe, or other instrument (see chapter 18). The changes in Central German organ building first appeared around 1700, and by 1720 or so the organs that Bach tested and inaugurated had a new orientation.

How were Central German organs different? Their features are well illustrated by three instruments from the late 1730s and the 1740s associated with Bach: the organ in the Castle Church in Altenburg (II/37), completed in 1739 by Tobias Heinrich Gottfried Trost and played by Bach that year; the specification proposed by Bach around 1742 for an organ, only partially realized, for St. Mary's Church in Bad Burka (II/28); and the organ in the Town Church of St. Wenceslas in Naumburg (III/53), completed in 1746 by Zacharias Hildebrandt and examined by Bach and Gottfried Silbermann that year (see the specifications in the Appendix). The dispositions of these instruments—one very progressive (Altenburg), one somewhat conservative (Naumburg), and one in the middle (Bad Berka)—illustrate the new currents in organ building that were taking hold in Central Germany.

Their main features, characteristic of Thuringian and Saxon instruments being constructed at the time, can be summarized as follows:[39]

1. High-pitched reeds—4' and 2'—were reduced in number. The builders focused instead on a Trompete 8' and Vox humana 8' in the manuals and a Posaune 16' in the pedal, as seen in all three organs. At the same time, they often retained a half-length Fagot 16' in the manuals, as in the Naumburg organ, that could be used as a substitute for a bassoon in concerted instrumental and vocal music, to reinforce the continuo line.

2. The builders introduced undulating celeste stops, most notably Unda maris 8', present in the Naumburg organ.

3. The builders exhibited a strong interest in the sound of the tierce, as a solo stop or within chorus mixtures, where it produced a dark and grave yet powerful and thrilling sound. This is evident in all three instruments: a Sesquialtera, Cornet, or combination of stops producing the same was available on every manual.

4. Pedal divisions were limited to a few essential 16' and 8' stops. Additional voices were sometimes provided by duplexing stops from the manuals, via wind couplers or transmissions, as in the Altenburg organ. This reflects the fact that in many cases, the pedal was intended to fulfill a continuo-like function.

5. Builders used progressive tunings that allowed the entire organ to be played in concerted music with voices and instruments. This was demonstrably the case in the Altenburg organ, whose tuning system allowed Bach to play the Creed chorale "Wir glauben all' an einen Gott" in E♭ minor (see chapter 15).

6. Builders placed great emphasis on the creation of an ensemble organ, an instrument in which divisions could be coupled together to produce special combinations or a unified plenum. The use of couplers and transmissions, both manual and pedal, increased during the course of the eighteenth century. In addition, the pipework was frequently contained in one large, deep case, without a Rückpositiv or the distinctive spatial separation of divisions that was common in North German organs. This unification is represented visually by the homogeneous facades of organs built by Gottfried Silbermann or Johann Scheibe, for instance (see plate 17-1).

7. Toy stops were quite popular: Zimbelsterns, Glockenspiels, Timpani, and others. The Altenburg organ contained a Glockenspiel, the Naumburg organ included a Cymbelstern.

8. The organs displayed a new and significant emphasis on weight and gravity—Gravität, in the word of the builders—resulting in an abundance of 16' and 8' stops. Both the Altenburg and Naumburg organs contained two 16' flue stops on the Hauptwerk, and the Altenburg instrument contained ten 8' flue stops on its two manuals and five 16' flue stops and a 32' Posaune in the pedal. The profusion of foundation stops, supported by improved winding systems, resulted not only in a deep, thick, majestic plenum but also in new exotic combinations of unison sounds. Bach's student Johann Friedrich Agricola alluded to the marvelous effect produced by using four unison 8' flue stops simultaneously, apparently on the Oberwerk of the Altenburg organ:

> Our ancestors believed that two stops of different scale at the same pitch level would of necessity sound bad if they were drawn together. But if such stops are well constructed and purely voiced, then one can refute our ancestors any day merely by drawing such stops and using them together. I have heard a

Lieblich Gedackt, Vugara, Quintadene, and Hohflöte played together on a certain organ, all at 8' and without any other stop, which produced a beautiful and strange effect.[40]

Agricola may have been referring to a combination used by Bach when he visited the Altenburg organ in 1739—a grouping of registers that surely would have frightened "many organ builders and organists . . . when they saw him draw the stops," as Johann Nicolaus Forkel put it.[41] The multitude of diverse unison stops at 16' and 8' pitch points forward to the German Romantic instruments of the nineteenth century.

9. The builders introduced new orchestral stops, deliberately patterned to duplicate the sounds of the instruments themselves. The most important were the Violone 16' (present in the pedal in the Altenburg and Naumburg organs), Viol di Gamba 8' (present in the Altenburg and Naumburg instruments), Flauto traverso 16', 8', or 4' (present at 16' pitch in the Altenburg organ), and Hautbois 8'. Builders and organists alike praised the imitative qualities of the new registers. Jacob Adlung described the Violone as a stop "with which one imitates the bowing of a violone," and "when it is exactly right, it buzzes like a violone."[42] The 8' gamba stop on Scheibe's organ for the St. Paul's Church in Leipzig was labeled "Viol di Gamb naturell," and the instrument also featured a second, highly unusual string register, a 1' Schweizerpfeife that had a "gentle, sharp, and viol-like sound," according to the builder.[43] Agricola, commenting on the Altenburg organ once again, observed that when the Querflöte 16' (i.e., Flauto traverso) and Gamba 8' were played together, "the combination produces a very beautiful effect, and the pleasant keenness that is found in these stops comes as close to the attack of a bowstroke on a stringed bass as it is possible to achieve with organ pipes."[44] Trost, in his 1733 proposal for the Altenburg organ, promised that the Gamba would "have a special voicing to sound similar to the real instrument" and that Hautbois 8' would be "a completely special stop—very similar to the natural oboe and also capable of being employed usefully in music-making when it [the natural oboe] is not available."[45]

It was this forward-looking instrument that inspired Bach's organ writing after 1723. As we shall see, its imitative stops, chamber-music qualities, and rich, orchestral-oriented plenum had a profound effect on the organ works Bach composed during the Leipzig years.

Notes

1. NBR, no. 32.
2. Johann Wolfgang von Goethe, *Dichtung und Wahrheit*, pt. 1, bk. 6, in *Goethes Sämtliche Werke* (Stuttgart: J. G. Cotta, n.d.), vol. 32, 37.

3. NBR, no. 306.
4. In modern times scholars have debated whether Bach actually composed five complete cantata cycles. The first three remain almost fully intact, and 11 works from a fourth cycle, set to texts by Christian Friedrich Henrici ("Picander"), survive. But the fifth cycle, if it existed, has disappeared completely. See the discussion in Wolff 2000, 269–286.
5. Christoph Wolff, in Wolff 2000, 315–317, has proposed that the Prelude and Fugue in B Minor, BWV 544, served as a tuning prelude for the main music of the memorial service, Cantata 198, *Lass Fürstin, lass noch einen Strahl* ("Trauer-Ode"), which was also set in B minor. The Scheibe organ in St. Paul's Church was tuned in Chorton, however, like the other church instruments in Leipzig. As a result, a tuning prelude for the cantata would have had to be in A minor. See Edwards Butler 2022, 146–147.
6. NBR, no. 150b.
7. NBR, no. 151.
8. NBR, no. 152.
9. George B. Stauffer, "Music for 'Cavaliers et Dames': Bach and the Repertoire of His Collegium Musicum," in *About Bach*, Gregory G. Butler, George B. Stauffer, and Mary Dalton Greer, eds. (Urbana: University of Illinois Press, 2008), 135; and Tatjana Schabalina, "Die 'Leges' des 'Neu aufgerichteten Collegium musicum' (1729)—Ein unbekanntes Dokument zur Leipziger Musikgeschichte," BJ 98 (2012), 107–120.
10. Michael Maul, "'Zwey ganzer Jahr die Music an Statt des Capellmeister aufführen, und dirigiren müssen'—Überlegungen zu Bachs Amtsverständnis in den 1740er Jahren," BJ 101 (2015), 75–97.
11. See Bach's indifferent response to the Town Council with regard to preparing Passion music for Good Friday in 1739, NBR, no. 208.
12. Johann Gottlob Harrer (1703–1755), who was auditioned on June 8, 1749, a full year before Bach's death. Harrer was subsequently appointed cantor of the St. Thomas School on August 7, 1750, just eight days after Bach's funeral.
13. NBR, no. 320.
14. Wolff and Zepf 2012, 49. The construction and tonal character of the St. Paul's organ is discussed in great detail in Edwards Butler 2022, 107–131.
15. Edwards Butler 2022, 150–195.
16. NBR, no. 151.
17. Walther 1732, 596.
18. NBR, no. 151.
19. Heinichen 1728, 10.
20. Quantz 1752, section XVIII, paragraph 87; translation from Johann Joachim Quantz, *On Playing the Flute: A Complete Translation*, Edward R. Reilly, trs. (London: Faber, 1966), 341.
21. See Wolfgang Hirschmann, *Studien zum Konzertschaffen von Georg Philipp Telemann* (Kassel: Bärenreiter, 1986), 143–147 and 202–208.
22. Such as the Concerto in G Major "alla polonese" for Strings and Continuo, TWV 43: G 7, composed before 1721. See Klaus-Peter Koch, *Die polnische und hanakische Musik in Telemanns Werk* (Magdeburg: Arbeitskreis Georg Philipp Telemann im Kulturbund der DDR, 1982–85), vol. 2, 8–29.

23. Beißwenger 1992a, 234–235.

24. On Bach's ability to juggle multiple national gestures in a single piece see also Robert L. Marshall's analysis of the opening chorus of Cantata 78, *Jesu, der du meine Seele*, in Marshall 1989a, 76–79.

25. The idea of a second synthesis was first proposed by Marshall, in Marshall 1989a, 74–79.

26. Bach owned a copy of the 1725 edition of *Gradus ad Parnassum* and most probably had a hand in Mizler's 1742 translation. The seminal study of the *stile antico* in Bach's music remains Wolff 1968.

27. Scholars have long speculated that Bach attended the premiere of *Cleofide* in 1731, which took place the day before his organ recital in St. Sophia's Church on September 14. But he probably attended a performance of *Alfonso* as well, which was running during his visit to Dresden in May 1738.

28. Quantz 1752, 329. Translation from NBR, no. 350.

29. Mattheson 1739, II Theil, Capitel 4, § 81 (p. 131).

30. See Ludwig Finscher, "Zum Parodieproblem bei Bach," in *Bach Interpretationen*, Martin Geck, ed. (Göttingen: Vandenhoeck & Ruprecht, 1969), 94–105, and Hans-Joachim Schulze, "The Parody Process in Bach's Music: An Old Problem Reconsidered," *BACH: The Journal of the Riemenschneider Bach Institute* 20 (1989), 7–21.

31. BDok I, no. 25; Schulze 1984, 17; and *Johann Sebastian Bach: Präludium und Fuge in G-Dur BWV 541. Faksimile nach dem Autograph* (Leipzig: Veröffentlichung der Neuen Bachgesellschaft, 1996), Hans-Joachim Schulze, ed., commentary.

32. Berlin State Library, *N. Mus.ms. 378*. Friedemann's handwriting appears at the top of the first page in the form of the remark "in the hand of the author," thus verifying that he owned the manuscript.

33. The changes were not picked up in later copies of the Prelude, which suggests once again that Bach gave the manuscript to Friedemann, who would have removed it from the Bach household when he departed for Dresden to accept the organist appointment there.

34. Both the notation of the revised version (modern G minor with two flats, rather than the dorian G minor with one flat of the initial version) and the nature of Bach's changes (the sharpening of rhythms, especially) point to a Leipzig reworking. The earliest source of the revised version, Berlin State Library, *P 804*, fascicle 55, dates from c. 1727 (Stinson 1992, 61).

35. Both Dietrich Kilian, in Kilian 1969, and I, in Stauffer 1980, 134, assumed that these three-movement experiments took place during the Weimar years, but more recent research by Kirsten Beißwenger, in Beißwenger 1992b, 29, has confirmed that they occurred in Leipzig, around 1729.

36. On the Trios in C Minor and G Minor see chapter 18 and Stauffer 2016, 53–54.

37. Hans Epstein, "Grundzüge in J. S. Bachs Sonaten schaffen," BJ 55 (1969), 23.

38. NBR, no. 336.

39. This description is drawn from Edwards 1991 and Stauffer 2011.

40. Johann Friedrich Agricola, review in Marpurg 1754–78, vol. 3, 503; translation from Faulkner 2008, 63.

41. Forkel 1802, 20; translation from NBR, 439.

42. Adlung 1768, Kapitel VII, § 205 (p. 153).

43. Johann Scheibe, cited in Edwards Butler 2022, 122.

44. Agricola, review in Marpurg 1754–78, vol. 3, 497.

45. Löffler 1932, 174.

18

Cantata and Passion Movements with Obbligato Organ and Miscellaneous Trios

Bach's intense involvement with cantata-writing during his initial years in Leipzig limited the amount of time he could devote to the organ. It was not long, however, before he returned to the instrument, approaching it in unorthodox ways.

The Obbligato Organ Repertory

The first hint that Bach was about to enter a new phase of organ composition appears in an account of his two concerts on the recently completed Gottfried Silbermann organ (II/30) in St. Sophia's Church in Dresden on September 19 and 20, 1725. According to the Hamburg *Relationscourier*:

> When the Capell-Director from Leipzig, Herr Bach, came here recently, he was very well received by the local virtuosos at the court and in the city, since he is greatly admired by all of them for his musical adroitness and art. Yesterday and the day before, in the presence of the same, he performed for over an hour on the new organ in St. Sophia's Church preludes and various concertos, with intervening soft instrumental music, in all keys.[1]

The term "preludes" points to improvised pieces, free and chorale-based, that Bach would have used to demonstrate the organ's various stops and stop-combinations as well as its modified meantone tuning,[2] which apparently could accommodate music "in all keys." As we noted in chapter 15, playing such preludes was a conventional feature of his organ recitals. But the phrase "concertos with intervening soft instrumental music" suggests something entirely new: a multimovement ensemble piece for strings and solo organ—that is, an organ concerto.

Precisely what Bach performed in Dresden is uncertain. He may have adapted a Cöthen instrumental concerto or composed a new piece altogether, possibly the Concerto in D Minor for Harpsichord and Strings, BWV 1052a,[3] or an early version of the Concerto in E Major for Harpsichord and Strings, BWV 1053, in

J. S. BACH. George B. Stauffer, Oxford University Press. © Oxford University Press 2024.
DOI: 10.1093/oso/9780195108026.003.0019

an organ arrangement. No matter what the case, the combination of solo organ with accompanying instruments points directly to the sinfonias, choruses, and arias with obbligato organ that emerged eight months later in Bach's third cantata cycle, in a series of works that had a decisive effect on his solo organ writing.

Bach had written concerted vocal music with obbligato organ before. In the soprano-tenor duet "Ich bin nun achtzig Jahr" from Cantata 71, *Gott ist mein König*, of 1708, the organ echoes select motives of the tenor on the Rückpositiv before breaking out with its own florid line. Later, in Weimar, Bach used the organ as a solo voice once again, to present a chorale cantus firmus in the opening alto aria of Cantata 161, *Komm, du süße Todesstunde*, of 1716.

These early experiments do not explain the sudden explosion of organ obbligato writing that appears in a series of six Leipzig cantatas written between May and November 1726, however, beginning with Cantata 146, *Wir müssen durch viel Trübsal in das Reich Gottes eingehen* (May 12); continuing with Cantata 170, *Vergnügte Ruh, beliebte Seelenlust* (July 28); Cantata 35, *Geist und Seele wird verwirret* (September 8); Cantata 47, *Wer sich selbst erhöhet* (October 13); and Cantata 169, *Gott soll allein mein Herze haben* (October 20); and concluding with Cantata 49, *Ich gehe und suche mit Verlangen* (November 3). The cantatas contain a total of 17 movements with obbligato organ, including five purely instrumental sinfonias that mirror the description of the Dresden music. After this concentrated engagement, Bach went on to use obbligato organ in another 12 cantata and Passion movements, creating an extensive repertory of 35 pieces (see table 18-1, at the end of this chapter).

Performance Considerations

Early writers attempted to link Bach's sudden interest in obbligato organ either with repairs made to the St. Thomas organ that supposedly rendered the Rückpositiv playable on an independent keyboard or with the availability of a portative instrument from the St. Thomas School.[4] The obbligato movements were not intended for an isolated Rückpositiv manual or a portative, however, but for a full-sized Central German instrument—the organs in the St. Blasius Church in Mühlhausen, the Court Chapel in Weimar, St. Sophia's Church in Dresden, and the St. Thomas and St. Nicholas churches in Leipzig. This practice is verified by notations in the early performance materials such as "Brustpositiv," "Rückpositiv: Sesquialtera," "Organo obligato à 2 Clav.," and "Orgel Baß: Posaune 16. Fuß." These indications point to large organs with multiple manuals and pedal.

Modern performances and recordings using small portative instruments with half-length 8' pipes present a very distorted view of Bach's obbligato movements. This is especially evident in a piece such as the opening chorus of Cantata 80, *Ein feste Burg ist unser Gott*, which calls for the use of a Posaune 16' pedal stop

to reinforce the lower voice of the two-part canon on the cantus firmus.[5] In recent recordings a regal is sometimes used instead of the Posaune, which results
in a caricature of the original sound. The modern use of portative instruments
creates a false gap between the organ of the obbligato movements and the organ
of the solo works. In Bach's practice, they were one and the same.

Bach's augmented use of obbligato organ in 1726 can be linked with his third
cantata cycle, assembled during the years 1725–1727. Of the three surviving
cycles, the third is by far the most heterogeneous and experimental. After writing
and revising cantatas steadily for two and a half years, Bach went through a four-
month dry spell, during which he used pieces by his Meiningen cousin Johann
Ludwig Bach instead of composing new works. When he returned to regular
composition, in May 1726, he made extensive use of preexisting instrumental
music from Cöthen, creating solo and chorus cantatas that display an unusually
wide range of vocal and instrumental colors. Obbligato organ, the innovative sonority that generated much excitement among connoisseurs in Dresden, fit perfectly into this pattern. Several of the cantatas with obbligato movements were
performed during the Leipzig fairs, in fact, providing Bach with another opportunity to showcase his skills as an organ virtuoso before large audiences of music
enthusiasts. Cantatas 47 and 169 were presented during the St. Michael's Fair in
1726, Cantata 146 during the Easter Fair in 1726 or 1727, and Cantata 188 during
the St. Michael's Fair in 1728.

The use of obbligato organ also served a practical purpose. From 1725 onward
Bach became increasingly concerned about the lack of skilled instrumentalists in
his church ensemble, finally appealing to the Town Council in his "Short But Most
Necessary Draft" of 1730 for the restoration of the honoraria that had formerly
been awarded to university students and other musicians playing in his church
ensemble.[6] In many of the cantata and Passion movements with obbligato organ,
the organ substitutes for an orchestral instrument (see table 18-1). Thus, the solo
organ parts reflect an element of necessity, and there is some evidence in the third
cycle that Bach used obbligato organ as a practical expedient when a particular instrumental soloist for whom the part was written was no longer available.[7]

The pragmatic use of the organ for actual instruments was facilitated by the
progressive Central German organ, which increasingly included imitative instrumental stops (see chapter 17). The development of such registers—Flaute
traverse 8', Hautbois 8', Viola da gamba 8', and others—underscored the close
ties between chamber music and organ music in Central Germany and enabled
the easy exchange of organ and instrumental voices in the performance of concerted music. If an oboist was not available, the organist could take over the part,
as Bach stipulated in a repeat performance of Cantata 194, *Höchsterwünschtes
Freudenfest*, around 1726 (= BWV[3] 194.4). It is also noteworthy that the large
organs in the St. Thomas (III/35) and St. Nicholas (III/36) churches were in

excellent condition, thanks to ongoing maintenance carried out by Leipzig organ builder Johann Scheibe.[8]

Bach was not alone in introducing obbligato organ into cantatas; a number of other Central German composers also used solo organ in their sacred vocal music.[9] The most prominent of these figures was Gottfried Heinrich Stölzel, whose cantata movements with obbligato organ for major church festivals in Gotha in the mid-1720s rival those of Bach. Stölzel's music appears in the Clavier-Büchlein albums for Anna Magdalena and Wilhelm Friedemann Bach, and Bach performed a series of his cantatas in the 1730s.[10] It is unclear which composer started the obbligato-organ craze, but most likely there was a friendly exchange of ideas about the new genre between Bach and Stölzel, similar to the earlier exchange in Weimar between Bach and Johann Gottfried Walther concerning canonic chorale settings and concerto transcriptions.

The best-known obbligato organ movements are the eight instrumental sinfonias. Dating from 1726 to 1731, they appear to be derived almost fully from preexisting instrumental works, either Cöthen concertos for violin, oboe, or other instruments that Bach later rearranged as harpsichord concertos for collegium musicum performances in the 1730s (Cantatas 146, 35, 169, 49, 188) or the Preludio from the Unaccompanied Violin Partita in E Major, BWV 1006 (Cantatas 120a and 29).[11] The obbligato organ parts stemming from violin solos display double stops, bariolage (playing in rapid alternation of two strings, one open and one stopped), and other gestures characteristic of string-writing, even though this sometimes produced keyboard figuration that was very awkward to play, as in the Sinfonia to Cantata 146 (example 18-1).

Bach handled the organ part in a similar way in all eight sinfonias: the left hand doubles the continuo line, thus fulfilling the traditional role of

Example 18-1 Cantata 146, *Wir müssen durch viel Trübsal in das Reich Gottes eingehen*, Sinfonia: obbligato organ part, mm. 74–76.

keyboard continuo, while the right hand plays the treble melody—a new, solo assignment. Metaphorically, this creates an instrumentalist with a split personality: continuo accompanist and obbligato "protagonist."[12] This may have translated into a divided performance on the organ as well, with the right hand playing on a *forte* manual with distinctive solo stops and the left hand playing on a *piano* manual with appropriate continuo registers. The use of two keyboards is evident in the Sinfonia and opening chorus of Cantata 146, where the high-ranging violin part of the original forced Bach to notate the organ solo an octave lower, to be played on a separate manual with a 4' stop—a registrational technique he had used earlier, in Weimar, for his transcription of Vivaldi's Grosso Mogul Concerto.[13] As was true in Bach's cantatas in general, continuo basses that did not move too quickly could be played on the pedalboard rather than a second keyboard. In the obbligato organ movements, continuo chords were normally realized by a second chordal instrument—harpsichord or lute—playing from a separate performance part (example 18-2).[14] This practice is sometimes obscured in modern scores, including those of the Bach-Gesamtausgabe and the Neue Bach-Ausgabe, which conflate the continuo and left hand of the organ obbligato and incorrectly assign the chords to the soloist.[15]

In the later harpsichord arrangements of this music, Bach treated the left hand of the keyboard differently, freeing it from its purely continuo function and giving it greater contrapuntal independence (example 18-3). In the cantatas, Bach labeled the solo organ part "obligato"; in the harpsichord concertos, he labeled the solo keyboard part "concertato." The term "concertato" may have implied a more encompassing solo role than "obligato." Stölzel and others wrote independent left-hand parts for the organ as a matter of course. Why Bach chose the middle ground for his organ obbligato movements is unclear. Perhaps he was laboring under time pressure and had to carry out the arrangement work in great haste. But it is also possible that he felt his church ensemble, performing in a

Example 18-2 Cantata 169, *Gott soll allein mein Herze haben*, Sinfonia: obbligato organ and continuo parts, mm. 13–15.

Example 18-3 Harpsichord Concerto in E Major, BWV 1053, movement 1: cembalo concertato and continuo parts, mm. 14–16, showing the same passage as example 18-2, now with an independent bass in the solo part.

very large space with a choir, needed all the continuo support it could get. Both the St. Thomas Church and the St. Nicholas Church could accommodate more than 2,000 people. This was a far cry from the 200 or so who could squeeze into Zimmermann's coffeehouse to hear the harpsichord versions of this music. By doubling the continuo bass line on the organ, Bach would have been able to provide his church ensemble with a clearer and stronger foundation, especially from registers such as a manual 16' Fagot or a pedal Subbaß 16' or Posaunenbaß 16', which were available on the St. Thomas and St. Nicholas organs in Leipzig.[16]

The solo organ parts in the cantata sinfonias are showy and demanding, calling for bravura technique and great concentration on the part of the player. In the surviving performance materials, the organ appears only in the composing score, where it is transposed down a whole step to accommodate the higher choir pitch of the organ. This means the soloist played from the score and was thus in the best position to lead the ensemble. These factors point to Bach himself as the player,[17] and it is not difficult to imagine the sensation this music must have caused in Leipzig. It gave congregants the opportunity to hear their legendary cantor during the morning worship service as organ soloist, displaying the talent that brought him great fame in Saxony and Thuringia—indeed, in all of Germany. The sinfonias with obbligato organ turned the St. Thomas and St. Nicholas churches into concert halls, blurring the boundary between sacred worship and secular entertainment. The performances allowed the "trophy organist" of Weimar to return to the spotlight.

Musical Style

The sinfonia arrangements opened new realms of organ-writing. The grand scale of the music (292 measures in Cantata 188/1; 395 measures in Cantata 49/1) paved the way for the "symphonic" dimensions of the Leipzig preludes and fugues, and the ritornello forms with large-scale da capo or del segno segments (Cantatas 169/1 and 188/1) provided an innovative prototype for the Six Sonatas as well as the Leipzig preludes and fugues. The obbligato sinfonias served as a critical structural model for the solo organ works that soon followed.

In chorus movements, Bach used obbligato organ mainly to present a chorale cantus firmus. His stop of choice for this procedure appears to have been the Sesquialtera, which is indicated in the opening chorus of the St. Matthew Passion and in the aria "Komm, du Süße Todesstunde" of Cantata 161. For the chorus "Wir müssen durch viel Trübsal in das Reich Gottes eingehen" of Cantata 146, Bach recycled the slow movement of the now-lost concerto from which the sinfonia of the work is derived,[18] assigning the solo instrumental line to the organ (to be played with the right hand on a 4' stop, as in the opening Sinfonia, so that it sounds at the correct pitch) and retaining the original string and continuo parts. Over this instrumental fabric he superimposed a newly written four-part chorus, which sings even during the intricate cadenza that concludes the organ solo (m. 74). The movement is a remarkable reimagining of the original instrumental score, with the organ solo weaving arabesques within a dense, 10-part vocal and instrumental texture.

As impressive as the sinfonias and chorus movements are, it was the aria movements with their finely nuanced textures and figuration that had the greatest impact on Bach's solo organ writing. The arias display most clearly the transfer of solo lines from violin, oboe, horn, and even lute to the organ, in the case of movements borrowed from instrumental pieces, and from the organ to violin, oboe, transverse flute, and even voice (in Cantata 161), in the case of movements that were reperformed with new solo forces. In the substitution process Bach experimented with using the Central German organ in a new way, as a full-fledged soloist in a chamber-music ensemble. For the alto aria "Wie jammern mich doch die verkehrten Herzen" from Cantata 170, for instance, he stipulated a unique quartet combination: alto, two treble organ parts (played "à 2 Clav."), and violins and violas in unison. The "bassetto" scoring (that is, with a high-pitched bass instrument only), in which the normal continuo line is omitted, emphasizes musically the disorienting, destabilizing anxiety described in the text: "How I surely pity the perverted hearts / That are so very contrary to You, my God!"[19] The two organ parts resemble the violin 1 and violin 2 lines in the "Et incarnatus" of the B-Minor Mass and are similarly marked with slurs intended to emphasize the chromatic sighs of the jagged melodic material. This was a new, highly expressive way of utilizing the organ.

In many arias Bach employed obbligato organ with a full ensemble of strings and continuo, with or without oboes, in the manner of the tutti scorings of the sinfonias. But in others he used the instrument more delicately, as an equal partner in fashionable trio and quartet textures. In the alto aria "Ich will nach dem Himmel zu" from Cantata 146, the organ solo appears as the topmost voice of a lengthy da capo trio, with intricate, well-articulated, violin-like figuration. The line may have been initially intended for violin, in fact, or later transferred to it.[20] In either case, the organist is required to play a highly nuanced solo part, with the subtlety of a violinist.

In the soprano aria "Wer ein wahrer Christ will heißen" from Cantata 47 and the bass aria "Ich geh und suche mit Verlangen" from Cantata 49, the obbligato organ participates in light, *galant* dance trios in 3/8 meter. In the latter movement, the melodic figuration in the upper voices moves subtly back and forth between triplet and duple figures, which are frequently juxtaposed in the two parts (example 18-4). This produces playful rhythmic shifts and skirmishes that are characteristic of Enlightenment flute trios, such as the opening movement of the Sonata in B Minor for Flute and Harpsichord, BWV 1030 (in which the right hand of the harpsichord takes the third part). The result is pure chamber-music writing, quite unlike anything found in Bach's pre-Leipzig organ works. These

Example 18-4 Cantata 49, *Ich geh und suche mit Verlangen*: bass aria "Ich geh und suche mit Verlangen," mm. 49–54.

compelling 3/8-meter dance movements, with their pliant melodic figures spinning out over a steadily pulsating continuo bass of eighth notes, point directly
to the *galant* finales of Sonata 3 in D Minor, BWV 527/3, Sonata 4 in E Minor
Sonata, BWV 528/3, and the aria transcriptions of the Schübler Chorales.

All this resulted in a lightening of the organ idiom. In the arias with obbligato organ parts Bach began to treat organ lines in a new, "instrumental" way,
calling for great delicacy and refinement. In addition, it is likely that these parts
were played with more articulation than we see on the page. The elaborate solo
organ part for the alto aria "Mir ekelt mehr zu leben" from Cantata 170 of 1726,
for example, contains no articulation marks. In a subsequent performance some
20 years later, Bach assigned the part to transverse flute. This time, presumably
because he was not playing the part himself, he marked the articulation very me-
ticulously, giving a better impression of the manner in which the line was to be
performed (example 18-5).[21] A similar sequence occurs in the soprano aria "Wer
ein wahrer Christ will heißen" from Cantata 47: the original obbligato organ part
displays no articulation; the later version for solo violin contains carefully marked
dots and slurs.[22]

The scores of Bach's solo organ works written in Leipzig show much more
articulation than those of his earlier pieces,[23] a change that can be seen quite

Example 18-5 Cantata 170, *Vergnügte Ruh, beliebte Seelenlust*: alto aria "Mir ekelt
mehr zu leben," mm. 6–8: (a) obbligato organ part of 1726, and (b) transverse flute
part of c. 1746–1747.

clearly in the Prelude in B Minor, BWV 544/1, the pedal setting of "Vater Unser im Himmelreich," BWV 682, from Clavier-Übung III, and the Six Sonatas. The increased appearance of instrumental articulation—dots, slurs, and wedges— coincides with the rise of imitative "orchestral" stops in the progressive Central German organ. The Leipzig solo organ works also display a host of meters commonly associated with instrumental music: 2/4, 3/4, 6/4, 3/8, 6/8, 9/8, and 12/8. This forms a sharp contrast with the chorale settings of the Orgel-Büchlein, which display an abundance of old-fashioned 3/2 and 4/4 meters. The shift in articulation and meter practices represents a pivotal change in Bach's organ writing—the adoption of chamber music style. This change first appeared in his innovative cantata and Passion movements with obbligato organ.

Writing about Bach's "Compositions for Organ and Orchestra" more than 50 years ago, Hermann Keller lamented that the obbligato organ movements remained a "little-cultivated field."[24] Unfortunately, the repertory is still not performed often, and when the pieces are played or recorded, the organ part is commonly assigned to a portative instrument, which does little to convey the full-bodied sound that characterized Bach's performances.[25] The use of a large organ is critical not just for the obbligato movements but also for the closing chorales of the Leipzig cantatas: When performed with doubling manual principals and 16' pedal stops in the continuo, the chorales suddenly take on the nature of the tutti opening choruses and become framing elements of equal weight. The cantata and Passion movements with obbligato organ served as an essential catalyst for the solo organ works that followed. But they also stand as a worthy repertoire in their own right.

Trio Transcriptions and Compositions

As we noted in chapter 10, Bach wrote lengthy chorale trios for two manuals and pedal in Weimar. These works explored the potential of three-part texture and carried the tradition of the pedal chorale-trio to new musical and technical heights. The "Trio super Allein Gott, in der Höh sei Ehr," BWV 664a, with its lengthy, virtuosic episodes in invertible counterpoint and its quasi-da capo form, pointed to a new style, based on the Italian trio sonata.

Bach's interest in transferring the trio sonata to the organ is even clearer in a series of miscellaneous trios that emerged in Leipzig around the same time as the obbligato organ movements.[26] Although small in size and number, and often overlooked by present-day organists, the pieces played an important role in Bach's transition back to solo organ music and his adoption of the Italian instrumental trio as a viable organ form. That Bach wrote additional free organ trios was first pointed out by Johann Nicolaus Forkel, who concluded his comments on the Six Sonatas in his Bach biography of 1802 by noting that "several individual pieces, which remain distributed here and there, may also be reckoned fine, though they do not equal the first-mentioned."[27]

Like the organ preludes and fugues, the miscellaneous trios are not passed down as a collected group. They are transmitted singly instead, in several source traditions:[28] various manuscripts associated with Bach followers Johann Peter Kellner, Johann Nicolaus Mempell, and Johann Gottlieb Preller; a now-lost compendium titled "35 Organ Trios of Sebastian Bach," which can be partly reconstructed;[29] and the nineteenth-century editions of Gotthilf Wilhelm Körner. These sources point to a group of 10 organ trios—eight transcriptions and two original works—stemming from Bach and his circle in the second half of the1720s.[30]

Four of the transcriptions display refinements that point to Bach as the arranger:

Trio in C Minor, BWV 585: a transcription of the first two movements of Johann Friedrich Fasch's four-movement "Trio a 2 Violini e Basso." Bach seems to have known the instrumental trio from a manuscript copy in the music library of the Dresden Court.[31]

Trio in G Major, BWV 586: a transcription of a lost trio-sonata movement, possibly the last movement of a sonata for two flutes and continuo by Georg Philipp Telemann.[32]

Trio in F Major (Aria), BWV 587: a transcription of the "Air gracieusement" movement of François Couperin's trio sonata *La Convalescente* (an early version of the sonata *L'impérale*, later published in the collection *Les Nations* of 1726). Bach appears to have known *La Convalescente* from a manuscript copy written by his Dresden colleague Johann Georg Pisendel, concertmaster of the Dresden Court orchestra.[33]

Trio in C Minor, BWV 21/1a: a transcription of the instrumental Sinfonia from Cantata 21, *Ich hatte viel Bekümmernis*, in its Leipzig form of June 1723 (= BWV^3 21.3). The organ trio is a distillation of the original, produced by drawing on the oboe, violin 1, and continuo parts of the Sinfonia while dropping the remaining string lines. Previously known only from a Körner nineteenth-century edition, the C-Minor Trio recently resurfaced in a pre-1750 manuscript copy of the Six Sonatas,[34] lending significant credibility to its claim to authenticity.

Four additional transcriptions stem from students or colleagues in Bach's circle who had access to his works and may have been working under his supervision:

Trio in G Minor, BWV 584 (= BWV^3 App C): a transcription of the A section of the quartet "Ich will an den Himmel denken" from Cantata 166, *Wo* *gehest du hin?* of 1724. In the organ arrangement the original violin part, which survives only in the organ trio, is amalgamated with the tenor part to produce a single line that is assigned to manual II.[35]

Trio in C Major, BWV 1014/3: a transcription of the third movement of the Sonata 1 in B Minor for Violin and Harpsichord, BWV 1014. The music has been transposed from D major to C major, and small changes have been made here and there to accommodate the range of a C–c''' keyboard and a C–c' pedalboard. Otherwise, the organ trio contains no significant alterations from the instrumental model.

Sonata in G Major, BWV 1039: a group of three independently transmitted transcriptions, of the first, second, and fourth movements of the Sonata in G Major for Two Flutes and Continuo, BWV 1039, or its model. The arrangements of the first and second movements are closely related and may be the work of Johann Peter Kellner.[36]

Trio in B Minor, BWV 790: a transcription of Three-Part Sinfonia 4 in D Minor, BWV 790, transposed to B Minor to accommodate the compass of eighteenth-century German organs. The arrangement may be the handiwork of Kellner or his student Leonhard Frischmuth.[37]

Finally, two miscellaneous trios appear to be original compositions, the first by Bach, the second by someone in his circle:

Trio in D Minor, BWV 583: this worthy piece, displaying idiomatic organ figuration, A B A form, imitative treatment, and a high degree of integration, closely resembles the idiom of the Six Sonatas. It is handed down with the early variants of three movements from the Sonatas in the "35 Organ Trios of Sebastian Bach" collection, and Bach may have initially intended to use it in the Six Sonatas but changed his mind as he assembled the collection.

Concerto in E♭ Major, BWV 597 (= BWV³ App B 46): this work appears to be the outer movements of a three-movement "Sonate auf Concertenart" (Sonata in the manner of a concerto), for which the middle movement would have been improvised, in the fashion of the middle movement of Brandenburg Concerto No. 3. It could be a transcription of an instrumental trio, but the pedal solo in the first movement and other features point to an original organ composition. The Trio's attribution to "Mons. Bach" in its only manuscript source[38] suggests a tie with Bach, but its unabashedly *galant* style and the inconsistent part-writing in the Gigue point beyond Sebastian to a composer of a younger generation, perhaps one of Bach's sons (a 15-year old Wilhelm Friedemann?) or students (Heinrich Nicolaus Gerber, who published a now-lost set of Concert-Trios in 1734?).

The Function of the Pieces

Surveyed as a group, the miscellaneous trios appear to reflect a period of concentrated interest in trio-writing leading up to the composition of the Six Sonatas, a time when Bach and his followers focused intensely on the free organ trio through transcription and composition. In terms of style, the free trios differ from the chorale trios of Weimar. The chorale trios sprang from hymn tunes, and their thematic material, imitative treatment, and formal structure were determined by phrases of a hymn melody. The free trios, by contrast, sprang from instrumental models. Their thematic material, imitative treatment, and formal structure were derived from the Italian instrumental trio, which Bach does not seem to have taken up in earnest until his Cöthen years.

Like the cantata and Passion movements for obbligato organ, the miscellaneous trios reflect Bach's growing interest in the 1720s in utilizing the Central German organ as a chamber instrument, one capable of reproducing the sounds of orchestral instruments. The trios call for a nuanced performance, with the slurs, dots, strategically placed rests, and other articulatory gestures associated with chamber music. As with the Six Sonatas, the articulations are not always marked in the score. In the case of the miscellaneous trios, the appropriate articulation can often be discerned from markings in the instrumental models upon which the transcriptions were based. The Trio in F Major (Aria), BWV 587, for instance, is passed down in an organ score lacking articulation marks. The original instrumental trio, by contrast, displays a host of slurs in the violin parts, suggesting that the lines should be performed in a highly expressive way (example 18-6).

The miscellaneous trios also mirror Bach's growing need for teaching material during his initial years in Leipzig, when the number of students seeking organ lessons increased dramatically. From a pedagogical standpoint, the miscellaneous trios and Six Sonatas were the organ equivalent of the Inventions and Sinfonias for keyboard: they offered instruction in the cantabile manner of performance, finger and foot independence, and composition. Moreover, in Bach's day, the improvisation of chorale trios was a common audition requirement for organist positions. Free trios provided appropriate practice in the skill of playing and extemporizing three independent parts on two manuals and pedal, one of the greatest challenges of organ performance. The miscellaneous trios are less difficult than the Six Sonatas, and most call for a slow tempo. It is possible that Bach's students used them as preparatory studies for the Six Sonatas.

Example 18-6 Trio in F Major (Aria), BWV 587, opening measures: (a) organ transcription, and (b) instrumental model.

a) Trio in F Major (Aria):

b) François Couperin, Sonata "La Convalescente," Air gracieusement:

Stylistic Aspects

From a stylistic standpoint, the miscellaneous trios exemplify the instrumental principles that Bach embraced in Cöthen. The Italian trio sonata was ideal for organ transcriptions, since it transferred to the instrument more readily than the Italian concerto. It did not involve the extensive rewriting normally required of concerto arrangements, and once transcribed, it served as ready service, concert, and teaching material. The eight transcriptions closely follow their originals, for other than rewriting pedal lines to bring them into the range of the organ pedalboard, little adjustment was needed. The two original organ trios mirror the style of contemporary chamber music, utilizing freely invented *galant* material and balanced structures.

In Weimar, Bach arranged concertos in friendly competition with Johann Gottfried Walther. In Leipzig, he seems to have arranged trio movements from his own music as well as that of his contemporaries in collaboration with colleagues and students.

Numerous aspects of the miscellaneous trios foreshadow the style of the Six Sonatas. The well-crafted themes, invertible counterpoint, and the periodic cadences of the two Trios in C Minor, BWV 585 and BWV 21/1a, and the Trio in G Minor, BWV 584, closely resemble the writing of the Six Sonatas. In the case of

Example 18-7 (a) Cantata 166, *Wo gehest du hin?*, tenor aria "Ich will an den Himmel denken," oboe, mm. 1–3, and (b) Trio in G Minor, BWV 584, manual I, mm. 1–3 (arrows point to additional ties that produce new syncopations).

the G-Minor Trio, the transcriber created a new, more highly syncopated version of the principal theme of the cantata aria by adding a tie to the repeated-note motive that appears in beats 3 and 4 of the first and third measures (example 18-7, arrows). In the middle of the trio, the transcriber dropped the tie to produce a contrasting section of more animated rhythmic activity.

The imitative binary forms of the Trio in G Major, BWV 586, and the Gigue of the Concerto in E♭ Major, BWV 597, point to the finale of Sonata 1 in E♭ Major. And the unison opening of movement 1 of the E♭-Major Concerto, a common concerto gesture implied in this case by the work's original notation,[39] resembles that of movement 1 of Sonata 6 in G Major.

The Trio in D Minor, BWV 583, with its tightly wrought design and high degree of thematic integration (blocks of repeated material either transposed or with treble parts exchanged, or both), is a movement worthy of the Six Sonatas:

Section	Mm.	Material	Description	Key
A	1–7	a1	Imitative theme	i
	7–13	a2	Imitative sequences, derived from a1	III
	13–19	a1	Treble parts exchanged	i
B	19–24	b1	Imitative theme derived from a2	VI
	24–25	b2	Imitative theme derived from a2	
	26–27	b3	Imitative theme derived from a2	
	28–29	b3	Treble parts exchanged, bass elaborated	
	30–35	b1	Transposed, treble parts exchanged	iv
	35–36	b2	Transposed, treble parts exchanged	
	37–38	b3	Transposed, treble parts exchanged	
	39–40	b3	Transposed, treble parts exchanged, bass elaborated	
A'	41–45	a1	Transposed (i)	
	45–50	a2	Transposed, treble parts exchanged	VI
	51–53	a1	Coda	i

This design closely resembles that of the *adagio e dolce* of Sonata 3 in D Minor (see chapter 19), hinting at the chronological proximity of the two movements and suggesting once again that Bach may have initially intended the D-Minor Trio for the Six Sonatas but changed his mind in the process of compiling the collection.

The miscellaneous trios, then, together with the cantata and Passion movements with obbligato organ, served as preparatory exercises for the Six Sonatas, as display pieces for demonstrating the instrumental qualities of the progressive Central German organ, and as pedagogical material for students such as Heinrich Nicholas Gerber, Johann Ludwig Krebs, and Gottfried August Homilius, who went on to compose organ trios of their own. The miscellaneous trios of Bach and his circle, while not equal to the Six Sonatas, may nevertheless be "reckoned fine," as Forkel put it. They remain excellent teaching pieces and merit greater study and performance today.

Notes

1. NBR, no. 118.
2. Wolff and Zepf 2012, 16.
3. Wolff 2016, 65–75.
4. Spitta 1873–80, vol. 2, 446–447; Wilhelm Rust, BG 22 (1875), xvi–xviii; and Richter 1908, 53–54.
5. The indication "Orgel Baß: Posaune 16. Fuß" appears in the Kittel-circle manuscript, Berlin State Library, *P 71*, which seems to be derived from the original, now-lost performance parts of the cantata. See NBA I/31, KB (Frieder Rempp, ed., 1988), 55–56, 74, and 82.
6. NBR, no. 151.
7. Butler 2010, 134–139.
8. Lynn Edwards Butler, in Edwards Butler 2022, 150–195, documents not only ongoing maintenance by Scheibe but also extensive repairs amounting to renovations of the St. Thomas organ in 1720-1721 and the St. Nicholas Organ in 1724-1725.
9. Matthew Cron, in Cron 2003, identifies more than 150 works, written by 15 Central German composers, that use obbligato organ.
10. Marc-Roderich Pfau, "Ein unbekanntes Leipziger Kantatentextheft aus dem Jahr 1735: Neues zum Thema Bach und Stölzel," BJ 94 (2008), 99–122, and Andreas Glöckner, "Ein weiterer Kantatenjahrgang Gottfried Heinrich Stölzels in Bachs Aufführungsrepertoire?" BJ 95 (2009), 95–116.
11. The sinfonias are discussed in Stauffer 1999. Possible models of the movements are considered in Küster 2002 and Wolff 2016.
12. Dreyfus 1986, 184–188.
13. Tagliavini 1986, 247. See also the discussion of the Grosso Mogul Concerto in Chapter 9.

14. Dreyfus 1987, 63–68.

15. See the score of Cantata 169 in NBA I/24, for instance.

16. The manual reed on the St. Thomas organ was a Krumbhorn 16' rather than a Fagot 16'. See the dispositions of both instruments in Wolff and Zepf, 50–54.

17. Bernhard Friedrich Richter, in Richter 1908, 58, proposed that the obbligato organ parts were performed by Wilhelm Friedemann Bach, a view later reiterated by Georg von Dadelsen, Alfred Dürr, and others. Laurence Dreyfus, in Dreyfus 1986, 174, notes that Wilhelm Friedemann left the Bach household to study violin with Johann Gottlieb Graun in Jena in June 1726 and did not return until April 1727. As a consequence, he was out of town when the bulk of the obbligato organ movements were performed.

18. The lost concerto can be seen in full form in the later Harpsichord Concerto in D Minor, BWV 1052.

19. Translation from Dürr 2005, 433.

20. NBA I/11.2, KB (Reinmar Emans, ed., 1989), 85–86.

21. He also presented the second two-thirds of the line an octave lower on the organ, to avoid the note d''' in the theme, which could be played on the flute but not on the organ, with its C–c''' manual range.

22. Reproduced in NBA I/23, 361 (obbligato organ version) and 345 (obbligato violin version).

23. See the discussion in Butt 1990, 177–179.

24. Keller 1967, 167.

25. Notable exceptions are John Eliot Gardner's recording of Cantata 146 in his *Complete Cantatas of J.S. Bach* series (SDG 107) and Joan Lippincott's recording *Sinfonia: Organ Concertos and Sinfonias by J.S. Bach* (Gothic Records: G 49130), which use large organs with several manuals and pedal. The recent videos of the Netherlands Bach Society also utilize full-size instruments.

26. On the dating of the repertoire, see Stauffer 2016.

27. Forkel 1802, 60.

28. The traditions are described and assessed in the Editorial Report of the Leupold Edition, vol. 7, 148–158.

29. NBA IV/7, KB (Dietrich Kilian, 1988), 58 and 113.

30. The ten works are published as a group in the Leupold Edition, vol. 7.

31. Schulze 1984, 87.

32. Karl Anton, in *Musik und Kirche* 1942, vol. 2, 47–49, claimed that the G-Major Trio is based on a work by Telemann contained in a manuscript volume dating from Telemann's years in Leipzig—that is, 1701-1705. The volume was destroyed in W.W. II, before Anton could publish his findings. The style of the work is consistent with that of Telemann's trio sonatas.

33. Delang 2007, 197–198.

34. Schwerin, Landesbibliothek Mecklenburg-Vorpommern, *Mus. 888a*, described in NBA IV/11, KB (Ulrich Bartels and Peter Wollny, 2004), 222 (Nachtrag). Facsimile in Leupold Edition, vol. 7, xxxv.

35. The complicated history of the G-Minor Trio is summarized in Alfred Dürr, "Verstummelt überlieferte Arien aus Kantaten J.S. Bachs," BJ 46 (1960), 28–31 and 39–41.
36. Stinson 1990, 38–40, 60–62.
37. Stinson 1990, 38–40.
38. Leipzig Town Library, Mempell-Preller Collection, *Peters Ms. 7*, fascicle 13.
39. The notation calls for a unison opening that is not realized in most modern editions. See Leupold Edition, vol. 7, xxxiii (facsimile), 94-97 (music) and 149-150 (Editorial Report).

Table 18-1 Bach's Cantata and Passion Movements with Obbligato Organ

---

Cantata 71, *Gott ist mein König*   February 4, 1708

  Movement 2—Soprano-tenor duet "Ich bin nun achtzig Jahr"

Cantata 161, *Komm, du süße Todesstunde* (solo cantata)   September 27, 1716

  Movement 1—Alto aria "Komm, du Süße Todesstunde"
  (organ presents cantus firmus "Herzlich tut mich
  verlangen"; part later assigned to soprano)

Cantata 70, *Wachet! betet! betet! wachet* (second   November 21, 1723
version = BWV^3 70.2)

  Movement 3—Alto aria "Wenn kömmt der Tag" (organ
  doubles the obbligato cello part—or plays it alone?)

Cantata 194, *Höchsterwünschtes Freudenfest* (fourth   June 16, 1726?
version = BWV^3 194.4)

  Movement 3—Bass aria "Was des Höchsten Glanz erfüllt"
  (organ replaces oboe 1 of 1724 version)
  Movement 7—Soprano-bass duet "O wie wohl ist uns
  geschehn" (formerly movement 10; organ replaces oboe
  2 of 1724 version)

Cantata 128, *Auf Christi Himmelfahre allein*   May 10, 1725

  Movement 4—Alto-tenor duet "Sein Allmacht zu
  ergründen" (obbligato instrumental part initially
  assigned to organ, then changed to oboe d'amore)

Cantata 146, *Wir müssen durch viel Trübsal in das Reich Gottes*   May 12, 1726
eingehen   (or 1727?)

  Movement 1—Sinfonia (music derived from same model
  as Harpsichord Concerto in D Minor, BWV 1052,
  movement 1)
  Movement 2—Chorus "Wir müssen durch viel Trübsal"
  (music derived from same model as Harpsichord
  Concerto in D Minor, BWV 1052, movement 2)
  Movement 3—Alto aria "Ich will nach dem Himmel zu"
  (obbligato organ line originally intended for violin, or
  later transferred to it?)

Cantata 170, *Vergnügte Ruh, beliebte Seelenlust* (solo cantata)   July 28, 1726

  Movement 3—Alto aria "Wie jammern mich doch die
  verkehrten Herzen" ("Organo obligato à 2 Clav.")
  Movement 5—Alto aria "Mir ekelt mehr zu leben" (organ
  obbligato part later assigned to transverse flute)

Table 18-1 Continued

Cantata 35, *Geist und Seele wird verwirret* (solo cantata)	September 8, 1726

Movement 1—Sinfonia to Part I (music derived from
same model as Harpsichord Concerto in D Minor,
BWV 1059, movement 1)
Movement 2—Alto aria "Geist und Seele wird verwirret"
(music derived from same model as Harpsichord
Concerto in D Minor, BWV 1059, movement 2?)
Movement 4—Alto aria "Gott hat alles wohlgemacht"
Movement 5—Sinfonia to Part II (music derived from
same model as Harpsichord Concerto in D Minor,
BWV 1059, movement 3?)
Movement 7—Alto aria "Ich wünsche nur, bei Gott zu leben"

Cantata 47—*Wer sich selbst erhöhet*	October 13, 1726

Movement 2—Soprano aria "Wer ein wahrer Christ will
heißen" (organ obbligato part later assigned to violin)

Cantata 169, *Gott soll allein mein Herze haben* (solo cantata)	October 20, 1726

Movement 1—Sinfonia (music derived from same model as
Harpsichord Concerto in E Major, BWV 1053, movement 1)
Movement 3—Alto aria "Gott soll allein mein Herze haben"
Movement 5—Alto aria "Stirb in mir, Welt" (music
derived from same model as Harpsichord Concerto in
E Major, BWV 1053, movement 2)

Cantata 49, *Ich geh und suche mit Verlangen* (Dialogue)	November 3, 1726

Movement 1—Sinfonia (music derived from same model
as Harpsichord Concerto in E Major, BWV 1053,
movement 3)
Movement 2—Bass aria "Ich geh und suche mit Verlangen"
Movement 6—Soprano-bass duet "Dich hab ich je und je
geliebet"

St. Matthew Passion, BWV 244 (= BWV[3] 244.1)	April 11, 1727

Movement 1—"Kommt, Ihr Töchter, helft mir klagen"
(organ carries cantus firmus)

Cantata 188, *Ich habe meine Zuversicht* (solo cantata)	October 17, 1728 (or November 6, 1729?)

Movement 1—Sinfonia (fragment; music derived from
same model as Harpsichord Concerto in D Minor, BWV
1052, movement 3)
Movement 4—Alto aria "Unerforschlich ist die Weise"

(continued)

Table 18-1 Continued

Cantata 120a, *Herr Gott, Beherrscher aller Dinge* (= BWV³ 120.2)	c. 1729
Movement 4—Sinfonia (fragment; music derived from Preludio of Unaccompanied Violin Partita in E Major, BWV 1006)	
Cantata 63, *Christen, ätzet diesen Tag* (reperformance)	December 25, 1729?
Movement 3—Soprano-bass duet "Gott, du hast es wohl gefüget" (organ replaces obbligato oboe of original version)	
Cantata 29, *Wir danken dir, Gott, wir danken dir*	August 27, 1731
Movement 1—Sinfonia (music derived from Preludio of Unaccompanied Violin Partita in E Major, BWV 1006) Movement 7—Alto aria "Halleluja, Stärk und Macht"	
Cantata 172, *Erschallet, ihr Lieder* (Leipzig C-major version = BWV³ 172.3)	May 13, 1731
Movement 5—Soprano-alto duet (organ replaces obbligato oboe d'amore and cello of original version)	
St. John Passion, BWV 245 (third version = BWV³ 245.3)	April 7, 1730?
Movement 19—Bass aria "Betrachte, meine Seele" (organ replaces obbligato lute of original version)	
Cantata 73, *Herr, wie du willt, so schicks mit mir* (reperformance)	1732–1735
Movement 1—Chorus/recitative complex "Herr, wie du willt, so schicks mit mir" (organ replaces horn of original version)	
Cantata 27, *Wer weiss, wie nahe mir mein Ende* (reperformance)	c. 1741–1742
Movement 3, Alto aria "Willkommen! will ich sagen" (organ replaces obbligato harpsichord part of original version)	
Cantata 80, *Ein feste Burg ist unser Gott* (third version = BWV³ 80.3)	Reformation Festival 1739?
Movement 1—Chorus "Ein feste Burg ist unser Gott" (organ carries cantus firmus, in pedal)	

19

The Six Sonatas

The Six Sonatas represent the culmination of several trends that emerged in Bach's writing during the Cöthen and early Leipzig years: his turn to lighter, dance-filled instrumental and vocal music; his growing interest in the new type of organ emerging in Central Germany; his use of the organ as an obbligato instrument in his third cantata cycle; and his transcription and composition of free organ trios between 1725 and 1730 or so. These developments led to the Six Sonatas collection, Bach's first large-scale organ project since the Orgel-Büchlein of the Weimar years.

As we have noted, Bach wrote lengthy chorale trios for two manuals and pedal in Weimar. But the Six Sonatas, composed a decade and a half later, raise the concept of the organ trio to an unprecedented plane. Based on instrumental writing rather than chorale elaboration, they represent a remarkable reimagining of solo organ music. They are closely related to the miscellaneous trios, but here Bach took the next step and grouped individual pieces into a three-movement sequence—fast-slow-fast—in the manner of a Vivaldi concerto. The very fact that the collection contains six sonatas and is thus an "opus" of pieces, underscores its instrumental roots. In a single flash of inspiration, Bach invented a new organ genre and provided its most sublime representatives.

At the same time, Bach increased the technical demands of organ-playing even beyond those of his Weimar works. The Six Sonatas, with their transparent and fiercely independent parts for right hand, left hand, and feet, offer the performer no place to hide. They were, and remain, the ultimate test of an organist's skill.

The Genesis of the Collection

The sole account of the Sonatas' origin comes from Johann Nicolaus Forkel's Bach biography of 1802:

> Six Sonatas, or Trios, for two claviers and obbligato pedal. Bach composed them for his eldest son, Wilhelm Friedemann, who by practicing them prepared himself for becoming the great performer on the organ that he afterward was. It is impossible to say enough of their beauty. They were composed when the author was in his most mature age and may be considered as his chief work of this description.[1]

J. S. BACH. George B. Stauffer, Oxford University Press. © Oxford University Press 2024.
DOI: 10.1093/oso/9780195108026.003.0020

Bach's autograph manuscript of the Sonatas, *P 271* in the Berlin State Library, supports Forkel's description.[2] It contains a watermark from the period 1727–1732,[3] and various characteristics of Bach's handwriting point more precisely to c. 1730,[4] a time when Bach was in his prime and Friedemann was 20 years old and ready for advanced organ study.

The manuscript is best described as a revision score. The writing is neat and orderly, with corrections and small improvements here and there.[5] There is very little compositional activity except for the first movement of Sonata 2 in C Minor, which displays several passages that appear to have been composed (or possibly recomposed) on the spot. The manuscript begins with Bach's customary invocation for composition projects, "J.J." or Jesu Juva (Jesus, come to my aid; plate 19-1, top left corner). The generally clean appearance of the manuscript and its well-planned layout suggest that Bach worked from sketches or preexisting scores as he filled in the text.

The survival of early versions of four movements of the Sonatas hints at the collection's prehistory:[6]

Trio in E♭ Major, BWV 525/1a → Sonata 1 in E♭ Major, movement 1
Trio in D Minor, BWV 527/1a → Sonata 3 in D Minor, movement 1
Trio in D Minor, BWV 528/2b → Sonata 4 in E Minor, movement 2
Trio in A Minor, BWV 529/2a → Sonata 5 in C Major, movement 2

Of these, only the Trio in D Minor, BWV 528/2b, appears to have been composed as an independent piece, without being earmarked for incorporation into the Six Sonatas. Bach refined its text slightly (BWV 528/2a) before appropriating it for use in Sonata 4 in E Minor. At that point he transposed the music from D minor to B minor, changed the manual notation from soprano to treble clef, and substantially revised the text.[7] The other variants display minor changes of detail only and seem to have been written with placement in the Six Sonata collection in mind. This view is supported by the fact that the earliest manuscript copies of the Trio in D Minor, BWV 527/1a, and Trio in A Minor, BWV 529/2a, date from c. 1725–1729—that is, from the period leading up to the completion of the Sonatas around 1730. It is possible that Bach was working from a sketchbook containing drafts of individual pieces that he subsequently grouped into three-movement sonatas as he worked on *P 271*. Several transposition mistakes in Sonata 5 in C Major and Sonata 6 in G Major hint that Bach was copying from versions of those works in which the right hand was notated in soprano rather than treble clef.

Two additional movements stem—or appear to stem—from preexisting instrumental trios. The first movement of Sonata 4 is a transcription of the Sinfonia that opens Part II of Cantata 76, *Die Himmel erzählen die Ehre Gottes*, from 1723. Written for oboe d'amore, viola da gamba, and continuo, in the fashion of a North

Plate 19-1 Sonata 1 in E♭ Major, BWV 525, beginning of movement 1. Bach's autograph score, c. 1730, with opening invocation "J.J." ("Jesu Juva," or Jesus, come to my aid) in the upper left corner.

German trio for one treble and two bass instruments,[8] the Sinfonia may itself be an arrangement of an earlier instrumental piece from Weimar.[9] Whether or not this is true, Bach seems to have used the cantata movement as his model for the first movement of Sonata 4, transcribing the music directly into the organ score and making adjustments in the process. The second movement of Sonata No. 3 in D Minor was most probably derived from an instrumental trio as well, a piece now lost but also used as the model for the middle movement of the Concerto in A Minor for Flute, Violin, Harpsichord, and Strings, BWV 1044.[10]

In the course of writing the Six Sonatas, then, Bach not only relied on early versions of many movements but also seems to have combed his shelves for pre-existing vocal or instrumental music that could be appropriated for the collection, just as he had done a few years before when compiling his third cantata cycle. Like the cantatas, the Six Sonatas show the increasing role of recycling and revision in Bach's compositional process in Leipzig.

How far back does the earlier material go? Although some writers have sought to trace various sonata movements to Bach's Weimar years,[11] there is no concrete evidence that any of the music (aside from the Trio in D Minor, BWV 528/2a and 2b, perhaps) dates from that time—at least as organ trios. The earliest manuscripts of both the miscellaneous trios and the variants from the Six Sonatas stem from Leipzig, and the chamber-music style of the works suggest that they were written after Bach's Cöthen tenure. Thus the composition of the Six Sonatas appears to have taken place in close proximity to the compilation of the autograph manuscript, most probably in the period 1725–1729.

In the Six Sonatas Bach established keyboard ranges of CD–$\hat{c}'''$ for the manuals and CD–d' for the pedal as his new personal standard for *pedaliter* organ music. The pedal range was two notes higher than that used for many of his Weimar works, CD–c', and the fact that the Trio in D Minor, BWV 528/2a and 2b, exceeds this compass, extending from CD to e♭', hints once again at its independent origin, perhaps going back to Weimar and the extended range of the pedalboard of the Palace Chapel organ.[12] When compiling the Sonata collection, Bach also seems to have considered arranging the pieces in a different order. An early version of Sonata 3 containing the first movement variant BWV 527/1a is transmitted with the title "Sonata 1" in two manuscripts,[13] and an early version of Sonata 5 containing the second movement variant BWV 529/2a is handed down with the title "Sonata 4" in one source.[14] Moreover, the fascicle structure of the autograph shows that Sonatas 2–6 were written as a collected group, while Sonata 1 in E♭ Major was composed as an independent piece and possibly added to the collection after the others were in place.[15] Thus Bach seems to have contemplated several organizational plans before settling on the order we know today.

A second important manuscript of the Six Sonatas, Wilhelm Friedemann Bach's personal copy of the collection, *P 272* in the Berlin State Library, displays further refinements of the text of Bach's autograph. It probably dates from 1733, the year Friedemann left the family household to take up the position of organist of St. Sophia's Church in Dresden. It is a composite manuscript: it appears to have originated as a complete copy of the Six Sonatas written by Anna Magdalena Bach, but for one reason or another, the first three sonatas were removed, perhaps to serve as a gift or a sales item. Friedemann then wrote out a new copy of Sonatas 1–3 to restore the collection to a complete state. Both Anna Magdalena and Friedemann used Bach's autograph as the model for their copies.

While the basic text of the Friedemann/Anna Magdalena manuscript is practically the same as that of Bach's autograph, the portion written by Anna Magdalena—Sonatas 4–6—contains a multitude of additional performance markings inserted by Bach. These markings include tempo indications, slurs, dots, and rhythmic clarifications (Example 19-1), and in a few instances Bach refined the text of the music as well. Such illuminating additions probably existed in Anna Magdalena's copy of Sonatas 1–3, and it is especially lamentable that the original front half of her manuscript is missing.

The Friedemann/Anna Magdalena score represents an important second stage in the genesis of the music, and all modern editions since the Peters Edition have adopted the additional markings it contains. At the same time, there are a number of changes in Bach's autograph that are not conveyed in the copy, presumably because Bach made them after *P 272* left the family household.[16] As is true with so many of Bach's keyboard works, the refinement of the Six

Example 19-1 Sonata 6 in G Major, BWV 530, movement 3 (Allegro), mm. 48–50: (a) Bach's autograph manuscript, and (b) Anna Magdalena Bach's copy, with performance nuances added by Johann Sebastian.

Sonatas appears to have been an ongoing process, brought to an end only by the composer's death.

Pedagogical Use

Although the Six Sonatas may have been written for Wilhelm Friedemann, as Forkel claimed, Bach appears to have assigned the music selectively to other Leipzig organ students as well. Copies of the Sonatas and Sonata movements can be linked to Johann Caspar Vogler, Bernard Christian Kayser, Johann Christian Kittel, Johann Philipp Kirnberger, Carl Philipp Emanuel Bach, and others who studied with Bach.

The Six Sonatas therefore represent a further contribution to the series of pedagogical keyboard collections that Bach assembled in the 1720s: the Inventions and Sinfonias, the French and English Suites, and the Well-Tempered Clavier, volume 1. For organ instruction Bach could turn to the Orgel-Büchlein, whose belatedly added title emphasizes its didactic purpose, as well as a large store of free works and other chorale settings from Weimar. The Six Sonatas broadened and updated this teaching repertory by adding new, fashionable pieces that took full advantage of the chamber-music qualities of the progressive Central German organ. The forward-looking style of the Sonatas would have made the music especially appealing to Bach's students, with their youthful interest in fashionably *galant* instrumental music.

Musical Style

That Bach took the time to gather the Six Sonatas in a handsome, carefully laid-out manuscript reflects the special nature of the works, which were deemed attractive by devotees of Bach's music even during the period 1750–1800, when many of his works fell from favor. Several distinctive features account for the Sonatas' broad appeal.

First, they are permeated with dance music, a feature verified by the profusion of dance and dance-like meters: 12/8, 6/8, 3/8, 3/4, 2/4, and non-alla breve ¢.[17] Bach's avoidance of straightforward ¢ in the Trio Sonatas is striking: it appears only twice in 18 movements, in the opening Adagio-Vivace and Andante of Sonata 4, both derived from preexisting pieces. The scarcity of ¢ time signals a distinct break from the seventeenth-century-oriented music of the Orgel-Büchlein, in which 42 of the 46 chorale preludes are written in the conservative meters of ¢ or 3/2. The use of lighter instrumental meters in the Six Sonatas represents a "galanticization" of Bach's organ writing.

Bach's wholehearted embrace of dance music in Cöthen spurred him to incorporate delicate dance meters into his music more often than before. The 3/8 meter of the closing movements of Sonatas 3 and 4, for example, was characterized by Bach's student Johann Philipp Kirnberger as having "the lively tempo of a passepied. It is performed in a light and almost playful manner and is widely used in chamber and theatrical music."[18] Elsewhere Kirnberger mentions that 3/8 has "a liveliness that is almost frolicsome." The finales of Sonatas 3 and 4 are frolicsome, indeed, and it is Bach's use of dance and dance-like meters throughout the Six Sonatas that gives the music much of its lightness and grace.

The melodic material exhibits fashionable tendencies as well. The themes of the fast movements lean toward crisp, tuneful melodic ideas that are organized into succinct, balanced phrases. This represents a move away from the melodic "spinning out" of the Baroque era to the periodic phrasing of the Classical period. Many of the themes are composed of small, cadentially closed phrases of 2, 4, or 8 measures. This stems in part from the dance roots of the music, but it also reflects Bach's desire to create more "natural" melodic ideas.

In a number of cases the themes are subdivided into small symmetrical units that are paired in dialogue fashion. The ritornello that opens movement 1 of Sonata 5, for instance, begins with a pair of two-bar units. In the first, the right hand presents a consonant, triadic solo motive (example 19-2, x) that is answered by the tutti (example 19-2, y). The left hand then presents the same motive an octave lower, which is again answered by the tutti, also an octave lower. This creates a dialogue between the two manual voices, much in the fashion of an amorous duet in the Neapolitan opera music of Bach's day. It also represents the kind of witty, conversational thematic material that was later valued by Classical composers—Haydn in his late string quartets, for example. The last movement of Sonata 1 and the first movements of Sonatas 2 and 6 begin in much the same

Example 19-2 Sonata 5 in C Major, BWV 529, movement 1 (Allegro): opening dialogue.

manner, with short, chatty, dialogue-like phrases that immediately engage the listener and lead to conversational development.

The slow movements of the Sonatas, by contrast, exhibit themes of great expressiveness, with chromaticism, syncopation, and rhythmic elasticity (that is, the use of a wide range of note values—8th notes, 16th notes, and 32nd notes—in the same theme). The melodic intricacies of the treble voices contrast sharply with the steady pulse and clear harmonic contour of the continuo-like bass lines. In the slow movements of Sonatas 1 and 6 this creates a siciliano-like texture— an elaborate melody over a straightforward, emphatic, repeated-note bass—that appears in Leipzig cantata arias and concerto movements [19] but is lacking in the Brandenburg Concertos or other Cöthen works.[20]

While the themes of the fast movements constantly stress the downbeat, the melodies of the slow movements commonly delay harmonic resolution until the very end of the phrase. This prolongation produces a sense of longing that appealed to the generation of composers that followed Bach. The slow movements of the Sonatas foreshadow the "sensitive style" of the late eighteenth century and require a new and more delicate type of organ articulation. The Lente from Sonata 6, for instance, is marked with an abundance of slurs and delicate detachments in Anna Magdalena's score (example 19-3). As John Butt has described it: "the detail of the two manuscripts *P 271* and *P 272*, although not comprehensive, suggests that Bach was educating his pupils in a livelier style of organ playing, one particularly suited to the music of BWV 525–530."[21] Among Bach's organ works, this kind of finely nuanced instrumental articulation surfaces in full form for the first time in the Six Sonatas.

The Six Sonatas also display the extensive use of invertible counterpoint and transposition as a means of expanding musical material and creating varied yet unified structures. As we noted in Part II, Bach experimented with the use of invertible counterpoint as early as the Arnstadt years, in the Reincken sonata arrangements; the fugues after Bononcini, Corelli, and Albinoni; and other keyboard works. By the time he arrived in Weimar, it had become part and parcel of his compositional style. With the Inventions and Sinfonias of the Cöthen period, however, he seems to have brought the technique to a new level of refinement, using invertible counterpoint and transposition to create balanced forms in which extensive blocks of musical material are repeated at new pitches with voices exchanged. At the same time, he did not hesitate to interrupt the invertible counterpoint with free writing, to "reanimate the theme," as he once said of the need for appropriate interludes in fugues.[22] The overall effect is much less severe than the canonic chorales of the Orgel-Büchlein or the permutation fugue of the Passacaglia in C Minor, in which very little contrapuntal relaxation takes place.

Bach used invertible counterpoint and transposition as a fundamental compositional device in the Sonatas. We can see this technique at work in movement

Example 19-3 Sonata 6 in G Major, BWV 530, movement 2 (Lente), opening
theme: (a) Bach's autograph manuscript, and (b) Anna Magdalena Bach's copy, with
additional performance nuances added by Johann Sebastian.

2, Adagio e dolce, of Sonata 3. The movement has a ternary A B A' structure,
composed entirely of small blocks of material that are repeated and altered, often
through invertible counterpoint and transposition. This is especially evident
in the A' section, where themes from the A and B sections are recapitulated in
transposed, contrapuntally varied forms, sometimes including stretto:

Section	Mm.	Material	Description	Key
A				
	1–2	a	Homophonic theme	I
	3–4	b	Imitative sequence, modulatory	
	5–6	c	Imitative sequence, related rhythmically to b	
	7–8	d	Cadential sequence, related to a, cadences in V	V
B				
	9–10	a	Treble parts exchanged, transposed to V	V
	11–12	e	Derived from m. 2 of a, imitative and modulatory	
	13–14	a'	Treble parts in original vertical order, but varied	vi
	15–16	f	Derived from m. 1 of b, cadences in vi	vi
	17–18	g	Derived from b, modulatory	
	19–20	h	Derived from c	
A'				
	21–22	a'	Treble parts exchanged and varied	I
	23–24	e	Transposed, treble parts exchanged	
	25–26	b	Transposed, treble parts exchanged, stretto	
	27–28	b	Transposed, treble parts in original order, stretto	
	29–30	c	Transposed, treble parts exchanged	
	39–32	d	Transposed, treble parts exchanged, cadences in I	I

Bach's reliance on balanced, two-bar phrases in the Adagio is clear, but it is the repetition of material through invertible counterpoint and transposition that gives the movement its high degree of symmetry and cohesion. Bach refined this method of construction in the Leipzig cantatas, where it served not only as a successful unifying device but also as a practical expedient, allowing him to repeat large sections of material once he had worked out the counterpoint. The use of invertible counterpoint is not generally associated with *galant* style. In the Six Sonatas, however, it leads to the repetition of material in a playful way. We can see why Bach returned to the music of the Adagio e dolce in the 1740s, adding a fourth part and recycling it as the middle movement of the Concerto in A Minor for Violin, Flute, and Harpsichord, BWV 1044, a work most probably performed by his collegium musicum in Zimmermann's coffee house. If Bach wrote music for Enlightenment tastes, this is it.

The Six Sonatas also display a new clarity of design. Bach cast the music in forms with balanced, clearly defined sections. Even the fugal third movements have da capo elements. The sole exception is the Largo of Sonata 2, which is through-composed:

Sonata 1 in E♭ Major

[Allegro]	ritornello form
Adagio	rounded binary form
Allegro	rounded binary form

Sonata 2 in C Minor

Vivace	ritornello form, with da capo element
Largo	through-composed
Allegro	fugal A B A B A form

Sonata 3 in D Minor

Andante	A B A da capo form
Adagio e dolce	rounded binary form
Vivace	fugal A B A da capo form

Sonata 4 in E Minor

Adagio-Vivace	fugal form (Adagio) → ritornello form (Vivace)
Andante	A B A B form
Un poc' allegro	fugal A B A form

Sonata 5 in C Major

Allegro	A B A da capo form
Largo	A B A B A form
Allegro	fugal da capo form/modified binary form

Sonata 6 in G Major

Vivace	ritornello form
Largo	rounded binary form
Allegro	fugal A B A B A da capo form

The ritornello forms show fewer and larger segments than those of the Weimar period, and the episodic sections within them tend to become larger and more developmental as the music proceeds. This type of ritornello design with expanded sections mirrors that found in the "symphonic" preludes from the Leipzig years (see chapter 20).

Finally, the Six Sonatas set a new technical standard. Bach had composed demanding trios "à 2 Clavier et Pedal" in Weimar—the trio settings of "Nun komm, der Heiden Heiland," BWV 659a, or "Allein Gott in der Höh sei Ehr," BWV 664a, for instance. These were very select pieces, however, presented as one option among others for preluding on a chorale tune. In the Six Sonatas, Bach employs trio texture as the standard for an extended multimovement work. There is no relief for the left hand, right hand, or feet. The player must perform three independent lines for as long as 15 minutes—a task calling for intense concentration.

These performance challenges extend to crossed-hand passages that reflect the virtuosic "Scarlatti style" hand-crossings that appear in several Bach keyboard

Example 19-4 Sonata 3, BWV 527, movement 3 (Vivace), mm. 108–112: crossed-hand passage.

works after 1725: the "Giga" from Partita I, BWV 825, the Fantasia in C Minor, BWV 906/1, and the Goldberg Variations. Passages such as measures 108–121 in the closing Vivace of Sonata 3, in which the hands cross in contrary motion in the highest treble range against an active pedal line (example 19-4), are exceedingly demanding by any standard, and the bravura element adds further to the music's exuberant nature—for the listener, at least.

We must also note how smoothly Bach blended rising technical challenges with rising musical development within movements. In the opening Vivace of Sonata 6 the initial episode contains a sequence of arpeggiated chords that appears three times during the course of the movement. The first time (mm. 37–52) the arpeggio figuration appears in the right hand; the second time (mm. 85–100) in the left hand; and the third time (mm. 137–152) in both hands in contrary motion, with syncopated pedal punctuation. In this way, Bach combined escalating performance demands with escalating musical complexity.

While the Six Sonatas are patterned after the Italian trio sonata with two independent treble voices and accompanying bass, they also display features of the "Sonate auf Concertenart," the "sonata written in the manner of a concerto" described by Johann Adolph Scheibe. According the Scheibe, sonatas composed this way have the three-movement sequence of a concerto (fast–slow–fast), their upper melodies do not have to be imitative in the opening fast movement, and their bass lines can be harmonic rather than thematic.[23] This description fits the opening movements of Sonatas 2, 5, and 6. Bach adopted other concerto elements in the Sonatas as well, such as tutti and solo themes, declamatory unison melodies, and ritornello forms. He seems to have had great interest in this type of amalgamative concerto-sonata design in Leipzig in the 1730s, to judge from the Gamba Sonata in G Minor, BWV 1029, and the Flute Sonatas in B Minor, E♭ Major, and A Major, BWV 1030–1032, which also show concerto elements.

The Six Sonatas, then, reflect Bach's reawakened interest in solo organ music in Leipzig. At the same time, they show his new expectations for the instrument, both technically and musically. He firmly established a new standard compass for the organ music: C to c''' for the manuals and C to d' for the pedals, carrying the expectations beyond the more restrictive C to c''' and C to c' range of most Saxon and Thuringian organs of the day. One can observe a similar trend in Bach's Leipzig harpsichord music, in which he gradually expanded the range of his pieces beyond the C to c''' standard at both ends of the keyboard.

But musically, too, Bach broadened the concept of organ music with the Six Sonatas, taking it into the realm of the chamber dialogue. Goethe defined the string quartet as a conversation among four intelligent people. One can say the same of Bach's Sonatas, which are a conversation among three equal participants—right hand, left hand, and feet. The melodic material of the Sonatas reflects this conversational approach, with delicate articulations that come close to the nature of speech—highly refined, highly nuanced speech. It is easy to see why this music continues to appeal to listeners today, with its wit, charm, and musical banter.

Performance Issues

A matter often raised with the Six Sonatas is the question of pedal registration: Should the pedal be based on a 16' or 8' pitch? The normal registration for organ trios in Bach's time appears to have been:[24]

Manual I:	8' foundation tone
Manual II:	8' foundation tone
Pedal:	16' foundation tone

Bach indicated this type of disposition in the chorale trio "Wachet auf, ruft uns die Stimme," BWV 645, and it appears in numerous trio settings for two manuals and pedal in Georg Friedrich Kauffmann's *Harmonische Seelen-Lust*, published in Leipzig in the 1730s.

The use of 16' tone in the pedal provides the bass line with clarity and gravity, especially in large spaces, where it produces great carrying power. In Baroque instrumental trios and concertos, the instrument of choice for 16' in the continuo was the violone, the Baroque equivalent of the double bass. As Bach's Hamburg contemporary Johann Mattheson explained:

> [The violone] is in the sixteen-foot range, and it provides an important basic foundation in concerted works, such as choruses and the like, but no less importantly in arias and even in recitatives in the theatre, since its thick sound carries further and can be heard more clearly than the keyboard or other bass instruments.[25]

Acoustically, a 16' instrument or organ stop achieves its penetration and clarity from the diffraction produced by the longer soundwaves it creates. The longer waves have the ability to flow around objects to a greater extent than the shorter soundwaves of 8' instruments, and they therefore arrive at the ear of the listener without substantial loss of intensity.[26] The emergence of the Violone 16' stop in the pedal divisions of Central German organs in the first decades of the eighteenth century coincided with the increased use of the organ as a chamber instrument and the rise of the free organ trio. It would appear to be an ideal pedal register for trios.

Sonatas 2, 5, and 6 are written in the concerto style, and as a consequence it is possible that the 16' tone should be retired in the pedal in the middle movement of these works, for the sake of contrast with the outer movements. This would follow the pattern of Brandenburg Concertos 2 and 5, in which the Violone is silent in the middle movements.

In terms of manual stops, Bach's registration in the opening movement of the Concerto in D Minor after Vivaldi, BWV 596—Principal 8' (or Octava 4' played an octave lower) and Principal 8' and Octava 4'—hints that straightforward unison sounds should be used for outer movements of the Sonatas, rather than combinations with mutation stops and mixtures. This approach is reflected in Kauffmann's registrations for chorale trios for two manuals and pedal, which commonly consist of Principal 8' (top voice), Principal 4' (middle voice, played an octave lower), and Sub-Baß 16' and Octaven-Baß 8' (pedal).[27]

In addition to using 8' Principals in the manuals for trios, Kauffmann advocated the practice of playing the left-hand part an octave lower, on a 4' stop, for ease of performance:

> On this topic [trio playing] I am also of the opinion that although two keyboards are available, one should draw two equal stops—e.g., Principals 8' and 4'—and play the second part on the 4' register an octave lower, if both parts are to sound in the same range. When performed this way, the parts have the same character, whether they are played on one keyboard or two.[28]

Playing the Six Sonatas with the left hand an octave lower, with a 4' registration, makes the performance of the works somewhat easier. This is especially true of crossed-hand passages, such as that in the last movement of Sonata 3.

Postscript

Unlike many of Bach's works, the Six Sonatas did not fall into eclipse after the composer's death in 1750. Written in a fashionable style, they matched the Enlightenment aesthetic of a younger generation of composers. As a consequence, they enjoyed wide distribution in Germany, Austria, and England in the second half of the eighteenth century. The Sonatas were strongly championed by Bach's sons Wilhelm Friedemann and Carl Philipp Emanuel and his student Johann Christian Kittel. All three provided manuscript copies to organ students, music collectors, and devotees. C.P.E. Bach seems to have been particularly fond of the works, sending a copy to Forkel together with a note emphasizing their timeless nature:

> The 6 Clavier Trios, which you will find among the enclosed, are among the best works of my late father. They still sound very good and give me great pleasure, even though they are over 50 years old. There are several *Adagii* within that one could not set today in a more singable manner.[29]

C.P.E. later used the Sonatas as an example of his father's best organ writing. In a spirited response to the claim of the English chronicler Charles Burney that Handel was a better organ composer than J. S. Bach, C.P.E. asked a friend: "Did Handel ever write trios for 2 manuals and pedal?!"[30] Shortly thereafter he expanded this line of thought in a published defense of his father:

> In addition to the chorale settings and variations J.S. wrote, and the preludes to them . . . various trios for the organ have become known, particularly six for two manuals and pedal that are written in such *galant* style that they still sound very good, and never grow old, but on the contrary will outlive all revolutions of fashion in music. All in all, no one has written so much beautiful music for the organ as J. S. Bach.[31]

These remarks were echoed in comments by Johann Friedrich Köhler, who studied theology at the University in Leipzig before taking up an appointment as minister at the St. Nicholas Church in Taucha. To Köhler, who is known for his description of Bach's disputes with Rector Johann August Ernesti in the 1730s, the Six Sonatas were "so beautiful, so new, and so richly inventive" that they would "never become old and rather outlive all changes in musical style."[32]

Also speaking to the broad appeal of the Six Sonatas was their performance in the influential music salons of Sara Levy in Berlin and Baron Gottfried van Swieten in Vienna in the 1780s and 1790s. The Berlin listeners heard all six works in a transcription for two cembalos.[33] The Vienna auditors were treated to three movements from Sonatas 2 and 3 arranged for string trio (violin, viola, and cello) by Mozart, who took part in van Swieten's Sunday afternoon musicales on a regular basis.[34] Thus the Sonatas were performed and studied in an un-broken chain extending from J. S. Bach through Wilhelm Friedemann Bach, Carl Philipp Emanuel Bach, and Mozart to the Bach Revival of the 1820s.

And the Sonatas remained *en vogue* in the nineteenth century. In London Samuel Wesley, a leader of the British Bach Revival between 1800 and 1835, expressed awe over the technical demands of the works. Obbligato pedal-playing was still uncommon in England at the time, and Wesley was greatly impressed with Bach's equal treatment of feet and hands:

> Mr. Horn has a vast quantity of [Bach's] Compositions that have never seen the light; among the rest, Stupendous Trios for the Organ, which he used to play thus: his right hand played the first part on the Top Row of the Clavier; his left the second part on the second Row, and he played the Bass *wholly* upon the Pedals. There are Allegro Movements among them, and occasionally very brisk notes in the Bass Part, whence it appears that he was alike dexterous both with hands and feet.[35]

With the publication of the Six Sonatas in the Peters Edition in 1844 and the Bach Gesamtausgabe in 1867, the works became part of the standard organ rep-ertory, rising above passing fashions to achieve universal acceptance—just as Köhler and C.P.E. Bach predicted they would.

Notes

1. Forkel 1802, 60; translation from NBR, 471–472.
2. The Sonatas are found in fascicle 1 of *P 271*.
3. No. 122 in NBA IX/1 (Wisso Weiss and Yoshitake Kobayashi, eds., 1985).
4. Dadelsen 1958, 104.
5. The characteristics of the manuscript are discussed in Butt 1988.
6. The list here is limited to the variants that can be confirmed. It does not include the hypothetical variants proposed by Hans Klotz, in Klotz 1950, 196, and Dietrich Kilian, in NBA IV/7, KB (Dietrich Kilian, ed.,1988), 66–88.
7. The three stages of the Trio in D Minor can be followed in the Breitkopf Edition, vol. 5, and the Leupold Edition, vol. 7. Both reprint all three versions of the movement.
8. Much like the trio arrangement of "Nun komm, der Heiden Heiland," BWV 660a (see chapter 10).
9. Dirksen 2003, 23.
10. Hans Epstein, "Grundzüge in J. S. Bachs Sonatenschaffen," BJ 55 (1969), 23.
11. Walter Emery, in Emery 1957, book IV, 102 (BWV 528/2a); Dietrich Kilian, in NBA IV/7, KB, 86 (BWV 529/2a); or Peter Williams, in Williams 2003, 24 (BWV 528/2a), for instance.
12. Dirksen 2003.
13. Berlin State Library, *P 1096*; and Leipzig Town Library, *Peters Ms. 1*, fascicle 5.

14. Leipzig Town Library, *Peters Ms. 1*, fascicle 4.

15. NBA IV/7, KB, 19–20.

16. The complete list of additions to *P 272* and the subsequent changes to *P 271* not conveyed in *P 272* are presented in the Leupold Edition, vol. 7, Editorial Report. They are summarized only in the NBA IV/7, KB.

17. That is, alla breve meter notated as black-note ¢ with 16th-note motion, implying a fast, well-articulated performance.

18. Kirnberger 1771–79, vol. 2, pt. I, 130.

19. The aria "Wenn kömmst du, mein Heil?," from Cantata 140, *Wachet auf, ruft uns die Stimme* (1731) or the *Alla siciliana* middle movement of the Concerto in D Minor for Three Harpsichords, Strings, and Continuo, BWV 1063 (c. 1730), for example.

20. Christoph Wolff, "Die Orchesterwerke J.S. Bachs: Grundsätzliche Erwägungen zur Repertoire, Überlieferung und Chronologie," in *Bachs Orchesterwerke*, Martin Geck, ed. (Witten: Klangfarben Musikverlag, 1997), 23.

21. Butt 1990, 179.

22. NBR, no. 357a.

23. Scheibe 1745, 675–683. See Jeanne R. Swack, "On the Origins of the *Sonate auf Concertenart*," *Journal of the American Musicological Society* 46 (1993), 369–414.

24. See Whiteley 2016 and Breig, 1999, 682–688.

25. Mattheson 1713, 285–286.

26. I am indebted to violonist David Chapman for this point.

27. In the trio settings "Jesus Christus unser Heiland" and "Wo Gott zum Haus nicht gibt sein Günst," from *Harmonishce Seelen-Lust*, for example.

28. Georg Friedrich Kauffmann, *Harmonische Seelen-Lust* (Leipzig: Boetius, 1733 and 1736), preface. See also the discussion of 4' left-hand registration in the Leupold Edition, vol. 7, xxvi–xxvii.

29. BDok III, no. 795. Hans-Joachim Schulze, editor of BDok III, suggests that the reference is to the Six Sonatas for Violin and Harpsichord, BWV 1014–1019. But the context, title of the works in question ("Claviertrio"), and stylistic description point to the organ sonatas.

30. Letter to J. J. Eschenburg of January 21, 1786. BDok III, no. 908.

31. NBR, no. 396.

32. BDok III, no. 820.

33. Preserved in a manuscript owned by Sara Levy's sister, Fanny von Arnstein, and now located in the Austrian National Library, *Mus.Hs. 5008*. The arrangements are described in Rebecca Cypess, "Duets in the Collection of Sara Levy," in *Sara Levy's World: Gender, Judaism, and the Bach Tradition in Enlightenment Berlin*, Rebecca Cypess and Nancy Sinkoff, eds. (Rochester, NY: University of Rochester Press, 2018), 186–187.

34. The movements are listed as K 404a in the Köchel Catalog. On the dating and authorship of the trio arrangements, see Christoph Wolff, "Mozart 1782, Fanny Arnstein und viermal Bach," *Mozart-Jahrbuch* 10 (2009), 147–148.

35. NBR, 496.

20

Free Works: Prelude-and-Fugue Pairs

The Six Sonatas were not the only beneficiary of Bach's concentrated involvement with cantata-writing during his initial years in Leipzig. The free organ works, too, profited from the great production of sacred vocal music, which resulted in new approaches to form and idiom that soon surfaced in a remarkable series of preludes and fugues.

An Unorthodox Transcription

It is best to begin, perhaps, with the **Prelude and Fugue in D Minor ("Fiddle"),** **BWV 539,** an anomalous piece that may have been the first of the Leipzig free organ works. The Fugue is derived from the second movement of Sonata 1 in G Minor, BWV 1001, from the Six Sonatas and Partitas for Unaccompanied Violin. Bach seems to have been especially fond of the music from this collection of solo violin music, transcribing the Fuga of Sonata 1 for lute (BWV 1000) as well as organ (BWV 539/2) and expanding the Preludio of Partita 3 in E Major into a cantata sinfonia for obbligato organ, first with accompanying strings, oboes, and continuo (Cantata 120a/4 of 1729) and then with additional trumpets and timpani (Cantata 29/1 of 1731; see chapter 18).

The Unaccompanied Sonatas and Partitas are dated 1720 in Bach's autograph manuscript, and the organ transcription of the G-Minor Fuga, transposed to D minor to better suit the keyboard compass of the organ, appears to stem from a few years after that. Dietrich Kilian noted that the text of the organ transcription reflects variants appearing in a copy of the violin music made by Anna Magdalena Bach around 1725,[1] and it is possible that the organ arrangement stems from 1725–1730 or so, the period when Bach focused on a number of trio transcriptions. Such a chronology must remain speculative, however, since the only eighteenth-century copies of the Prelude and Fugue in D Minor date from after Bach's death and contain the Fugue only.[2]

The Prelude does not appear in the source materials until 1802, when it surfaces in Johann Nicolaus Forkel's Bach biography. There it is listed in the inventory of Bach's organ works, paired with the Fugue transcription.[3] The two pieces next appear together in an anonymous copy of c. 1820–1839 and a manuscript owned by Mendelssohn from the same period.[4] While scholars have

J. S. BACH. George B. Stauffer, Oxford University Press. © Oxford University Press 2024.
DOI: 10.1093/oso/9780195108026.003.0021

generally accepted the Prelude as authentic, they have questioned whether it was paired with the Fugue by Bach and whether it is truly an organ work, rather than an appropriated harpsichord or clavichord piece.

Looking first at the Prelude: it is written in *style brisé*, the stroked style associated with lute and harpsichord music. Bach used *style brisé* now and then in organ works such as the Orgel-Büchlein chorale "Nun komm der Heiden Heiland, BWV 599, the Partita "Christ, der du bist der helle Tag," BWV 766 (variation 7), and the Fugue in C Major, BWV 547/2 (mm. 47–48). Thus the Prelude's *style brisé* idiom does not preclude it from being an organ piece. Nor does its *manualiter* setting mean that Bach would not have paired it with a *pedaliter* fugue: Manual and pedal movements sit comfortably side by side in the Partita "Sei gegrüßet, Jesu gütig," BWV 768, the Pastorella in F Major, BWV 590, and other organ works.

In terms of structure, the Prelude is a da capo form, with the main thematic material appearing in the tonic at the beginning and end:

Mm. 1–6	Main theme in the tonic, ending on v
Mm. 7–15	Main theme in the dominant, parts exchanged, ending on V/v
Mm. 15–24	Sequence 1, ending with a full cadence in v
Mm. 24–33	Sequence 2, ending on V/i
Mm. 34–43	Main theme in the tonic, ending with a full cadence in I
	(= mm. 1–6 and 22–24)

This results in a straightforward, balanced design that forms a pleasing contrast with the complex, through-composed Fugue. The exchange of parts in the repeat of the main theme (mm. 7–15) and the note-for-note return of the main theme in the tonic at the end are characteristic of Bach's Leipzig style.

These factors suggest that the Prelude is an organ piece, and that its pairing with the D-Minor Fugue by Forkel may reflect a tradition that stemmed from Bach himself.[5] Another possibility is that the Prelude was composed and added to the Fugue by Carl Philipp Emanuel Bach, who wrote a similarly short, tranquil *Einleitung* for the Credo portion of his father's B-Minor Mass when he performed it for a benefit concert in Hamburg in 1786.[6] Authentic or not, the Prelude works well as a pacific preface to the animated Fugue.

Now to the Fugue: there have been questions about its pedigree, too. Its unconventional part-writing and unusual figuration have troubled a number of writers,[7] and Ulrich Siegele has even gone so far as to dismiss it as a "school exercise" by an anonymous student.[8] The violin fugue itself is unorthodox, with expositions that feature subdominant rather than dominant answers to the subject in the first exposition and sequential, circle-of-fifth entries of the subject in the second, third, and fourth expositions. The episodes, too, are unusual, since they contain segments of unique, discontinuous material (mm. 35–42, 64–68, etc.).[9] The transcription mirrors these unusual features, and as a result it has a structure and idiom quite unlike that of any other organ fugue.

The organ transcription is two measures longer than the violin model and contains additional entries of the subject in the first three expositions:

	Violin fugue		Organ transcription	
	Mm.	Subject entries	Mm.	Subject entries
Exposition 1	1–5	i iv iv i	1–6	i iv iv i i
Episode	5–14	cadencing in i	6–15	cadencing in i
Exposition 2	14–18	i iv VII III	15–19	i iv VII I III
Episode	18–24	cadencing in v	19–25	cadencing on v
Exposition 3	24–30	i iv VII	25–31	i iv VII v
Episode	30–55	cadencing in iv	31–57	cadencing in iv
Exposition 4	55–58	VII III III	57–60	VII III III
Episode	58–82	cadencing in III	60–84	cadencing in i
Exposition 5	82–87	i (extended)	84–89	i (extended)
Close	87–94	close in i	89–96	close in i

It is difficult to imagine anyone other than Bach making the changes that occurred in the process of transcribing the violin fugue. The opening exposition, for instance, is artfully reimagined: The third entry of the subject is now accompanied by new counterpoint derived from the subject; the fourth entry of the subject now appears an octave higher than its original range; a fifth entry has been added in the bass, establishing the five–part texture that is maintained in the tutti sections of the arrangement; and a new quasi–entry in the soprano leads to the first episode. In the second exposition a new entry of the subject in tonic major has been inserted (m. 17), producing a stretto with the previous entry.

The insertion of new obbligato voices into the D–Minor Fugue is similar to the production of new obbligato voices in the Prelude in G Major, BWV 541/1, when Bach revised the Weimar version of the work in Leipzig (see chapter 17). In addition, melodic lines in the violin Fuga requiring no change have been newly animated in the organ Fugue through lively diminutions, bold syncopations, emphatic upbeat chords, and thematic counterpoint (example 20–1).

The episodic material has also been rewritten with great invention, transforming violin lines into figurations that are effective on the organ (mm. 44–49, 60–63, and 71–76). Measures 44–49 of the transcription are especially telling: in the violin version, the harmonic movement is intensified by accelerating

Example 20-1 (a) Sonata 1 in G Minor for Unaccompanied Violin, BWV 1001, Fuga, mm. 76–78 (transposed to D minor for comparison), and (b) Fugue in D Minor, BWV 539/2, mm. 78–80.

the figural pattern of the arpeggiated 16th notes, from a change every measure (mm. 44–46) to a change every half measure (m. 47) to a change every quarter note (m. 48).[10] In the organ transcription, both the note–motion and the texture of the accompaniment increase accordingly, reinforcing the harmonic crescendo that leads to the dramatic pedal-point of measure 49. The skillful realization of the hidden harmonies of the solo violin fugue in the organ transcription matches Johann Friedrich Agricola's description of Bach playing the Unaccompanied Sonatas and Partitas on the keyboard:

> Their composer often played them on the clavichord, adding as much in the nature of harmony as he found necessary. In so doing, he recognized the necessity of a sounding harmony, such as in a composition of this sort he could not fully achieve.[11]

As with the cantata sinfonias derived from the Preludio of Partita 3 for solo violin, Bach produced something quite different from a conventional fugue when he transcribed the Fuga from Violin Sonata 1 for the organ. Walter Blankenberg once referred to Bach's transformation of secular cantatas into sacred works as "awakening the sleeping potential" of the original music.[12] We might say that something similar has happened here. In the organ transcription, Bach has awakened the sleeping potential of the violin fugue's part-writing, creating a highly unusual, fleshed-out keyboard arrangement that grants the music new life in a new context.

Four Monumental Works

Of an entirely different nature are four large, highly refined preludes and fugues that are bound together by their preludes' similar structures:

Prelude and Fugue in B Minor, BWV 544
Prelude and Fugue in E Minor ("Wedge"), BWV 548
Prelude and Fugue in C Minor, BWV 546
Prelude and Fugue in E♭ Minor ("St. Anne"), BWV 552

Although there is no evidence that Bach ever gathered the four pieces into a collection,[13] we can see him using the same design in each of the preludes, which he then paired with strikingly different fugues.

Spitta termed the Prelude and Fugue in E Minor a "two-movement symphony,"[14] and this description is appropriate for all four compositions. They are of symphonic proportions (the E-Minor Prelude and Fugue runs to 368 measures) and foreshadow the orchestral organ works of Max Reger, César Franck, Charles-Marie Widor, and Louis Vierne written a century-and-a-half later. It was surely not by chance that Bach wrote this series of monumental preludes and fugues as the new aesthetic principles of the Central German organ were taking hold. The emphasis on "gravity" achieved through an abundance of 16' and 8' stops, pedal divisions geared to simpler bass lines, and tuning systems that could accommodate modulations to very distant keys parallels perfectly the new idiom and breadth of the four works. Hermann Keller aptly remarked that the sequences in the E-Minor Prelude seem to "raise and lower the musical structure like the hull of an enormous ship pounding through the waves of the sea."[15]

The four works can be assigned to the period c. 1727–1739. The Prelude and Fugue in B Minor is passed down in a fair-copy autograph dating from 1727–1732,[16] and the Prelude and Fugue in E Minor is transmitted in a manuscript from the same time, jointly copied by Bach and Johann Peter Kellner.[17] The original materials for the Prelude and Fugue in C Minor do not survive; the earliest copy is a manuscript in Kellner's hand that most probably stems from the 1730s.[18] And the Prelude and Fugue in E♭ Major can be dated 1739 on the basis of its appearance in the original print of Clavier-Übung III, issued that year.

The four preludes are based on a similar concerto-derived design. They begin with a lengthy ritornello in the tonic, followed by a series of increasingly complex episodes that are separated by segments of ritornello material in related keys. They end with the return of the ritornello in the tonic, either in its entirety (Preludes in C Minor and E♭ Major) or in an abbreviated form (Preludes in B Minor and E Minor). The opening ritornellos are much more substantial than those in the Weimar concerto-derived preludes, ranging in length from 16 measures (Prelude in B Minor) to 32 measures (Prelude in E♭ Major). In addition, the ritornellos are composed of the traditional three segments—introduction, extension, and conclusion—and the segments contain distinctive but closely related melodic material. In the middle of the work, the ritornellos appear either in full or fragmentary form.

Bach's structural model for these preludes appears to have been the opening choruses of his Leipzig cantatas, which commonly begin with a lengthy instrumental ritornello that subsequently appears in full or partial form between phrases of the chorale. This can be seen in the opening chorus of Cantata 140, *Wachet auf, ruft uns die Stimme*, for instance, a work written in 1731 to fill a gap in the chorale-cantata cycle of 1724–1725. The ritornello is composed of the usual Vivaldian segments: introduction (r1), extension (r2), and conclusion (r3):[19]

Mm.	Thematic material	Harmonic station
1–16	Ritornello (complete): r1 (mm. 1–4), r2 (mm. 5–8), r3 (mm. 9–16)	I–I
17–53	Chorale phrases 1–3 (Stollen)	
53–68	Ritornello (complete): r1, r2, r3	I–I
69–105	Chorale phrases 1–3 (repeat of the Stollen)	
105–116	Ritornello (abbreviated): r2, r3	I→V
116–189	Chorale phrases 4–9 (Abgesang), with fragments of the ritornello	
189–205	Ritornello (complete): r1, r2, r3	I–I

The most striking aspects of this form are: (1) the ritornello's substantial length, (2) its limited number of appearances (generally no more than four—fewer than in a typical Vivaldi string concerto), and (3) the tendency, especially apparent in Bach's works from the 1730s and 1740s, to create symmetrical ritornello structures: 8 [4 + 4] + 8 measures in the *Wachet auf* chorus; 12 + 12 measures in the C-Minor Prelude; and 16 + 16 measures in the E♭-Major Prelude. In such music, Bach moved away from the atomistic *Fortspinnung* of the Baroque period and toward the balanced periodic phrases of the Classical era.

The **Prelude and Fugue in B Minor, BWV 544,** appears to be the first work in the series. The somber character of the Prelude is similar to that of the opening choruses of the St. John and St. Matthew Passions and Cantata 198 ("Trauer-Ode"), which Bach recycled as the first movement of the St. Mark Passion. Bach labeled the opening chorus of Cantata 198 "Tombeau de S.M. la Reine de Pologne" (Lament for Her Majesty the Queen of Poland), and the B-Minor Prelude has the character of a tombeau, or lament, as well.[20] The expressive appoggiaturas and suspensions, the chromatic harmonies and sigh motives, the inexorable piling up of dissonant chords followed by deceptive cadences, and the imitative tension in the episodic segments create an atmosphere of anguish and mourning. The idiom, with its continuous 32nd-note figuration, resembles that of a recitative, with the implied expressivity that goes with a free vocal line. What better way for Bach to break with the Vivaldi-oriented motor rhythms of the Weimar preludes? The Hamburg theorist Johann Mattheson described the key of B minor as "seldom-used" and "bizarre, morose, and melancholy."[21] That is the tone here: elegiac.

The Prelude's structure is quite similar to that of the Cantata 140 chorus:

Mm.	Thematic material	Harmonic station
1–17	Ritornello (complete): r1 (mm. 1–7), r2 (mm. 7–13), r3 (mm. 14–17)	i
17–27	Episode: e, plus bridge (mm. 23–26)	
27–43	Ritornello (complete): r1, r2', r3	v
43–50	Episode: e (parts exchanged)	
50–73	Ritornello (segments reordered): 2", r1, r2'''	III, iv
73–78	Episode: e (parts in contrary motion)	
78–85	Ritornello (abbreviated): r2', r3	i

As the Prelude unfolds, both the ritornello and episode material are subjected to constant—and often astonishing—development and reinterpretation. For instance, the theme of the imitative episodes is derived from three motivic fragments appearing in the ritornello: the upward scale of measures 8 and 10, the syncopated pedal octave of measure 4, and the soprano flourish of measure 16 (example 20-2). In the initial episode, the imitative entries of this theme appear in the order alto-soprano-bass-soprano. In the second episode, the order changes: bass-alto-soprano-bass. In the third episode, the initial order of the entries is restored, but the voices now move in contrary motion: alto-soprano (inverted)-bass-soprano (inverted). Such transformations and exchanges take place throughout the Prelude.

The Fugue is the perfect complement to the Prelude. The serene subject, consisting of stepwise-moving 8th notes only, forms an immediate contrast with the animated leaping figures of the Prelude. It is nevertheless foreshadowed in the Prelude, in the soprano flourish of the penultimate measure (m. 16) of the ritornello (example 20-2, a). The Fugue contains no augmentation, diminution, inversion, or stretto. Rather, Bach focused solely on the subject, the three countersubjects that accompany it, and the great variety that can be produced by the manipulation of these themes. The subject itself appears in three guises: a tonally closed form, a modulating form that leads to circle-of-fifths sequences,

Example 20-2 Prelude in B Minor, BWV 544/1: (a) motives in the initial ritornello, and (b) imitative theme of the episodes.

and an elongated, stepwise form. The three countersubjects contrast with the subject and with each other: The first contains angular leaps, the second nonstop 16th notes, and the third an emphatic upbeat *suspirans* motive (example 20-3).

The countersubjects are introduced one at a time in the Fugue's three sections, and in the climatic third section, countersubjects 1 and 3 are combined with the subject in triple counterpoint, as can be seen from the following summary:

Mm.		Key of fugue subject entries
A (*pedaliter*)		
1–11	Subject with countersubject 1	i v i v
12–28	Short episodes plus subject in modulatory form	i iv III VII v
B (*manualiter*)		
28–58	Subject in modulatory form with countersubject 2 and free counterpoint, alternating with short, playful episodes (mm. 32–34, 37–40, 50–53)	v i iv II v III
C (*pedaliter*)		
59–75	Subject with countersubjects 1 and 3.	i v ii iv
76–78	Subject in step-wise form (derived from mm. 32–34)	III
79–88	Subject in modulatory form in pedal, creating circle-of-fifths progression to final statement in the tonic	v i iv i

This results in a tripartite structure steeped in the ongoing manipulation and embroidering of the fugue subject. Most episodes are no more than two or three measures long; the longest is eight measures, leading up to the beginning of the C section. The emphatic appearance and reappearance of the subject produces

Example 20-3 Fugue in B Minor, BWV 544/2: the three forms of the subject and three countersubjects.

Fugue subject:

Normal form

Modulating form

Step-wise form

Fugue countersubjects:

Countersubject 1

Countersubject 2

Countersubject 3

great intensity, even in the lighter middle section. This intensity builds to the final climactic statement of the subject, with the subject and third countersubject appearing in the outermost voices (m. 85).

Bach's evident pride in the Prelude and Fugue in B Minor can be sensed in the elegant calligraphy of his fair-copy autograph (plate 20-1), which Anna Magdalena Bach presented to her youngest surviving son, Johann Christian, after her husband's death.[22] Johann Christian had received "three claviers with a set of pedals" from his father at an earlier point,[23] and he may have been the best organist among the Bach sons next to Wilhelm Friedemann.

The **Prelude and Fugue in E Minor ("Wedge"), BWV 548,** can be viewed as the companion piece to the Prelude and Fugue in B Minor, since the Prelude is constructed along the same lines. It also opens similarly with an expressive soprano melody consisting of upward leaps (each an *exclamatio*, or exclamation, in Baroque terminology), turning figures, and upward-resolving appoggiaturas, accompanied by emphatic upbeat chords and pedal octaves. As Peter Williams described it: "the lines are no longer traditional like BWV 545

Plate 20-1 Prelude and Fugue in B Minor, BWV 544, first page of Bach's fair-copy autograph.

Morgan Library & Museum, New York

[Prelude and Fugue in C Major] or motivically single-minded like BWV 547 [Prelude and Fugue in C Major, "9/8"] but much more original, new to the corpus of organ music."[24]

From these five gestures—three melodic, two accompanimental—plus a series of descending scales, Bach forged a highly unified, organic ritornello form of 137 measures. While the general structure is similar to that of the B-Minor Prelude, the episodes are nonfugal and much more complex, consisting of four different segments of material that evolve naturally from the opening ritornello and from each other. In addition, the opening melody returns in a modulatory form (mm. 59–60, 69–75) in the episodes:

Mm.	Thematic material	Harmonic station
1–19	Ritornello (complete): r1, r2, r3, r4	i
19–33	Episode: e1, e2, e3	
33–51	Ritornello (complete): r1, r2, r3, r4	v
51–81	Episode: e4, e1, r1', e4, e1, r1', e3	
81–90	Ritornello (abbreviated): r1, r1	III, iv
90–125	Episode: e4, e2, e3, e1, e1, e4, e1	
125–137	Ritornello (abbreviated): r3, r4	i

Key:

e1 (mm. 19–23) = based on the turn, leap, and pedal figure (mm. 5–6) of the ritornello

e2 (mm. 24–26) = based on the turn, manual 16th-note figure (m. 5), and up-beat chords of the ritornello

e3 (mm. 27–32) = based on the turn, appoggiatura, and pedal figure (m. 5) of the ritornello

e4 (mm. 51–54) = based on the manual figure (m. 14) and appoggiatura semi-tone of the ritornello

Part-exchange, inversion, and melodic variation appear everywhere. In the *manualiter* episodic segment (e4), for instance, we can observe the same type of parts-manipulation that occurs in the episodes of the B-Minor Prelude. On its first appearance (mm. 51–54), the ascending dotted figures appear in the soprano and tenor, with the undulating minor second (derived from the appoggiatura of the ritornello) in the alto (example 20-4, a). On its second appearance (mm. 61–64), the whole has been transposed down a fifth to the tonic, and the part assignments remain the same. But the soprano has been moved up a fourth, to create a new, more capacious texture (example 20-4, b). On the third appearance (mm. 90–93), the original texture returns, but the three figures have been inverted—making the

Example 20-4 Prelude in E Minor, BWV 548/1: four forms of the *manualiter* episodic segment (a–d) and the ritornello motive from which the segment was derived ("x" in e).

dotted figure's derivation from the opening ritornello evident for the first time (example 20-4, "x" in c and e)—and the dotted figure is presented in imitation, at the octave (example 20-4, c). And on the fourth appearance (mm. 115–120), the dotted figure appears in both upright and in contrary motion, against a new, more highly animated accompaniment (example 20-4, d). This virtuosic manipulation of the material, with parts being transposed, treated imitatively, and inverted, is typical of the entire Prelude: its various segments are subjected to almost obsessive variation. Walter Frisch has characterized Brahms's compositional style as continuous "developing variation."[25] We find a similar procedure in Bach's Preludes in B Minor and E Minor, composed a century and a quarter earlier.

Example 20-5 Fugue in E Minor, BWV 548/2: fugue subject (a) with the descending chromatic tetrachord (b) and the ascending chromatic fifth (c) that it forms.

The "Wedge" Fugue is so named because of its splaying subject, ingeniously derived from a descending, chromatic tetrachord—the Italian-lament bass—combined simultaneously with an ascending, chromatic fifth (example 20-5). Bach used the descending tetrachord in its traditional ground-bass form in many works, from the "Lamento" of the Capriccio on the Departure of a Dearly Beloved Brother, BWV 992, to the opening chorus of Cantata 78, *Jesu, der du meine Seele*, to the "Crucifixus" of the B-Minor Mass. In those works, it is used expressively to portray the *affect* of mourning. (The Capriccio movement is labeled "Adagiosissimo [*sic*], a universal lamenting of the friends.") In the Wedge Fugue, the tetrachord is transformed through a steady stream of 8th notes into an animated, toccata-like theme. The alla breve meter makes the 8th notes equivalent to the 16th notes of the Prelude, thus uniting prelude and fugue with a uniform pulse.

The E-Minor Fugue is Bach's longest and most virtuosic fugue. It is also his only fugue in which the subject appears on all seven degrees of the scale, thus breaking the conventional restriction of using only the six most closely related keys in a single movement. Its gigantic structure can be diagrammed as follows:

	Mm.	Material	Subject entries
A	1–60	Exposition	i v i v i i v i
B	60–68	Episode: e1	
	69–71	Subject (abridged)	i
	72–80	Episode: e1	
	81–83	Subject (abridged)	v
	84–88	Episode: e2	
	89–93	Subject	VII
	93–107	Episode: e2, e3	
	108–112	Subject	III
	112–136	Episode: e2, e3, e4, e1, e4, e1, e4	

	137–141	Subject	ii
	141–155	Episode: e3'	
	156–160	Subject	VI
	160–176	Episode: e2, e4'	
A'	172–231	Exposition (da capo)	i vi vi i vi

Key:

  e1 (mm. 60–68) = based on an upbeat semitone

  e2 (mm. 84–88) = based on the scales of m. 59

  e3 (mm. 98, 100, 102) = based on exposition countersubject

  e4 (mm 120–123) = a semitone converted into a *suspirans* figure

The Fugue combines a wide variety of procedures, structures, and styles: fugue procedure, aria form (A B A da capo), concerto form (with the fugue subject serving as the ritornello), toccata style, and North German praeludium style (e4). In some cases, these elements bump against one another in ingenious ways, as in the remarkable pivot of measures 172–176, which serves both as a close to the final episode of the ritornello form and the beginning of the repeat of the A section of the da capo form. Bach's model here was the opening choruses of the Leipzig chorale cantatas, once again, where the last phrase of the chorale, sung by the chorus, sometimes overlaps with the beginning of the final return of the instrumental ritornello.[26]

The symmetry of the da capo form clashes with the through-composed nature of fugue procedure. Yet the idea of a da capo fugue was something that clearly attracted Bach's interest in his late years, for it appears not only in the "Wedge" Fugue but also in the Duetto in F Major, BWV 803, from Clavier-Übung III and the fugues of the Fantasia and Fugue in C Minor, BWV 537, and the Prelude, Fugue, and Allegro in E♭ Major for Lute or Harpsichord, BWV 998. In fugue writing, too, Bach's constant quest to find new approaches to old genres led him into the realm of Classical style, with its balanced phrases and structures. And the great emphasis on semitone figuration in both the Prelude and Fugue serves to unite the two movements motivically.

Of special relevance for the Wedge Fugue are Bach's comments on maintaining variety in fugue composition, as recorded by his champion Friedrich Wilhelm Marpurg from a conversation that took place in Leipzig:

I myself once heard him . . . pronounce the works of an old and hardworking contrapuntist dry and wooden, and certain fugues by a more modern and no less great contrapuntist—that is in the form in which they are arranged for clavier—pedantic; the first because the composer stuck continuously to his principal subject, without any change; and the second because, at least in the

Example 20-6 Fugue in E Minor, BWV 548/2: three forms of the fourth episodic segment.

fugues under discussion, he had not shown enough fire to reanimate the theme by interludes.[27]

In the E-Minor Fugue, Bach demonstrated how to sustain interest by not sticking continuously to the subject. At the same time, he also created interludes that not only reanimate the subject but take on a life of their own. In the three versions of the fourth episodic segment (e4) of the Fugue, for instance, he has systematically moved the semitone motive upward, from the tenor (mm. 120–123) to the alto (mm. 126–129) to the soprano (mm. 132–135; example 20-6). This closely resembles the methodical manipulation of the dotted figure in the Prelude or the arpeggiated figure in the episodes of the first movement of Sonata 6 in G Major, BWV 530 (see chapter 19).

If the Prelude and Fugue in B Minor can be compared with the B-minor opening chorus of Cantata 198, then the Prelude and Fugue in E Minor can be compared to the E-minor opening chorus of the St. Matthew Passion, as Werner Breig has proposed.[28] The deeply expressive idiom and the immense sweep are much the same

The Prelude and Fugue in C Minor and the Prelude and Fugue in E♭ Major represent a second stage in the evolution of the four monumental preludes and fugues. They appear to have been written at a somewhat later date than the E Minor and B Minor works, and their preludes display still longer ritornellos, more strongly developmental episodes, and more markedly symmetrical designs. In addition, both preludes explore new tonal areas—D♭ major and G♭ major in the Prelude in C Minor and E♭ minor and B♭ minor in the Prelude in

E♭ Major—that were facilitated by the well-tempered tunings introduced in the progressive Central German organ.

The first work, the **Prelude and Fugue in C Minor, BWV 546,** has been viewed since the time of Spitta as a mismatched pair—a superb prelude paired with a humdrum fugue.[29] As we noted in chapter 12, the Fugue dates from Weimar and was originally paired with the Fantasia in C Minor, BWV 562/1a. In Leipzig Bach removed it from the Fantasia and paired it instead with the newly composed C-Minor Prelude. We find similar marriages of convenience among the prelude-fugue pairs of the second volume of the Well-Tempered Clavier, compiled around 1740.[30]

The majestic Prelude is a creation on the same high plane as the *pedaliter* settings of Clavier-Übung III. It has an almost perfectly balanced structure: the 24-measure ritornello frames sections of 24, 48, and 24 measures, to create a strikingly symmetrical plan:

Length	Mm.	Material	Segment	Harmonic station
24 mm.	1–25	Ritornello (complete	r1, r2, r3	i
24 mm.	25–49	Episode	e	
48 mm.	49–53	Ritornello (abbreviated)	r1	v
	53–70	Episode	e	
	70–78	Ritornello (abbreviated)	r2	v
	78–85	Episode	e	
	85–97	Ritornello (abbreviated)	r3	iv
24 mm.	97–120	Episode	e	
24 mm.	120–144	Ritornello (complete)	r1, r2, r3	i

The ritornello of the Prelude is itself a work of art, with its three segments springing spontaneously from one another. The initial segment (r1, mm. 1–4) consists of a dialogue-like alternation of three-part chords over a tonic pedal. It is quite like the opening section of the double-chorus motet *Komm, Jesu, Komm,* which features alternating 4-voice choirs, or the opening chorus of Cantata 47, *Wer sich selbst erhöhet, der soll erniedriget werden,* which features a string band alternating with two oboes. In the organ Prelude, two sets of chords in different ranges—one high, the other low—achieve the same double-choir effect. This is followed by the second segment (r2, mm. 5–12) that begins with a *suspiratio,* or sigh motive, picked up from the slurred second in the first segment (m. 2). The second segment ends with triplet figuration over a dominant pedal point; the emphatic chords hark back to those in the first segment. The closing segment (r3, mm. 13–25) begins with a pedal motive derived from the second segment (m. 5). It moves to an ascending 16th-note motive on a Neapolitan sixth chord (D♭

major!) over a subdominant pedal point, and finally concludes with the triplet figures from the second segment.

The natural movement from long note values to short (♩→♪→♫→♪♫→♫♫) creates a compelling accelerando, while the cross-reference of motives binds the three sections into a single, unified whole. Similar writing appears in the pedal setting of "Dies sind die heiligen zehn Gebot," BWV 678, of Clavier-Übung III, in which the ritornello moves smoothly from quarter notes to 8th notes to 16th notes. The elasticity of the figuration in the Prelude in C Minor underscores once again just how far Bach had come from the mechanistic motoric rhythms of the Vivaldi-derived organ preludes of the Weimar years. The ritornello of the C-Minor Prelude is a world apart from those of the D-Minor Toccata ("Dorian"), BWV 538/1, or the Prelude in G Major, BWV 541/1. The new, freer idiom stemmed from Bach's cantata- and motet-writing experience in Leipzig.

The episodes are also distinctive. They display fugal development, with a motive that climbs to a fifth in half notes and then quickly returns to the initial pitch in quarter notes, echoing the acceleration found in the ritornello. The episodic motive appears in parallel thirds in the second and third episodes (mm. 53 and 82) and parallel sixths in the fourth episode (m. 97), creating a mounting sense of tension. All this is bound together by triplet figuration, which emerges naturally from the triplets that appeared in the second and third segments of the opening ritornello. In the middle of the Prelude the ritornello appears only in fragmentary forms, which serve as brief respites from the powerful forward movement of the fugue-like episodic material, which becomes the main point of focus.

We discussed the Fugue in C Minor in Chapter 12, where we noted that it was an ambitious if not fully successful attempt on Bach's part to write a large five-part fugue. Several features make it an appropriate partner for the C-Minor Prelude, despite its shortcomings. First is its alla breve idiom, which seems to have been of particular interest to Bach in the 1730s, as part of his general study of the *stile antico*. The second attractive aspect may have been the Fugue's compound theme, which combines several motives in the same manner as the Prelude's ritornello. And the third element may have been the symmetrical structure of the fugue itself, which complements the symmetrical design of the C-Minor Prelude. Finally, there is the Neapolitan chord at the close (m. 151), which echoes the Neapolitan close of the Prelude's ritornello. Bach must have felt that these advantages outweighed the prospect of writing a new fugue altogether. Like the four Short Mass settings, BWV 233–236, of c. 1740, the Prelude and Fugue in C Minor reflects Bach the pragmatist rather than Bach the uncompromising composer of Clavier-Übung III.

The **Prelude and Fugue in E♭ Major ("St. Anne"), BWV 552,** whose sobriquet comes from the coincidental resemblance of its first fugue subject to William

Croft's hymn tune of the same name, is the last member of this extraordinary series of monumental works. The Prelude and Fugue are printed separately in Clavier-Übung III, where they appear as the first and last pieces, respectively, of the collection. The two were first united in the Peters Edition of 1845 by its editor, Friedrich Conrad Griepenkerl, who stated that he was pairing the two "not arbitrarily, but according to an old tradition imparted to me by Forkel some forty years ago."[31]

The Prelude shows the same type of construction as the previous preludes, but its three main elements—a ritornello and two kinds of episodic material—are now starkly distinguished from one another, and the fugal development of the second episodic segment is even more intense than that of the C-Minor Prelude.

The ritornello is cast in the idiom of a French overture—the perfect curtain-raiser for the Clavier-Übung III collection. The cut-time meter, dotted rhythms, and five-part texture all point to the opening grave portion of an overture. Yet within the Prelude, the segment functions as a ritornello, appearing at the beginning and end in the tonic and in between in the dominant and subdominant. In treating the material this way, Bach achieved a remarkable stylistic synthesis, reconciling in one movement the Italian concerto and French overture, the two archetypal forms that he separated by a tritone (the "devil in music") in Clavier-Übung II of 1735. In addition, the material is balanced in a way that the grave sections of overtures are not: in its full form, the ritornello falls into two equal segments of 16 measures each: the first moves to the dominant, the second returns to the tonic. The Prelude thus carries the principle of symmetry seen in the ritornello of the Prelude in C Minor a step further.

The first episodic segment appears to be something entirely different: a placid echo exchange, also characteristic of French style. But in truth it is derived from the falling scale and appoggiatura of the ritornello. The second episodic segment appears to be something different still: an imitative, animated fugue. Its theme, too, is based on the falling scale and appoggiatura of the ritornello, plus the syncopated rhythm that initially appears in the second half of episode 1 (example 20-7).

While the ritornello returns in abbreviated form (the first highly embellished) in the middle of the prelude and in full form at the end (though beginning, startlingly, in C minor before turning quickly to the "right" key, E♭ major), it is the fugal development that takes place in episode 2 that dominates the piece, just as the episodic fugal development dominated the Prelude in C Minor. Episode 2 first appears as a lengthy three-part *manualiter* segment, touching on C minor and G minor as well as E♭ major and B♭ major. Upon the episode's return at measure 130, the texture is increased to four parts with the addition of the pedal, and the subject touches on expected keys, E♭ major and B♭ major, once again. But beginning in measure 143, the entries become more frequent, with the pedal

Example 20-7 Prelude in E♭ Major, BWV 552/1: ritornello theme with derived episodes.

finally picking up the fugue theme in a virtuosic, modified form (example 20-7). The pedal then drops out, and the music appears to spin out of control harmonically, modulating to B♭ minor, then F minor, and finally C minor, marked by a run to the bottom of the keyboard (m. 169), before coming back to the ritornello. The proceedings of the Prelude can be summarized in the following way:

Mm.	Material	Segment	Harmonic station
1–32	Ritornello	r1 (mm. 1–16), r2 (mm. 17–32)	I
33–50	Episode	e1 (echo motive)	
51–71	Ritornello	r1 (embellished, then extended)	V → vi
71–98	Episode	e2 (3-part *manualiter* fugue; subject entries: vi iii vi I V)	
98–111	Ritornello	r2 (parts exchanged)	IV
112–174	Episode	e1 (transposed to IV)	
		e2 (4-part *pedaliter* fugue; subject entries: I V I V vi V IV)	
		e2 (3-part *manualiter* fugue; subject entries: v ii vi)	
175–205	Ritornello	r1, r2	vi → I

The exotic nature of the excursions to E♭ minor (mm. 123–128) and B♭ minor (mm 161–163) is lost to a certain extent to modern ears when the Prelude is played on an organ tuned in equal temperament. In Bach's time, E♭ minor and B♭ minor were very foreign keys—so much so that Mattheson omitted them completely in his discussion "Musical Tonalities: Their Nature and Effect in

Expressing Musical Affects" in *Das neu-eroffnete Orchestre* of 1713.[32] They were literally off the charts. It would not be surprising if Bach played the Prelude during his Sunday morning performance on the Trost organ of the Castle Church in Altenburg in September 1739, just a month before the release of Clavier-Übung III at the St. Michael's Fair. As we know from the eyewitness account of Bach's Sunday morning performance, the Trost organ was specifically capable of accommodating E♭ minor (see chapter 15).

The tripartite Fugue in E♭ Major is sui generis among Bach's works. While the E♭-Major Prelude represents a synthesis of national styles, the E♭-Major Fugue represents a synthesis of historical styles: it contains three distinct sections patterned after music from three different eras. The first section, in 4/2 meter with a slow-moving subject in white notes, is in sixteenth-century Renaissance vocal style, or *stile antico*. The second, in 6/4 meter time with a conjunct subject in continuous 8th notes, is in seventeenth-century instrumental style. And the third, in 12/8 time with a leaping, animated subject, is in eighteenth-century dance style. Bach combined the first subject with the subjects of the second and third sections but did not combine all three in triple counterpoint.

The E♭-Major Fugue displays even more symmetries than the Wedge Fugue: the first and third sections are *pedaliter*, five-part, and contain 36 measures each. The middle section is *manualiter*, four-part, and contains 45 measures that are divided into two equal portions of 22½ measures each: in the first half, the second subject is presented alone, in its own exposition; in the second half, it is joined by the subject of the first fugue in double counterpoint:

	Length	Mm.	Material	Fugue subject
A	36 mm.	1–37	5-part *pedaliter* fugue	Subject 1
B	22½ mm.	37–59	4-part *manualiter* fugue	Subject 2
	22½ mm.	59–82	4-part *manualiter* fugue	Subject 2 + 1
C	36 mm.	82–117	5-part *pedaliter* fugue	Subject 3 + 1

Bach wrote other double and triple fugues, but in no other work did he change meters with the introduction of each new theme, in the manner of a seventeenth-century canzona or ricercar. In a sense, the metrical progression is a tribute to the music of Frescobaldi and Froberger. And in no other work was Bach as free with the subjects, altering the 4/2-meter first subject metrically to produce syncopated versions in 6/4 and 12/8, and altering the second subject melodically to fit with the first subject (example 20-8). Breig has termed this "thematic metamorphosis,"[33] and it is a far cry from the rigid counterpoint of the permutation fugue of the Passacaglia in C Minor or the chorale canons of the Orgel-Büchlein of the Weimar years. The counterpoint in the "St. Anne" Fugue becomes increasingly free as the music progresses. The second subject is pushed out of shape in

Example 20-8 Fugue in E♭ Major, BWV 552/2: (a) subject 1, (b) subject 2, alone and in combination with subject 1, and (c) subject 3, alone and in combination with subject 1.

the second half of the middle section, and in the third section, only snippets of the third subject appear against the first subject. The entire 12/8 section takes on the effect of a free improvisation on the first and third fugue subjects, rather than a strict fugue. This freedom, too, stems from the more relaxed counterpoint of the Leipzig cantatas, in which Bach seemed to be more concerned with pleasing a congregation than satisfying the rules of Johann Theile or Johann Joseph Fux.

The increase in note motion inherent in the metric progression of 4/2 to 6/4 to 12/8 creates a natural crescendo in the Fugue. This is supplemented by the remarkable climactic effect of the chain of entries of the third subject at measure 111—soprano 2, alto, tenor—leading to the final tonic entry of the first subject in the lowest register of the pedal three measures later. The double turn and trill in contrary motion that Bach added to the final measure in the London copy of the original Clavier-Ubung III[34] seems to underscore his own sense of joy in this remarkable and highly imaginative Fugue.

A number of writers have seen Trinitarian symbolism in the Prelude and Fugue in E♭ Major, in its notation (the three flats of E♭ major, an unusual organ key at the time), in the three themes of the Prelude, and the three sections of the Fugue.[35] There is surely something to this, given the work's strategic placement in Clavier-Übung III, a collection devoted to Luther's Catechism and

Trinitarian doctrine (see chapter 22). But to link specific thematic shapes with specific members of the godhead (Rudolf Steglich saw the descent and diffusion of the Holy Spirit in the theme of episode 2 of the Prelude) probably goes too far. What is most significant musically is that in this extraordinary work, Bach developed both the prelude and the fugue to the point of complete self-sufficiency. The second episode of the Prelude provides it with an imitative component characteristic of a fugue, and the tripartite structure of the Fugue provides it with an episodic component characteristic of a prelude. It is not surprising that the Prelude in E♭ Major and Fugue in E♭ Major appear as independent pieces in the original Clavier-Übung edition, separated from one another by 60 pages of chorale settings.

Ironically, in these two pieces Bach brought the organ prelude and the organ fugue full circle, back to the independent, multi-sectional praeludium of Buxtehude and the North Germans.

Notes

1. NBA IV/5–6, KB (Dietrich Kilian, 1978–79), 354.
2. Berlin State Library, *P 213*, fascicle 4, and *Am.B. 606*, both written between 1760 and 1780 by Carl August Hartung. Dating from Bach digital.
3. Forkel 1802, appendix, figure 16, no. 7.
4. Berlin State Library, *P 517*, and the Bodleian Library of Oxford University, *Ms. Deneke Mendelssohn, c 70*, fascicle 1, a manuscript written by Mendelssohn's sister, Fanny Hensel. Dating from Bach digital.
5. Forkel received much of the information for his biography directly from Bach's sons Wilhelm Friedemann and Carl Philipp Emanuel. The pairing of the Prelude and Fugue could reflect such information.
6. Stauffer 2003, 183–185.
7. See Kilian 1961 or Williams 2003, 72–74, for instance.
8. Ulrich Siegele, *Kompositionsweise und Bearbeitungstechnik in der Instrumentalmusik Johann Sebastian Bachs* (Neuhausen-Stuttgart: Hänssler-Verlag, 1975), 86–87. Siegele termed the transcription "Schulmäßig."
9. See Joel Lester's highly detailed analysis of the solo violin version of the Fugue, in Lester, *Bach's Works for Solo Violin: Style, Structure, Performance* (New York: Oxford, 1999), 56–86.
10. Lester, *Bach's Works for Solo Violin*, 81.
11. NBR, 447.
12. Walter Blankenburg, *Einführung in Bachs h-moll Messe*, 3rd ed. (Kassel: Bärenreiter, 1974), 97–98.
13. Nonetheless, it is noteworthy that six large preludes and fugues, BWV 543–548, are handed down as a group in Berlin manuscripts emanating from the circle of Carl Philipp Emanuel Bach and Johann Philipp Kirnberger after 1750: Berlin State

Library, *Am.B 54*, fascicle 3 (c. 1760–1789), and *Am.B 60*, fascicles 1–6 (after 1754). This grouping is noted in BWV³, 13, as one of the "Original printed and manuscript collections."

14. Spitta 1873–80, vol. 3, 209–210.

15. Keller 1967, 97.

16. New York City, Pierpont Morgan Library, Robert Owen Lehmann Collection, *B1184, P 898*.

17. Berlin State Library, *P 274*, fascicle 2. Bach copied the Prelude and mm. 1–20 of the Fugue; Kellner copied the remainder of the Fugue.

18. Berlin State Library, *P 286*. Dating from Stinson 1990, 25.

19. Cantata 140 was written for the twenty-seventh Sunday after Trinity, which occurred only twice during Bach's tenure in Leipzig: 1731 and 1742.

20. Christoph Wolff, in Wolff 2000, 315–317, has suggested that the Prelude in B Minor may have served as a tuning prelude for Cantata 198 at its performance in St. Paul's Church in 1727. The Chorton pitch of the organ would have made such a pairing unlikely, however, since the B-Minor Prelude would have sounded in C♯ minor. See chapter 17, n. 5.

21. Mattheson 1713, 250–251.

22. NBA IV/5–6, KB, 35. The cover page of the autograph includes the annotation "Christel" in Anna Magdalena's handwriting.

23. NBR, no. 279.

24. Williams 2003, 121.

25. Walter Frisch, *Brahms and the Principle of Developing Variation* (Berkeley: University of California Press, 1984).

26. As in Cantata 113, *Herr Jesu Christ, du höchstes Gut*, of 1724, for instance. In the opening chorus, mm. 78–80 serve simultaneously as the final cadence of the chorale and the return of the opening ritornello.

27. NBR, no. 357a.

28. Breig 1999, 692.

29. Spitta 1873–80, vol. 3, 208.

30. An independent Fughetta in D Minor, BWV 875/2a, was appropriated for the Prelude and Fugue in D Minor, BWV 875, and a Praeludium in C Major, BWV 872/1a, was transposed and appropriated for the Prelude and Fugue in C♯ Major, BWV 872, for instance. See NBA V/6.2 (Alfred Dürr, ed., 1995), 356–357 and 344–345.

31. Peters Edition, vol. 3, i.

32. Mattheson 1713, 253.

33. Breig 1999, 700.

34. Stauffer 2010, 49. The double ornament is reproduced in the Leupold Edition, vol. 8.

35. Rudolf Steglich, *Johann Sebastian Bach* (Potsdam: Akademische Verlagsgesellschaft Athenaion, 1935; rpt. Laaber, Laaber-Verlag, 1980), 146; Keller 1967, 159; and Humphreys 1994, 41–64.

21

Free Works: Singular Pieces and Late Prelude-and-Fugue Pairs

In addition to writing an inventive transcription and four symphonic prelude and fugues during the Leipzig years, Bach composed two contrasting but equally remarkable singular works and three further interpretations of the prelude-and-fugue pair. We will also consider here the Pedal Exercitium, a unicum whose authorship is not fully certain.

Three Unique Compositions

The **Pastorella in F Major, BWV 590**, has been received unevenly by Bach scholars and champions over the years. Philipp Spitta, without citing evidence, stated that its three *manualiter* movements did not belong with the opening *pedaliter* movement, whose A-minor close he found disturbing as well.[1] These concerns were echoed later, first by Hermann Keller, who thought it improbable that Bach played all four movements in direct succession, and then by Peter Williams, who questioned the authenticity of the four-movement form.[2] Felix Mendelssohn knew better, however, and included the Pastorella with other masterpieces in his groundbreaking all-Bach organ recital in the St. Thomas Church on August 6, 1840, to raise funds for the first Bach memorial in Leipzig.[3] Robert Schumann, reviewing the concert in the *Neue Zeitschrift für Musik*, praised the Pastorella as being "mined from the deepest depths in which a composition of this nature may be found."[4]

The reservations of Spitta, Keller, and Williams may have stemmed from that fact that in some nineteenth-century manuscripts, movements from the Pastorella are handed down individually.[5] The Pastorella is transmitted fully intact in its three earliest sources, however: a copy from c. 1730 by Johann Peter Kellner, a copy from the Berlin circle of Carl Philipp Emanuel Bach, and a copy by an Amalian Library scribe working under Johann Philipp Kirnberger.[6] Thus there is no reason to believe the Pastorella was not originally intended as a four-movement work, and the notation of the three early manuscripts points to a Leipzig origin: the right hand is written in treble clef throughout, and the third movement is notated in C minor with three flats (modern notation) rather than

J. S. BACH. George B. Stauffer, Oxford University Press. © Oxford University Press 2024.
DOI: 10.1093/oso/9780195108026.003.0022

two (dorian notation). Both are notational habits that Bach adopted during the Leipzig years.

As a genre, the pastoral first appeared in Italy toward the beginning of the seventeenth century before spreading northward to other Catholic countries, notably Austria, Poland, and South Germany. It was a Christmas piece, associated with the three shepherds coming to see the newborn Christ. Written for voices and instruments, instruments alone, or organ, the pastoral was characterized by a moderate tempo, unaffected keys (most commonly F, G, or C major), consonant harmonies (with parallel thirds and sixths), and triple meter (most often 12/8, 3/2, 6/4, or 6/8). Its soothing melodies and lilting rhythms were associated with the swaying of animals in the manger or with the music used by shepherds to calm their flocks. Drones were also a common feature, to mimic bagpipes played outdoors by the shepherds.

Organ pastorals were exceedingly popular in Bach's time, both in Italy (works by Girolamo Frescobaldi, Bernardo Pasquini, Domenico Zipoli, and others) and Austria and South Germany (works by Franz Xaver Murschhauser, Georg and Gottlieb Muffat, Valentin Rathgeber, and others).[7] They appeared in a great number of forms, from one-movement, song-like pieces to elaborate multi-sectional works. Zipoli's "Pastorale" from *Sonate d'intavolatura* (Rome, 1716), for instance, displays a ternary structure: A (12/8 meter), B (4/4 meter), A (12/8 meter).

The pastoral idiom first appeared in Bach's works during the Cöthen years, when he began to incorporate dance idioms into his secular cantatas and instrumental pieces in a significant way. His use of the idiom culminated in the Sinfonia to Part II of the Christmas Oratorio, BWV 248, an orchestral pastoral in G major and 12/8 meter for strings, two flutes, two oboes d'amore, two oboes da caccia, and continuo. First performed on the second day of Christmas 1734, it sets the stage for the text "And there were in the same country shepherds abiding in the fields."

Bach's organ Pastorella in F Major is an ingenious four-movement dance suite, along the lines of Zipoli's multi-sectional form. The first movement is a pastorale (here using the Italian term) in 12/8 meter, the second movement a musette in ¢ meter,[8] the third movement an air in 3/8 meter, and the fourth movement a gigue in 6/8 meter.[9] Unlike conventional dance suites, in which the movements are in the same key (or the parallel major or minor, in trios), the Pastorella displays a multi-key scheme that creates a continuous whole: the opening pastorale, in F major, ends in an open-ended fashion, in A minor. This leads to the musette, which begins and ends in C major, the dominant of F major. The air begins in C minor, the parallel minor of the musette's key, and ends, via a Picardy third, in C major, the dominant of the closing F-major gigue. This sequence of cadences and keys produces a harmonic design that fuses the four movements into a united sequence:

        Pastorale (12/8)   F → a
       Musette (¢)   C → C
       Air (3/8)   c → C (Picardy third)
        Gigue (6/8)   F → F

In addition, the pastorale and musette both display drones; the musette and the air have thematic ties (the air is an extended riff on the main notes of the musette's tune);[10] and the gigue's theme is an embellishment of the fourteenth-century German Christmas carol "Joseph lieber, Joseph mein" (Dear Joseph, my Joseph; example 21-1).

In no other dance suite does Bach show such concern for unifying transitions, motives, and themes, and it is this aspect that most marks the Pastorella as a Leipzig work. Similar cyclical tonal arrangements appear in the Fantasia and Fugue in C Minor, BWV 537; the manuscript version of the Art of Fugue (where Contrapunctus 2 ends on the dominant, leading to Contrapunctus 3); and, most strikingly, in the Credo portion of the Mass in B Minor, in which several movements are joined through open-ended cadences and recurring motives. One should not be deceived by the apparent simplicity of the Pastorella. As Schumann rightly concluded, it is drawn "from the deepest depths" of Bach's imagination.

In what context was the Pastorella performed? Christoph Wolff has suggested that Bach might have composed the work for a prince or duke whose chapel or chamber contained a small organ only.[11] This would explain the Pastorella's intimate nature and its modest use of the pedal. But nothing would have prevented it from being performed in Leipzig during the Christmas season, when it could have served as a prelude or as Communion music in the worship service.

The **Allabreve in D Major, BWV 589,** stands in stark contrast to the Pastorella. As a single, ongoing movement for full organ, it is a four-part Italian update of

Example 21-1 Pastorella in F Major, BWV 590: derivation of the theme of the gigue (movement 4) from the German carol "Joseph, lieber Joseph mein."

the five-part French Gravement section of Pièce d'Orgue, BWV 572. Spitta paired the Allabreve with the Canzona in D Minor, BWV 588, and similarly assigned it to the Weimar period[12]—a lead followed by many writers since. The Allabreve's notation (treble rather than soprano clef), masterful handling of counterpoint and stretto, and kinship with Renaissance vocal style point rather to the Leipzig years. The work's provenance also suggests a Leipzig origin: its earliest source is a manuscript from around 1742 written by "Anonymous O," a son, student, or assistant of Bernhard Christian Kayser, who studied with Bach first in Cöthen and then in Leipzig until 1730 or so.[13] There is evidence that Kayser remained in contact with Bach until Bach's death, obtaining new works as they appeared.[14] The Allabreve may have been one of these.

The Allabreve is written in what is commonly termed "alla breve style," an instrumental adaption of motet writing used in the seventeenth century by Girolamo Frescobaldi, Johann Jacob Froberger, Johann Caspar Ferdinand Fischer, and others. The style calls for ¢ meter and white-note themes, melodic movement largely by step, abundant suspensions, and frequent use of double themes and stretto. Alla breve style is similar to *stile antico*, the ancient vocal style of Palestrina, but it displays critical differences: its harmonies are tonal and chord-based rather than modal, its phrase structure is often periodic, its rhythms and episodic development reflect instrumental principles rather than vocal, and it often contains intervalic and harmonic twists (such as the sudden lurch to a Neapolitan sixth chord toward the conclusion of the Allabreve) that would be unthinkable in true *stile antico*.[15] Bach used alla breve style in a host of vocal and instrumental works, ranging from opening choruses in cantatas (Cantata 38, *Aus tiefer Not*, or Cantata 144, *Nimm, was dein ist*) to fugues in the Well-Tempered Clavier (Fugue in E♭ Major and Fugue in B Major in volume 2) to the Six-Part Ricercar from the Musical Offering.

The Allabreve in D Major features continuously unfolding motivic variation, held together by the carefully prepared entries of the main theme. The main theme and its countersubject provide all the motive material necessary for almost 200 measures of exuberant spinning out: the rising diatonic fourth and twisting quarter-note idea of the main theme and the descending third and upward leaping fourth of the countersubject. The harmonic movement through keys is concerto-like, touching on D major and its dominant, A major; A major and its dominant, E major; and B minor and its minor dominant, F♯ minor. These stations are reached through episodes based mostly on the quarter-note motive of the main theme and its chromatic manipulation.

Strettos abound in the Allabreve, occurring at the distance of one measure (mm. 55 and 174), two measures (mm. 43, 97, 134, and 185), three measures (mm. 40, 150), and even zero measures (at m. 167, as parallel 3rds[16]). Equally remarkable is Bach's playful twisting of the main theme through chromatic

Example 21-2 Allabreve in D Major, BWV 589, principal theme: original form
(a) and chromatic alterations (b) and (c).

alteration (example 21-2), ultimately setting the stage for the Neapolitan shock that opens the curtain for the final act, the concluding pedal point. The organ, with its ability to sustain tones, is an ideal medium for the vocal lines and harmonic suspensions of alla breve style. Bach maximized this potential in the Allabreve in D Major, creating a work in which variety and unity are in perfect balance.

Bach often set to paper a single, extraordinary example of a particular type of piece, producing an *exemplum classicum*—a classic example—before moving on to other things. Both the Pastorella and Allabreve reflect this propensity. They serve as singular illustrations of their genres, in which Bach summarized what came before but at the same time demonstrated new compositional possibilities.

The **Pedal-Exercitium, BWV 598** (= BWV[3] App C), an incomplete fragment of 28 measures, is transmitted in a single manuscript sketch, hastily written by Carl Philipp Emanuel Bach, sometime before 1734.[17] The title and author (simply "Bach") appear to have been added by Carl August Thieme,[18] a student at the St. Thomas School from 1735 to 1745 with close ties to the Bach family.[19] The authenticity of the Exercitium has been questioned, and in BWV[3] it has been moved to Appendix C, "Works with false or no attribution."

A number of stylistic features point to Emanuel's authorship: the periodic nature of the melodic material, the symmetrical repetition of the principal theme and sequential motives, the stormy character of the harmonic scheme, and the hurried handwriting and small revisions that give the impression of compositional activity. One could view the piece as the pedal equivalent of Emanuel's well-known Solfeggio in C Minor, Wq. 117/2.

But other qualities point to Johann Sebastian as the composer: the drama created by the extended dominant pedal-point, the movement to a climactic expanding figure that eventually exploits the extremes of the pedalboard, the chamber-music-like articulatory nuance set up by the accent indication in measure 16, and the systematic coverage of a wide range of pedal techniques, including the use of alternate feet, the execution of leaps, the use of the same toe for adjacent notes, the rapid shifting required for repeated notes with different toes, and the performance of varied articulations and scales.[20] Such comprehensive coverage of technical matters is characteristic of Bach's pedagogy. The incomplete nature of the Pedal-Exercitium is also reminiscent of Bach's habit, seen in the family albums, of leaving small study pieces unfinished, presumably for his sons to complete.

One can envision a scenario in which Emanuel carried out a compositional exercise under the watchful eye of his father.[21] But one can also imagine Johann Sebastian orally dictating or physically demonstrating certain ideas and Emanuel writing them down, making refinements to the material here and there as he worked. This would explain the hurried handwriting, the frequent use of repeats for measures,[22] and the missing beat in measure 14 (something less likely to happen if Emanuel were composing). No matter what the true origin of the Pedal-Exercitium, we are fortunate to have this unique example of a pedal étude from Bach's circle, illustrating how the most important gestures in pedal-playing can be practiced.

The Prelude and Fugue: Final Directions

Where could Bach go with the organ prelude and fugue after the four symphonic works of 1727–1739? With his restless creative energy, he appears to have moved forward with the following three additional pieces that point to still further compositional possibilities:

Prelude and Fugue in C Major ("9/8"), BWV 547
Fantasia and Fugue (incomplete) in C Minor, BWV 562
Fantasia and Fugue in C Minor, BWV 537

In the case of the **Prelude and Fugue in C Major ("9/8"), BWV 547**, Bach's autograph has not survived, and one must turn to other means to determine a date of composition. The earliest source of the work is a manuscript copy written by Johann Peter Kellner sometime after 1730.[23] Stylistically, the methodical manipulations of the subject in the five-part Fugue seem to reflect Bach's concentrated exploration of fugal and canonic techniques in works from the 1740s: the Art of Fugue, the Canonic Variations on "Vom Himmel hoch," the Musical Offering, and the Mass in B Minor (the "Confiteor," in particular). Thus, a date of 1740 or so seems possible.

The Prelude is a lilting dance in 9/8 meter cast in a Vivaldian concerto form, with an eight-measure ritornello that touches on the tonic (mm. 1–8); dominant (mm. 13–20); submediant and supertonic (mm. 31–39); subdominant, tonic, and dominant (mm. 48–60); and tonic (mm. 80–88). Ostensibly this represents an extension of the ritornello practices of the Toccata in F Major, BWV 540/1, and Toccata in D Minor ("Dorian"), BWV 538/1, from the Weimar years.

But the construction and presentation of the ritornello is far more subtle. The ritornello consists of a chain of four one-measure motives (example 21-3, a–d)— two scalar and two triadic—that are inverted and combined contrapuntally in every possible way. Added to these succinct ideas is a carillon-like pedal motive, derived from an inverted form of "b," that recurs throughout the piece in the manner of an ostinato, not unlike the pedal theme in the *pedaliter* setting of "Wir glauben all an einen Gott," BWV 680, from Clavier-Übung III. All this makes for an ongoing, exuberant medley of vertical and horizontal combinations and sequences. We might view the Prelude as an update of the permutation technique of Bach's early years, now liberated and raised to a new level of polyphonic give-and-take.

Bach also upped the ante by methodically introducing additional contrapuntal elements as the piece progresses. At measure 31, when motive "a" and the pedal ostinato appear in the submediant, they are joined by a new off-beat twisting motive (example 21-3, e), derived from "c," that further animates the texture with its 16th notes. At measure 48, when "a" arrives in the subdominant, it is accompanied by yet another off-beat motive in descending 16ths (example 21-3, f), derived from a motive that accompanied "d" in measure 6, creating new counterpoint in contrary motion. And from measure 50 onward, "a" appears in parallel thirds and sixths, in inversion and contrary motion, with "e" and "f" providing contrapuntal coloring. All this is tossed off with apparent ease.

After an exuberant return of the ritornello in the tonic in measure 54, in newly animated forms, an episode leads to a darkening of the harmony and a flirtation

Example 21-3 Prelude in C Major, BWV 547/1, ritornello: original form (with motives a–d) and with additional countersubjects (b inverted, and e and f).

with C minor over a dominant pedal point. Dramatic chords, punctuated by rests, lead to a tonic pedal point and the final return of the ritornello in C major, which seems all the brighter for the chromatic digression that preceded it. The opening motives are revisited a final time before a unison close—an emphatic gesture learned from Vivaldi. The carefully calculated structural control, with counterpoint, harmonic colorings, and chromaticism used for dramatic ends, links the Prelude in C Major with the "Fughetta super Dies sind die heiligen zehn Gebot," BWV 679, and Duetto 2 in F Major, BWV 803, from Clavier-Übung III, both dance-derived pieces that work in a similar way.

The astonishing five-part fugue that follows the Prelude is arguably Bach's most sophisticated art fugue—that is, a fugue in which the contrapuntal manipulation of the subject takes precedence over episodic elaboration, in four- or five-part texture.[24] The succinct but sophisticated subject, which incorporates both scalar (notes 1–6) and triadic (notes 6–9) elements like the "royal theme" of the Musical Offering, is modulatory and appears almost 50 times in all conceivable forms: upright, inverted, chromatically altered, augmented (upright and inverted), and stretto. The pedal, which appeared without a break in the Prelude, is now withheld until measure 49, when it enters dramatically with the fugue subject in augmentation.

Structurally, the Fugue can be divided into five main expositions followed by a coda:

Mm.	Exposition	Texture	Procedure
1–15	Exposition 1	4-part, *man.*	Subject upright, 9 entries, cadence in I
15–27	Exposition 2	4-part, *man.*	Subject upright, 7 entries with new countersubjects, half-cadence on V
27–34	Exposition 3	4-part, *man.*	Subject inverted, 4 entries, half-cadence on V/vi
34–48	Exposition 4	4-part, *man.*	Subject upright and inverted, 13 entries, in stretto in contrary motion, chromatic intensification, half-cadence on V, *style brisé* bridge
48–66	Exposition 5	5 part, *ped.*	Pedal finally enters, with subject in augmentation. Subject upright, inverted, and in augmentation, 10 entries, in stretto and contrary motion, chromatic intensification, resolution in I
66–72	Coda	5-part, *ped.*	Subject upright and inverted, 4 entries, in stretto in contrary motion, over tonic pedal point

While this sketch shows the growing complexity of the expositions, it gives little sense of the drama created by the progressive harmonic and contrapuntal intensity of expositions 4 and 5, where the subject is increasingly stretched out of shape by chromatic alterations. This process reaches a climax in measures 56–57, where a tenor entry of the subject beginning in D minor resolves, via diminished-seventh harmonies, in B major! And this is followed by an alto entry of the subject beginning in B major that resolves, via diminished-seventh harmonies once again, in F minor—a tritone away![25] B major and F minor are far afield from C major, and the long tonic pedal point that follows the suspension of motion by the diminished chords in measures 64–65 is necessary to restore harmonic order through sunny diatonic entries in the subdominant and tonic.

Bach unites the Prelude and the Fugue of this work with remarkable subtlety and sophistication. Although the two pieces appear to be very different on the surface, the use of increasing chromaticism to create tension, the sudden suspension of note-motion through a series of detached chords (dominant-seventh chords in the Prelude, diminished-seventh chords in the Fugue), and the restoration of the rhythmic pulse and original theme over a tonic pedal at the end are the same in both. So is the short cutoff at the conclusion: a quarter note in the Prelude, and an 8th note in the Fugue. While the Prelude and Fugue in C Major may lack the symphonic grandeur of the four monumental preludes and fugues, it is arguably Bach's most contrapuntally sophisticated free organ work and a fitting inhabitant of the rarified realm of Clavier-Übung III, the Musical Offering, and the Art of Fugue.

The **Fantasia and Fugue (incomplete) in C Minor, BWV 562,** points in the same direction—albeit somewhat enigmatically. As we observed in chapter 12, Bach composed the Grigny-inspired five-part Fantasia in Weimar, where he paired it with the five-part Fugue, BWV 546/2a. In Leipzig, he removed the Fugue, refined its text, and paired it with the newly composed Prelude in C Minor, BWV 546/1. For many years he preserved the Fantasia as an independent piece, revising its text at least once before writing it out anew around 1743–1745 in a fair-copy autograph,[26] leaving space for a fugue. In 1747–1748 or so he returned to the manuscript[27] and added the Fugue in C Minor, BWV 562/2, which appears as a composition score. Unfortunately, the Fugue breaks off at the bottom of a verso page after 26½ measures, just after the beginning of a second exposition (m. 22), in which the theme appears in dense stretto. Custi (directs) appear at the end of the last measure (m. 27a), suggesting that the music continued on a now-lost page (or pages).[28]

The surviving fragment is intriguing. Like the five-part Fugue in C Major, BWV 547/2, the new Fugue is clearly an art fugue and reflects in a similar way Bach's late interest in learned contrapuntal devices. Two aspects set it apart from the C-Major Fugue, however. The first is the use of 6/4 time, a dance meter that Bach employed in only two other keyboard fugues: the Fugue in F# Minor, BWV 859/2, from the Well-Tempered Clavier, volume 1, and the middle section of the "St. Anne" Fugue in E♭ Major, BWV 552/2. As a meter, 6/4 is characterized by frequent metrical shifts between two large beats per measure and three large beats per measure—that is, between 6/4 and 3/2. This results in temporary hemiolas that are characteristic of courantes written in 3/2 meter. As Bach's Weimar colleague Johann Gottfried Walther put it, "the courante meter, or more precisely, the rhythm that the courante demands as a dance, is the most serious that one can find."[29] Bach seems to have been interested in bringing this seriousness to the C-Minor Fugue.

The second unusual feature is the appearance of stretto after just 22 measures. This suggests that other artful manipulations of the subject were to follow. But what would they have been? Stretto appears at a very early point in the Fugue in D Major, BWV 874/2, and the Fugue in E Major, BWV 878/2, both from the Well-Tempered Clavier, volume 2. In the D-Major Fugue the initial stretto is followed by still-narrower versions; in the E-Major Fugue the initial stretto is followed by versions with the subject in diminution. Both techniques would be difficult to accomplish in the Fugue in C Minor, since its stretto is already extremely narrow and the 6/4 meter makes diminution improbable. More likely possibilities would be: (1) a section with the theme inverted,[30] (2) a B section on new subject, which would subsequently be combined with the original theme to produce a double fugue,[31] or (3) a B section on a new subject followed by a da capo of the A section.[32] But Bach carried out these plans in other organ fugues,[33] and he rarely repeated himself. So perhaps he had still another contrapuntal manipulation in mind. We are regrettably deprived of the outcome because of the lost continuation in the autograph manuscript.

The last piece pointing in a new direction is the **Fantasia and Fugue in C Minor, BWV 537**. Like the Pastorella in F Major, it has been a misunderstood work. Spitta and Hans Klotz assigned it to the Weimar period,[34] instead of the Leipzig years, where it rightly belongs,[35] and John O'Donnell proposed that the da capo fugue was completed by Johann Ludwig Krebs,[36] a claim that ignores the remarkable nature of the fugue's conclusion as well as the limits of Krebs's compositional abilities.[37]

There are good reasons to believe, in fact, that the Fantasia and Fugue may be Bach's final statement on the prelude and fugue. Viewed as a whole, the work is more compact than the other Leipzig preludes and fugues, and it contains an unusually large number of elements that unite its two portions. This closely mirrors the distillation and unification process that took place in the Credo portion of the Mass in B Minor, which Bach compiled toward the very end of his life,

1748–1749. In addition, unlike other preludes and fugues completed in Leipzig, the Fantasia and Fugue is passed down in just one early copy,[38] an accurate, neatly written manuscript jointly penned by Johann Tobias Krebs and his son Johann Ludwig, dated "January 10, 1751"—that is, approximately six months after Bach's death. The only other known early copy, a now-lost manuscript used by Gotthilf Wilhelm Körner for his editions of the work in the 1840s and 1850s,[39] appears to have stemmed from the circle of Johann Christian Kittel,[40] who studied with Bach between 1748 and 1750. If the piece had been written earlier, it probably would have been transmitted in copies by the "usual suspects": Johann Peter Kellner, Carl Gotthelf Gerlach, Bernhard Christian Kayser, Johann Fredrich Agricola, and other students and colleagues writing out Bach's free organ works in Leipzig between 1723 and 1740 or so.

In terms of structure, the Fantasia has the same clear, balanced A B A B form that appears in the "Et incarnatus" of the Mass in B Minor, one of the work's most progressive movements and one of the few that appears to have been newly composed.[41] The Fantasia's design can be summarized as follows:

Mm.	Section	Event
1–11	A	Theme 1, in imitation, initially over a tonic pedal point but then taken up by the pedal
12–21	B	Theme 2, in imitation, leading eventually to 16th–note figuration
21–31	A	Theme 1, in imitation, initially over a dominant pedal point but then taken up by the pedal
31–47	B	Theme 2, in imitation, both upright and inverted, leading eventually to 16th note figuration
47–48	Bridge	Closing bridge, much like that of an instrumental concerto slow movement, leading to a half cadence

Both A sections close with half cadences that foreshadow the Fantasia's concluding half cadence, and all four sections move smoothly to 16th-note motion at the close, creating a rhythmic crescendo in each case. The meandering 16th-note motives at the end of the B sections, in particular, resemble instrumental motives in Leipzig cantatas, such as the flute writing in the opening chorus of Cantata 46, *Schauet doch und sehet, ob irgendein Schmerz sei* (which served as the model for the "Qui tollis peccata mundi" movement of the B-Minor Mass). While the second A section closely echoes the first A section, with parts appearing in a different order, the second B section is an extended development of the first B section, with the principal motive appearing in upright and inverted forms and in parallel sixths and thirds.

Example 21-4 Fantasia in C Minor, BWV 537/1: thematic material.

Perhaps the most impressive feature of the Fantasia is the expressive nature of its vocal-derived themes. The main theme of the A section begins with an *exclamatio*, the upward leap of a minor sixth that Wagner used so effectively a century later in the Prelude to *Tristan und Isolde* (example 21-4, a). Walther described the *exclamatio* as "a rhetorical figure used when one calls out somewhat agitatedly, which in music can be produced very effectively through the upward-leaping minor sixth."[42] The main theme of the B section also contains an *exclamatio* in the form of an upward-leaping octave, which works equally well when inverted (example 21-4, b). The leaping octave of the B section is followed by a weeping motive of slurred, falling seconds that appears in Passion settings such as the Orgel-Büchlein chorale "O Lamm Gottes, unschuldig," BWV 618, or the chorus "O Mensch bewein dein Sünde gross" from the St. John Passion. In the Fantasia Bach elaborated and extended these gestures with consummate mastery.

The expressive melodic material of the Fantasia has nothing to do with the mixture-filled *plenum* normally used for free organ works. It seems tailor-made instead for the doubling of 8' foundation stops that was a feature of the progressive Central German organ (see chapter 17).

The Fugue is an A B A' da capo design also based on contrasting themes: a compound subject for the A section that combines an ascending fifth and diminished triad with a descending scalar tail, much like the royal theme of the Musical Offering, and an ascending chromatic scalar subject for the B section. The Fugue's structure can be summarized as follows:

Mm.	Section	Event
1–29	A	Four-part exposition of subject 1 (mm. 1–18), followed by sequences (mm. 18–24) and an alto entry in i
28–49		Three-part manual episode, with intermittent entries of the subject in v (tenor, m. 37) and i (soprano, m. 45)
49–57		Reentry of the pedal with subject 1 in i, move to a half cadence

57–78	B	Four-part exposition of subject 2 (mm. 57–69), with counter-subject derived from three-part manual episode of A
78–104		Subject 2 in stretto, leading to a double–trill[43] and half-cadence
104–123	A	Return of subject 1, with a literal repeat of mm. 1–23
124–130		Dominant pedal, final entry in the alto, in i, then close

In addition to being equally succinct and dramatic, the Fantasia and the Fugue display an unusually high degree of unification: the Fugue's second subject is anticipated in the rising chromatic alto line in the last measure of the Fantasia; the countersubject of the B section of the Fugue is likewise anticipated in the Fantasia as well as in the A section of the Fugue; the half-cadence serves as a critical structural device, within both the Fantasia and the Fugue, where it connects sections in a forceful way, and within the work as a whole, where it compellingly connects the Fantasia with the Fugue.[44] These cyclical and cadential factors take the Fantasia and Fugue in C Minor to a level of unity found most strikingly in the Credo portion of the B-Minor Mass, where Bach used half-cadences and interrelated motives to connect movements in an organic, dramatic way. And the compression of the A' section of the da capo Fugue lends great intensity to the work's conclusion.

When seeing the Fantasia and Fugue in C Minor into print in the Peters Edition, Friedrich Conrad Griepenkerl termed it "one of the most splendid works of Bach's yet discovered."[45] Given the Fantasia and Fugue's progressive, expressive elements, it is not surprising that Mendelssohn, as champion of the St. Matthew Passion in the nineteenth-century Bach Revival, owned a copy of the work.[46] And it is understandable that in the twentieth century Richard Strauss and Edward Elgar, sensing the Fantasia and Fugue's orchestral qualities, agreed to team up to transcribe the piece for symphony orchestra.[47]

Together with the four "symphonic" preludes and fugues, the Fantasia and Fugue in C Minor foreshadows the Romantic style of the nineteenth century. It is a distillation of Bach's earlier free organ works, much as the Credo portion of the B-Minor Mass is a distillation of his earlier cantata writing. The Fantasia and Fugue may represent Bach's final engagement with the prelude and fugue, the genre that was so central to his evolving concept of organ music in a time of stylistic change.

Notes

1. Spitta 1873–80, vol. 3, 213, n. 398.
2. Keller 1967, 197; Williams 2003, 197.

3. *Ein Denkstein für den alten Prachtkerl: Felix Mendelssohn Bartholdy und das alte Bach-Denkmal in Leipzig*, Peter Wollny, ed. (Leipzig: Evangelische Verlagsanstalt, 2004), 12–21.

4. *Neue Zeitschrift für Musik*, vol. 13, no. 14 (August 15, 1840), cited in BDok VI, no. C150.

5. See Bach digital, under BWV 590.

6. Berlin State Library, *P 287*, fascicle 6; *P 290*; and *P 277*, respectively.

7. See the discussion in Stauffer 1983.

8. Not an allemande, as proposed by Ernst Naumann, in BG 38, xlii, and Williams 2003, 198. An allemande would have an upbeat, and as a courtly dance it has little to do with shepherds. The only other musette in the Bach repertory is the Musette in D Major, BWV Anh. 126, that appears in the Clavier-Büchlein for Anna Magdalena Bach of 1725. Most probably written by Carl Philipp Emanuel Bach, it is in 2/4 meter with pedal-point drones and a recurring *corta* figure—gestures that occur in the Pastorella musette.

9. Not an Italian giga, as proposed in Williams 2003, 197. A giga would be more homophonic and lack the imitative entries at the beginning of both halves, which are characteristic of a gigue.

10. Stauffer 1983, 55.

11. Christoph Wolff, discussion with the author.

12. Spitta 1873–80, vol. 1, 422–423.

13. Berlin State Library, *P 1106*. On Anonymous O see Talle 2003, 162–163.

14. Talle 2003, 163–167.

15. Wolff 1968, 119–126.

16. This technique can also be observed in variation 22, labeled "allabreve," of the Goldberg Variations.

17. Berlin State Library, *P 491*, where the text appears on the reverse side of an abandoned performance part of an aria, also in Emanuel's hand, from a lost cantata. Dating from BWV[3].

18. Schulze 1984, 125–127. See, however, Bernd Koska's comments in Koska 2019, 60.

19. Thieme also penned the title page to the handwritten copy of Bach's "Precepts and Principles for Playing the Thorough-Bass," BWV[3] 1134, of c. 1738.

20. The application of these techniques within the context of contemporary pedal playing is discussed in Yearsley 2012, 261–263.

21. See Ulrich Bartels' comments along similar lines in NBA IV/11, KB (Ulrich Bartels and Peter Wollny, eds., 2004), 86.

22. The original abbreviated notation, with repeated measures marked as such, is reproduced in the Leupold Edition, vol. 1A and 1B, 35.

23. Berlin State Library, *P 274*, fascicle 1. Dating from Stinson 1990, 24.

24. See the discussion of art fugues in Stauffer 1986b, 148–150.

25. See Peter Williams' discussion of this extraordinary passage, in Williams 2003, 116.

26. Berlin State Library, *P 490*.

27. Kilian 1962, 127–135.

28. See facsimile in NBA IV/5, x, or Bach digital, under BWV 562.

29. Walther 1732, 189.

30. As suggested by Williams, in Williams 2003, 148.

31. As suggested by Keller, in Keller 1967, 127.

32. As suggested by Harry Overholtzer, cited in Williams 2003, 148.

33. The Fugue in C Major, BWV 547/2, the Fugue in F Major, BWV 540/2, and the Fugue in C Minor, BWV 537/2, respectively.

34. Spitta 1873–80, vol. 1, 591–592, and Klotz 1950, 199.

35. Stauffer 1980, 118–119.

36. O'Donnell 1989.

37. See Stauffer 2020.

38. Berlin State Library, *P 803*, fascicle 15.

39. *Musicalische Aehrenlese*, band I, no. 1 (c. 1845); *Der Orgel-Virtuos*, heft 125 (c. 1846); and *Sämmtliche Orgel-Compositionen von Joh. Sebastian Bach*, heft 3 (c. 1852).

40. NBA IV/5–6, KB (Dietrich Kilian, ed., 1978–79), 331–332.

41. Stauffer 2003, 116–120.

42. Walther 1732, 233.

43. The double-trill in mm. 101–102 leading to the abridged da capo of the A section has often been compared to the similar passage that leads to the conclusion of the Passacaglia in C Minor. Although the Passacaglia was written many years earlier, in Weimar, Bach used the piece throughout the Leipzig years for teaching purposes and may have had the sound in his ears as he composed the Fantasia and Fugue.

44. See the more detailed discussion in Stauffer 2020, 84–86.

45. Peters Edition, vol. 3, ii.

46. Oxford, Bodleian Library, *MS. B Deneke Mendelssohn c. 10*, fascicle 1, a copy of the Krebs manuscript.

47. Strauss agreed to transcribe the Fantasia and Elgar the Fugue. Elgar completed his task in 1921, publishing the Fugue as op. 86. Strauss never finished his portion, however, and Elgar ended up orchestrating the Fantasia as well, publishing it as the second part of op. 86 in 1922.

22

Clavier-Übung III

The Third Part of the Clavier-Übung, sometimes called the "German Organ Mass," is Bach's single greatest accomplishment in the realm of organ composition. Written when Bach was 54 and at the peak of his creative powers, it contains works that point back to the Renaissance as well as works that point forward to the pre-Classical era. And it covers a vast array of styles in between. The collection represents some of Bach's most technically and intellectually demanding organ music, and some of his most rewarding as well.

The Clavier-Übung Series

It was not until 1726, at age 41, that Bach began to bring his keyboard works to print, in a series titled "Clavier-Übung"—"Keyboard Practice" or "Keyboard Exercise." In his day, the phrase served as a general title for German publications that encompassed a wide range of music for harpsichord, clavichord, or organ. The term was used by Johann Krieger for his *Anmuthige Clavier-Übung*, a collection of preludes, fugues, ricercars, and other contrapuntal pieces, printed in Nuremberg in 1698. It was also employed by Vincent Lübeck for his *Clavier Übung*, an album containing a prelude, fugue, dance suite, and chorale-based chaconne, published in Hamburg in 1728. The German publication with the closest ties to Bach was the *Neue Clavier-Ubung* of his predecessor as cantor of the St. Thomas School, Johann Kuhnau (1660–1722). Kuhnau's collection was issued in two installments, in 1689 and 1692, each consisting of seven dance suites.

Bach began his own Clavier-Übung series with the Six Partitas, BWV 825–830. Issued singly at first, starting in 1726, the Six Partitas appears to have been modeled after Kuhnau's publication, especially since Bach initially announced that his series would contain seven works, in the manner of the *Neue Clavier-Ubung*. In the end, he published only six suites, gathering the single prints into a collected edition issued in 1731 as "Opus 1." This was followed four years later by Clavier-Übung II, which contained the French Overture, BWV 831, and the Italian Concerto, BWV 971, both for two-manual harpsichord. Next came the organ works of Clavier-Übung III in 1739, and finally Clavier-Übung IV, the "Goldberg" Variations, BWV 988, for two-manual harpsichord, in 1741. It is also possible that the Art of Fugue, published posthumously in 1751, was intended as Clavier-Übung V.[1]

J. S. BACH. George B. Stauffer, Oxford University Press. © Oxford University Press 2024.
DOI: 10.1093/oso/9780195108026.003.0023

Bach used the volumes of the Clavier-Übung series to explore various keyboard genres in an exhaustive, encyclopedic way. In Clavier-Übung I, for instance, he prefaced each dance suite with a different type of prelude: Praeludium, Sinfonia, Fantasia, Ouverture, Praeambulum, and Toccata. He also notated the five gigues (Partita 2 concludes with a capriccio rather than a gigue) in five different meters: C, 12/8, 9/16, 6/8, and ¢. In Clavier-Übung II he presented keyboard arrangements of the two principal genres for instrumental ensemble, the Italian concerto and French overture, separating them by a tritone (F major and B minor), the *diabolus in musica* (devil in music), to emphasize the stylistic gulf between the two national styles. And in Clavier-Übung IV Bach worked his way through the various figurations, meters, and canonic permutations that were available to the improviser or composer of a variation set, from Renaissance alla breve motet (variation 22) to Italian giga (variation 7) to German fughetta (variation 10) to Scarlatti-like *esercizio* (variations 14 and 28).

Bach's methodical, comprehensive examination of compositional possibilities in the Clavier-Übung was unparalleled and reflects his unquenchable thirst for new invention as a "learned musician," the epithet coined by Christoph Wolff in his monumental Bach biography.[2] Within Bach's organ music, we find these learned interests at work par excellence in Clavier-Übung III.

The Genesis of the Original Print

The origins of Clavier-Übung III lie very much in the dark. In the case of Clavier-Übung I and Clavier-Übung II, Bach drew heavily on preexisting works that had been composed years before the prints appeared. The music of Clavier-Übung III, by contrast, seems to have sprung out of the blue. There are no early variants of the pieces,[3] and all extant manuscript copies are derived from the original edition.[4] Gregory G. Butler, author of a full-length study of the Clavier-Übung III print, has proposed that Bach may have begun composition of the music as early as 1736—that is, three years before the edition appeared.[5] It is tempting, for instance, to link the music of Clavier-Übung III with Bach's recital on the new Silbermann organ in the Church of our Lady in Dresden (frontispiece), presented before an audience of distinguished guests in December 1736. There is no evidence for this hypothesis, however. It seems more likely, given the lack of any manuscript or documentary proof to the contrary, that Bach wrote the music shortly before—and possibly during—the printing process.[6]

The first reference to the project appears in a letter written by Johann Elias Bach, Bach's cousin and house-guest turned personal secretary, on January 10, 1739, to Cantor Johann Wilhelm Koch in Ronnenberg, near Hanover:

Thus it happens also that my good Cousin will bring out some clavier pieces that are mostly for organists and exceedingly well composed. They will probably be ready for the upcoming Easter Fair, and they make altogether some 80 folios. If my Brother can obtain some subscribers for them, he will get them at a discount. Others, later, will have to pay more.[7]

The publication was not finished in time for the Easter Fair in April, however, and it was not until the next Leipzig fair, the St. Michael's Fair in October, that it was finally placed on sale. As Elias Bach confirmed in another letter to Koch dated September 28, 1739: "The work engraved in copper of my honored Cousin is finished and may be purchased from the same for 3 Reichstaler."[8] Two days later the local *Leipziger Zeitung* announced the availability of the print: "Lovers of Bach's Clavier-Übung are hereby given the friendly news that the third part of the series is finished and can now be purchased directly from the author in Leipzig for 3 taler."[9]

The Clavier-Übung III edition was a remarkably ambitious undertaking. The complexity of the engraving process, the collection's great length (it is Bach's largest print), and the fact that Bach published the work on his own surely contributed to the delay in its completion. Butler has proposed that Bach started the printing process by engaging the services of Leipzig copper-plate engraver Johann Gottfried Krügner, who had carried out the work on Clavier-Übung I. Although Krügner seems to have enlisted the help of two assistants, he nevertheless found it necessary to call in yet another engraver to complete the project, Balthasar Schmid of Nuremberg,[10] who later engraved the plates for the Goldberg Variations and the Canonic Variations on "Vom Himmel hoch."

The Krügner shop was known more for its pictorial engravings than for its music prints, and the plates it produced for Clavier-Übung III closely resemble what must have been Bach's fair-copy manuscript (see plate 22-1).[11] Schmid, by contrast, took the mechanical approach of a professional musical engraver and produced stylized pages with a more generic appearance. Once the plates were engraved, Bach would have taken them to a copper-plate press for printing. It is likely that he had the press produce approximately 200 copies of Clavier-Übung III, in at least two major "pulls."[12] In the course of selling copies from his house, Bach or an assistant added handwritten corrections and improvements to the texts. Twenty-two copies of the print survive today;[13] of these, 14 contain minor changes.[14] Two additional copies—one in the British Library and one at Princeton University[15]—were emended more extensively than the others, and the refinements they contain, recognized only recently as the handiwork of Bach himself, represent important updates to the standard text.[16]

Lorenz Christoph Mizler, who later invited Bach to join his Corresponding Society of Musical Sciences, praised the recently issued collection in the *Neu*

Plate 22-1 "Vater unser im Himmelreich," BWV 682, mm. 1–14: page from the 1739 edition of Clavier-Übung III, engraved by Johann Gottfried Krügner and having the appearance of Bach's own handwriting. The words "Choral" at the entrances of the chorale canon were added by Bach after the printing.
British Library, London

eröffnete musicalische Bibliothek, under the rubric "New and Noteworthy Music Publications":

> The work consists of 77 copper plates in folio, very cleanly engraved and neatly printed on good strong paper. The price is 3 Reichstaler. The author has here given new proof that in this field of composition he is more practiced and more fortunate than many others. No one will surpass him in it, and few will be able to imitate him.[17]

The Music

Clavier-Übung III was Bach's first and most extensive printed collection of organ music, and he seems to have wished to cover as many aspects of organ composition as possible: pedal pieces, manual pieces, chorale preludes, free works, and two-part inventions. The title reads as follows:

> Third Part of the Clavier-Übung, consisting of various preludes on the Catechism and other hymns, for the organ. For music lovers, and especially

for connoisseurs of such work, for the refreshment of the spirit. Composed by Johann Sebastian Bach, Royal Polish and Electoral Saxon Court Composer, Capellmeister and Director of the Music Choirs in Leipzig. Published by the Author.

The city of Leipzig celebrated two special Reformation events in 1739: the bicentennial of Luther's sermons in the Pleissenburg Castle and St. Thomas Church that took place on May 24 and 25, 1539, and the bicentennial of the town's acceptance of the Augsburg Confession (that is, its embrace of Protestantism), which occurred on August 12, 1539. Bach's original goal of having the edition ready for the Easter Fair in April suggests that he may have intended the collection to be part of the festivities commemorating Luther's visit to Leipzig two centuries earlier. The focus in Clavier-Übung III on the Small Catechism and early Reformation chorales appears to reflect the Luther-related events in Leipzig the year the collection was published.

At the heart of Bach's collection stand the "Catechismus-Lieder" on the five articles of Luther's Small Catechism:

The Ten Commandments: "Dies sind die heiligen zehen Gebot" (These are the Holy Ten Commandments)
The Creed: "Wir glauben all an einen Gott" (We all believe in one God)
The Lord's Prayer: "Vater unser im Himmelreich" (Our Father in Heaven)
The Sacrament of Baptism:: "Christ, unser Herr, zum Jordan kam" (Christ our Lord to the Jordan Came)
Holy Communion: "Jesus Christus unser Heiland, der von uns den Zorn Gottes wand" (Jesus Christ, Our Savior, Who Turned the Wrath of God away from Us)

Also included in the group is Luther's "Buß-Gebet" (Prayer of Repentance) on Psalm 130, "Aus tiefer Not schrei ich zu dir" (Out of the Depths I Cry to Thee), which was included as part of the Catechism in many contemporary hymnals.[18] The texts of all six chorales stem from Luther, who is sometimes credited with writing the melodies of "Christ, unser Herr, zum Jordan kam" and "Aus tiefer Not schrei ich zu dir" as well.

These central chorales are prefaced by chorale preludes on "other hymns"—the Kyrie and Gloria melodies that were sung at the beginning of the Lutheran worship service. Both tunes were derived from early Latin chant, and the Kyrie, based on "Kyrie fons bonitatis" (Kyrie II in the *Liber Usualis*, the book of commonly used Gregorian chants compiled by the monks of the Abbey of Solesmes in France in 1896), retains the medieval trope (here in German) that was later dropped by the Roman Catholic Church during the Counter- Reformation:[19]

Kyrie, Gott Vater in Ewigkeit (Lord, God Father in Eternity)
Christe, aller Welt Trost (Christ, Comfort of All the World)
Kyrie, Gott heiliger Geist (Lord, God Holy Spirit)

Four duets follow the chorales, and the whole is framed by an immense prelude and an immense fugue.

It is incorrect, and misleading, to call the Third Part of the Clavier-Übung a "German Organ Mass." The collection is more broadly cast and represents Bach's own interpretation of the French *Livres d'Orgue* of Jacques Boyvin, Nicolas de Grigny, Pierre du Mage, Guillaume Gabriel Nivers, and André Raison, which he admired, studied, and in some cases copied out during his Weimar years (see chapter 7). These organ miscellanies, published in Paris and widely promulgated, present diverse examples of liturgical pieces for performance and study. Grigny's *Livre d'Orgue*, for instance, contains works for the Mass and the principal feasts of the year, and several of the fugues, dialogues, and versets display dense five-part texture distributed over two manuals and pedal that is echoed in the five- and six-part settings of Clavier-Übung III. Bach's collection, while bearing a German title and containing works based on Lutheran hymns, reflects the French tradition.

The melodies of Clavier-Übung III date from the early years of the Reformation. Written between 1522 and 1541, they are among the most important "founding hymns" of the Lutheran faith. The Catechism chorales embody the fundamental premises of Lutheran doctrine, while the Kyrie and Gloria hymns reflect the opening liturgy of the *Hauptgottesdienst*, the principal weekly worship service. The melodies offered Bach the opportunity to pay tribute to Luther and his church, but at the same time they allowed him to explore the possibilities of modal counterpoint and thereby expand the more traditional tonal vocabulary he had used exhaustively in his earlier organ works.

In *Die Kunst des reinen Satzes* (The Art of Strict Musical Composition) Bach's student Johann Philipp Kirnberger stressed the need for understanding and utilizing church modes when writing music:

> Knowledge of the old church modes and their proper treatment is necessary not only because correct fugue writing cannot be learned without them . . . but also because the old style of writing has real advantages that are missing in the new style. We have numerous old hymns that are so full of feeling and expression that they cannot be reworked in the new style without noticeably diminishing their value. Moreover, the old modes have more variety of harmony and modulation than the newer style permits in such simple hymns, where generally only the tonic and its dominant and subdominant chords are used.[20]

Kirnberger noted with pride Bach's use of modal harmony in the Clavier-Übung chorales: "I can also state that the finest of the more recent composers,

J.S. Bach, held the method of writing according to the old church modes as necessary, as can be seen in his Catechism chorales, so many of which are set in this manner."[21] Kirnberger then listed the chorales, together with their modes:

"Dies sind die heiligen zehen Gebot" [pedal setting] mixolydian
"Dies sind die heiligen zehen Gebot" [manual setting] mixolydian
"Wir glauben all an einen Gott" [pedal setting] dorian
"Wir glauben all an einen Gott" [manual setting] dorian, transposed to E
"Vater unser im Himmelreich" [pedal setting] dorian, transposed to E
"Vater unser im Himmelreich" [manual setting] dorian
"Christ, unser Herr, zum Jordan kam" [pedal setting] dorian, transposed to C
"Christ, unser Herr, zum Jordan kam" [manual setting] dorian
"Aus tiefer Not schrei ich zu dir" [pedal setting] phrygian
"Aus tiefer Not schrei ich zu dir" [manual setting] phrygian, transposed to F♯
"Jesus Christus, unser Heiland [pedal setting] dorian
"Jesus Christus, unser Heiland" [manual setting] dorian, transposed to F

In Clavier-Übung III, these works form a strong contrast with pieces in the "new style"—that is, pieces written in a tonal rather than modal idiom: the Prelude and Fugue in E♭ Major, the three "Allein Gott in der Höh sei Ehr" settings, and the four Duetti. Bach appears to have desired not only to honor Luther but also to summarize the course of music over the 200 years that followed the Reformation.

The stylistic diversity of the works points in the same direction. Bach paid homage to the Catholic roots of the Lutheran church by including an unusually large number of pieces written in *stile antico*, the sixteenth-century Renaissance motet style of Palestrina: the *pedaliter* Kyrie-Christe-Kyrie complex, the *pedaliter* "Aus tiefer Not schrei ich zu dir" setting, and the opening section of the Fugue in E♭ Major. These works are characterized by alla breve meter, conjunct white-note themes, and vocal imitation. They also display thick textures: four-part, in "Kyrie, Gott Vater in Ewigkeit" and "Christe, aller Welt Trost"; five-part, in "Kyrie, Gott heiliger Geist" and the E♭-Major Fugue; and six-part, in "Aus tiefer Not." The five- and six-part settings are performed *organo pleno*, to match the sound of a full vocal chorus. This type of "organ motet" was Bach's invention. There was nothing quite like it before its appearance in Clavier-Übung III, and it reflects Bach's study of the *stile antico* and his performances of Palestrina's music in the Leipzig worship service in his final years.[22]

In the *pedaliter* "**Kyrie, Gott heiliger Geist**," BWV 671, the chorale melody appears as a cantus firmus in the pedal over a web of imitative counterpoint based on the first two phrases of the chorale tune, presented in contrary motion and stretto. In the final measures, the smooth flow of the music is interrupted by a turn to dark, dissonant chromatic writing, most probably to reflect the misery that is relieved by death, as described in the last line of the chorale trope:

Kyrie, Gott heiliger Geist
Tröst, stärk uns im Glauben allermeist,
Daß wir am letzten End,
Frölich uns scheiden aus diesem Elend.
Eleison.

Kyrie, God, Holy Spirit,
Comfort and strengthen us above all in faith,
So that we, at our death,
Gladly depart from this misery.
Eleison.

Astonishingly, the *pedaliter* "Aus tiefer Not schrei ich zu dir," BWV 686, goes beyond the "Kyrie, Gott heiliger Geist" setting. Written in the Renaissance motet tradition, it features an augmented tenor cantus firmus, here assigned to the right foot of the double pedal part. Each phrase of the cantus is preceded by fore-imitation in five voices, four played on the manual and one played by the left foot on the pedalboard. Bach proudly labeled the setting "à 6, in Organo pleno con Pedale doppio" in the original print, and in the British Museum copy he marked the entrance of each phrase of the cantus firmus "Choral," to confirm the procedure that is taking place. "Aus tiefer Not" is his densest organ work, matched in his keyboard music only by the six-part Ricercar of the Musical Offering, BWV 1079/2. The use of double pedal harks back to his youthful admiration of North German organ works such as Nicolaus Bruhns's Praeludium in G Major (see chapter 2). But in this case, Bach employed it not for virtuosic purposes but to create an organ motet that took organ performance beyond previous standards, eclipsing even the five-part Mass settings of Grigny.

At the opposite end of the stylistic spectrum, Bach honored the eighteenth-century Italian instrumental trio in the first two arrangements of "Allein Gott in der Höh sei Ehr" and the large "Jesus Christus, unser Heiland, der von uns den Zorn Gottes wand," and he acknowledged the eighteenth-century Italian ritornello form in the *pedaliter* settings of "Dies sind die heiligen zehen Gebot," "Vater unser im Himmelreich," and "Christ, unser Herr, zum Jordan kam."

"Jesus Christus, unser Heiland," BWV 688, may be the most bizarre trio ever written for the organ. Its leaping, twisting wedge-shaped theme, presented in the two manual voices, seems to reflect either the wrath of God or the pain of hell mentioned in the first verse of Luther's text, in which humankind is ensnarled by sin. One way or the other, what it portrays is clearly not benevolent:

> Jesus Christus, unser Heiland,
> Der von uns den Gottes Zorn wand,
> Durch das bitter Leiden sein,
> Half er uns aus der Höllen-Pein.

> Jesus Christ, our Savior,
> Who turned God's wrath from us,
> By his bitter suffering,
> Saved us from the pain of hell.

The trio is written in ritornello form, and the leaping theme appears in four guises: upright, inverted, retrograde (that is, backward), and retrograde inverted (example 22-1). It also appears in stretto as well, at the beginning and end of the setting. Bach developed the ritornello theme throughout, during the introduction, conclusion, and interludes and during the four phrases of the cantus firmus, which appears as a tenor voice (implying an 8' solo stop) in the pedal. While the structure appears to be straightforward, the evolution of the ritornello material is far from it:

Example 22-1 "Jesus Christus, unser Heiland, der von uns den Zorn Gottes wand," BWV 688: forms of the ritornello theme.

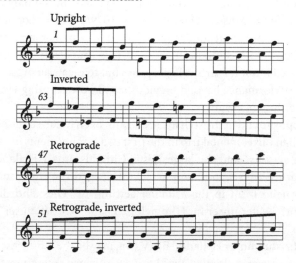

Mm.	Material
1–18	Ritornello theme upright
18–29	Phrase 1 of the chorale; ritornello theme upright, in stretto
29–47	Ritornello theme upright
47–58	Phrase 2 of the chorale; ritornello theme retrograde and retrograde-inverted
58–73	Ritornello theme inverted, against retrograde-inverted
73–82	Phrase 3 of the chorale; ritornello theme retrograde-inverted
82–99	Ritornello theme retrograde and retrograde-inverted, then upright and inverted
99–112	Phrase 4 of the chorale; ritornello theme retrograde-inverted
112–118	Coda; ritornello theme inverted and retrograde-inverted, then in stretto, then inverted against the countersubject, syncopated

The contrapuntal manipulation of the ritornello theme in "Jesus Christus, unser Heiland" matches anything in the Art of Fugue. In fact, it may even go beyond it, since all four forms of the principal theme—upright, inverted, retrograde, and retrograde inverted—are brought into play within the course of a single setting.

"Christ, unser Herr, zum Jordan kam," BWV 684, illustrates well Bach's approach to the ritornello chorale, the most progressive method of chorale preluding at the time. The complex, Vivaldi-derived ritornello has three elements: a 16th-note running bass, a triadic figure treated in imitation, and a syncopated close. The three elements are developed and extended throughout, both between and during phrases of the chorale, which appears in the pedal. As in "Jesus Christus, unser Heiland," there is no note-for-note recapitulation of the ritornello at the end. The conclusion consists rather of an unwinding of previously developed material over a pedal point, in a dorian-mode close.

The stark contrast between instrumental style and motet style is evident in Bach's notation. Works in motet style are devoid of articulation markings (Example 22-2, a), while works in instrumental style display an abundance of slurs, detachment marks, and ornaments (Example 22-2, b). Each style calls for a particular mode of performance, with motet style, derived from choral singing, requiring little or no embellishment and a heavier, less-articulated touch, and instrumental style, derived from string, oboe, and flute-playing, requiring ornamentation and a lighter, more highly articulated touch. As we noted in the discussion of the Six Sonatas, during the Leipzig years Bach increased the use of articulation marks in organ works written in instrumental style.[23]

In the large settings "Dies sind die heiligen zehen Gebot," BWV 678, and "Vater unser im Himmelreich," BWV 682, Bach also explored canonic procedure. "Vater unser im Himmelreich" closely mirrors the dense, five-part pieces of Grigny that call for the use of two manuals, with two voices on each, and pedal. In

Example 22-2 (a) "Kyrie, Gott heiliger Geist," BWV 671, mm. 1–3, illustrating the neutral notation of motet-style works in Clavier-Übung III, and (b) Duetto IV in A Minor, BWV 805, mm. 17–20, illustrating the articulated notation of instrumental-style works in Clavier-Übung III, with dots, slurs, and ornaments.

the setting the chorale appears in canon at the octave, assigned to the upper voice in the right hand and the lower voice in the left hand. The other two manual parts are devoted to a ritornello theme derived from the chorale but dressed in the garb of a French instrumental line, complete with fashionable short-long Lombardic rhythm (Example 22-3) and lightly articulated triplets. The pedal acts as a continuo bass, providing harmonic support for what amounts to be a ritornello trio. In this unprecedentedly cosmopolitan piece, Bach combined techniques from Germany (chorale tune, canon, obbligato pedal), Italy (ritornello, trio, Lombardic rhythm), and France (ornaments indicated by symbols, *galant* triplets)—eight gestures from three countries! So complex are the goings-on that he labeled the canonic voices "Choral" as an afterthought in the British Library copy of the original print, to highlight their entries in the dense texture (see plate 22-1).

Fugue is well covered in the collection, too, in the *pedaliter* "Wir glauben all in einen Gott," BWV 680; the *manualiter* "Fuga super Jesus Christus, unser

Example 22-3 "Vater unser im Himmelreich," BWV 682: chorale tune and ritornello theme derived from it.

Heiland," BWV 689; and the Fugue in E♭ Major ("St. Anne"), BWV 552/2. Each represents a different approach to fugal counterpoint. "Wir glauben all an einen Gott" is, in essence, a three-part manual fugue with a pedal ostinato that marks each harmonic station. "Jesus Christus, unser Heiland" is a dense, four-part manual fugue that features stretto entrances of the principal subject (derived from the first phrase of the chorale) at different intervals. It reaches a climax in the final measures, where the subject appears in augmentation in the tenor. And as we noted in chapter 20, the "St. Anne" Fugue is a triple fugue, featuring three themes and three meters.

The manual settings in Clavier-Übung III similarly display a great variety of forms and genres:

French overture	"Fughetta super Wir glauben all an einen Gott," BWV 681
Fughetta	"Fughetta super Allein Gott in der Höh sei Ehr," BWV 677
Fugue	"Fuga super Jesus Christus, unser Heiland" BWV 689
Dance fugue	"Fughetta super "Dies sind die heiligen zehen Gebot," BWV 679
Cantus firmus	"Vater unser im Himmelreich," BWV 683
Cantus firmus in contrary motion	"Christ, unser Herr, zum Jordan kam," BWV 685
Trio	"Allein Gott in der Höh sei Ehr," BWV 675
Instrumental motet	"Kyrie, Gott Vater in Ewigkeit," BWV 672
	"Christe, aller Welt Trost," BWV 673
	"Kyrie, Gott heiliger Geist," BWV 674
Vocal motet	"Aus tiefer Not schrei ich zu dir," BWV 687

Finally, the **"Fughetta super Dies sind die heiligen zehen Gebot,"** BWV 679, and **Duetto II in F Major, BWV 803** (which we will examine shortly) point to the progressive pre-Classical style of Bach's sons and students. As light, entertaining pieces, they are at the opposite end of the spectrum from the works in Renaissance motet style and lighter in nature than the works in Baroque ritornello style.

The music of Clavier-Übung III epitomizes the grand synthesis that Bach achieved during the late Leipzig years. On the one hand the works display the amalgamation of national styles—that is, the merging of German, French, and Italian idioms. On the other hand they display the amalgamation of historical styles—that is, the joining of Renaissance, Baroque, and pre-Classical idioms.[24] Both syntheses are at work in the magnificent Prelude and Fugue in E♭ Major ("St. Anne"), which we examined at length in chapter 20. While the modal writing of the chorale settings gives Clavier-Übung III a retrospective stamp, the remarkable synthesis of national and historical styles points to the internationalism of the future.

The Structure of the Collection

Like a number of Bach's late printed collections, Clavier-Übung III displays an organizational scheme with many layers of symmetries, progressions, and interconnections (table 22-1). The overall shape of the collection—large free prelude *pro Organo pleno*, smaller pieces with varying registrations, and large fugue *pro Organo pleno*—reflects the general scheme of Bach's organ recitals (see chapter 15). As the early biographer Johann Nicolaus Forkel explained, when Bach performed for audiences outside the worship service, he began with a prelude and fugue on the full organ, continued with smaller works to "show the art of using the stops," and concluded with a fugue, on the full organ once again.[25] According to Forkel, Bach improvised on the same theme throughout. While Bach did not limit himself to one theme in Clavier-Übung III, the progression of pieces and the framing element of a large free work played on the full organ match Forkel's description.

The three inner groups of pieces—Kyrie and Gloria hymns, Catechism chorales, and duets—suggest the tripartite nature of the Trinity that stands at the center of Lutheran belief. The three-times-three grouping of the Kyrie and Gloria hymns points in the same direction. Within the Catechism chorales, the pairs of settings fall into two groups of three, in terms of procedure, with the large settings of "Dies sind die heiligen zehen Gebot" and "Vater unser im Himmelreich" (both with cantus firmus in canon) framing an *organo pleno* work (the large "Wir glauben all an einen Gott") in the first, and the large settings of "Christ, unser Herr, zum Jordan kam" and "Jesus Christus unser Heiland" (both with cantus firmus in the pedal) likewise framing an *organo pleno* work (the large "Aus tiefer Not schrei ich zu dir") in the second. And Bach's choice of a key with three flats, E♭ major, for the Prelude and Fugue that bookends the collection may represent Trinitarian symbolism as well.

At the same time, the three "Allein Gott in der Höh sei Ehr" settings and four duets are arranged in sequences of ascending keys: F major → G major → A major for the "Allein Gott" chorale preludes and E minor → F major → G major → A minor for the duets. By contrast, the cantus firmus in the initial Kyrie group is organized in a descending pattern: soprano → tenor → bass.

It is unlikely that Bach intended Clavier-Übung III to be played in its entirety, as a cycle. It is too long, too dense, and too intense to be comprehended

Table 22-1 The Structure of Clavier-Übung III

Preludium pro Organo pleno	¢ meter
Kyrie, Gott Vater in Ewigkeit (*pedaliter*)	4/2 meter; cantus firmus in soprano
Christe, aller Welt Trost (*pedaliter*)	4/2 meter; cantus firmus in tenor
Kyrie, Gott heiliger Geist (*pedaliter*)	4/2 meter; cantus firmus in bass
Kyrie, Gott Vater in Ewigkeit (*manualiter*)	3/4 meter
Christe, aller Welt Trost (*manualiter*)	6/8 meter
Kyrie, Gott heiliger Geist (*manualiter*)	9/8 meter
Allein Gott in der Höh sei Ehr (*manualiter*)	3/4 meter; F major
Allein Gott in der Höh sei Ehr (*pedaliter*)	6/8 meter; G major
Fughetta super Allein Gott (*manualiter*)	4/4 meter; A major
Dies sind die heiligen zehen Gebot (*pedaliter*)	6/4 meter; cantus firmus in canon
Fughetta super Dies sind (*manualiter*)	12/8 meter
Wir glauben all an einen Gott (*pedaliter*)	2/4 meter; in organo pleno
Fughetta super Wir glauben (*manualiter*)	4/4 meter
Vater unser im Himmelreich (*pedaliter*)	3/4 meter; cantus firmus in canon
Vater unser im Himmelreich (*manualiter*)	6/8 meter
Christ, unser Herr, zum Jordan kam (*pedaliter*)	4/4 meter; cantus firmus in pedal
Christ, unser Herr, zum Jordan kam (*manualiter*)	3/4 meter
Aus tiefer Not schrei ich zu dir (*pedaliter*)	4/2 meter; in organo pleno
Aus tiefer Not schrei ich zu dir (*manualiter*)	2/4 meter
Jesus Christus, unser Heiland (*pedaliter*)	3/4 meter; cantus firmus in pedal
Fuga super Jesus Christus (*manualiter*)	4/4 meter
Duetto I	3/8 meter; E minor
Duetto II	2/4 meter; F major
Duetto III	12/8 meter; G major
Duetto IV	¢ meter; A minor
Fuga pro Organo pleno	4/2, 6/4, 12/8 meters

well as a whole in one sitting—then or now. Instead, the organizational plan allows the player to choose from various "mini-cycles": the *pedaliter* chorales alone or the *manualiter* chorales alone, framed by the prelude and fugue; the

Kyrie and Gloria hymns alone; the duets alone; the prelude and fugue alone; and so forth.

The Duets

The four Duetti are often neglected in discussions of Bach's organ music. Coming at the very end of Clavier-Übung III and written for manual performance, they seem to stand apart from the chorale preludes and the prelude and fugue, and it is sometimes questioned whether they are organ music at all. In the Schmieder catalog they are placed among the clavier works rather than the organ pieces.

Bach may have chosen the term "Duetto" rather than "Bicinium" or "Invention" for the duets because of their ties with chamber music—ties underscored by the pieces' instrumental meters. Bach's Weimar colleague Johann Gottfried Walther defined Duetto as follows:

> Duetto, plural Duetti (Italian), the diminutive of Duo, denotes: 1) a short song for two singing voices (without taking into account the continuo-bass that goes with them), and 2) a similar Piece for two instrumental parts (NB: in this instance the bass part is assimilated within the two voices).[26]

Bach's duets reflect the instrumental genre, observable in works such as Georg Philipp Telemann's Sei duetti for two treble instruments, TWV 40: 130–135, or Wilhelm Friedemann Bach's three duets for two violas, F 60–62. The duets of Clavier-Übung III represent a keyboard rendering of the instrumental form, much like the French Overture and Italian Concerto of Clavier-Übung II.

The four duets appear to have been an afterthought on Bach's part. Without the duets, the harmonic sequence leading from the last chorale prelude in the collection, "Fuga super Jesus Christus unser Heiland," to the concluding Fugue in E♭ Major is compelling: the closing F-major chord of the chorale serves as the dominant of the first note of the Fugue, b♭.[27] When the duets are inserted, this sequence is disrupted by the unrelated keys that begin and end the set of four pieces: E minor and A minor, respectively. That the four duets were composed independently and inserted into a preexisting scheme is also suggested by the fact that the copper plates upon which they were etched appear to have been produced at the very end of the engraving process by Schmid,[28] who, as we noted earlier, was called in to assist the Krügner team after the project was under way.

The rising key sequence of the duets reflects the ascending keys of the "Allein Gott in der Höh sei Ehr" settings earlier in the collection, but it also hints at the pieces' pedagogical kinship with the Inventions and Sinfonias and the Well-Tempered Clavier, which are organized in a similar fashion. The duets are a logical extension of the Inventions, since they also demonstrate the possibilities of two-part invertible counterpoint. They are considerably larger and more sophisticated, however, and resemble more closely the expansive two-part preludes of the Well-Tempered Clavier, volume 2 (the Preludes in E♭ minor, E minor, F♯ major, A minor, and B minor) and the two-part canons of the Art of Fugue. The duets thus represent a second stage of Bach's interest in two-part writing, one that emerged in the late 1730s.

Like the chorale preludes in Clavier-Übung III, the four duets are calculatedly diverse. In addition to being written in four different keys, they are cast in four different meters: 3/8, 2/4, 12/8, and ¢. Notably absent are the more common meters of 4/4 and 3/4. The pieces also show a wide range of characters: the E-minor and G-major duets are dance-like, the F-major duet is markedly *galant*, and the A-minor duet resembles an alla breve instrumental fugue. Most significant, each work illustrates a different method of contrapuntal elaboration. In **Duetto I, BWV 802**, a subject and countersubject, presented together at the outset, are developed through modulation and invertible counterpoint. In **Duetto II, BWV 803**, two subjects are developed independently through

Example 22-4 Duetto II in F Major, BWV 803: (a) subject 1 of the A section, and (b) subject 2 of the B section (above), showing the derivation of subject 2 from subject 1 (below).

stretto, chromaticism, mode shifts, and invertible counterpoint. In **Duetto III, BWV 804**, a subject and a free countersubject are developed in a diatonic context through extension and invertible counterpoint. And in **Duetto IV, BWV 805**, a subject and three distinct episodic segments are developed independently through invertible counterpoint.

Of these four extraordinary contrapuntal studies, **Duetto II in F Major** is perhaps the most remarkable of all. Its structural framework is a straightforward A B A (da capo) design, an opera-aria format that Bach used in a number of forward-looking Leipzig organ works. The A section unfolds innocently enough, with thematic expositions of a sprightly, diatonic F-major subject (subject 1, example 22-4, a) that alternate with episodes derived from a triadic motive in the initial counterpoint (example 22-4, a, x).

In the B section, however, all expectations of normal da capo aria proceedings—the straightforward presentation of the main subject in minor mode, for example—are dashed. Bach introduced instead a new, odd-sounding, across-the-bar chromatic subject containing the jarring melodic intervals of an augmented second and diminished seventh. While seemingly unrelated to what has come before, subject 2 is actually a reimagining of the first eight notes of subject 1 of the A section (example 22-4, b). Presented in canon at the fourth, subject 2 unwinds, twisting and turning, for eight measures.

Bach then proceeded to alternate expositions of subject 2 with newly wrought expositions of subject 1, presented in the related minor keys of D minor and A minor, as expected, but in odd-sounding strettos with the dominant of each key. In the second half of the B section, subject 1 is presented in minor again, but this time in the minor tonic and minor dominant (F minor and C minor)—a bold switch of modes. Most shocking of all, perhaps, is a short exposition of subject 1 in the very middle of the B section, (mm. 68–81), where the theme is restored to lighter, nonstretto counterpoint (though with a new chromatic counpersubject) in F major and then, inverted, in F minor. This is followed by alternating expositions of subject 1 in stretto and subject 2 in canon, once again. The B section leads to a return of the A section, da capo.

Viewed as a whole, Duetto II has a perfectly balanced design, with the special exposition of subject 1 in the B section standing at the exact center of the piece, framed by mirroring portions of B and A material:

	Structural element	Mm.	Contrapuntal activity (S1=subject 1, S2=subject 2)
A	Exposition of S1	1–9	S1 in I (RH) and V (LH)
	Episode	10–16	Imitative and parallel treatment of x
	Exposition of S1	17–21	S1 in IV
	Episode	22–28	Imitative and parallel treatment of x
	Exposition of S1	29–37	S1 in I
B →	Exposition of S2	38–45	S2 in canon, at the interval of the 4th
	Exposition of S1	46–52	S1 in stretto at the 4th, vi and its dominant
	Exposition of S2	53–60	S2 in canon, at the interval of the 5th (= 38–45, parts exchanged)
	Exposition of S1	61ss–67	S1 in stretto at the 5th, iii and its dominant (= 46–52 parts exchanged)
	Exposition of S1	68–81	S1 in I (LH) and i (inverted, RH)
	Exposition of S2	82–89	S2 in canon, at the interval of the 5th
	Exposition of S1	90–96	S1 in stretto at the 5th, i and its dominant
	Exposition of S2	97–104	S2 in canon, at the interval of the 4th (= 82–89, parts exchanged)
	Exposition of S1	105–112	S1 in stretto at the 4th, v and its dominant (= 90–96, parts exchanged)
A	Exposition of S1	113–116	Lead-in, then da capo
	Episode	10–16	
	Exposition of S1	17–21	
	Episode	22–28	
	Exposition of S1	29–37	

Structurally, Duetto II is chiastic, or cross-like—a design Bach favored in two other late works: the Credo portion of the B Minor Mass, where the "Crucifixus" movement stands at the center of a nine-movement complex with arias and choruses radiating outward in a symmetrical way,[29] and the manuscript version of the Canonic Variations on "Vom Himmel hoch," BWV 769a, where the most complex variation, "Canto fermo in Canone alla Sesta e all' roverscio," stands in the center of the set, preceded by two three-voice variations and followed by two four-voice variations (see chapter 23). How very far this perfectly balanced form stands from the "spinning out" procedures of Bach's Arnstadt/Mühlhausen and Weimar fugues! Clearly the concept of perfectly balanced structures was on Bach's mind in the late 1730s and 1740s.

Some writers, pointing to the liturgical nature of Clavier-Übung III, have suggested that the four duets were intended to serve as Communion music.[30] It is more likely that Bach viewed the pieces purely as keyboard exercises—published companions to the two-part preludes of the Well-Tempered Clavier, volume 2—that might increase the sales potential of the collection. The fact that the upper and lower parts of the duets never cross one another makes the works ideal for one-manual performance, not only on the organ but also on the harpsichord or clavichord. It is lamentable that the duets are not performed in concert more frequently today, since they show Bach at the very height of his musical and contrapuntal powers.

The Reception of the Music

The print of the Third Part of the Clavier-Übung appears to have sold well during Bach's lifetime and in the years following his death. The price of 3 talers was very high—approximately equal to the cost of a viola da gamba or a small spinet harpsichord.[31] This probably placed the print beyond the reach of all but the most serious buyers. Still, sales seem to have been successful, so much so that Carl Philipp Emanuel Bach was able to tell Forkel in 1774 that the supply of printed editions had run out, and that nothing remained except his father's composition manuscript and personal copy of the original edition.[32]

The ambitious pieces of Clavier-Übung III were not for everyone, however. While Mizler praised the music when it appeared in 1739, others found it overly artful and technically trying. One early owner of the printed edition embellished the title-page remark "zur Gemüths Ergezung" (for the refreshment of the spirit) with the comment "und Ohren Verletzung" (and the injury of the ears).[33] And Georg Andreas Sorge, Bach's colleague and fellow member of Mizler's Corresponding Society, noted in the preface to his *Erster Theil der Vorspiele vor bekannten Choral-Gesängen* (First Part of Preludes on Well-Known Chorale Melodies) of 1750:

> Nothing is more necessary to the organist than he be adroit in preluding on the various chorales, according to their particular content, so that the congregation will be stimulated to sing the subsequent chorale with appropriate devotion. The preludes on the Catechism Chorales by Herr Capellmeister Bach in Leipzig are examples of this kind of keyboard piece that deserve the great renown they enjoy. But works such as these are so difficult as to be all but unusable by young beginners and others who may lack the considerable proficiency they require.[34]

Sorge went on to recommend instead the eight simple preludes in his edition, which posterity did not treat as favorably as Bach's works, despite the preludes' user-friendliness.[35]

Bach seems to have written the music of Clavier-Übung III solely for the printed edition, and once it was issued, he does not appear to have used the pieces for instructional purposes. Johann Nicolas Mempell, an avid collector of Bach's music, and Kirnberger, who studied with Bach between 1739 and 1741, owned copies of the edition or music from it.[36] But there are no student copies containing early variants or revised versions of the pieces, as there are for the Orgel-Büchlein, the Six Sonatas, the Well-Tempered Clavier, and other collections used for teaching.

It may be, then, that the fame Bach earned from Clavier-Übung III cited by Mizler and Sorge was achieved chiefly through intellectual contemplation of the music. Most of the works could be played from the print, and in certain pieces Bach and his engravers went out of their way to provide convenient page turns. But performers would have found some passages problematic to decipher: the final measures of the *pedaliter* "Kyrie, Gott heiliger Geist" and the voice crossings in the *pedaliter* "Jesus Christus, unser Heiland" are so crowded that the printed scores are extremely difficult to read.[37] In addition, the performance technique required by many of the large settings would have been beyond all but a handful of players at the time—chiefly Bach's students, who do not seem to have studied the pieces.

Parts I, II, and IV of the Clavier-Übung cycle were dedicated to "Liebhaber"— lovers of music. Clavier-Übung III was dedicated to a different audience: "Liebhaber," once again, but also "besonders denen Kennern"—to connoisseurs, especially. Whether performed or simply studied, the Third Part of the Clavier-Übung was Bach's most sophisticated statement on organ composition, celebrating Martin Luther and the art of modal counterpoint.

Notes

1. It is less likely that the chorales of the Leipzig Portfolio (the "Great Eighteen" Chorales) were intended as part of the series (see chapter 25).
2. Wolff 2000.
3. Manfred Tessmer, editor of Clavier-Übung III for the NBA, printed the variants "Allein Gott in der Höh sei Ehr," BWV 676a, and "Vater unser im Himmelreich," BWV 683a, in the KB. But as he admitted, both have a corrupt text, and it is unlikely that either stems from Bach. See NBA IV/4, KB (Manfred Tessmer, ed., 1974), 33–34.
4. NBA IV/4, KB, 25–26.
5. Butler 1990, 3–20.
6. The incomplete Art of Fugue print demonstrates that Bach was willing to begin the engraving process for a publication before he had finished the music. In the case of Clavier-Übung III, he may have delayed the composition of the four duets and the *manualiter* Catechism chorales until the etching of the copperplates was under way. Several of the *manualiter* chorales seem to have been written with the amount of free space available at the end of the corresponding *pedaliter* setting in mind.
7. NBR, no. 205.
8. *Die Briefentwürfe des Johann Elias Bach (1705–1755)*, Evelin Odrich and Peter Wollny, eds. (Hildesheim: Georg Olms, 2000), 118–119.
9. BDok II, no. 456.
10. Butler 1990, 21–37.

11. This led a number of early writers, most notably Georg Kinsky, in *Die Originalausgaben der Werke Johann Sebastian Bachs* (Vienna: Herbert Reichner Verlag, 1937), to believe that Bach himself took part in the engraving process.

12. Stauffer 2010, 50–51.

13. The 19 copies listed in the KB of NBA IV/4 plus three copies that have surfaced recently: Princeton University Library, *(Ex) M3.1 B2C5 1739q*; Berlin, Private Collection; and Lawrenceville, NJ, Private Collection (=A 20 in NBA IV/4, KB). See Bach digital, under BWV 552.

14. The changes and exemplars are listed in NBA IV/4, KB, 14–16.

15. British Library, *K 10 a 42*, and Princeton University Library, *(Ex) M3.1 B2C5 1739q*.

16. Stauffer 2010. The readings were printed for the first time in the Leupold Edition, vol. 8.

17. NBR, no. 333.

18. Its various classifications are given in Bighley 2018, 34.

19. The full text of the trope is given in Bighley 2018, 165.

20. Kirnberger 1771–79, vol. 2, pt. I, sec. 1, 47; translation from Johann Philipp Kirnberger, *The Art of Strict Musical Composition*, David Beach and Jurgen Thym, trs. (New Haven: Yale University Press, 1982), 319–320.

21. Kirnberger 1771–79, vol. 2, pt. I, sec. 1, 49.

22. The performances included the Kyrie and Gloria portions of Palestrina's *Missa Ecce sacerdos magnus, Missa sine nomine*, and other works. The complete list of Palestrina Masses arranged by Bach is given in BWV³, 657.

23. Butt 1990, 164–179.

24. The concept of Bach's "double synthesis" was first raised in Marshall 1989a, 74–79.

25. Forkel 1802, 22. The full quotation is given here in chapter 15.

26. Walther 1732, 218–219.

27. In a similar fashion, at the beginning of the collection the conclusion of the Prelude in E♭ Major leads logically to the opening b♭′ of "Kyrie, Gott Vater in Ewigkeit."

28. Butler 1990, 19, 77.

29. Friedrich Smend, "Bachs h-moll-Messe. Entstehung, Überlieferung, Bedeutung," *Bach-Jahrbuch* 34 (1937), 52, and Stauffer 2003, 141–142.

30. This was first proposed in Keller 1967, 198.

31. To judge from the appraisal of Bach's estate, in which his viola da gamba and spinet harpsichord were each valued at 3 Reichstaler. See NBR, no. 279.

32. NBR, no. 393c. Bach's manuscript has disappeared, but his personal copy of the print appears to have survived as the exemplar in the Princeton University Library, *(Ex) M3.1 B2C5 1739q*.

33. Handwritten remark on the title page of the copy of the 1739 edition of Clavier-Übung III in the Sibley Music Library, *Vault: M3.3B 118c*.

34. BDok V, no. B595a; translation from Wolff 1991g, 115.

35. Only two copies of Sorge's collection are known to have survived: Yale Music Library, *LM 4630*, and Lawrenceville, NJ, Private Collection.

36. Kirnberger cited music from Clavier-Übung III in *Die Kunst des reinen Satzes*; Mempell's manuscript copy of "Allein Gott in der Höh sei Ehr," BWV 676, survives as *Peters Ms. 7*, fasc, 26, in the Leipzig Town Library.

37. See the facsimiles in Bach digital, under BWV 671 and 688.

23

Canonic Variations on
"Vom Himmel hoch, da komm ich her"

If Clavier-Übung III shows Bach as the supreme master of national and historical styles, the Canonic Variations on "Vom Himmel hoch, da komm ich her" display him as the consummate master of contrapuntal artifice. Dating from his final years, the Canonic Variations summarize the art of composing chorale canons for the organ, a centuries-long tradition that Bach admired, studied, and furthered. Far from dry contrapuntal exercises, the "Vom Himmel hoch" Variations display the exuberance and bravado of a star Olympian, striding confidently into the arena of learned musicians and vanquishing all competitors with his canonic skills.

The Canonic Variations Project

There may, in fact, be something to the Olympics metaphor, for according to the Obituary of 1750, the Canonic Variations were written in collegial competition with a number of Bach's most distinguished musical peers:

> [Bach] joined the Society of Music Sciences in the year 1747, in the month of June, at the suggestion of Chief Counselor Mizler, whose good friend he was and to whom he had given instruction in clavier playing and composition while the latter was still a student in Leipzig. Our lately departed Bach did not, it is true, occupy himself with deep theoretical speculations on music, but was all the stronger in the practice of the art. To the Society he furnished the chorale *Vom Himmel hoch, da komm ich her* fully worked out, which was thereupon engraved on copper.[1]

This account, the only reference to the origin of the Canonic Variations, was added to the conclusion of the Obituary by Lorenz Christoph Mizler (1711–1778), who founded the Corresponding Society of Musical Sciences in 1738.[2] With Mizler serving as its permanent secretary, the Society eventually consisted of 19 members, including Georg Philipp Telemann, Gottfried Heinrich Stölzel, Carl Heinrich Graun, George Frideric Handel (as an honorary member), Bach,

J. S. BACH. George B. Stauffer, Oxford University Press. © Oxford University Press 2024.
DOI: 10.1093/oso/9780195108026.003.0024

and other distinguished musicians. Membership was limited to 20, and in 1755 an invitation was extended to Leopold Mozart to join as the final member. The Society disbanded shortly thereafter, however, apparently due to Mizler's relocation in Warsaw.

According to the Society's principles, published in Mizler's *Neu eröffnete Musikalische Bibliothek*, members received by post a circulating packet containing news, essays, and practical and theoretical works contributed or solicited by the membership, to stimulate discussion on philosophical and musical topics.[3] The packets were to be sent out twice a year, around Easter in the spring and St. Michael's Day in the fall, but we know from Mizler's accounts that they were circulated far less frequently than that.[4] Bach's contributions to the packets consisted of the six-part canon, BWV 1076,[5] the Canonic Variations, and possibly the Musical Offering.[6] He "undoubtedly would have contributed much more," Mizler noted in the Obituary, "had not the shortness of time—he was a member for only three years—prevented him from doing so."[7]

The Canonic Variations have been passed down in two primary sources: a printed edition and a fair-copy autograph manuscript. The printed edition (plate 23-1) was published by the Nuremberg music engraver Balthasar Schmid, who may have studied with Bach while enrolled at the University in Leipzig in 1727.[8] Schmid had assisted with the engraving of the first three volumes of the Clavier-Übung series,[9] and he served as the publisher of the Goldberg Variations. The Schmid print of the Canonic Variations is arguably the most beautiful and accurate of the editions issued under Bach's supervision. Twenty-two copies survive, and the exemplar of the University of the Arts in Berlin[10] contains changes and additions in red ink in Bach's hand.[11] Similar markings, also made by Bach in red ink, appear in copies of the original editions of Clavier-Übung III, the Goldberg Variations, and the Six Partitas. It seems that Bach retained such specially marked prints for his own use. The Berlin print of the Canonic Variations contains only four emendations—a testament to the meticulous precision of Schmid's engraving.

According to Mizler, the six-part canon, BWV 1076, appeared in the Society's fall packet for St. Michael's Day 1747.[12] Thus it is likely that the Canonic Variations were written for one of the Society's packets the following year, 1748, and engraved by Schmid shortly after the submission.

Bach's composition manuscript and the manuscript that was circulated in the packet of the Society of Musical Sciences have not survived. The composition manuscript must have contained the canons fully written out, while the packet manuscript probably presented the first three canons in enigmatic notation— that is, with the *dux*, or leader, of each canon fully written out, and the *comes*, or follower, indicated by an incipit only. This notation, used in the engraved edition (plate 23-1), was impractical for performance purposes, but it boldly highlighted

Plate 23-1 Canonic Variations on "Vom Himmel hoch," BWV 769: print of c. 1747–1748, variation 1 and beginning of variation 2.

Universität der Künste Berlin, Universitätsbibliothek

Bach's contrapuntal skill, underscoring the fact that the three canons were truly strict.[13] The notation of variation 4 in the print also emphasizes the theoretical over the practical: the four parts are written in open score, on four staves, like the notation of the Art of Fugue, to show the contrapuntal intricacy of the music in the clearest possible way. Only the fifth variation is notated in straightforward organ-trio score, on three staves. It would make sense that the packet manuscript shared with the members of Mizler's Society used the same notation as the Schmid print, since it emphasized the learned nature of the work.

The surviving fair-copy autograph manuscript of the Canonic Variations (plate 23-2) appears in the Leipzig chorale portfolio containing the "Great Eighteen" Chorales, BWV 651–668.[14] The Canonic Variations appear toward the end of the portfolio, between "Komm, Gott Schöpfer, heiliger Geist," BWV 667, entered by Bach's son-in-law Johann Christoph Altnikol, and the final piece, "Vor deinen Thron tret ich hiermit," BWV 668, a fragment, entered by an unidentified scribe. The Canonic Variations autograph, which can be dated c. 1747–1748 on the basis of handwriting analysis,[15] is the last entry in the portfolio in Bach's hand. Unlike the print version, it is a practical performance score, with all five variations written out in full, in three-staff organ notation.

Various refinements in the music text of the manuscript version suggest that it was written after the completion of the printed edition. The final variation, "L'altra Sorte del' Canone all'rovercio," appears in the middle of the set rather than at the end, followed by variations 3 and 4, which now serve as the conclusion. (We will return to this new ordering shortly.) In addition, the free voice of the cantabile variation, variation 3 in the print but now variation 4, has been fully rewritten, and passages throughout the work have been improved here and there.[16] The revised version of the Canonic Variations, listed as BWV 769a in BWV[2], is generally accepted as Bach's last word on the piece and is more commonly performed today than the original print version, BWV 769. In all likelihood, Bach did not intend the revised version of the Canonic Variations to stand as an independent work, like the print version, but viewed it as part of the chorale settings in the Leipzig portfolio (see chapter 25).

There has been much speculation about the precise dating and compositional process of the Canonic Variations. Philipp Spitta was the first to question Mizler's account of things. Using the plate numbers of Schmid's publications as a guide, he suggested that Bach published the first three variations, at least, by 1746, and then presented them to the Society of Musical Sciences once he joined, in June 1747.[17] Hans Klotz, editor of the Neue Bach-Ausgabe, proposed that Bach wrote variations 1–4 before entering the Society, and then added variation 5 as a culminating afterthought.[18] And more recently, Gregory G. Butler has proposed that Bach wrote variations 1–3 as early as 1745, with variation 5 added later that year, possibly in conjunction with the service of thanksgiving that marked the signing of

Plate 23-2 Canonic Variations on "Vom Himmel hoch," BWV² 769a: autograph manuscript of c. 1748, variation 1.

Staatsbibliothek zu Berlin—Preußischer Kulturbesitz, Musikabteilung mit Mendelssohn-Archiv

the Peace of Dresden, held in the St. Nicholas Church in Leipzig on Christmas Day, December 25, 1745.[19] In Butler's view, variation 4 was completed last, in 1746 or 1747. There are also traces of a lost revision manuscript that contained a version of the Canonic Variations that stood midway between the print version and the fair-copy autograph. Its text appears to be echoed in an early nineteenth-century manuscript and a Breitkopf & Härtel edition published in 1803.[20]

In the end, the precise genesis of the Canonic Variations is uncertain, and the evidence against Mizler's sequence of events and Bach's composing the canons as a set in one go remains hypothetical. What seems clear is that Bach presented the Canonic Variations to the Society of Musical Sciences in some form after becoming a member in June 1747, and that the work's sophisticated canonic writing was a good match with the didactic interests of its members.

No matter what the precise date of composition, publication, and revision, the Canonic Variations reflect Bach's intense occupation in the last decade of his life with creating works that focused on the principles of monothematicism and canonic development. This interest emerged in the Goldberg Variations of 1741, a composition based on a single sarabande aria and featuring a series of nine canons at ever widening intervals placed among the 30 variations. It continued with the Fourteen Canons, BWV 1087, derived from the first eight notes of the Goldberg Variations bass, and the Musical Offering of the fall of 1747, in which Bach demonstrated the potential of Frederick the Great's "Royal Theme" through two ricercars, a trio sonata, and 10 canons. And in the Art of Fugue, commenced around 1740 and left incomplete in the midst of the engraving process a decade later, Bach explored in an exhaustive way the treatment of a single theme through 12 fugues and four canons. It is as if Bach wanted to demonstrate in each case how an infinite amount of music could be produced from a finite amount of melodic material.[21]

The Canonic Variations—Bach's examination of the canonic potential of Martin Luther's highly popular 1534 Christmas chorale "Vom Himmel hoch, da komm ich her,"[22] arranged for organ in a chorale-partita-like format—was part of this late obsession with counterpoint.

The Music

Bach displayed a lifelong interest in chorale canons, evident in the Neumeister Chorales of c. 1695–1705, the Orgel-Büchlein of the early Weimar years, and Clavier-Übung III of 1739. This interest came to full fruition in the Canonic Variations, which can be viewed as a compact compendium of canonic practices.

For variation 1 (here and elsewhere using the numbering of the print version), the introduction to the set, Bach chose the gentle 12/8-idiom of a pastoral, perhaps to symbolize the shepherds who visited the Christ child in Bethlehem. Variation 1 is a trio, with the canonic voice based on the falling fourth of the first and last phrases of the chorale, the upward leap of a fourth in the third phrase, and the C-major triad of the second phrase (example 23-1, x, y, and z). The canonic material, appearing in the manuals, serves as a type of fore-imitation to the cantus firmus itself, which appears unembellished in the pedal. The C-major triad is immediately repeated in diminution, foreshadowing the diminution that takes place at the conclusion of variation 5. The descending motive may well depict the descent of the angel from heaven with the good news of Christ's impending arrival:

> Vom Himmel hoch, da komm ich her,
> Ich bring euch gute neue Mähr,
> Der guten Mähr bring ich so viel,
> Davon ich singn und sagen will.

> From heaven on high I come here,
> And bring you good, new tidings,
> I bring so many good tidings,
> Of which I want to sing and speak.

The initial entry of the *dux* and *comes* is recapitulated in the tonic in measure 13, giving shape and balance to an otherwise through-composed form.

Variation 2, labeled "Alio modo," or "in another manner," in the print, is a duple-meter riff on variation 1. Like variation 1, it is a fore-imitation trio, with

Example 23-1   (a) Chorale "Vom Himmel hoch, da komm ich her," and (b) Canonic Variations on "Vom Himmel hoch," BWV 769, variation 1: canonic voice, with intervals drawn from the chorale marked.

the free canonic voices in the two manuals and the cantus firmus in the pedal. The *comes* now follows the *dux* at the interval of the fifth instead of the octave. The opening motive of the canon is similarly based on the descending fourth that appears in the first and last phrases of the "Vom Himmel hoch" melody. The triad of the second phrase of the chorale tune also comes into play, though not until measure 9, when it echoes the cantus firmus in the pedal. And once again the opening canonic material is recapitulated in C major, in measures 16–17, lending balance to the otherwise through-composed canonic material. In this case, the opening motive is varied, however, through syncopation and embellishment (example 23-2). Thus variation 2 is a variation on a variation: it forms the perfect complement to variation 1 while taking the canonic procedure to the next level of complexity.

Variations 3 and 4, both in four-part texture, form a second complementary pair. Variation 3 is an inverted version of variations 1 and 2: the canon, at the interval of the seventh, now appears in the lower voices: tenor (left hand, on manual II) and bass (pedal), with the cantus firmus appearing at the top, in the soprano (right hand, on manual I). The *dux* of the canon is based on the full first phrase of "Vom Himmel hoch," which is presented in a series of sequences. This block of sequential material recurs throughout the variation, separated by interludes. The florid free voice, presented in the alto (also right hand, on manual I), is the object of the *cantabile* label. It is a melismatic, highly embellished voice, decorated with appoggiaturas and 32nd notes, much in the manner of a florid-melody organ chorale. The free voice occasionally hints at the chorale melody (mm. 3, 7, 10, etc.) and takes on the air of an expressive, improvised tune in an otherwise strict canonic texture. In the fair-copy autograph Bach revised the free voice, making it more embellished still (adding triplets in m. 6, for instance). Yet certain passages in the autograph version are simpler than those in the print, hinting that Bach may have been working from the composition score of the set rather than the improved print version.

Variation 4, also a quartet, is a canon at the octave, in augmentation. The cantus firmus returns to the pedal in a slightly more elaborate form than in the

Example 23-2 Canonic Variations on "Vom Himmel hoch," BWV 769, variation 2: (a) *dux* of the canon in m. 1, and (b) *dux* upon its "reprise" in m. 16.

previous variations, and the alto functions as a free line, filling in the harmony where necessary. The canon takes place between the soprano and the tenor and represents one of Bach's most remarkable contrapuntal feats: the soprano *dux*, with its 16th- and 32nd-note flourishes, sounds like the cantabile melody of a concerto middle movement or the soprano of a florid-melody organ chorale, while the tenor *comes*, derived from the soprano and sounding in augmented note values, serves as a bass for the other three voices. The soprano becomes especially ornate once its canonic function is finished at measure 21, beat 3, and no longer serves as the feeder for the tenor. Bach was understandably proud of his handiwork and marked this pivotal spot with a red fermata in the University of the Arts copy of the original print, to underscore the musical miracle that is taking place. All three manual voices refer to the chorale melody (the allusions are clearest in the augmented figures of the tenor), making this variation what Peter Williams termed "a dense tissue of allusions."[23]

Variation 5, labeled "Other kinds of canons, in contrary motion" in the print, is what we might call a "potpourri" variation, covering techniques (contrary motion, diminution, stretto) and intervals (sixth, third, second, and ninth) not unleashed in the other variations. All are dutifully marked in the original print. The canons are now based on the chorale tune itself, and the inverted *comes* answers are real, without the tonal adjustments of the previous canons. In this culminating variation Bach revealed at last the full potential of the "Vom Himmel hoch" melody not only to produce free canons from motives borrowed from its phrases (variations 1-4) but also to be subjected to all sorts of canonic treatment itself (variation 5). This was the true raison d'être of the work, now unveiled. It is interesting to note that Bach had touched on the potential contrapuntal juxtapositions of Luther's tune some 30 years earlier, in his manual fughetta setting of "Vom Himmel hoch," BWV 701 (see chapter 11).

Variation 5 is a tour de force. The canons at the sixth and third are trios, with the canonic voices in manuals I and II and the pedal serving as a walking bass. The canons at the second and ninth are quartets, with the canonic voices in the pedal and tenor (canon at the second) and the pedal and soprano (canon at the ninth). In the original print, the canon at the ninth is marked forte; in the fair-copy autograph, both the canon at the second and the canon at the ninth carry this indication. The addition of stops adds to the growing sense of climax, which reaches its highest point in the final five measures with the introduction of diminution (m. 52) and stretto (m. 54). The ingenuity of the last three measures, in which Bach combined all four phrases of the chorale in stretto together with fragments of the melody in diminution, while at the same time increasing the number of parts to six, was already noted in 1787 by Daniel Gottlob Türk, who published an analysis of this remarkable passage in his widely circulated treatise on organ playing (example 23-3).[24]

Example 23-3 Canonic Variations on "Vom Himmel hoch," BWV 769, variation 5: final three measures, as analyzed by Daniel Gottlob Türk in *Von den wichtigsten Pflichten eines Organisten* (1787).

a) The first phrase of the melody.
b) The second phrase of the same.
c) The third phrase, in augmentation, with a slight embellishment.
d) The fourth phrase.
e) The first phrase, in inversion and diminution, with slight embellishment.
f) The same phrase, treated the same way.
g) The first phrase, in diminution.

Bach's choice of "Vom Himmel hoch, da komm ich her" for contrapuntal treatment in the Canonic Variations may have reflected seasonal interests, if the Society packet containing it was circulated in the fall, shortly before Christmas. But it is more probable that he picked the chorale because of its imitative potential and the close relationship of phrase 1 to phrase 4 and phrase 2 to phrase 3. It was this potential that he examined to the fullest in the Canonic Variations, providing clear labels in the print, especially, for each procedure. One can understand why Mizler used the phrase "fully worked out" ("vollständig ausgearbeitet") to describe Bach's treatment of the chorale in this extraordinary, learned work.

The Organizational Schemes

Although the music in the print and the fair-copy autograph of the Canonic Variations is fundamentally the same, the different ordering of the canons provides a study in contrasting organizational aesthetics.

In the print, the variations appear in a developmental sequence of increasing length and complexity. Three simple canons at ever widening intervals—octave, fifth, and seventh—are followed first by an augmentation canon and then by a "potpourri canon" that covers all remaining intervals except the fourth, in contrary motion ("all' rovercio"). In the first four variations, the canonic voices are newly composed and surround the cantus firmus, which is preserved intact. In the final variation, the chorale itself is subjected to canonic treatment, unleashing at long last, as we have noted, its contrapuntal potential (which Bach obviously recognized from the start). The dynamics are increased to forte at m. 39 of variation 5, for the canon at the ninth, and the music concludes with diminution and stretto, both climactic gestures in fugues and canons. The canonic intervals, diminution, and stretto are precisely labeled in the print, as if the work were an illustration in a didactic treatise by Friedrich Wilhelm Marpurg or Johann Philipp Kirnberger. In this case, it was surely intended for the benefit of the members of Mizler's Society of Musical Sciences. The number of parts grows incrementally in the set, from three voices (variations 1 and 2) to four voices (variations 3 and 4), to five and then six voices (the concluding measures of variation 5). This methodical buildup creates an inexorable sense of increasing complexity and excitement:

	Length	Voices	Nature of canon
Variation 1	18 mm.	3	Canon at the octave
Variation 2	23 mm.	3	Canon at the fifth
Variation 3	27 mm.	4	Canon at the seventh
Variation 4	42 mm.	4	Canon at the octave, in augmentation
Variation 5	56 mm.	4–6	Canons at the sixth, third, second, etc.

In the fair-copy autograph, Bach shifted variation 5 to the middle of the set, placing it between variations 2 and 3. This created an axial plan, with the variation that treats the chorale as a canon "in various ways" serving as the center of the design. Variation 5 is labeled "Canto fermo in Canone—alla Sesta è all' roverscio" in the autograph manuscript and marked forte twice: at measure 27, in the right hand, for the canon at the second, and in measure 39, in the left hand, for the canon at the ninth. Variation 5 is framed by two three-part canons (variations 1 and 2) and two four-part canons (variations 3 and 4), all containing canons on newly composed material, with the chorale melody preserved. The complicated augmentation canon (variation 4) now closes the work, with the treble line ascending to the highest note of Bach's keyboard, c''', at the very end. The reorganization shifts the focus to the middle of the set, rather than to the end:

	Length	**Voices**	**Nature of canon**
⌐ Variation 1	18 mm.	3	Canon at the octave
⌐ Variation 2	23 mm.	3	Canon at the fifth
→ Variation 5	56 mm.	4-6	Canons at the sixth, third, second, etc.
⌐ Variation 3	27 mm.	4	Canon at the seventh
⌐ Variation 4	42 mm.	4	Canon at the octave, in augmentation

A year or two later Bach made a similar architectural change in the Credo portion of the B-Minor Mass. In this instance, he inserted, as a second thought, the newly composed movement "Et incarnatus est" into an eight-movement complex, shifting the "Crucifixus" to the middle and creating a chiastic plan with mirroring groups of a chorus, an aria, and two connected choruses radiating outward on each side.[25] The result is a palindromic plan similar to that of the reconfigured Canonic Variations:

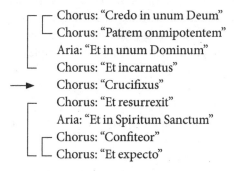

    Chorus: "Credo in unum Deum"
    Chorus: "Patrem onmipotentem"
    Aria: "Et in unum Dominum"
    Chorus: "Et incarnatus"
→   Chorus: "Crucifixus"
    Chorus: "Et resurrexit"
    Aria: "Et in Spiritum Sanctum"
    Chorus: "Confiteor"
    Chorus: "Et expecto"

In the 1740s Bach seems to have engaged in this type of structural reimagining with increased frequency. It appears not only in the Canonic Variations and the B-Minor Mass but also in Sonata 6 in G Major for Violin and Harpsichord, BWV 1019 (version 1019.3 in BWV³); the Art of Fugue; and the chorale partita "Sei gegrüßet, Jesu gütig," BWV 768, a Weimar work in which he switched the order of variations 6 and 7, most likely while reviewing it during the course of organ instruction (see chapter 10).

In the case of the Canonic Variations, both structures, that of the print and that of the fair-copy autograph, have convincing validity. The revision of the free voice in variation 3 and other, smaller refinements in the autograph may be a reason to prefer the manuscript version, but that advantage is counterbalanced by the climactic progression of the five variations in the print version. Thus, in the improvisatory spirit of the time, Bach provided two equally viable options for performance.

As we noted, the contrapuntal ingenuity of the Canonic Variations on "Vom Himmel hoch" was already recognized by Türk in the 1780s. Writing in 1800 about organ music of the past, the German composer, writer, and pedagogue Johann Gottlieb Karl Spazier went further and underscored the preeminent standing of the work:

> One has, of course, the printed collection titled *Bible des Noëls*, to which several famous French organists—le Begue, Dandrien, and Corette, for instance—have contributed pieces edited for the clavier or organ. The works are like the chorale preludes of our protestant organists: here the melody is in the soprano, here in the bass or in a middle voice, here is it used for a duo, trio, quartet, or a fugue, built out of a part of the same. But our Sebastian Bach's Vom Himmel hoch leaves all this far behind.[26]

Within 50 years of Bach's death the Canonic Variations themselves had become canonized.

Notes

1. NBR, no. 306.
2. NBR, no. 395.
3. Two lengthy reports in the *Bibliothek* serve as the chief source of information about the Society's goals, members, and activities. They appear in band 3, part 2 (Leipzig, 1746, covering 1738–1745), 346–362, and band 4, pt. 1 (Leipzig, 1754, covering 1746–1752), 103–123. The latter report contains the famous Bach Obituary.
4. In 1754 Mizler published the six-part canon, BWV 1076, in the *Bibliothek* with the remark that Bach had circulated it earlier in the Society's fifth packet, which appeared in 1747 (BDok III, no. 665). This suggests that the packets went out every two years or so.
5. The canon is one of the 14 "Goldberg Canons," BWV 1087, and is featured in the two versions of the famous Haussmann portrait of Bach, painted in 1746 and 1748, respectively.
6. To judge from Mizler's letter to member Meinrad Spiess of September 1, 1747. See NBR, no. 247.
7. NBR, no. 306.
8. Koska 2019, 54.
9. Butler 1990, 33–34.
10. Berlin, Universität der Künste, Universitätsbibliothek, *Rara 0439*.
11. Stauffer 2017.
12. NBR, no. 241.
13. Except for the adjustment of accidentals. See the Editorial Report in the Leupold Edition, vol. 9, 130–131.
14. Berlin State Library, *P 271*, fascicle 2.
15. Kobayashi 1988, 60.

16. These changes were first discussed in detail in Smend 1933. They are listed in NBA IV/2, KB (Hans Klotz, 1957), 90–98.
17. Spitta 1873–80, vol. 3, 219, 294–295.
18. NBA IV/2, KB, 86–87.
19. Butler 1990, 91–116, and 104–105, in particular.
20. NBA IV/2, KB, 87–98.
21. See the discussion in Wolff 2020, 268–274.
22. Luther described the chorale as "A children's song for Christmas of the Baby Jesus, drawn from the second chapter of the Evangelist St. Luke." Bighley 2018, 220.
23. Williams 2003, 521.
24. Daniel Gottlob Türk, *Von den wichtigsten Pflichten eines Organisten* (Leipzig: Schwickert, 1787), 236–237.
25. Friedrich Smend, "Bachs h-moll-Messe. Entstehung, Überlieferung, Bedeutung," *Bach-Jahrbuch* 34 (1937), 52, and Stauffer 2003, 141–142.
26. BDok III, 597.

24

The Schübler Chorales

The "Schübler" Chorales, named after the printer who published them, occupy an odd place in the late organ works. The music represents Bach at his Leipzig best, and the individual settings bring delight to the performer and listener alike. But the flawed nature of the engraved edition calls into question the extent of Bach's involvement with the project, and if it were not for the survival of two copies of the print containing his handwritten corrections, we would be hard pressed to know what to make of the error-filled, riddle-ridden text.

The Problematic Original Print

The chorales first appeared in a small, engraved edition of 14 pages, issued in the late 1740s by Johann Georg Schübler (1720–1755) in Zella (now Zella-Mehlis), a village in Thuringia approximately 90 miles southwest of Leipzig. The title page reads as follows:

> Six Chorales of Various Sorts, to be performed on an Organ with 2 Manuals and Pedal, composed by Johann Sebastian Bach, Royal Polish and Electoral Saxon Court Composer and Capellmeister and Director of Musical Choirs in Leipzig. Published by Johann Georg Schübler in Zella in the Thuringian Forest. Available from Herr Capellmeister Bach in Leipzig, from his Sons in Berlin and Halle, and from the Publisher in Zella.[1]

Schübler and his brothers Johann Jacob Friedrich and Johann Heinrich, Jr., served as music engravers for Bach and his sons for a number of projects, including the Musical Offering in the summer of 1747 and the Art of Fugue two years later.[2] The Schübler Chorales appear to have been an intermediary undertaking, most probably issued between 1747 and 1748. The edition contains six works:

Wachet auf, ruft uns die Stimme, BWV 645
Wo soll ich fliehen hin, oder Auf meinen lieben Gott, BWV 646
Wer nur den lieben Gott lässt walten, BWV 647
Meine Seele erhebt den Herren, BWV 648
Ach bleib bei uns, Herr Jesu Christ, BWV 649
Kommst du nun, Jesu, vom Himmel herunter, BWV 650

J. S. BACH. George B. Stauffer, Oxford University Press. © Oxford University Press 2024.
DOI: 10.1093/oso/9780195108026.003.0025

The music of five of the settings can be traced to movements from Bach's chorale-cantata cycle of 1724–1725; the source of the remaining setting, "Wo soll ich fliehen hin," is less certain. (We will return to this shortly.) A comparison of the organ chorales with the cantata settings shows that only minor details were changed in the transcription process. Unlike Bach's Weimar organ arrangements of Vivaldi and Johann Ernst concertos, which are imaginative reworkings of their instrumental originals, the Schübler Chorales are mostly note-for-note clones of their cantata models.

The mechanical adoption of the cantata music hints at Bach's limited participation in the Schübler project, and there is some evidence that he may have relied on an assistant or student to transcribe the music directly from the cantata scores.[3] There is little doubt that Bach selected the pieces, proposed their order of appearance, and designated a number of critical alterations in the musical text (the deletion of the second verse of the chorale in "Ach bleib bei uns, Herr Jesu Christ," for instance). But at some point, he appears to have dropped out of the production process and failed to proofread the engraved pages, leaving many obvious errors in place and numerous performance issues unresolved. These matters could have been rectified if Bach had marked up a set of proof sheets, but for some reason he did not. The result is a flawed print quite unlike the other editions of his works issued during his lifetime.

Other aspects of the edition are peculiar as well. The wording on the title page is different from that of Bach's other prints,[4] and the fact that only six copies of the edition survive suggests that it may have had an unusually small run or may have been withdrawn from circulation.[5] Moreover, Bach's son Carl Philipp Emanuel later treated the print with a certain air of disdain, giving his copy containing his father's handwritten corrections to Forkel at no cost, while at the same time charging for an unannotated copy of Clavier-Übung III.[6]

All of this suggests that the "Six Chorales of Various Sorts" may have been an undertaking initiated and carried out by Johann Georg Schübler, rather than Bach. According to his brother Johann Heinrich, Schübler "studied music in Leipzig with the famous Bach" and later, to judge from church records, worked in Zella as an "assiduous practitioner of the organist's art."[7] Bach seems to have had limited control over the production process, so much so that one wonders if he might have stepped in afterward and stopped distribution of the edition, once he realized the degree to which its music text was flawed.

The Hand-Corrected Copies

Bach, and perhaps Schübler himself, attempted to rectify the problematic print by inserting handwritten corrections and improvements. Of the six surviving copies of the edition, three contain handwritten changes. The exemplar in the British Library in London displays 30 alterations.[8] They are in faded ink and may have been added by Johann Georg Schübler or his brother Johann Heinrich. Two other copies, the first preserved in the Princeton University Library,[9] the second in the Austrian National Library in Vienna,[10] display extensive changes made by Bach himself. The Princeton exemplar was once owned by Carl Philipp Emanuel Bach, who confirmed to Johann Nicolaus Forkel that the "inscribed annotations are from the hand of the late author."[11] It was used as the basis for the text of the Peters, Bach-Gesamtausgabe, Neue Bach-Ausgabe, and Breitkopf editions. The importance of the Vienna exemplar (plate 24-1) was not recognized until recently, since the changes it contains were long attributed to an early owner, Johann Christoph Oley, rather than to Bach himself.[12] Its readings have been incorporated into the Leupold Edition.

The London copy displays fundamental corrections and clarifications (such as providing the missing second ending of the Stollen in "Wachet auf") and may reflect a printer's errata list of basic emendations, now lost. The Princeton and London copies, corrected by Bach, underscore his discontent with Schübler's engraving and his determination not only to correct the mistakes of the original edition but also to improve the musical text and clarify matters of performance.

Plate 24-1 "Ach bleib bei uns, Herr Jesu Christ," BWV 649, mm. 36–46, and "Kommst du nun, Jesu, vom Himmel herunter," BWV 650, mm. 1–6: Vienna copy of the original print with Bach's handwritten corrections and improvements.
Österreichische Nationalbibliothek, Musikabteilung

His handwritten alterations in the two exemplars are extensive: the Princeton copy, which has lacked its first page since the 1880s,[13] contains 109 changes; the Vienna exemplar 125. The alterations concern the correction of printing errors, the insertion of additional ornaments and slurs, the clarification and sharpening of rhythms, and the provision of missing accidentals, ties, and ledger lines. The sharpening of rhythms, in particular, is typical of Bach's revision process during the Leipzig years.

Even more important, the handwritten insertions in the Princeton and Vienna prints show Bach rewriting various passages and adding instructions to aid in the performance of the settings.[14] While there is a certain degree of overlap in the alterations, Bach seems to have annotated the copies independently, with the result that each contains unique changes that are of great importance for interpreting the text. The most striking unique insertion in the Princeton print is the addition of manual, pedal, and pitch indications in "Wachet auf," "Meine Seele," and "Kommst du nun, Jesu." The most striking unique insertion in the Vienna print is the provision of additional slurs and performance details in "Meine Seele."

In the case of "Kommst du nun, Jesu," Bach turned Schübler's engraving mistakes to good advantage in both the Princeton and Vienna exemplars, not only fixing the mangled ritornello of the original engraving but refining the opening of the theme beyond its cantata model (example 24-1). In the Vienna exemplar he indicated that this improved reading should be maintained when the ritornello returns in the dominant in measure 44.[15] In both copies Bach also sharpened the rhythm of the cantus firmus (example 24-2, a) and clarified that duple figures appearing in the cantus firmus should be absorbed into the triplet figures of the bass, when the two appear simultaneously (example 24-2, b).[16]

Example 24-1 "Kommst du nun, Jesu, vom Himmel herunter," BWV 650, mm. 1–2: (a) Cantata 137, movement 2, Violin 1 solo, (b) Schübler print, uncorrected, and (c) Schübler print, as revised by Bach in the Princeton and Vienna copies.

Example 24-2 "Kommst du nun, Jesu, vom Himmel herunter," BWV 650: (a) cantus firmus, mm. 13–15, with rhythms sharpened in the corrected print, and (b) cantus firmus, mm. 16–8, with clarification in the corrected print that the duplet figures are to be absorbed into the triplet figures of the bass.

In the Princeton print Bach indicated that the middle voice of "Kommst du nun, Jesu"—the cantus firmus—is to be performed in the pedal, an octave lower than written, and with a 4' stop. He did not make this change in the Vienna print, however, even though he made extensive revisions to the setting's text. This opens the possibility that when he marked up the Vienna copy, he still considered the printed score to correctly indicate the distribution of the parts—that is, that the ritornello figure is to be taken by the right hand on manual I (top staff in the print, in treble clef), the cantus firmus by the left hand on manual II (middle staff in the print, in alto clef), and the bass line by the feet on the pedalboard (lower staff in the print, in bass clef; see plate 24-1). This was not a perfect scheme, since the bass line contains an e' (in m. 42), a note seldom found on the pedalboards of Bach's day. But the note occurs in the pedal parts of several other works, and from a technical standpoint, the bass line is performable by the feet, however challenging.[17]

Viewed together, the Princeton and Vienna copies of the original edition present an ambiguous picture with regard to the assignment of the cantus firmus in "Kommst du nun, Jesu." Bach's instruction in the Princeton print to play the chorale melody in the pedal, long considered definitive, is contradicted by his acceptance in the Vienna print of playing the cantus firmus in the left hand and taking the animated bass line in the pedal. The two sources appear to give players the option of picking their pedal poison: difficult ornaments, if the pedal carries the cantus firmus, or difficult leaps, if the pedal carries the bass line.[18]

Another apparently spontaneous performance decision can be observed in the Vienna print, at the well-known "thumbing" spot in measure 13 of "Meine Seele," where the right hand is required to sustain the last note of a cantus firmus phrase on manual I while simultaneously playing notes 2–4 of the accompaniment on manual II (example 24-3, a). In the Vienna print, Bach changed the cantus firmus note from a dotted half note to a dotted quarter note and a dotted quarter-note rest and added a slur over notes 3–4 of the alto in the accompaniment (example 24-3, b). This appears to indicate that the right hand is to play simultaneously on manual I and manual II for just one note in the first half of the measure and then move to manual II in the second half of the measure to realize the slurred figure in the accompaniment. This change does not appear in the Princeton exemplar.

We have gone into some detail about the Princeton and Vienna copies of the original edition because they not only illustrate Bach's desire to resolve the printing problems of the Schübler Chorales but also show his unending quest to improve the text of his works. And they provide a rare glimpse of Bach the organist grappling with practical issues of performance as well: How *is* one to play these technically challenging settings, which are so elegant in their original cantata form but somewhat awkward when transferred to the organ? Bach seems to have been sorting this out on the fly, offering different solutions at different moments as he corrected copies of the print. For Bach, performance was an open-ended undertaking, sometimes calling for bold, improvised

Example 24-3 "Meine Seele erhebt den Herren," BWV 649, m. 13: (a) Schübler print, uncorrected, and (b) Vienna copy of the print, with Bach's handwritten revisions.

strokes of invention. For this reason, we must regret that only six copies of the Schübler print have survived. Lost exemplars might have reinforced the singular indications found in the Princeton and Vienna prints—or they might have presented still other options!

The Music

Despite the claim on the title page that the Schübler Chorales are "of Various Sorts," the six settings share a similar formal design. In each case, the chorale melody appears as a simple cantus firmus within a well-rounded ritornello form. The ritornello, which appears in full at the beginning and end of the setting (with the exception of "Wachet auf," where it occurs only at the beginning), follows the three-part Vivaldian model that we observed in the Leipzig "symphonic" organ preludes: an initial segment establishing the key is followed by a middle segment of sequential material, which leads to a closing cadential segment. Portions of the ritornello, sometimes transposed, appear between the phrases of the chorale tune, much in the fashion of concerto episodes. The ritornello appears in altered form against the tune as well.

The ritornello establishes the mood for each setting. It functions almost independently from the cantus firmus, and portrays in a general way the character, or *affect*, of the choral text. The bass line, derived from the continuo of the cantata-aria model, is mostly nonthematic and proceeds steadily from beginning to end. Nowhere does Bach pause to highlight individual words or phrases associated with the chorale text, as he does in several settings in the "Great Eighteen" Collection. The strong, constant presence of the ritornello theme and the uninterrupted movement of the bass make for a highly unified, homogeneous accompanimental fabric that clothes the chorale melody as it sounds in stark simplicity. The instrumental roots of the Schübler Chorales are reflected in the fact that the collection contains six settings, the number of pieces commonly associated with an instrumental opus.

The use of a fully developed, well-rounded ritornello form was a new approach to chorale preluding at the time. Bach explored the potential of ritornello procedure in his Leipzig cantatas before adopting it for several chorale settings in Clavier-Übung III (see chapter 22). In the Schübler Chorales, he appropriated it directly from the arias of his chorale-cantata cycle. With its clear structure, attractive tunes, and balanced phrases, the ritornello chorale was a progressive genre that was warmly embraced by Bach's sons and students, who viewed it as a stylish update to chorale preluding. Johann Ludwig Krebs, Gottfried August Homilius, Johann Friedrich Doles, and other composers of the younger generation turned enthusiastically to writing chorale settings in this new way—so much so that Carl Philipp Emanuel Bach, inheriting his father's Orgel-Büchlein album, transformed the old-fashioned melody chorale "Ich ruf zu dir, Herr Jesu Christ," BWV 639, into an up-to-date ritornello chorale (BWV² Anh. II 73) by inserting a newly composed ritornello theme at the beginning and end of the chorale tune and between its phrases as well.[19] By the 1730s, the ritornello chorale was the form of the future—a *galant* approach to organ improvisation and composition that lent an operatic air to the venerable practice of preluding on a hymn tune. Bach may have agreed to publish the Schübler Chorales to show that he, too, could write chorale preludes in this way.

Bach's choice of chorales for the Schübler settings was also progressive. In contrast to the modal Reformation melodies that served as the basis for Clavier-Übung III, the chorales of the Schübler settings were almost all tonal products of the post-Reformation period—highly popular, tuneful melodies created in the late sixteenth and seventeenth centuries. Even the ancient Magnificat tune, based on the *tonus peregrines* of Gregorian chant, appears within a dance idiom in updated D minor, notated with one flat:

Schübler setting	Chorale source
Wachet auf, ruft uns die Stimme	Philipp Nicolai, 1599
Wo soll ich fliehen hin	Melchior Vulpius, 1609
Wer nur den lieben Gott lässt walten	Georg Neumark, 1641
Meine Seele erhebt den Herren	Psalm tone IX[20] (*tonus peregrinus*)
Ach bleib bei uns, Herr Jesu Christ	Seth Calvisius, 1594
Kommst du nun, Jesu, von Himmel herunter	Stralsund hymnal, 1665

The trio and quartet writing of the Schübler Chorales, however, is what most sets the pieces apart from Bach's other organ works. The counterpoint is markedly accessible and attractive, with a distinctly modern ring. One can play the ritornello themes and bass lines without the cantus firmus melodies and still have an engaging piece (albeit with gaps, where the chorale tune occurs alone with the bass). The ritornello figures are so independent and universally attractive that Bach did not hesitate to remove them from the specific imagery of their original texts, be it of a verse ("Wachet auf," "Wer nur den lieben Gott," and "Meine Seele") or of an entire chorale ("Kommst du nun, Jesu"). With the possible exception of "Wo soll ich fliehen hin," the music was originally intended for church congregants in Leipzig, to draw them into the message of the cantata. This gives the Schübler Chorales an unusually broad, public appeal.

Although there are many attractive trio and quartet settings with chorale cantus firmus in the cantatas, Bach's choices were surprisingly limited when it came to selecting pieces that could be transferred to the organ without significant rearranging. The alto trio "Erbarm dich mein in solcher Last" (tune: "Herr Jesu Christ, du höchstes Gut") from Cantata 113, for instance, is sufficiently tuneful, but it is cast in F♯ minor, an awkward key for the organ in Bach's day, and its continuo line ascends three times to e'—a note unavailable on most German pedalboards of the time, as we noted earlier. Or the soprano trio "Du Friedefürst, Herr Jesu Christ" from Cantata 143 is an engaging ritornello form, but its continuo line is too active and too high for pedal performance and its soprano part is too high for the pedal, if the continuo line were to be taken by the left hand. One by one the pieces fall away, leaving the five movements from the chorale-cantata cycle of 1724–1725 as the most viable selections (table 24-1).

"Wachet auf, ruft uns die Stimme," BWV 645, is derived from the central Choral movement of Cantata 140, *Wachet auf, ruft uns die Stimme*, written for the twenty-seventh Sunday after Trinity in 1731, the first time during Bach's tenure that this final Sunday in the church year occurred. The Choral is a trio setting for unison tenors, unison strings (violins and violas), and continuo of the second verse of Nicolai's famous hymn. The leaping ritornello figure may mirror the leaping and animated mirth described in the verse's opening lines:

> Zion hört die Wächter singen,
> Das Hertz tut ihr für Freuden springen,
> Sie wachet und steht eilend auf.

> Zion hears the watchmen singing,
> Her heart leaps for joy,
> She wakes and quickly rises.

With its slurred appoggiaturas, melodic jumps, syncopations, and ornamental slides (several of which were added in the Princeton and Vienna prints), the ritornello is about as jazzy as Bach can get. It is also a riff on the opening triad of Nicolai's tune: measures 1–4 are an extended embellishment of the notes e♭' and g', and measures 5–12 an extended embellishment of the note b♭'. All this is foreshadowed in measures 1–2 of the pedal, where the opening triad of Nicolai's melody is presented in a more concise form. Six years lay between the composition of Cantata 140 and the other chorale cantatas that provided material for the Schübler settings, and in the interim Bach continued to evolve different types of ritornello structures. The ritornello of "Wachet auf" reflects this ongoing exploration, for it concludes unusually, in open-ended fashion, by cadencing in the dominant rather than the tonic. Hence it could not be repeated note-for-note at the end of the piece, like the ritornellos of the other Schübler settings, but had to be rewritten to conclude in the tonic.

There is also the remarkable foreshortening of the ritornello segment in C minor in the second half of the setting (mm. 35–44), to accommodate the third phrase of the Abgesang of the chorale, and the climactic animation of the ritornello and bass at the end of the movement. All this, plus the masterful

Table 24-1 The Schübler Chorales: Summary

Title	Texture	Key	Location of cantus firmus	Source
Wachet auf, ruft uns die Stimme, BWV 645	Trio	E♭ Major	LH (8')	Cantata 140, *Wachet auf, ruft uns die Stimme* (1731, 27th Sunday after Trinity), mvt. 4, "Zion hört die Wächter singen"
Wo soll ich fliehen hin, oder Auf meinen lieben Gott, BWV 646	Trio	E minor	Ped. (4')	Organ chorale setting?
Wer nur den lieben Gott lässt walten, BWV 647	Quartet	C minor	Ped. (4')	Cantata 93, *Wer nur den lieben Gott lässt walten* (1724, 5th Sunday after Trinity), mvt. 4, "Er kennt die rechten Freudenstunden"
Meine Seele erhebt den Herren, BWV 648	Quartet	D minor	RH (8')	Cantata 10, *Meine Seel erhebt den Herren* (1724, Visitation of the Virgin), mvt. 5, "Er denket der Barmherzigkeit"
Ach bleib bei uns, Herr Jesu Christ, BWV 649	Trio	B♭ major	RH (8')	Cantata 6, *Bleib bei uns, denn es will Abend werden* (1725, 2nd day of Easter), mvt. 3, "Ach bleib bei uns, Herr Jesu Christ"
Kommst du nun, Jesu, vom Himmel herunter, BWV 650	Trio	G major	LH (8') or Pedal (4')	Cantata 137, *Lobe den Herren, den mächtigen König der Ehren* (1725, 12th Sunday after Trinity), mvt. 2, "Lobet den Herren, der alles so herrlich regieret."

interweaving of the ritornello and the cantus firmus phrases, has led with good reason to the modern nickname "The King of Chorales."

"Wo soll ich fliehen hin, oder Auf meinen lieben Gott," BWV 646, has no identifiable model, but one can imagine it being drawn from a now-lost cantata aria for alto (= cantus firmus, pedal, 4'), violin (= ritornello, manual I, 8'), and continuo (= bass, manual II, 16'). This would explain the range, style, and clefs of the three parts. One finds similarly angular, concise, restless violin writing in the opening chorus of Cantata 26, *Ach wie flüchtig, ach wie nichtig* of 1724. The turning motive of the ritornello, reinforced by Bach's systematic addition of handwritten turns at the four principal cadences in the Vienna exemplar of the original print,[21] suggests that the music may have been a setting of "Auf meinen lieben Gott," the anonymous 1603 text also set to Vulpius's melody, whose penultimate line includes the word *wenden*—"to turn."

> Auf meinen lieben Gott
> Trau ich in Angst und Not,
> Der kann mich allzeit retten
> Aus Trübsal, Angst und Nöten
> Mein Unglück kann er wenden,
> Steht all's in seinen Händen.

> In my beloved God
> I trust in anguish and need,
> He can rescue me at all times
> From distress, hardship, and dire straits.
> He can turn away my misfortune,
> For everything stands in his hands.

On the other hand, several factors point in the direction of an original organ piece rather than a transcription. First, the dual title of the setting resembles those found in several organ chorales of the Orgel-Büchlein. It would seem to apply to an organ piece rather than a texted cantata aria, where there would be only one chorale source. Second, the relatively error-free text of the setting suggests the absence of a transcriber/assistant, who seems to have introduced mistakes into the other settings. Third, a variant reading, transmitted in a copy of the setting written after Bach's death,[22] and titled "Praeludium über Wo soll ich fliehen hin?," hints at the existence of a now-lost early version of the piece, which would imply an organ-chorale origin rather than a cantata-aria model. The variant concerns only a single four-note figure, however.[23] These factors must be weighed against the overall pattern of borrowing in the Schübler collection.[24]

The ritornello theme is a highly embellished version of the first two phrases of the chorale melody: measures 1–2 reflect the ascending fifth of the first phrase, and measures 3–5 reflect the descending fourth of the second phrase twice, first at the distance of two beats, then at the distance of a single beat (example 24-4). Such ingenious invention, together with the imitation between the ritornello theme and the bass, gives the short setting a remarkably cohesive and tightly knit structure.

"**Wer nur den lieben Gott lässt walten,**" BWV 647, is a transcription of the fourth movement of Cantata 93, *Wer nur den lieben Gott lässt walten*, a vocal duet for soprano and alto with cantus firmus (performed by unison strings)

Example 24-4 "Wo soll ich fliehen hin, oder Auf meinen lieben Gott," BWV 646: (a) Chorale melody, and (b) ritornello figure, with related melodic steps marked.

and continuo on the fourth verse, "Er kennt die rechten Freudenstunden," of Neumark's hymn "Wer nur den lieben Gott lässt walten" of 1641. The ritornello, derived from the first six notes of the chorale, creates a somber atmosphere, yet at the same time its animated 16th-note figures may reflect the moments of joy mentioned in the text ("He knows the right times for joy").

The crossing lines of the vocal parts in the cantata aria make for awkward keyboard writing, despite Bach's handwritten improvements in the Princeton and Vienna copies of the original print. One small but important change not reflected in the Peters, Bach-Gesamtausgabe, Neue Bach-Ausgabe, or Breitkopf editions occurs in measure 13, where Bach altered the third note in the left hand from B-flat to B-natural, creating a jarring cross-relationship with the B-flat of the cantus firmus that appears simultaneously in the pedal (example 24-5). The B-flat/B-natural clash echoes the tonal/modal ambiguity of the chorale tune and may have been intended to highlight the phrase "in allem Kreuz" (as one bears the cross) that appears at that spot in the first verse of the chorale. There is no doubt that Bach intended this striking dissonance as the final reading: it appears as a handwritten change in the London, Princeton, and Vienna prints. In modern editions it is reproduced only in the Leupold Edition.

"Meine Seele erhebt den Herren," BWV 648, is a transcription of the fifth movement of Cantata 10, *Meine Seel erhebt den Herren*, a vocal duet for alto and tenor with cantus firmus (performed by the oboes and trumpet) and continuo on the fifth and sixth lines of the Magnificat text (Luke 1:46-55): "Er denket der Barmherzigkeit und hilft seinem Diener Israel auf." (He remembers his mercy and helps his servant Israel.) As in "Wer nur den lieben Gott," the independent voice lines make for awkward performance on the keyboard, especially when the alto and tenor parts diverge to the point that they cannot be played by the left hand alone but require "thumbing" from the right hand (mm. 13 and 24). The music is a gentle dance of supplication in 6/8 meter, in which the semitone

Example 24-5 "Wer nur den lieben Gott lässt walten," BWV 647, mm. 12b–14: Bach's alteration, in the Vienna and Princeton copies of the print, of the third note of the bass (LH) in m. 13 to create a clashing false relation with the first note of the cantus firmus (pedal).

Pedal 4'

Example 24-6 "Ach, bleib bei uns, Herr Jesu Christ," BWV 649: (a) chorale melody, and (b) ritornello figure, with related melodic steps marked.

appoggiatura is emphasized all the more in the Vienna and Princeton copies of the original print through Bach's handwritten insertion of additional slurs.

"Ach bleib bei uns, Herr Jesu Christ," BWV 649, is a transcription of the third movement of Cantata 6, *Bleib bei uns, den es will Abend werden*, a chorale trio for soprano, violoncello piccolo, and continuo. In the cantata version, the soprano sings the first two verses of Calvisius's hymn; in the organ setting, the music is abridged to one verse. The virtuoso violoncello line, which is ingeniously derived from the first phrase of the chorale melody (example 24-6), may express the soul's "jumping for joy" in anticipation that the bright light of Christ's divine word will offer protection against the approaching darkness of death:

> Ach bleib bei uns, Herr Jesu Christ,
> Weil es nun abend worden ist,
> Dein göttlich Wort, das helle licht,
> Laß ja bei uns auslöschen nicht.

Oh, stay with us, Lord Jesus Christ,
For it has now become evening.
Let not your divine word, that bright light,
Be extinguished among us.

In the organ arrangement, the obbligato cello part is assigned to the left hand. The leaps are idiomatic for a string instrument but present great challenges for the performer when transferred to the keyboard of an organ. Although a transcription of a vocal trio, the setting is not unlike that of the bicinium "Allein Gott in der Höh sei Ehr," BWV 711, which contains an equally leap-filled, string-like left-hand part under a simple cantus firmus.

The music for the last Schübler chorale, "**Kommst du nun, Jesu, vom Himmel herunter auf Erden**," BWV 650, comes from the Cantata 137, *Lobe den Herren, den mächtigen König der Ehren*, of 1725. It is a cantata *per omnes versus*, in which Bach used the five verses of Joachim Neander's 1680 hymn text word for word as the libretto for a five-movement work. The Schübler music is derived from the second movement, a trio for alto, solo violin, and continuo based on the second verse of the hymn "Lobe den Herren, der alles so herrlich regieret":

Lobe den Herren, der alles so herrlich regieret,
Der dich auf Adelers Fittichen sicher geführet,
Der dich erhält,
Wie es dir selber gefällt.
Hast du nicht dieses verspüret?

Praise to the Lord, who governs all things so magnificently,
Who bears you safely on eagle's wings,
Who preserves you
As you yourself wish.
Have you not perceived this?

The contour of the obbligato violin line, taken by the right hand in the organ arrangement, is derived from the opening triad of the chorale tune, and its rapidly rising and falling 16th notes may reflect the beating of the eagle's wings mentioned in the verse. As we noted earlier, in the Princeton and Vienna copies of the original print Bach used the task of correcting the error-filled music text of the organ transcription to improve the ritornello and, in the Princeton exemplar, to present the performance option of playing the cantus firmus, sung by the alto in the cantata movement, on the pedal instead of the manual. In the violin part of the cantata, the ritornello figure is strongly articulated (example 24-1)—a nuance that is not transmitted in the organ score but can be realized to good effect in performance.

Why Bach renamed his transcription of "Lobe den Herren" after Caspar Friedrich Nachtenhöfer's five-verse chorale "Kommst du nun, Jesu, vom Himmel herunter auf Erden" is not fully clear. In contemporary hymnals Nachtenhöfer's 1667 text is listed as appropriate for Advent or Christmas and sung to the melody "Lobe den Herren."[25] In the Schübler setting, the joyful dance idiom in 9/8 meter captures the mirth of Christ's anticipated arrival just as well as the joy of God's glory, and the possible cantata imagery of eagle's wings might now allude to the eternal soaring mentioned in the final verse of Nachtenhöfer's hymn:

> Führe mich endlich, O Jesu, ins ewige Leben
> Welches du allen, die gläuben, versprochen zu geben
> Da ich bey Gott,
> Ohne Not, Jammer und Tod
> Ewig in Freuden kann schweben.

> Lead me at last, O Jesus, into the eternal life
> Which you have promised to grant to all who believe
> So that with God,
> Without misery, distress, and death,
> I am able to soar eternally in joy.

If the Schübler edition was offered for sale in the fall, Bach might have changed the text of "Lobe den Herren" to spur sales at the annual St. Michael's Fair in Leipzig, a three-week event that began the first week in October or so. A setting based on "Kommst du nun, Jesu" would have added market value to the collection, as a potential gift for Advent or Christmas.

The Structure of the Collection

When Bach assembled the Orgel-Büchlein and Clavier-Übung III, he began with an organizational principle—the Lutheran hymnbook for the former, the Lutheran ritual and Catechism for the latter—and then composed pieces to fit the preconceived framework. With the Schübler Chorales, he seems to have done the opposite. He appears to have selected an opus of six preexisting cantus firmus pieces on the basis of technical considerations—their potential as organ trios and quartets—and then placed them a logical order according to compositional features. While some writers have attempted to see a theological plan at work in the Schübler collection, such as a believer seeking divine grace or a celebration of feast days,[26] one must stretch matters considerably to perceive a liturgical pattern at work.[27] The six chorales have diverse liturgical functions, and the cantatas in which five of them appear are represented out of their sequence in the church year.

It is far more likely that Bach, once having chosen his six transcriptions, placed them in an order that emphasized the balanced placement of the cantus firmus (left hand–pedal, pedal–right hand, right hand–left hand) and the symmetrical grouping of textures (trio, trio–quartet, quartet–trio, trio):

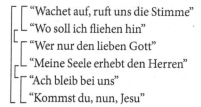

"Wachet auf, ruft uns die Stimme"	Trio, cantus firmus in the left hand
"Wo soll ich fliehen hin"	Trio, cantus firmus in the pedal
"Wer nur den lieben Gott"	Quartet, cantus firmus in the pedal
"Meine Seele erhebt den Herren"	Quartet, cantus firmus in the right hand
"Ach bleib bei uns"	Trio, cantus firmus in the right hand
"Kommst du, nun, Jesu"	Trio, cantus firmus in the left hand

This assumes that "Kommst du, nun, Jesu" was intended to be played as originally printed, with the cantus firmus performed by the left hand on manual II and the bass line by the feet on the pedalboard. The resulting format of the Schübler print underscores the methodical treatment of an unembellished cantus firmus in diverse ways (the "various sorts" of the title) and resembles the nuanced, multilayered designs of Bach's other late keyboard collections, most notably the order of Clavier-Übung III, where the treatment of an unadorned cantus firmus (in canon and as a pedal voice) serves as an organizational principle within the *pedaliter* Catechism settings (see table 22-1 in chapter 22).

Two other organizational aspects of the Schübler Chorales hark back to the Six Trio Sonatas of c. 1730. The first is the key scheme, which similarly begins with the "heroic" key of E♭ Major, continues with three pieces in minor mode, and ends with two pieces in major mode. The second is the technical progression, in which performance demands similarly increase as the player moves through the collection, culminating with the most difficult works, "Ach bleib bei uns" and "Kommst du nun, Jesu." These are also the most animated pieces, producing a musical and technical climax to the collection.

The Significance of the Settings

Coming nearly a decade after the retrospective settings of Clavier-Übung III, the Schübler Chorales put Bach back on the organ-music market with a collection of progressive, modern pieces—catchy, fashionable cantus firmus settings of popular hymns holding appeal for the next generation of organists. The Schübler

Chorales may have been the aging cantor's response to the varied settings of Georg Friedrich Kauffmann's *Harmonische Seelenlust*, issued in installments in Leipzig between 1733 and 1736. Kauffmann's publication included the full gamut of chorale prelude types, from simple congregational harmonizations to fore-imitation chorales to progressive ritornello settings to arrangements for oboe and organ. It also contained instructions for registration and the distribution of parts to specific divisions of the organ (plate 24-2)—performance aids that Bach uncharacteristically adopted in the Schübler edition, in "Wo soll ich fliehen hin" and "Wer nur den lieben Gott lässt walten" in the original print and in "Wachet auf, ruft uns die Stimme" "Meine Seele erhebt den Herren," and "Kommst du nun, Jesu, vom Himmel herunter" in the emended Princeton exemplar.

Harmonische Seelenlust brought the published organ chorale into the *galant* era in Germany, with performable settings of broad appeal. As we mentioned earlier, Bach may have wished to demonstrate that he, too, could produce such pieces, not only to win over younger organists but perhaps also in belated response to Johann Adolph Scheibe's criticism in 1737 that his compositional style was bombastic, confused, and, in general, too artful and unnatural.[28] To refute

Plate 24-2 Georg Friedrich Kauffmann, opening measures of "Wie schön leuchtet der Morgenstern," for organ and oboe, from *Harmonische Seelenlust*.
Staatsbibliothek zu Berlin—Preußischer Kulturbesitz, Musikabteilung mit Mendelssohn-Archiv

Scheibe's claims, one of Bach's defenders, Lorenz Christoph Mizler, pointed to the fashionable style of a vocal work performed at the Easter Fair the year before by the Collegium Musicum.[29] Bach's supporters could have similarly noted the up-to-date style of the Schübler Chorales, had they been in print, even though most, of not all, of the "new" settings were derived from music that was already more than two decades old.

The Schübler Chorales may also have been a product of Bach's general review of his sacred vocal works in the late 1730s and 1740s, a process that resulted in the recycling of earlier cantata material in the four Short Masses and the Mass in B Minor. In these vocal works Bach took preexisting choruses and arias, inserted the Latin Mass Ordinary text, and revised the scores to give the music new life in a broader context. In a similar fashion, rearranging the five arias—or six, depending how we view "Wo soll ich fliehen hin"—from his annual cycle of chorale cantatas gave the music a new life outside the Lutheran worship service, where it would have been performed no more than once every few years. As organ chorales, the pieces could have been played more generally within the service, as organ preludes to the hymn tunes whenever they were sung, or outside the service, as music for recitals.

In the case of the Masses, Bach sometimes compromised the music, abandoning specific word imagery and using just select portions of movements. In the case of the Schübler Chorales, he sometimes abandoned specific text and verse imagery in a similar fashion and shortened the setting in the case of "Ach bleib bei uns." He also sacrificed the chordal support provided by the continuo, a feature that led Walter Emery to declare that the arrangements are "much less effective than the originals, and it is hard to see why Bach published them."[30] The ongoing popularity of the works has vindicated Bach's decision, which lifted the music out of the Leipzig worship service and placed it in a more public arena.

There is evidence that Bach performed Cantatas 6, 10, and 137 once again in the 1740s.[31] This raises the possibility that he presented the entire chorale cycle at that time, and that this music—his greatest accomplishment in the realm of cantata writing—was very much on his mind. It is even possible that Johann Georg Schübler heard the works while studying with Bach, or heard his teacher perform a transcription of a favorite aria in the cycle, giving rise to the idea of a published collection of trios and quartets. But this is speculation only. We simply don't know the precise impetus for the project.

That said, the Schübler Chorales illustrate Bach's remarkable inventiveness in the realm of transcription, displaying the same "technical-demands-be-damned" approach seen in the concerto transcriptions of the Weimar period. "With his two feet, he could play things on the pedals that many not unskillful clavier players would find it bitter enough to have to play with five fingers," said the Obituary of 1750.[32] This is well illustrated in Bach's suggestion in the Princeton exemplar to play the cantus firmus of "Kommst du nun, Jesu" in the pedal rather than the left hand. His addition of trills to the line was sheer bravado.

Finally, we cannot overlook the affinity of the Schübler settings with chamber music. The bass lines are literally continuo lines, and the upper parts literally instrumental or vocal parts. What better way to illustrate the versatility of the forward-looking Central German pipe organ, with its chamber music orientation and progressive stops designed to imitate the oboe, transverse flute, gamba, violone, and other instruments? The settings bring Bach's Leipzig output full circle, back to the miscellaneous trios and the Six Sonatas of the first decade. We are fortunate to have the Schübler Chorales, whether they were initiated by Schübler or by Bach himself.

Notes

1. Translation adapted from NBR, no. 238.
2. Gregory G. Butler, "Schübler," in *Bach Companion*, Malcolm Boyd, ed. (London: Oxford University Press, 1999), 441, and "The Printing History of J. S. Bach's Musical Offering: New Perspectives," *Journal of Musicology* 19 (2002), 306–331.
3. Wolff 1991c, 184–185.
4. Schulze 2008, 303.
5. By comparison, Bach's other editions have been passed down in quantities ranging from 16 to 24 copies. See the figures in Stauffer 2010, 50–51.
6. BDok, no. 794.
7. BDok III, no. 745, and Günther Kraft, "Johann Georg Schübler: Bachs Notenstecher und Verleger," in *Johann Sebastian Bach in Thüringen: Festgabe zum Gedenkjahr 1950*, Heinrich Besseler, ed. (Weimar: Thüringer Volksverlag, 1950), 186.
8. British Library, *K 12 a 23*.
9. Princeton University Library, Special Collections, William H. Scheide Library, *26.2*.
10. Austrian National Library, Anthony von Hoboken Collection, *SH J.S. Bach 40*.
11. NBR, no. 389a.
12. Stauffer 2015.
13. Wolff 1991c, 180. The first page was present when Wilhelm Rust edited the BG in the 1870s but missing by the time Spitta attempted to discern the copy's provenance in the 1880s.
14. For details of the changes in the Princeton exemplar, see Wolff 1991c, 184–185. For details of the changes in the Vienna exemplar, see Stauffer 2015, 181–186.
15. In NBA IV/1, 101, this important change is presented as an ossia and mistakenly credited to Oley rather than Bach.
16. To be more precise: The rhythmic sharpening in m. 13 appears in the Princeton, Vienna, and London prints; the sharpening in m. 14 appears in the London print only. The assimilation of the duplet figures into the bass triplets appears in all three corrected prints.

17. See also the comments in Yearsley 2012, 56–58.

18. Both versions of "Kommst du nun, Jesu" are presented in the Leupold Edition, vol. 9.

19. C.P.E. Bach's version is reproduced in *Carl Philipp Emanuel Bach: The Complete Works* (Los Altos, CA: Packard Humanities Institute, 2005–), I/9 (*The Organ Works*, Annette Richards and David Yearsley, eds., 2008), 82–83, and the Leupold Edition, vol. 1A, 137–139.

20. As classified in the *Liber Usualis*, the book of commonly used Gregorian chants compiled by the monks of the Abbey of Solesmes in France in 1896.

21. Over the fourth 8th note in mm. 6, 14, 24, and 33. See the text in the Leupold Edition, vol. 9.

22. Berlin State Library, *P 566*, in the hand of Gottfried Heinrich Möhring (1749–1825).

23. See NBA IV/1, KB (Heinz-Harald Löhlein, ed., 1987), 149 and 169.

24. The best summary of this complex issue appears in Kube 1999, 607–608.

25. Bighley 2018, 160.

26. W. M. Taesler 1969 or Bighley 1991, for instance.

27. As in Williams 2003, 319, where a liturgical plan is proposed by considering the settings in reserve order.

28. NBR, no. 343.

29. The cantata *Willkommen! Ihr herrschenden Götter der Erden*, BWV[3] 1161, whose text survives but music is lost.

30. Walter Emery, quoted in Williams 2003, 317.

31. Bach Compendium, 247, 537, 735.

32. NBR, no. 306.

25

Nineteen Large Chorales of Various Sorts

In addition to publishing the Third Part of the Clavier-Übung in the fall of 1739, Bach began to focus on two other large-scale projects involving keyboard music. The first was volume 2 of the Well-Tempered Clavier, which he and his wife Anna Magdalena wrote out in a series of sheets in orchestral format around 1739–1742,[1] probably for collegium musicum performances at Zimmermann's Coffee House and Coffee Garden. In assembling the set, Bach used earlier preludes and fugues whenever possible, revising, expanding, and transposing the pieces as necessary.[2] He then filled the gaps with new compositions. Bach appears to have had a dual goal in mind as he worked on the project: first, to compile a second book of 24 preludes and fugues to complement volume 1 of the Well-Tempered Clavier, and second, to clear the shelves of worthy pieces that could be recycled in a useful way. The result was an update of the Well-Tempered Clavier: the preludes and fugues of volume 2 are more progressive than those of volume 1, displaying a much richer array of idioms and meters. Stylistically, some pieces verge on the *galant*, and a number of preludes are cast in rounded-binary formats that foreshadow Pre-Classical style.

The Leipzig Chorale Portfolio

Bach's second undertaking was quite different: a portfolio of large, retrospective *pedaliter* organ chorales, derived almost exclusively from works written earlier in Weimar. Widely known today as the "Great Eighteen" Chorales, the collection is preserved together with the Six Sonatas and the Weimar version of the trio on "Nun komm, der Heiden Heiland," BWV 660a, in the autograph miscellany *P 271* in the Berlin State Library.[3] If the Well-Tempered Clavier, volume 2, looked to the future, the chorale portfolio, by contrast, pointed to the past, preserving a tradition of preluding on hymns that had mostly gone out of style by the 1730s and 1740s.

The portfolio contains 19 works, in the following order:

Fantasia super Komm, heiliger Geist, Herre Gott, BWV 651
Komm, heiliger Geist, Herre Gott, BWV 652
An Wasserflüssen Babylon, BWV 653

J. S. BACH. George B. Stauffer, Oxford University Press. © Oxford University Press 2024.
DOI: 10.1093/oso/9780195108026.003.0026

Schmücke dich, o liebe Seele, BWV 654

Trio super Herr Jesu Christ, dich zu uns wend, BWV 655

O Lamm Gottes unschuldig, BWV 656

Nun danket alle Gott, BWV 657

Von Gott will ich nicht lassen, BWV 658

Nun komm der Heiden Heiland, BWV 659

Trio super Nun komm der Heiden Heiland, BWV 660

Nun komm der Heiden Heiland, BWV 661

Allein Gott in der Höh sei Ehr, BWV 662

Allein Gott in der Höh sei Ehr, BWV 663

Trio super Allein Gott in der Höh sei Ehr, BWV 664

Jesus Christus, unser Heiland, der von uns den Gotteszorn wand, BWV 665

Jesus Christus, unser Heiland, der von uns den Gotteszorn wand, BWV 666

Komm, Gott Schöpfer, heiliger Geist, BW 667

Vom Himmel hoch, da komm ich her (Canonic Variations), BWV 769a

Vor deinen Thron tret ich hiermit (fragment), BWV 668

Bach started to assemble the collection around the same time he compiled Well-Tempered Clavier II—that is, c. 1739–1742, to judge from the nature of his handwriting.[4] In this case he returned to the same paper he had used a decade or so earlier for the Six Sonatas.[5] Thus it seems that when he wrote out the Sonatas around 1730, he set aside a large batch of paper with a still larger project in mind—perhaps an encompassing compendium of organ works that would illustrate various compositional genres. The cleanly written autograph of the Prelude and Fugue in B Minor, BWV 544, and the partial fair-copy autograph of the Prelude and Fugue in E Minor ("Wedge"), BWV 548, are handed down on the same paper, raising the possibility that they, too, might have been part of this project.

Bach began the chorale collection by invoking Christ's help, writing "J.J." ("Jesu Juva," or Jesus help me) at the top of the first page (plate 25-1). He therefore viewed the endeavor as a significant compositional undertaking, much like the Six Sonatas, which display a similar opening invocation. Bach then proceeded to write out 13 settings, beginning with "Fantasia super Komm, heiliger Geist," BWV 651, and ending with the second "Allein Gott in der Höh sei Ehr," BWV 663.[6] He appears to have entered the first 12 pieces in one go, since he ruled their pages with the same rastrum, or staff ruler.[7] This suggests that he began the cho- rale portfolio with a cache of a dozen settings that were revised and ready for entry. The second "Allein Gott" setting—the thirteenth piece—seems to have been added at a slightly later point, since Bach used a different rastrum to com- plete its text.[8]

Plate 25-1 Leipzig chorale portfolio, first page, with beginning of "Fantasia super Komm, heiliger Geist," BWV 651, and "J.J." ("Jesu Juva," or Jesus, come to my aid) in the upper left corner.

Staatsbibliothek zu Berlin—Preußischer Kulturbesitz, Musikabteilung mit Mendelssohn-Archiv

After writing out the second "Allein Gott" setting, Bach set the project aside for several years, picking it up again around 1746–1747 to add two more settings: the "Trio super Allein Gott in der Höh sei Ehr," BWV 664, and "Jesus Christus, unser Heiland," BWV 665.[9]

What happened after this is open to debate. The portfolio continues with "Jesus Christus, unser Heiland, alio modo," BWV 666, and "Komm, Gott Schöpfer, heiliger Geist," BWV 667, entered neatly on four pages by Johann Christoph Altnickol (1719–1759), Bach's son-in-law and former student.[10] The chorales added by Altnickol are followed on a new page by the revised version of the Canonic Variations on "Vom Himmel hoch, da komm ich her," BWV 769a, in Bach's hand once again. The entry dates from around 1747–1748, a year or so after his addition of the "Allein Gott" trio and the first "Jesus Christus, unser Heiland" setting.[11] And the Canonic Variations are followed immediately by "Vor deinen Thron, tret ich hiermit," BWV 668, entered by the unidentified scribe known in Bach scholarship as "Anonymous Vr," a copyist who worked for Bach between 1743 and 1750 (plate 25-2).[12] "Vor deinen Thron" breaks off after 25½ measures at the bottom of a verso page. The *custi*, or directs, at the end of the last measure hint that "Vor deinen Thron" continued on another page, and the folio structure of the manuscript suggests that such a page once existed and is now missing.[13]

Hans Klotz, editing the chorales for the Neue Bach-Ausgabe in the 1950s, before the appearance of the groundbreaking handwriting studies of Georg von Dadelsen and Yoshitake Kobayashi,[14] speculated that Bach assembled the entire chorale portfolio only at the very end of his life, beginning possibly as late as 1749.[15] Klotz assumed that the Canonic Variations were a separate project from the other chorale settings, and that Bach purposely left four pages blank between the first "Jesus Christus, unser Heiland" setting and the Canonic Variations in order to set the Variations apart from the other pieces. Then, according to Klotz, Bach asked Altnickol to add "Jesus Christus, unser Heiland, alio modo" and "Komm, Gott Schöpfer" to the collection. "Komm, Gott Schöpfer" is designated "in organo pleno," and in Klotz's view it represented an appropriate framing element with the opening piece in the portfolio, "Fantasia super Komm, heiliger Geist," which also calls for a plenum registration. Klotz believed that "Vor deinen Thron," in the hand of an anonymous scribe, was added at a later point, possibly after Bach's death.

To Klotz, then, the Leipzig portfolio consisted of three distinct, unrelated elements: a closed group of 17 chorales, the Canonic Variations, and the "deathbed" chorale "Vor deinen Thron," dictated "to a friend" by the blind, bedridden Bach shortly before his death.[16] With this view of the contents in mind, Klotz rechristened the collection—known since the publication of the Bach-Gesamtausgabe in the nineteenth century as "The Eighteen Chorales"[17]—as "The Seventeen Chorales."[18]

Plate 25-2 Leipzig chorale portfolio, last page, containing the conclusion of "Vom Himmel hoch, da komm ich her" BWV 769a, and the beginning of "Vor deinen Thron tret ich hiermit," BWV 668.

More recently, Peter Wollny proposed that Anonymous Vr added "Vor deinen Thron" to the manuscript after Bach's unsuccessful eye operation in March 1750, either before or soon after Bach's death, but that Altnickol entered "Jesus Christus, unser Heiland, alio modo" and "Komm, Gott Schöpfer" well beyond that—in 1751 or even later.[19] Wollny based his hypothesis on the nature of Altnickol's handwriting, which has characteristics that seem to point to a period following his Leipzig years. Russell Stinson, in his monograph on the Great Eighteen Chorales, subsequently accepted Wollny's view and underscored the separate nature of the Canonic Variations:

> It follows that Bach left blank the four pages between the fifteenth chorale and the Canonic Variations simply as a means of separating the latter work—which is unquestionably an independent composition—from the preceding fifteen. Accordingly, Altnickol was careful in choosing two works of relatively modest size that would not exceed the available space.[20]

But if this scenario is correct, and Altnickol only added the alio modo setting of "Jesus Christus, unser Heiland" and "Komm, Gott Schöpfer" a year or so after Bach's death, one must ask why Anonymous Vr entered "Vor deinen Thron," presumably before Bach's death or shortly thereafter, awkwardly in the left-over three-staff systems at the end of the Canonic Variations (see plate 25-2) rather than writing it in the free space after the first "Jesus Christus, unser Heiland" setting. The views of Klotz, Wollny, and Stinson all rest on the assumption that Bach left four pages blank between the first setting of "Jesus Christus, unser Heiland" and the Canonic Variations and that he viewed the Canonic Variations as a separate project.[21]

This assumption can be questioned, however, for when Bach resumed work on the portfolio in 1747–1748 to enter the Canonic Variations, he seems to have begun by ruling the four pages in question with two-staff systems, in anticipation of adding one or two two-staff chorale settings, before ruling six and a half pages with three-staff systems for the Canonic Variations, which he proceeded to enter. That Bach, rather than Altnickol, ruled the four pages containing "Jesus Christus, unser Heiland, alio modo" and "Komm, Gott Schöpfer" is confirmed by the fact that the staves for the two chorale settings and the staves for the Canonic Variations were drawn with the same rastrum.[22]

It appears, then, that Bach planned from the start to insert additional pieces between the first "Jesus Christus, unser Heiland" setting and the Canonic Variations, and that he did not view the Variations as an independent project but as a continuation of the assembled settings. This intention is reflected in the Variations' title, which Bach changed from "Einige canonische Veränderungen über das Weynacht-Lied: Vom Himmel hoch da komm ich her. vor die Orgel mit

2 Clavieren und dem Pedal. von Johann Sebastian Bach"—the title in the printed edition—to "Vom Himmel hoch, da komm ich her. per Canones. à 2 Clav. et Pedal. di J. S. Bach"—the title in the chorale portfolio. The new heading mirrors precisely those of the other portfolio settings: chorale name, procedure, medium, and composer ("di J. S. Bach").

Since Bach ruled the four pages preceding "Vom Himmel hoch" with two-staff systems, it follows that he had specific settings—or types of settings—in mind. The alio modo arrangement of "Jesus Christus, unser Heiland," BWV 666, would have been a logical choice to follow the initial setting of the same chorale, since the two had already been paired in Weimar, to judge from the surviving sources from that time.[23] And "Komm, Gott Schöpfer" would have been a logical choice for a second work, since it already existed as an enlarged version of a Weimar piece, the Orgel-Büchlein chorale, BWV 631. As a double setting with the chorale melody treated in two different ways, the expanded "Komm, Gott Schöpfer" would have formed a logical bridge to "Vom Himmel hoch," in which the chorale tune is treated in five canons.

That both the alio modo setting of "Jesus Christus, unser Heiland" and "Komm, Gott Schöpfer" appear in the portfolio in revised form suggests that Bach was working on them with the intention of adding them to the collection, and that Altnickol was carrying out his wishes, most probably after March 1750, when Bach was blind and bedridden. Whether Altnickol entered the pieces while Bach was alive, or shortly after his death, as Wollny has proposed, is difficult to determine with certainty. The fact that Altnickol was mentioned with regard to the deathbed dictation of "Vor deinen Thron" (see below) and that he added the title "Die Kunst der Fuge" to the autograph manuscript of the Art of Fugue[24] suggests that he was present during Bach's last days and involved with setting the dying cantor's final musical matters in order. That "Vor deinen Thron," which also required only two staves, was placed after the Canonic Variations rather than before seems to confirm that the Altnickol entries were in place before Bach's death or soon afterward, when the "deathbed chorale" was entered into the manuscript by Anonymous Vr.

Viewing the Canonic Variations as an integral part of Bach's collection of revised chorales alters our perception of the whole. By positioning the Variations at the end of the portfolio, Bach may have intended the work as the culminating setting of the collection, covering the one retrospective technique not addressed in the earlier pieces: the art of the chorale canon. Although the Variations had been composed only recently, in Leipzig, rather than in Weimar, they preserved a genre that Bach had explored in the Orgel-Büchlein and that harkened back to the contrapuntal manipulations so admired by his North German predecessors and codified in Johann Theile's *Musicalisches Kunstbuch*. In addition, the manuscript version of the Canonic Variations is a performance score, unlike the printed edition with its enigmatic notation, and therefore matches the performance scores of the other settings in the portfolio, which contain a number of calculatedly convenient page turns.

It is also critical to discern that Bach planned to enter chorale settings on the pages before "Vom Himmel hoch," and that he most probably instructed Altnickol to add the "Jesus Christus, unser Heiland, alio modo" and "Komm, Gott Schöpfer" settings. This strengthens the case that their presence in the portfolio reflects Bach's wishes.

Whether or not he also intended "Vor deinen Thron" to be included cannot be decided definitively. As Christoph Wolff notes in his study of the piece,[25] the setting utilizes the same procedure as "Komm, Gott Schöpfer"—the expansion of an Orgel-Büchlein chorale—and like the other works in the portfolio, it represents the sophisticated treatment of a traditional genre, the fore-imitation chorale. It is quite possible that Bach indicated to Altnickol, to whom refinements were allegedly dictated, or to Anonymous Vr that "Vor deinen Thron" should be entered into the portfolio, where it formed a closing benediction to the collection. As Wolff has speculated, it may have been Bach's final offering to God.[26]

If this is true, then all four final settings—"Jesus Christus, unser Heiland, alio modo," "Komm, Gott Schöpfer," "Vom Himmel hoch," and "Vor deinen Thron"—were not random additions but part of an evolving, overarching plan determined by Bach. Thus the various titles proposed for the collection in the past—"Eighteen Large Chorales of Various Sorts" (Wilhelm Rust, in the Bach-Gesamtausgabe), "Eighteen Chorales" (shorter version of Rust's title, commonly used today in Germany and England), " 'Great Eighteen' Chorales" (E. Power Biggs, apparently, in concert programs),[27] and "Seventeen Chorales" (Hans Klotz, in the Neue Bach Ausgabe)—do not describe accurately the scope of the project.

A more appropriate title might be "Nineteen Chorales," or, following Rust's lead drawn from the title of the Schübler Chorales, "Nineteen Large Chorales of Various Sorts." This covers the full contents of the Leipzig portfolio and may best represent Bach's own thoughts on the revised works that he wished to be part of his final collection of organ music, dedicated to the art of setting a chorale.

Why These Chorale Settings?

What factors determined Bach's choice of pieces for the Leipzig portfolio, as he surveyed his earlier organ chorales?

Most obviously, all the works are substantial pedal settings, ranging in length from 199 measures (the second "Komm, heiliger Geist" setting) to 26 measures ("Komm, Gott Schöpfer"). They were either large from the start or had potential for expansion (the "Fantasia super Komm, heiliger Geist," "Komm, Gott Schöpfer," and "Vor deinen Thron"). Eleven of the 19 call for the use of two manuals and pedals—the mark of colorful chorale settings in Bach's time—and 12 of the 19 are written on three staves, a notation reserved for pieces with unusually complex, independent parts. All this points to the works' sophisticated nature.

Unlike the chorale settings of Clavier-Übung III, which are based on the founding hymns of the Lutheran church, the works of the Leipzig portfolio cover a wide historical range of hymn melodies, from derivatives of medieval chants ("Allein Gott, in der Höh sei Ehr" and "O Lamm Gottes") to sixteenth-century adaptations of Martin Luther ("Nun komm, der Heiden Heiland" and "Vom Himmel hoch") to seventeenth-century original tunes of Johann Crüger ("Schmücke dich" and "Nun danket alle Gott"). In the Orgel-Büchlein, Bach intended to set all the chorales of the liturgical year; in the Leipzig portfolio, he turned to just a handful of the most popular melodies.

Some settings may have had a special meaning for Bach, as pieces that represented bold compositional experiments from the Weimar years. As we noted in chapter 10, a number of settings were breakout works: the third "Nun komm, der Heiden Heiland" setting represented a stunning stylistic amalgamation, combining cantus firmus technique with complex fugal writing; the "Trio super Herr Jesus Christ" was one of Bach's first forays into Torelli's concise concerto style; the "Trio super Allein Gott in der Höh sei Ehr" foreshadowed the idiom of the Six Sonatas; and the "Fantasia super Komm, heiliger Geist" was one of Bach's initial adaptations of Vivaldi's forceful motoric rhythms.

Other settings may have held special significance as "crowd pleasers" in recitals. Pieces such as "Schmücke dich," with its sweet parallel thirds and sixths and gentle sarabande rhythms, or "Komm, Gott Schöpfer," with its powerful, jazzy, off-beat syncopations, must have impressed listeners greatly. "Vom Himmel hoch," with its complex but appealing variations, would have given Bach the opportunity to demonstrate his unparalleled contrapuntal wizardry in a public forum. In some instances, one also has a sense of Bach trying to outdo his predecessors: as we noted in chapter 10, the remarkable ending of the first "Nun komm, der Heiden Heiland" setting appears to be a riff on the pedal-point close of Buxtehude's chorale prelude on the same tune, BuxWV 211.

Bach also seems to have been especially concerned with the handling of the chorale melody, treating it as a simple cantus firmus in nine settings and a highly embellished line in seven others. He appears to have been equally concerned with the melody's placement, covering all possibilities in these settings—soprano, alto (in the second verse of "O Lamm Gottes"), tenor, and bass. In eight settings Bach specifically stipulated the location of the "canto fermo," much as he did in many settings of Clavier-Übung III. In "Nun danket alle Gott," the second "Jesus Christus, unser Heiland" setting, and "Vor deinen Thron," the cantus firmus is specifically labeled "Choral."

Within the portfolio, Bach approached the issue of *affect*—of not treating the chorales "merely offhand but according to the sense of the words," as his student Johann Gotthilf Ziegler put it[28]—in various ways. Some pieces display an old-fashioned, seventeenth-century localized approach, which called for the special highlighting of a single word or phrase of the text. In verse 3 of "O Lamm Gottes," for example, the line "sonst müsten wir verzagen" (Otherwise we would have to despair; mm. 101–105) is underscored by a sudden turn to dark chromaticism, climaxing in a move to five-part texture in contrary motion. More commonly, figuration used throughout a piece sets a general tone: the use of rushing 16th notes in the "Fantasia super Komm, heiliger Geist" to portray the rustling wind of the Holy Spirit, for instance.[29] In other cases, Bach focused on contrapuntal procedures such as fore-imitation in a more or less neutral environment: the embellishment of the chorale melody against a placid accompaniment in "An Wasserflüssen Babylon," for example.

In terms of compositional style, the settings of the portfolio are markedly old-fashioned. The popular ritornello chorale that appears in Clavier-Übung III and the Schübler Collection, settings in which attractive ritornello and episodic material functions almost independently of the cantus firmus, is not found here. Nor is the innovative *stile antico* organ motet that occurs in Clavier-Übung III. Aside from a few forward-looking pieces based on instrumental style, such as "Fantasia super Komm heiliger Geist" and "Komm, Gott Schöpfer," Bach focused on methods of chorale preluding that were in vogue in the seventeenth and early eighteenth centuries: the Central German fore-imitation chorale, chorale trio, and chorale partita (in "Vom Himmel hoch") and the North German florid-melody chorale. These types of settings represented the art that Reincken thought dead in 1720 but declared still alive after hearing Bach play for the St. James' Church audition in Hamburg. In the portfolio project, Bach seemed determined to preserve this tradition.

Although the Leipzig portfolio is a miscellany, compiled over time, Bach clearly wished to illustrate as many approaches to chorale preluding as possible. While the settings are generally retrospective, they nevertheless pushed the boundaries of conventional formats and procedures in unconventional ways, as we noted in chapter 10. As a result, the art of chorale preluding praised by Reincken was not only well preserved, but masterfully extended. The settings of the Leipzig chorale portfolio appear to have been Bach's personal favorites, works he had played in recital or the worship service over the years and thoroughly enjoyed.

The Revisions

More than any other keyboard collection, the Leipzig chorale portfolio reveals Bach's late obsession with revising earlier works. All but two of the pieces ("Vom Himmel hoch" and "Vor deinen Thron") can be traced to Bach's Weimar years, and all but one ("Vom Himmel hoch") represent fundamental compositional concepts from that period. What gives the works a Leipzig stamp are the changes Bach made to the music—expansions, revisions, and refinements that reflect his final thoughts on form, contrapuntal texture, motivic unity, and metrical notation. Bach's meticulous revisions show that the portfolio was far more than a repository: it was a compendium in which he sought to preserve earlier chorale-preluding practices in the best possible way.

Aside from Bach's autograph of "Nun Komm, der Heiden Heiland," BWV 660a, handed down with the portfolio, the original manuscripts of the Weimar chorales are lost. The settings are transmitted instead in secondary copies preserved mostly in three sources: the large collection of chorale preludes compiled by Johann Gottfried Walther and Johann Tobias Krebs during Krebs's years of study with Walther and Bach in Weimar,[30] the large collection of chorale preludes compiled by Walther in the late 1730s,[31] and the group of manuscripts written by Johann Gottlieb Preller in the 1740s.[32]

Also of importance are copies of the Weimar chorales made in Leipzig in the 1730s and 1740s by a number of Bach students: Johann Caspar Vogler, Johann Friedrich Agricola, Johann Christian Kittel, and "Anonymous X," the yet-unidentified individual writing under Bach's watchful eye in the early 1740s.[33] The copies of Vogler, Agricola, Kittel, and Anonymous X show several chorales in a state of transition, midway between the Weimar and the portfolio versions. This suggests that Bach revised some of the portfolio settings little by little, over time, to the point where he accumulated 12 pieces to launch the project (see the foregoing discussion).

Let us look at the revisions of the individual settings.

"Fantasia super Komm, heiliger Geist. canto fermo in Pedal. in Organo pleno," BWV 651. In an extraordinary rethinking of the Fantasia for the Leipzig portfolio, Bach more than doubled the size of the Weimar setting, expanding the text from 48 to 106 measures. His overarching goal was to achieve a complete statement of the lengthy chorale tune, which sounds as a cantus firmus in the pedal. In the Weimar version, the 10-phrase melody appears in an abbreviated form of four phrases. In the Leipzig version, Bach supplied the missing phrases through ingenious carpentry, inserting two sizable segments of new material (mm. 44–54 and 89–103) and repeating a lengthy passage that appeared toward the beginning (mm. 12–43; figure 25-1).[34]

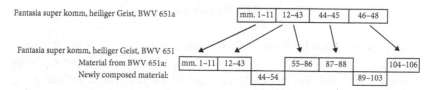

Figure 25-1 "Fantasia super Komm heiliger Geist, Herre Gott" BWV 651a and BWV 651: Bach's expansion of the work.

In the first new segment, the principal accompanimental theme, an arpeggiated motive derived from the first phrase of the chorale, appears in the alto, surrounded by chordal accompaniment in the soprano and tenor (m. 47). This introduces a textural variant into what might have become, in the expanded version, an overly homogeneous contrapuntal fabric (such as that of the Toccata in F Major, BWV 540/1, perhaps). In the second new segment, a concise new 16th-note figure (m. 89, beats 1–2), derived from the concluding Hallelujah phrase of the chorale tune, adds more variety still. And in the closing measures of the piece (mm. 98–106), all the key thematic elements of expanded work—old and new—are brought together in five- and six-part texture: the pedal cantus firmus, the principal accompanimental theme, the new concise 16th-note figure, and the suspension motives from the interludes. As Werner Breig has pointed out, this uniting of ideas is quite similar to the "alla stretta" (in stretto) close of the "Canto fermo in Canone" variation of "Vom Himmel hoch," and it reflects perfectly Walther's definition of stretto: "one or several voices are brought together in a very short space, and follow smartly one upon the other."[35] In its monumental revised form, the "Fantasia super Komm, heiliger Geist" represented a majestic invocation to Bach's chorale portfolio project.

"**Komm, heiliger Geist. alio modo. à 2 Clavier et Pedal,**" BWV 652. The most significant change to the Weimar version is the expansion of the cadences to phrases 2–4 and 6–8 of the chorale by one measure each, making them more active and substantial and making a very long setting (193 mm.) even longer (199 mm.). In the process, Bach unified the cadences to phrases 2, 3, and 7 by introducing the same material in the accompanying voices. He also simplified the ornamentation of the Weimar version—or at least notated it in a more straightforward way (he dropped the small notes and almost all the *pincé* c's)—and he changed an occasional half note or dotted quarter note and 8th note in the lower voices to a dotted quarter note and two 16th notes, to make the figures more animated. Finally, for one reason or another, Bach omitted the sigh-motive slurring in the accompaniment to the final Hallelujah phrase (mm. 165 and 178 of the Weimar version) that is present in both the Krebs and Preller manuscripts.

"An Wasserflüssen Babylon. à 2 Clavier et Pedal," BWV 653. Bach appears to have had a special interest in this chorale tune, on which he improvised "at great length (for almost half an hour) and in different ways" during the Hamburg audition of 1720. Already in Weimar he reworked the initial five-part double-pedal version of this setting, BWV 653b, into a four-part single-pedal version, BWV 653a, shifting the highly embellished melody line from the soprano to the tenor to create the effect of a French *tierce en taille*. For the Leipzig portfolio Bach revised the four-part version further, improving many details. He sharpened rhythms everywhere, turning ♩♫ figures into ♩. ♫, and he refined the part-writing. Most important, he added a new six-measure conclusion, in part to compensate for the lost tenor part of the original five-part version.[36] The inserted conclusion places stronger emphasis on the subdominant and includes a final quotation of the initial phrase of the chorale tune, first in the pedal and then in the soprano (see example 17-2), thus connecting the end of the setting with the beginning, much like the Leipzig revision of the Fantasia in C Minor, BWV 562/1 (see chapter 12).

"Schmücke dich, o liebe Seele. à 2 Clavier et Pedal," BWV 654. In this case Bach made only minor changes to the Weimar version. He sharpened rhythmic figures here and there (in measure 17 the alto rhythm ♩♪♪♪ is changed to ♩♪♪. ♪, much like the handwritten changes in "Wer nur den lieben Gott lässt walten," BWV 647, in the Schübler Chorales), and in measures 71–72 he altered the tied dotted half notes in the pedal to quarter note–rest–quarter note, to improve the rhythmic profile of the passage. In addition, he dropped the ornaments embellishing the first two notes of the cantus firmus as well as the sigh-motive slurring in measures 88 and 89.

"Trio super Herr Jesu Christ, dich zu uns wend. à 2 Clavier et Pedal," BWV 655. The most striking refinement to the Weimar version is Bach's revision of the countersubject to the main theme, making it less repetitive and more contrapuntally compelling. He also added the leap of a fourth that appears in the first measure of the main theme (example 25-1, a). Carried over to the final measure, the new countersubject produces a more interesting and finely nuanced closing cadence (example 25-1, b). Elsewhere, Bach changed 8th notes into pairs of 16th notes to create more rhythmic activity (mm. 15 and 55) and altered pedal figures to strengthen the sense of syncopation (mm. 22–24) or to create attractive contrary motion with the left hand (mm. 31 and 50).

"O Lamm Gottes unschuldig. 3 Versus," BWV 656. This setting is passed down in three versions: an early Weimar version reflected in Krebs's copy, a revised Weimar version reflected in Preller's copy, and the final version of the Leipzig portfolio.[37] The Preller text foreshadows the portfolio text in a number of details but does not seem to have been Bach's direct model. It may represent a Weimar revision that was no longer in his possession by the late 1730s.

Example 25-1 "Trio super Herr Jesu Christ, dich zu uns wend," BWV 655a and BWV 655: (a) change to the countersubject, and (b) revision of final cadence.

In verse 1 of the Leipzig version, Bach introduced several octave transpositions to improve the counterpoint. In verse 2 he greatly altered the ending of the first half by adding a measure and introducing new 8th-note motion. In the Krebs copy, verse 3 begins with an isolated upbeat pedal note, in a separate 9/8 measure. The overlapping start of verse 3, with the pedal entrance occurring within the last measure of verse 2, appears first in the Preller text, which also contains the indication *vivace* for the new figure that appears in imitation to mark the beginning of the Stollen of the chorale in verse 3 (m. 82 of the Preller version; m. 88 of the Leipzig version).

Most significant, in the Leipzig version Bach changed the meter of verse 3 from 9/8, with 8th notes as the basic pulse, to the very unusual signature 9/4, with quarter notes as the basic pulse. To judge from his student Johann Philipp Kirnberger, this may have stemmed from Bach's desire to have verse 3 flow more naturally from the

3/2 meter of verse 2 and to signify that the opening of verse 3 is to be played more broadly and with a weightier articulation than if it were notated in 9/8:

> The 9/4 meter of [three] triple beats that is derived from 3/2 occurs rarely, since 9/8 is used instead. But it is easily understood that the two meters are very different with respect to the performance and tempo that they specify. In church style, where a ponderous and emphatic execution is generally combined with a subdued and slow tempo, 9/4 meter is preferable by far to 9/8, since a melody that assumes a serious expression in the former meter can easily appear playful in the latter.[38]

The use of 9/4 also makes for a smoother return to 3/2 meter at measure 101 for the striking chromatic passage on the text phrase "Sonst müsten wir verzagen." In addition, it creates a greater contrast with the 8th-note motion that begins at measure 106 for the final line of verse 3, "Gib uns dein'n Fried, O Jesu" (Grant us Thy peace, O Jesus), which would be played with greater lightness and more animation than the 9/4 section (once again according to Kirnberger). Bach sometimes doubled the note values of cantata movements that he later adopted for Mass movements, to give the music additional weight.[39] That appears to be the case here.

"Nun danket alle Gott. à 2 Clavier et Pedal. canto fermo in Soprano," BWV 657. Bach did little more than add a few trills to the Weimar version. Hence one cannot really speak of an early version and a late version—they are one and the same.

"Von Gott will ich nicht lassen. canto fermo in pedal," BWV 658. The pedal cantus firmus remains the same in the Leipzig version of this setting, except for the creation of passing tones in measures 6, 20, and 22 (half notes to dotted quarter and 8th notes), thus adding an element of unification to the first, fourth, and fifth phrases of the chorale. The manual voices, by contrast, display a host of refinements: rhythms are sharpened, note-motion is increased, the counterpoint is touched up to improve contrary motion, and note values are altered to create additional syncopation (most strikingly at m. 24 of the alto, where ♫♩♫ in the Weimar version becomes ♪·♩♪· in the Leipzig version). Bach also seems to have been especially concerned with producing more punctuated cutoffs, changing the concluding quarter notes of many figures to 8th note and 8th-note rests (e.g., LH, mm. 14 and 15)—much as he had done in the revision of the Prelude in G Major, BWV 541/1, a decade earlier (see example 17-1). He also dropped "Fantasia" from the title of the Weimar setting, perhaps because his concept of what constituted a chorale fantasia changed after his revision of "Fantasia super Komm, heiliger Geist" at the beginning of the portfolio.

"Nun komm, der Heiden Heiland. à 2 Clavier et Pedal," BWV 659. Here, too, Bach dropped the Weimar rubric "Fantasia super" when revising the setting for the Leipzig portfolio. He also changed many details of the ornamented cantus firmus: he clarified the execution of the cadential figures with written-out slurs and trills; he created additional rhythmic variety by altering the recurring figure ♪♫♫ → ♪♫♫ or ♫♫ here and there; and he fully rewrote measures 22–23 to produce more 32nd-note motion. Moreover, he added slurs to sigh motives that appear in both the cantus and the accompanimental manual voices in the third phrase of the chorale (mm. 19–27), probably to give special expressivity to the words "des sich wundert alle Welt" (the whole world marvels) of the chorale text.

"Trio super Nun komm, der Heiden Heiland. à due Bassi è canto fermo," BWV 660. In this single case Bach's autograph manuscript of the Weimar version has survived, as an appendix to the Six Sonatas and chorale portfolio that was probably added after his death.[40] Comparing its text with that of the Leipzig revision, we can see that Bach added the phrase "à due Bassi è canto fermo" to the title, most likely to emphasize the unique nature of this trio setting, and he changed the meter from ¢ to the more straightforward C, perhaps to indicate a slightly slower tempo, with a pulse of four beats per measure rather than two.

Bach also altered a host of details. He further animated the right-hand cantus firmus by subdividing the half notes in measures 8 and 9 into 16th or 32nd notes, by making a number of figures more rhythmically incisive, and by rewriting the florid figure in measure 26 completely, adding the upward leap of an augmented fifth to create a more harmonically rich approach to the cadence. In the accompanimental voices he added the turn marking the concluding cadence of the ritornello (m. 7, and again in m. 37), much as he added turns to the cadences to "Wo soll ich fliehen hin," BWV 646, in the Vienna copy of the Schübler Chorale print (see chapter 24). And in the pedal he introduced additional syncopation by replacing the initial note of a four-note group with a rest (mm. 24 and 34). Most striking is the change of the final chord of the setting, from a picardy-third G major in the Weimar version (to match the D major chord in measure 15) to G minor in the Leipzig version. Did Bach simply forget to add the B natural, or did he want the more dramatic G minor close, perhaps to contrast with the picardy-third endings of the framing "Nun komm" settings in the portfolio? No matter what the case, he also omitted the slurring that appeared in the cantus firmus in the Weimar version (mm. 9, 25–26, and 36) as well as the arpeggio indication before the cadential chords in measures 15 and 42, a gesture that is fully appropriate for the cello- or gamba-like writing of the manual parts.

"Nun komm der Heiden Heiland. in Organo pleno. canto fermo in Pedal," BWV 661. Here, as in the third verse of "O Lamm Gottes," Bach altered the metrical notation, in this case from C with the 16th note as the smallest unit to ¢ with the 8th note as the smallest unit. This creates the visual effect of an augmentation, and it doubles the length of the setting, from 46 to 92 measures. Bach may have carried out this change to make the piece easier to read on the page or to make its plenum cantus firmus move in stately half notes, like that of the "Fantasia super

Komm, heiliger Geist," BWV 651, also a plenum piece. But taken literally, the alla breve meter would call for a weightier tempo and more emphatic performance than straightforward 𝄵 time, to judge from Kirnberger, once again:

> 2/2 meter, or rather *alla breve*, which is always designated by 𝄵 or 𝟤, is most often used in church pieces, fugues, and elaborate choruses. It is to be noted about this meter that it is very serious and emphatic, yet is performed twice as fast as its note values indicate, unless a slower tempo is specified by the adjectives *grave*, *adagio*, etc.[41]

Bach also made many small changes to the music text. The most important is his reshaping throughout of the last four notes of the countersubject, changing the figure from a conjunct descending scale to a disjunct angular motive that creates additional contrary motion and better reflects the jagged nature of the principal theme (example 25-2). Elsewhere Bach improved the counterpoint here and there, sometimes to create more animation (tenor, m. 24, and soprano, m. 91 of the revised version) but sometimes to create less (alto, mm. 35 and 84 of the revised version). He also confirmed in the title that the setting should be played "in Organo pleno."

"Allein Gott in der Höh sei Ehr. à 2 Clavier et Pedal. canto fermo in Soprano," BWV 662. When revising this setting in Leipzig, Bach added the rubric "adagio" but otherwise changed very little. The few revisions that occur appear mainly in the soprano cantus firmus, where he replaced Lombardic figures with still-more-fashionable triplets (m. 14) and the conventional figure ♪♪♪♪♪ with the more syncopated ♪♪♪♪♪ (m. 36). He seemed chiefly concerned with clarifying and filling out the ornamentation, mostly in the accompanimental voices but occasionally in the florid cantus firmus as well (mm. 12 and 36).

"Allein Gott in der Höh sei Ehr. à 2 Clavier et Pedal. canto fermo in Tenore," BWV 663. Here, too, Bach adjusted only small details when revising the Weimar

Example 25-2 "Nun komm der Heiden Heiland," BWV 661a and BWV 661: change to the countersubject.

BWV 661a

BWV 661

version. At several spots he clarified the precise length of held notes and cutoffs, much as he had done in "Von Gott will ich nicht lassen." He also rewrote the rhythmically free transitional measure (m. 63 of the Weimar version), expanding it to two measures and bringing the cadenza and Adagio bridge into the strict metrical context of 3/2 meter. He also added a few ornaments to the tenor cantus firmus and expanded existing embellishments, replacing a simple *trillo* with a more nuanced *doppelt cadence* (turn and trill; mm. 17, 33, and 83). On the other hand, Bach did not eliminate the additional accompanimental voice that appears briefly here and there (mm. 44, 70, and 72) before entering in a sustained way at the close (m. 89 to the end). He apparently viewed this early contrapuntal "sin" as acceptable, given the free style of the piece.

   "Trio super Allein Gott in der Höh sei Ehr. à 2 Clavier et Pedal," BWV 664. This setting is passed down in three versions: an initial Weimar version, represented by the manuscripts of Krebs and Preller; an intermediate Leipzig version, represented by the manuscript of "Anonymous X" from the early 1740s; and the final Leipzig version, represented by Bach's autograph in the Leipzig portfolio.[42] A comparison of measures 88b–90 in the three versions illustrates the evolution of the text (example 25-3).

   The final version of this Trio marked Bach's return to the chorale portfolio project after a hiatus of several years, and it is not altogether surprising that he focused his attention on this progressive setting, which, when written in Weimar, pointed forward to the extraordinary Six Sonatas that were to come more than a decade later in Leipzig. Although he retained the basic text of the "Allein Gott" trio in his later revisions, adding no measures, he made a greater number of small refinements than in any other work in the collection.

Example 25-3 "Trio super Allein Gott in der Höh sei Ehr," BWV 664, mm. 88b–90, evolution of the text: (a) Weimar version, BWV 664a, (b) refinement appearing first in Leipzig, c. 1740, and (c) refinement appearing solely in the Leipzig portfolio.

On a detailed level, he added mordents on off-beats to accent syncopations (RH, mm. 1 and 2, for instance) and trills to create more embellishment (the chain of trills in mm. 41–42 and 61–64, for example). He also sharpened the rhythm in the pedal at several spots (♩♪♪♪→♩♪♪♪), adjusted the manual counterpoint (especially to create more contrary motion), and refined the part-writing here and there. Most notably, he thoroughly revised the two most important structural "joints" of the setting. The first is the recapitulation of the ritornello in the tonic (mm. 79–80), where he added animated 32nd notes to the right-hand part and extended the left-hand part to subtly disguise the return of the theme (example 25-4). He used similar overlapping passages to disguise recapitulations in the opening choruses of many Leipzig cantatas and the da capo fugues of the Prelude and Fugue in E Minor ("Wedge"), BWV 548, and Fantasia and Fugue in C Minor, BWV 537. The second key structural moment is the preparation for the entry of the chorale tune in the pedal (mm. 83–84), where he eliminated the two-measure pedal-point of the Weimar version and replaced it with an animated pedal line that serves as a better contrast with the long-held notes of the cantus firmus, which enters in the next measure.

Bach also rewrote almost every measure of the manual parts in the concluding cantus firmus section (m. 85 to the end), improving and animating the voices

Example 25-4 "Trio super Allein Gott in der Höh sei Ehr," BWV 664a and BWV 664, mm. 79–80: change to produce overlap in the return of the embellished ritornello in the tonic.

(the soft 8th-note resolution of the soprano appoggiatura in m. 2 now becomes disjunct 16th notes in the alto, in m. 91) and creating more contrary motion. Bach clearly admired his original concept of this piece: an A B A instrumental trio, followed by an abbreviated statement of the cantus firmus underneath the trio material. But he wanted to improve the part-writing and create still greater drama at the setting's critical moments of transition.

"Jesus Christus, unser Heiland. sub Communione. pedaliter," BWV 665. Bach changed small details only in the text of this setting: in the third phrase of the chorale (mm. 27–38) he created a new, syncopated 32nd-note motive in the countersubject (mm. 28, 31, 34, 36) that foreshadows the 32nd-note motion of the fourth phrase; he sharpened the cutoff of the final note of the chorale tune (alto, m. 29; soprano, m. 32); and he revised the part-writing at various spots. The most notable change is the substitution of the subtitle "sub Communione. pedaliter" for the instruction "In Organo pleno" found in the Weimar version.[43] Might this imply the use of softer stops?

"Jesus Christus, unser Heiland. alio modo," BWV 666. Bach appears to have revised this "alio modo" setting at an early point, since manuscript copies written in Leipzig around 1740 by Agricola and Anonymous X already display the port-folio changes to the Weimar text, which is preserved in a copy by Walther.[44] These changes include the omission of the important slurs in measure 1, which indicate that the 8th-note figure is to be performed with a dance-like lilt (♪♪♪), the clarification of cutoffs here and there, octave adjustments to the bass voice (m. 20), and the alteration of the twisting 16th-note figure that first appears in the top voice in measure 26, making it less repetitive.

"Komm, Gott Schöpfer, heiliger Geist. in Organo pleno con Pedale obligato," BWV 667. An early copy by Walther or (possibly Krebs) and an early fragment by Krebs confirm that Bach had already created this expanded version of his Orgel-Büchlein setting, BWV 631, in Weimar.[45] A later manuscript, written by Walther around 1736,[46] confirms that Bach began to refine the enlarged setting in Leipzig at least a decade before Altnickol entered it in the portfolio.

In addition to making normal Leipzig revisions (changing 8th-note pairs to dotted 8th- and 16th-note figures, clarifying cutoffs and holds, animating voices through diminutions), Bach improved the initial Orgel-Büchlein segment (mm. 1–8) by inserting additional off-beat pedal notes and 16th notes, dressing up the cadences with more animated lines, and converting disjunct figures into conjunct. All these changes helped to foreshadow the move to continuous 16th notes in the newly composed second segment (mm. 9–26). Within this segment, he corrected quarter notes representing one full beat to dotted quarter notes, in accordance with the 12/8 meter.

"Vom Himmel hoch, da komm ich her. per Canones. à 2 Clavier et Pedal," BWV 769a. As we noted in chapter 23, in the Leipzig portfolio Bach not only wrote out a performance version, BWV 769a, of the Canonic Variations on "Vom Himmel hoch," BWV 769, which had appeared earlier in an engraved print issued by Balthasar Schmid around 1748, he also made substantial revisions to the text. Most strikingly, he shifted variation 5 ("L'altra Sorte del' Canone all' rovercio"— Other kinds of canons, in contrary motion), which concluded the set in the print, to the middle of the piece, creating an axial structure that radiated out from a climactic central movement. This contrasts with the order of the print, where the variations become increasingly complex with each succeeding variation. Bach also rewrote the free voice of the cantabile variation (variation 3 in the print), making it more ornate and inserting additional motivic references to the chorale. In addition, he improved small details in the other canons (see chapter 23).

"Vor deinen Thron tret ich hiermit" (incomplete), BWV 668. There is no Weimar source for the early version of "Vor deinen Thron," the setting "Wenn wir in höchsten Nöten sein," BWV 668a, which is handed down solely in the first edition of the Art of Fugue that was published after Bach's death in 1751. As Philipp Spitta first observed,[47] "Wenn wir in höchsten Nöten sein" is derived from the Weimar arrangement of the same chorale, BWV 641, which Bach entered into the "General Use" portion of the Orgel-Büchlein around 1711–1713. It appears there as a nine-measure florid-melody chorale for two manuals and pedal, without interludes.

In a remarkable reworking of the Orgel-Büchlein setting, Bach reduced the florid melody to a lightly embellished cantus firmus, introduced segments of fore-imitation material before each phrase of the chorale tune, greatly revised the three accompanimental parts, and added a new conclusion.[48] The result was a completely transformed, greatly enlarged 45-measure setting. The architectural changes, made by the insertions of fore-imitation material (figure 25-2),[49] resemble those in the "Fantasia super Komm, heiliger Geist, Herre Gott," BWV 651 (figure 25-1), which opens the Leipzig portfolio.

Since only the first half—measures 1-26a—of "Vor deinen Thron" survives, we have a limited view of Bach's revisions to the expanded "Wenn wir in höchsten Nöten sein." To judge from the surviving portion of the portfolio entry, Bach made small refinements only, sharpening the rhythm of two 8th-note pairs (♪♪→♪♪; pedal, m. 9; alto, m. 26), heightening the effect of a phrase ending by introducing a deceptive cadence (m. 10), and animating the tenor line with *corta*

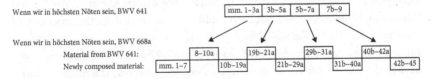

Figure 25-2 "Wenn wir in höchsten Nöten sein," BWV 641 and BWV 668a: Bach's expansion of the work.

figures (m. 7). And he changed the title to "Vor deinen Thron tret ich hiermit," in reference to Bodo von Hodenberg's text of 1646:

> Fur deinem Thron tret ich hiermit,
> O Gott, und dich demüthig bitt:
> Wend dein genädig Angesicht
> Von mir Blut-armen Sünder nicht.

> I come now before your throne saying this,
> O God, and humbly ask you,
> "Do not turn your gracious countenance
> From me, a weak sinner."

Whether Bach also modified the conclusion of the piece, a type of revision he carried out in several other portfolio settings, must remain an open question. No matter what the case, as an expanded and refined version of an Orgel-Büchlein chorale, "Vor deinen Thron" served both as an appropriate companion to "Komm, Gott Schöpfer" and a compositional bookend to "Fantasia super Komm, heiliger Geist, Herre Gott."

How far back does the model for "Vor deinen Thron" go? According to a notice in the first edition of the Art of Fugue, "Wenn wir in höchsten Nöten sein" was dictated by Bach "in his blindness . . . on the spur of the moment to the pen of a friend."[50] The early Bach biographer Johann Nicolaus Forkel, who had gathered information from the Bach sons, expanded this account:

Bach dictated it ["Wenn wir in höchsten Nöthen sein"] a few days before his death to his son-in-law, Altnickol. Of the art displayed in this Chorale, I will say nothing; it was so familiar to the author that he could exercise it even in his illness. But the expression of pious resignation and devotion in it has always affected me whenever I have played it.[51]

Wolff has proposed that the expanded version of "Wenn wir in höchsten Nöten sein" was composed before Bach's eye operations, either in Weimar or Leipzig, and that the dictation described in the Art of Fugue and Forkel's biography involved only the refinements to its text that resulted in "Vor deinen Thron."[52] Wolff based this assumption on his belief that Bach could not have carried out the expansion of an Orgel-Büchlein setting while blind. It should be noted, however, that in modern times the blind organist Helmut Walcha (1907–1991) learned Bach's complete solo keyboard works through dictation. It does not seem beyond the realm of possibility that Bach carried out the expansion of the Orgel-Büchlein setting while on his deathbed, when he was gravely ill and "in deepest need." Thus, "Wenn wir in höchsten Nöten sein," BWV 668a, may date from Bach's final months, together with "Vor deinen Thron." This would explain the lack of earlier copies of the "Wenn wir in höchsten Nöten" setting.

Bach's revisions in the chorale portfolio preserve and honor the bold, experimental qualities that appear in many of his Weimar works. At the same time, they give the selected settings the higher degree of motivic and structural integration that was characteristic of his Leipzig compositions. They are Weimar-like in style, but Leipzig-like in refinement.

Unanswered Questions

Finally, we must ask why Bach assembled the Leipzig chorale portfolio. There are several possibilities.

Did Bach intend the chorales for pedagogical use, like the Six Sonatas that are also transmitted in the miscellany? Several Bach students—Johann Tobias Krebs, Johann Caspar Vogler, Johann Friedrich Agricola, and Anonymous X—copied Weimar versions of the chorales as part of their organ studies with Bach. There can be no doubt, then, of the settings' instructional merit, especially since they demonstrate a wide range of stylistic and technical approaches to preluding on a chorale.

But at the same time, there are no student copies of the revised settings. For one reason or another, Bach kept the collection to himself in his final decade. Moreover, in the portfolio manuscript, the chorales are not arranged in a technically graduated order, as in the Six Sonatas and Schübler Chorales. The 19 chorales are also cast in an antiquated style, for the most part. This contrasts strongly with the Six Sonatas, the Schübler Chorales, and volume 2 of the Well-Tempered Clavier, which contain forward-looking music that would have appealed to the more modern tastes of Bach's sons and students.

Did Bach intend the chorales for liturgical use? Most of the settings are too long to have served as preludes to congregational singing, and, to judge from contemporary accounts, the organ preludes and postludes performed before and after the service consisted of free pieces or free improvisations played on the full organ rather than music based on hymn tunes. Several of the chorales could have been used as communion music, however, as confirmed by the rubric added to the first "Jesus Christus, unser Heiland" setting: "sub Communione." Bach's instructions for a substitute organist in Leipzig on the first Sunday in Advent 1723, state that during Communion, after the performance of a concerted piece (probably the second part of the cantata of the day or another work altogether), the remaining time was to be filled with "alternate preluding and singing of chorales until the end."[53]

The chorales "Jesus Christus, unser Heiland" and "Schmücke dich, o liebe Seele" were specifically associated with Holy Communion in contemporary hymnals.[54] The Eucharistic ties of the other melodies appearing in the chorale portfolio are more tenuous. As we noted earlier, when Bach added the subtitle "sub Communione" to the first "Jesus Christus" setting in the portfolio, he dropped the instruction "in Organo pleno" that appears in all copies of the Weimar version of the piece. This may imply that if one plays "Jesus Christus" during the Eucharist, one should use a smaller registration.

Did Bach intend the chorales for recital use? As we noted in chapter 15, organ recitals in Bach's time normally consisted of improvised pieces, and according to Forkel, when Bach played outside the worship service, he often extemporized for "two hours or more."[55] But on occasion he clearly used existing compositions as well. At St. Sophia's Church in Dresden in 1725 he performed a piece with instrumental ensemble—something that could not have been improvised—and at St. Martin's Church in Kassel he played the Toccata and Fugue in D Minor ("Dorian"), BWV 538 (see chapter 12). It also appears that Bach prepared a copy of the Prelude and Fugue in G Major, BWV 541, for his son Wilhelm Friedemann to use for his audition at St. Sophia's Church in Dresden in 1733. Thus, on occasion, he and his sons played from the written page.

The portfolio chorales would have represented masterful recital pieces, and the layouts of "Schmücke dich" and "Trio super Herr Jesu Christ," which leave empty space at the bottom of right-hand pages to accommodate convenient page-turns, together with the remark "VS volti" (Jump to the reverse side!; plate 25-3), suggest that the portfolio was to be used in performance rather than serving simply as a reference copy. This is also true of the score of the Canonic Variations in the portfolio: in their new "Vom Himmel hoch" form, the enigmatic canons are fully written out, ready to be played. The Leipzig portfolio may have served as a recital resource that Bach reserved for himself.

Did Bach intend the settings to serve as an organized compendium of chorale preludes? The portfolio displays a number of obvious groupings: the "alio modo" pairs of the "Komm, heiliger Geist" and "Jesus Christus" settings and the three-fold clusters of "Nun komm, der Heiden Heiland" and "Allein Gott in der Höh sei Ehr" arrangements. In addition, the "Fantasia super Komm, heiliger Geist" and "Vor deinen Thron" represent appropriate framing elements for the collection. Otherwise, there is no unambiguous organizing principle at work, such as key, cantus firmus or canonic procedure, or liturgical year, despite the attempts of several scholars to see such underlying plans.[56] In Johann Gottfried Walther's late collections of chorale settings, assembled after 1736, the pieces are grouped by liturgical function and hymn tune.[57] The settings in the Leipzig portfolio, by contrast, appear to have been entered in a spontaneous manner.

Did Bach intend to publish the set, perhaps as an extension of the Clavier-Übung series? Possibly, since the entries in the portfolio are fair copies, and therefore ready for printing. But in the Clavier-Übung series and other late keyboard publications, Bach used carefully calculated organizational plans. This is especially evident from 1739 onward: Clavier-Übung III, Clavier-Übung IV

Plate 25-3 Leipzig chorale portfolio: manageable page turn, with "VS volti" (Jump to the reverse side!), in "Schmücke dich, o liebe Seele," BWV 654.

Staatsbibliothek zu Berlin—Preußischer Kulturbesitz, Musikabteilung mit Mendelssohn-Archiv

(Goldberg Variations), and the Art of Fugue, especially, display well-worked-out, multifaceted organizational schemes. Even if the 19 chorales in the portfolio were reshuffled, it is difficult to see how they could be organized in a similarly sophisticated way. In addition, "Vom Himmel hoch" had already been issued in print, as the Canonic Variations. It is unlikely that Bach would have published it again, even in a revised form with practical layout.

Did Bach view the Leipzig chorale portfolio solely as a miscellany, a collection of his favorite settings from the past, assembled for occasional performance in concert but essentially for his own pleasure? Viewed this way, the portfolio would resemble the Bach family albums, the Clavier-Büchlein for Wilhelm Friedemann and Anna Magdalena, in which pieces were entered intermittently, in a random order except for occasional groupings (of preludes destined for volume 1 of the Well-Tempered Clavier, for instance). Bach's "Jesu Juva" inscription above the "Fantasia super Komm, heiliger Geist" does not preclude this possibility, since Friedemann's Clavier-Büchlein begins with a similar invocation, "I.N.J." ("In nomine Jesu," In the name of Jesus).[58] Bach may have viewed the portfolio as another project to be kept within the family.

Except for an apple-like doodle and several rastrum testings, the front page of the Leipzig chorale portfolio remains blank.[59] There is no title, such as those Bach added to the Clavier-Büchlein for Wilhelm Friedemann Bach, the Clavier-Büchlein for Anna Magdalena Bach of 1722, and the Orgel-Büchlein. Thus Bach's final intention for his last compilation of organ works remains unclear. We can speculate that with the insertion of "Vor deinen Thron" by Anonymous Vr, Bach, on his deathbed, may have considered the portfolio complete. If he had lived longer, however, he might have continued the project, adding such worthy Weimar settings as "Wir Christenleut haben jetzund Freud," BWV 710 (45 mm.); "Wo soll ich fliehen hin," BWV 694 (91 mm.); or "Valet will ich dir geben," BWV 735 (64 mm.). He had already revised and expanded all three. Or he might have considered including the magisterial partita "Sei gegrüßet, Jesu gütig," BWV 768, which Anonymous X copied out in a revised form around 1740.[60] There is no reason to think that he would not have added more works.

The Search for Musical Perfection

The Leipzig chorale portfolio was Bach's last and possibly largest unfinished project, more open-ended still than the Art of Fugue, for which a conclusion was planned, if not fulfilled. Bach viewed music composition as a statement of faith, as the constant and unshakable focus of his life as a Lutheran organist, capellmeister, and cantor. His works were gifts to God. This is affirmed in his organ music by his invocation of Christ's help at the beginning of large projects and in his turn to a chorale setting, "Vor deinen Thron tret ich hiermit," as his final statement in the realm of composition.

As the organ works show, Bach was an indefatigable composer, writing pieces steadily from youth to old age, methodically blending national and historical styles with his own unique contrapuntal idiom. And as the refinement of preexisting pieces in Leipzig demonstrates, he was an equally indefatigable reviser, determined to update and improve earlier works, even when they were admirable in their original form. It is highly symbolic, then, that Bach died while compiling the Leipzig chorale portfolio, in the midst of bringing worthy compositions to an even higher level of refinement. The portfolio vividly reflects his lifelong creed—the unending search for musical perfection.

Notes

1. British Library, *Add. MS 35021*.
2. The revisions and borrowings are summarized in NBA V/6.2, KB (Alfred Dürr, ed., 1996), 201–209.
3. The chorale portfolio is fascicle 2 of the miscellany.
4. Kobayashi 1988, 45.
5. The paper is characterized by a distinctive watermark, a middle-size "MA" (no. 122 in NBA IX/1, *Wasserzeichen-Katalog*). Bach used this type of paper mostly for works written between 1727 and 1732.
6. Kobayashi 1988, 45.
7. Stauffer 2023, 220–221.
8. Stauffer 2023, 221.
9. Kobayashi 1988, 56–57.
10. Altnickol studied with Bach from 1744 to 1748 and married his daughter Elisabeth Juliana Friderica in January 1749.
11. Kobayashi 1988, 60.
12. No. 231 in NBA IX/3 (*Die Kopisten Johann Sebastian Bachs: Katalog und Dokumentation*). As this book goes to press, Peter Wollny has identified Anonymous Vr as Christoph Transchel, who served as a copyist for Bach in the late 1740s and his son Carl Philipp Emanuel after his death. See Wollny, "Neuerkenntnisse zu einigen Bach-Kopisten der 1740er Jahre—Biographische und quellenkundliche Ermittlungen," BJ 109 (2023), 76–90.
13. A diagram of the folio structure, presented in NBA IV/7, KB (Dietrich Kilian, ed., 1988), 21, shows that a final page was most probably torn off.
14. Dadelsen 1958, Kobayashi 1988, and NBA IX/2 (*Die Notenschrift Johann Sebastian Bachs: Dokumentation ihrer Entwicklung*, Yoshitake Kobayashi, ed., 1989).
15. NBA IV/2, KB (Hans Klotz, ed., 1957), 13.
16. NBA IV/2, KB, 13.
17. BG 25.2 (Wilhelm Rust, ed., 1878).

18. NBA IV/2, KB, 58.

19. Wollny 2016a, 8–9. As Wollny points out, this possibility was already raised by Yoshitake Kobayashi, in Kobayashi 1988, 57.

20. Stinson 2001, 34.

21. Dietrich Kilian, when discussing the structure of the chorale portfolio while editing the Six Sonatas for the NBA, also espoused this view and even speculated further that Bach might have intended to use the blank page before the Canonic Variations as a title page for the Variations. See NBA IV/7, KB, 18.

22. Stauffer 2023, 222–223.

23. The two settings of "Jesus Christus, unser Heiland" are paired in Berlin State Library, *P 802* (Johann Gottfried Walther, 1714–1717) and other Weimar-related manuscripts, where the second setting is already labeled "alio modo."

24. NBA VIII/2, KB (Klaus Hofmann, ed., 1996), 23.

25. Wolff 1991f.

26. Wolff 2000, 449–450.

27. Stinson 2001, 65.

28. NBR, no. 340.

29. The most complete summary of the imagery perceived by modern writers in the settings of the portfolio chorales can be found in Leahy 2011.

30. Berlin State Library, *P 802*.

31. Berlin State Library, *Mus.ms. 22541 I* and *Mus.ms. 22541 II*; dating from Beißwenger 1992b, 30.

32. Leipzig Town Library, *Peters Ms. 7*; dating from Schulze 1974, 119–120.

33. See introduction, n. 50.

34. Diagram adapted from Breig 1986b, 105.

35. Breig 1986b, 107; Walther 1732, 582.

36. Breig 1986b, 117.

37. The NBA presents the Krebs and *P 271* versions only. The Preller version can be found in the Breitkopf and Leupold editions.

38. Kirnberger 1771–79, vol. 2, pt. I, 128–129. Translation from Johann Philipp Kirnberger: *The Art of Strict Musical Composition*, David Beach and Jurgen Thym, trs. (New Haven: Yale University Press, 1982), 395.

39. Wolff 1968, 133–134. The two examples cited are the conversion of the chorus "Darzu ist erschienen der Sohn Gottes" from Cantata 40 into the "Cum sancto Spiritu" of the Mass in F Major and the chorus "Jauchzet, ihr erfreuten Stimmen" from Cantata 120 into the "Et expecto" of the Mass in B Minor.

40. Both Bach's handwriting and the paper watermark (No. 36 in NBA IX/1) of the autograph of the early version confirm its Weimar origin. It appears to have been in place as fascicle 3 of the *P 271* miscellany by the time of Carl Philipp Emanuel's death in 1788.

41. Kirnberger 1771–79, vol. 2, pt. I, 118. Translation from Johann Philipp Kirnberger: *The Art of Strict Musical Composition*, 386.

42. Berlin State Library, *P 801*, fascicle 3 (Johann Tobias Krebs); Leipzig Town Library, Mempell-Preller Collection, *Ms. 7* (Preller); and Leipzig Town Library, Becker Collection, *III.8.8* (Anonymous X).

43. Berlin State Library, *P 802* (Johann Gottfried Walther); Leipzig Town Library, *Peters Ms. R 16* (Johann Friedrich Agricola); and Leipzig Town Library, Becker Collection, *III.8.11* (Anonymous X).

44. Leipzig Town Library, *Peters Ms. R 16* (Agricola); Leipzig Town Library, Becker Collection, *III.8.11* (Anonymous X); and Berlin State Library, *P 802* (Walther).

45. Berlin State Library, *P 802* and *P 801*, fascicle 30, respectively.

46. Berlin State Library, *Mus.ms. 22541 III*. Dating from Beißwenger 1992b, 30.

47. Spitta 1873–80, vol. 3, 274–275.

48. Bach's carpentry work and revisions are discussed in great detail in Wolff 1991f.

49. Diagram adapted from Wolff 1991f, 288.

50. NBR, no. 284.

51. Forkel 1802, 53; translation from NBR, 466.

52. Wolff 1991f, 288.

53. NBR, no. 113.

54. Bighley 2018, 153 and 212.

55. Forkel 1802, 22.

56. In Williams 2003, 339–340; Leahy 2011, xxiv–xxv; or Stinson 2001, 66–73, for instance.

57. Berlin State Library, *Mus.ms. 22541 II* and *Mus.ms. 22541 III*. The contents are given in NBA IV/2, KB (Hans Klotz, ed., 1957), 30–35. Dating from Beißwenger 1992b, 30.

58. It appears above the "Applicatio," BWV 994 (= BWV[3] Suppl 1), the first piece of music in the album. See facsimile in NBA V/5, VIII.

59. See facsimile in Wollny 2016a or on Bach digital, under BWV 651.

60. Leipzig Town Library, Becker Collection, *III.8.17*.

Three Representative Central German Organs

Altenburg: Castle Church of St. George

Built by Tobias Heinrich Gottfried Trost, 1733–1739

Hauptwerk

* Groß-Quintadena	16'
* Flaute traverse	16'
Principal	8'
* Bordun	8'
Spitzflöte	8'
Viol di Gamba	8'
Rohrflöte	8'
* Octave	4'
Kleingedackt	4'
Quinte	3'
Superoctave	2'
Blockflöte	2'
Sesquialtera	II
* Mixtur	VI-IX
Trompete	8'
Glockenspiel (c-c''')	
Tremulant	

Oberwerk

Geigenprincipal	8'
Lieblich Gedackt	8'
Vugara	8'
Quintadena	8'
Hohlflöte	8'
Gemshorn	4'
Flaute douce II	4'
Nasat	3'
Octave	2'
Waldflöte	2'
Superoctava	1'
Cornet	V
Mixtur	IV-V
Vox humana	8'
Tremulant	

*Wind coupler (Pedal transmission)

Pedal

Principalbaß	16'
Violonbaß	16'
Subbaß	16'
Groß-Quintadena (T)	16'
Flute traverse (T)	16'
Octavenbaß	8'
Bordun (T)	8'
Octave (T)	4'
Mixtur (T)	VI-IX
Posaune	32'
Posaune	16'
Trompete	8'

Hauptwerk/Oberwerk
Hauptwerk/Pedal
Compass: Manual: C→c'''
Pedal: C→c'

Bad Berka: St. Mary's Church

Disposition by J. S. Bach, c. 1742

Hauptwerk		Brustwerk		Pedal ("Bäβe")	
Quintadena	16'	Quintadena	8'	Suppaβ	16'
Principal	8'	Gedackt	8'	Principal	8'
Flöte	8'	Principal	4'	Hohlflöte	4'
Gedackt	8'	Nachthorn	4'	Posaun Baβ	16'
Gemshorn	8'	Quinte	2⅔'	Trompete	8'
Octave	4'	Octave	2'	Cornett	4'
Gedackt	4'	Waldflöte	2'	Brustwerk/Hauptwerk	
Quinta	2⅔'	Terz ("Tritonus")	1⅗'	Hauptwerk/Pedal	
Naβat	2⅔'	Cimpel	III		
Octave	2'				
Seβquialter	II				
Mixtur	V				
Trompete	8'				

Naumburg: Church of St. Wenzel

Zacharias Hildebrandt, 1746

Hauptwerk		Oberwerk		Rückpositiv		Pedal	
Principal	16'	Bordun	16'	Principal	8'	[Untersatz	32']
Quintathen	16'	Principal	8'	Quintadehn	8'	Principal	16'
Octava	8'	Hollflött	8'	Rohr Floete	8'	Violon	16'
Spitzflöte	8'	Unda maris	8'	Viol de Gamba	8'	Subbaβ	16'
Gedackt	8'	Praestant	4'	Praestanta	4'	Octav	8'
Octav	4'	Gemshorn	4'	Vagara	4'	Violon	8'
Spitzflöte	4'	Quinta	3'	Rohrflött	4'	Octav	4'
Sesquialtera	II	Octav	2'	Nasat	3'	Octava	2'
Quinta	3'	Waldflöte	2'	Octava	2'	Mixtur	VII
Weit Pfeiffe	2'	Tertia	1⅗'	Rausch Pfeife	II	Posaune	32'
Octav	2'	Quinta	1½'	Mixtur	V	Posaune	16'
Cornett	IV	Sif-Floete	1'	Fagott	16'	Trompet-Bass	8'
Mixtur	VIII	Scharff	V			Clarin-Bass	4'
Bombart	16'	Vox humana	8'	Tremulant			
Trompet	8'	Trumulant		Cymbelstern		Rückpositiv/Hauptwerk	
				Compass: Manual: CD → c'''		Oberwerk/Hauptwerk	
				Pedal: CD → d'		Hauptwerk/Pedal	

Source: Wolff and Zepf 2012.

Bibliography

Documents

Bach-Dokumente Bach-Archiv, Leipzig, ed. (Kassel: Bärenreiter, 1963–2008), 7 vols.
The New Bach Reader. Hans T. David, Arthur Mendel, and Christoph Wolff, eds. (New York: Norton, 1998).

Editions

Johann Sebastian Bach's Kompositionen für die Orgel. Friedrich Conrad Griepenkerl and Ferdinand Roitzsch, eds. (Leipzig: C. F. Peters, 1844–52), 9 vols.
Johann Sebastian Bachs Werke [Bach-Gesamtausgabe = BG] (Leipzig: Breitkopf und Härtel, 1851–99), 46 vols.
Johann Sebastian Bach. Neue Ausgabe sämtlicher Werke [Neue Bach-Ausgabe = NBA] (Kassel and Leipzig: Bärenreiter, 1954–2007), 112 vols.
Johann Sebastian Bach: The Complete Organ Works (Colfax, NC: Wayne Leupold Editions, 2010–).

Primary Sources

Adlung, Jacob. 1758. *Anleitung zur musicalischen Gelahrtheit* (Erfurt: Johann David Jungnicol, 1758).
Adlung, Jacob. 1768. *Musica mechanica organoedi* (Berlin: Birnstiel, 1768; rpt. Kassel: Bärenreiter, 1961).
Forkel, Johann Nicolaus. 1802. *Über Johann Sebastian Bachs Leben, Kunst und Kunstwerke* (Leipzig: Hoffmeister and Kühnel, 1802; rpt. Kassel: Bärenreiter, 1999).
Heinichen, Johann David. 1728. *Der General-Bass in der Composition* (Dresden: author, 1728).
Kircher, Athanasius. 1650. *Musurgia Universalis sive Ars Magna Consoni et Dissoni* (Rome: Ex Typographia Hæredum Francisci Corbelletti, 1650; rpt. Hildesheim: Georg Olms Verlag, 1970).
Kirnberger, Johann Philipp. 1771–79. *Die Kunst des reinen Satzes in der Music,* 2 vols. (Berlin: Christain Friedrich Voß, 1771–79; facs. rpt. Hildesheim: Georg Olms, 1968).
Marpurg, Friedrich Wilhelm. 1754–78. *Historisch-Kritische Beyträge zur Aufnahme der Music,* Friedrich Wilhelm Marpurg, ed. (Berlin: Gottlieb August Lange, 1754–78; rpt. Hildesheim: Georg Olms, 1970).
Mattheson, Johann. 1713. *Das neu-eröffnete Orchestre* (Hamburg: der Autor und Benjamin Schillers Wittwe, 1713).

Mattheson, Johann. 1717. *Das beschützte Orchestre* (Hamburg: Schillerischen Buchladen, 1717).

Mattheson, Johann. 1719. *Exemplarische Organisten-Probe* (Hamburg: Schiller und Kißner, 1719).

Mattheson, Johann. 1722–25. *Critica musica* (Hamburg: auf Unkosten des Autoris, 1722–25; rpt. Laaber: Laaber Verlag, 2003).

Mattheson, Johann. 1728. *Der musicalische Patriot* (Hamburg: n.p., 1728).

Mattheson, Johann. 1731. *Grosse General-Baß-Schule, oder Der exemplarischen Organisten-Probe*, 2nd ed. (Hamburg: Johann Christoph Kißner, 1731; rpt. Hildesheim: Georg Olms, 1968).

Mattheson, Johann. 1739. *Der vollkommene Capellmeister* (Hamburg: Christian Herold, 1739; rpt. Kassel, Bärenreiter, 1954).

Mattheson, Johann. 1740. *Grundlage einer Ehren-Pforte* (Hamburg, In Verlegung des Verfassers, 1740; rpt. Berlin, Liepmannssohn, 1910).

Praetorius, Michael. 1619. *Syntagma Musicum*, Book II, *De Organographia* (Wolfenbüttel: Elias Holwein, 1619; rpt. Kassel: Bärenreiter, 1958).

Quantz, Johann Joachim. 1752. *Versuch einer Anweisung die Flöte traversiere zu spielen* (Berlin: Johann Friedrich Voß, 1752).

Scheibe, Johann Adolph. 1745. *Der Critische Musicus. Neue, vermehrte und verbesserte Auflage* (Leipzig: Bernhard Christoph Breitkopf, 1745).

Walther, Johann Gottfried. 1708. *Praecepta der musicalischen Composition* (manuscript, 1708), Peter Benary, ed. (Leipzig: Breitkopf & Härtel, 1955).

Walther, Johann Gottfried. 1732. *Musicalisches Lexicon* (Leipzig: Wolfgang Deer, 1732; facs. rpt. Kassel: Bärenreiter, 1953).

Secondary Literature

Beißwenger, Kirsten. 1992a. *Johann Sebastian Bachs Notenbibliothek* (Kassel: Bärenreiter, 1992).

Beißwenger, Kirsten. 1992b. "Zur Chronologie der Notenhandschriften Johann Gottfried Walthers." In *Acht kleine Präludien und Studien über BACH: Festschrift für Georg von Dadelsen* (Kassel: Breitkopf & Härtel, 1992), 11–39.

Belotti, Michael. 2001. "Johann Pachelbel als Lehrer." In *Bach und seine mitteldeutschen Zeitgenossen*, Rainer Kaiser, ed. (Eisenach: Karl Dieter Wagner, 2001), 8–44.

Bighley, Mark. 1991. "The Schübler Chorales as Cycle: A Liturgical and Theological Perspective." *Organ Yearbook* 22 (1991), 97–118.

Bighley, Mark. 2018. *The Chorales of Bach's Organ Works: Tunes, Texts, and Translations* (Colfax, NC: Wayne Leupold Editions, 2018).

Billeter, Bernhard. 2007. "Wann sind Johann Sebastian Bachs Choralfughetten (BWV 696–699 und 701–704) und die sogenannten 'Arnstädter Gemeinde-Choräle' (BWV 726, 715, 722, 732, 729 und 738) entstanden?" *Bach-Jahrbuch* 93 (2007), 213–221.

Blanken, Christine. 2013a. *Bach 'Nürnberger Art': Die einzigartige Notensammlung des Organisten Leonhard Scholz (1720–1798)"* (Leipzig: Bach-Museum Leipzig, 2013). Published in conjunction with an exhibition of the same title at Bach-Museum Leipzig, September 19, 2013–February 9, 2014.

Blanken, Christine. 2013b. "Ein wieder zugänglich gemachter Bestand alter Musikalien der Bach-Familie im Verlagsarchiv Breitkopf & Härtel, *Bach-Jahrbuch* 99 (2013), 79–128.

Blanken, Christine. 2019. "Johann Sebastian Bach, die Bach-Familie und die Breitkopfs." In *Breitkopf & Härtel: 300 Jahre europäische Musik- und Kulturgeschichte*, Thomas Frenzel, ed. (Wiesbaden: Breitkopf & Härtel, 2019), 45–62.

Breig, Werner. 1986a. "Bachs freie Orgelmusik unter dem Einfluß der italienischen Konzertform." In *Johann Sebastian Bachs Traditionsraum* (= Bach-Studien 9), Reinhard Szeskus, ed. (Leipzig: VEB Breitkopf & Härtel Musiksverlag Leipzig, 1986), 29–43.

Breig, Werner. 1986b. "The 'Great Eighteen' Chorales: Bach's Revisional Process and the Genesis of the Work." In *J. S. Bach as Organist: His Instruments, Music, and Performance Practices*, George B. Stauffer and Ernest May, eds. (Bloomington: Indiana University Press, 1986), 102–120.

Breig, Werner. 1986c. "J. S. Bachs Orgeltoccata BWV 538 und ihre Entstehungsgeschichte." In *Festschrift Martin Ruhnke zum 65. Geburtstag*, Mitarbeiter des Instituts für Musikwissenschaft der Universität Erlangen-Nürnberg, eds. (Neuhausen-Stuttgart: Hänssler, 1986), 56–67.

Breig, Werner. 1987. "Bachs Orgelchoral und die italienische Instrumentalmusik." In *Bach und die italienische Musik*, Wolfgang Osthoff and Reinhard Wiesend, eds. (Venice: Centro Tedesco de studi veneziana, 1987), 91–107.

Breig, Werner. 1990. "Textbezug und Werkidee in Johann Sebastian Bachs frühen Orgelchorälen." In *Musikkulturgeschichte—Festschrift für Constantin Floros zum 60. Geburtstag*, Peter Petersen, ed. (Wiesbaden: Breitkopf & Härtel, 1990), 167–182.

Breig, Werner. 1992. "Formprobleme in Bachs frühen Orgelfugen." *Bach-Jahrbuch* 78 (1992), 7–21.

Breig, Werner. 1995. "Versuch einer Theorie der Bachschen Orgelfuge." *Die Musikforschung* 48 (1995), 14–52.

Breig, Werner. 1998. "Bach und Marchand in Dresden. Eine überlieferungskritische Studie." *Bach-Jahrbuch* 84 (1998), 45–56.

Breig, Werner. 1999. "Freie Orgelwerke." In *Bach Handbuch*, Konrad Küster, ed. (Kassel: Bärenreiter, and Stuttgart: J. B. Metzler, 1999), 613–712.

Breig, Werner. 2000. "Bach und Walther." In *Der junge Bach, weil er nicht aufzuhalten . . .*, Reinmar Emans, ed. (Plauen: Sebald Sachsendruck, 2000), 309–321.

Breig, Werner. 2001. "'. . . Das Fehlerhafte gut, das Gute besser und das Bessere zum Allerbesten zu machen': Zu Umarbeitungsprozeß in einigen Orgelkompositionen Bachs (BWV 535, 572, und 543)." In *"Die Zeit, die Tag und Jahre macht": Zur Chronologie des Schaffens von Johann Sebastian Bach*, Martin Staehelin, ed. (Göttingen: Vandenhoeck und Ruprecht, 2001), 121–141.

Breig, Werner. 2006. "Bachs kompositorische Erfahrungen mit der norddeutschen Musikkultur." In *Lübeck und die nordeutsche Musiktradition*, Wolfgang Sandberger, ed., 2nd ed. (Kassel: Bärenreiter, 2006), 27–42.

Burba, Otto-Jürgen. 1994. "Bachs Choralfughetten aus der Kirnbergerschen Sammlung." *Musik und Kirche* 64 (1994), 87–94.

Butler, Gregory. 1981. "Borrowings in J. S. Bach's Klavierübung III." *Canadian University Music Review* 4 (1981), 204–217.

Butler, Gregory. 1990. *Bach's Clavier-Übung III: The Making of a Print* (Durham, NC: Duke University Press, 1990).

Butler, Gregory. 2010. "'Instrumente Mangel': Leipzig Cantata Movements with Obbligato Organ as a Reflection of Bach's Performing Forces." *Keyboard Perspectives* 3 (2010), 131–146.

Butt, John. 1988. "Bach's Organ Sonatas BWV 525–530: Compilation and Recomposition." *Organ Yearbook* 19 (1988), 80–90.

Butt, John. 1990. *Bach Interpretation: Articulation Marks in Primary Sources of J. S. Bach* (Cambridge: Cambridge University Press, 1990).

Chailley, Jacques. 1974. *Les chorals pour orgue de J.-S. Bach* (Paris: Alphonse Leduc, 1974).

Claus, Rolf, Dietrich. 1995. *Zur Echtheit von Toccata und Fuge d-moll BWV 565* (Cologne: Verlag Dohr, 1995).

Claus, Rolf, Dietrich. 1999. *Johann Peter Kellner: Studien zu Leben und Werk nebst einem thematisch-systematischen Verzeichnis seiner musikalischen Werke* (diss., Rostock University, 1999).

Cron, Matthew. 2003. *The Obbligato Organ Cantatas of J. S. Bach in the Context of 18th-Century Practice* (diss., Brandeis University, 2003).

Czubatynski, Uwe. 1993. "Choralvorspiel und Choralbegleitung im Urteil J. S. Bachs." *Bach-Jahrbuch* 79 (1993), 223.

Dadelsen, Georg von. 1958. *Beiträge zur Chronologie der Werke Johann Sebastian Bachs* (Trossingen: Hohner-Verlag, 1958).

Dadelsen, Georg von. 1963. "Zur Entstehung des Bachschen Orgelbüchleins." In *Festschrift Friedrich Blume*, Anna Amalie Abert and Wilhelm Pfannkuch, eds. (Kassel: Bärenreiter, 1963), 74–79.

Daw, Stephen. 1976. "Copies of J. S. Bach by Walther and Krebs: A Study of the Mss. P 801, P 802, and P 803." *Organ Yearbook* 7 (1976), 31–58.

Delang, Kerstin. 2007. "Couperin-Pisendel-Bach. Überlegungen zur Echtheit und Datierung des Trios BWV 587 anhand eines Quellenfundes in der Sächsischen Landesbibliothek." *Bach-Jahrbuch* 93 (2007), 197–204.

Dirksen, Pieter. 2002. "Bach's 'Acht Choralfughetten.' Ein unbeachtetes Leipziger Sammelwerk." In *Bach in Leipzig—Bach und Leipzig. Konferenzbericht Leipzig 2000*, Ulrich Leisinger, ed. (Hildesheim: Georg Olms, 2002), 155–182.

Dirksen, Pieter. 2003. "Ein verschollenes Weimar Kammermusikwerk Johann Sebastian Bachs? Zur Vorgeschichte der Sonate e-Moll für Orgel (BWV 528)." *Bach-Jahrbuch* 89 (2003), 7–36.

Dirksen, Pieter. 2019. "Johann Sebastian Bach's Chorale Partita 'Ach, was soll ich Sünder machen,' BWV 770." *Organ Yearbook* 48 (2019), 88–109.

Douglass, Fenner. 1995. *The Language of the Classical French Organ*, 2nd ed. (New Haven: Yale University Press, 1995).

Dreyfus, Laurence. 1986. "The Metaphorical Soloist: Concerted Organ Parts in Bach's Cantatas." In *J. S. Bach as Organist*, George Stauffer and Ernest May, eds. (Bloomington: Indiana University Press, 1986), 172–189.

Dreyfus, Laurence. 1987. *Bach's Continuo Group: Players and Practices in his Vocal Works* (Cambridge, MA: Harvard University Press, 1987).

Dürr, Alfred. 1977. *Studien über die frühen Kantaten Johann Sebastian Bachs* (Wiesbaden: Breitkopf & Härtel, 1977).

Dürr, Alfred. 1986. "Kein Meister fällt von Himmel—Zu Johann Sebastian Bachs Orgelchorälen der Neumeister-Sammlung." *Musica* 40 (1986), 309–312.

Dürr, Alfred. 2005. *The Cantatas of J. S. Bach*. Richard D. P. Jones, trs. Rev. ed. (Oxford: Oxford University Press, 2005).

Edskes, Cornelius H. 2016. "The Organs and Façades of Arp Schnitger." In *Arp Schnitger and His Work*, Cornelius H. Edskes and Harald Vogel, eds. (Bremen: Edition Falkenberg, 2016), 1–105.

Edwards, Lynn. 1991. "The Thuringian Organ 1702–20: ' . . . Ein wohlgerathenes gravitätisches Werk.'" *Organ Yearbook* 22 (1991), 119–150.

Edwards Butler, Lynn. 2022. *Johann Scheibe, Organ Builder in Leipzig at the Time of Bach* (Urbana: University of Illinois Press, 2022).

Eggebrecht, Hans Heinrich. 1965. "Das Weimarer Tabulaturbuch von 1704." *Archiv für Musikwissenschaft* 22 (1965), 115–125.

Eller, Rudolf. 1957. "Zur Frage Bach-Vivaldi." In *Kongressbericht Hamburg 1956*, Walter Gerstenberg, Heinrich Husmann, and Harald Heckmann, eds. (Kassel: Bärenreiter, 1957), 80–85.

Emery, Walter. 1957. *Notes on Bach's Organ Works* (London: Novello, 1957).

Emery, Walter. 1966. "Some Speculations on the Development of Bach's Organ Style." *Musical Times* 107 (1966), 596–603.

Ernst, H. Peter. 1987. "Joh. Seb. Bachs Wirken am ehemaligen Mühlhäuser Augustinerinnenkloster und das Schicksaal seiner Wender-Orgel." *Bach-Jahrbuch* 73 (1987), 75–83.

Faulkner, Quentin. 2008. *The Registration of J. S. Bach's Organ Works* (Colfax, NC: Wayne Leupold Editions, 2008).

Fischer, Wilhelm. 1915. "Zur Entwicklung des Wiener klassischen Stils." *Studien zur Musikwissenschaft* 3 (1915), 24–84.

Fock, Gustav. 1950. *Der junge Bach in Lüneburg. 1700 bis 1702* (Hamburg: Merseburger, 1950).

Fock, Gustav. 1974. *Arp Schnitger und seine Schule: Ein Beitrag zur Geschichte des Orgelbaues im Nord- und Ostseeküstengebiet* (Kassel: Bärenteiter, 1974).

Forst, Inge. 1990. "Johann Sebastian Bachs Orgelkonzert d-moll: Vorlage und Endform." In *Beiträge zur Geschichte des Konzerts: Festschrift Siegfried Kross zum 60. Geburtstag*, Reinmar Emans and Matthias Wendt, eds. (Bonn: Gundrun Schröder Verlag, 1990), 77–86.

Friedrich, Felix. 1989. *Der Orgelbauer Heinrich Gottfried Trost: Leben, Werk, Leistung* (Wiesbaden: Breitkopf & Härtel, 1989).

Friedrich, Felix. 2000. "Der Orgelbau in Thüringen zur Bachzeit." In *Der junge Bach, weil er nicht aufzuhalten . . .* , Reinmar Emans, ed. (Plauen: Sebald Sachsendruck, 2000), 60–84.

Golon, Peter. 2016. "On the Life and Work of Arp Schnitger." In *Arp Schnitger and His Work*, Cornelius H. Edskes and Harald Vogel, eds. (Bremen: Edition Falkenberg, 2016), xxiv–xxvi.

Górny, Tomasz. 2019. "Estienne Roger and His Agent Adam Christoph Sellius. New Light on Italian and French Music in Bach's World." *Early Music* 47 (2019), 361–370.

Grapenthin, Ulf. 2003. "Bach und sein 'Hamburgischer Lehrmeister' Johann Adam Reincken." In *Bachs Musik für Tasteninstrumente—Bericht über das 4. Dortmunder Bach-Symposion 2002*, Martin Geck, ed. (Dortmund: Klangfarben-Musikverlag, 2003), 9–50.

Grattoni, Maurizio. 1983. "Una scoperta vivaldiana a Cividale del Friuli." *Informazione e studie vivaldiani* 4 (1983), 3–19.

Grychtolik, Alexander Ferdinand. 2013. "Anmerkungen zu den Aùfführungsstätten J. S. Bachs in Weimar." *Bach-Jahrbuch* 99 (2013), 309–318.

Heller, Karl. 2006. "Überlegungen zur Datierung der Reinken-Fugen Johann Sebastian Bachs." In *Bach, Lübeck und die norddeutsche Musiktradition*, Wolfgang Sandberger, ed. (Kassel: Bärenreiter, 2006), 231–244.

Hiemke, Sven. 2007. *Johann Sebastian Bach: Orgelbüchlein* (Kassel: Bärenreiter, 2007).

Hill, Robert. 1985. "The Lost Clavier Books of the Young Bach and Handel." In *Bach, Handel, Scarlatti: Tercentenary Essays*, Peter Williams, ed. (Cambridge: Cambridge University Press, 1985), 161–171.

Hill, Robert. 1987. *The Möller Manuscript and the Andreas Bach Book: Two Keyboard Anthologies from the Circle of the Young Johann Sebastian Bach* (diss., Harvard University, 1987).

Hill, Robert. 1995. "Johann Sebastian Bach's Toccata in G Major BWV 916/1: A Reception of Giuseppe Torelli's Ritornello Concerto Form." In *Das Frühwerk Johann Sebastian Bachs*, Karl Heller and Hans-Joachim Schulze, eds. (Cologne: Studio, 1995), 162–175.

Hofmann, Klaus. 1995. "Zum Bearbeitungsverfahren in Bachs Weimar Concerti nach Vivaldis 'Estro Armonico' op 3." In *Das Frühwerk Johann Sebastian Bachs*, Karl Heller and Hans-Joachim Schluze, eds. (Cologne: Studio, 1995), 176–202.

Hofmann, Klaus. 2000a. "Bach in Arnstadt." In *Der junge Bach, weil er nicht aufzuhalten…*, Reinmar Emans, ed. (Plauen: Sebald Sachsendruck, 2000), 239–255.

Hofmann, Klaus. 2000b. "Bach in Mühlhausen." In *Der junge Bach, weil er nicht aufzuhalten…*, Reinmar Emans, ed. (Plauen: Sebald Sachsendruck, 2000), 261–272.

Horn, Victoria. 1986. "French Influences in Bach's Organ Works." In *J. S. Bach as Organist: His Instruments, Music, and Performance Practices*, George B. Stauffer and Ernest May, eds. (Bloomington: Indiana University Press, 1986), 256–273.

Humphreys, David. 1982. "The D Minor Toccata BWV 565." *Early Music* 10 (1982), 216–217.

Humphreys, David. 1994. "'Und besonders für Kenner von dergleichen Arbeit': A Study of the Symbolic Aspects of Bach's 'Dritter Theil der Clavierübung.'" *Organ Yearbook* 24 (1994), 41–64.

Jauernig, Reinhold. 1950a. "Bachs erster Aufenthalt in Weimar." In *Bach in Thüringen*, Landeskirchenrat der Evangelisch-Lutherischen Kirche in Thüringen, ed. (Berlin: Evangelische Verlagsanstalt, 1950), 69–70, 77–84.

Jauernig, Reinhold. 1950b. "Johann Sebastian Bach in Weimar." In *Johann Sebastian Bach in Thüringen: Festgabe zum Gedenkjahr 1950*, Heinrich Besseler and Günter Kraft, eds. (Weimar: Thüringer Volksverlag, 1950), 49–105.

Kaiser, Rainer. 2000. "Bachs Konzerttranskriptionen and das 'Stück in Goldpapier'. Zur Datierung der Bach-Abschriften P 280 and Ms. R 9." *Bach-Jahrbuch* 86 (2000), 307–312.

Kaiser, Rainer. 2001. "Johann Christoph Bachs 'Choräle zum Präambulieren'— Anmerkungen zu Echtheit und Überlieferung." *Bach-Jahrbuch* 87 (2001), 185–189.

Keller, Hermann. 1967. *The Organ Works of Bach*, Helen Hewitt, trs. (New York: C. F. Peters, 1967).

Kilian, Dietrich. 1961. "J. S. Bach, Präludium und Fuge d-Moll, BWV 539: Ein Arrangement aus dem 19. Jahrhundert?" *Musikforschung* 14 (1961), 323–328.

Kilian, Dietrich. 1962. "Studie über J. S. Bachs Fantasie und Fuge c-moll (BWV 562)." In *Hans Albrecht in Memoriam*, Wilfried Brennecke and Hans Hasse, eds. (Kassel: Bärenreiter, 1962), 127–135.

Kilian, Dietrich. 1969. "Dreisätzige Fassungen Bachscher Orgelwerke." In *Bach-Interpretationen*, Martin Geck, ed. (Göttingen: Vandenhoeck & Ruprecht, 1969), 12–21.

Kilian, Dietrich. 1983. "Zu einem Bachschen Tabulaturautograph." In *Bachiana et alia musicologica: Festschrift Alfred Dürr zum 65. Geburtstag am 3. März 1983*, Wolfgang Rehm, ed. (Kassel: Bärenreiter, 1983), 161–167.

Klein, Hans-Günter. 1970. *Der Einfluss der Vivaldischen Konzertform im Instrumental-Werk Johann Sebastian Bachs* (Baden-Baden: Heintz, 1970).

Klotz, Hans. 1950. "Bachs Orgeln und seine Orgelmusik." *Musikforschung* 3 (1950), 189–203.

Klotz, Hans. 1975. *Über die Orgelkunst der Gotik, der Renaissance und des Barock*, 2nd ed. (Kassel: Bärenreiter, 1975).

Kobayashi, Yoshitake. 1983. "Der Gehrener Kantor Johann Christoph Bach (1673–1727) und seine Sammelbände für Tasteninstrumente." In *Bachiana et alia Musicologica*, Wolfgang Rehm, ed. (Kassel: Bärenreiter, 1983), 168–177.

Kobayashi, Yoshitake. 1988. "Zur Chronologie der Spätwerke Johann Sebastian Bachs: Kompositions- und Aufführungstätigkeit von 1736 bis 1750." *Bach-Jahrbuch* 74 (1988), 7–72.

Koska, Bernd. 2012. "Bach-Schüler bei der Organistenwahl zu Schleiz 1727/28." *Bach-Jahrbuch* 98 (2012), 225–234.

Koska, Bernd. 2017. "Die Berliner Notenkopisten Johann Gottfried Siebe und Johann Nicolaus Schober und ihre Bach-Abschriften." *Bach-Jahrbuch* 103 (2017), 149–184.

Koska, Bernd. 2019. "Bachs Privatschüler." *Bach-Jahrbuch* 105 (2019), 13–82.

Kraft, Günter. 1950. "Johann Georg Schübler: Notenstecher und Verleger." In *Johann Sebastian Bach in Thüringen*, Heinrich Besseler and Günter Kraft, ed. (Weimar: Thüringer Volksverlag, 1950), 183–188.

Krüger, Elke. 1970. *Stilistische Untersuchungen zu ausgewählten frühen Klavierfugen Johann Sebastian Bachs* (Hamburg: Karl Dieter Wagner Musikalienhandlung, 1970).

Krumbach, Wilhelm. 1985. "Sechzig unbekannte Orgelwerke von Johann Sebastian Bach: Ein vorläufiger Fundbericht." *Neue Zeitschrift für Musik* 146 (1985), 4–12.

Krummacher, Friedhelm. 1985. "Bach und die norddeutsche Orgeltoccata: Fragen und Überlegungen." *Bach-Jahrbuch* 71 (1985), 119–134.

Kube, Michael. 1993. "'. . . Daß man cantabel setzen soll': Anmerkungen zu Pachelbels Fugenstil." *Ars Organi* 40 (1993), 124–131.

Kube, Michael. 1994. "Pachelbel, Erfurt und der Orgelchoral." *Musik und Kirche* 64 (1994), 76–82.

Kube, Michael. 1999. "Choralgebundene Orgelwerke." In *Bach-Handbook*, Konrad Küster, ed. (Kassel: Bärenreiter-Verlag, 1999), 541–612.

Kube, Michael. 2001. "Modelle und Lösungen. Überlegungen zu den Choralbearbeitungen über 'Wie schön leuchtet der Morgenstern' von Pachelbel, Buttstett/Armsdorf und Bach." In *Bach und seine mitteldeutschen Zeitgenossen*, Rainer Kaiser, ed. (Eisenach: Karl Dieter Wagner, 2001), 190–198.

Kube, Michael. 2003. "Satztyp und Kontrapunkt: Einige Anmerkungen (nicht nur) zu Bachs Choralbearbeitungen über Vom Himmel hoch, da komm ich her." In *Bachs Musik für Tasteninstrumente*, Martin Geck, ed. (Dortmund: Sackmann, 2003), 309–322.

Küster, Konrad. 1996. *Der junge Bach* (Stuttgart: Deutsche Verlags-Anstalt, 1996).

Küster, Konrad. 2002. "Konzertvorlage oder Originalkomposition? Zu den obligaten Orgelanteilen in Bachs Kantaten aus dem Jahr 1726." In *Bach in Leipzig—Bach und Leipzig: Konferenzbericht Leipzig 2000*, Ulrich Leisinger, ed. (Hildesheim: Georg Olms Verlag, 2002), 45–58.

Leahy, Anne. 2011. *J. S. Bach's "Leipzig" Chorale Preludes: Music, Text, Theology*, Robin A. Leaver, ed. (Lanham, UK: Scarecrow Press, 2011).

Leaver, Robin A. 1985. "Bach and Hymnody: The Evidence of the *Orgelbüchlein*." *Early Music* 13 (1985), 227–236.

Leaver, Robin A. 2009. "Religion and Religious Currents." In *The Worlds of Johann Sebastian Bach*, Raymond Erickson, ed. (New York: Amadeus Press, 2009), 105–139.

Leisinger, Ulrich, and Peter Wollny. 1997. *Die Bach-Quellen der Bibliotheken in Brüssel— Katalog* (Hildesheim: Georg Olms Verlag, 1997).

Lobenstein, Albrecht. 2015. "Gottfried Albin de Wette als Gewährsmann für Orgeldispositionen der Bach-Zeit in Weimarer Landgebiet." In *Bach-Jahrbuch* 101 (2015), 273–304.

Löffler, Hans. 1931. "G. H. Trost und die Altenburger Schloßorgel." *Musik und Kirche* 4 (1932), 171–176 and 280–285.

Löffler, Hans. 1953. "Die Schüler Johann Sebastian Bachs." *Bach-Jahrbuch* 50 (1953), 5–28.

Luther, Martin. 1955–86. *Luther's Works: American Edition*, Jaroslav Pelikan and Helmut Lehman, eds. (St. Louis: Concordia, 1955–86).

Marissen, Michael. 2021. "Bach against Modernity." In *Rethinking Bach*, Bettina Varwig, ed. (New York: Oxford University Press, 2021), 315–335.

Marshall, Robert L. 1989a. "On Bach's Universality." In *The Music of Johann Sebastian Bach: The Sources, the Style, the Significance*, Marshall, ed. (New York: Schirmer Books, 1989), 65–79.

Marshall, Robert L. 1989b. "Tempo and Dynamics: The Original Terminology." In *The Music of Johann Sebastian Bach: The Sources, the Style, the Significance*, Marshall, ed. (New York: Schirmer Books, 1989). 255–269.

Marshall, Robert L. 2001. "Chorale Settings." In *The New Grove Dictionary of Music and Musicians*, Stanley Sadie, ed., vol. 5, 2nd ed. (London: Macmillan, 2001), 747–763.

Marshall, Robert L., and Traute M. Marshall. 2016. *Exploring the World of J. S. Bach: A Traveler's Guide* (Urbana: University of Illinois Press, 2016).

May, Ernest. 1974. *Breitkopf's Role in the Transmission of J. S. Bach's Organ Chorales* (diss., Princeton University, 1974).

May, Ernest. 1996. "Connections between Breitkopf and J. S. Bach." In *Bach Perspectives 2: J. S. Bach, the Breitkopfs, and Eighteenth-Century Music Trade*, George B. Stauffer, ed. (Lincoln: University of Nebraska Press, 1996), 11–26.

Maul, Michael. 2004. "Frühe Urteile über Johann Christoph und Johann Nikolaus Bach, mitgeteilt anläßlich der Besetzung der Organistenstelle an der Jenaer Kollegienkirche (1709)." *Bach-Jahrbuch* 90 (2004), 157–168.

Maul, Michael, and Peter Wollny. 2007. *Weimarer Orgeltabulatur Johann Sebastian Bach*, Michael Maul and Peter Wollny, eds. (Kassel: Bärenreiter, 2007).

Neubacher, Jürgen. 2001. "Johann Ernst Bernhard Pfeiffer und die Organistenproben." In *Critica musica: Studien zum 17. und 18. Jahrhundert: Festschrift Hans Joachim Marx zum 65. Geburtstag*, Nicole Ristow, Wolfgang Sandberger, and Dorothea Schröder, eds. (Stuttgart: Metzler, 2001), 221–232.

Neumann, Werner. 1953. *J. S. Bachs Chorfuge*, vol. 3 of *Bach-Studien*, 3rd ed. (Leipzig: VEB, 1953).

O'Donnell, John. 1989. "Mattheson, Bach, Krebs and the Fantasia & Fugue in C Minor BWV 537." *Organ Yearbook* 20 (1989), 88–95.

Oefner, Claus. 2000. "Musik und Musikleben in Thüringen um 1700." In *Der junge Bach, weil er nicht aufzuhalten . . .* , Reinmar Emans, ed. (Plauen: Sebald Sachsendruck, 2000), 33–41.

Over, Berthold. 2017. "Eine ubekannte Quelle zu BWV 531 aus dem Besitz von Johannes Ringk." *Bach-Jahrbuch* 103 (2017), 93–108.

Pfau, Marc-Roderich. 2008. "Ein unbekanntes Leipziger Kantatentextheft aus dem Jahr 1735—Neues zum Thema Bach und Stölzel." *Bach-Jahrbuch* 94 (2008), 99–122.

Pirro, André. 1907. *J. S. Bach* (Paris: F. Alcan, 1907).

Ponsford, David. *French Organ Music in the Reign of Louis XIV* (Cambridge: Cambridge University Press, 2011).

Power, Tushaar. 2001. *J. S. Bach and the Divine Proportion* (diss., Duke University, 2001).

Rasch, Rudolf. 1996. "La famosa mano di Monsieur Roger: Antonio Vivaldi and His Dutch Publishers." *Informazione e studi vivaldiani* 17 (1996), 89–135.

Rasch, Rudolf. 2019. "Roger, Bach and Walther: Musical Relations between Amsterdam and Weimar." In *Tijdschrift van de Koninklijke Vereniging voor Nederlandse Musiekgeschiedenis* 69 (2019), 75–90.

Rempp, Frieder. 2000. "Johann Sebastian Bach in Eisenach," 2000. in *Der junge Bach, weil er nicht aufzuhalten . . .* , Reinmar Emans, ed. (Plauen: Sebald Sachsendruck, 2000), 161–186.

Rich, Norman. 2009. "The Historical Setting: Politics and Patronage." In *The Worlds of Johann Sebastian Bach*, Raymond Erickson, ed. (New York: Amadeus Press, 2009), 67–104.

Richter, Bernhard Friedrich. 1908. "Über Seb. Bachs Kantaten mit obligater Orgel." *Bach-Jahrbuch* 5 (1908), 49–63.

Roth, Hermann. 1915. "Bachs c-Moll Passacaglia und die verwandten Werke Dietrich Buxtehudes." *Monatsschrift für Gottesdienst und kirchliche Kunst* 20 (1915), 18–29.

Sackmann, Dominik. 1998. "Johann Sebastian Bachs vermeintliche 'Arnstädter Gemeindechoräle." *Schweizer Jahrbuch für Musikwissenschaft* 18 (1998), 229–250.

Sackmann, Dominik. 2000. *Bach und Corelli—Studien zu Bachs Rezeption von Corellis Violinsonaten op. 5 unter besonderer Berücksichtigung der "Passagio-Orgelchoräle" und der langsamen Konzertsätze* (Munich: Musikverlag Katzbichler, 2000).

Sackmann, Dominik. 2003. "Konzerte des/für den Prinzen. Zur Funktion und Datierung von Bachs Konzert Bearbeitung BWV 595/984." In *Bachs Musik für Tasteninstrumente*, Martin Geck, ed. (Dortmund: Sackmann, 2003), 133–143.

Schering, Arnold. 1926. *Musikgeschichte Leipzigs 1650 bis 1723* (Leipzig: Fr. Kistner & C. F. W. Siegel, 1926).

Schiffner, Markus. 1985. "Johann Sebastian Bach in Arnstadt." In *Beiträge zur Bachforschung* 4 (1985), 5–22.

Schneider, Matthias. 1999. "Johann Sebastian Bach und der Fantasiestil—Zur Choralbearbeitung BWV 718 Christ lag in Todesbanden." In *Bach und die Stile—Bericht über das 2. Dortmunder Bach-Symposion*, Martin Geck, ed. (Dortmund: Klangfarben Musikverlag, 1999), 205–217.

Schrammek, Winfried. 1985. "Johann Sebastian Bachs Stellung zu Orgelpedalregistern im 32-Fuß-Ton." *Bach-Jahrbuch* 71 (1985), 147–154.

Schrammek, Winfried. 1988. "Orgel, Positiv, Clavicymbel und Glocken der Schloßkirche zu Weimar 1658 bis 1774." In *Bach-Händel-Schütz-Ehrung 1985 der Deutschen Demokratischen Republik. Bericht über die Wissenschaftliche Konferenz zum V. Internationalen Bachfest der Neuen Bachgesellschaft*, Winfried Hofmann and Armin Schneiderheinze, eds. (Leipzig: VEB Deutscher Verlag für Musik, 1988), 99–111.

Schulenberg, David. 2006. *The Keyboard Music of J. S. Bach*, 2nd ed. (New York: Routledge, 2006).

Schulze, Hans-Joachim. 1972. "J. S. Bach's Concerto Arrangements for Organ—Studies or Commissioned Works?" *Organ Yearbook* 3 (1972), 4–13.

Schulze, Hans-Joachim. 1974. "Wie entstand die Bach-Sammlung Mempell Preller?" *Bach-Jahrbuch* 60 (1974), 104–122.

Schulze, Hans-Joachim. 1983. "Telemann—Pisendel—Bach. Zu einem unbekannten Bach-Autograph." In *Die Bedeutung Georg Philipp Telemanns für die Entwicklung der europäischen Musikkultur im 18. Jahrhundert*, Günter Fleischhauer, ed. (Magdeburg: Zentrum für Telemann-Pflege und -Forschung, 1983), 73–77.

Schulze, Hans-Joachim. 1984. *Studien zur Bach-Überlieferung im 18. Jahrhundert* (Leipzig: Edition Peters, 1984).

Schulze, Hans-Joachim. 1985. "Johann Christoph Bach (1671 bis 1721), 'Organist und Schul Collega in Ohrdruf.'" *Bach-Jahrbuch* 71 (1985), 55–83.

Schulze, Hans-Joachim. 1991. "Bach und Buxtehude. Eine wenig beachtete Quelle in der Carnegie Library zu Pittsburgh/PA." *Bach-Jahrbuch* 77 (1991), 177–181.

Schulze, Hans-Joachim. 1995. "Die Handhabung der Chromatik in Bachs frühen Tastenwerken." In *Das Frühwerk Johann Sebastian Bachs*, Karl Heller and Hans-Joachim Schulze, eds. (Cologne: Studio, 1995), 70-86.

Schulze, Hans-Joachim. 2008. "'Die 6 Choräle kosten nichts'—Zur Bewertung des Originaldrucks der 'Schübler-Choräle.'" *Bach-Jahrbuch* 94 (2008), 301–304.

Schweitzer, Albert. 1905. *J. S. Bach le Musician-Poète* (Leipzig: Breitkopf and Härtel, 1905). Citations from the English edition, *J. S. Bach*, Ernest Newman, tr. (New York: Macmillan, 1925; rpt. New York: Dover, 1966).

Seiffert, Max. 1920. "Das Plauener Orgelbuch von 1708." *Archiv für Musikwissenschaft* 2 (1920), 371–393.

Siegele, Ulrich. 1981. "Bachs Ort in Orthodoxie und Aufklärung." *Musik und Kirche* 51 (1981), 3–14.

Smend, Friedrich. 1933. "Bachs Kanonwerk über 'Vom Himmel hoch da komm ich her.'" *Bach-Jahrbuch* 30 (1933), 1-29

Snyder, Kerala J. 2002. "Organs as Historical and Aesthetic Mirrors." In *The Organ as a Mirror of Its Time: North European Reflections, 1610–2000*, Kerala J. Snyder, ed. (Oxford: Oxford University Press, 2002) 1-22.

Snyder, Kerala J. 2007. *Dieterich Buxtehude: Organist in Lübeck*, rev. ed. (Rochester, NY: University of Rochester Press, 2007).

Spitta, Philipp. 1873–80. *Johann Sebastian Bach* (Leipzig: Breitkopf und Härtel, 1873–80); Citations from the English ed., *Johann Sebastian Bach*, Clara Bell and J. A. Fuller-Maitland, trs. (London: Novello, 1889; rpt. New York: Dover, 1952).

Stahl, Wilhelm. 1942. *Die Totentanz-Orgel der Marienkirche zu Lübeck,* 2nd ed. (Mainz: Rheingold, 1942).

Stauffer, George B. 1980. *The Organ Preludes of Johann Sebastian Bach* (Ann Arbor: UMI Research Press, 1980).

Stauffer, George B. 1983. "Bach's Pastorale in F—A Closer Look at a Maligned Work." In *Organ Yearbook* 14 (1983), 44–60.

Stauffer, George B. 1986a. "Bach's Organ Registration Reconsidered." In *J. S. Bach as Organist: His Instruments, Music, and Performance Pracctices*, George B. Stauffer and Ernest May, eds. (Bloomington: University of Indiana Press, 1986), 198–200.

Stauffer, George B. 1986b. "Fugue Types in Bach's Free Organ Works." In *J. S. Bach as Organist: His Instruments, Music, and Performance Pracctices,* George B. Stauffer and Ernest May, eds. (Bloomington: Indiana University Press, 1986), 133–156.

Stauffer, George B. 1993. "Boyvin, de Grigny, and D'Anglebert and Bach's Assimilation of French Style." *Early Music* 21 (1993), 83–98.

Stauffer, George B. 1994. "J. S. Bach as Organ Pedagogue." In *The Organist as Scholar: Essays in Memory of Russell Saunders*, Kerala J. Snyder, ed. (Stuyvesant, NY: Pendragon Press, 1994), 25–44.

Stauffer, George B. 1999. "Die Sinfonien." In *Die Welt der Bach Kantaten*, Christoph Wolff, ed. (Kassel: Bärenreiter, and Weimar: Metzler, 1999), vol. 3, 157–175.

Stauffer, George B. 2003. *Bach: The Mass in B Minor* (New Haven: Yale University Press, 2003).

Stauffer, George B. 2008. "Bach's Cantata and Passion Movements with Obbligato Organ." In *Festschrift Ewald Kooiman*, Hans Fidom, Jan R. Luth, and Christoph Wolff, eds. (Veenhuizen, Netherlands: Boejenga Music, 2008), 19–41.

Stauffer, George B. 2009. "Bach and the Lure of the Big City." In *The Worlds of Johann Sebastian Bach*, Raymond Erickson, ed. (New York: Amadeus Press, 2009), 243–266.

Stauffer, George B. 2010. "Ein neuer Blick auf Bachs 'Handexemplare': Das Beispiel Clavier-Übung III." *Bach-Jahrbuch* 96 (2010), 129–152.

Stauffer, George B. 2011. "Bach's Late Works and the Central German Organ." *Keyboard Perspectives* 3 (2011), 113–130.

Stauffer, George B. 2015. "Noch ein 'Handexemplar': Der Fall der Schübler-Choräle." *Bach-Jahrbuch* 101 (2015), 177–192.

Stauffer, George B. 2016. "Miscellaneous Organ Trios from Bach's Leipzig Workshop." In *Bach Perspectives 10: Bach and the Organ*, Matthew Dirst, ed. (Urbana: University of Illinois Press, 2016), 39–59.

Stauffer, George B. 2017. "Von Bach korrigierte Exemplare der Originaldrucke seiner Tastenwerke—ein weiterer Fall." In *Bach-Jahrbuch* 103 (2017), 211–218.

Stauffer, George B. 2020. "Bach's Fantasia and Fugue in C Minor, BWV 537: Further Thoughts." *Organ Yearbook* 49 (2020), 77–92.

Stauffer, George B. 2023. "Bachs 'Neunzehn Choräle'? Ein neuer Blick auf die Leipziger Sammelmappe." *Bach-Jahrbuch* 109 (2023), 217–230.

Stinson, Russell. 1985. "Bach's Earliest Autograph." *Musical Quarterly* 71 (1985), 235–263.

Stinson, Russell. 1990. *The Bach Manuscripts of Johann Peter Kellner and His Circle* (Durham, NC: Duke University Press, 1990).

Stinson, Russell. 1992. "Ein Sammelband aus Johann Peter Kellners Besitz: Neue Forschungen zur Berliner Bach-Handschrift *P 804*." *Bach-Jahrbuch* 78 (1992), 45–64.

Stinson, Russell. 1996. *Bach: The Orgelbüchlein* (New York: Schirmer Books, 1996).

Stinson, Russell. 2001. *J. S. Bach's Great Eighteen Organ Chorales* (Oxford: Oxford University Press, 2001).

Stinson, Russell. 2012. *J. S. Bach at His Royal Instrument: Essays on His Organ Works* (Oxford: Oxford University Press, 2012).

Synofzik, Thomas. 2001. "Johann Gottlieb Preller und seine Abschriften Bachscher Clavierwerke—Kopistenpraxis als Schlüssel zur Afführungspraxis." In *Bach und seine mitteldeutschen Zeitgenossen*, Rainer Kaiser, ed. (Eisenach: Karl Dieter Wagner, 2001), 45–64.

Taesler, W. M. 1969. "Von Zusammenhang in einigen zyklischen Orgelwerken Johann Sebastian Bachs—Beobachtungen eines Orgel-spielers." *Musik und Kirche* 39 (1969), 184–187.

Tagliavini, Luigi Ferdinando. 1986. "Bach's Organ Transcription of Vivaldi's 'Grosso Mogul' Concerto." In *J. S. Bach as Organist: His Instruments, Music, and Performance Practices*, George B. Stauffer and Ernest May, eds. (Bloomington: Indiana University Press, 1986), 240–255.

Talle, Andrew. 2003. "Nürnberg, Darmstadt, Köthen—Neuerkenntnisse zur Bach-Überlieferung in der ersten Hälfte des 18. Jahrhunderts." *Bach-Jahrbuch* 89 (2003), 143–172.

Tell, Werner. 1938. "Das Formproblem der Passacaglia Bachs." *Musik und Kirche* 10 (1938), 102–112.

Vogelsänger, Siegfred. 1967. "Passacaglia und Chaconne in der Orgelmusik." *Musik und Kirche* 27 (1967), 14–24.

Walker, Paul. 1989. "Die Entstehung der Permutationsfuge." *Bach-Jahrbuch* 75 (1989), 21–41.

Weiß, Ulman. 2000. "Die Thüringer Bach-Städte. Ein Überblick." In *Der junge Bach, weil er nicht aufzuhalten . . .* , Reinmar Emans, ed. (Plauen: Sebald Sachsendruck, 2000), 14–32.

Whiteley, John Scott. 2016. "Historische Belege zur Registrierungspraxis in den Sechs Sonaten BWV 525–530. Eine Neubewertung." *Bach-Jahrbuch* 102 (2016), 11–44.

Williams, Peter. 1981. "BWV 565: A Toccata in D Minor for Organ by J. S. Bach?" *Early Music* 9 (1981), 330–337.

Williams, Peter. 1982. "J. S. Bach: Orgelsachverständiger unter den Einfluß Andreas Werckmeisters?" *Bach-Jahrbuch* 68 (1982), 131–142.

Williams, Peter. 2003. *The Organ Music of J. S. Bach,* 2nd rev. ed. (Cambridge: Cambridge University Press, 2003).

Wolf, Uwe. 2000a. "Musik-Organisation und Musiker-Ausbildung im frühen 18. Jahrhundert." In *Der junge Bach, weil er nicht aufzuhalten . . .* , Reinmar Emans, ed. (Plauen: Sebald Sachsendruck, 2000), 42–60.

Wolf, Uwe. 2000b. "Von Ohrdruf bis zu Bachs erster Anstellung in Weimar." In *Der junge Bach, weil er nicht aufzuhalten . . .* , Reinmar Emans, ed. (Plauen: Sebald Sachsendruck, 2000), 193–205.

Wolff, Christoph. 1968. *Der stile antico in der Musik Johann Sebastian Bachs: Studien zu Bachs Spätwerk* (Wiesbaden: Franz Steiner Verlag, 1968).

Wolff, Christoph. 1986. "Johann Valentin Eckelts Tabulaturbuch von 1692." In *Festschrift Martin Ruhnke zum 65. Geburtstag,* Klaus-Jürgen Sachs, ed. (Neuhausen-Stuttgart: Hänssler, 1986), 44–62.

Wolff, Christoph. 1991a. "The Architecture of the Passacaglia." In *Bach: Essays on His Life and Music,* Wolff, ed. (Cambridge, MA: Harvard University Press, 1991), 306–316.

Wolff, Christoph. 1991b. "Bach and Johann Adam Reinken: A Context for the Early Works." In *Bach: Essays on His Life and Music,* Wolff, ed. (Cambridge, MA: Harvard University Press, 1991), 56–71.

Wolff, Christoph. 1991c. "Bach's Personal Copy of the Schübler Chorales." In *Bach: Essays on His Life and Music,* Wolff, ed. (Cambridge, MA: Harvard University Press, 1991), 178–186.

Wolff, Christoph. 1991d. "Buxtehude, Bach, and Seventeenth-Century Music in Retrospect." In *Bach: Essays on His Life and Music,* Wolff, ed. (Cambridge, MA: Harvard University Press, 1991), 41–55.

Wolff, Christoph. 1991e. "Chronology and Style in the Early Works: A Background for the Orgel-Büchlein," in *Bach: Essays on His Life and Music,* Wolff, ed. (Cambridge, MA: Harvard University Press, 1991) 297–305.

Wolff, Christoph. 1991f. "The Deathbed Chorale: Exposing a Myth." In *Bach: Essays on His Life and Music,* Wolff, ed. (Cambridge, MA: Harvard University Press, 1991), 282–294.

Wolff, Christoph. 1991g. "The Neumeister Collection of Chorale Preludes from the Bach Circle." In *Bach: Essays on his Life and Music,* Wolff, ed. (Cambridge, MA: Harvard University Press, 1991), 107–127.

Wolff, Christoph. 1991h. "Vivaldi's Compositional Art, Bach, and the Process of 'Musical Thinking.'" In *Bach: Essays on His Life and Music,* Wolff, ed. (Cambridge, MA: Harvard University Press, 1991), 72–83.

Wolff, Christoph. 1997. "Zum Quellenwert der Neumeister-Sammlung: Bachs Orgelchoral 'Der Tag der ist so freudenreich.'" *Bach-Jahrbuch* 83 (1997), 155–162.

Wolff, Christoph. 2000. *Johann Sebastian Bach: The Learned Musician* (New York: Norton, 2000).

Wolff, Christoph. 2002a. "Bach's Organ Toccata in D Minor and Its Authenticity." In *Perspectives on Organ Playing and Musical Interpretation: Pedagogical, Historical, and Instrumental Studies. A Festschrift for Heinrich Fleischer at 90*, Heinrich Fleischer Festschrift Committee, ed. (New Ulm, MN: Graphic Arts, Martin Luther College, 2002), 85–107.

Wolff, Christoph. 2002b. "Zum nortdeutschen Kontext der Orgelmusik des jungendlichen Bach: Das Scheinproblem der Toccata d-Moll BWV 565." In *Bach, Lübeck und die norddeutsche Musiktradition*, Wolfgang Sandgerger, ed. (Kassel: Bärenreiter, 2002), 154–160.

Wolff, Christoph. 2016. "Did J. S. Bach Write Organ Concertos? Apropos the Prehistory of the Cantata Movements with Obbligato Organ." In *Bach Perspectives 10: Bach and the Organ*, Matthew Dirst, ed. (Urbana: University of Illinois Press: 2016), 60–75.

Wolff, Christoph. 2020. *Bach's Musical Universe: The Composer and His Work* (New York: Norton, 2020).

Wolff, Christoph, and Markus Zepf. 2012. *The Organs of Johann Sebastian Bach: A Handbook*. Lynn Edwards Butler, trs. (Urbana: University of Illinois Press, 2012).

Wollny, Peter. 2005. "Über die Hintergründe von Johann Sebastian Bachs Bewerbung in Arnstadt." *Bach-Jahrbuch* 91 (2005), 83–94.

Wollny, Peter. 2013. "Eine unbekannte Bach-Handschrift und andere Quellen zur Leipziger Musikgeschichte in Weißenfels." *Bach-Jahrbuch* 99 (2013), 129–170.

Wollny, Peter. 2015. "Vom 'apparat der auserleßensten kirchen Stücke' zum 'Vorrath an Musicalien, von J. S. Bach und andern berühmten Musicis'—Quellenkundliche Ermittlungen zur frühen Thüringer Bach-Überlieferung und zu einigen Weimarer Schülern und Kollegen Bachs." *Bach-Jahrbuch* 101 (2015), 99–154.

Wollny, Peter. 2016a. *Johann Sebastian Bach: Die Achtzehn Großen Orgelchoräle BWV 651–668 und die Canonische Vernderungen über "Vom Himmel hoch" BWV 769*. Peter Wollny, ed. (Laaber: Laaber-Verlag, 2016).

Wollny, Peter. 2016b. "Neuerkenntnisse zu einigen Kopisten der 1730er Jahre." *Bach-Jahrbuch* 102 (2016), 63–113.

Wollny, Peter. 2018. "Der Schleizer Organist Johann Jacob Kieser und seine Abschriften von Werken Johann Sebastian Bachs." *Bach-Jahrbuch* 104 (2018), 81–93.

Yearsley, David. 2002. *Bach and the Meanings of Counterpoint* (Cambridge: Cambridge University Press, 2002).

Yearsley, David. 2012. *Bach's Feet: The Organ Pedals in European Culture* (Cambridge: Cambridge University Press, 2012).

Zehnder, Jean-Claude. 1988. "Georg Böhm und Johann Sebastian Bach. Zur Chronologie der Bachschen Stilentwicklung." *Bach-Jahrbuch* 74 (1988), 73–110.

Zehnder, Jean-Claude. 1991. "Giuseppe Torelli und Johann Sebastian Bach. Zu Bachs Weimarer Konzertform." *Bach-Jahrbuch* 77 (1991), 33–95.

Zehnder, Jean-Claude. 1995. "Zu Bachs Stilentwicklung in der Mühlhäuser und Weimarer Zeit." In *Das Frühwerk Johann Sebastian Bachs*, Karl Heller and Hans-Joachim Schulze, eds. (Cologne: Studio, 1995), 311–338.

Zehnder, Jean-Claude. 1997. "Zum späten Weimarer Stil Johann Sebastian Bachs." In *Bachs Orchesterwerke*, Martin Geck, ed. (Witten: Klangfarben Musikverlag Martin Hartmann, 1997), 89–124.

Zehnder, Jean-Claude. 1999. "'Des seeligen Unterricht in Ohrdruf mag wohl einen Organisten zum Vorwurf gehabt haben'—Zum musikalischen Umfeld Bachs in Ohrdruf, insbesondere auf dem Gebiet des Orgelchorals." In *Bach und die Stile—Bericht über das 2. Dortmunder Bach-Symposion*, Martin Geck, ed. (Dortmund: Klangfarben Musikverlag, 1999), 186–187.

Zehnder, Jean-Claude. 2001. "'Phantastisches' beim jungen Bach." In *Bach und seine mitteldeutschen Zeitgenossen*, Rainer Kaiser, ed. (Eisenach: Karl Dieter Wagner, 2001), 127–145.

Zehnder, Jean-Claude. 2007. "Weitere Überlegungen zur Datierung der Choralfughetten." *Bach-Jahrbuch* 93 (2007), 223–227.

Zehnder, Jean-Claude. 2009. *Die frühen Werke Johann Sebastian Bachs, Stil—Chronologie—Satztechnik* (Basel: Schwabe Verlag, 2009).

Zehnder, Jean-Claude. 2013a. "Die Passaggio-Orgelchoräle—Neue Perspektiven." *Bach-Jahrbuch* 99 (2013), 223–242.

Zehnder, Jean-Claude. 2013b. "Zur Überlieferung von Bachs Passacaglia c-Moll BWV 582." In *A Fresco, Mélanges offerts au Professeur Etienne Darbellay*, B. Boccadoro and G. Starobinski, eds. (Berlin: Peter Lang, 2013), 183–202.

Zietz, Hermann. 1969. *Quellenkritische Untersuchungen an den Bach-Handschriften P 801, P 802, und P 803* (Hamburg: Karl Dieter Wagner, 1969).

Ziller, Ernst. 1935. *Johann Heinrich Buttstedt (1666–1727)* (Halle/Salle: Buchhandlung des Waisenhauses, 1935; rpt. Hildesheim, Georg Olms, 1971).

Zitellini, Rodolfo. 2013. "Das 'Thema Legrenzianum' der Fuge BWV 574—ein Fehlzuschreibung?" *Bach-Jahrbuch* 99 (2013), 243–259.

General Index

Index of Bach's Works

For the benefit of digital users, indexed terms that span two pages (e.g., 52–53) may, on occasion, appear on only one of those pages.

Tables and figures are indicated by t and f numbers, respectively.